Ladies in the Laboratory II

West European Women in Science, 1800–1900
A Survey of Their Contributions to Research

Mary R. S. Creese

with contributions by Thomas M. Creese

The Scarecrow Press, Inc.
Lanham, Maryland, and Oxford
2004

SCARECROW PRESS, INC.

Published in the United States of America
by Scarecrow Press, Inc.
A wholly owned subsidary of The Rowman & Littlefield Publishing Group, Inc.
4501 Forbes Boulevard, Suite 200, Lanham, Maryland 20706
www.scarecrowpress.com

PO Box 317
Oxford
OX2 9RU, UK

British Library Cataloguing in Publication Information Available

Library of Congress Cataloging-in-Publication Data

Creese, Mary R. S., 1935–
  Ladies in the laboratory II : West European women in science.
1800–1900 : a survey of their contributions to research / Mary R. S.
Creese with contributions by Thomas M. Creese.
     p.   cm.
  Includes bibliographical references and index.
  ISBN 0-8108-4979-8 (alk. paper)
  1. Women in science—Europe, Western-History-19th century.   2. Women
scientists-Europe, Western-Biography.   I. Title: Ladies in the
laboratory 2.   II. Title: Ladies in the laboratory two.   III. Creese,
Thomas M.   IV. Title.
Q141 .C693   2004
500′.82′09409034-dc22   2003020846

To the memory of P., a dear friend. Her example of gentle, patient resignation through long suffering is always with me.

> The all of thine that cannot die
> Through dark and dread Eternity
> Returns again to me,
> And more thy buried love endears
> Than aught except its living years.

—Lord Byron

Acknowledgments

I would like to thank the following archivists and librarians for the invaluable help they have most generously given me in completing this part of the survey: Gordon Anderson, University of Kansas Libraries; Tone Birkemoe, Biologisk Bibliotek, Blindern (Oslo); Jens Blecher, Archives, University of Leipzig; Linda Greenwood, Belfast Public Libraries; Maria Paola Invernizzi, Biblioteca Universitaria, Pavia; David Kessler, Bancroft Library, University of California, Berkeley; Dr. Kessler, University Archives, Ruprecht-Karls-Universität, Heidelberg; Christine Knueppel, Universitätsbibliothek, Christian-Albrechts-Universität, Kiel; Frau L. Kuenstling, Information Division, University of Leipzig; Rena Lohan, College Archives, University College Dublin; Thomas Maisel, Archiv der Universität, Wien; Mona Malmkvist, Swedish Museum of Natural History; Sean Phillips, Librarian, University College Dublin; Kate Russell, Special Collections, Vancouver Public Library; Armin Schlechter, Universitäts Bibliothek, Heidelberg; Gordon Squires, Cavendish Laboratory Museum, Cambridge University; and Sarina Wyant, Special Collections, University of Rhode Island Libraries. I am especially grateful to Dr. Leo von Euler, of Bethesda, Maryland, for sharing with me his memories of his grandmother, Astrid Cleve von Euler, and for most patiently answering my many questions. I would also like to thank Annette Vogt, MPI for the History of Science, Berlin, and Michael Serafin, editor, *Oberhessische Naturwissenschaftliche Zeitschrift*, for their generous help.

Even more than in the preparation of the first part of this survey (*Ladies in the Laboratory?*), I have relied on the help of the interlibrary loan staff of the University of Kansas libraries. Their assistance has been essential.

Several specialists have written to me following the publication of *Ladies in the Laboratory?* to give new information or point out errors. I would especially like to thank David Damkaer, Monroe, Washington; Bernard Lightman, York University, Toronto; and Rudolf Schmid, University of California, Berkeley.

Thomas Creese prepared the special bibliography of scientific journal articles, 1800–1900, from lists collected from the Royal Society's nineteen-volume *Catalogue of Scientific Papers*, 1800–1900. He also drew the graphs included in most chapters and assisted with the material on mathematicians, particularly the discussion of the work of Sophie Germain and Cornelia Fabri. In addition he provided a great deal of general help and encouragement throughout the course of the work. Anna Creese helped with a number of finer points in translations from both French and German.

The staff of the College of Liberal Arts and Sciences Word Processing Center, University of Kansas, especially Paula Courtney, Pam LeRow, and Lynn Porter, typed the manuscript with great skill and patience; we are once more much indebted to them.

Any errors are my responsibility.

Mary Creese
Lawrence, Kansas
March 2003

Contents

Figures

x   *Figures*

Introduction

This volume continues a survey of nineteenth-century women whose journal publications are listed in the London Royal Society's *Catalogue of Scientific Papers,* 1800–1900,[1] the major index of scientific journal literature for the period. The first part of the survey, *Ladies in the Laboratory?,* concerned American and British women, who together constitute about two thirds of all the women authors identified in the *Catalogue.*[2] This volume focuses on 177 European women working in the following twelve countries: Austria-Hungary, Belgium, Denmark, Finland, France, Germany, Ireland, Italy, the Netherlands, Norway, Sweden, and Switzerland.[3] The contributions of these 177 make up about 20 percent of the articles by women indexed in the *Catalogue* (Figure 0-1). For many of them, fairly full biographical sketches are given; others, about whom information is lacking or inaccessible to me at the present time, are mentioned only briefly.

Organization is by nationality. Each country covered has a separate chapter except for two regions, Scandinavia and Belgium/the Netherlands, where individual countries have separate sections within single chapters. For each country, workers are generally grouped according to area of activity—biological and medical sciences, mathematical and physical sciences, and social sciences. This arrangement, rather than a simple alphabetical ordering, perhaps leads toward a fuller overall picture of women's activity in any one area in a given country. Pie graphs accompanying most chapters offer quantitative data on choice of fields and productivity within fields for each country.

A bibliography of the women's pre-1901 papers extracted from the Royal Society *Catalogue* is included. Here also, organization is by country and within each country by area of activity. The information on which biographical sketches are based came largely from the now considerable and ever-expanding body of works on early women scientists by European writers and historians. Of the currently readily available sources, which range from recent biographies and collections of shorter essays to updated national biographical lexicons, those dealing with German, Norwegian, and Irish subjects are especially notable. Some of the women discussed,

a. Authors   b. Papers

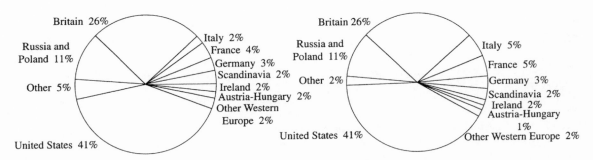

Figure 0-1.   Distribution of women authors and their scientific journal publications (all fields), by country or region, 1800–1900. The sectors "Other Western Europe" represent authors and papers from the following countries: Belgium, Netherlands, Switzerland, and Serbia. The sectors "Other" represent authors and papers from the following countries: Australia, Canada, China, India, Japan, Mexico, New Zealand, South Africa, and Unidentified. Data from the Royal Society *Catalogue of Scientific Papers.*

particularly in the French and German groups, will already be fairly well known to American readers, but the work of many more has been brought to light here.

With some important exceptions, especially in Italy, most began their research careers in the late 1880s or the 1890s, when university-level education was becoming more generally accessible to women. Many came from solid, middle-class backgrounds; they were the daughters of businessmen, school teachers, professors, doctors, clergymen, or government officials. However, a few belonged to the aristocracy or even royalty and, at the other end of the social scale, there were one or two daughters of farmers, low-ranking army officers, and even a Paris slum shopkeeper. Two of them, a French physician and a German chemist, were outspoken social activists, socialist or communist in their political allegiance, the causes they championed being equal rights for women and the fair treatment of working-class people. A number of others were very much left-wing liberals; a few were actively involved in politics. Although almost all of those whose stories are known strongly supported the feminist movement, some confined themselves to doing so by example, that is, by proving themselves capable of carrying out valuable scientific research. Bar graphs showing numbers of authors and papers per decade are included in most chapters.

The two world wars inevitably marked the lives and careers of these women to a far greater extent than was the case with their relatively sheltered contemporaries in Britain and the United States. Many were able to resume their research after the upheavals of 1914–1918, but the economic collapse of Germany in the 1920s left most members of that country's scientific community, men as well as women, with considerable difficulties to face. Again in the 1930s, as a result of the political events that led up to the Second World War, the German women in this survey who were still professionally active suffered greatly; they were required to give up their jobs and in some cases had to flee the country. Early retirement was also thrust upon Italy's outstanding woman biologist with the coming to power of that country's fascist government.

As well as adding to the historical record of early work by women in science, this volume offers information on a number of people about whom a very limited amount has been written outside their native countries. Looking back on them one discovers more than a few vivid and colorful personalities, wonderfully energetic and purposeful women whose accomplishments, given the handicaps of the era, were sometimes remarkable: among them we meet a Bavarian royal princess working her way up the Rio Negro collecting rare Brazilian flora and fauna; a hardworking Danish agricultural entomologist making her rounds of the farming community by bicycle; a German-Lithuanian bacteriologist challenging the practices of powerful commercial dairy interests in the 1900 "Berlin milk war"; a Dutch botanist collecting algae along the coral reefs and in the deep ocean basins of the Malaysian Archipelago. Not only were these women pioneers, leading the way for female entry into hitherto segregated fields of endeavor, but they succeeded in making notable contributions to research despite significant disadvantages and handicaps. Further, although one must allow for a modicum of the glamour imparted by distance, they give every appearance of having led extremely full, interesting, and satisfying lives.

This book is not intended to be a biographical dictionary but rather to offer a selected and ordered series of pictures of the lives and careers of many of the most notable nineteenth-century women of science in Western Europe. Their stories to a large extent have been neglected, general interest being more inclined to focus on women in other fields of human endeavor. Nevertheless their achievements constitute, I feel, a considerable fraction of the high points in women's history for the period.

Notes

1. Royal Society, London, comp., *Catalogue of Scientific Papers, 1800–1900,* 19 volumes (Cambridge: Cambridge University Press, 1867–1925).

2. Mary R. S. Creese, *Ladies in the Laboratory? American and British Women in Science, 1800–1900* (Lanham, Md.: Scarecrow Press, 1998). The appendix at the end of this volume offers updated information about a few American and British women collected since the publication of *Ladies in the Laboratory?*

3. Remarks concerning the one woman identified as Serbian appear in a footnote to the chapter on Austro-Hungarians.

Chapter 1

SCANDINAVIA: BALTIC DIATOMS, SNOW-LINE PLANTS, INSECTS OF THE OATFIELDS

The bibliography lists pre-1901 work by twenty-nine women from the Scandinavian countries, sixteen from Sweden, five from Norway, five from Denmark, and three who were either from Finland or studied and worked there (Figure 1-2a). The greater part of their research was in the biological sciences, especially botany and zoology (Figure 1-2, c and d). In part, this choice reflected the outstanding opportunities for original investigations on northern plants (including work on such topics as the adaptation of forms to Arctic conditions), and the tremendous interest at the time in the rich microscopic animal and plant life of the waters of the North Atlantic. In both Norway and Sweden women made notable, in some cases outstanding, contributions in botany (including palaeobotany) and zoology; Denmark, a country in which agriculture was especially important, had a leading woman agricultural entomologist. University-level training was opened to Scandinavian women in the 1870s and early 1880s. However, as in most other countries, the lack of secondary schools for girls was a serious handicap initially.

Sweden

From 1853, Swedish women were accepted as teachers in primary schools. By the early 1860s they had access to teacher training colleges, and by 1870 they had the right to take university entrance examinations and to train in the faculty of medicine. Three years later, they were granted entrance to all university faculties except theology and law.[1]

This relatively early opening to women of educational opportunities and teaching careers in Sweden has been attributed not to a particularly strong feminist movement but rather to the demographic situation in the country in the nineteenth century and to the social and economic changes that followed Sweden's increasing industrialization; a large surplus of women in the population meant that those of the middle class had to be given some means of supporting themselves outside marriage.[2] Thus, although there were a number of prominent women activists and many ardent supporters of higher education for women,[3] there was no well-organized push for university-level training for women.[4] In fact, until after 1900 only a few came forward to take advantage of the opportunities available to them. Most of those who did enrolled at Uppsala University, the older and larger of Sweden's two universities (founded as an ecclesiastical institution in 1477). The first woman entered in 1873, the first doctorate given a woman was conferred in 1883, and by the turn of the century the institution had about fifty women students (2 percent of the total student body).[5]

Also prominent in the education of Sweden's earliest women scientists was the Stockholm Högskola, now Stockholm University. Nearly all of the thirteen women discussed here who carried out pre-1901 research studied there at some time during their training.[6] Independent, radical-liberal in general outlook, and financed by private donations and municipal grants, Stockholm Högskola opened in the expanding industrial capital city in 1878 and offered higher education in the sciences and mathematics. Although it was not granted the right to confer degrees until 1904 and its financial resources were limited, its academic standards were comparable to those at the two state universities (Uppsala and Lund). Lectures were open to the public, women as well as men, for a nominal entrance fee; by the turn of the century women made up ten percent of the total student body of about 400.[7] Programs of study placed a strong emphasis on original research.[8]

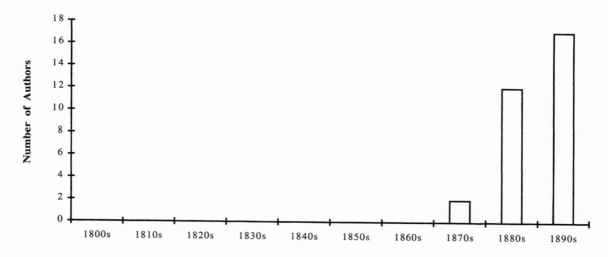

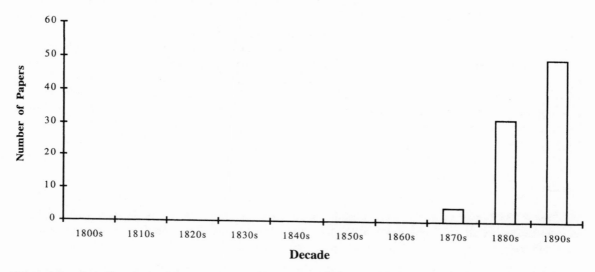

Figure 1-1.   Scandinavian authors and papers, by decade, 1800–1900. Data from the Royal Society *Catalogue of Scientific Papers.*

The largest contribution of the Swedish women discussed here was in botany, where six authors published a total of twenty-two pre-1901 papers. Work in zoology was also notable, with three authors bringing out thirteen papers.

ASTRID CLEVE VON EULER[9] (1875–1968), whose scientific contributions ranged over three fields—botany, chemistry, and Quaternary geology—and who was active in research for seven decades, was perhaps the most distinguished member of this Swedish group. She was born in Uppsala on 22 January 1875, the oldest of the three daughters of Per Teodor Cleve and his wife Caralma (née Öhbom). Per Cleve (1840–1905), chemist, geologist, oceanographer, and professor of chemistry at Uppsala University, was widely recognized for his plankton studies and for his work on the rare earth elements. His wife Caralma, usually called Alma, was one of the first girls in Sweden to complete studies at the gymnasium level. Active in ongoing debates on women's issues, Alma Cleve wrote pamphlets and letters to the press and, although less radical in her views about women's place in society than the most prominent of Swedish women activists of the time,[10] she was a strong believer in the value of higher education for women. Having earlier worked as a governess in well-to-do families, she gave her daughters their early education at home. All three of them went on to professional careers.[11]

At age eleven Astrid Cleve was sent to a boarding school in Lausanne for two years, where she learned French and German. Thereafter she continued her education at home. She spent much time in her father's

a. Authors, by country

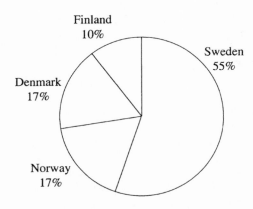

b. Papers, by country

c. Authors, by Field

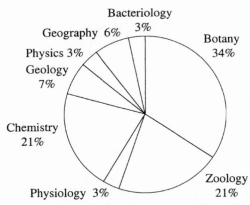

d. Papers, by field

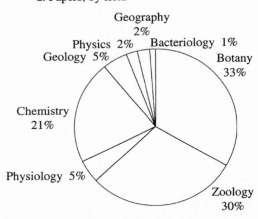

Figure 1-2.   Distribution of Scandinavian authors and papers, by country and by field, 1800–1900. (In c., an author contributing to more than one field is counted in each.) Data from the Royal Society *Catalogue of Scientific Papers.*

chemical laboratory, housed in the same building as the family's dwelling quarters. Indeed it was he who gave her her basic scientific training, introducing her at an early age to the study of diatoms when she was assisting him in his work on plankton. She passed her baccalaureate examinations at the age of sixteen as an external student at the Uppsala public secondary school and in the autumn of 1891 entered Uppsala University, where she studied natural sciences. Following the award of her *kandidat filosofie* (bachelor) degree in January 1894 she went on to concentrate on botany.

Astrid Cleve was one of the pioneers in investigations of the diatoms of the Swedish mountain lakes in Lule Lappmark, where she first carried out field studies in 1895 and 1896. In the summer of 1895 she and her friend Lilly Paijkull walked across the mountains of northern Sweden passing along the shores of Lake Virihaure (about 67° 20′N) and reaching Saltenfjord on the Norwegian coast near the town of Bodø. Clad in ankle-length skirts and carrying packs filled with botanical collecting equipment as well as camping necessities, they often had to pick their own route as best they could across the treeless high country, help from Lapp guides not always being available. At night they frequently slept on the bare ground, wrapped in blankets.[12] Again in 1896, Astrid Cleve spent the whole summer in the high mountains of Lule Lappmark continuing botanical fieldwork. Her reports on the then unknown diatom flora of the Arctic lakes were among her earliest published work; they were well illustrated with excellent drawings of the new varieties and forms she found.[13] About this time she also carried out a broad ecological study of plant life in these northern upland regions with a focus on adaptation to environment.[14] At the age of twenty-three, in May 1898, she successfully defended her doctoral dissertation, studies on the germinating time and maturation period of some Swedish plants.[15] She was the second woman to receive a *filosofie doktor* degree from a Swedish university and the first in the natural sciences.

A person of wide scientific outlook with tremendous energy and purposefulness, as a graduate student, Astrid Cleve carried out several studies in the university's chemical laboratory—work done in addition to her botanical research. Under the general supervision of Karl Oskar Widman she prepared a number of organic compounds containing nitrogen, both straight chain and cyclic structures, materials then of particular interest to Widman. Four papers published between 1896 and 1898 reported the work (see bibliography), which was noteworthy for its careful, painstaking execution. Two more papers on chemical research she carried out at Uppsala University appeared in 1901 and 1902.[16] Of these, her 1901 report of the determination of the atomic weight and some of the properties of the rare earth element ytterbium (one of the lanthanides) was especially notable. Most likely carried out under her father's guidance, the work was again thorough and painstaking; her value of 173.11 for the atomic weight compares favorably with later determinations (173.04). This area of inorganic chemistry was very much to the fore at the time, the possibility of fitting the rare earth elements into a single zone of closely related individuals occupying one space in the periodic table being under consideration.[17]

After receiving her degree in 1898, Astrid Cleve moved to Stockholm Högskola. There she held an assistantship in the chemistry department until 1902 when she married Bavarian-born Hans von Euler-Chelpin, professor of chemistry. Between 1903 and 1907, although she no longer had a formal position at the Högskola, she worked along with her husband and coauthored a succession of about sixteen papers and notes in Swedish and German journals; during the same four years, the first three of her five children were born.[18] The von Eulers's joint research covered synthetic studies on organic systems containing nitrogen, investigations of metal-ammonia complexes and chemicals isolated from resin, some notable work on the condensation of formaldehyde to form simple carbohydrates (ketoses), and enzyme and alcoholic fermentation studies (work relating to the commercial production of industrial alcohol).[19] Hans von Euler's pioneering investigations of the fermentation process were recognized with the award in 1929 of the Nobel prize in chemistry (shared with Sir Arthur Harden of the Lister Institute in London). By then, however, the Cleve–von Euler partnership had ended, their having divorced in 1912.

Between 1911 and 1917, Astrid Cleve von Euler taught in Stockholm schools—at Anna Sandströms women teachers seminary (1911–1917),[20] at the Högere Realläroverket (secondary modern school) in the district of Norrmalm (1912–1914), and at the Nya Elementarskolan (New High School) for girls (1912–1916). By about 1910 she had also returned to plankton studies, her first research interest, and over the next few years she published several investigations of waters near Stockholm. Her papers of 1910 and 1912 were especially notable;[21] they remain of interest as a unique source of information on diatomaceous plankton in waters of the Stockholm region in the pre-pollution era. From 1913 to 1917 she was a biological assistant with the Swedish Hydrographical Biological Commission. Her comprehensive monograph on plankton research in the Skagerak appeared in 1917.[22]

That year she and her five children moved to the province of Värmland, where she became head of the Skoghallsverkens Forskningslaboratorium, a forestry research laboratory of the Uddeholm Company on the northern shore of Lake Vänern. Although largely concerned with administration, while at Skoghall she carried out a series of investigations on forest products, particularly the lignin by-products from the sulfite pulp–manufacturing process. About twenty-one papers and notes published between 1920 and 1925 reported her studies, which included analyses of pine and spruce needles, attempts to find commercially viable ways of separating valuable materials from pulp industry by-products, and examinations of methods for determining the lignin content of woods. In addition she wrote on the more theoretical topic of carbon dioxide absorption and metabolism in plants.[23] About this time she also coauthored a basic textbook in applied biological chemistry, wrote a short book for general readers on the element selenium, and published two papers on petroleum and coal.[24]

From about 1920 Astrid Cleve von Euler concentrated more and more on diatom studies, the work for which she is widely remembered. She became the country's foremost expert on both fossil and living forms of Baltic region diatoms. Her paleobotanical studies continued for four decades and, looking toward a broad, comprehensive picture, she also sought to fit her observations into a more general theoretical framework. This led her to the problem of late– and post–Ice Age water-level changes in the Baltic, a complex question because of the interplay in the region of several factors: these are the isostatic uplift of the land following the retreat of the Scandinavian ice sheet, the eustatic (climate-controlled) rise of the sea level, and the fact that, during parts of this period, the Baltic was an independent lake, cut off from the ocean, with its own water-level fluctuations.[25] The Quaternary stages of the Baltic have been described as "intervals of either open or closed connection with the ocean,"[26] and the consequences of this opening and closing are reflected in, among other things, the biostratigraphical changes in Baltic sediments. Although Astrid Cleve von Euler's boundary analyses, based for the most part on diatom investigations, were at times pushed further than her data might fully justify (many of the postglacial sediments tend to be poor in diatoms and often contain redeposited or inwashed taxa[27]), she entered into debates and defended her interpretations vigorously, both in print and in a number of lectures she gave to the Stockholm Geological Society. The details of the location and course of development of the drainage passageways of the independent lake stages, points of much discussion during her time and later, were subjects of special interest to her; she did not agree with the theory that the Ancylus Lake[28] was at a higher level than the ocean. She also found herself in opposition to many Swedish and Finnish geologists over the so-called oscillation theory, about periodically repeated movements of the land masses, which she favored but which was never generally accepted.[29]

These points acknowledged, it remains the case that Astrid Cleve von Euler's great output of taxonomic and systematic work was outstanding. Particularly notable were the major monographs she published between 1932 and 1955.

Her 1932 report of the diatom flora (recent and fossil) of the Tåkern basin in Östergötland presented descriptions of 535 species and varieties of which 184 were new for Sweden. Lake Tåkern, heavily fertilized by the masses of birds for which it was famous, had a rich eutrophic microflora, partly relic and of southern and central European origin.[30] Following a "minor expedition" in the summer of 1932 to the lakes of Finnish Lapland during which she collected 118 soil samples, she published a comprehensive systematic and comparative account of the then little known diatom flora of northern Finland (1934). A considerable number of the 673 species and varieties she identified in this study were new; further, on the basis of diatom associations established by examination of distribution, frequency, ecology, and taxonomy, she also drew conclusions about a number of puzzling questions concerning the pre- and postglacial floras of northern Europe. This led to a second paper in 1934 on the Quaternary geology of northern Finland,[31] a subject she was to return to in subsequent papers, not always agreeing with the views held by Finnish geologists.

About 1940 Astrid Cleve von Euler started work on her great, comprehensive diatom Flora, "Die Diatomeen von Schweden und Finnland." Published between 1951 and 1955 in five parts, it covered the greater part of the Baltic Sea region—Sweden, especially its northern and central parts, and all of Finland. It listed almost 1,600 species, freshwater, brackish, and marine, both fossil and living (and many varieties and forms in addition). Bringing together her enormous and detailed knowledge of the field, it included not only taxonomy but also ecology, current distribution, and fossil occurrence. Several illustrations were provided for every taxon. The flora has remained a standard reference for Quaternary geologists working in the region.[32]

She published many additional papers on the diatom flora of Sweden and Finland. These regularly contained reports of species and varieties new to the Baltic region as well as detailed notes on distribution (geologic and geographic), frequency, ecology, and taxonomy. Some of her studies led her to propose complete revisions and redefinitions of existing genera and to suggest new subspecies and forms.[33]

Except for the five-year period when she was head of the Skoghallsverkens research laboratory, she supported her family by high school teaching. One of her striking qualities was her warm sense of responsibility for her children; she gave her large family strong and capable guidance under difficult circumstances. For three years, beginning in 1923, they lived in Uppsala. In 1933 Astrid moved the family home to the small town of Lindesberg, about ninety miles west of Uppsala, where she bought a farm, Limnäs, located along a lake. She raised sheep and had some assistance with the work but did much of it herself.[34] One might imagine that the farm, despite its demands, brought her considerable satisfaction, the lifestyle it entailed blending well with her strong sense of closeness to nature—the soil, the rocks, and the plants. During her years in Lindesberg, she taught at the local *realskola* (nonclassical secondary school) and in addition carried out a considerable amount of diatom analyses of postglacial sediments for Quaternary geologists working on the Geological Survey of Sweden.

Botanist, chemist, teacher, independent research worker, for a time farmer, Astrid Cleve von Euler was an extraordinarily versatile person. She was always constrained, however, by limited financial resources and the many demands on her time. Further, coming from an academic background, she was fully conscious of the handicap of never having a university position from which to carry out her scholarly work. Her chances of finding such a post in the 1920s and 1930s (her midlife years) were probably reduced by the fact that her scientific views and theories did not always fit in with the majority opinion. This would almost certainly have told against her with the often very conservative university faculty members and administrators of the time. By the 1950s, when her great *Flora* was published, she was in her seventies and beyond the age of taking up a teaching post. Nevertheless she had many students and collaborators with whom she kept in close contact over the years. Both at her farm and later in Uppsala, diatomologists, Swedish and foreign, visited her for consultation, discussion, and instruction, sometimes staying with her for extended periods, some receiving their first real instruction on diatoms from her. One friend and fellow scientist, herself inspired by Astrid Cleve von Euler's teaching, wrote, "On leaving her beautiful and pleasant home, one always had the feeling of having taken part in something interesting, and something outside everyday experience."[35] A good-looking woman of great personal charm and a generous host, she had a wide spectrum of interests that ranged well beyond her immediate professional concerns. These included philosophy, religion (she converted to Catholicism in 1949), current French literature, and the Stone Age prehistory of the Baltic region, particularly the dating of the earliest settlements in central Sweden. On the latter topic, a natural extension of her Quaternary studies, she published a number of papers and essays.[36]

In 1945 she returned to Uppsala, where she was active in the university's geology division, often discussing ideas concerning Quaternary water-level changes in the Baltic, particularly theories about the outflow from Ancylus Lake.[37] She gave a comprehensive course of lectures on diatomology at the Institute of Plant Ecology at Uppsala University over two terms in 1947–1948. In 1948, the fiftieth anniversary of the awarding of her degree, she become Sweden's first woman Jubilee Doctor of Philosophy (*jubeldoktor*). In 1955, when she was eighty, she was made professor *honoris causa* in appreciation of her extensive work on diatoms. Physically weakened by a hernia operation but still mentally vigorous and in close touch with her family, Astrid Cleve von Euler spent the last months of her life in a nursing home in Västerås, about fifty miles west-northwest of Stockholm. She died there on 8 April 1968, at age ninety-three.

The five other Swedish women mentioned here who carried out pre-1901 botanical research—Andersson, Lewin, Lovén, Olbers Wester, and Söderström—were students at Stockholm Högskola in the 1880s and 1890s. For the most part their work was done at the Högskola's Botanical Institute and their results published in the appendices of the Royal Swedish Academy of Sciences' *Handlingar*.[38]

SIGRID ANDERSSON (1868–1918), the daughter of Nils Johan Andersson and his wife Anna Elisabet Amanda (née Tigerhielm), was born in Stockholm on 2 January 1868. Her father, professor of botany at Lund University, later worked at the Riksmuseum in Stockholm. A student at the Högskola from 1885 to 1888, Sigrid Andersson published her work on monocotyledon anatomy in 1887. For a time she held a position as histological preparator at the Karolinska Institute. In 1895 she married John G. Rissler later chief of the Sabbatsberg hospital in Stockholm. She died in Stockholm on 31 October 1918.

Born in Stockholm on 30 July 1859, MARIA LEWIN studied at the Wallinska high school for girls and passed the qualifying examination for elementary school teachers in 1881. She entered Stockholm Högskola in 1884 and attended classes there for at least three years, completing training as a teacher of science and mathematics. From 1891 she taught at the Wallinska school. Her research at the Botanical Institute, published in 1887 and 1888, included work on monocotyledon anatomy and a study on algae.

HEDVIG LOVÉN (1867–?), daughter of physiologist Otto Christian Lovén of the Karolinska Institute, Stockholm, and his Finnish wife Elisabeth Johanna Emilia (née von Julin), was born in Stockholm on 13 December 1867. A student at the Högskola from 1885, she published three botanical papers, including plant respiration studies, between 1888 and 1892. She married professor of medicine and pharmacologist Carl Gustav Santesson of the Karolinska Institute in 1892.

ALIDA OLBERS (1842–1912) was born on 13 October 1842 in the historic town of Marstrand on a small island about twenty miles north of Göteborg. Famous for its ancient fortifications and as the site of the coronation of King Kristian of Oldenburg in 1449 (when the region was part of Norway), the town is now a popular summer seaside resort and sailing center.

The earliest of the Swedish women botanists in this survey, Alida Olbers studied at the higher seminar for women teachers in Stockholm and then worked as a private teacher in Stockholm until 1904. During the 1880s and 1890s she carried out research in plant anatomy and morphology at the Högskola's Botanical Institute. Eight papers and notes reported her studies of flower and fruit anatomy in a number of families including the Caryophyllaceae (pinks), the Labiatae (mints), Geraniaceae (geraniums), and Rosaceae (roses). Alida Olbers married M. Wester in 1897. She died in Marstrand on 29 October 1912 at the age of seventy.

EDLA SÖDERSTRÖM (1868–?), whose 1889 plant anatomy paper is listed in the bibliography, was born in Stockholm on 30 August 1868. The daughter of C. C. Söderström, a wealthy Stockholm merchant and government official, she studied at the Högskola in the late 1880s specializing in algae. In 1894 she married her former instructor Johan Echard Fredrik af Klercker, a *docent* in botany at the Högskola. Her algae studies continued for a number of years but she was also interested in eighteenth century British social life and customs.[39]

The three early women zoologists listed in the Swedish section of the bibliography—Ärnbäck-Christie-Linde, Carlsson, and Westling[40]—all studied and worked at least for a time at Stockholm Högskola's Zoological Institute. Both Ärnbäck-Christie-Linde and Carlsson became well known for their many contributions to their areas and are discussed here.

AUGUSTA ÄRNBÄCK-ANDERSSON[41] (1870–1953) was born on 28 March 1870, the daughter of Anders Andersson and his wife Augusta (née Larsen). The Anderssons were farmers in the district of Södermanland, south of Stockholm. After taking her university matriculation examinations in the town of Örebro in 1888 Augusta Ärnbäck-Andersson studied at Uppsala University. When she graduated in 1892 she went to Stockholm, where she first worked as a school teacher. However, in 1896 morphologist and taxonomist Wilhelm Leche, director of the Zoological Institute, offered her a teaching assistantship that continued until 1899 and was renewed for the years 1900–1901. About 1898 she married Edvard Eilert Christie-Linde, a lawyer. Her teaching appointment at the institute was the first such taken up by a woman and, although she was remembered as pleasant and competent, not all her colleagues found themselves able to welcome her presence in their midst. The resentment not infrequently aroused when an outsider moves into a previously well-defined and long-established professional group was not absent here. For some, Ärnbäck-Andersson's arrival disrupted the comfortable, unconstrained atmosphere of what had until then been an all-male preserve.[42]

She published her first paper, an anatomical study of the brain in lower vertebrates, in 1900. Her master's degree (*filosofie licentiat*) was awarded in 1908 and she received a doctorate in 1909. For twenty-four years (1916–1940), she held a nonpermanent position as assistant zoologist at the Swedish National Museum (Riksmuseum), where for a time she also served as curator. During these years she was notably productive, bringing out over twenty papers in British, German, and Swedish journals.

In her doctoral research, morphological studies on small mammals, she concentrated particularly on the Soricidae (shrews) carrying out a detailed examination of tooth development, an area of special interest to Wilhelm Leche.[43] Thereafter, however, she focused almost exclusively on marine fauna except for a brief return to tooth development studies at Stockholm University in the 1940s, after she had retired from the Riksmuseum.[44]

Ärnbäck-Christie-Linde's work at the museum concerned ascidians, a class of primitive marine chordates in the subphylum Tunicata. Ascidians are free-floating, filter-feeling animals, some of which are especially important in ocean food chains because of their ability to trap cellular plankton, which cannot be harvested by most other animals. Her papers included several monographic accounts of collections brought back to the Riksmuseum by Swedish expeditions to the Arctic and Antarctic; in these, she frequently incorporated taxonomic reviews and discussions of geographical and depth distribution, and described many new, rare, or poorly established species.[45] A somewhat shorter monograph brought out in 1929 discussed antarctic and subantarctic tunicates (including new species) from the waters around the Guaitecas Islands off the coast of Chile.[46] In addition, she contributed a number of taxonomy and morphology notes and papers on individual species and genera.[47]

She made a number of field trips to collect marine fauna, mainly tunicates, along the Norwegian coasts and the Swedish west coast. Her taxonomic and morphological account of the tunicate fauna of Norway appeared in 1925, and a monograph on ascidians collected off Göteborg was published in 1923;[48] her specimens are held at the Swedish Museum of Natural History. She is credited with being the first zoologist to carry out a thorough and extensive investigation of ascidians in Swedish waters.[49] Her last work, completed in 1952 but not published until 1971, was a study of ascidian collections brought back in 1927 by a Danish expedition to the Faroe Islands.[50]

A member of the Swedish Biological Association from 1900, Augusta Ärnbäck-Christie-Linde was widely known among her fellow marine biologists and she had an active correspondence (preserved in the archives of the Swedish National Museum) with scientists in many countries. She died in 1953 when she was about eighty-three. The species *Polycarpa aernbaeckae* F. Monniot, 1964 and *Preudodistoma arnbacki* Pérès, 1959, commenmorate her name.

ALBERTINA CARLSSON[51] (1848–1930), who was known internationally for her studies in vertebrate morphology, was born in Stockholm on 12 June 1848, the daughter of Anders Petter Carlsson and his wife Anna Maria (née Jönsson). She studied at the higher training college for women teachers in Stockholm, passing the final examinations in 1868, and for thirty-seven years taught in Stockholm schools for girls, first at the C. G. Paulis school (1870–1881) and later (1881–1907) at Södermalm's higher institution.

Encouraged by morphologist Wilhelm Leche of the Stockholm Högskola's Zoological Institute, she developed a lifelong interest in zoology and over the course of more than forty years, under Leche's guidance, carried out a succession of notable studies of specimens (including fossils) in the institute's collections. Her first research, work on the anatomy of water birds, was published in the supplement of the Royal Swedish Academy of Sciences' *Handlingar* in 1884 as a forty-four page monograph; it won her an Academy of Sciences prize the following year.

Albertina Carlsson concentrated especially on insectivores and carnivores from tropical southeast Asia and Australia but her investigations covered a wide range of topics, from early anatomical work on residual limb appendages of snakes and tooth development studies in bony fishes to morphological research on the Tragulidae (chevrotains), the small, herbivorous ungulates of the tropics.[52] An able morphologist, she published at least twenty-five papers, some of them short monographs, and was well known for her contributions to embryological anatomy, phylogenetics, and systematics. Several of her publications dealt with ancestral forms and living members or close relatives of the Viverridae (the family that includes the civet and mongoose), the Canidae (dog family), and the Procyonidae (racoons and allies);[53] others reported systematic work on insectivorous animals of the tropics,[54] and studies on marsupial anatomy.[55]

She retained a lively interest in vertebrate studies into her old age and on numerous occasions in radio broadcasts encouraged public support of the work of the Högskola's Zoological Institute. Although she never pursued an academic degree, she was awarded an honorary doctorate by Stockholm Högskola in 1927. She died in Stockholm on 25 December 1930 at the age of eighty-two.

In addition to botany and zoology, chemistry, and analytical chemistry in particular, was an area that attracted a number of early women scientists in Sweden. Astrid Cleve's early research in the field and her assistantship in the chemistry department at Stockholm Högskola in the late 1890s has been noted above. By then, however, women students had already been working in the Högskola's chemical laboratory for at least a decade, probably encouraged by the lively and enthusiastic Sven Otto Pettersson, head of the department from 1881 and well known for his work in chemical analysis.

The most prominent of the early Stockholm women chemists was NAIMA SAHLBOM[56] (1871–1957), who made an important contribution to the development of mineralogical research in Sweden. Born in Stockholm on 15 May 1871, she was the daughter of Gustav Valfrid Sahlbom and his wife Charlotte (née Hallin). After passing the university matriculation examinations in 1893 she studied at both Uppsala University and Stockholm Högskola, graduating in 1896. Her first paper (1897) reported a mineral analysis done in Stockholm of rocks from Alnö island;[57] a second, on the fluoride content of Swedish phosphorites, published jointly with geologist Johan Andersson of Uppsala University, appeared in 1900 (see bibliography). Over a period of several years, she built up a broad background in mineral analysis while working at a number of geological institutions—in Helsinki, Heidelberg, Basel, and the Swedish national mineralogical museum. She received a doctorate in chemical physics from Neuchâtel University in 1910 having presented a dissertation on the analysis of colloidal solutions, work carried out under the direction of Swiss chemist Carl Fritz Fichter of Basel University.[58] In 1914 she opened her own laboratory in Stockholm and for several decades provided a highly valued service, carrying out rock, mineral, and water analyses for Swedish workers in petrography and mineralogy.

Her publications were not many, but she did bring out a notable study on the relationship between the radioactivity of the waters in Swedish springs and the nature of the rocks through which they flow. The work was of considerable interest at the time, the investigations of Curie, Rutherford, and others having only shortly before brought radioactivity to the forefront of scientific research. Sahlbom's first report of her findings (1907), published jointly with Hjalmar Sjögren of the mineralogical division of the Swedish national museum, discussed their study of springs in central and southern Sweden. A second paper (1916) presented Sahlbom's very considerable extension of the work to about 400 deep-bored wells and open drinking springs from different geological regions throughout Sweden. It confirmed the earlier finding that high activity is associated with flow through primary rocks, particularly granites, but springs in regions of sedimentary rocks generally show low activity.[59]

For twenty-five years (1919–1944), Naima Sahlbom was an enthusiastic and hardworking member of the Swedish section of the International Women's Association for Peace and Freedom; in 1935 she served as section president. The Swedish award for meritorious service, the Illis Quorum Medal, conferred on her in 1946, recognized her public work. She died in a private nursing home in Stockholm on 29 March 1957, two months before her eighty-sixth birthday.

The other three chemical analysts in this group were Rudbeck, Palmqvist, and Troili-Peterson.

SOFIA RUDBECK's reports of mineral analyses carried out at the Swedish mineralogical institute appeared in 1893 and 1895 (see bibliography). Both AUGUSTA PALMQVIST and GERDA TROILI-PETERSSON worked on atmospheric analysis in Stockholm Högskola's chemical laboratory. Palmqvist, a student of Otto Pettersson, published mainly in the 1880s and early 1890s reporting research on the measurement of atmospheric carbon dioxide and on the design of equipment needed for such analyses. She also collaborated in a marine investigation with Pettersson who, in addition to being widely recognized as a chemist, had an international reputation for his work in hydrography. Palmqvist's marine research, carried out in the summer of 1890, was a study of water at various depths in the Gullmars fjord in the Skagerrak; salt content, acidity, and the concentrations of oxygen and nitrogen were among the variables measured (see bibliography).

Gerda Troili-Petersson was born in the old port city of Västervik about 125 miles south of Stockholm on 24 May 1878.[60] A student at Stockholm Högskola in the late 1890s, she, too, collaborated with Pettersson in his investigations of carbon dioxide measurement techniques, but her special interest was bacteriology. She went on to a post at a bacteriological station at Åtvidaberg, Östergotland, about thirty miles northwest of Västervik. Between 1903 and 1914 she brought out nine papers and notes in two areas—the bacteriology of dairy products and sewage treatment by means of chemical disinfectants (especially for typhoid and cholera control). Her work on dairy products included extensive studies on bacterial classification in addition to investigations of the cheese ripening process. She also collaborated with public health physician and bacteriologist Ernst Bernhard Almquist of the Karolinska Institute in writing a general bacteriology text, *Mikroorganismena i Praktiska Livet* (1901).[61] Gerda Troili-Petersson became Almquist's second wife in 1916.[62]

Norway

Norway's geographical position and physical conditions make it, like Sweden, a natural laboratory for research in a number of fields including marine biology and botany, two areas in which Norwegian women in this survey were prominent. For marine biologists the whole Norwegian west coast, with its abundant plant and animal life that results from the warming effects of the Gulf Stream, provided outstanding research opportunities, while for botanists the spectrum of environments, from the boreal region of south Norway to the mountain glaciers and arctic tundra, offered a wide range of problems. In addition, with its communities of peasant families living for many generations in the country's isolated valleys, Norway, in the early years of the twentieth century, offered scope for studies in human inheritance and genetics, fields in which one of the biologists discussed here (Bonnevie) made important contributions.[63]

Kongelige Frederiks Universitet in Kristiania (Royal Frederiks University—Oslo University from 1939) was founded in 1811 by King Frederik VI of Denmark, Norway then being under Danish control; instruction began two years later. Until 1870 the great majority of the students were being trained for careers as clergymen, lawyers, government officials, public servants, and medical doctors. The few who studied science were for the most part destined for grammar school teaching. Norway's only university for many years, it opened to women in 1882, nine years after the Swedish universities (see above) and seven years after Copenhagen (see below). By the turn of the century women made up about 10 to 15 percent of the matriculation candidates, the majority planning to study medicine; for some time they continued to choose teacher-training institutions and commercial training colleges rather than the university.[64] Of the five Norwegian women covered here, two held teaching posts at the Kongelige Frederiks Universitet and one was conservator at Kristiania's zoological museum.

The most prominent of the group, both in her profession and in public life, was zoologist KRISTINE BONNEVIE (1872–1948),[65] Norway's first woman professor. Born in Trondheim on 8 October 1872, she was the daughter of Jacob Aall Bonnevie and his wife Anne Johanne (née Daae). Following the death of her mother when she was four, her father married Susanne Byrne. Kristine was the fifth of nine children. The Bonnevie family, descended from Honoré Bonnevie who emigrated from Antibes, Provence, to Norway in the early years of the eighteenth century, had by Kristine's time a tradition of public work that went back several generations. Her grandfather, Honoratus Bonnevie, business secretary in the government Department of Church and Education, was later mayor of Trondheim. Her father, a science graduate, was a teacher, educationist, author of mathematics textbooks, and politician, who served as a member of the Storting (parliament) for seventeen years (1880–1897); a member of the Department of Church and Education and of several parliamentary committees, he was very active in educational work and went to great effort to enhance the position of science and mathematics in Norwegian schools. Kristine Bonnevie's half-brother, Carl Bonnevie, a lawyer and a pacifist with special interests in social matters, played a prominent part in a number of governmental organizations, both national and international.

Not much is known about her childhood other than that she went to school in Trondheim and then in Kristiania after the family moved to the capital in 1886. She took the school intermediate examination in 1888 and continued her studies for university entrance at a two-year gymnasium while also teaching mathematics and physics. It is said that about this time she had access to a microscope and quickly became an expert in its use.[66] In 1892 she passed the science matriculation examination and entered the university.

She arrived at an opportune time for studies in biology, her special interest. The traditional focus on systematics was beginning to shift and, starting about 1893, subjects such as microscopy and comparative anatomy, with a strong emphasis on individual laboratory work, were being introduced. Instruction in the life sciences was still split between the faculties of medicine and mathematics–natural sciences. Her initial studies were in the former but before long she switched faculties, becoming a student of Johan Hjort, the person then laying the foundations of the biology modernization program; Hjort was also head of the Norwegian Fisheries Survey and a pioneer in the exploration of ocean currents and the biology of the North Atlantic. Within a short time, Bonnevie had begun a research project under Hjort's direction examining ascidians and hydroids brought back by the Norwegian North Atlantic Expedition of 1876–78. A joint paper with Hjort published in 1895, barely three years after she had entered the university, reported her investigations of ascidian reproductive processes. She then went on to a series of systematics studies.[67] Over the course of this work, she extended her knowledge of living forms, especially of hydroids, spending her leisure time at biological stations along the coasts[68] or with fishermen out among the islands and skerries. In 1895–1896 she substituted as conservator in the university's zoological museum and in 1900 she was formally appointed to that position.

Although her research started in the traditional area of ascidian and hydroid studies, she soon moved on to cellular-level work, the area that was to be her major interest throughout most of her scientific career. She learned cytological technique with anatomist Arnold Lang at the Zurich Federal Polytechnikum (1898–1899) and with Theodor Boveri at Würzburg University (1900–1901). Boveri (1862–1915), a superb microscopist, was known for his pioneering investigations of chromosomes, work that laid the foundation for a physical explanation of Mendel's law of heredity; he had an especially important influence on Bonnevie's biological thinking.[69] A little later (1906–1907), she spent some time in Edmund Wilson's laboratory at Columbia University, New York; Wilson also was engaged in chromosome studies.

Throughout these years, Bonnevie focused especially on sex cell development, particularly the problem, then a subject of intense debate, of how the chromosome number in the sex cells is reduced to half during the process of meiotic cell division (meiosis). Although the two Norwegian cytologists Alette and Kristian Schreiner had already suggested the process of conjugation (the parallel lining up and pairing of homologous chromosomes, or synapsis), this interpretation was by and large rejected in favor of an alternative concept of fusion. In her doctoral work, a study of germ cell development in the parasitic sea snail *Enteroxenos östergreni* (1906), Bonnevie generally favored the idea of "conjugative fusion" rather than the Schreiners's interpretation that, as developed by them in a series of classic papers, was later shown to be correct. But she stuck to her explanation and believed that she found support for it in studies she carried out subsequently on other material.

Bonnevie also investigated the problem of how chromosomes behave during the process of mitosis (the partitioning of hereditary material between two daughter cells in normal cell division) another topic then under much discussion. Here she found, among other things, that at certain stages in the process the chromosomes could be distinguished as fine spiral threads. These threads were considered by many to be an artifact, but twenty-five years later, when the existence of the spiral threads was confirmed, Bonnevie's interpretation of the picture and of the processes taking place was shown to be correct. Her successor Bjørn Føyn remarked, "Our view of chromosome behavior at the interphase stage is in the main Bonnevie's interpretation of 1908. With her publications of that year she became one of the founders of the modern idea of chromosome structure."[70] Her key papers were cited in the literature for decades.[71] It is perhaps worth pointing out that cell level research in Bonnevie's time was done with only the light microscope with its limited resolving power; the work was demanding and required tremendous skill. Not until the 1930s did the electron microscope become available and when it did it opened a new window into cell structure.

In 1910, four years after she had taken her doctoral degree, she applied for a vacant teaching position at the Bergen Museum which had begun to offer university-level instruction in 1907. However, in 1912, at the urging of the two senior zoology professors at the Kongelige Frederiks Universitet, Robert Collett and Georg Sars,[72] the Storting passed a resolution allowing women to hold official positions; the same year Kristine

Bonnevie became professor *extraordinarius* and head of the zoological laboratory at Kongelige Frederiks Universitet, the first woman professor in Norway. In 1919, following the retirement of Sars, she was appointed professor *ordinarius* (full professor), the post she held until she reached the age limit in 1937.

When Johan Hjort returned from the "Michael Sars" North Atlantic Deep Sea Expedition of 1910, he recruited Kristine Bonnevie to help with the analysis of collections brought back. Her two reports, both important phylogenetic contributions, appeared in 1913 (on Pteropoda) and 1919 (on Heteropoda).[73] By 1914, however, she was moving into a new field—human inheritance studies. She recognized that because the communities in the Norwegian mountain districts were still relatively isolated, their populations constituted valuable material for such study. Further, she was well aware of the fact that the conditions of life that had persisted in these communities for centuries were about to change with the development of transportation and communications, and that the research opportunity, if not promptly taken up, would be lost beyond recall. To provide an institutional base for the work, which would require considerable time to complete, she founded in 1916 the university's Institute for Inheritance Research, now the Genetics Institute; this she directed for twenty-two years. The most extensive of her inheritance investigations that used data from the mountain districts was her study, in collaboration with Aslaug Sverdrup, of genetic predisposition for fraternal twin births, a trait she demonstrated to be recessive. She also examined predisposition for particular physical abnormalities, including polydactyly (having too many fingers or toes) and dwarfed stature.[74]

By the early 1920s, Bonnevie had begun her study of the inheritance of finger papillary patterns (fingerprints), a subject that occupied her intensely over the next ten years and brought her name into the foremost ranks of workers in the field. Interest in fingerprint patterns had arisen among administrative authorities in the latter part of the nineteenth century because of the increasingly pressing problem of keeping track of habitual criminals in rapidly expanding populations of industrial cities. Fingerprints, being unique to a given individual and normally unchangeable, appeared to offer a means, constant across time and geographical location, whereby habitual offenders could be identified, provided a practical system of classification and record keeping was devised. At the same time scientists, particularly morphologists and statisticians, were impressed by the fact that fingerprints can be grouped into distinct, regular patterns and that these patterns are not restricted to humans but are found in a number of other animal species as well. This suggested that they might well contain information about evolutionary paths and human inheritance, an aspect of fingerprint research largely forgotten once the field became primarily the preserve of criminal justice officials.

Modern scientific studies in the area[75] were founded in large part on the work of British statistician Sir Francis Galton (1822–1911) who, in the course of his search for a reliable somatic indicator of inheritance in his biometric investigations, took the first steps toward devising a system of classification for fingerprint patterns. He designated three basic types (whorls, loops, and arches) and carried out the first statistical treatment on a sample of 500 individuals.[76] His work with siblings, particularly twins, demonstrated that papillary patterns are inherited and that some function as Mendelian dominants. However, his scheme did not allow him to accommodate borderline cases and he gradually extended it from the original three types to fifty-three. Consequently the problem of systematically distinguishing between types became frustratingly difficult and he put the work aside.

To solve the classification difficulties that had so troubled Galton, Kristine Bonnevie set about quantifying patterns by ridge counting,[77] a technique first used by Colonial Office official Sir Edward Henry in British India in the 1890s. She also greatly increased the sample size using fingerprints from 24,518 individuals (giving ten times that number of digits) supplied by the Kristiania Office of Identification. Her method gave a rational and standardized subdivision of Galton's three basic types; refinement according to "shape-index" and "twisting tendency" allowed further subdivision. The results produced a bell curve of quantitative values for this huge data collection and generally confirmed and reinforced the findings of Galton and others concerning the inheritance of pattern types. She then went on to detailed analyses of the various patterns of individuals within family groups, further demonstrating and elucidating the inherited nature of basic pattern types. Indeed, Bonnevie is said to have "accomplished more than any other person in analyzing the inheritance of fingerprint characteristics."[78]

These studies led her to the underlying question of how inherited characteristics manifest themselves at the earliest stages of an individual's development, that is, in the embryo, and the interaction of genetics with embryological environment.

Among her human embryonic finger samples she found some with vesicle- or bubble-type thickening of the epidermis of the fingerballs. This observation she connected with similar findings made by the American workers Bagg, Little, and Murray in investigations of abnormal embryonic eye and limb development in a strain of mice, descendants of animals subjected to X-ray treatment that appeared to have produced hereditary, recessive anomalies.[79] Working from the conjecture that these abnormalities followed as secondary effects from an anomaly in brain development that caused an overproduction of cerebro-spinal fluid (pockets of which could accumulate in developing extremities), she went on to a series of detailed and extensive studies on how inherited conditions, including hydrocephalus and eye, foot, and ear abnormalities, manifest themselves at the foetal stage in the mouse.[80] These were problems that occupied her for the rest of her life; even after reaching retirement age in 1937, she continued to work in the zoological laboratory, her investigations on hydrocephalus going on through much of the 1940s. A congenital endocrine disorder in man (which gives rise to a number abnormalities including dwarfed stature) is known today as the Bonnevie-Ullrich syndrome.

Kristine Bonnevie was associated with the university in Kristiania (Oslo) for her whole life from the age of twenty. In 1900, when Johan Hjort left for a position in Bergen and Bonnevie became conservator in the university's zoological museum, she took over the task begun by Hjort of modernizing the instructional program in zoology. Neither of the two senior zoologists (Collett and Sars) being especially inclined to the work, they were not loath to leave it to the young and vigorous Bonnevie. She was a good lecturer and a very dedicated teacher. Under her leadership individual laboratory work in microscopy and comparative anatomy was further expanded, and over time greatly increased laboratory space developed. She put particular emphasis on fieldwork so that students could experience "free living nature" rather than having to limit themselves to books and museum collections; she often led excursions and spent much time with students at the Drøbak Biological Station.[81]

The place of biology in the secondary school curriculum was one of her major concerns; she felt that the subject was important in awakening in everyone a sense of responsibility for the environment. Her high school biology textbook, which first came out in 1902, had its tenth edition in 1940.[82] Lectures throughout the country and the publication of books and popular articles were part of her extensive effort to bring biology to the general public. In her popular writing, she dealt not only with her own research but also covered topics in field biology such as freshwater animal life (*Dyreliv i Ferskvann*, 1934) and life along the seashore (*Dyreliv i Sjøens Strand-belter*, 1934). The task of updating and bringing out the first Norwegian edition of Alfred Brehm's great multi-volume classic, *Thierleben* (*Dyrenes Liv*, 3 vols., 1928–31) was another of her undertakings. As chair of the university broadcasting committee from 1927 to 1937, she gave many radio talks on biological topics.

Impressive as Kristine Bonnevie's academic accomplishments are, her activities were by no means confined to that sphere. She had great social commitment both within the university community and beyond. The general well-being of students, a matter the university took minimal interest in during the early decades of the century, was one of her special concerns. She felt that if they were to work successfully students needed adequate food and housing. Her efforts to improve matters in this area were of especially great value during the last years of the First World War when food scarcities were acute and many students, who had little money, were living under very difficult conditions. She had temporary living quarters established in a vacant area in the university and also worked for more permanent accommodations, including the "Study home" for girls founded in 1916 in Geitmyrsveien and a student residence in Schultz gate. In 1917 a university "Committee on Scarcity" was set up under her chairmanship and on her initiative student cafeterias were opened in basements of university buildings, first in the old city-center university area in Karl Johans gate and later at the new Blindern complex. A leader of the women students' choral union from 1897, she was also a strong supporter of the women students' club (Kvinnelige Studenters Klub) from its founding in 1902. Bonnevie played an important role in the national organization of women in higher education, the Norske Kvinnelige Akademikeres Landsforbund (NKAL, later the Norske Kvinnelige Akademikere, NKA), which was founded in Kristiania in 1920; she served as its first chairwoman.[83]

Again in the Second World War, although then retired, she took on food distribution responsibilities. In 1940 she chaired a women's committee assisting with the securing of food for Norwegian prisoners of war. When Oslo University was closed in 1943 she continued the distribution of Danish relief organization food shipments, first from her own home and later from a basement area at Blindern; the academic community and banned groups were her particular concerns. The work, which was not without considerable risk, was of tremendous importance, especially for those in hiding during this time of German occupation. Supplementing the food supply directly by growing quantities of potatoes and vegetables in fields set aside for the purpose and in her own garden was another of her contributions to the national effort.

Active in the political life of her country, Kristine Bonnevie belonged to the Frisinnede Vestre (Independent Liberals), a party that separated from the main Liberal Party (Venstre) in 1908;[84] the Frisinnede Venstre put great emphasis on individualism and intellectual freedom. Bonnevie was a director of the party, and from

1908 until 1919 its representative on the Kristiania city council; from 1916 to 1918 she served as substitute member of the Storting.[85] However, she later remarked that she had never wanted to take up political work; she felt more comfortable dealing with scientific facts than accepting the necessary compromises of party politics.[86] One of the Norwegian delegates to the first five assemblies of the League of Nations (1920–1924), she was for several years a hardworking member of the League's International Committee on Intellectual Co-operation.[87] Here she made many international contacts and came to know, among others, Marie Curie and Albert Einstein.

After the early death of her sister Honoria Bonnevie Bjerknes in 1928, Kristine Bonnevie shared a house with her brother-in-law, the eminent meteorologist Vilhelm Bjerknes. "Tante Tinni" referred to herself as the family's grandfather. She had tremendous energy and enthusiasm for work, a strong will, and a great sense of purpose. Every day was filled with activity and when one job was completed she went on with undiminished vigor to the next. Her output of scientific works is impressive by any standard (see notes 70, 74, and 80), and all of her contributions, including her popular writings, bear the stamp of her tremendous pleasure in having a part in the progress of science. Although she enjoyed both administration and teaching, she tried to find at least some time each day for research, the central theme of her life. Even when she lay in hospital in 1948 she was engrossed in her scientific work and the day before her death returned the proof sheets of her last paper.[88] Her standards for herself were demanding but she looked after her students with warmth and care and was liked and respected in turn.[89]

She enjoyed dancing, was reluctant to miss a good concert, and took pleasure in housekeeping and handcrafts, particularly sewing and embroidery, arts in which many Norwegian women excel. Her dearly loved hill farm, "Snefugl," near Mysuseter about 150 miles north of Oslo was a place often visited by friends and former students. Her view of life was strongly influenced by her technical background which she felt had given her an independent outlook not bound by conventional patterns of thought. She put her emphasis on human interests. Nevertheless, despite her truly exceptional commitment to social and civic work, she was not a "women's issues" person in the usual sense; her role in the women's movement was as her country's first female professor—a role she filled superbly.[90]

Kristine Bonnevie received the King's Gold Medal of Merit in 1920 for her work for student welfare. In 1946 she became Knight First Class of the Order of St. Olaf for her work of food distribution during the war. She was the first woman member of the Norwegian Academy of Science (elected 1911) and also belonged to several foreign academies. In 1935 she received the Academy of Science's Fridtjof Nansen award in recognition of her genetics studies. The biology building at Oslo University, Blindern, is called "Kristine Bonnevie hus." She died in Oslo on 30 August 1948, shortly before her seventy-sixth birthday. The Royal Norwegian Scientific Society's commemorative medal for 1990, its 230th year, carries her portrait; she was the society's second woman member. Marine species that bear her name include *Plumularia bonnevieae* Billard, 1907, *Cladocarpus bonneviaei* Jäderholm (1909), and *Cephalobrachia bonnevii* Massy (1917).

Zoologist EMILY ARNESEN[91] (1867–1928), the second Norwegian woman to receive a doctoral degree, was born in Kristiania on 14 June 1867, the daughter of Johannes Arnesen, a builder, and his wife Josephine Albertine (née Johnsen). Although her scientific contributions were far fewer than those of her contemporary, Kristine Bonnevie, Emily Arnesen was none the less a notable zoologist.

Her scientific education did not come easily; for the most part she had to combine her studies with work to earn her living. After passing the school intermediate examination with distinction she went on to prepare for the university matriculation examination while at the same time holding a translator's post in the Norwegian Intelligence Office. From 1889 to 1891, the matriculation hurdle being then behind her, she was governess at the parsonage in the town of Seljord in the Telemark, about 100 miles southwest of Kristiania. She also continued her studies, preparing for further examinations. For a year (1891–1892) she managed to attend the university in Kristiania where she studied science, but she then returned to a governess post, this time in the family of Otto Blehr, Norwegian minister in Stockholm.[92] While in Stockholm she took classes in zoology and botany. On her return to Kristiania she taught in various schools and also took private pupils but spent all her spare time over the next three years studying zoology at the university under Johan Hjort's guidance. She made a visit to Berlin in 1894 in an effort to gain admission to studies in a zoological laboratory there but had no success. After a further year as a governess in Spain in 1896–1897 she continued studies at the zoological laboratory in Kristiania while also teaching in Kristiania schools. Grants enabled her to get practical experience during summers at the Norwegian coastal biological stations[93], where she took part in ongoing dredging operations collecting material for coastal fauna studies. A more substantial scholarship awarded in 1901 permitted her to go to Zurich, where, as a student of anatomist Arnold Lang, she carried out a doctoral study on the fine structure of the blood vessel system in the leech[94]—basically a histological project using microscopical sections, a popular technique at the time.

After she received her doctorate in 1903 Emily Arnesen was offered a position at a German research station in Egypt but she declined in favor of spending four months at the zoological museum in Amsterdam. There, under the direction of Max Weber, head of the museum,[95] she had responsibility for part of the museum's collection of sponges, animals in which she had been especially interested since her earlier Norwegian coastal water studies. She became acting conservator of the Kristiana zoological museum in 1905; from 1911, until she retired because of poor health in 1926, she was conservator.

Emily Arnesen's research was somewhat outside the main line of Norwegian zoological investigations. Having taught herself modern microscopic technique, she initially studied the anatomy and taxonomy of some corals, publishing her first paper in 1898 (see bibliography). However it was the sponges, even today one of the less well known groups of marine invertebrates,[96] that became her primary interest. She was probably the first Norwegian worker to carry out research on this group, and because few of her countrymen have concentrated on the area since her time her contributions remain especially valuable. Her systematic papers on Norwegian sponges appeared between 1901 and 1903, that of 1903 being a particularly important contribution to the overall picture of the geographical distribution of sponges.[97] She brought out a report on budding in *Polymastia mammilaris*, Bow in 1917 and a systematic work on sponges from the 1910 "Michael Sars" North Atlantic Deep-Sea Expedition in 1920.[98]

A capable teacher, Arnesen lectured on invertebrates and animal geography at the Kongelige Frederiks Universitet from 1906 to 1913. Her guidebook for the zoological museum, the first ever published (*Zoologisk Museum. De hvirvelløse Dyr. I*, 1912), covered many invertebrate groups and presented information about collections displayed. In 1902 she brought out a short high school zoology text, *Lærebog i Zoologi for Gymnasiet*, a work that emphasized Darwinian principles, particularly the idea of the ongoing evolution of animal life. She believed strongly in the importance of starting students on independent work and problem-solving exercises from an early age, an outlook undoubtedly moulded by her own experience.

Museum work occupied much of Emily Arnesen's time and in her later years she was considerably handicapped by illness. Consequently her scientific production was not extensive. Nevertheless she was clearly a gifted and capable biologist, reliable and painstaking in her work; although "undervalued" by her fellow Norwegian zoologists during her lifetime,[99] later sponge specialists have recognized the importance of her contributions. She frequently contributed to newspapers and periodicals, writing on professional matters and travel as well as current social issues. Active in academic women's circles and a member of the executive committee of the Norwegian Women's Union, she was particularly concerned with the economic status of women and with the suffrage issue.[100]

She died in Oslo on 13 August 1928, at the age of sixty-one. Although there is still a considerable amount of confusion in sponge taxonomy and revisions are frequent, at least two species would seem to be accepted as having been discovered by Arnesen—*Gellius arnesenae* Arndt (1927) and *Anchinoe arneseni* Topsent (1913).

BIRGITHE ESMARK[101] (1841–1897) is generally considered the first Norwegian woman zoologist; she was also the first woman to receive some financial support for her work from the Kongelige Frederiks Universitet. A malacologist, she made a number of useful contributions in the 1880s to knowledge of the country's land and freshwater mollusks, both modern and fossil, particularly mollusks of the Arctic regions. The daughter of parish minister, mineralogist, and palaeontologist Hans Morten Thrane Esmark and his wife Ulrike Benedicte (Wiborg), she was born on 13 October 1841 in Brevik, about 100 miles south of Oslo on the west side of the Oslo Fjord. Her family had close connections with the university in Kristiania; her grandfather Jens Esmark, geologist, mining engineer, and professor of mining science, was one of its early faculty and her uncle, Laurits Esmark, for long conservator at the zoological museum, was professor of zoology.

Often ill as a girl, Birgithe Esmark spent some time at a health resort in Sandefjord, where she met an English woman, Mrs. Fearnley. Fearnley is said to have awakened her interest in Christian social work, a field in which she was later very active. When she was about twenty-seven she went to Madeira for two years as a cure for tuberculosis, and while on the island began to study mollusks. On her return to Norway, although she could not enroll at the university in Kristiania, which was still closed to women, she developed her interest in mollusks into a program of serious study, obtaining help from Laurits Esmark. Between 1880 and 1887 she published six papers, several of them lengthy; one (1886) was written in collaboration with Zacharias Hoyer, then conservator at the university zoological museum. Esmark was always careful to record soil type for every one of her mollusk find locations, a clear indication that she had a sense, unusual for her time, of the importance of this factor in determining species occurrence. Her one specialized paper discussed fossil mollusks of the little-studied Pisides group (the fingernail clams) collected in southern Norway. Widely distributed fresh water mollusks often found along shorelines, these animals have thin, fragile shells and can be difficult to study, some species being minute. Specimens she described came mostly from the collections of Olaf Jensen, then at the Bergen Museum, but she also carried out fieldwork herself for this study, traveling from the southern tip of Norway up the western coasts of the Skagerrak and the Oslo Fjord to Kristiania and then north through southern Gubrandsdal to northern Osterdal; she collected from limestone, gneiss, and schist formations. Her 1882 paper lists ten species and two varieties, increasing previous counts of this group by six species and one variety.

However, Birgithe Esmark was known to the general public more as a philanthropist than as a zoologist. During the late 1880s and the 1890s social reform and the amelioration of the living conditions of the working class were matters under much discussion in society and in the country's legislative bodies.[102] Esmark's efforts were focused on the working class districts of Kristiania; a talented organizer, she joined forces with Countess Ida Wedel Jarlsberg in the founding of a succession of institutions to help the poor. These included a school for needy children in Piperviken, Kristiania's dock area, and a mission to the poor with house visits and prayer meetings in neighboring parts of the city. In 1889, urged by her English friend Mrs. Fearnley, she established the Norwegian section of the Young Women's Christian Association; three years later she founded the Norwegian Women's Temperance League and for a time served as secretary for both groups. In 1893, when prohibition was becoming a major national issue, she toured the country lecturing on temperance and morality, and most likely also recruiting league members. Birgithe Esmark died in Kristiania on 2 April 1897 of cancer at age fifty-five. In 1908 a memorial statue was placed at her grave in Vor Freslers cemetery, Kristiania.

The remaining two of the five Norwegian women biologists in this survey are botanists Sophie Møller and Thekla Resvoll.

Møller collaborated with British bryologist Rev. Charles Binstead collecting mosses with him in the summer of 1886. The region they explored, around the hill-lodge of Maristuen on the western slopes of the Filefjeld, near the head of the Sognefjord, might have been expected to yield a variety of alpine species. Their total of 210 mosses found (and listed in their joint paper of 1890) was considered poor in the rarer species, but the shortfall was due in part, they felt, to bad weather and shortness of collecting time.

THEKLA RESVOLL[103] (1871–1948) was remembered especially for her exploration of the development and life cycles of arctic and alpine plants. Both she and her younger sister Hanna, also a notable botanist, held positions at the Kongelige Frederiks Universitet in Kristiania in the early years of the twentieth century. Only Thekla Resvoll is discussed fully here because only her work is listed in the Royal Society *Catalogue*; Hanna Resvoll-Holmsen did not begin to publish until 1913. Although recently rescued from obscurity, the Resvoll sisters were to a large extent forgotten for many years. However, both left an important imprint on Norwegian botany; they were both pioneers, decades ahead of their time.[104]

Thekla Resvoll was born on 22 May 1871 in Vågå, a town in the high country of inland Norway about 200 miles north and west of Oslo. Her parents were Hans Resvoll, who came from an old Vågå family, and his wife Julie Martine (née Deichmann). The Resvolls moved to Kristiania in 1878 when Hans Resvoll took a position as clerk in the Ministry of Justice, but though Thekla Resvoll lived in the capital for the rest of her life she always felt strongly tied to her native district and to the mountains.

After passing the school intermediate examination she became governess in the family of V. A. Wexelsen, parish minister in Overhalla, about 100 miles north of Trondheim; in 1892, having by then taken the university matriculation examination, she resumed her governess post in the same family but this time in Stockholm, Wexelsen having been appointed Norwegian minister in the Swedish capital. Her months in Stockholm were important, the city's lively intellectual milieu fostering and stimulating her own broad interests.

On her return to Kristiania in 1893 Resvoll began science studies at the university, concentrating on botany. The teacher who fired her imagination was Axel Blytt, well known for his work on Norwegian flora and his theories of plant immigration and adaptation through postglacial climate changes. Blytt's field excursions were legendary. He knew how to give the process of plant discovery a plant-geographical cohesion that was especially inspiring for his students; besides that he was jovial and companionable in a way that was unusual for professors at the time. Resvoll graduated, becoming *kandidat real*, in 1899 and immediately after spent a year in Copenhagen as a student of Eugenius Warming, for many decades a leader in the investigation of the flora of the Arctic and a founder of the science of the relationship between plants and their environment.[105] Her detailed morphological and anatomical study of species of the genus Ranunculus—of the buttercup family—(see bibliography), collected from all round the Arctic from Greenland to Novaya Zemlya, was carried out at Copenhagen University's botanical laboratory and at the Copenhagen botanical museum. The year in Denmark was a formative one for Thekla Resvoll; it was largely Warming's influence and this early study that led her several years later to her own research specialty—the alpine plants of the snow-line.

In 1903–1904 she studied in Munich with Karl von Göbel and in Zurich with Carl Schröter. Göbel, one of Germany's outstanding botanists, was a pioneer in work on the development of plant form and structure, particularly the modifications that particular organs can undergo as a result of change in physiological function. The equally well known Schröter, with whom she studied ecology, was at the time working on his great book *Das Pflanzenleben der Alpen*[106] which in many ways introduced a new era of plant geography. The annual excursions he led to the high Alps were a tremendous source of inspiration for his students; Thekla Resvoll ("die Thekla," as Schröter called her), with her lively intelligence and sparkling humor, became his special favorite during the two summers she spent with him in Switzerland. Her 1904 paper presented a condensed account of the vegetation, including cultivated plants, trees, and grasses, of the Swiss and northern Italian Alpine and sub-Alpine regions.[107] Much of the work was done in the Zurich and Vierwaldstätter Lake region, the Bernese Oberland, and the Rhone valley above Lake Geneva, but she also made a long, ambitious excursion over the St. Gotthard Pass and down the southern slopes of the Alps to Lakes Maggiore and Lugano.

Throughout her undergraduate years Thekla Resvoll worked as a schoolteacher. In 1901, however, thanks to help from J. N. F. Wille, professor of botany in Kristiania from 1893, she received an assistantship in the university's botanical laboratory which had been established in rented space only six years previously on Wille's initiative. In 1902 she was appointed to the newly created position of *amanuensis* (roughly equivalent to assistant professor in American terminology), the post she held until she reached the age limit and retired in 1936.

As a young woman she was considered something of a radical, in part because she wore her hair short.[108] Although never combative, she was a strong advocate of equality for women, social, political, and financial. She continued her support for the women's cause throughout her life and occasionally contributed articles to the press on women's concerns, speaking out strongly and clearly. In 1895 she married her student friend, geologist Andreas Holmsen,[109] later a mining engineer and mine inspector. They had one son, Dag. Thelka followed her husband's geographical and geological work and he shared her botanical interests; both went on Axel Blytt's field excursions and the collections they made laid the foundations of a fine herbarium in the Oslo botanical museum. They belonged to the same scientific circles at the university and their home became a meeting place for a succession of young research workers who later played an important role in Norwegian scientific and university life.

Thekla Resvoll's scientific production was not particularly extensive because of her heavy commitment to teaching, but nevertheless her major publications reported important work, meticulously and thoroughly carried out. Much of the botanical research in Kristiania in her time dealt with marine organisms; Wille, the professor, was an algologist (Axel Blytt had died unexpectedly in 1898). However, Resvoll, like her younger sister after her, chose an entirely different area, the flora of polar and Alpine regions, particularly the morphology of snowline plants in relation to the extremely short growing season. Here her contributions were groundbreaking. They are beginning to be cited in current literature, although, because she published her main monograph in Norwegian without a foreign language abstract, her findings did not receive the notice they deserved for a remarkably long time.[110]

With her background of excellent training with Warming, Schröter, and Göbel in ecology, plant geography, and morphogenesis and her own outstanding problem-solving abilities Thekla Resvoll came to her work very well prepared. However, her major undertaking was, by its very nature, a long, drawn-out project that stretched over many years of patient, demanding labor, both in the field and at the microscope; results, therefore, were necessarily slow in coming. Her work site was the upper slopes of Knutshø, a 5,545-foot peak in the Dovrefjel mountain region about ninety miles south of Trondheim and about forty miles north of Vågå, her birthplace. Year after year she spent her summers in a mountain cottage near the town of Kongsvoll, following the same regular routine, working in all weather on the highest slopes, measuring with tape and wooden pegs the retreat of the snow edge, registering the resurgence of plant life, and following its development during the short growing season. Between field measurements came days of microscope work until the next set of data and specimens had to be collected.

The well-illustrated monograph, *Om Planter som Passer til kort og kald Sommer,*[111] presented her study of fifty-six species of snow-line plants, their particular sprouting, blooming, and ripening characteristics. By scrupulously examining the minutest details of individual plants she demonstrated how they had adapted to survive the extreme conditions of their environment by acquiring a specific set of characteristics: slow growth over several years; very often a many-year maturation period before flower buds are set (for example in *Ranunculus glacialis* accumulation of carbohydrates and nutrients in the vegetative plant parts goes on over several years of photosynthesis until the surplus available energy is enough for flower production. Sometimes it can even take more than one year from bud initiation to flowering[112]); fast development of the flower shoot from the bud in the flowering year; brief flowering; fast seed ripening (a snow-line plant can bloom five days after its snow cover has melted and disperse its ripened seed seventeen days later). Resvoll defended this research as a doctoral dissertation in 1918 and received her degree the same year.

A number of additional publications described investigations along similar lines, such as her 1909 paper on mountain willows, where she demonstrated that buds set two and a half years before their opening.[113] Two especially notable papers reported another many-year study, this one on *Rubus chamaemorus* L., or arctic cloudberry, the small, herbaceous bramble common in subarctic peat bogs all across the northern hemisphere. For long a prized dessert berry in Norway and especially valuable because of its high vitamin C content, the cloudberry has been developed as a commercial crop over the last few decades, demand having far outpaced the supply from wild sources.[114] Resvoll's cloudberry study, published in 1925 and 1929,[115] was the initial, basic investigation of this dioecious plant. Another pioneering undertaking, it established a pattern for research in the area. In addition to providing a morphological and anatomical description (here again bud development is spread over more than one year), Resvoll dealt with the special peculiarities of the male and female forms, for instance the greater hardiness of the male flowers which are more resistant to frost and downpours than the female flowers, and the fact that a specially rich year weakens female plants so that they fail to blossom the following year, but male plants can bloom year after year. She stressed the necessity of many-year investigations in the same locality during the blooming period.

Thekla Resvoll's focus on individuals in a chosen population followed a tradition not found in Norwegian botany. Her contemporaries and most of the botanists who came after her were more concerned with the main lines of development of vegetation and vegetative types as a whole. As late as 1988 an international committee evaluating Norwegian botany pointed out that work in plant ecology was least well developed in individual- and population-based studies, exactly the area Thekla Resvoll pioneered. One of her biographers wondered if that was because the strongest promoter and interpreter of the field was a woman or if people were of the opinion that Thekla Resvoll had exhausted the entire topic![116]

Resvoll has the honor of having discovered at Aursundsjøen, about seventy miles south of Trondheim, a plant new to the Scandinavian peninsula, *Aster sibiricus*. Now *Aster subintegerrimus* (Trautw.) Ostenf. et Resv., it was described in 1916 by Danish professor C. H. Ostenfeld in a joint paper with Resvoll.[117] The discovery created a sensation at the time, the nearest known location for other specimens being Finland, although the plant is not uncommon to the east in the Russian Arctic. Plant geographers, despite much discussion, were unable to produce a satisfactory explanation for the isolate.

In 1923–1924, along with her son, she went on a study trip to Java, where she spent some time at the Buitenzorg Botanical Gardens and also made excursions into the tropical rain forest and to the island's volcanic peaks. Later, in the circle of her friends who came to Kongsvoll during the summers—a wide circle that included artists as well as scientists and students—she often talked of this trip, her most memorable experience. Her descriptions of life in the tropics, particularly the fascinating sounds and calls of the tropical nights, were long remembered. The Java trip was also the subject of a number of formal addresses and popular lectures.[118]

Her botanically most notable contribution from Java concerned her observations on a species of evergreen oak. An expert on the winter buds of the native trees of Norway,[119] which include two species of the oak family, she had a particular interest in the winter bud forms of the rain forest oak species. Much to her surprise, she discovered that one of these has small, tight, scale-covered winter buds, similar to those of species from the temperate zone. (The arrangement provides defense against frost and water loss in the temperate zone, where the oaks are considered to have originated.) Her observation was the first of scale-covered buds on trees of the tropical forest, and it raised interesting questions concerning plant migration and the retention of characteristics superfluous in a new location.[120]

Thekla Resvoll's popular writing covered a wide range of topics. For more than twenty years she was Amund Helland's botanical collaborator in the publication of his great multivolume *Norges Land og Folk*.[121] A massive work covering eighteen counties and two cities (Bergen and Kristiania), the project had been started by others but by the time the first five counties were completed all the members of the original team were either dead or exhausted! Helland undertook to finish the task—a project of twenty years involving the preparation of thirty-nine volumes. Thekla Resvoll's carefully prepared and easily read sketches of plant life in the thirteen Norwegian counties she covered did much to further the growing interest in botany throughout the country, especially among school teachers. Based partly on existing literature and partly on her own research, these sketches dealt for the most part with plant topography and flowers but also touched on ecological concerns. Geologist Helland, one of the prominent people in the university community, had a very high opinion of Resvoll's scientific abilities; he is reported to have said that he never would have believed a woman could go so far.[122] Her botany textbook for secondary schools, *Biologi for Gymnasiet. 1: Botanik,* first appeared in 1902 and ran to ten editions, the last published in 1934. She also wrote a short work for nonspecialist readers, *Norske Fjellplanter* (Norwegian Mountain Plants, 1934). Especially popular was the long series of botanical articles she brought out in the newspapers *Aftenpost* (1913–1923) and *Tidens Tegn* (1924–1929). Written in a pleasant and personal style, these reached a wide audience; her notes on spring plants were particularly well received.

As *amanuensis* in the Botanical Laboratory, Thekla Resvoll was responsible for microscopy instruction in plant anatomy for science students. Her courses were models of good planning and careful preparation, but more than that she brought to her teaching, both in the laboratory and on the many field excursions she led, her own distinct liveliness and sparkle. Her enthusiasm for her subject was catching and although she never directed students specializing in botany, she all the same over a period of many years had a central role as popular mentor in practical work in botany; her influence on the next generation of professional botanists and on a vast number of the country's high school science teachers was very great. For many years she also had charge of microscopy courses for medical and pharmacy students. In fact she was responsible for all the botanical instruction and examination of pharmacy students for a considerable period. Following the opening in 1932 of the new Pharmaceutical Institute at Blindern she taught some of the institute's botany laboratory courses. From 1935, when the university's botanical laboratory moved to its Blindern building, she had charge of the two large plant anatomy laboratories that accommodated the ever-increasing numbers of science students. From 1932 to 1938 she served as an examination judge (*sensor*).

Not of a very robust constitution, she was in poor health when she retired in 1936 but the farewell party held for her at Blindern the following year was long remembered by friends and colleagues, several of them her former students, who came to salute her with speeches and song. An outstanding teacher and an innovative and productive research botanist,[123] Thekla Resvoll, an unassuming person, well deserved her place in the Kristiania university community, then only just beginning to open to women academics. Indeed, one of her obituarists remarked that her obvious research talent had clearly been misemployed in elementary teaching.[124] She did, however, become a member of the Norwegian Academy of Science. After retiring she still spent her summers in the mountains at Kongsvoll, often visiting the small botanical garden of mountain plants that she herself had laid out and for many years cared for at the Kongsvoll mountain railway station. She died at her home in Bestun, in the parish of Ulleren about thirty miles northeast of Oslo on 14 June 1948, shortly after her seventy-seventh birthday, following a year of severe illness. In 1954 a group of her friends and admirers had a memorial stone in her memory placed in the Kongsvoll station garden. Carved from light, almost jade-green steatite, it was patterned after a plant leaf design on a tombstone from the 1790s in the churchyard at Vågå, her birthplace.

Currently, a century after Resvoll began her work on plants of the snow line, arctic ecosystems are of special interest because of the need to understand the impact of environmental changes, such as global warming and the "greenhouse" effect.[125] However, even some recent studies that follow the same pattern as that set by Resvoll and by and large come to the same conclusions about the life cycles of arctic and alpine plants omit reference to her work;[126] the language barrier would seem to be not yet entirely overcome.

Denmark

The ancient University of Copenhagen, inaugurated in 1479, began, like Uppsala University, as a foundation of the Roman Catholic church, a typical late-mediaeval university with the traditional four faculties—theology, law, medicine, and arts. Following a hiatus in the early sixteenth century because of the upheavals of the Reformation, it was reestablished in 1537 as the ideological center of the new Danish Lutheran State Church, its most important function for the next two centuries being the training of ministers for that church. Much of the work of the arts faculty consisted of preparing students for studies in the other three faculties, especially the faculty of theology. Changes introduced in the late eighteenth century formed the framework for the transformation from a classical university to a modern institution for education and research. Although the Polyteknisk Laeranstalt (now the Technical University of Denmark) was founded in 1829, Copenhagen University remained the country's only university until the twentieth century.[127] All of its faculties except theology opened to women students in 1875; the event appears to have proceeded smoothly without problems of harassment.[128] However, as in most other countries at the time, girls had to overcome the hurdle of no gymnasia being open to them. Hence the number of women entering the university was very low until about 1890, although it grew at an increasing rate from then on.[129]

Five Danish women who published articles in technical journals before 1901 are included in this survey—entomologist Sofie Rostrup, physicist and science historian Kirstine Bjerrum Meyer, geographical commentator Astrid Andersen, botanist Emma Hallas, and chemist Dagmar Schou.

SOFIE ROSTRUP,[130] née JACOBSEN (1857–1940), was one of the most distinguished and productive of Denmark's early women scientists. For all practical purposes she might well be described as the founder of agricultural entomology in Denmark. Working during the closing years of the nineteenth century and the first quarter of the twentieth, she laid a solid foundation that served as the base for all later advances in the field.

She was born at Sønderholm by Nibe in Nordjylland on 7 August 1857, the daughter of parish minister Frederik Theodor Jacobsen and his wife Pouline Elisabeth Cathrine (née Blicher) who came from the family of the much-honored early nineteenth-century Danish poet Steen Steensen Blicher. From an early age Sofie was an eager student; her father taught her Latin and Greek and she grew up with a broad, humanistic outlook and a wide range of interests. As a young woman she knew many of the leading Danish literary figures of the 1880s. Nevertheless, the subject that most attracted her attention was natural history.

She trained first for a career in teaching, passing the qualifying examinations for community school teachers in 1879. Continuing her studies, she took the gymnasium leaving examinations in 1884 and enrolled at the university. She concentrated on biology, particularly insect studies, and under the guidance of the distinguished entomologist Jørgen Christian Schiødte acquired a sound basic training. Her degree (*magisterkonferens*) in natural history with zoology as major subject was awarded in 1889; it was the first given to a woman in Denmark.[131] While a student at the university she taught in Copenhagen schools, an outstanding and well-liked instructor. Her teaching continued until 1919 and she also served over a long period as examiner in the preliminary examinations for university external students (*privatister*).

In 1883 she married zoologist H. J. Hansen but was divorced seven years later; she remarried in 1892. Ove George Rostrup, her second husband, was the son of botanist Emil Rostrup of the Copenhagen Veterinary College.[132] An internationally recognized expert on agricultural plants, Emil Rostrup brought out over a period of twenty years (1885–1905) a series of annual reports on disease and insect damage to farm crops.[133] Under his influence Sofie Rostrup, whose earlier studies were on insect galls (see bibliography), became interested in applied agricultural entomology.

With some state support and continuing help from her father-in-law she undertook, from about 1896, a pioneering program of investigations. Traveling the country by bicycle (her favorite conveyance) and train, observing the details of local conditions, she studied problems in the field and established the close contact between farmers and research workers that would be fundamental to successful pest control efforts. Such collaboration between academically trained biologist and farmer was new and innovative at the time; she had to find her own way and build up her knowledge slowly.[134] These being the days before the introduction of chemical insecticides, her advising had to be based on a thorough knowledge of the insects involved. Patient, persistent, and endowed with outstanding powers of observation, she was very much a field biologist; on her rounds she filled her record books with notes and her jars with specimens that she studied at home. Always direct, clearly capable, and very practical in her approach, rather than a "learned lady" from Copenhagen, she won the confidence of farmers and was accepted by them as a friend and helper, one of themselves who, although there to advise them, was also eager to get their views and benefit from their experience and insight.

By the early years of the century, partly because of unusually serious insect depredations in 1905, the Danish farming community was becoming increasingly conscious of the serious threat insects posed. This realization led to the establishment in 1907 by the Danish farmers' cooperative association of an Experiment Station for plant pathology with mycological and zoological consultants. These were respectively, M. L. Mortensen (botanist) and Sofie Rostrup. Rostrup continued as zoological consultant when the organization was taken over by the state in 1913. The work of the group was limited however, facilities consisting of a couple of rooms in a large house in the township of Lyngby, just north of Copenhagen, and a small experimental plot. Sofie Rostrup did most of her indoor work in her own home. She was appointed head of the organization's zoological section in 1919. By 1922 a spacious, modern building was provided for the station near the Sorgenfri Palace in Lyngby[135] and thereafter activities were expanded greatly.

For many years, circumstances were difficult for Sofie Rostrup because of her need to earn an income by school teaching, but nevertheless she brought tremendous energy and enthusiasm to her entomological work and in it found great enjoyment. Year round she received inquiries from farmers and agriculturalists, all of which she answered with scrupulous care. While schools were in session, her consulting, research, and writing was done in the early mornings and in the evenings; as soon as the school year was over, she set out on her rounds of the country. She took part in the whole range of activities of the agricultural community—plant-breeding congresses, field trips, courses, and expositions—always with great interest and unflagging energy. She remained head zoologist at the state Experiment Station until she retired in 1927 at age seventy.

Although much of her work was advising and consulting, over the course of about three decades Sofie Rostrup published at least fifty technical papers, a number of more popular articles, information booklets, and the very important book, *Vort Landbrugs Skadedyr* . . . (*Insects and other Agricultural Pests*), which was brought out in 1900 in the Royal Danish Association for Rural Economy series of publications for farmers and agriculturalists. *Landbrugs Skadedyr* was based largely on her early field investigations; a comprehensive, well-organized, and clearly written manual, it presented information on the occurrence and habits of species injurious to agricultural crops in Denmark, together with methods for their control. It was well illustrated and easy to use, giving both systematic and common names. Groups such as gastropods (snails), nematodes (round worms), and myriapods (centipedes) were included. Interest in the field being already considerable, the book was well received. A second edition was brought out in 1904 and a third in 1907; a revised, much expanded fourth edition appeared in 1928.[136] In 1931, when a German translation of the fourth edition appeared, it reached a much wider audience; hailed as the best book in the field, it brought its author international recognition. A fifth and final edition appeared in 1940.

Among the investigations Sofie Rostrup carried out to answer questions about insect life history and control were several that were specially important. One of the first insects she studied in detail was the frit fly (*Oscinis frit*, now *Oscinella frit*), which in 1904 was the major cause of the drop in value by twelve and a half million krone of the Jutland oat crop. As early as 1897 she reported her observation that wild oats are more resistant to attack than the cultivated varieties, and in 1907 she pointed out that sowing time greatly affects the severity of the onslaught; further, she demonstrated that the insect overwinters, not as a pupa in seed as had been assumed, but in the larval stage in pastureland plants. Her work on *Hylemya coarctata* (the wheat bulb fly, now *Delia coarctata* [Fallen]) showed that the species did not, as had been thought, lay its eggs on plants but in earth, especially on fallow ground, and on this basis she suggested control measures which in practice gave excellent results. She also carried out life cycle studies and explored control measures during the serious infestations of the cabbage moth (*Plutella cruciferarum*, probably the diamondback moth) in 1905, 1911, and 1914. Her experiment of spraying with tobacco leaf extract to control attacks (1911 and 1914) on beets, beans, and a number of other crops and ornamentals by the aphid *Aphis papaveris* (now *Aphis fabae* Scopoli, the black bean aphid[137]) was especially noteworthy. Life cycle studies on the foxtail midge (*Oligotrophus alopecuri*, now *Dasineura alopecuri*) and the cabbage fly larvae (Chortophila spp.), and her demonstration that the "carrot psylid" *Trioza viridula* (Psyllidae family) was the cause of carrot leaf curl, were likewise very valuable contributions.

Although agricultural concerns occupied most of her time, after 1917, when horticultural investigations were incorporated into the work of the state Experiment Station, she also studied problems in this area. These included the control of fruit tree infestations by modern winter spraying methods, measures which led to a notable increase in Danish fruit production from about 1925.

Typically Sofie Rostrup's papers presented not only life histories but also information about a whole range of factors influencing the resistance of plants; these included weather, soil type, degree and duration of attack, and cultivation method.[138] Solidly based on her considerable biological insight and wide knowledge, many were classic studies, important from the point of view of the development of the field as a whole. However, because almost all of her publications were in Danish without, until latterly, a foreign language abstract, her work did not become widely known outside Scandinavia until after the German edition of her book appeared in 1931.[139] In addition to her studies on particular insects she brought out, from 1905 until the early 1920s, a series of annual surveys of insect damage to agricultural crops in Denmark.[140]

A sociable woman with a good sense of humor, Sofie Rostrup was an excellent contact person between the research institutions and the farming community. That the state Experiment Station had from the beginning a particularly close working relationship with the country's farmers was in large measure due to her. She joined the Copenhagen Entomological Society in 1906 and often presented papers at its meetings, including her annual surveys of the situation in agricultural entomology. Her talks were regularly received with great interest by the group's academic entomologists as well as those working primarily on the applied side. In 1937, on her eightieth birthday, she was given honorary membership in the society in recognition of her many contributions to the field. The Stockholm Entomological Society made her an honorary member in 1928. On her retirement in 1927 the state recognized Sofie Rostrup's service to Danish agriculture and through that to the country as a whole by awarding her the gold medal of merit, the highest distinction that could be conferred on a woman. At that time she also received the Tagea Brandts Reiselegat, an award for outstanding women in Denmark;[141] she used this to visit the Mediterranean countries whose natural beauties and art she much admired but had never until then had the time and means to visit. Sofie Rostrup died in Frederiksberg (a district of Copenhagen) on 25 January 1940 at age eighty-two, after a year of illness. Her large collection of insect galls was donated to the zoological museum.

KIRSTINE BJERRUM[142] (1861–1941), the daughter of Niels Janniksen Bjerrum, a farmer, and his wife Christiane (née Degn), was born in Skærbæk, North Schleswig, on 12 October 1861. When she was nineteen, both her parents by then dead, she moved to Copenhagen to live with her brother Jannik Bjerrum and his family. Jannik Bjerrum was an ophthalmologist, later professor.

Kirstine Bjerrum studied at Nathalie Zahle's teachers' seminary[143] and in 1882 passed the women teachers' examination (*lærerinde examen*). She had developed a strong interest in the sciences, stimulated by the frequent presence in her brother's home of a number of his young academic friends, among whom was the physicist Adolph Meyer. By means of a tuition arrangement organized by Zahle she, along with a few other young Copenhagen women, continued studies and prepared for the university entrance examinations. Coming from southern Jutland and considered "peasant born," Kirstine Bjerrum initially encountered some prejudice among the young ladies from the capital,[144] but she quickly became a close friend of fellow student Hanna Adler, forming a relationship that was to have an important influence on much of her later career. She and Adler both passed the entrance examinations in the summer of 1885 and enrolled at the university. She married Adolph Meyer in November of the same year.

Bjerrum Meyer and Adler were the first Danish women to take the university course in physics. Their teachers included a number of influential men—the astronomer Thorvald Nicolai Thiele, physicist Christian Christiansen, known particularly for his broad understanding and appreciation of the history and development of his field, and geometer Hieronymus Zeuthen, who wrote a history of mathematics in the sixteenth and seventeenth centuries that is still considered a useful work. Kirstine Bjerrum Meyer's strong interest in the history of natural philosophy and physics most likely had its origin in her early contacts with these men. She received her degree (*magisterkonferens*) in physics in 1892.[145]

Her scientific and scholarly work falls into three fairly distinct parts: first, early studies in thermodynamics, in particular the laws governing change of state; second, general considerations of the concept of temperature and the history of the development of temperature measurement, investigations that followed directly from her thermodynamics work; third, studies of the lives and work of natural philosophers and physicists of the past.

Her first paper, published in 1900 in *Zeitschrift für Physikalische Chemie* (see bibliography), resulted from her entry to a competition set in 1894 by the Danish Academy of Sciences. The subject was the laws representing the behavior of gases, namely the van der Waal's equation of state for real gases and the generalized Law of Corresponding States which follows from it; these had been put forward by Dutch physicist Johannes van der Waals in 1873 and 1881. The competition called for a demonstration of the validity of the law and an explanation of the exceptional behaviour of some materials using already-available data. Bjerrum Meyer's entry won the gold medal. She developed the subject further in a second paper published ten years later—a study of standardized vapor pressure curves for a number of organic compounds.[146] Using a modification she proposed, she effectively demonstrated that the Law of Corresponding States holds at the lowest temperatures.[147]

The examination of temperature measurement from a historical perspective, Bjerrum Meyer's doctoral dissertation research carried out under the guidance of Christian Christiansen, was published in 1904.[148] Her full study of the topic, completed in 1909, was widely regarded as an important contribution to the history of physics and merited a German translation (1913).[149] She also brought out in 1909 and 1910 several shorter papers reporting parts of her doctoral research, including discussions of the contributions to temperature measurement of the seventeenth-century Danish scholar Ole Rømer.[150] Rømer, best known for his work in astronomy and the theory of light, was one of the subjects of Bjerrum Meyer's later studies as well.[151]

In 1920, in collaboration with the Royal Danish Scientific Society, she brought out a three-volume work on the life and contributions of Hans Christian Ørsted (1777–1851),[152] professor of physics at Copenhagen University, for some years secretary of the Danish Academy of Sciences, and a leader in bringing science to the general public. Bjerrum Meyer's account marked the centenary of Ørsted's 1820 publication of his observations linking electricity to magnetism, work which set the stage for the subsequent rapid development of the field of electromagnetism.[153] Her 1931 essay in *Nature*[154] discussed the importance of Ørsted's work on the scientific thinking of British physicist Michael Faraday and the influence that Faraday in turn had on Ørsted. Ørsted was particularly impressed by the impact made by Faraday's Royal Institution lectures presenting the latest scientific discoveries to the general public; these inspired Ørsted to take up his own extensive educational work. Bjerrum

Meyer's last major publication was her short biography of the seventeenth-century Danish geometer and natural philosopher Erasmus Bartholin, widely known for his studies on the double refraction of light and for his writings introducing and explaining to a wider audience the new geometrical methods of René Descartes.[155]

For almost half a century, Kirstine Bjerrum Meyer was much involved in the development of the Danish educational system, first as a student in the 1880s, pioneering university education for women in the sciences, then as a science teacher, especially in girls' schools, and as a leader in the practical training of specialist teachers. The early years of her career coincided with a period of considerable adjustment in the secondary school system, including teacher training; a major curriculum reorganization was required following the addition, in 1883, of modern languages, history, and sciences to what had previously been a program centered on the study of classical languages and culture. From 1885 until 1909 (except for 1892–1893) she taught in the various divisions of Zahle's school (in 1892–1893 in other Copenhagen schools). Between 1900 and 1939 she was an instructor in the school founded and led by her long-time friend Hanna Adler, a soundly academic and very progressive institution, the first in Denmark to offer common instruction for both boys and girls; Bjerrum Meyer taught mathematics and physics at the upper level (university entrance),[156] but her interests and her influence on the development of teaching methods reached far beyond her specialty. Her 1902 book *Lille Naturlære* broke new ground in early science teaching. A *censor* (external examiner) for teacher training colleges, she was also a gymnasium inspector and from 1919 until 1923 a member of the schools' examination commission; in 1928 she served as chairperson of the external examiners committee and as *censor* in physics for the university entrance examinations. Her award of the King's gold medal of merit came in 1920 in recognition of this work.

Although her physicist husband died in 1896, Bjerrum Meyer remained closely integrated into the Copenhagen physics research community whose members included some very distinguished figures. Her connections were not only professional, through her scholarly writings, but social through her colleague Hanna Adler, aunt of physicist Niels Bohr, and through her nephew, physical chemist Niels Bjerrum.[157] One of the group that founded the journal *Fysisk Tidsskrift* (1902), she edited that publication until 1913. Kirstine Bjerrum Meyer died in Hellerup, Copenhagen, on 28 September 1941, a month before her eightieth birthday.

Little information has been collected about the remaining three Danish women in this survey—Andersen, Hallas, and Schou.

Astrid Andersen's 1897 paper in the journal of the Swedish Society for Anthropology and Geography (see bibliography) reported observations made during a seven-week, 500-mile trip in the summer of 1893 when she accompanied her father on his annual official tour as inspector for north Greenland. That year he visited settlements in the region of the island of Disko, which they sailed round, and Umanaks fjord, almost 300 miles north of the Arctic Circle on Greenland's west coast. Astrid Andersen presented a day-by-day diary-style account of the trip, describing the country in its summer beauty, the small coastal settlements, and the Eskimo inhabitants. Emma Hallas[158] (1849–1926) was born in Copenhagen on 1 June 1849. A specialist in cryptogamic botany, she published occasional taxonomic notes on new species.[159] She died on 16 March 1926. Dagmar Schou's 1897 paper on organo-platinum compounds reported work done in the laboratory of the Farmaceutisk Læreanstalt (College of Pharmacy) in Copenhagen.

Finland

Work by three women from Finland (then part of imperial Russia) is listed in the bibliography; they were Lidiia Sesemann, a chemist; Maria Øhberg, whose contributions were in geography and mathematics education; and Nanny Lagerborg, Baroness Cedercreutz, who studied physics and mathematics at the Stockholm Högskola in the late 1880s.

Like a considerable number of the young, middle class Russian women of her generation, LIDIIA SESEMANN, who was from Viborg, went to Switzerland for her advanced education. A student in Zurich from 1869 to 1874,[160] she was probably the first woman (from any country) to receive a doctoral degree in chemistry. Hers was awarded by Zurich University in the spring of 1874, following presentation of a dissertation on dibenzylacetic and homotoluic acids (see bibliography).[161]

Sesemann is mentioned briefly in the memoirs of Franziska Tiburtius, a German medical student at Zurich in the 1870s. Tiburtius described her as a sensible Finlander, blonde, very cultured and well-educated, a bit stiff and pedantic, but possessing a good sense of humor; she remembered particularly Sesemann's leave-taking party at which most of the guests were Russian.[162] Little is known about her later career, except that she was in Leipzig from at least 1877 until 1888, working at the physical chemistry laboratory there, and by 1889 had moved to Florence, Italy.[163]

MARIA ÖHBERG[164] (b. 1873) studied at the University of Helsingfors in the 1890s. Her detailed analytical correlation of water height at Kronstadt with sunspot activity over the years 1841–1886 appeared in the journal of the Finnish Geographical Society; the work, published in 1894, was a contribution to investigations into the rising or falling of the Gulf of Finland coastline. The same year she brought out a lengthy paper on solutions of differential equations in the annual publication of the Helsingfors high school for boys and girls (see bibliography).

NANNY LAGERBORG[165] (1866–1950) was born in Cannes on 19 March 1866, the daughter of Captain Alexander Vilhelm Lagerborg and his wife Nanny Franzén. The Lagerborgs were an old Finno-Swedish family, prominent over the course of several centuries in the military and in government. Nanny had a cosmopolitan education studying in her late teens and early twenties at Geneva University, Stockholm Högskola, and the Sorbonne. At the Högskola in the late 1880s, she was a student of physicist Knut Ångstrom in the Institute of Physics; two papers, one on the variation of refractive index with temperature (1888) and the other on the problem of the motion of a solid body about a fixed point (1890), reported her research under his guidance. In 1892 she married Baron Emil Valdemar Cedercreutz and from then lived much of the time in Helsingfors.

Between 1912 and 1944 Baroness Cedercreutz published a succession of literary works, some under pseudonyms (Ala and Bengt Ivarson). These included collections of short stories, poems, and tales for young people. Her stories have the special interest of being written in Finländssvenska, an old Scandinavian dialect of which she was very fond. She also brought out articles and books on travel and natural history, such as her *Från Alp och Hav* on the flora of her childhood home, the French Riviera, which she knew well and greatly loved. Her easy, elegant style won praise from contemporary reviewers.[166] Baroness Cedercreutz died in Helsingfors on 8 December 1950 in her eighty-fifth year.

Summary

Of these twenty-nine early Scandinavian women scientists, seven (24%) were active in research over many years and made notable contributions to their fields. Particularly outstanding were Kristine Bonnevie, the Norwegian zoologist; Astrid Cleve von Euler, the Swedish palaeobotanist; Thekla Resvoll, the Norwegian botanist; and Sofie Rostrup, the Danish agricultural entomologist. The original research contributions of both Bonnevie and Resvoll were of lasting value, Cleve von Euler's great diatom flora of Sweden and Finland remains a basic reference work for research in the area, and Rostrup's insect pests manual, a pioneering work, was in use for half a century after its first publication. The two Swedish zoologists Augusta Ärnbäck-Christie-Linde and Albertina Carlsson were also productive scientists who had admirable publication records, as had Danish physics historian and educationist Kirstine Bjerrum Meyer. Norwegian sponge specialist Emily Arnesen, Swedish mineral analyst Naima Sahlbom, and her fellow countrywoman Gerda Troili-Petersson, although they published less than the seven already mentioned, also made very creditable contributions, especially Arnesen.

Of the ten, two—Bonnevie and Resvoll—had university teaching posts, Bonnevie as full professor and Resvoll as *amanuensis* (assistant professor); the third Norwegian—Arnesen—also had a formal position, as conservator in the Kristiania zoological museum. Two of the Swedish women carried out their work at research institutions, Ärnbäck-Christie-Linde in a "non-permanent" capacity at the Riksmuseum, Carlsson, somewhat informally at the Zoological Institute at Stockholm Högskola although for much of her career she also worked as a high school teacher; Cleve von Euler did her research without institutional backing, earning a livelihood for the most part by high school teaching; Sahlbom established her own commercial laboratory; Troili-Petersson was employed by a non-university laboratory. Of the two Danes, entomologist Rostrup held a government research position in the latter part of her career, although for most of her life she, too, earned a living as a schoolteacher; physics historian Bjerrum Meyer, although very much a part of the Copenhagen academic community, was a secondary school teacher and educationist.

Scandinavian women began to take their place in the science research community in the last decades of the nineteenth century (Figure 1-1), mainly in the 1880s and 1890s when university-level training to the doctorate level became more accessible. More than half of those whose careers began before 1900 were Swedish; they produced two thirds of the papers. Norwegians and Danes produced about 17 percent and 10 percent respectively (Figure 1-2, a and b). By far the largest contribution was in the biological sciences, particularly botany and zoology, which together make up almost two thirds of the total. Work in chemistry, much of it chemical analysis, accounts for another 21 percent (Figure 1-2d).

Notes

1. Sif Johansson, "The University of Stockholm at the Turn of the Century—A Chance for Female Students," *Proceedings of the International Conference on the Role of Women in the History of Science, Technology and Medicine in the 19th and 20th Century*, Veszprém, Hungary, August 15–19, 1983, vol. 2, 53–57.

2. Johansson, "University of Stockholm," 53. There was also a considerable need for teachers, a Swedish law of 1842 having mandated that all children, boys and girls, receive primary education in reading and writing.

3. See for instance the works of writer Ellen Key, one of the leading and more radical Swedish social reformers and feminists of the time, in *Lexikon der Frau*, 2 vols. (Zürich: Encyclios Verlag A. G., 1953), vol. 2, 207; and Ronald William DeAngelis, "Ellen Key: A Biography of the Swedish Social Reformer," Ph.D. diss., University of Connecticut, 1978 (University Microfilms International, Ann Arbor, Michigan, 1979).

4. Remaining restrictions that significantly limited Swedish women's professional work for several decades typically were removed by pressure from female professional organizations (such as the Female Doctors' Association), rather than by the action of feminist groups; see Johansson, "University of Stockholm," 54.

5. Johansson, "University of Stockholm"; Sten Lindroth, *A History of Uppsala University 1477–1977*, trans. Neil Thomkinson (Stockholm: Uppsala University, 1976), especially 172–73.

6. An additional pre-1900 woman research worker, perhaps Swedish but not discussed here, was Julia Maria Brinck. Brinck is listed as having a home address of "Helsingborg, Sweden" (Hälsingborg, Sweden?) when she was a medical student at Bern University in 1886 (Barbara Bachmann and Elke Brendenahl, "Medizinstudium von Frauen in Bern 1871–1914," Inaugural diss., Medical Faculty, Bern University, 25 June 1990). It was earlier assumed that Brinck was British. She studied under the direction of Hugo Kronecker, head of the Physiological Institute at Bern, and received her degree in 1887. Her three papers on muscle nutrition and synthetic processes in cells appeared in British and German journals in the late 1880s. In 1890 she received a British Medical Association research award, the first given to a woman; see Mary R. S. Creese, *Ladies in the Laboratory? American and British Women in Science, 1800–1900: A Survey of Their Contributions to Research* (Lanham, Md.: Scarecrow Press, 1998), 174, 399.

7. Johnsson, "University of Stockholm," 54.

8. Sif Johansson, "Stockholms Högskola för 100 år sedan—ett naturvetenskapligt universitet med plats för kvinnor," *Kvinno-vetenskaplig Tidskrift*, no. 4, (1984), 42–47; and Fredric Bedoire and Per Thullberg, *Stockholm University: A History*, trans. Alan Tapsell (Stockholm: Stockholm University, 1987). Notable research was done at Stockholm Högskola before the turn of the century in mathematics by Gösta Mittag-Leffler and Sofia Kovalevskaia, in chemistry and physics (electrolytic dissociation) by Svante Arrhenius, and in hydrography by Otto Pettersson. Some financial responsibility for the institution was assumed by the state from 1940, and it was nationalized in 1960. It is now the largest of Sweden's universities.

9. Maj-Britt Forin, "Astrid Cleve von Euler," *Svensk Botanisk Tidskrift* 62, no. 4 (1968): 549–64; obituary, *Geologiska Föreiningen i Stockholm, Förhandlingar* 90 (1968): 327–28 (Proceedings); Inge Fischer-Hjalmars, "Women Scientists in Sweden," in *Women Scientists: The Road to Liberation*, ed. Derek Richter (London: Macmillan, 1982), 118–35, on 121–22; *Svenska Män och Kvinnor: Biografisk Uppslagsbok*, vol. 2, (1944), 112; *Lexikon der Frau*, vol. 1, 659; Johansson, "Stockholm's Högskola," 43–44; and private information from Dr. Leo von Euler, grandson of Astrid Cleve von Euler.

10. See for instance the works of writer Ellen Key, one of the leading and more radical Swedish social reformers and feminists of the time, in *Lexikon der Frau*, 2 vols. (Zürich: Encyclios Verlag A. G., 1953), vol. 2, 207; and Ronald William DeAngelis, "Ellen Key: A Biography of the Swedish Social Reformer," Ph.D. diss., University of Connecticut, 1978 (University Microfilms International, Ann Arbor, Michigan, 1979).

11. The middle daughter, Agnes Cleve Jon-And, became an artist whose paintings remain in moderate demand at current art auctions in Stockholm; the youngest, Célie Cleve Brunius, became a journalist in Stockholm.

12. See Astrid Cleve and Lilly Paijkull, "Genom Lule Lappmark" [Through Lule Lappmark], *Svenska Turistförening Årsskrift* (1896): 227–40.

13. See bibliography and also "Beiträge zur Flora der Bären-Insel. 1. Die Diatomeen," *Bihang till Kongl. Svenska Vetenskaps-Akademiens Handlingar* 26, afd. 3 (1901), no., 10, 25 pp.

14. "Zum Pflanzenleben in nordschwedischen Hochgebirge. Einige ökologische und phänologische Beiträge," *Bihang till Kongl. Svenska Vetenskaps-Akademiens Handlingar* 26, afd. 3 (1901), no. 15, 105 pp. Cleve returned to problems of adaptation to environment in upland regions in a 1911 paper, "Till frågen om jordmånens betydelse för fjällväxterna" [On the question of the significance of soil type for high mountain plants], *Svensk Botanisk Tidskrift* 5 (1911): 402–10.

15. *Studier öfver några svenska växters groningstid och förstärkningstadium* (Uppsala: Akademisk Avhandling, 1898).

16. "Contributions to the knowledge of ytterbium," *Öfversigt af Kongl. Vetenskaps-Akademiens Förhandlingar* 58 (1901): 573–618; *Zeitschrift für Anorganische Chemie* 32 (1902): 129–63; and "On organic peroxides. A brief report," *Svensk Kemisk Tidskrift* 14 (1902): 94–97.

17. J. R. Partington, *A History of Chemistry,* 4 vols. (London: Macmillan, 1964), vol. 4, 908–9.

18. The von Eulers's five children were Sten (b. 1903), Ulf (b. 1905), Karin (b. 1907), Georg (b. 1908), and Birgit (b. 1910). Ulf von Euler was awarded the 1970 Nobel Prize in medicine and physiology (jointly with Julius Axelrod and Sir Bernard Katz). Karin von Euler translated into Swedish a considerable number of works of fiction from several languages.

19. See "Ueber die Einwirkung von Amylnitrit auf ß-Aminocrotonsäureester," *Berichte der Deutschen Chemischen Gesellschaft* (hereafter *Ber.*) 36 (1903): 4246–53; "Ueber die Bildung hydrirter Osotriazole," *Ber.* 36 (1903): 4253–56; "Ueber α Isonitroso-ß-nitrosaminobuttersäureester," *Ber.* 37 (1904): 47–49; "Notizen über ammoniakalische Platinverbindungen," *Ber.* 37 (1904): 2391–95; "Über die Bildung von aliphatischen Isonitrosoverbindungen und Osotriazolen aus ß-Aminocrotonsäureester," *Arkiv för Kemi* 1 (1904): 111–26; "Über die Konstitution unserer Isonitroso-nitrosamine Verbindungen und deren Derivate," *Arkiv för Kemi* 1 (1904): 159–66; "Zur Kenntnis der Assimilationsvorgänge. 2. Kondensationsprodukte des Formaldehyds," *Arkiv för Kemi* 1 (1904): 347–55; "Enzymologische Notizen," *Arkiv för Kemi* 1 (1904): 365–69; "Zur Kenntnis des Formaldehyds und der Formiatbildung," *Ber.* 38 (1905): 2551–60, "Nachtrag," *Ber.* 39 (1906): 36–39; "Zur Kenntnis der Zuckerbildung aus Formaldehyd," *Ber.* 39 (1906): 39–45, *Arkiv för Kemi* 2 (1906), no. 10, 11 pp.; and *Arkiv för Kemi* 2 (1906), no. 15, 7 pp; "Über die Bildung von i-Arabinoketose aus Formaldehyd," *Ber.* 39 (1906): 45–51; "Naphtochinon-anile und Derivate derselben," *Ber.* 39 (1906): 1041–45; "Fermentreaktionen im Presssaft fettreicher Keimlinge," *Zeitschrift für Physiologische Chemie* 51 (1907): 244–58; and "Alkohole und Harzsauren im Blattfirnis von *Alnus glutinosa,*" *Ber.* 40 (1907): 4760–64.

20. Anna Maria Sandström (1854–1913), a well-known Swedish educationist, founded and directed a school, Sandströms Skola, and a seminary for training women high school teachers (*Lexikon der Frau,* vol. 2, 1139).

21. "Das Bacillariaceen-Plankton in Gewässern bei Stockholm," *Archiv für Hydrobiologie und Planktonkunde* 6 (1910): 209–12; "Das Bacillariaceen-Plankton in Gewässern bei Stockholm. 2. Zur Morphologie und Biologie einer pleomorphen Melosira," *Archiv für Hydrobiologie und Planktonkunde* 7 (1911–12): 119–39, 230–61; "Das Bacillariaceenplankton in Gewässern bei Stockholm. 3. Über Geminden des schwachsalzigen Wassers und eine neue Charakterart derselben," *Archiv für Hydrobiologie und Planktonkunde* 7 (1912): 500–14; and "Vattnet i sjöar och vattendrag inom Stockholm och i des omgivningar II. Planktonundersökningar: Diatomacéplankton," *Bihang Stockholms stads Hälsovårdsnämnds årberättelse, 1911* (1912), 59–133.

22. "Quantitative plankton researches in the Skagerrak. Pt. 1," *Kungl. Svenska Vetenskaps-Akademiens Handlingar* 57, no. 7 (1917): 1–130. See also the three Swedish Hydrographical Biological Commission plankton research reports: *Svenska Hydrografisk Biologiska Kommissionens berättelse för arbetsåret 1 Maj 1915–30 April 1916. Speciella undersökningar II. Planktonundersökningar* (Göteborg, 1916); *Sv. Hydrog. Biol. Komm. berättelse för arbetsåret 1 Maj 1916–30 April 1917. Rapport öfver de planktonbiologiska arbetena* (Göteborn, 1917); and *Sv. Hydrog. Biol. Komm. berattelse for arbetsåret 1 Maj 1917–30 April 1918. Planktonundersökningar* (Göteborg, 1918).

23. See for example the following (titles are given in English as listed in the American Chemical Society's *Chemical Abstracts*): "Relation to lignin of crude resin and tannic acid in spruce needles," *Svensk Pappers-Tidning* 24 (1921): 191–95; "Chemical constituents of pine leaves II," *Teknisk Tidskrift* 51 (1921): 35–38, 47–52; "Constitution of cellulose and cellobiose," *Chemiker Zeitung* 45 (1921): 977–78, 998; "The lignin-like resins and tannins of spruce-needles," *Cellulosechemie* 2 (1921): 123–35, and 3 (1922): 1–7; "Some experiments on the separation of fatty acids and resin acids in the liquid resin from the sulfite (pulp) process," *Arkiv för Kemi, Mineralogi och Geologi* 8 (1921), no. 4, 21 pp; "The carbon dioxide problem," *Svensk Kemisk Tidskrift* 34 (1921): 119–35; "Quantitative composition of carboniferous woods," *Cellulosechemie* 4 (1923): 1–11; and "Sources of error in the determination of the lignin content of wood by the method of Schmidt and Graumann," *Svensk Kemisk Tidskrift* 35 (1923): 100–107. Additional lignin studies were reported in the Forestry Association journal *Skogsvårdsförening Tidskrift* 21 (1923): 112–32; 346–59.

24. (With I. Bergh) *Kemien och dess Tillämpningar, kortfattad Lärobok för den grundläggande Undervisningen och för Självstudium. II. Djur- och Växtkemi* (Stockholm, 1918); "Petroleum och stenkol," *Svensk Kemisk Tidskrift* 31 (1919): 190–93; "Petroleum och stenkol. II," *Svensk Kemisk Tidskrift* 32 (1920): 30–32; and *Det underbara Grundämnet Selen* (Uppsala: n.p., 1925).

25. The retreat of the last (Weichselian) ice sheet from Estonia and southern Sweden was followed by the formation of an ice-dammed lake, the Baltic Ice Lake, which covered parts of southern and eastern Sweden and extended as far north as Lake Ladoga in Russia; successive outlets were through the valleys of southern Sweden to the ocean on the west. The Baltic Ice Lake's final drainage (about 12,700 years before the present) via the Lake Vänern basin in southern Sweden was followed by an influx of salt water into the Baltic giving the Yoldia Sea stage with a lower shore line. Subsequent land uplift narrowed the connection to the ocean leading to the formation (about 9,500 B.P.) in Sweden and Finland of a second freshwater lake, Ancylus Lake; the latter also had an opening to the west, first through south-central Sweden and then further to the south and southeast. Finally, the fall in the lake level via its more southerly outlets coupled with the rise in ocean level produced a Baltic-ocean connection and the marine Litorina Sea stage began (about 8,000 to 8,500 B.P.); this gradually evolved into the contemporary Baltic Sea—see Joakim Donner, *The Quaternary History of Scandinavia* (Cambridge: Cambridge University Press, 1995), especially chapter 13. For recent estimates of dates for the stages of the breakup and retreat of the major ice masses, see M. J. Siegert, J. A. Dowdeswell, J.-I. Svendsen, and A. Elverhøi, "The Eurasian Arctic during the last Ice Age," *American Scientist* 90 (2002): 32–39.

26. H. Hyvärinen, "Definition of the Baltic Stages," in *Problems of the Baltic Sea History*, eds. J. Donner and A. Raukas (Helsinki: Suomalainen Tiedeakatemia, 1988), 7–11, on 7.

27. Hyvärinen, "Definition of the Baltic Stages," 9.

28. See Joakim Donner, *The Quaternary History of Scandinavia* (Cambridge: Cambridge University Press, 1995), especially chapter 13. For recent estimates of dates for the stages of the breakup and retreat of the major ice masses, see M. J. Siegert, J. A. Dowdeswell, J.-I. Svendsen, and A. Elverhøi, "The Eurasian Arctic during the last Ice Age," *American Scientist* 90 (2002): 32–39.

29. Astrid Cleve von Euler's writings on the history of land–sea relations during the Quaternary era include the following: "Försök till analys av Nordens senkvartära nivåförändringar," *Geologiska Föreiningen i Stockholm, Förhandlingar* (hereafter *Geol. För. Stockholm, Förh.*) 45 (1923): 19–107; "Svar på Lektor U. Sundelius inlägg i frågen om nivåförändringarna i Kalmartraken," *Geol. För. Stockholm, Förh.* 45 (1923): 448–52; "Våra kvartärgeologer och de senkvartära landrörelserna. Ett svar på kritiken av mitt inlägg i oscillationsfrågan," *Geol. För. Stockholm, Förh.* 46 (1924): 516–33; "On ice-lake discharges and shorelines at Mt. Billingen," *Uppsala. Geological Institution. Bulletin* 19 (1925): 245–47; "Skalbankar och nivåförändringar i Skageracksområdet," *Geol. För. Stockholm, Förh* 48 (1926): 321–56; "'Baltiska issjöns tappning'. Några anmärkningar till Dr. Simon Johanssons avhandling med denna titel," *Geol. For. Stockholm, Förh.* 48 (1926): 463–77; (with A. L. Backman) "Om Litorinagränsen i Haapavesi och diatomacéfloran på Suomenselkä," *Acta Societatis pro Fauna et Flora Fennica* 60 (1937): 209–44; "Alleröds och senglacial utveckling i det södra Östersjöområdet," *Geol. För. Stockholm, Förh.* 61 (1939): 424–28; "Das letztinterglazia Baltikum und die Diatomeenanalyse," *Beihefte zum Botanischen Centralblatt*, abt. B, 60, no. 3 (1940): 287–334; "Natur und Alter der Strandflächen Finnlands. Eine spätquartäre Rekonstruktion," *Zeitschrift für Geschiebeforschung und Flachlandsgeologie* 18 (1943): 139–227; "Die Diatomeen als quartärgeologische Indikatoren. Eine kritische Übersicht," *Geol. För. Stockholm, Förh.* 66 (1944): 383–410; *Om den sista landisens bortsmältning från södra Sverige, den s.k. Baltiska issjön, tappningarna vid Billingen och Degerfors samt Vätterns historia. Jämte ett tillägg om norska isgränser* (Stockholm: privately printed, 1946); "Zur Geographie der Eiszeit und zur spätglazialen Entwicklung des Nordens, besonders Schonens," *Uppsala. Geological Institution. Bulletin* 32 (1948): 65–104; "Was war der Svea älv?," *Regiae Societas Scientiarum Upsaliensis, Nova Acta* s. 4, 17 (1957): 1–54; "Det tvetydiga Yoldia havet. Ett avskedsord till Nordens geologer" [The questionable Yoldia Sea. A farewell word to Scandinavian geologists], *Institute of Quaternary Geology, Uppsala*, stencilled manuscript, (1965), 8 pp.

30. "Die Kieselalgen des Tåkernsees in Schweden," *Kungl. Svenska Vetenskaps-Akademiens Handlingar* 11 (1932): 1–254.

31. See "The diatoms of Finnish Lapland," *Societas Scientiarum Fennica Commentationes Biologicae* 4, no. 14 (1934): 1–154; and "Det Gotiglaciala havets utbredning samt maximihöjd i Nordfinland och i trakterna omkring Vita havet," *Terra* (*Geografiska Sällskapets i Finland Tidskrift*) 46 (1934): 91–112.

32. "Die Diatomeen von Schweden und Finnland, I," *Kungl. Svenska Vetenskaps-Akademiens Handlingar* s. 4, 2 (1951), 162 pp.; "Die Diatomeen . . . , V," *Kungl. Svenska Vetenskaps-Akademiens Handlingar* s. 4, 3 (1952), 153 pp.; "Die Diatomeen . . . , III," *Kungl. Svenska Vetenskaps-Akademiens Handlingar* s. 4, 4 (1953), 255 pp.; "Die Diatomeen . . . , II," *Kungl. Svenska Vetenskaps-Akademiens Handlingar* s. 4, 4 (1953), 158 pp.; "Die Diatomeen . . . , IV," *Kungl. Svenska Vetenskaps-Akademiens Handlingar* s. 4, 5 (1955), 232 pp. For fairly recent references to these monographs, see, for instance, Barbara Thulin, *Diatoms and Palaeoenvironment at Ottenby, Southern Öland, Southeastern Sweden*, Striae monograph series, ed. Lars-König Königsson (Uppsala: Societas Upsalensis pro Geologia Quaternaria, 1987).

33. "New contributions to the diatomaceous flora of Finland," *Arkiv för Botanik* (Uppsala, Stockholm) 14 (1915): 1–81; (with A. L. Backman) "Die fossile Diatomeenflora in Österbotten," *Acta Forestalia Fennica* 22 (1922): 1–74; "Om diatomacévegetationen och dess förändringar i Säbysjön, Uppland, samt några dämda sjöar i Salatrakten," *Sveriges Geologiska Undersökning* s. C, 309 (1922): 49–76; "Diatomacéerna i Öresjö vid Borås," *Svensk Botanisk Tidskrift* 29 (1935): 45–56; "Subfossila diatomacéer från Åland," *Memorandum. Societatis pro Fauna et Flora Fennica, 1933–34* 1 (1935): 289–322; "Undersökningar över Öresund, 24. Sundets Plankton. 1. Sammansättning och fördelning," *Lunds Universitets Årsskrift* n. f. 2, 33 (1937): 1–50; "Våra sjöars *Melosira*-plankton," *Botaniska Notiser* (1–3) (1938): 143–70; "Bacillariaceen-assoziationen im nördlichsten Finnland," *Acta Societatis Scientiarum Fennicae* n.s. B 2 (1939), no. 2, 41 pp.; "Zur fossilen Diatomeenflora Österbottens in Finnland," *Acta Societatis pro Fauna et Flora Fennica* 62 (1939): 1–22; "Svenska sötvattensformer av diatomacésläktet *Rhizosolenia* Ehrenberg," *Botaniska Notiser* (1940): 77–96; "*Fragilaria Du Rietzi* nov. sp., eine neue Aufwuchsalge der Schären Södermanlands," *Botaniska Notiser* (1940): 247–52; "Alttertiäre Diatomeen und Silicoflagellaten im inneren Schwedens, gefunden und gezeichnet von Åke Berg, beschreiben von Astrid Cleve-Euler," *Palaeontographica* 92 (1941): 165–200; "*Coscinodisci* et *Thalassiosirae* Fennosoeciae. Eine kritische Übersicht," *Botaniska Notiser* (1942): 231–78 (this work led to a revision and redefinition of these two genera); "Vad år *Melosira moniliformis* (Mill.) Ag.?," *Arkiv för Botanik* 30 (1942): 1–8; "List of Diatoms from Lago Frey," appendix to paper by B. Collini, *Uppsala. Geological Institution. Bulletin* 30 (1943): 221–25; "Süsswasserdiatomeen aus dem Feuerland. Von Prof. V. Auer gesammelt," *Acta Geographica* (Helsingfors) 10 (1948): 1–61; (with I. Hessland) "Vorläufige Mitteilung über eine neuentdeckte Tertiärablagerung in Süd-Schweden," *Uppsala. Geological Institution. Bulletin* 32 (1948): 155–82; "Litoral Diatoms from Tristan da Cunha," *Norwegian Scientific Expedition to Tristan da Cunha, 1937–38* 18 (1949): 1–30; and (with I. Th. Rosenquist and I. Hessland) "Über einige Diatomitablagerungen und weissliche minerogene Feinsedimente aus den Südlichen Skanden," *Regiae Societas Scientiarum Upsaliensis, Nova Acta* s. 4, 15 (1951): 1–44.

34. A son-in-law recalled that the first time he saw Astrid Cleve was on top of a full hay wagon.

35. Forin, "Cleve von Euler," 555.

36. See, for example, "Om tiden för den första bebyggelson i Scandinavien" [On the time of the first settlement in Scandinavia], *Ymer* 49 (1929): 135–52; "Viken—urhemmet i Norden" [The inlet—original home in Scandinavia], *Göteborgs Handels och Sjöfartstidning,* 7 October 1935; "Sverige återbefolkas efter sista istiden" [Post-Ice Age repopulation of Sweden], *Dagsposten* (Stockholm), 22 June 1950; "På dristig vikingafärd i okänt Sverige" [On bold Viking expeditions into unknown Sweden], *Dagsposten* (Stockholm), 30 August 1950; and *Istider och manniskor i Norden* [The Ice Age and Man in Scandinavia] (Uppsala: privately printed, 1960). For additional publications by Cleve von Euler, both scientific and popular, see Florin, "Cleve von Euler," Bibliography, 556–64.

37. See Joakim Donner, *The Quaternary History of Scandinavia* (Cambridge: Cambridge University Press, 1995), especially chapter 13. For recent estimates of dates for the stages of the breakup and retreat of the major ice masses, see M. J. Siegert, J. A. Dowdeswell, J.-I. Svendsen, and A. Elverhøi, "The Eurasian Arctic during the last Ice Age," *American Scientist* 90 (2002): 32–39.

38. Biographical information about these five botanists came mainly from Th. O. B. N. Krok, *Bibliotheca Botanica Suecana* (Uppsala and Stockholm: Almqvist and Wiksells, 1925). For Andersson, see also *Svenska Män och Kvinnor,* vol. 1, (1942), 102 (entry for Nils Johan Andersson); for Lovén *Svenska Män och Kvinnor,* vol. 5, (1949), 79–80 (entry for Otto Christian Lovén) and *Svenska Män och Kvinnor,* vol. 6, (1949), 522–23 (entry for Carl Gustav Santesson); for Söderström, *Svenskt Författarlexikon, 1900–1940,* vol. 1 (1942), 410 (entry for Johan Echard Fredrik af Klercker), and A[xel] Klinckowström, *Klinckans Minnen; skildringar och erinringar från mitt forskar- och färdeliv i när och fjärran* (Stockholm: Albert Bonniers Förlag, 1933), 2 vols., vol. 1, 204; and for Olbers Wester, *Svensk Botanisk Tidskrift* 6 (1912): 931.

39. Edla Söderström af Klercker, *Vett och dårskap; kulturskilnigar från 1700-talets England* (Stockholm: H. Geber, 1918).

40. Charlotte Westling was a student of morphologist and taxonomist Wilhelm Leche at the Stockholm Zoological Institute in the 1880s. She published a notable paper on peripheral nerve systems in 1884 and an anatomical study on echidna (spiny anteaters of Australia and New Zealand) in 1890. She does not appear to have published further work under the name Westling.

41. *Svenska Män och Kvinnor,* vol. 2 (1944), 98–99; Swedish Museum of Natural History, Stockholm, Archives and Department of Invertebrate Zoology.

42. Baron Axel Klinckowström wrote in his memoirs published in 1933 of how, after returning to a docent position at the Zoological Institute after some years' absence, he found that Ärnbäck-Andersson's mere presence as a colleague on the teaching staff spoiled the atmosphere. The valued old camaraderie had gone and talk had to be a little more circumspect. For Baron Axel, the change was no small matter. ["Hon var både hygglig och kunnig och varken så ung eller vacker att det nämnvärt störde, men hon var i alla fall fruntimmer, och antingen hon nu ville eller inte—jag ä alldeles säker om att hon *inte* ville—rubbade hennes blotta närvaro totalt våra cirklar. Med den gamla fria, octvungna samtalstonen var det förbi . . . kort sagt, det var inte längre gemytligt som förr och i längden blev också arbetet lidande därav." (She was both pleasant and competent and neither young enough nor beautiful enough to disturb, but still she was a woman, and whether she wanted to or not—I am quite sure that she did not—her very presence completely changed our group. The old free tone of discussions was gone . . . in short, it was no longer as genial and sociable as before and ultimately the work also suffered as a result.)]—Klinckowström, *Minnen,* vol. 1, 216–17. For another specific example of this kind of difficulty during the initial stages of female entry into academic laboratory settings, see the case of physiologist Marion Greenwood at Cambridge University in the 1880s and 1890s (W. G. Hardy, "Mrs G. P. Bidder," *Nature* 130 (1932): 689–90). Similar strong reactions to the arrival of women are well known in the story of medical training—see for instance the cases of Blanche Edwards and Augusta Klumpke in the chapter on Frenchwomen.

43. Augusta Ärnbäck-Christie-Linde, "On the Development of the Teeth of the Soricidae; An Ontogenetical Inquiry," *Annals and Magazine of Natural History* s. 8, 9 (1912): 609–25—reprinted in the multivolume collection *Teeth of Mammals—Structure and Development* (1865–1931); "Der Bau der Soriciden und ihre Beziehungen zu anderen Säugetieren. Pt. 2," *Gegenbauer's Morphologisches Jahrbuch* 44 (1912): 261–96 (dissertation research). While a student of Leche, she also published, "A collection of bats from Formosa," *Annals and Magazine of Natural History* s. 8, 2 (1908): 235–38.

44. "On the first premolar in *Talpa europaea,*" *Acta Zoologica* 25 (1944): 251–62.

45. "Northern and Arctic invertebrates in the collection of the Swedish State Museum (Riksmuseum). 8. Tunicata. 1. Styelidae and Polyzoidae," *Kungl. Svenska Vetenskaps-Akademiens Handlingar* 63 (1922), no. 2, 62 pp.; "Northern and Arctic invertebrates in the collection of the Swedish State Museum (Riksmuseum). 9. Tunicata. 2. Botryllidae; reproductive organs of *Metrocarpa* (n. gen.) *leachi* Savigny and *Botryllus scholosseri* Pallas," *Kungl. Svenska Vetenskaps-Akademiens Handlingar* 63 (1923). no. 9, 25 pp.; "Northern and Arctic invertebrates in the collection of the Swedish State Museum (Riksmuseum). 11. Tunicata. 3. Molgulidae and Pyuridae," *Kungl. Svenska Vetenskaps-Akademiens Handlingar* s. 3, 4 (1928): 1–101; "Northern and Arctic invertebrates in the collection of the Swedish State Museum (Riksmuseum). 12. Tunicata. 4. Cionidae, Ascidiidae, Agnesiidae, Rhodosomatidae," *Kungl. Svenska Vetenskaps-Akademiens Handlingar* s. 3, 13 (1934): 4–91; "Asidiacae. I," *Further Zoological Results, Swedish Antarctic Expedition, 1901–1903* 3 (1938): 1–54; and "Ascidiacae, II," *Further Zoological Results, Swedish Antarctic Expedition, 1901–1903* 4 (1950): 3–41.

46. "Chilean tunicates. Ascidians from the Guaitecas Islands," *Arkiv för Zoologi* (Stockholm) 21A, no. 6 (1929): 1–27.

47. These include the following: "A new styelid tunicate from Norway," *Bergens Museum Aarbog, 1919–1920, Naturvid Raekke* (1920): 3; "On the reproductive organs of the ascidian *Kükenthalia borealis* (Gottschaldt)," *Proceedings of the*

Zoological Society (1921): 187–96; "A remarkable styelid tunicate from Spitzbergen," *Annals and Magazine of Natural History*
s. 9, 7 (1921): 347–52; "A remarkable pyurid tunicate from Novaya Zemlya," *Arkiv för Zoologi* (Stockholm) 16, no. 15
(1924), 7 pp.; "Notes on *Botrylloides aurea* M. Sars," *Nyt Magazin för Naturvidenskaberne* (Kristiania) 61 (1924): 285–93;
"On the generic names *Botrylloides* Milne Edwards and *Metrocarpa* Ärnbäck," *Arkiv för Zoologi* 17B, no. 12 (1925), 5 pp.;
"On the Genus Tylobranchion Herdm. with Supplementary Notes on *Rhopalaea norvegia* Ärnb.," *Arkiv för Zoologi* 18A,
no. 35 (1927), 20 pp.; "On *Styela nidrosiensis* Ärnb.," *Arkiv för Zoologi* 18A, no. 36 (1927), 5 pp.; "Further Notes on
Metrocarpa aurea Sars," *Arkiv för Zoologi* 21A, no. 17 (1930), 4 pp.; "Notes on *Cnemidocarpa mortenseni* Hartm. and
Molgula kiaeri Hartm.," *Arkiv för Zoologi* 22A, no. 1 (1931), 10 pp.; "A New Styelid Tunicate from the Bohuslän Coast,"
Arkiv för Zoologi 22A, no. 12 (1931), 6 pp.; "On *Xenomolgula mira*, gen. et sp. n., and *Lithonephrya complanata* Alder and
Hancock," *Arkiv för Zoologi* 23A, no. 5 (1931), 14 pp.; (with P. Brien) "Remarques au sujet du post-abdomen des
Cionidae," *Annales de la Société Royale Zoologique de Belgique* 63 (1932): 41–53; "A Notable Case of Relation in Perophora,"
Arkiv för Zoologi 28B, no. 9 (1936), 6 pp.; "On the Reproductive Organs of *Holozoa cylindrica* Lesson," *Discovery Reports*
25 (1949): 109–11; and "On the Situation of the Heart in Tylobranchion," *Annals and Magazine of Natural History* s. 12,
3 (1950): 977–81.

48. "Contributions to the tunicate fauna of Norway; with notes on *Polycitor giganteus* Sleuiter," *Arkiv för Zoologi* 18A,
no. 1 (1925), 22 pp.; and "A list of ascidians collected off Gothenburg," *Göteborgs Kungl. Vetenskaps- och Vitterhetssamhälles
Handlingar* s. 4, 27, no. 2 (1923), 19 pp.

49. *Svenska Män och Kvinnor,* vol. 2 (1944), 98.

50. "Tunicata, Ascidiacae" (1952), in *Zoology of the Faroes,* 3 vols., eds. R. Spärck and S. L. Tuxen (Copenhagen: Andr.
Fred. Høst and Søn, 1928–71), vol. 3, pt. 1 (1971), article 61, 52 pp.

51. *Svenska Män och Kvinnor,* vol. 2 (1944), 34.

52. See bibliography and "Ueber die Tragulidae und ihre Beziehungen zu den übrigen Artiodactyla," *Acta Zoologica*
(Stockholm) 7 (1926): 69–100.

53. See "Ueber die systematische Stellung von *Eupleres goudoti*," *Zoologische Jahrbücher. Abt. für Systematik, Geographie
und Biologi der Thiere* 16 (1902): 217–36; "Ist *Otocyon caffer* die Ausgangsform des Hundegeschlechts oder nicht?" *Zoologische Jahrbücher. Abt. für Systematik, Geographie und Biologi der Thiere* 22 (1905): 717–54; "Die genetischen Beziehungen
der Madagassischen Raubtiergattung Galidia," *Zoologische Jahrbücher. Abt. für Systematik, Geographie und Biologi der Thiere*
28 (1910): 559–602; "Uber *Cryptoprocta ferox*," *Zoologische Jahrbücher. Abt. für Systematik, Geographie und Biologi der Thiere*
30 (1911): 419–70; "On the fossil carnivores *Cynodictis intermedius* and *Cynodon gracilis* from the phosphorites of Quercy,"
Proceedings of the Zoological Society (1914): 227–29; "Ueber *Arctictis binturong*," *Acta Zoologica* (Stockholm) 1 (1920):
337–80; "Ueber *Ailurus fulgens*," *Acta Zoologica* (Stockholm) 6 (1925): 269–305.

54. "Die Macroselididae und ihre Beziehungen zu den übrigen Insectivoren," *Zoologische Jahrbücher, Abt. für Syst. Geog.
und Biol . . .* 28 (1910): 349–400; and "Über die Tupaiidea und ihre Beziehungen zu den Insectivora und den Prosimiae,"
Acta Zoologica 3 (1922): 227–70.

55. "Antomie der Marsupialregion bei den Beutelthieren," *Zoologische Jahrbücher, Abt. für Anatomie und Ontogenie der
Thiere* 18 (1903): 489–506; "Zur Anatomie des *Notoryctes typhlops*," *Zoologische Jahrbücher, Abt. für Anatomie und Ontogenie
der Thiere* 20 (1904): 81–122; "Über *Dendros lagus dorianus*," *Zool. Jahrbücher, Abt. für Syst., Geog. und Biol . . .* 36 (1914):
547–617; "Zur Morphologie des Hypsiprymnodon moschatus," *Kungl. Svenska Vetenskaps-Akademiens Handlingar* 52, no.
6 (1915); and "Ueber den Bau des *Dasyuroides byrnei* und seine Beziehungen zu den übrigen Dasyuridae," *Acta Zoologica*
(Stockholm) 7 (1926): 249–75.

56. *Svenska Män och Kvinnor,* vol. 6, (1949), 465; Stockholm Stadsarkiv.

57. Much later, Sahlbom published a second paper reporting early work done at the Stockholm Mineralogical Institute,
"Analysen von swedischen Glaukoniten," *Uppsala Geological Institution Bulletin* 15 (1917): 211–12.

58. Naima Sahlbom, "Die Kapillaranalyse kolloider Losungen," Thèse, Neuchâtel University (Dresden: T. Steinkopff,
1910), also published in *Kolloidchemische Beihefte* 2 (1910): 79–140, and jointly with F. Fichter in *Verhandlungen der Naturforschenden Gesellschaft in Basel* 21 (1910): 1–24.

59. Naima Sahlbom (with H. Sjögren), "Undersökningar af radioaktiviteten hos svenska källvatten," *Arkiv för Kemi,
Mineralogi och Geologi* 3, no. 2 (1907), 28 pp.; and "Om radioaktiviten hos svenska källvatten och dess samband med de
geolgiska förhållandena," *Arkiv för Kemi, Mineralogi och Geologi* 6, no. 3 (1916), 52 pp. Sahlbom's first publication on
radioactivity in thermal springs was probably her short note with University of Berlin chemist Friedrich Willy Hinrichsen
on investigations of springs in Aachen, "Notiz über die Radioaktivität der Aachener Thermalquellen," *Berichte der Deutschen
Chemischen Gesellschaft* 39 (1906): 2607–8.

60. Krok, *Bibliotheca Botanica Suecana.*

61. *Mikroorganismena i Praktiska Livet. Bacteriologiens Utveckling och Nutida Ståndpunkt* [*Microorganisms in Practical
Life: The Development and Present Position of Bacteriology*], (Stockholm: Palmquist, 1901). Troili-Petersson's post-1900
journal articles include the following: "Studien über die Mikroorganismen des schwedischen Güterkäses," *Centralblatt für
Bakteriologie, Parasitenkunde und Infektionskrankheiten* abt. 2, 11 (1903): 120–43; "Bemerkungen zu der Arbeit von A.
Rodella, 'Einiges über die Bedeutung der direkten mikroskopischen Präparate für das Studium des Käseriefungsprozesses',"
Centralblatt für Bakteriologie, Parasitenkunde und Infektionskrankheiten abt. 2, 15 (1905): 430; (with Ernst Almquist) "Quan-
titative Desinfektionsversuche," *Centralblatt für Bakteriologie, Parasitenkunde und Infektionskrankheiten* abt. 1, 39 (1905),

Originale: 477–82; "Studien über das Wachstum des *Bakterium typhosum* und des *Vibrio cholerae* in sterilisierten und nicht-sterilisierten Abfallstoffen und Abwässern," *Centralblatt für Bakteriologie, Parasitenkunde und Infektionskrankheiten* abt. 1, 45 (1907), Originale: 5–15; "Fortgesetzte Studien über das Wachstum einiger pathogener Bakterien in sterilisierten und nichtsterilisierten Abfallstoffen," *Centralblatt für Bakteriologie, Parasitenkunde und Infektionskrankheiten* abt. 1, 48 (1908), Originale: 129–35; "Studien über in Käse gefundene glycerinvergärende und lactatvergärende Bakterien," *Centralblatt für Bakteriologie, Parasitenkunde und Infektionskrankheiten* abt. 2, 24 (1909): 333–42; "Experimentelle Versuche über die Reifung und Lochung des schwedischen Güterkases," *Centralblatt für Bakteriologie, Parasitenkunde und Infektionskrankheiten* abt. 2, 24 (1909): 340–60; "Zur Kenntnis der schleimbildenden Bakterien. Das auf *Drosera intermedia* gefundene *Bakterium droserae*," *Centralblatt für Bakteriologie, Parasitenkunde und Infektionskrankheiten* abt. 2, 38 (1913): 1–8; and "Einzelkultur von langsam wachsende Bakterienarten, speziell der Propionsäurebakterien," *Centralblatt für Bakteriologie, Parasitenkunde und Infektionskrankheiten* abt. 2, 42 (1914): 526–28.

62. *Svenska Män och Kvinnor,* vol. 1, (1942), 66–67 (entry for E. B. Almquist).

63. See Kristine Bonnevie, "Introduction," in *Natural Science in Norway* (Geneva: League of Nations Committee on Intellectual Co-operation, 1923), 2nd series. *Intellectual life in various countries: Norway.*

64. Ida Blom, "'. . . uden dog at overskride sin naturlige Begrænsning'—kvinner i Akademia 1882–1932," in *Alma Maters Døtre: Et Århundre med Kvinner i Akademisk Utdanning,* eds. Suzanne Stiver Lie and Maj Birgit Roslett (Oslo: Pax Forlag A/S, 1995), 19–32, on 19 (the first woman student at the university in Kristiania was Cecilie Thorensen, who matriculated on 8 September 1882). See also John Peter Collett, "Vendepunkter i norsk universitetshistorie," in *Universitet, Samfunn og Politikk: 18 Innlegg om Universitets- og Vitenskapshistorie,* eds. A. F. Andersen and Guri Hjeltnes (Olso: Forum for Universitetshistorie, Universitetet i Oslo, 1997), 91–106, on 98.

65. *Norsk Biografisk Leksikon,* vol. 2 (1925), 85 (see also other Bonnevie family entries, 79, 80, 81–84); Bjørn Føyn, "Minnetale over Professor Kristine Bonnevie," *Det Norske Videnskaps-Akademi i Oslo. Årbok 1949,* (Oslo: Jacob Dybwad, 1950), 71–84; Hjalmer Broch, *Zoologiens Historie i Norge: till Annen Verdenskreig* (Oslo: Akademisk Forlag, 1954), 123–27; Gunnar Sundnes, "Kristine Bonnevie (1872–1948)," *Det Kongelige Norske Vitenskabers Selskab, Forhandlinger* (1990): 29–33; Rasmus Lyngnes, "Professor Dr. Kristine Bonnevie," *Naturen* (Bergen), no. 2 (1961): 67–73; Anette Bonnevie Wollebæk, "Kristine Bonnevie (1872–1948): vår første kvinnelige professor," in *Alma Maters Døtre* 183; Arne Semb-Johansson, "Bonnevie, Kristine Elisabeth Heuch," in *Norsk Biografisk Leksikon,* vol. 1, (1999), 402–3; *Lexikon der Frau,* vol. 1, 479; and *Das Frauenstudium an den Schweizer Hochschulen,* ed. Schweizerischer Verband der Akademikerinnen (Zürich: Rascher & Cie, 1928), 45–46.

66. Sundnes, "Kristine Bonnevie," 29.

67. See bibliography and also "Ascidiae simplices og Ascidiae compositae. Fra Nordhavs Expeditionen," *Den Norske Nordhavs Expedition 1876–1878, Zoologi* (Kristiania: Grøndahl & Søn, 1896), 23, 16 pp.; "Om Knopskydningen hos Distaphia magnilarva og Pyrosoma elegans," *Den Norske Nordhavs Expedition 1876–1878, Zoologi,* 23, 15 pp.; and "Hydroida," *Den Norske Nordhavs Expedition 1876–1878, Zoologi,* 26, 103 pp.

68. One of these stations was at Drøbak on Oslo Fjord; another, run by the Bergen Museum, which even then was known internationally for its work in marine biology, was on the small island of Herdla, just north of Bergen.

69. Boveri had a number of women students about this time, including two Americans, Marcella O'Grady (1863–1950) and Nettie Maria Stevens (1861–1912). Stevens, a notable cytologist who went on to carry out important studies on the chromosomal determination of sex, was in Würzburg in 1901–1902. O'Grady, who worked in Boveri's laboratory in 1896–1897, was his first female student; following their marriage in 1897, she continued to collaborate in his research. She returned to the United States some years after his death, and from 1927 until 1943 led the science department at Albertus Magnus College in New Haven, Connecticut (then an undergraduate college for women)—see Margaret R. Wright, "Marcella O'Grady Boveri (1863–1950); her three careers in biology," *Isis* 88 (1997): 627–52. For Stevens, see Patricia C. Gross and John P. Steward, "Nettie Maria Stevens, cytologist," *Sandstone & Tile* (Stanford Historical Society) 17 (1993): 3–12.

70. Føyn, "Minnetale," 73 ["Vårt syn på kromosomenes forhold i interfasekjernen er i dag i hovedsaken Bonnevie's oppfatning fra 1908. Med sin avhandling fra dette år har hun vaert med på å grunnlegge den moderne oppfatning av kromosomenes struktur."] Bonnevie's publications from this period include: "Über Chromatindiminution bei Nematoden," *Jenaischen Zeitschrift für Naturwissenschaft* 36 (1901): 275–88; "Abnormitäten in der Furchung von *Ascaris lumbriocoides,*" *Jenaischen Zeitschrift für Naturwissenschaft* 37 (1902): 83–104; "Zur Kenntnis der Spermiogenese bei den Gastropod, *Enteroxenos östergreni,*" *Biologisches Centralblatt* 24 (1904): 267–310; "Das Verhalten des Chromatins in den Keimzellen von *Enteroxenos östergreni,*" *Anatomischer Anzeiger* 26 (1905): 373–87, 497–517; "Undersøgelser over kimcellerne hos *Enteroxenos östergreni,*" *Archiv for Mathematik og Naturvidenskab* 27, no. 12 (1906) (doctoral diss., abbreviated version); "Physiologische Polyspermie," *Archiv for Mathematik og Naturvidenskab* 27, no. 13 (1906); "De nyere tiders opfatning af hermaphroditismen," *Archiv for Mathematik og Naturvidenskab* 27, no. 14 (1906); "Untersuchungen über Keimzellen. I. Beobachtungen an den Keimzellen von *Enteroxenos östergreni,*" *Jenaischen Zeitschrift für Naturwissenschaft* 41 (1906): 229–428 (doctoral dissertation, full monograph); "Untersuchungen über Keimzellen. II. Physiologische Polyspermie bei Bryozoen," *Jenaischen Zeitschrift für Naturwissenschaft* 42 (1907): 567–98; "'Heterotypical' mitosis in *Nereis limbata* (Ehlers)," *Biological Bulletin* 13 (1907): 57–83; "Chromosomenstudien. I. Chromosomen von Ascaris, Allium und Amphiuma. Ein Beitrag zur Lehre der Chromosomenindividualität," *Archiv für Zellforschung* 1 (1908): 450–514; "Chromo-

somenstudien. II. Heterotypische Mitose als Reifungscharacter. Nach Untersuchungen an *Nereis limbata* (Ehlers), *Thalassema mellita* Conn. und *Cerebratulus lacteus* Hubr.," *Archiv für Zellforschung* 2 (1908): 201–79; "Uber die Rolle der Centralspindel während der indirekten Zellteilung," *Archiv für Zellforschung* 5 (1910): 1–35; "Chromosomenstudien. III. Chromatinreifung in *Allium cepa* (♂)," *Archiv für Zellforschung* 6 (1911): 189–253; and "Über die Struktur und Genese der Ascarischromosomen," *Archiv für Zellforschung* 9 (1913): 433–57.

71. See for instance, Franz Schrader, *Mitosis; the Movements of Chromosomes in Cell Division* (New York: Columbia University Press, 2nd ed., 1953), 13, 45; and K. R. Lewis and B. John, *Chromosome Marker* (Boston: Little, Brown & Co., 1963), 165.

72. Broch, *Zoologiens Historie.*

73. "Pteropods from the 'Michael Sars' North Atlantic Deep-Sea Expedition 1910," in *Report on the scientific results of the "Michael Sars" North Atlantic Deep-Sea Expedition,* 3, pt. 1 (1913), 87 pp.; and "Heteropoda," 3, pt. 2 (1919), 15 pp. Sir John Murray and Johan Hjort (Bergen: Trustees of the Bergen Museum, 1913–).

74. Bonnevie's human inheritance studies include the following: "Arvelighetsundersøkelser i Norge," *Norsk Magazin for Lægevidenskab* 76 (1915): 1177–222; "Inledning till diskussion om arvelighet hos mennesker; forskningens maal og midler," *Forhandlinger ved det 16 Skandinaviske Naturforskeres møte i Kristiania, 10–15 juli 1916,* Kristiania (1918), 857–63; "Polydaktyli i norske bygdeslekter," *Norsk Magazine for Lægevidenskab* 80 (1919): 601–32; "Om tvillingfødslernes arvelighet. Undersøkelse over en Norsk bygdeslegt," *Norsk Magazine for Lægevidenskab* 80 (1919): 847–68; "Arvelighetsundersøkelser i norske bygdeslekter," *Naturens Verden,* København, (July 1920): 317–26; "Om arvelig disposition till tvillingfødsler," *Naturen* 50 (1926): 11–24; (with Aslaug Sverdrup) "Hereditary predisposition to dizygotic twin-births in Norwegian peasant families," *Journal of Genetics* 16 (1926): 125–88; and "Arv hos menneskene," *Folkehelseforeningens Tidsskrift* 11, no. 7 (1931).

75. For discussions of the history of papillary pattern studies, see Edward R. Henry, *Classification and Uses of Finger Prints* (London: H. M. Stationery Office, 1905), 3rd ed.; William J. Herschel, *The Origin of Finger-printing* (New York: AMS Press, 1974—reprint of the 1916 ed., Oxford University Press, London); Gerald Lambourne, *The Fingerprint Story* (London: Harrap, 1984), especially chapters 1–3; and Simon A. Cole, *Suspect Identities: A History of Fingerprinting and Criminal Identification* (Cambridge, Mass.: Harvard University Press, 2001).

76. Francis Galton, *Finger-prints* (London: Macmillan, 1892).

77. The skin ridges that produce the patterns have a largely mechanical function; that is, they constitute friction ridges, providing traction. Friction ridge skin, however, is a highly specialized organ with additional functions including that of heightening the sense of touch by virtue of its specially generous endowment of nerve endings—see James F. Cowger, *Friction Ridge Skin: Comparison and Identification of Fingerprints* (New York: Elsevier, 1983), "Introduction," 1–7; and also Bonnevie, "Studies of Papillary Patterns on Human Fingers," *Journal of Genetics* 15 (1924): 1–112.

78. Harold Cummins and Charles Midlo, *Finger Prints, Palms and Soles: An Introduction to Dermatoglyphics* (Philadelphia: Blakiston Co., 1943), 21.

79. H. J. Bagg and C. C. Little, "Hereditary Structural Defects in the Descendents of Mice Exposed to Roentgen Ray Irradiation," *American Journal of Anatomy* 33 (1924): 119–46; H. J. Bagg, "Hereditary Abnormalities of the Limbs, Their Origin and Transmission. II. A Morphological Study . . . in the Desendents [sic] of X-rayed Mice," *American Journal of Anatomy* 43 (1929): 167–220; W. S. Murray, "Studies of Developmental Anomalies in the Descendents of X-rayed Mice," *Papers of the Michigan Academy of Science, Arts, and Letters* 10 (1929): 509–87.

80. Bonnevie's papillary pattern and embryological studies include the following: "Zur Analyse der Vererbungsfaktoren der Papillarmuster," *Hereditas* (Lund) 4 (1923): 221–30; "Main results of a statistical investigation of 'fingerprints' from 24,518 individuals," *Eugenics, Genetics and Family* 1 (1923): 198–211; "Studies of papillary patterns . . . ," *J. of Genetics* 15 (1924): 1–112; "Die ersten Entwicklungsstadien der Papillarmuster der menschlichen Fingerballen," *Nyt Magazin for Naturvidenskaberne* 65 (1927): 19–56; "Lassen sich die Papillarmuster der Fingerbeere für Vaterschaftsfragen praktisch verwerten?" *Zentralblatt für Gynäkologie* 51 (1927): 539–43; "Det materielle grunnlag for papillarmønstrenes arvelighet," *Det 18 Skandinaviske Naturforskermøde, 26–31 august 1929 i København,* København, 7 pp.; "Recherches nouvelles sur les dessins papillares des doigts humains" (résumé of results)," *Bulletin de la Société d'Étude des Formes Humaines* 7, nos. 3–4 (1929): 371–92; "Was lehrt die Embryologie der Papillarmuster über ihre Bedeutung als Rassen- und Familiencharakter?" *Zeitschrift für induktive Abstammungs- und Vererbungslehre* 50 (1929): 219–74, and 59 (1931): 1–60; "Zur Mechanik der Papillarmusterbildung. I. Die Epidermis als formativer Faktor in der Entwicklung der Fingerbeeren und der Papillarmuster. II. Anomalien der menschlichen Finger- und Zehenbeeren, nebst Diskussion über die Natur der hier wirksamen Epidermispolster," *Archiv für Entwicklungsmechanik der Organismen* 117 (1929): 384–420, and 126 (1932): 348–72; "Vererbbarer Cerebrospinaldefekte bei Mäusen, mit sekundären Augen- und Fussanomalien, nebst Turmschädelanlage," *Norske Vistenskaps-Akademi i Oslo,* 1 Mat.-naturv. kl., *Avhandlinger* 13 (1930); "Øien og fotanomalier samt tårnskalle som ledd i et arvelig kompleks," *Naturen* 55 (1931): 215–24; "Die Papillarmuster der menschlichen Fingerbeeren," *Eugenics* 2 (1932): 145–68; "Die vererbbaren Kopf- und Fussanomalien der Little und Bagg'schen Mäuserasse in ihren embryologischen Bedingtheit," *Zeitschrift für induktive Abstammungs- und Vererbungslehre* 62 (1932): 73–84; "Papillarmuster bei Linkshändigen," *Hereditas* 18 (1933): 129–39; "Embryological analysis of gene manifestation in Little and Bagg's abnormal mouse tribe," *Journal of Experimental Zoology* 67 (1934): 443–520; "Pseudencephalie als spontane (recessive?) Mutation bei der Hausmaus," *Norske Videnskaps-Akademi i Oslo, Mat.-naturv. kl., Skrifter,* 1, no. 9 (1936); "Abortive differentiation of the ear vesicles following

a hereditary brain anomaly in 'short-tailed waltzing mice'," *Genetica* 18 (1936): 105–25; (in part with Alf Brodal and Wilhelm Harkmark) "Hereditary hydrocephalus in the house mouse," (in 4 parts) *Norske Videnskaps-Akademi i Oslo, Mat.-naturv. kl., Skrifter* 1, no. 4 (1943), 1, no. 8 (1944) and 1, no. 10 (1944); and "The development of cerebellar anomalies during foetal life with notes on the normal development of the mouse cerebellum," *Norske Videnskaps-Akademi i Oslo, Mat.-naturv. kl., Skrifter* 1, no. 4 (1946).

81. One of these stations was at Drøbak on Oslo Fjord; another, run by the Bergen Museum, which even then was known internationally for its work in marine biology, was on the small island of Herdla, just north of Bergen.

82. *Zoologi* (*Biologi for Gymnasiet*), 1902. An expanded, illustrated edition, coauthored by botanist Rolf Nordhagen and authorized by the Department of Church and Education, was published in 1943 and reissued in 1946.

83. Anne Holden Rønning, "Kvinner organiserer seg—75 år med norske kvinnelige akademikere," in *Alma Maters Døtre*, 117–28.

84. Bernt A. Nissen, *Political Parties in Norway: An Introduction to Their History and Ideology*, trans. R. Hammerschlag and T. Bergaust (Oslo: n.p., 1949), 24.

85. Norwegian women were granted voting rights in national elections on the same basis as men in 1913; universal suffrage in municipal elections was granted in 1901 (Nissen, *Political Parties in Norway*, 20).

86. Sundnes, "Kristine Bonnevie," 32–33.

87. For one of Bonnevie's League of Nations publications, see Kristine Bonnevie, "Introduction," in *Natural Science in Norway* (Geneva: League of Nations Committee on Intellectual Co-operation, 1923), 2nd series. *Intellectual life in various countries: Norway.* The League Committee on Intellectual Co-operation, one of the main predecessors of the present UNESCO organization, met in Geneva throughout the period 1922–1946.

88. "New facts on mesoderm formation and proamnion derivatives in the normal mouse embryo," *Journal of Morphology* 86 (1950): 495–533. As a footnote (495–96) to this posthumously published paper, Bonnevie's friend L. C. Dunn appended a brief account of her life and work, one of the few in English readily available. For a full listing of Bonnevie's publications see Føyn, "Minnetale," 78–84.

89. She would, however, insist that rules be obeyed to the letter. The following story is told of an incident during a field trip near Trondheim: the women students of the group were living on board the vessel *Gunnerus* moored a short distance offshore while the men were housed at the nearby biological station, the party assembling daily for breakfast on board. One morning the gentlemen, despite a heroic rowing effort, slipped to their places at table a little after the appointed hour. Silence reigned. Then Kristine Bonnevie stood up, rapped on the table, and spoke: "When breakfast is at eight o'clock it is at eight o'clock precisely, neither earlier nor later." The saloon clock was at barely one minute after eight (Sundnes, "Kristine Bonnevie," 32).

90. Wollebæk, "Kristine Bonnevie."

91. *Norsk Biografisk Leksikon*, vol. 1 (1923), 241; Broch, *Zoologiens Historie*, 121–22 (port. opp. 129); Arne Semb-Johansson, "Arnesen, Emily," in *Norsk Biografisk Leksikon*, vol. 1 (1999), 130–31.

92. Between 1814 and 1905 there was an especially close relationship between Norway and Sweden, that being the period of the dual kingdom of Norway and Sweden.

93. One of these stations was at Drøbak on Oslo Fjord; another, run by the Bergen Museum, which even then was known internationally for its work in marine biology, was on the small island of Herdla, just north of Bergen.

94. *Uber den feineren Bau der Blutgefässe der Rhynchobdelliden mit besonderer Berücksichtigung des Rüchengefässes und der Klappen* (Jena: G. Fisher, 1904); and *Jenaische Zeitschrift für Naturwissenschaft* 38 (1904): 771–806.

95. See the discussion of Anna Weber-van Bosse in the section on Dutch women.

96. See *Taxonomy of Porifera. From the N. E. Atlantic and Mediterranean Sea*, eds. Jean Vacelet and Nicole Boury-Esnault, Proceedings of the NATO Advanced Research Workshop on Taxonomy of Porifera . . . , Marseille, September 22–27, 1986, NATO ASI Series (Berlin, Heidelberg: Springer, 1987), Preface.

97. "Spongien von der norwegischen Küste II. Monaxonida: Halichrondrina," *Bergens Museums Aarbog for . . . Afhandlinger og Aarsberetning* afh. 1 (1903), 30 pp.; for a contemporary appreciation see *Zoological Record* 40 (1903), section 17, Spongae, "Introduction," 4; for recent references to the paper, see W. H. de Weerdt and R. W. M. van Soest, "A Review of North-Eastern Atlantic *Hemigellius* (Niphatidae, Haplosclerida)," in *Taxonomy of Porifera* 309–20, on 314, 315.

98. "Brutknospenbildung bei *Polymastia mammilaris* (O. F. Müller) Bow. (*Rinaldia arctica* Merej)," *Skrifter vedkommende Norske Selskab* (1917) (1920), no. 1, 1–24; and "Spongia . . . ," Report on the Scientific results of the "*Michael Sars*" *North Atlantic Deep-Sea Expedition, 1910*, 3, pt. 2 (1920), no. 3. Sir John Murray and Johan Hjort Bergen: Trustees of the Bergen Museum, 1913–).

99. Broch, *Zoologiens Historie*, 122.

100. Norwegian women were granted voting rights in national elections on the same basis as men in 1913; universal suffrage in municipal elections was granted in 1901 (Nissen, *Political Parties in Norway*, 20).

101. *Norsk Biografisk Leksikon*, vol. 3 (1921), 591–92 (see also other Esmark family entries, 592–96); and Broch, *Zoologiens Historie*, 134 (portr. opp. 129); Lie and Roslett, eds., *Alma Maters Døtre*, 226 (portr.).

102. Nissen, *Political Parties*, 19–20.

103. *Norsk Biografisk Leksikon*, vol. 11 (1952), 398–99; Rolf Nordhagen, "Minnetale over amanuensis Thekla Resvoll," *Det Norske Videnskaps-Akademi i Oslo. Årbok 1949* (Oslo: Jacob Dybwad, 1950), 29–37; Ove Arbo Høeg, "Thekla Resvoll.

1871–1948," *Blyttia: Norsk Botanisk Forenings Tidsskrift,* no. 4 (1948): 57–61; Inger Nordal, "Thekla Susanne Ragnhild Resvold [*sic*] (1871–1948) og Hanna Marie Resvold-Holmsen [*sic*] (1873–1943): 'Grønnstrømper' og pionerer," in *Alma Maters Døtre,* 185–86; Finn-Egil Eckblad, "Thekla Resvoll og Hanna Resvoll-Holmsen, to glemte?—pionerer i norsk botanikk," *Blyttia* 49 (1991): 3–10; "Litt om Hanna Resvoll-Holmsen og Thekla Resvoll—med mere," interview of Knut Fægre by Inger Nordal, 5 May 1995 (transcript in Biology Library, Oslo University); Rolf Nordhagen, "Minnesmerke over dr. Thekla Resvoll," *Blyttia* 12 (1954): 32.

104. Hanna Resvoll (1873–1943), two years younger than her sister, was very different from her in personality and scientific style. In contrast to the sociable and popular Thekla, Hanna was impersonal and difficult to get along with. Students found her lectures uninspiring. Deeply involved in a range of botany-related matters, she took on powerful opponents, such as the forestry industry, and fought for conservation measures that were half a century ahead of the thinking of her time. Her early research on the isolated Svalbard Islands in the far north (1907, 1908) resulted in the first *Svalbards Flora* (1927). She was particularly interested in the use of statistical methods for the study of plant communities and pioneered the introduction of this technique to Norway. Often ill as a child, she matriculated only in 1902; classical studies were her first interest but she took a science degree, becoming *kandidat real* in 1910. She married geologist Gunnar Holmsen in 1909. Much of her work was done at the botanical museum, but she received a university scholarship in 1915. In 1921, although lacking a doctorate, she became docent in plant geography—probably in part thanks to the influence of Kristine Bonnevie. She held that position (about equivalent to associate professor in the United States) until she reached pension age and retired in 1938. She was a member of the Norwegian Academy of Science.

105. The publication in 1895 of Warming's *Plantesamfund* [Plant Communities] is widely regarded as marking the beginning of the field of plant ecology—see A. G. Morton, *History of Botanical Science* (London: Academic Press, 1981), 433.

106. *Das Pflanzenleben der Alpen: eine Schilderung der Hochgebirgsflora,* 4 vols. (Zürich: Albert Raustein, 1905).

107. "Vegetationen i Schweizeralperne," *Naturen* (Bergen) 28 (1904): 97–108.

108. Many years later, her son stated that her short hair had absolutely nothing to do with her views on women's issues. As a girl she had long, thick hair. However, she suffered from headaches. Hearing that having short hair relieved the problem, she got a sheepherder in her home district to cut hers with his shears. That helped, and so she never let it grow again. (Eckblad, "Thekla Resvoll og Hanna Resvoll-Holmsen," 9).

109. Andreas Holmsen was the older brother of geologist Gunnar Holmsen, who married Thekla Resvoll's younger sister Hanna (see n. 104).

110. For recent references to Resvoll's work, see for instance F. E. Wielgolaski, "Fennoscandian Tundra," in *Polar and Alpine Tundra* (Amsterdam: Elsevier, 1997), 27–83; K. Rapp, S. K. Næss, and H. J. Schwartz, "Commercialization of the Cloudberry (*Rubus chamaemorus* L.) in Norway," in *New Crops,* "Proceedings of the Second National Symposium NEW CROPS—Exploration, Research, and Commercialization, Indianapolis, Indiana, October 6–9, 1991 . . . American Society for Agronomy . . ." eds. Jules Janick and James E. Simon, (New York: Wiley, 1993), 524–26.

111. *Om Planter som Passer til kort og kald Sommer* [Plants that adapt to short, cold summers] (Kristiania: M. Johansen, 1917); reprinted from *Archiv for Mathematik og Naturvidenskab, B* 35, no. 6 (1917): 1–224.

112. See also Wielgolaski, "Fennoscandian Tundra," 64.

113. "Über die Winterknospen der norwegischen Gebirgsweiden," *Nyt Magazin for Naturvidenskaberne* 47 (1909): 299–368.

114. Rapp, Næss, and Schwartz, "Commercialization of the Cloudberry."

115. "*Rubus chamaemorus* L. Die geographische Verbreitung der Pflanze und ihre Verbreitungsmittel," *Festschrift Carl Schröter* (Zürich: n.p., 1925); and "*Rubus chamaemorus* L. A morphological-biological study," *Nyt Magazin for Naturvidenskaberne* 67 (1929): 55–130.

116. Nordal, "Thekla Susanne Ragnhild Resvold [*sic*]," 185.

117. (With C. H. Ostenfeld) "Den ved Aursunden fundne *Aster subintegerrimus,*" *Nyt Magazin for Naturvidenskaberne* 54 (1916): 149–64.

118. "Skoger på Java," *Tidsskrift for Skogbruk* 33 (1925): 499–512; *Tidsskrift for Skogbruk* 34 (1926): 96–99, 291–306; "Kratervegetasjon på Java," *Naturen* 53 (1929): 321–39; "Fra tropiske urskoger," *Universitetets Radioforedrag* ser. A, no. 4 (1931): 31–43.

119. Resvoll's short monograph, *Vinterflora: Vore vildvoksende Løvtraer og Busker i Vinterdragt* (Kristiania: n.p., 1911), was a popular practical manual for the identification of deciduous trees and bushes in winter.

120. "Beschuppte Laubknospen in den immerfeuchten Tropenwäldern Javas," in *Festschrift zum 70. Geburtstage von Karl von Goebel* (Jena: n.p., 1925); *Flora,* N.F.B., nos. 18–19 (1924): 409–20.

121. Amund Theodor Helland and Johan Ludvig Vibe, *Norges Land og Folk: Topografisk-statistisk Beskrevet* (Kristiania: Aschehoug and other publishers, 1885–1906).

122. Eckblad, "Thekla Resvoll," 7.

123. Botanical papers by Resvoll not already listed include the following: "Den nye vegetation paa lerfaldet i Værdalen," *Nyt Magazin for Naturvidenskaberne* 41 (1903): 369–96; "Pflanzenbiologische Beobachtungen aus dem Flugsandgebiet bei Røros im inneren Norwegen," *Nyt Magazin for Naturvidenskaberne* 44 (1906): 235–302; "Vegetationen paa flyvesanden ved Røros," *Naturen* 31 (1907): 321–28; "Litt om blomstens bygning og bestøvning hos *Neottia nidus avia,*" in *Biologiske*

Arbeider tilegnede Eug. Warming (København: 1911), 159–65; "Bundvegetationen i vore skoger," *Tidsskrift for Skogbruk* 21 (1913): 327–34, 416–25, and 22 (1914): 12–25, 153–62; "Plantebiologiske undersøkelser fra norske høifjeld," *Forhandlinger ved det 16 Skandinaviske Naturforskers møte i Kristiania 10–15 juli 1916*, Kristiania (1918), 582–89; "En utpreget selvbestøver," *Nyt Magazin for Naturvidenskaberne* 56 (1919): 131–35; "Gentiana acaulis," *Haveddyrkeren. Organ for det praktiske Landbruk* 4 (1922): 59; "Litt om plantebastarder," *Tidsskrift for Skogbruk* 28 (1920): 143–54; "Litt om utbredelsen av *Salix polaris* Wahlenb. i Rørostrakten og henimot Sylene," *Nyt Magazin for Naturvidenskaberne* 60 (1922): 131–36; "Om trichomene hos *Matricaria chamonilla* L.," *Norsk Farmaceutisk Tidsskrift* 21 (1923): 244–47; "Litt om sneleier og deres plantevekst," *Norges Apotekerforenings Tidsskrift* 44 (1936): 20–25, 52–58, 66–70; "Gule bjerker på Dovrefjell i sommer," *Tidsskrift for Skogbruk* 45 (1937): 390–92; and "Kloverblader med røtter fra bladstilken," *Naturen* 65 (1941): 127.

124. Nordhagen, "Minnetale," 35.

125. Philip A. Wookey and Clare R. Robinson, "Responsiveness and resilience of high Arctic ecosystems to environmental change," in *Variation and Evolution in Arctic and Alpine Plants. Proceedings of VI International Symposium of IOPB*, eds. Liv Borgen and Bengt Jonsell, *Opera Botanica (Nordic Journal of Botany*, monograph series), 132 (1997): 215–32.

126. Catherine M. Pickering, "Reproductive strategies and constraints of alpine plants as illustrated by five species of Australian alpine Ranunculus," in *Variation and Evolution*, 101–8.

127. Svende Erik Stybe, *Copenhagen University: 500 Years of Science and Scholarship*, trans. Reginald Spink (Copenhagen: Royal Danish Ministry of Foreign Affairs, 1979).

128. The first women students were Nielsine Mathilde Nielsen and Johanne Marie Gleerup who passed the entrance examinations in 1877 and received medical degrees in 1884 and 1885 respectively. The first woman to receive a doctorate (1893) was historian Anna Hude (Stybe, *Copenhagen University*, 170–74).

129. From 1886 a course set up by Danish pedagogue Nathalie Zahle (1827–1913) in connection with her girls' school and women teachers training college prepared girls directly for university entrance. Zahle, an influential figure in women's education in Denmark, also established (1867) a school for housewives whose cooking department set standards for countrywide reforms in the culinary arts (see *Lexikon der Frau*, vol. 2, 1670).

130. *Dansk Biografisk Leksikon*, vol. 12 (1982), 413; Kai L. Henriksen, "Oversight over dansk entomologisk historie," *Entomologiske Meddelelser* 15, hf. 1–12 (1922–37): 1–578, on 308–13; K. L. Henriksen, "Sofie Rostrup: Æresmedlem af entomologisk forening," *Entomologiske Meddelelser* 20, hf.2 (1938): 65–66; Prosper Bovien, "Sofie Rostrup," *Entomologiske Meddelelser* 20, hf.7 (1940): 593–96; Mathais Thomsen, "Sofie Rostrup: in memoriam," *Tidsskrift for Landøkonomi* 3 (1940): 176–80; and L. O. Howard, "A history of applied entomology," *Smithsonian Miscellaneous Collections* 84 (1930): 1–545, on 279. George Byers, professor emeritus, University of Kansas, and Glen Salsbury, state survey entomologist, Kansas Department of Agriculture, helped in identifying several of the species Rostrup studied.

131. The peculiarly Danish *magisterkonferens* degree was, at the time of its introduction in 1884, typically awarded in "new" fields, such as natural history, in which a formal examination had not been established. It was roughly equivalent in level to a Ph.D.

132. Ove Georg Frederik Rostrup (1864–1933) received a *magisterkonferens* degree in botany in 1890 and was director of the Danish seed inspection office from 1891 until 1902. After that, he did not have any steady employment but made occasional contributions to the records of Danish cryptogamic flora, also one of his father's strong interests; Ove Rostrup had an unusual ability for finding rare fungi—see *Dansk Biografisk Leksikon* (København: J. H. Schultz, 1933–1944), vol. 20 (1941), 202 (footnote to article on Emil Rostrup).

133. Emil Rostrup's surveys ("Oversigter") appeared in *Tidsskrift for Landøkonomi* (vols 4–12, 1885–93) and in *Tidsskrift for Landbrugets Planteavl* (vols. 1–13, 1894–1905).

134. For an account of another pioneering woman agricultural entomologist from this period, see the discussion of Eleanor Ormerod in Creese, *Ladies in the Laboratory?*, 75–78. Although their circumstances and methods of operation were somewhat different, there are several noteworthy parallels between the careers of these two notable contributors to this emerging field.

135. The Sorgenfri Slot (Palace), whose original structure dates back to 1705–1706, although it was rebuilt and remodeled more than once, was for long used as a residence by the Danish royal family. A large, elegant building in the style of a country mansion surrounded by a spacious park and gardens, it is now owned by the state—see the Sorgenfri Slot website, www.ses.dk/ses_web/html/dk_slotte/sorgenfrisl.htm (in Danish; last accessed 5 February 2000).

136. *Vort Landbrugs Skadedyr blandt Insekter og andere lavere Dyr* (København: Hovedkommission, Schulbothe, 1900–1940); 1928 ed. coauthored by Mathias Thomsen; 1940 ed. by Thomsen and Prosper Bovien; and German tr. of 1928 ed., *Die tierischen Schädlinge des Ackerbaues*, trans. Hans Bremer and R. D. L. Langenbuch (Berlin: Parey, 1931).

137. R. L. Blackman and V. F. Eastop, *Aphids on the World's Crops: an Identification and Information Guide* (New York: Wiley, 1984), 224; A. Balachowsky and L. Mesnil, *Les Insects Nuisibles aux Plantes Cultivées: leurs moeurs, leurs destruction*, chapter 4, "Insectes nuisibles aux plantes potagéres et industrielles" (Paris: Ministère de l'Agriculture, 1936), 1277–84.

138. See, for example, "Fritfluens levenis og optræden i Danmark samt midler imod den" [Habits, occurrences and control of the frit fly in Denmark], *Tidsskrift for Landbrugets Planteavl. Hovedorgan for Statens Forsøg og Undersøgelser vedrørende Markens Avlsplanter* (the Copenhagen journal for plant-breeding research; hereafter, *Tids. Landbr. Planteavl*) 10 (1903): 350–60; "Fritfluen" [*Oscinis frit*.; life history and harmfulness to agriculture], *Meddelelser vedrørende Insektangreb paa Markafgrøder i Jylland 1905* (1906): 75–83; "Kaalmøllet" [*Plutella cruciferarum* (cabbage moth)], *Meddelelser vedrørende*

Insektangreb paa Markafgrøder i Jylland 1905 (1906): 84–94; "Undersøgelser over fritfluens overvintringsforhold" [Investigations into overwintering habits of the frit fly], *Tids. Landbr. Planteavl* 14 (1907): 170–90; "Die Lebensweise der *Hylemya coarctata* in Dänemark," *Zeitschrift für Pflanzenkrankheiten* (Stuttgart) 21 (1911): 385–87; "Bedelusangrebet i 1911 og dettes bekæmpelse" [The 1911 *Aphis papaveris* attack in Denmark], *Tids. Landbr. Planteavl* 19 (1912): 193–213; "Kløveraalens optræden i Lucerne, samt nogle iagttagelser over stængelaalen" [Appearance of clover eelworm (*Tylenchus devastatrix*—a nematode) on alfalfa, and observations on stem-eelworms], *Tids. Landbr. Planteavl* 20 (1913): 731–43; "Forsøg med sprøjtemidler mod Bedelus (*Aphis papaveris*)" [Control of *Aphis papaveris* by spraying with tobacco-leaf extract], *Tids. Landbr. Planteavl* 22 (1915): 234–56; (with K. Iversen) "Forsøg vedrørende kloveraalens smitteveje" [Modes of infection of *Tylenchus devastatrix*], *Tids. Landbr. Planteavl* 23 (1916): 424–41; "Undersøgelser over kaalfluen: dens levevis og bekæmpelse" [Life history and control of cabbage maggot] *Tids. Landbr. Planteavl* 25 (1918): 256–313; "Rævehalemyggens (*Oligotrophus alopecuri*) optræden i Danmark og forsøg med midler til dens bekæmpelse" [Distribution of fox-tail midge and experiments in control methods], *Tids. Landbr. Planteavl* 26 (1919): 38–51; "Jordloppeangrebet i 1918. Jordloppernes levevis og forsøg med deres bekæmpelse" [Life history and control of flea-beetles], *Tids. Landbr. Planteavl* 27 (1919): 216–86; "Gulerods-krusesyge; foraarsaget af gulerods-bladloppen (*Trioza viridula*)" [Carrot leaf curl caused by *Trioza viridula*], *Tids. Landbr. Planteavl* 27 (1919): 618–30; (with Mathias Thomsen) "Bekæmpelse af tæger paa æbletræer samt bidrag til disse tægers biologi" [Control of Miridae (plant-bugs) on apple trees and contributions to their biology], *Tids. Landbr. Planteavl* 29 (1923): 396–461; "Kronets blomsterflue (*Hylemya coarctata*) i Danmark 1903–23. Undersøgelser over dens levevis og bekæmpelse," *Tids. Landbr. Planteavl* 30 (1924): 713–59; "Forsøg vedrørende kløveraalens (*Tylenchus devastatrix*); levedygtidhed i renbrakket jord og nogle andre undersøgelser angaaende kløveraalen" [Clover eelworm investigations], *Tids. Landbr. Planteavl* 32 (1926): 762–73; and "Attack of *Contarinia nasturtii* and *Miris dolabratus* on cruciferous cultivated plants." *Entomologiske Meddelelser* (København) 16, no. 3 (1928): 120–21.

139. By 1930 American entomologist L. O. Howard, in his review of the field, was commenting on the outstanding breadth and thoroughness of Rostrup's work (Howard, "History," 279).

140. These surveys were published in *Tids. Landbr. Planteavl* 12 (1905): 108–29; 13 (1906): 298–314; 14 (1906): 311–21; 15 (1908): 145–58; 16 (1909): 283–302; 17 (1910): 306–31; 20 (1913): 249–80; 21 (1914): 188–222; 23 (1916): 398–423; 24 (1917): 229–54; and 27 (1920): 399–450 (many of those from 1910 on were coauthored with F. Kølpin Ravn and Jens Lind, those of 1908 and 1910 with Ravn, Lind, and M. L. Mortensen, and that of 1920 with C. Ferdinandsen). Sofie Rostrup's more general articles appeared in the zoological numbers of the Experiment Station's newsletter for farmers, *Meddelelser fra Statens plantepatologiske Forsøg,* and in the zoological sections of the *Maanedsoversigter,* both of which were publications started in 1906 in response to the need for prompt information about current insect attacks. Among her other works was her manual on diseases of garden plants, *Haveplanternes Sygdomme og deres Bekæmpelse,* coauthored with C. Ferdinandsen and F. Kølpin Ravn (København, 1921). For a full listing of her publications, see Henriksen, "Oversight," 310–13.

141. The Tagea Brandts Reiselegat (Tagea Brandt Travel Legacy) was an award for women for study or recreational travel established in 1905 by Morten Vilhelm Brandt (1854–1921), of the Brandt cloth manufacturing family in Copenhagen. The award was in memory of his wife Tagea Rovsing (1847–1882), a strong supporter of the women's movement in Denmark. Recipients were selected from a wide range of fields—science, literature, and the arts—the charter having specified that distribution of the fund be "in a liberal spirit"; see *Dansk Biografisk Leksikon,* vol. 4 (1934), 1–2.

142. *Dansk Biografisk Leksikon,* vol. 9 (1981), 549–50; Mogens Pihl, "Kirstine Meyer," *Fysisk Tidsskrift* 40 (1942): 175–91; J. C. Poggendorf, *Biographisch-Literarisches Handwörterbuch zur Geschichte der exacten Wissenschaften . . .* (Leipzig: J. A. Barth, 1863–), vol. 4 (1904), 1003; *Hanna Adler og hendes Skole* (København: G. E. C. Gad Forelag, 1959), especially 38–47; and *Salmonsens Konversations Leksikon,* ed. Chr. Blangstrup (København: J. H. Schultz Forlagsboghandel, (1915–1930), vol. 16 (1924), 1059–60.

143. From 1886 a course set up by Danish pedagogue Nathalie Zahle (1827–1913) in connection with her girls' school and women teachers training college prepared girls directly for university entrance. Zahle, an influential figure in women's education in Denmark, also established (1867) a school for housewives whose cooking department set standards for countrywide reforms in the culinary arts (see *Lexikon der Frau,* vol. 2, 1670).

144. *Hanna Adler og hendes Skole,* 38.

145. The peculiarly Danish *magisterkonferens* degree was, at the time of its introduction in 1884, typically awarded in "new" fields, such as natural history, in which a formal examination had not been established. It was roughly equivalent in level to a Ph.D.

146. "Über korrespondierende Zustande der Stoffe," *Zeitschrift für Physikalische Chemie* 71 (1910): 325–36.

147. See also J. Timmermans, "Density of liquids below 0°," *Scientific Proceedings of the Royal Dublin Society* 25 (1912): 310–74.

148. "Zur Geschichte der Antiperistasis," *Annalen der Naturphilosophie,* 3 (1904): 413–41, also published in Danish in *Oversigt over det Kongelige Danske Videnskabernes Selskabs Forhandlinger, 1903,* no. 6 (1904): 573–604.

149. *Temperaturbegrebets Udvikling gennem Tiderne* (København: n.p., 1909); *Die Entwickelung des Temperaturbegriffs im Laufe der Zeiten sowie dessen Zusammenhang mit der wechselnden Vorstellung über die Natur der Wärme,* trans. Irmgard Kolde, Vorwort von Eilhard Wiedemann (Braunschweig: F. Vieweg, 1913), also published in Bd. 48 of *Die Wissenschaft;* [The

development of the idea of temperature and its connection with the changing views as to the nature of heat; doctoral disputation, Copenhagen, 1909.]

150. "Ole Römer und das Thermometer," *Archiv für die Geschichte der Naturwissenschaften und der Technik* 2 (1910): 323–49, also published in Danish in *Fysisk Tidsskrift* 7 (1909): 201–28; "Von welchen Voraussetzungen muss man ausgehen, um den Begriff 'Temperatur' definieren zu können?," *Zeitschrift für den physikalischen und chemischen Unterricht* 23 (1910): 162–63; also published in Danish in *Fysisk Tidsskrift* 8 (1910): 118–20; "Ole Römer," *Fysisk Tidsskrift* 9 (1910): 8–12.

151. See for example *Om Ole Rømer's Opdagelse af Lysets Tøven* (København: A. F. Høst, 1915), and *Ole Rømer . . .* (København: J. Jørgensen & Co., 1918)—a presentation on the unveiling of a Rømer statue. Working in 1676 from observations of eclipses of Jupiter's satellites, Rømer realized that light was taking time to travel and deduced its speed. However, this idea was not accepted until confirmed in 1725 by J. Bradley, Astronomer Royal at Greenwich; see Sir James Jeans, *The Growth of Physical Science* (Cambridge: Cambridge University Press, 1951), 199, 241.

152. The first two volumes consisted of Ørsted's collected works, *Ørsteds naturvidenskabelige Skrifter,* 1797–1808 and 1808–1851; the third was Bjerrum-Meyer's account of Ørsted's work in the community and his popular scientific writings for the period 1798–1851, *Ørsteds Arbeidsliv i det danske Samfund; blandede naturvidenskabelige Afhandlinger skrevne af H. C. Ørsted for hans Landsmænd 1798–1851* (København: A. F. Høst, 1920).

153. Ørsted discovered that a freely swinging magnetic needle was deflected from its position when an electric current was flowing in its vicinity, a key observation that led not only to the technology of the electric telegraph but also directly to the work in electromagnetism of Ampère and the great discoveries of Michael Faraday.

154. Kirstine Meyer, "Faraday and Ørsted," *Nature* (supp.) 128 (1931): 337–39.

155. *Erasmus Bartholin: et Tidsbillede* (København: Levine og Munksgaard, 1933).

156. Hanna Adler (1859–1947) founded in 1893 and headed until 1927 the Hanna Adler *fællesskole* (coeducational community school), later the Sortedams Gymnasium. Adler gave her school to the city of Copenhagen in 1918 (*Lexikon der Frau,* vol. 1, 34; *Hanna Adler og hendes Skole*).

157. Niels Bjerrum, professor at the Royal Veterinary and Agricultural College, Copenhagen, was well known for his studies in a number of areas including electrochemistry, the theory of acids and bases, and the theory of infrared spectra (Partington, *History of Chemistry,* vol. 4, 682).

158. John Hendley Barnhart, comp., *Biographical Notes upon Botanists,* 3 vols. (Boston, G. K. Hall, 1965), vol. 2, 115; and *Botanisk Tidsskrift* (København) 39 (1926): 216.

159. See bibliography and also "Nye arter af Oedogonium fra Danmark" [New species of Oedogonium from Denmark], *Botanisk Tidsskrift* (København) 26 (1905): 397–410; and "Om *Oedogonium inclusum* Hirn," *Botanisk Tidsskrift* (København) 28 (1907): 211–13.

160. *Ebenso neu als kühn; 120 Jahre Frauenstudium an der Universität Zürich,* Verein Feministische Wissenschaft Schweiz (Zürich: Verein Feministische Wissenschaft Schweiz, Schriftenreihe, 1988), 202; and J. M. Meijer, *Knowledge and Revolution: the Russian Colony in Zurich (1870–1873)* (Assen: Internationaal Instituut voor Sociale Geschiedenis, 1955), 204, n. 71.

161. Later the same year, the Russian Iuliia Lermontova received a doctorate in chemistry from Göttingen University after passing the required oral examination. Lermontova had previously studied privately at Heidelberg and Berlin universities (see Mary R. S. Creese, "Early Women Chemists in Russia: Anna Volkova, Iuliia Lermontova and Nadezhda Ziber-Shumova," *Bulletin for the History of Chemistry,* no. 21 (1998): 19–24.

162. Franziska Tiburtius, *Erinnerungen einer Achtzigjährigen* (Berlin: C. A. Schwetschke, 1929), 3rd. ed., 148–49.

163. Membership lists, Deutsche Chemische Gesellschaft, *Berichte der Deutschen Chemischen Gesellschaft,* 1877–1889. No mention of Lidiia Sesemann was found in University of Leipzig records for the period 1870–1890 (Archives, University of Leipzig). It would seem probable, therefore, that she was there as a private research worker.

164. G. Eneström, "Note bibliographique sur les femmes dans les sciences exactes," *Bibliotheca Mathematica* 10 (1896): 73–76, on 75.

165. G. Valentine, "Die Frauen in den exacten Wissenschaften," *Bibliotheca Mathematica* 9 (1895): 65–76, on 72; Alphonse Rebière, *Les Femmes dans la Science. Notes recueilles* (Paris: Nony et Cie, 1895), 52; *Svenskt Författarlexikon 1910–1940,* vol. 1, (1942), 137, and vol. 4, *1941–1950* (1953), 113; *Svenska Män och Kvinnor,* vol. 4 (1948), 411.

166. Baroness Cedercreutz's books include the following: *Arabellas resor*—stories for young people, under the pseudonym Ala (Helsingfors: n.p., 1912); *Från Alp och Hav* [From Alps and Sea], (Helsingfors: n.p., 1914), reviewed by R. F. V. Willebrand, *Finska Tidskrift* 77 (1914): 447–49; *Gåbbar och Gummor* [Old Men and Old Women], under the pseudonym Bengt Ivarson (Helsingfors: n.p., 1917); *Fröken Milla Lund och Fiken, hennes Hund* [Miss Milla Lund and Fiken, Her Dog], a rhyming story from the troubled year 1916, with silhouette illustrations by Emil Cedercreutz (Helsingfors: n.p., 1919); *Snällt och ilakt* [Kind and Evil], under the pseudonym B. Ivarson (Helsingfors: n.p., 1925); *Bidrövlit och glatt* [Sad and Joyful], poems, under the pseudonym B. Ivarson (Helsingfors: n.p., 1932); *Hemma och ute* [At Home and Abroad], poems (Helsingfors: n.p., 1934); *Vandringslust* (Helsingfors: n.p., 1935); and *Oenhetligt* (miscellaneous poems) (Helsingfors: n.p., 1944).

Chapter 2

IRELAND: MOSSES, MOLLUSKS, AND MIGRATING BOULDERS

Botany, geology, conchology, entomology, and marine biology were the fields in which nineteenth-century Irish women or women working in Ireland made their largest contributions as measured by papers indexed in the Royal Society *Catalogue*.[1] Their combined output constituted about 8 percent of the total for pre-1901 journal articles published by Western European women (excluding those working in Britain), a figure comparable to that for Swedish women (see Figure C-1). In botany seven authors published fifteen pre-1901 papers, while in geology the eight reports by one author, Sydney Mary Thompson, stand out; four workers contributed eight conchology articles, seven papers or notes discussed topics in entomology, and in marine biology three women students at the Royal College of Science Dublin—Glascott, Maguire, and Shackleton—authored or coauthored several substantial publications (Figure 2-2). Only three early papers in astronomy are listed in the bibliography although a considerable body of pre-1901 work in this field was carried out by Irish women or women with close connections to Ireland, in particular Margaret Huggins, Agnes Clerke, and Mary Proctor. Because their work was done in Britain (or, in Proctor's case, largely in the United States) their careers have been discussed in an earlier volume on British and American women scientists.[2]

With the exception of five papers by Mary Ward, which came out in the 1860s and an 1846 report by Mary Ball published by her brother Robert Ball, all of the Irish work listed in the bibliography appeared in the last two decades of the century, most of it in the 1890s (Figure 2-1). The period was one of remarkable activity in natural history studies in Ireland, particularly in the prosperous upper- and middle-class, mainly Protestant section of the community—people with leisure and mobility. Interest was stimulated in part by the expansion of the Irish railway network, which made possible the exploration of the west of the country. It has also been suggested that natural history studies were part of the cultural expression of the settler community in the process of embedding itself more deeply into the fabric of its adopted country by taking possession of its botany, geology, paleography, and antiquarianism. Further, these studies offered a secular sphere of action when the Protestant-Catholic religious divide was increasing.[3] Field clubs thrived in Belfast, Dublin, Cork, and Limerick, all important cultural centers.[4] Belfast, then increasingly prosperous, largely because of its important and rapidly expanding linen industry, supported the earliest of these clubs, the Belfast Naturalists' Field Club (BNFC). Founded in 1863, it was one of the first to fully accept women members[5] and was a group with an impressive range of activities; Sydney Mary Thompson's notable work in glacial geology was done as part of its program and botanist Matilda Knowles's early studies were inspired by her BNFC contacts. Likewise the Dublin Naturalists' Field Club helped marine biologist Annie Massy when she was starting her work on mollusks.

Two Early Naturalists

The two mid-century naturalists, Mary Ball and Mary Ward, the earliest of the Irish women discussed here,[6] made their main contributions in entomology and microscopy respectively; Ward was also known for her scientific writing and illustrating.

MARY BALL[7] (1812–1898) was born at Cove of Cork, County Cork, in 1812, the younger of two daughters among the four surviving children of Bob Stawell Ball and his wife Mary (née Green) of Youghal, County Cork. Their Ball forebears, from Bampton, Devonshire, had first settled in Youghal, a town about twenty-five miles north along the coast from Cork Harbour, in 1674. Although not wealthy the Balls were

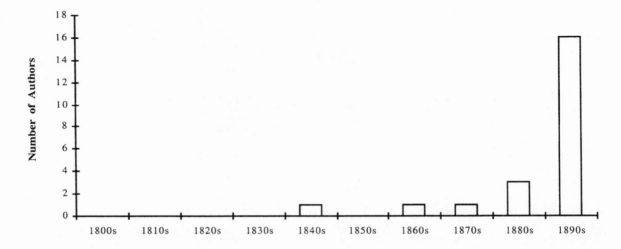

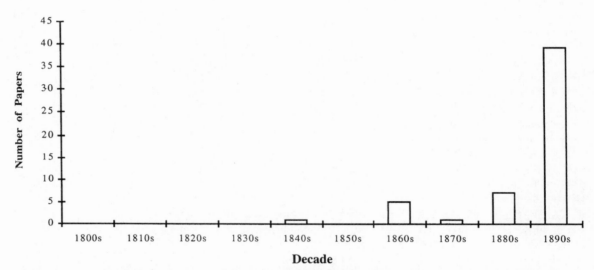

Figure 2-1.   Irish authors and papers, by decade, 1800–1900. Data from the Royal Society *Catalogue of Scientific Papers.*

comfortably off. Bob Stawell Ball was a customs official and at the time of Mary's birth the family lived at Cove of Cork. The father's poor health caused them to return to Youghal in 1815; some years later they moved to Dublin.

A quiet, cultivated man, Bob Stawell Ball enjoyed natural history and encouraged his children's interests in the subject. Three of them, Mary, her sister Anne, and her older brother Robert became naturalists; Robert, who held an administrative post in Dublin Castle, was elected honorary secretary of the Zoological Society of Ireland in 1837 and director of the Dublin Museum in 1844. Mary and Anne were probably educated at home. As children they followed Robert's example by collecting specimens, especially seaweeds and shells along the Youghal shores and insects in the surrounding countryside. By their twenties, both were competent naturalists in their chosen areas, Anne in algology and Mary in entomology. Few textbooks or manuals were then available, but by 1835 Mary Ball owned a copy of James Francis Stephens's *Systematic Catalogue of British Insects* (1829) given her by her brother; it was in the margins of that book that she recorded the original observations of stridulation, the production of sounds under water by insects, that form her most important contribution to biology.[8]

Mary Ball is considered to be the original discoverer of the stridulation of the Corixidae (water-bugs), the main source of underwater sound in lakes. Although now clearly recognized as an insect communication

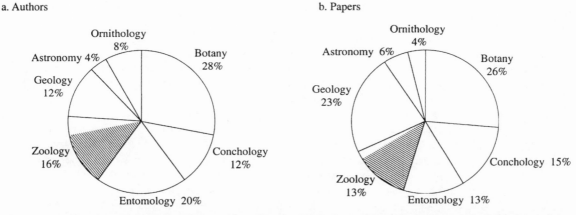

Figure 2-2.   Distribution of Irish authors and papers, by field, 1800–1900. Shaded sectors represent work in marine biology. (In a., an author contributing to more than one field is counted in each.) Data from the Royal Society *Catalogue of Scientific Papers.*

phenomenon involved in reproduction, it has proved to be unexpectedly complicated and the full details of its function were still being investigated more than a century and a half after Mary's time.[9] She herself made fairly detailed observations on a captured insect kept alive in a basin of water indoors over a period of six weeks in the spring of 1840, and she extended her study using other captures in the summer of 1844 and the autumn of 1845. She recorded the daily and seasonal periodicity of the sounds, temperature dependence, and the fact that there are two kinds of sounds, a chirp and a grinding; she also observed how long a sound-burst lasted and suggested that at least some of it was made by movements of the insect's anterior legs, although the precise way in which it is produced eluded her (and all other nineteenth-century workers as well). She identified the insect involved as *Corixa striata,* now *Sigara dorsalis* (Leach), which would seem "very reasonable."[10] Although some of her determinations are uncertain her work was notable, particularly considering the limited amount of reference material available to her and the complexities of the Western European Corixidae family.

Mary Ball did not publish her observations under her own name but in the second of three short notes by her brother Robert reporting her findings she was clearly identified as the original observer, Robert also stating that he had himself heard "this remarkable sound." Robert Ball's third note is, except for the first paragraph, a transcription of his sister's account;[11] it has been suggested that of all his numerous published writings on Irish natural history this third note on stridulation of the Corixidae was perhaps his most interesting single contribution.[12]

The Corixidae were not Mary Ball's only natural history interest. She also studied Irish flora, made observations on moths and butterflies, and assembled noteworthy collections of dragonflies and mollusks. Irish entomologist Alexander Henry Haliday cited her work in his writings on Lepidoptera and her dragonfly collection was an important enough source of Irish material to attract the attention of Baron de Selys-Longchamps, the leading mid-nineteenth-century European expert on the group. He visited her and used her records in his 1846 paper on Odonata of the British Isles.[13] Mary was the first to observe *Libellula depressa* L. in Ireland. Several of her mollusk finds also were the earliest recorded in Ireland; fourteen species, mostly taken around Youghal, were listed by her friend William Thompson in his *Natural History of Ireland.*[14] Thompson named the snail *Rissoa balliae* in her honor.

With the death of her brother Robert in 1857 the last of Mary Ball's male mentors was gone, her father having died in 1841 and William Thompson in 1852. She and her sister Anne remained in Dublin, sharing a house, although they did not get along very well with each other. Neither did any further scientific work.[15] For a time they very successfully followed the fashionable pastime of growing ferns, using the basement of their house; when they moved to another house, each had her own garden. Mary died in 1898, when she was eighty-six, outliving her sister by twenty-six years.

MARY WARD[16] (1827–1869), the Hon. Mrs. Ward, was one of the noted women writers on scientific topics of her time, publishing two very successful books, one on microscopy and one on astronomy. In addition she brought out a number of articles reporting original observations in natural history and astronomy.

Born in Ballylin, on the outskirts of Ferbane, County Offaly (then King's County), in central Ireland on

24 April 1827, Mary was the youngest child among the three daughters and one son of the Rev. Henry King and his wife Harriette (née Lloyd). The Lloyds were a distinguished King's County family and Ballylin was a large and gracious country residence surrounded by well-tended parkland. Taught at home by a governess and by her mother, Mary was encouraged to develop her early interest in natural history; she collected plants and insects and learned to make accurate drawings of her specimens. She also read extensively on her own using the various reference works and periodicals in the Ballylin library, and she soon began to assemble her own collection of scientific books. A list of these, particularly the works on microscopy, astronomy, and natural history,[17] provides ample evidence of the serious and ambitious nature of her studies.

Throughout her teens and early twenties she was much influenced by her frequent contact with her first cousin William Parsons, third Earl of Rosse, who lived only fifteen miles from Ballylin at Birr Castle, Parsonstown (now Birr). A noted astronomer, Lord Rosse was twenty-seven years older than Mary but he and his wife were her close friends and he took great interest in her scientific studies.[18] Between 1840 and 1845 a huge construction project was carried out at Birr Castle, the building of the Leviathin of Birr, a reflecting telescope which until 1919 was the largest in the world. The casting of the six-foot-diameter mirror (using a peat-fired forge), its grinding and polishing, and the building of the fifty-eight-foot-long tube were all carried out in the castle grounds by the Earl and a team of local men. Mary King recorded the progress of the work in notes and drawings, and she was one of the first to climb up to the telescope's gantries and galleries.[19] She later told of how she had "more than once stood in bitter frost long after midnight" to view the heavens through its lens.[20]

The many distinguished scientists who came to visit Lord Rosse and view his telescope were frequently received at Ballylin as well and so Mary had opportunities to discuss her scientific interests and show her sketches. In 1845, when she was eighteen, English astronomer Sir James South saw her making drawings of small objects with the aid of a single-lens magnifying glass. Following his suggestion that she be provided with a good microscope, the best then available in London was bought, an instrument by Andrew Ross. With this she carried out a long series of notable microscopical studies. Scottish physicist Sir David Brewster, another frequent visitor at Ballylin, was so favorably impressed by her powers of observation and artistic abilities that over the course of many years he had her prepare illustrations for his publications. These included drawings of Newton's telescope and Lord Rosse's telescope for his *Memoirs* of Sir Isaac Newton[21] as well as a number of microscopical illustrations. Indeed the finest of Mary Ward's microscopical illustrations appear in Brewster's papers; her series showing the colored patterns observable in old glass undergoing devitrification (a process then being studied by Brewster and others) are particularly impressive in their painstaking attention to precision and detail.[22]

In 1854 Mary King married Rugby-educated Henry William Crosby Ward, son of the third Viscount Bangor, a commissioned officer in the 43rd. Regiment who had served in the Crimea, reaching the rank of captain.[23] One year after their marriage Henry Ward resigned his commission. Thereafter he had no regular employment but, in the accepted manner for an aristocrat, devoted himself to hunting, sport, and attending social gatherings. The ancestral lands being entailed, Henry as the second son had little or no income; his family was supported mainly by the interest from Mary's holding of railway shares, which after a time declined significantly in value.

Over the next fifteen years, Mary Ward gave birth to eight live infants and had three miscarriages; six of the children survived to adulthood. Over these same fifteen years she carried out a remarkable amount of scholarly work, usually doing her writing late at night when her children were in bed. Her first effort to place her work before a wider audience came in 1856 when she prepared a twenty-page, home-printed article entitled "A Windfall for the Microscope"; a careful, detailed description of her investigation of the development of what proved to be caddisflies, from jelly-like egg mass to the larvae-in-case stage, it was a lively story told with enthusiasm, meant for circulation among family and friends. Included were five pages of attractive, hand-colored illustrations, the whole produced by the lithographic process. Subsequent papers, including an expanded version of that first home-printed work, appeared mainly in *Recreative Science* and *The Intellectual Observer*.[24] These reported more natural history investigations (on toads, moths, and insect development) and observations in astronomy (comets, shooting stars, and aurorae). An 1864 *Intellectual Observer* article on the Irish natterjack toad was reprinted in full in the *Irish Times* with very favorable editorial comments; English naturalist Sir Richard Owen requested a copy of the accompanying painting for the British Museum collection.

Her first book, *Sketches with the Microscope* (1857), was a collection of short letters to a friend describing the structure of common objects seen through a microscope accompanied by colored lithographed illustrations. The initial 250 copies printed privately in nearby Parsonstown sold within a few months by private subscription, but in 1858 the copyright was bought by a London publisher (for £15 plus 100 copies of the published work) and the book reissued under a new title.[25] A third edition, revised and expanded, followed a year later. Clearly written in the simple, direct style she had adopted in her 1856 paper, the work was essentially a manual on the use of the compound microscope in the examination of a whole variety of readily obtained tiny objects from the natural world, insect wings, fish scales, feathers, crystals, and the microscopic animal life of ponds and lakes. Well illustrated with many of Mary Ward's own delicate and accurate drawings, most of them colored, it did much to increase general interest in microscopical work; sales were brisk and reviews favorable. Later editions, much expanded, were brought out under the title *Microscope Teachings.*

Telescope Teachings, Mary Ward's second book, appeared in 1859 and was equally popular.[26] Again skillfully illustrated with her own sketches, it dealt especially with observations that could be made with a small telescope, including a method for safely viewing sunspots. She also discussed recent work done with powerful instruments. Of particular interest is her detailed description of Donati's Comet whose changing appearance she observed, both with the naked eye and using her two-inch telescope, over the period 10 September to 16 October 1858. She recorded this spectacular event in a special diary and illustrated her narrative with a set of outstanding complementary drawings. Her 1859 book would appear to be the only place where this work was published.[27] A third book, *Entomology in Sport; and Entomology in Earnest,* coauthored with her sister Lady Jane Mahon, also appeared in 1859. Written in an informal, lighthearted style, less rigorous than her other books, this short work was brought out specially to awaken the interest of young readers in natural history—a goal in which it succeeded admirably.

The publication of *Microscope Teachings* and *Telescope Teachings* established Mary Ward's reputation as an author of popular but reliable, plainly written and beautifully illustrated scientific works at the introductory level. Although by no means the first introductory works on microscopy and astronomy of the nineteenth century, hers appeared at a particularly opportune time. The audience for educational books was expanding quickly and London's commercial book production was in its mid-century boom. Further, affordable instruments were by then available and microscopy and astronomy were becoming fashionable hobbies. Mary Ward, recently described as "the best known nineteenth century writer on the use of the microscope and telescope,"[28] saw her opportunity in a mass market and was remarkably successful.

Because it was often difficult for her to obtain current journals, she kept up to date with developments in astronomy and microscopy by corresponding with the leading workers in these fields. Astronomer Hamilton and physicist Brewster continued to help her over the years; Hamilton lent her his copies of *Monthly Notices of the Royal Astronomical Society* and in 1859 requested the society to include her in its list of eminent people entitled to receive these *Notices.* She was one of only three women in the British Isles accorded the privilege; the others were Queen Victoria and Mary Somerville, the Scottish translator of Laplace's *Méchanique Céleste.* When attending the International Exhibition in London in 1862 she was allowed, after much effort on her part, to visit the Royal Observatory at Greenwich as an "exceptional case," despite the strict rules against the admission of women then in force. She made full use of the privilege, sketching equipment and instruments and taking many notes.

Much of Mary Ward's original work in microscopy and entomology was done during visits to Castle Ward, a large, eighteenth-century house on an estate of 700 acres on the shores of Strangford Lough, County Down, land owned by the Ward family since the late sixteenth century. Temple Water, one of the small lakes on the estate, was a source of specimens for her microscopical studies.

Mary died at the age of forty-two, on 31 August 1869. Although suffering from exhaustion and by then in poor health, she had gone with her husband to Birr so that they might pay their last respects at the grave of Lord Rosse, who had died two years previously. While riding on a steam road locomotive designed and built by Lord Rosse, she was thrown from her seat and killed when the vehicle went over a piece of rough road.

Ireland has not forgotten Mary Ward. Her achievements, despite the handicaps faced by mid-nineteenth-century women of scientific inclination, earned her the friendship and respect of some of the leading male scientists of her time. In 1986 Ulster Television produced a documentary, "The Wonderful World of Mary Ward," in which her first article "A Windfall for the Microscope" (a scientific detective story) was reenacted. An exhibition, "William and Mary: King's County Cousins: Another Glorious Revolution," curated by Owen Harry, was held at Birr Castle in 1991. In 1950, on the death of Mary's son Maxwell, Castle Ward was taken over by the National Trust. Her drawings of the house and surroundings were used in a recent restoration of the building and gardens; many of her books, illustrations, slides, and instruments are on display in the house.

Botanists

Among the Irish women botanists whose papers are listed in the bibliography is MATILDA KNOWLES[29] (1864–1933), a noted lichen specialist. Knowles's many publications and the extensive herbarium collections she amassed during the early years of the twentieth century form an important baseline contribution to the cryptogamic botany of Ireland and western oceanic Europe. A colleague of Thomas Johnson, professor of botany at the Royal College of Science Dublin and Keeper of Botany at the Irish National Museum, she was formally a technical assistant at the museum's herbarium for over thirty years. After Johnson's retirement in 1923 she became in effect the acting curator for the Botanical Section.

Born on 31 January 1864 in Ballymena, County Antrim, Matilda was one of three daughters of William James Knowles, an insurance agent, antiquarian, and amateur archaeologist known for his investigations of the Stone Age kitchen middens of Antrim and his large collections of prehistoric implements. Matilda probably received her early education at home and at a local academy for girls. Her father encouraged her early interests in natural history, especially plants; she and her sisters accompanied him to meetings of the Belfast Naturalists' Field Club and she acquired early experience in field botany on the club's excursions in northeast Ireland.

As a girl she knew Robert Lloyd Praeger (1865–1953), who often came to visit her father and study his Stone Age collections.[30] By the 1890s Praeger was probably the leading figure in Irish natural history studies, particularly botany. He enlisted Matilda Knowles's help in collecting material from Antrim and Londonderry for the first supplement (1895) to Stewart and Corry's 1888 *Flora of the North-east of Ireland*,[31] work in which she collaborated with Mary Isabella Leebody, a very experienced field botanist from Londonderry (p. 44). From there she went on to compile a flora of County Tyrone, a little-explored region for which she listed over 300 species. Published as part of Praeger's major work *Irish Topographical Botany* (1901), this collection was also the subject of her first botanical note, "Flowering Plants of Tyrone" (1897).

Sometime between 1896 and 1900 Matilda Knowles, along with one of her sisters, moved to Dublin, where she attended classes at the Royal College of Science. In 1902 she began working as a temporary technical assistant (later as a "non-pensionable assistant") under the direction of Thomas Johnson in the Botanical Section of the Museum of Science and Art (later the National Museum) Dublin. Many collections were then being acquired and she was much involved in the laborious routine work of mounting and the preparation of the materials for public display and teaching purposes. She entered fully into Dublin scientific life, attending lectures, participating in field trips and providing information and assistance to the many biologists who visited the herbarium. With considerable experience of her own by then, especially in field exploration and topographic botany, she often helped regional field clubs with questions about identification and distribution.

She continued her own fieldwork, which included a notable investigation in the region of the Shannon estuary, where she collaborated with botanist Charlotte O'Brien and her nephew Robert O'Brien; the results appeared in three papers in the *Irish Naturalist*.[32] About this time she also published a study of nonnative plants resulting from the casual importation of seeds in grain shipments and found in remarkable variety near flour mills at Straffan, County Kildare;[33] her efforts in this area have provided an important record of species present in the early years of the twentieth century (see also Hensman, below).

Knowles collaborated closely with Johnson in a number of studies including the work of compiling his *Hand-list of Irish Flowering Plants and Ferns* (1910). She and Rachel Hensman assisted Johnson and Henry Hanna in an investigation of the economically important Phaeophyceae, or brown algae, of Irish coastal waters, carried out in the late 1890s for the Flora and Fauna Committee of the Royal Irish Academy; Knowles examined material from the southeast coasts. Her 1903 joint paper with Johnson, her first on her herbarium work, dealt with the herbarium's holding of ferns from India and Ceylon collected by H. C. Levinge of Knock Drin Castle, County Westmeath.[34] Her high standards in identifying and filing did much to ensure the excellent quality of the herbarium's many acquisitions of this period.

In 1908, when the Clare Island Survey was organized under Praeger's leadership by the Royal Irish Academy, Matilda Knowles was invited to take part. The aim of this ambitious project was a systematic study of the geology, climate, agriculture, flora and fauna, and even the archaeology and folklore of Clare Island. Rugged and sparsely inhabited, this little island of six and a third square miles lies about three miles off the coast of County Mayo. Representing as it does a largely discrete but fairly extended region on the western edge of the European continent, its full, detailed study was of great interest to biologists and naturalists. Hilly over much of its surface with a peak of 1,520 feet in the northwest, it offered considerable altitude variation. Much of its western half was hill and moor, in places with a thin covering of peat; areas of glacial drift deposits and later detritus and hill wash were common. The small population of crofters was pretty much confined to the lower lying, fairly fertile, central valley.

The survey's biological investigations, by far the largest section, were extended to include both the adjacent mainland (from Achill south to Killary Harbour and inland as far as Castlebar) and the seas from Blacksod Bay to Ballynakill Harbour out to fifty fathoms. Published in sixty-eight reports, the results remain an important reference standard in Irish natural history studies and are a testimony to the abilities and initiative of Irish biologists of the period. The collections assembled are now in the Irish National Herbarium in Dublin and the British Museum.[35]

For some time especially interested in lichens, a group that had previously received little attention in western Ireland, Matilda Knowles joined lichen specialist Annie Lorrain Smith of the British Museum[36] in working out this section of the survey flora. Cryptogams (fungi, algae, lichens, and bryophytes) were abundant throughout the region and about 280 lichens identified of which more than thirty were new to Ireland.[37] In her 1911 report on the work Annie Smith referred to Matilda Knowles's "exceptional ability as an observer and collector."[38] Knowles spent parts of three summers on the island (1909–1911) surveying flowering plants as well as lichens, and in addition she collaborated with Annie Smith in the work of examination and identification.

From then on lichens became Knowles's major area of investigation, particularly the lichen flora of the sea coast. With little available literature on the subject, she began with an intensive, three-year exploration of the marine and maritime species of the Howth peninsula on the north side of Dublin Bay, paying careful attention to the area's geology and plant ecology. She was the first to examine in detail the pronounced vertical zoning in the coastal lichen colonies on rocky, noncalcareous shores—a lower zone of black lichens submerged at high tide, an intermediate zone where orange forms predominate, and above that a grey zone consisting largely of the genus Ramalina. In her lengthy 1913 paper she reported in detail the species composition of all three zones; of the 181 species, 135 subspecies, and twenty-five varieties she found, twenty-five were new to Ireland and three new to science.[39] Included in the paper were line drawings of the reproductive organs and spores by Eileen Barnes, one of Ireland's outstanding scientific artists of the time, although now largely forgotten.[40]

In 1929 Matilda Knowles's comprehensive 255-page monograph "The lichens of Ireland" appeared in the *Proceedings of the Royal Irish Academy*. Its preparation involved the examination, and wherever possible the verification, of earlier records from the few areas where lichens had been studied previously, in addition to the collecting of new material either by Knowles herself or by correspondents; the crucial work she did almost singlehandedly. Of the forty botanical divisions of Ireland (initially adopted for Praeger's *Irish Topographical Botany*) she personally collected lichens in twenty-six—a remarkable achievement, especially considering that travel was still very difficult in many districts. The work added over twenty accepted species to the country's flora and extended the range of many others. Praeger described it as "one of the finest pieces of work ever carried out in any section of the Irish flora."[41] Until her death she continued to collect records for a supplement.[42]

These investigations, and other studies, were carried on alongside her regular curatorial duties at the National Herbarium. Among her responsibilities was the arranging of special exhibitions, such as one on the drift seeds from the West Indies that wash up on Ireland's west coast and serve as important indicators of long-range dispersal of seeds by ocean currents. She also had charge of the library associated with the herbarium, an important and expanding collection of taxonomic and systematic works, as well as botanical art. In her free time she led field trips of the Dublin Naturalists' Field Club.

After Thomas Johnson retired from the museum in 1923, Matilda Knowles became responsible for the work of the botanical section; in effect she was acting curator until her death ten years later. Over these years she greatly increased the collections, building toward what became an outstanding reference index. Notable among her acquisitions (all obtained by exchange for Irish specimens, item by item) were materials from Newfoundland and eastern Quebec, California, Bulgaria, Sweden, and Russia, the latter two countries supplying lichens.

Although in her later years lichen studies dominated her research, they were not her only investigations during this period. In 1928 she published a summary of the history and distribution of the orchid Irish Lady's Tresses (*Spiranthes romanzoffiana* Cham.), widespread in northern North America but at the time known in Europe only from Ireland.[43] Her last paper was on the strange algal growths known as moorballs found on the shores of some loughs.[44]

An energetic botanist and an accurate and careful archivist, Matilda Knowles had a wide knowledge of systematic botany and a breadth of view and tolerance of divergent opinion in scientific matters. Humorous and sympathetic, she was also a forthright person who spoke her mind and defended her position and the interests of the herbarium in a multidisciplinary museum. Her biographer recounts that in later life, when she used an ear trumpet because of partial deafness, she would bring to an end a debate that had become offensive by removing the trumpet and placing it firmly on her desk![45] During her years in Dublin she most likely shared an apartment with her sister Margaret, an artist whose work had been exhibited at the Royal Hibernian Academy. Matilda Knowles died in Dublin on 27 April 1933 at the age of sixty-nine, of pneumonia.

Another institution-based botanist whose papers are listed in the bibliography is RACHEL HENSMAN. Hensman attended botany lectures and laboratory sessions as an "occasional student" at the Royal College of Science Dublin in 1892 and 1893.[46] She then joined Thomas Johnson and others, including Matilda Knowles, on investigations of the Phaeophyceae, or brown seaweeds of the Irish coasts, economically important plants both because of their use as agricultural fertilizer and because of the western kelp industry (the plants were burned and the ashes sold as a source of iodine). Hensman's other early studies on algae from Irish waters carried out in collaboration with Johnson included investigations of the Corallinaceae and an examination of algae collected from Belfast Lough by the Belfast Naturalists' Field Club (see bibliography).

Rachel Hensman went on to a position as assistant to G. H. Pethybridge at the Seed Testing Station of the Department of Agriculture and Technical Instruction. She also continued to collaborate with Johnson who had charge of the work of this station, the first, and for some years the only official seed-testing station in the United Kingdom, although by then there were several on the Continent, particularly in Germany. A 1910 paper by Johnson and Hensman discussed the work of this station,[47] work that was becoming increasingly necessary as seed buyers everywhere were recognizing the need for testing of seeds offered for sale. As well as examining for deliberate contamination with sand or gravel, the station investigated place of origin; some non-European seeds were of little value in Europe for various reasons such as susceptibility to fungal diseases. The best indicators of origin, the weed seeds, also constituted a significant addition to the alien flora of Ireland, one of Johnson's particular interests.

Among Ireland's women naturalists whose papers are listed in the Royal Society *Catalogue* are four contributors of botanical papers who were probably all independent workers rather than being institution-based—Leebody, Joyce, Swan, and Hart.

MARY ISABELLA LEEBODY[48] (d. 1911) was known for her extensive explorations of the flora of northern Ireland, particularly of Antrim, Londonderry, and Donegal, and for her efforts to encourage others in botanical work. Born in Portaferry, County Down, she married J. R. Leebody of Foyle College, Londonderry, and lived most of her life in that city. An outstanding field botanist and an enthusiastic supporter of the Belfast Naturalists' Field Club, she rarely missed any of its excursions to places within reach of Londonderry. However, somewhat diffident in personality, she resisted Robert Lloyd Praeger's attempts to persuade her to set up a Derry Field Naturalists' Club.[49]

In the early 1890s she worked with Praeger and Matilda Knowles, collecting material for Praeger's 1895 supplement to *The Flora of the North-east of Ireland*; she provided a great many contributions of Derry plants. She also made a number of important finds of rare plants, particularly in County Donegal. These included *Glyceria aquatica* (a perennial grass whose American relative is known as *Manna Grass*) found near Ballyshannon; *Dryas octopetala* (a dwarf evergreen of the rose family); *Stachys betonica* (a member of the mint family) at Portsalon; and *Malaxis paludosa* on Slieve Snaght. Her discovery of the rare orchid *Spiranthes romanzoffiana* at Kilrea demonstrated that it had a wider range than previously thought. She is also credited with being the discoverer of *Teesdalia nudicaulis* in Ireland (1896—at Lough Neagh). Active in botanical work to almost the end of her life, she died in Londonderry on 19 September 1911.

MARGARET JOYCE and LILIAN SWAN each published notes in the *Irish Naturalist* in the late 1890s (see bibliography). Mrs. Joyce, of Craughwell, County Galway, explored mainly in her home county. She corresponded about her finds with Alexander Goodman More, a notable figure in British and Irish natural history studies in the late nineteenth century. She had met More about 1892 when he visited her region; he was especially interested in the locations of her finds.[50] Lilian Swan, from Dundalk, reported a find of *Sisyrinchium angustifolium* near Schull on the south coast of County Cork, the identification being done by Thomas Johnson. Again location was a matter of special interest, this specimen being a long way from the only other two places in Ireland where the plant had been observed.

J. B. HART carried out her natural history studies in and near Bombay, India, where she and her husband W. E. Hart lived from the 1870s until about 1891. With its unrivalled position on the shores of the Arabian Sea and its magnificent harbor, Bombay, the western gateway to India and already one of the major cities of the East, was for long the eastern headquarters of the British East India Company. Important for its cotton manufacturing, engineering works, trading, and shipping industries, it was also a cultural and administrative center with many public institutions, including Bombay University (established in 1859 with a Medical College founded in 1845), several technical colleges, hospitals, museums, a mint, and a high court. Mrs. Hart was active in the Bombay Natural History Society in its earliest days;[51] she served on its managing committee and published five papers in its *Journal* between 1886 and 1891 (see bibliography); these reported fossil finds and her observations on insects as well as plants. W. E. Hart, who was from the Londonderry region, was also a naturalist and from 1875 a member of the British Association for the Advancement of Science. He published articles in the Bombay Natural History Society's journal on entomological topics and on the geology of the Bombay area and surrounding regions.

Evidently well acquainted with works on the flora of India, Mrs. Hart brought out her first botanical paper in volume 1 of the journal in 1886, a report on a tree root parasite she observed when living in Mahableshwar, south and inland from Bombay. She considered the plant to be a Balanophora; hers was the first report of its presence in the Bombay Presidency. In her note of the same year on tubular fossils she suggested that these were derived from burrowing mollusks of the family Pholididae rather than being calcareous casts of mangrove stems and roots. Other reports described rearing butterflies in her Bombay home from larvae collected nearby, observations of protective mimicry in butterflies (also a topic of particular interest to her husband), and an account of branching in palm trees. By 1892 the Harts had returned to Ireland and were living in County Donegal, near Londonderry. Mrs. Hart does not appear to have published further work in natural history although W. E. Hart's notes on Donegal plants, insects, and birds continued to appear in the *Irish Naturalist* for at least the next two decades.

Marine Biologists

Louisa Glascott, Katherine Maguire, and Alice Shackleton, the three women whose papers in marine biology are listed in the bibliography, were all students or coworkers of zoologist and anthropologist Alfred Court Haddon, professor at the Royal College of Science Dublin and one of the leading figures in the Dublin Naturalists' Field Club.

Glascott, who was from New Ross, Wexford, studied Rotifera, a class of microscopic freshwater worms. Her paper published in the *Scientific Proceedings* of the Royal Dublin Society in 1893 reported 158 species collected in Wexford, Waterford, Dublin, Carlow, and Kerry. Of these she described twenty-four as being new to science. Writing in 1947, R. L. Praeger noted that later workers had not been able to confirm her new species.[52] Louisa Glascott also collaborated with biologist Gerald Barrett-Hamilton over the course of three years (1887–1889) on field studies of flowering plants in counties Wexford, Waterford, and Kilkenny. Their area of investigation was the tidal portion of the Barrow river from New Ross south to the estuary, much of the work in County Waterford being done by Glascott alone. Their findings were reported as annotated lists in two joint papers in the *Journal of Botany* in 1889 and 1890.

Alice Shackleton, from Foxrock, Dublin, took classes in zoology, botany, and practical physics as an occasional student at the Royal College of Science Dublin between 1885 and 1889. She was awarded a first prize in botany (special course) in 1888 and received her B.A. degree the same year.[53] She and Dr. Katherine Maguire both collaborated with Hadon during the 1890s in his research on sea anemones (Actiniaria), an area in which he was one of the major investigators. As well as British species they studied materials collected by Haddon in 1888 and 1889 in the Torres Straits between Australia and New Guinea. Their results, which included descriptions of new species from the Torres Straits, were reported in a series of lengthy papers in the *Proceedings* and *Transactions* of the Royal Dublin Society; Shackleton's work appeared in joint papers with Haddon.

The best-known and by far the most productive of the early women marine biologists in Ireland was Annie Massy[54] (1867–1931), a mollusk expert of international reputation, despite her lack of formal academic credentials. Only her first paper, an 1899 report on land shells from County Limerick, is listed in the bibliography (conchology section).

Annie Massy was the third of four children of Hugh Deane Massy of southeastern County Limerick and his wife Annie. An Anglo-Irish family, the Massys were Cromwellian settlers who came from England in the early part of the seventeenth century. Annie's ancestor, General Hugh Deane Massy, settled in Duntryleague, County Limerick, in 1641 and over the years the family acquired substantial land holdings in the county. Her father's home, Stagdale, now in ruins, was a fine country mansion in its day.

Annie Massy grew up near Malahide, a few miles north of Dublin, although she also spent some of her early years in Enniskerry, County Wicklow. She was most likely educated at home. Living close to the coastal region around Malahide known as the *Velvet Strand*, "that classical collecting ground of the old conchologists,"[55] she became especially knowledgeable about mollusks at an early age; she was also very interested in birds and flowers. Her contacts with other naturalists in the Dublin Naturalists' Field Club, of which she was an enthusiastic member, probably helped her focus her studies. Her first notable observation, verified and reported by Charles William Benson, was a nesting of the European redstart in County Wicklow in 1885, the first recorded in Ireland.[56] She was then eighteen. The work brought her to the attention of naturalists as a careful and competent observer, although she did not actually publish anything of her own for another fourteen years. In 1901 she began work as a temporary employee in the Fisheries Division of the recently organized Department of Agriculture and Technical Instruction where she remained for the rest of her life.

A great deal of biological material was being collected around the Irish coasts at this time by the extensive dredging, trawling, and tow-netting exploratory surveys underway. A considerable fraction came from the deep waters of the Rockall Trough off the Atlantic slope, a region little explored until then. When working over these collections Annie Massy became especially interested in two types of mollusks, the pteropods (members of the snail family) and the cephalopods (the class which includes cuttlefish, octopi, and squid). A preliminary report of her work on cephalopods, collected over the period 1901–1907 by the fisheries steamer for marine patrols and research *Helga*, appeared in 1907.[57] Three of the six species she discussed were new to science—*Polypus profundicola, Polypus normani,* and *Heliocranchia pfefferi.* Her comprehensive detailed report of the Dibranchiata subclass of the Cephalopoda of Ireland was published in 1909 and four additional studies on the mollusks of Irish coastal waters appeared as Fisheries Ireland publications in the period up to 1913. These included a detailed survey of Irish Sea trawling grounds along the north-central section of the Irish east coast (1912) and descriptions of eight species of pteropods and heteropods never before recorded along British coasts; among them was one new to science, a member of the genus *Clione.*[58] Other investigations of mollusks of Irish coastal waters appeared at intervals in various journals up to the time of her death.[59]

A careful, critical worker who took pains to verify any doubtful points with leading experts on the Continent and at the British Museum as well as at the museum in Dublin, Annie Massy soon became known internationally for her accurate and detailed investigations. Her studies of mollusks brought back by the 1910 British Antarctic ("Terra Nova") Expedition came out in two papers published in 1916 and 1920, the first on Cephalopoda, the second on Euteropoda and Pterota.[60] The year 1916 also saw the appearance of her paper on Cephalopoda of the Indian Museum, Calcutta, which included her identification of a new species of cuttlefish. Cephalopods from South African waters collected by the government trawler S.S. *Pieter Fauve* were discussed in a 1927 paper; here again she described specimens new to science (two species of cuttlefish, whose type specimens are now in the British Museum).[61] Her last investigation concerned pteropods collected on another expedition to Antarctica, work she was occupied with at the time of her final illness.

A member of the Conchological Society of Great Britain and Ireland, Annie Massy was also a founding member of the Irish Society for the Protection of Birds (forerunner of the Irish Wildlife Conservancy). In 1926, as the society's honorary secretary, she almost singlehandedly saved it from dissolution; her efforts made possible its work, which culminated in the passage of the Wild Birds Protection Act of 1930. Throughout her life she remained an enthusiastic bird watcher and continued to publish notes on birds from time to time in the *Irish Naturalist* and the *Irish Naturalists' Journal.*[62] Although her work brought her many international contacts, she was a somewhat retiring person living most of her life in or near Dublin, latterly in Howth, near Malahide, to the north of the city. She kept a well-tended poultry yard, and her garden was always full of birds and other wildlife—"The shearwaters are great company to me at night, and the ravens by day."[63] She died unexpectedly at age sixty-four, on 16 April 1931, at her home in Howth, and is buried at St. Andrew's Church, Malahide, County Dublin.

Three conchologists—Galwey, Tatlow, and Warren—whose pre-1900 papers are listed in the Royal Society's *Catalogue* were probably independent workers.[64] Their combined contributions of annotated shell lists from northern and western Ireland, where beaches were well known for their remarkable richness and variety of marine life, were significant additions to the records of the period.[65]

Honoria Galwey, a member of the Conchological Society, published in the society's journal a list of more than fifty shells collected in the summers of 1886 and 1887 on Magilligan Strand, a long, sandy beach open to the Atlantic on the coast of County Londonderry. An enthusiastic and knowledgeable collector, she assembled a cabinet of specimens and was well acquainted with strands in the Dublin area as well.

EMILY TATLOW, of County Dublin, collected in southwest Donegal and also in Wexford. Her annotated list of Donegal shells appeared in the *Irish Naturalist* in 1899.

AMY WARREN, from Moy View, Ballina, County Mayo, brought out her first paper in *The Zoologist* in 1879. An annotated list of land and freshwater mollusks from Counties Mayo and Sligo, it appears to have been the first published catalogue of mollusks for her area. Her extensive list of marine Molluska from Killala Bay, near her home, appeared in the *Journal of Conchology* in 1892; this was followed by seven notes in the *Irish Naturalist* over the next four years, mainly describing rare or interesting species, some from Killala Bay. Amy Warren's interest in natural history was shared by at least one other member of her household. Robert Warren, also of Moy View, contributed many notes and papers on his regional ornithological observations first to *The Zoologist* and later to the *Irish Naturalist* over a period of at least forty years, beginning about 1875.

One other naturalist and marine biologist, MAUDE JANE DELAP[66] (1866–1953), is discussed here even though she did not publish her first paper until 1901 and so is not included in the Royal Society *Catalogue*. She is notable for her fairly extensive collaboration in the 1895–1896 biological survey of Valentia Harbour, and also for her contributions to the work of elucidating the details of the life cycles of a number of species of Hydrozoa in which generations alternate between free-swimming medusae (tiny jellyfishes) and attached polyps.

Maude Delap was born at Templecrone Rectory on the northwest coast of County Donegal on 7 December 1866, the fifth daughter among the ten children (six girls and four boys) of the Rev. Alexander Delap, a Church of Ireland clergyman, and his wife Anna Jane (née Goslett). In 1874, when Alexander Delap was appointed rector of Valentia Island and Cahirciveen, County Kerry, the family moved to Valentia, then sixty miles from the nearest railhead.

A small island community at the extreme western edge of the European land mass, far from large population centers, Valentia's people were in the main poor tenant farmers and fishermen. However, there was another Valentia. From the middle of the nineteenth century the island was a major international communications station, its geographical position having led to its selection as the European terminal for the first trans-Atlantic telegraph cable (running from Valentia to Heart's Content, Newfoundland). For many years, every message crossing the Atlantic went through the Valentia Cable Station. Operated by the Anglo-American Cable Company from 1866 until 1911, when it was taken over by the Western Union Company, it was manned twenty-four hours a day, 365 days a year, and it employed a sizeable permanent staff of well-paid electrical engineers, electricians, and instrument clerks; its impact on the island's economy was considerable.[67] Valentia, again because of its position, was also the site chosen for a climatological and geomagnetic observatory, established by the Royal Society in 1867. In addition, a radio broadcasting station was set up there by Marconi in the 1890s; taken over by the British Post Office in 1909, it was manned until 1921 by the Royal Navy.[68] And so, despite its isolation and the primitive conditions in which most of its population lived, this island to which Maude Delap came as a child of eight and on which she spent the rest of her life was by no means cut off from the scientific world.

Maude and her sisters were educated at the island school and by their father, an enthusiastic naturalist who brought out notes on his local observations in the *Irish Naturalist* and other journals[69] and contributed specimens to the Dublin natural history museum. Maude's own correspondence with the Dublin museum began in 1894 when she sent to naturalist Robert Francis Scharff a specimen of the woodlouse *Armadillo vulgaris*, the first found on the west coast. However, much of her early work, done with her father and her sister Constance, concerned the marine fauna of Valentia Harbour, the bay between the northern shore of Valentia Island and the adjacent mainland, open to the Atlantic but at the same time relatively well sheltered. Like the west coast of Ireland as a whole, the bay was a particularly interesting hunting ground for marine naturalists, both for its own peculiar fauna and because of the presence of rare Atlantic species.

On account of its suitable dredging ground and good tide from the ocean, and perhaps also in part because of the Delaps's earlier work, Valentia Harbour, the most westerly port in Europe, was chosen in the mid 1890s as the site for a detailed biological study, a forerunner of the Clare Island Survey. Nine British biologists, including Edward Browne of University College London, worked there in 1895 and 1896 and received a considerable amount of help from the Delap sisters, especially in the tow-netting operations carried out to collect planktonic fauna from the sea's upper layers.[70] After the British party left in October 1896, Maude and Constance continued the surface tow-netting for more than two years and the specimens they preserved and sent to London were the basis of several of the survey's reports.[71] Browne, in his paper on the medusae of Valentia Harbour, acknowledged the Delaps's contributions and complimented them warmly; he was indebted to them and he wrote, "not only for specimens, but also for valuable notes and drawings. I must take the responsibility for the contents of this Report and the identification of the species; but it is chiefly owing to the

Misses Delap that the Medusoid fauna of Valentia Harbour is now better known than that of any other locality within the British area." This is all the more remarkable because Browne began his report with the statement, "Very few species of Medusae have been recorded for the west coast of Ireland; and, owing to the vagueness of the descriptions given to these forms, the records are now in most cases of little value."[72] Filling this very considerable gap in the knowledge of British medusae was one of the main goals of the expedition.

Three other biologists from the British group, Isaac Thompson, F. W. Gamble and W. I. Beaumont, who, respectively, worked on Copepoda (small crustaceans), Chaetognatha (marine worms), and Lucernaridae (a family of medusae), expressed their appreciation in their reports for the Delaps's help. The bulk of the material described by both Thompson and Gamble was collected and forwarded to them by Maude and Constance Delap.[73]

After the completion of the British team's survey Maude and Constance continued their investigations of Valentia Harbour fauna, building up a record of monthly distribution figures for Hydrozoa and other pelagic animals which, combined with the 1895–1898 data from the British study, covered a period of ten years (1895–1905). The few gaps in their tables were caused by such problems as the severe gales and heavy seas during the winter of 1902–1903, which not only made collecting difficult but reduced the numbers of pelagic organisms in the area. They did their work from an open boat but Maude was a strong and skillful oarswoman—"Aunt Maude was remarkably tough, and enjoyed handling a boat in the dangerous, remote sea caves on Doulus Head."[74] The results of their 1899–1905 studies were published by Fisheries Ireland in two papers, which appeared in 1905–1906.[75]

While still involved with the investigation of the fauna of Valentia Harbour, Maude Delap also began her lifecycle studies of jellyfish, work in which she received help and guidance from Edward Browne; indeed she had a long friendship with Browne, keeping in contact for forty years until his death in 1937. She focused her attention on species that went through two forms, fixed polyp and free-swimming medusa. Starting with the fixed polyps (collected on their rock attachments), she observed specimens through a full life cycle in her home aquaria recording the asexual budding of the polyp to give medusae, which in turn reproduce sexually producing ova and sperm from the union of which the polyp form again develops. Her studies were a significant contribution toward establishing several polyp–medusa relationships.[76] Apart from a microscope she worked with little in the way of equipment and the task of keeping her tanks and bell jars supplied with fresh sea water was no small matter. Not all species did well in her small aquaria, but she demonstrated that the hydroids of *Laodicea undulata* and *Dipleurosoma typicum* were species of *Cuspidella* and she also reared the medusa *Dipurena ophiogaster* from a previously unknown Conynid hydroid. Sometime before 1906 she was offered a position at the Marine Biological Laboratory in Plymouth, but she did not accept this, her father having strong objections to any of his daughters leaving home except on marriage. Maude was then about forty.

Apart from one further report in 1924,[77] Maude Delap published no work in marine biology after 1906 but she continued to collect enthusiastically and supplied rare species to many other workers. Stephensen, in the preface to the 1928 volume of his monograph on British sea anemones, mentioned her specially among the people who had collected for him and he went on to comment, "Miss Delap's skill and persistence in collecting rare species are indefatigable." In recognition of her work he suggested that an undescribed species of *Edwardsia* that she discovered on the Valentia shore be named after her—*Edwardsia delapiae*.[78]

From time to time until about 1922 Maude brought out natural history notes in the *Irish Naturalist*. These reported bird sightings and botanical observations in particular.[79] In his *Flora of County Kerry*, Reginald Scully specially acknowledged her local notes and also her extensive fieldwork, carried out by bicycle over considerable distances and extremely rough roads.[80] She was also much interested in local history and archaeology; her well-illustrated account of holy wells in Kerry published in 1911 included a detailed discussion of associated religious practices, patron saints, and folklore.[81]

During the 1920s and 1930s, Maude Delap was one of a team, organized by the British Museum, of official recorders of whale strandings on British coasts; books and notes on how to identify species were provided to team members. Maude's responsibilities in this undertaking could on occasion involve her in an extraordinary amount of manual labor. Sometime in the 1920s when a whale carcass was washed ashore on Valentia, Maude identified it as a True's Beaked Whale, a species previously known only from one incomplete specimen found in North Carolina in 1913. When she notified the staff of the museum in Dublin she was asked to send them the head and flippers of the sixteen-foot animal (which weighed over a ton) and to bury the rest in a safe place. A couple of years later, when a request came from Dublin for the remaining bones, these were retrieved from the depths of Maude's asparagus bed, their temporary resting place, and duly dispatched. Unfortunately for the asparagus roots, the museum staff found that two small but important vestigial pelvic bones were missing. A second session of excavating and sieving ended only when the museum ascertained that the species does not possess vestigial pelvic bones. Some years later Maude Delap found the skeleton of a second of these exceedingly rare beaked whales on the Kerry coast.

After the Rev. Delap's death in 1906, Maude, her sisters Constance and Mary, and their mother moved to Reenellen, a large house in Knightstown, the community at the eastern end of the island. Granted for their use during their lifetimes by the Knight of Kerry, a major landowner on the island, the house was of the old style, heated by turf fires and lit by oil lamps and candles; it also had its full share of the problems of wood-rot and moulds, which increased over the years. Hardworking and virtually self-sufficient, the Delap women kept two cows and grew their own vegetables and fruits, including grapes and peaches that, thanks to Valentia's mild climate, Maude could produce in her tumble-down greenhouse; the edible seaweed carrageen (Irish moss) was also part of their diet. Money was in short supply, however. Expenses that Maude incurred in her scientific work (sending specimens to the Dublin museum) were carefully recorded and she was later reimbursed. She earned a little money by supplying in season a small quantity of arum lilies and a variety of white gladiolus to the Dublin market. Despite their limited means, the Delap sisters were remembered in Valentia for their charity. They did a tremendous amount of work in the management of both the small island hospital, which took care of injured seamen as well as local people, and Fisherman's Hall; the latter was a social center mainly for men from the many fishing fleets, navy patrols, and other ships which frequently put in to Valentia Harbour, a place of great activity throughout the nineteenth century. During summer vacations Reenellen was a second home for "successive waves of nieces and nephews."[82]

Maude Delap's contributions to biology were recognized by the Linnean Society in 1936 when she was made an associate, a notable honor. She died on 23 July 1953 at age eighty-six, the last surviving member of the Reenellen household. Burial was on Valentia Island. Unfortunately her large collections of specimens, mainly jellyfish, were lost; during her old age she had not been able to renew the necessary preservative in her bottles and jars.

Geologists

Papers in geology by two Belfast women—Sydney Mary Thompson (later Madame Christen) and Mary K. Andrews—are listed in the bibliography. Both were prominent and active members of the Belfast Naturalists' Field Club.

SYDNEY MARY THOMPSON[83] (1847–1923), a niece of the well-known Irish naturalist William Thompson (1805–1852),[84] was born in the village of Whitehouse, about three miles north of Belfast on the shore of Belfast Lough. The Thompsons were engaged in the then-thriving linen business and Sydney Mary's parents were comfortably off. She had at least three siblings. Later her family home was at Macedon Point, a promontory on the shore of the lough, less than a mile north of Whitehouse; a large old house surrounded by an extensive garden, it commanded fine views. She described her childhood as "amphibious"; a large part of every summer was spent with her brother on the water, exploring the neighboring coastline from their small boat, an experience that could well have stimulated her interest in geology. In an 1895 paper she described some geological features of the area (cross-dyke basalt intrusions) and "the delightful excitement when our small punt ran aground, even at full tide, on these familiar cross-reefs, and threatened to tilt us over into the water."[85] She developed broad interests in natural history, keeping an aquarium for which she collected specimens along the same shore and also studying botany.

Little is known about her education in early childhood except that for three years, while living in Dresden, she attended a local school and acquired a fair knowledge of German. Her formal training was in art. In 1870, when she was twenty-three, she began studies at the Belfast Government School of Art, an institution recently established in the city to further progress in the linen industry. She won many prizes and went on to more advanced training at the South Kensington art school. An active and enthusiastic member of two local art groups, the Belfast Ramblers' Sketching Club and the Belfast Art Society, she shared a studio with her sister in the garden of their Macedon Point home.

At the time Sydney Mary Thompson was growing up in Belfast, a number of organizations offered encouragement and considerable help in natural history studies, her other special interest. An Academy Natural History Society and a School Museum, organized by the Belfast Academy, dated back to the early part of the nineteenth century. By the 1830s the society's meetings were well attended by both men and women, particularly people from the city's middle-class business families; many girls attended the academy's classes. Mineralogy was a popular lecture topic and the museum's mineral collection was outstanding. The founding of the Belfast Naturalists' Field Club (BNFC) in 1863 resulted directly from the enormous public interest in geology and antiquities. Further, the Belfast museum, which also had important holdings of Irish and foreign plants and shells, insects, birds, snakes, and lizards, served as the model for Irish natural history societies.[86]

Sydney Mary Thompson became a strong supporter of the BNFC. For many years she was active in both its botanical section, to which she donated substantial plant collections, and its geological undertakings. By 1894 she was one of the ten officers of the club's Ordinary Committee, a position she held until 1899. Club membership by that time was over 500, with women well represented, but Thompson was the only woman on the committee. A short time before she had been appointed honorary secretary of the Geological Committee, a group formed in response to a request for information on local glacial phenomena from the Erratic Blocks Committee of the British Association for the Advancement of Science.

The distribution of erratic blocks is important because these boulders, transported by ice action across long distances from their places of origin, serve as indicators of how far a particular glacier penetrated into adjacent regions. Although glacial theories and the concepts of an Ice Age in Ireland were not accepted by the Irish geological community until the 1860s, in the succeeding decades a great deal of work was carried out—work that moved the Quaternary history of Ireland "from the realm of religious myth to that of a science of an increasingly exact nature."[87]

The Belfast group's work during the 1890s, the period when Sydney Mary Thompson was most actively involved, was a major contribution to studies of Ireland's glacial geology. Thorough, detailed, and accurate, it went well beyond the investigation of just erratics and provided a complete study of drift deposits and their contents at several selected sites with photographs illustrating the features examined. Indeed in the work of photographing geological features, the Irish contribution to the British Association's effort was greater than that of Scotland and Wales combined and came mainly from the BNFC.[88] The committee's reports, prepared by Sydney Mary Thompson, were well received by the British Association geologists;[89] they have remained useful baseline documents for present-day workers. Further, "the splendid work of the Belfast Naturalists' Field Club in investigating the distribution of 'erratics' in the drifts of the north of Ireland" was held in high regard by fellow scientists working in Ireland.[90]

In addition to preparing the Geological Committee's reports throughout the period 1893–1898, Sydney Mary Thompson did much of the organizing of both winter lecture courses and practical work dealing with stratigraphy and petrography. She also regularly brought exhibits of rock specimens, fossils, and microscopic sections to club meetings. A very sociable person with broad interests, she made her father's house at Macedon Point a well-known meeting place for geologists and other naturalists.

Her own fieldwork on the erratics and other glacial features was considerable, much of it published as part of the club's annual reports. Two of her papers, "A bit of foreshore," delivered at a December 1894 club meeting, and her March 1899 talk on a bed of white lias at Macedon Point (see bibliography) discussed the area she had known intimately since childhood; she dealt particularly with the ongoing changes brought about by storm erosion of the shoreline over the years. The white lias bed, protected by two surrounding basaltic dykes, had recently been exposed, revealing features not visible when the Irish branch of the Geological Survey had made its maps of the region. Its discovery was important because it suggested the need for a possible reevaluation of the details of the sedimentary deposits of the area; although assigned by the survey to a lower division of the Triassic period designated Bunter beds (predominantly red sandstone), club members had always considered these sedimentary layers to be an extension of the overlying Keuper marls. Sydney Mary Thompson's observations were considered to provide strong support for the club's opinion—which later work confirmed.[91]

In 1900 she married artist Rodolphe Christen, a native of St. Imier in northwest Switzerland, and from then on her association with the BNFC was somewhat reduced. She first met Christen in 1893 when he came to teach art classes in Dublin; she helped organize a course taught by him in Belfast.

For about two years following their marriage the Christens wandered the Continent, drawing and painting in France, Spain, Italy, Switzerland, and Germany. In Saxony, Mme. Christen made several excursions collecting samples of geological or archaeological interest, rhyolites, brown volcanic glasses, "chalk fossils,," and flint tools. Then, following a visit to western Ireland where she returned to investigations of glacial deposits, they settled in a house they built near Ballater in the Scottish Highlands. There they established a fine rock garden with both Mediterranean and northern plants. Rodolphe Christen's time in Scotland was short however; he died in 1906.

Sydney Mary Christen stayed on in her Ballater home and remained interested and active in geological work, including the distribution of erratic blocks in Ireland. Her find (sometime between 1907 and 1910) of a specimen of Ailsa Craig granite erratic at Moys, three miles south-southwest of Limavady, County Londonderry, pushed the limit of penetration of the Scottish glacier some twenty miles further west than previously designated.[92] She also made many geological trips to the Continent, her last to the volcanoes of the Auvergne in 1922. During the First World War, when she was in her late sixties, she worked with the War Comforts Association for Aberdeenshire. Her ties with Ireland, and especially the Belfast region, remained very close. She became a patron of the Belfast Art Society in 1921 and over the course of several years corresponded with Belfast local historian F. J. Bigger, supplying him with information for his family history studies. She felt that "Ireland deserves all her activities recorded."[93] Sydney Mary Christen died in Llandudno, Wales, on 16 July 1923, when she was about seventy-six.

MARY K. ANDREWS[94] (1852–1914), one of the six children (four girls and two boys) of Thomas Andrews and his wife Jane (née Hardie), was born in Belfast in 1852. Thomas Andrews (1813–1885), a physician and chemist remembered especially for his research on the liquefaction of gases and the discovery of the critical constants, was a leading figure in Belfast's academic life in the mid years of the nineteenth century. Appointed one of the first professors in the collegiate department of the Belfast Academical Institution (the first university-level institution in the north of Ireland), he later became professor of chemistry and then vice principal of Queen's College, Belfast.

A friend of Sydney Mary Thompson and Thompson's colleague on the BNFC Geological Committee from its establishment in 1893, Mary Andrews was active in the club's geological work throughout the 1890s when the investigation of local glacial features was very much to the fore. To a large extent her contributions, like those of Sydney Mary Thompson, were incorporated into the *Reports* of the Geological Committee. Part of the fieldwork she undertook was the photographing of features of special interest, a contribution greatly appreciated by the British Association geologists with whom the club was collaborating[95] (see discussion of Thompson, p. 50). She also did much of the trimming, mounting, and labelling of collections of Irish rock and erratic samples donated by members to the club's holdings. Her own exhibits included rock specimens and microscope sections; from time to time she also presented reports on geological topics at club meetings.

Her first published papers (1893 and 1894) dealt with postglacial denudation at Cultra on the south shore of Belfast Lough, and observations on dykes in Antrim and Down (see bibliography). In 1897 and again in 1903 she discussed in club talks her studies on granites and other rocks in the region of Newcastle on the Down coast; her investigation of coastal erosion appeared in the *Irish Naturalist* in 1901.[96] She also studied formations in the high country of northwest Wales in the early 1890s. Her findings of shells and foraminifera in a sand and gravel bed on Moel Tryfaen, an outlier of Snowdon, were presented at a winter meeting of the BNFC in 1894. The Welsh site was famous for a shell bed some 1,350 feet above sea level that, when first discovered in 1831, was a matter of intense interest to the geological community; the idea of land uplift to that extent was not then universally accepted. Andrews's shells and foraminifera were new discoveries in the bed she investigated. Mary Andrews died in 1914 when she was about sixty-two.

Summary

Of the twenty-one Irish women discussed here, two—Knowles and Massy—received international recognition, five were known nationally—Delap, S. M. Thompson, Ward, Leebody, and Warren—and at least five others made worthy contributions to the scientific work of the time—Andrews, Hensman, Galwey, Tatlow, and Ball. Among these twelve were three—Hensman, Knowles, and Massy—who had institutional bases, but nine (75 percent) were "amateurs" who for the most part worked independently, in partnership with professionals, or under the umbrella of scientific clubs. Because club membership included professionals who were very often glad to have the assistance and collaboration of independent workers, the latter generally enjoyed considerable support and encouragement. In addition, club reports and proceedings, which were brought out regularly, provided a place where the nonprofessional women could publish their observations.

Botany, marine biology including conchology, and geology, the major areas of activity of the group, were those into which the Irish naturalist societies and the country's scientific community were putting considerable effort at the time. There was no single field toward which the women gravitated.

The research in marine biology of Massy, Maguire, Shackleton, and Delap has parallels with the work of a number of American and Scandinavian women biologists of the time who were engaged in analysis of materials collected by marine exploratory expeditions undertaken by their countries.[97] The contributions of women to

Irish conchology reflect the great wealth of material available along the Irish Atlantic coasts to the knowledgeable amateur; here again a comparison might be drawn with the work of American women conchologists, in particular those active in the rich hunting grounds along their country's Pacific coast.[98]

In botany the work of Irish women was largely in field exploration. They joined in the topographical botany projects being conducted at the time, the preparation or expansion and updating of county floras, and the systematic exploration of less well investigated divisions of the field, particularly cryptogamic botany. Ireland's most notable early woman botanist, Matilda Knowles, made her name in the latter area, hardly one of the most popular branches of the field with the leading professionals but the niche in which a number of American and British women of the time were also extremely prominent.[99]

In geology, the contributions of Sydney Mary Thompson and Mary K. Andrews were very much part of the wider investigations of Irish glacial geology, and indeed British glacial geology, that were going on at the time.[100]

Notes

1. Papers by twenty women whose names appear in the Royal Society *Catalogue* and who have been identified as Irish are listed in the bibliography; an additional paper by Robert Ball has been added because, although published under his name only, it was almost entirely a direct quotation of observational records of his sister Mary Ball.

2. Mary R. S. Creese, *Ladies in the Laboratory? American and British Women in Science, 1800–1900: A Survey of Their Contributions to Research* (Lanham, Md.: Scarecrow Press, 1998), 237–42, 410–12. Had the work of Clerke, Huggins, and Proctor been discussed here, the paper count associated with this chapter would have almost doubled and astronomy would have held a very prominent position.

3. Sean Lysaght, "Science and the Cultural Revival, 1863–1916," in *Science and Society in Ireland: The Social Context of Science and Society in Ireland 1800–1950,* eds. Peter J. Bowler and Nicholas Whyte (Belfast: Institute of Irish Studies, Queen's University of Belfast, 1997), 153–65.

4. Helena C. G. Ross and Robert Nash, "The Development of Natural History in Early Nineteenth-Century Ireland," in *From Linnaeus to Darwin: Commentaries on the History of Biology and Geology,* eds. Alwyne Wheeler and James H. Price (London: Society for the History of Natural History, 1985), 13–27, on 13, 15.

5. Mary Robinson, "Foreword," in Women in Technology & Science (WITS), *Stars, Shells and Bluebells: Women Scientists and Pioneers* (Dublin: Women in Technology & Science [WITS], 1997), 10–11.

6. They were not the first women to make notable contributions to Irish natural history. See for instance the work in cryptogamic botany of Ellen Hutchins (1785–1815) of Ballylickey near Bantry on Ireland's then remote southwest coast. Ellen assembled outstanding collections of algae, liverworts, and lichens, many of them new to science, and was in close contact with several of the leading British and Irish botanists of her time. A number of species are named after her. She never published, but the major part of her specimen collections and her drawings and water colors are still extant, housed at the Royal Botanic Gardens, Kew (Helena C. G. Chesney, "The Young Lady of the Lichens," in Women in Technology & Science, *Stars, Shells and Bluebells,* 29–39).

7. G[eorge] E[velyn] Hutchinson, "The Harp that Once . . . A Note on the Discovery of Stridulation in the Corixid Water-Bugs," *Irish Naturalists' Journal* 20 (1982): 457–66, and *A Treatise on Limnology,* vol. 4, *The Zoobenthos* (New York: Wiley, 1993), 670, 714–15, 719, 722–23; and Jane Hanly and Patricia Deevy, "Stepping Stones in Science," in Women in Technology & Science, *Stars, Shells and Bluebells,* 41–44.

8. Mary Ball's copy of Stephens's *Catalogue* is now in the library of the National Museum, Dublin (see Hutchinson, "Harp that Once," 464).

9. Hutchinson, "Harp that Once," 458; and *Zoobenthos,* 722.

10. Hutchinson, "Harp that Once," 457.

11. Robert Ball's first note was "On the Sounds Produced by One of the Notonectidae under Water," *Annals and Magazine of Natural History* 16 (1845): 129; the second, in which he credited "Miss M. Ball" as being the original and major observer, was "On Noises Produced by One of the Notonectidae," *Reports of the British Association for the Advancement of Science,* Cambridge, 1845 (1846): 64–65 (Notices and Abstracts section); for the third note, see bibliography.

12. Hutchinson, "Harp that Once," 461.

13. E. De Selys-Longchamps, "Revision of the British Libellulidae," *Annals and Magazine of Natural History* 18 (1846): 217–27.

14. William Thompson, *The Natural History of Ireland,* vol. 4, *Mammalia, Reptiles and Fishes. Also Invertebrata,* ed. R. Patterson (London: H. G. Bohn, 1856).

15. The topic of stridulation in Corixidae was discussed again by an Irishwoman, Mary Thompson, in two short notes in the *Irish Naturalist* in 1894 and 1895 (see bibliography). Mrs. Thompson, from Cork, had been invited by the journal editors to describe her observations made while keeping a *Corixa* in a jar of water for several days; they considered her

report of special interest. Her work was one of the first confirmations of Mary Ball's findings and was apparently made independently.

16. Owen Harry, "The Hon. Mrs. Ward (1827–1869); A Wife, Mother, Microscopist and Astronomer in Ireland 1854–1869," in *Science in Ireland 1800–1930: Tradition and Reform*, eds. J. R. Nudds, N. D. McMillan, D. L. Weaire, and S. M. P. McKenna-Lawlor (Dublin: Trinity College Dublin, 1988), 187–97; Owen Harry, "The Hon. Mrs Ward and 'A Windfall for the Microscope' of 1856 and 1864," *Annals of Science* 41 (1984): 471–82; Ita Kavanagh, "Mistress of the Microscope," in Women in Technology & Science, *Stars, Shells and Bluebells,* 57–65; Susan McKenna-Lawlor, *Whatever Shines Should Be Observed,* Samton Historical Studies (Blackrock, Co. Dublin: Samton Ltd., 1998), 29–55; *Burke's Peerage and Barontage,* 106th ed., ed. Charles Mosley (Crans, Switzerland: Burke's Peerage, 1999), vol. 1, 182.

17. Mary King's scientific library included the following works: Henry Baker, *The Microscope Made Easy* (1743) and *Employment for the Microscope* (1753); David Brewster, *Treatise on Optics* (1853); Robert Grant, *History of Physical Astronomy* (1852); John Herschel, *Treatise on Astronomy* (1833) and *Astronomy* (1837); George Airy, *Six Lectures on Astronomy* (1851); Robert Patterson, *Introduction to Zoology* (1848); William Carpenter, *Zoology* (1848); William Kirby, *Introduction to Entomology* (1843); and William Jardine, *The Naturalist's Library* (1852).

18. The earl's wife, also named Mary, was a noted photographer. Her darkroom in Birr Castle is said to be the oldest fully equipped photographic laboratory in existence. She used both the popular daguerreotype plates and other processes then becoming available (McKenna-Lawlor, *Whatever Shines,* 22–24).

19. Along with the daguerreotype photographs taken by the countess of Rosse, Mary King's notes and drawings were crucial for the recent restoration of the Leviathin at Birr Castle (Kavanagh, "Mistress of the Microscope," 60).

20. Ward to Sir William Rowan Hamilton, Ireland's Astronomer Royal, quoted by Harry, "Hon. Mrs. Ward," 191.

21. David Brewster, *Memoirs of the Life, Writings and Discoveries of Sir Isaac Newton* (Edinburgh: T. Constable, 1855).

22. David Brewster, "On the Structure and Optical Phenomena of Ancient Decomposed Glass," *Transactions of the Royal Society of Edinburgh* 23 (1864): 193–204. See also Ward's illustrations in Brewster's, "On the Existence of Acari between the Laminae of Mica in Optical Contact," *Transactions of the Royal Society of Edinburgh* 23 (1864): 95–96, and "On Certain Vegetable and Mineral Formations in Calcareous Spar," *Transactions of the Royal Society of Edinburgh* 23 (1864): 97–98.

23. Henry Ward succeeded to the title, becoming the fifth viscount Bangor, on the death of his older brother Edward in 1881, twelve years after Mary's death. Mary's son Maxwell succeeded to the title in 1911, and her great-grandson William became the eighth viscount Bangor in 1993 on the death of his father Edward.

24. A now largely forgotten general journal, *Recreative Science,* began publication in London in 1859, changed its title to *The Intellectual Observer* in 1862, underwent a second title change in 1868 (to *Student and Intellectual Observer of Science, Literature and Art*), and ceased publication in 1871. Its stated interests included in particular natural history and microscopical science.

25. Mary Ward, *A World of Wonders Revealed by the Microscope; A Book for Young Students with Coloured Illustrations* (London: Groomsbridge, 1858, and several later editions), initially printed as Mary Ward, *Sketches with the Microscope* (Parsonstown: Shields, 1857).

26. *Telescope Teachings: A Familiar Sketch of Astronomical Discovery, Combining a Special Notice of Subjects Coming within the Range of a Small Telescope . . .* (London: Groomsbridge, 1859, and two additional printings).

27. Excerpts from the diary and some of the drawings have been reproduced in McKenna-Lawlor, *Whatever Shines,* 43–49.

28. Lawlor, *Whatever Shines,* 52. For a discussion of earlier popular introductory works on these subjects see John R. Issitt, "Jeremiah Joyce: Science Educationist," *Endeavour* 26 (2002): 97–101. Joyce (1763–1816) brought out *The Wonders of the Microscope or An Explanation of the Wisdom of the Creator in Objects Comparatively Minute, Adapted to the Understanding of the Young* (London: Tarbert and Phillips, 1805), and *The Wonders of the Telescope or Display of the Starry Heavens Calculated to Promote and Simplify the Study of Astronomy* (London: Tarbert and Phillips, 1805).

29. Maura Scannell, "Inspired by Lichens," in Women in Technology & Science, *Stars, Shells and Bluebells*, 85–97; R. Lloyd Praeger, *Some Irish Naturalists: A Biographical Notebook* (Dundalk: W. Tempest, 1949), 116, and obituaries by him in *Irish Naturalists' Journal* 4 (1933): 191–93 and *Journal of Botany* 71 (1933): 230–31.

30. Matilda Knowles was also interested in materials from the Neolithic era and published two papers on archaeological finds in County Clare—see bibliography and "Kitchen Middens of County Clare," *Journal of the Limerick Field Club* 2 (1901–04): 34–42.

31. S. A. Stewart and R. Lloyd Praeger, "A Supplement to *The Flora of the North-east of Ireland* of Stewart and Corry," *Annual Report and Proceedings of the Belfast Naturalists' Field Club* 4 (1901): 136–236.

32. "Notes on the Additions to the Flora of County Limerick," *Irish Naturalist* 12 (1903): 249–53; (with C. G. O'Brien) "The Flora of the Barony of Shanid," *Irish Naturalist* 16 (1907): 185–201; and (with R. D. O'Brien) "A Botanical Tour of the Islands of the Fergus Estuary and Adjacent Mainland," *Irish Naturalist* 18 (1909): 57–68.

33. "A Contribution towards the Alien Flora of Ireland," *Irish Naturalist* 15 (1906): 143–50.

34. "The Levinge Herbarium," *Scientific Proceedings of the Royal Dublin Society* 10 (1903): 122–32.

35. James White, "Clare Island off the County Mayo Coast," in *Some People and Places in Irish Science and Technology,* eds. Charles Mollan, William Davis, and Brendon Finucane (Dublin: Royal Irish Academy, 1985), 94–95.

36. See Creese, *Ladies in the Laboratory?*, 36–37, 385.

37. Annie Lorrain Smith, "Lichens (Clare Island Survey, Pt. 14)," *Proceedings of the Royal Irish Academy* 31 (1911): 1–14; see also M. C. Knowles, "Notes on West Galway Lichens," *Irish Naturalist* 21 (1912): 29–36, and "Lichens," in G. P. Farran, "Results of a Biological Survey of Blacksod Bay, County Mayo," *Scientific Investigations: Fisheries Branch, Ireland, 1914* 3 (1915): 1–72.

38. Smith, "Lichens," 2.

39. "The Maritime and Marine Lichens of Howth," *Scientific Proceedings of the Royal Dublin Society* 14 (1913): 79–143. The new species were *Acarospora benedarensis* Knowles (now *A. amaragdula*), *Lecania atrynoides* Knowles, and *Verrucaria lorrain-smithii* (now *V. sandstedei*).

40. Maura Scannell, "A Work of Special Value," in Women in Technology & Science, *Stars, Shells and Bluebells*, 165–72.

41. Praeger, obituary, 192.

42. This material was published in 1948 by Cork-based lichenologist Lillian Porter, along with some of Porter's own work—see Lillian Porter, "The Lichens of Ireland (Supplement)," *Proceedings of the Royal Irish Academy* 51, B (1948): 347–86.

43. "On the Irish *Spiranthes romanzoffiana*," *Irish Naturalists' Journal* 2 (1928): 2–6.

44. "Moorballs," *Irish Naturalists' Journal* 4 (1933): 170–73. For a full listing of Knowles's thirty-two publications, see Scannell, "Inspired," 95–96.

45. Scannell, "Inspired," 93–94.

46. Register of occasional and nonassociate students, Royal College of Science Dublin (1867–1906), College Archives, University College Dublin.

47. T. Johnson and R. Hensman, "Agricultural Seeds and Their Weed Impurities. A Source of Ireland's Alien Flora," *Scientific Proceedings of the Royal Dublin Society* 12 (1910): 446–62. See also T. Johnson and R. Hensman, "Six Years of Seed Testing in Ireland," *Reports of the British Association for the Advancement of Science,* York, 1906, (1907): 744.

48. Obituary, *Irish Naturalist* 20 (1911), 218; Praeger, *Some Irish Naturalists*, 118.

49. Lysaght, "Science and the Cultural Revival."

50. *Life and Letters of Alexander Goodman More*, ed. C. B. Moffat (Dublin: Hodges, Figgis & Co., 1898), 377–81, 393–94.

51. Founded in 1883 by the British community in Bombay for the purpose of exchanging notes on natural history and exhibiting specimens, the Bombay Natural History Society is today a major organization, the largest in the subcontinent engaged in conservation and in education and research in natural history. For a general view of the early history of Bombay, see *The Bombay Presidency, the United Provinces, the Punjab, etc: Their History, People, Commerce, and Natural Resources,* comp. Somerset Playne (London: Foreign and Colonial Compiling and Publishing Co., 1917–20).

52. Praeger, *Some Irish Naturalists,* 86.

53. Calendar of the Royal University of Ireland; Register of occasional and nonassociate students, Royal College of Science Dublin (1867–1906).

54. Obituaries, *Nature* 123 (1931): 59; G. P. Farran and C. B. Moffat, *Irish Naturalists' Journal* 3 (1931): 215; Anne Byrne, "Bringing a Shy Biologist Out of Her Shell," in Women in Technology & Science (WITS), *Stars, Shells and Bluebells,* 111–19; and Praeger, *Some Irish Naturalists,* 128. Few details about Annie Massy's family have been found. She had at least one brother, Colonel Godfrey Massy, G.M.G. (Byrne, "Bringing a Shy Biologist," 112).

55. Obituary, *Nature.*

56. Rev. Charles William Benson, *Our Irish Songbirds* (Dublin: Hodges, Figgis, 1886).

57. "Preliminary Notice of New and Remarkable Cephalopods from the Southwest Coast of Ireland," *Annals and Magazine of Natural History* s. 7, 20 (1907): 377–84.

58. "The Cephalopoda Dibranchiata of the Coasts of Ireland," *Fisheries Ireland. Scientific Investigations 1907* 1 (1909): 1–39; "The Pteropoda and Heteropoda of the Coasts of Ireland," *Fisheries Ireland. Scientific Investigations 1907* 2 (1909): 1–52; "Report of a Survey of Trawling Grounds on the Coasts of Counties Down, Louth, Meath and Dublin. Pt. 3: Invertebrate fauna," *Fisheries Ireland. Sci. Invest. 1911* 1 (1912): 1–225; "Further Records of the Cephalopoda Dibranchiata of the Coasts of Ireland," *Fisheries Ireland. Sci. Invest. 1912* 5 (1913): 1–12; and "Notes on the Evidence of Age Afforded by the Growth Rings of Oysters," *Fisheries Ireland. Sci. Invest. 1913* 2 (1914): 1–12.

59. "Molluska and Brachiopoda of the Irish Atlantic Slope," *Journal of Conchology* 15 (1916): 45–61; "The gymnosomatous Pteropoda of the Coasts of Ireland," *Scientific Proceedings of the Royal Dublin Society* n.s. 15 (1917): 223–44; "The Holothuroidea of the Coasts of Ireland," *Scientific Proceedings of the Royal Dublin Society* n.s. 16, no. 4 (1920); "Note on a New Cephalopod, *Cirroteuthis* (*Cirrotheuthopis*) *massyae* Grimpe," *Annals and Magazine of Natural History* s. 9, 14 (1924): 127–30; "The Cephalopoda of the Irish Coast," *Proceedings of the Royal Irish Academy* B, 38, 2 (1928): 25–37; "Molluska (Pelecypoda, Scaphopoda, Gastropoda, Opisthobrancia) of the Irish Atlantic Slope, 50–1,500 fathoms," *Proceedings of the Royal Irish Academy* B, 39, 13 (1930): 231–342; and "Gastropoda, Thecosomata and Gymnosomata," [Posth.] *Discovery Reports* 3 (1932): 267–96.

60. "Molluska. Pt. II. Cephalopoda: British Antarctic ('Terra Nova') Expedition, 1910," *British Museum (Natural History), London: Natural History Reports, Zoology* 2 (1916): 141–75; and "Molluska. Pt. III. Euptteropoda (*Pteropoda theco-*

somata) and Pterota (*Pteropoda gymnosomata*): British Antarctic ('Terra Nova') Expedition, 1910," *British Museum (Natural History), London: Natural History Reports, Zoology* 2 (1920): 203–32.

61. "The Cephalopoda of the Indian Museum," *Records of the Indian Museum,* Calcutta, 12, Pt. 5 (1916): 185–247; (with G. C. Robson) "On a Remarkable Case of Sex-Dimorphism in the Genus *Sepia*," *Annals and Magazine of Natural History* s. 9, 12 (1923): 435–42; "On the Cephalopoda of the Natal Museum," *Annals of the Natal Government Museum,* Pietermaritzburg, 5, Pt. 2 (1925): 201–29; and "The Cephalopoda of the South African Museum," *Annals of the South African Museum,* Capetown, 25 (1927): 151–67.

62. "Black Redstart on Hill of Howth," *Irish Naturalist* 31 (1922): 56; "Kestrel Feeding while Hovering," *Irish Naturalists' Journal* 1 (1926): 113; "Crossbill on Howth," *Irish Naturalists' Journal* 1 (1927): 255; and "Redstart on Howth Hill," *Irish Naturalists' Journal* 2 (1929): 246. Massy also published notes on flowers: "New Locality for *Paludestrina jenkinsi*," *Irish Naturalist* 10 (1902): 19; and "Red Cowslips," *Irish Naturalist* 32 (1923): 63.

63. Massy, in a letter dictated three days before her death, quoted by Byrne, "Bringing a Shy Biologist," 117.

64. Two other naturalists, Lena Gyles and Frances O'Connor, were most likely also independent workers, although not in marine biology. Gyles, a bird observer from Dublin, reported her sightings of *Iynx torquilla,* the wryneck, in 1898. The first record of the bird in Ireland had been made only in 1877. O'Connor, from Ballycastle, Antrim, contributed a note on spider behavior to the *Irish Naturalist* in 1896.

65. The papers by Galwey, Tatlow, and Warren listed in the bibliography are included in "Important Works and Papers Referring to Irish Marine Mollusca," in A. R. Nichols, "List of Marine Mollusca of Ireland," *Proceedings of the Royal Irish Academy* s. 3, 5 (1900): 477–662, on 483, 488, 490.

66. Anne Byrne, "Untangling the Medusa," in Women in Technology & Science, *Stars, Shells and Bluebells,* 99–109; N. F. McMillan and W. J. Rees, obituary, *Irish Naturalists' Journal* 12 (1958): 221–22; Nellie O'Cleirigh, *Valentia. A Different Irish Island* (Dublin: Portobello Press, 1992); and Praeger, *Some Irish Naturalists,* 200.

67. Since the 1866 cable was stranded copper (insulated, armored, and strengthened) and lacked the repeater units incorporated into later installations, messages had to be recorded at Valentia and then reentered into the system for transmission across the Atlantic stretch (or after being received from Newfoundland). Hence the need for the large staff of instrument clerks; messages were visually read and recorded letter by letter, a process requiring skill and speed. By the 1880s Valentia had three cables, one in direct communication with Emden in the north of Germany through which all Continental messages were routed. The station remained in operation until 1966. Undersea repeaters were first used in an Anglesey to Isle of Man cable in 1943; the first transatlantic repeatered coaxial telephone cable system was installed in 1956—from Oban, Scotland, to Clarenville, Newfoundland. See E. T. Mottram, R. J. Halsey, J. W. Emling and R. G. Griffith, "Transatlantic Telephone Cable System: Planning and Overall Performance," in *Proceedings of the Institution of Electrical Engineers, Pt. B, Supplement No. 4, Transatlantic Telephone Cable* 104 (1957): 3–10, on 4, 5.

68. Now run by the Irish government, the Valentia Radio Station remains an important facility. It broadcasts weather bulletins, forecasts, and navigation warnings and provides telegraph and telephone service for shipping of all kinds as well as oilrigs. In addition it is an integral part of marine rescue services, maintaining a twenty-four-hour watch on international distress frequencies.

69. See for instance Alex H. Delap, "*Tricomanes radicans* in Co. Tyrone," *Journal of Botany* 30 (1892): 121; "Additional localities for Irish land and freshwater Molluska," *Irish Naturalist* 2 (1893): 84; "The tree mallow (*Lavatera arborea*) in Ireland," *Irish Naturalist* 2 (1893): 112.

70. Maude Delap's biographer concluded that Constance Delap, although she worked with Maude in the Valentia Harbour studies, did not have the same overall commitment as Maude to scientific work (Byrne, "Untangling the Medusa," 102).

71. E. T. Browne, I. Thompson, F. W. Gamble, et al., "The Fauna and Flora of Valentia Harbour on the West Coast of Ireland," *Proceedings of the Royal Irish Academy* s. 3, 5 (1900): 667–854.

72. E. T. Browne, "Report on the Medusae (1895–98)," *Proceedings of the Royal Irish Academy* s. 3, 5 (1900): 694–736 on 694. It is worth noting that the waters of the south and west of Ireland, and Valentia in particular, are especially rich in these fauna—see T. A. Stephensen, *The British Sea Anemones,* 2 vols. (London: The Ray Society, 1928, 1935), vol. 1, 83.

73. Isaac C. Thompson, "Report on the Free-Swimming Copepoda (1895–98)," *Proceedings of the Royal Irish Academy* s. 3, 5 (1900): 737–44; F. W. Gamble, "The Chaetognatha," *Proceedings of the Royal Irish Academy* s. 3, 5 (1900): 745–7; and W. I. Beaumont, "Report on the Lucernaridae," *Proceedings of the Royal Irish Academy* s. 3, 5 (1900): 806–11.

74. Peter Delap, Maude Delap's nephew, quoted by Byrne, "Untangling the Medusa," 103. Doulus Head, the westernmost point of the mainland on the northern shore of Valentia Harbour inlet, is fully open to the Atlantic.

75. (With Constance Delap) "Notes on the Plankton of Valencia Harbour, 1899–1901," *Annual Report of the Fisheries of Ireland 1902–03* pt. 2, appendix I (1905): 3–19; and (with Constance Delap) "Notes on the Plankton of Valencia Harbour 1902–05," *Report on the Sea and Inland Fisheries of Ireland for 1902 and 1903. Pt. 2 Scientific Investigations 1905* 7 (1906): 3–26.

76. "Notes on the Rearing of *Chrysaora isosceles* in an Aquarium," *Irish Naturalist* 10 (1901): 25–28; "Notes on the Rearing, in an Aquarium, of *Cyanea Lamarcki* Peron et Lesueur," *Annual Report of the Fisheries of Ireland 1902–03,* pt. 2, appendix 1 (1905); (with Constance Delap) "Notes on the Rearing, in an Aquarium, of *Aurelia aurita* L. and *Pelagia perla*

(Slabber)," *Report on the Sea and Inland Fisheries of Ireland for 1902 and 1903, Pt. 2, Scientific Investigations 1905* 5 (1906): 22–26.

77. "Further Notes on the Plankton of Valentia Harbour," *Irish Naturalist* 33 (1924): 1–6.

78. Stephensen, *British Sea Anemones,* vol. 1, Preface, x.

79. "Birds of the Skelligs," *Irish Naturalist* 14 (1905), 134; "New Localities for *Geomalacus maculosus, Irish Naturalist* 15 (1906): 190; "Early Appearance of *Macroglossa stellaturum,*" *Irish Naturalist* 18 (1909): 140; "Drift on the Kerry Coast," *Irish Naturalist* 30 (1921): 40; "The Breeding of the Fulmar Petrel in Ireland" *Irish Naturalist* 31 (1922): 130; and "Swans in Valentia Harbour," *Irish Naturalist* 31 (1922): 140.

80. Reginald W. Scully, *Flora of County Kerry: Including the Flowering Plants, Ferns, Characeae, etc.* (Dublin: Hodges, Figgis, 1916), Preface, v.

81. "Some Holy Wells in Valencia and Portmagee," *Kerry Archaeological Magazine* 7 (1911): 403–14.

82. McMillan and Rees, obituary, 221.

83. Obituaries, G. A. J. C[ole], *Geologists' Magazine* (1923): 478–79; *Irish Naturalist* 32 (1923): 108; Kate Newman, *Dictionary of Ulster Biography* (Belfast: Queen's University, 1993), 253; Mary R. S. Creese and Thomas M. Creese, "British Women Who Contributed to Research in the Geological Sciences in the Nineteenth Century," *British Journal for the History of Science* 27 (1994): 23–54, on 32–3; Sydney Mary Thompson (Mme Christen), *Rodolphe Christen: The Story of an Artist's Life* (London: Longmans Green, 1910).

84. William Thompson, *The Natural History of Ireland,* vol. 4, *Mammalia, Reptiles and Fishes. Also Invertebrata,* ed. R. Patterson (London: H. G. Bohn, 1856).

85. See bibliography ("A Bit of Foreshore," 211).

86. Ross and Nash, "Development of Natural History," 16; and Timothy Collins, "Some Irish Women Scientists," *UCG Women's Studies Centre Review* 1 (1992): 39–53.

87. Kevin J. Edwards and William P. Warren, "Quaternary Studies in Ireland," in *The Quaternary History of Ireland,* eds. K. J. Edwards and W. P. Warren (London: Academic Press, 1985), 1–16, quotation on 6. There was a considerable amount of general interest in recent geological deposits because these were considered by many to have the most direct bearing on man's appearance in the region. The tremendous importance to Neolithic societies of erratic blocks, especially the more exotic stones of granite and quartz, has been discussed by Warren and coauthors. These blocks were used as raw material for the manufacture of the huge ceremonial rock monuments left by the early peoples. "It would seem that the site and even the design of their circles and alignments were dictated by the supply of the desired stones that had been transported by the ice to within a convenient distance." (William P. Warren, Michael O'Meara, Eugene P. Daly, Michael J. Gardiner, and Edward B. Culleton, "Economic Aspects of the Quaternary," in Edwards and Warren, eds., *Quaternary History,* 309–52, on 310).

88. *Annual Reports and Proceedings of the Belfast Naturalists' Field Club* 4 (1901): 598.

89. "Erratic Blocks of England, Wales, and Ireland—Twenty-Third Report of the Committee Consisting of E. Hull (Chairman) . . .," *Reports of the British Association for the Advancement of Science,* Oxford, (1895): 426–27.

90. T. Hallissy, "Geology," Clare Island Survey, pt. 7, *Proceedings of the Royal Irish Academy* 31 (1911–15): 1–22 on 9.

91. See Geological Survey of Northern Ireland, 1971; and Geology of Belfast and District; Special Engineering Geology Sheet. The stratigraphic sequence of Irish Quaternary deposits (which cover over 90 percent of the land surface) is especially complex and was still being studied long after Thompson's time (see Edwards and Warren, "Quaternary Studies," 6).

92. Hallisy, "Geology," 9. The post-1901 geological reports published by Sydney Mary Christen herself include "Investigations into the Glacial Drifts of the N.E. of Ireland, Conducted by the Naturalists' Field Club," *Irish Naturalist* 11 (1902): 275–76; "A Summary of the [B.N.F.] Club's Recent Glacial Work," *Irish Naturalist* 15 (1906): 80–81 (a review of work done several years earlier).

93. Sydney Mary Christen to F. J. Bigger, June 10, 1918 (S. M. Christen letters, Belfast Public Libraries archives).

94. *Dictionary of National Biography,* supplement 1, vol. 1 (1901), 49–51, entry for Thomas Andrews; and Newman, *Dictionary of Ulster Biography,* 5.

95. See for instance "Sixty Years Denudation; Cultra, near Holywood, Down," (Photographs of Geological Interest in the United Kingdom), *Reports of the British Association for the Advancement of Science* 1 (1902): 541.

96. "Notes on the Granite and Other Rocks at Newcastle," *Report of the Geological Section, 1897–98, Annual Reports and Proceedings of the Belfast Naturalists' Field Club* 4 (1901): 432 (title only); "Erosion at Newcastle, Co. Down," *Irish Naturalist* 10 (1901): 114; and "Notes on Some Igneous Rocks in Down and Antrim," *Reports and Proceedings of the Belfast Natural History and Philosophical Society, 1902–03* (1903): 51–57.

97. For the Americans, see Creese, *Ladies in the Laboratory?,* 85–88; for the Scandinavians, see chapter 1 of the present volume. Work of this kind was also being done by British women at the time (Creese, *Ladies in the Laboratory?,* 108), but not as much as in the United States or in Scandinavia.

98. Creese, *Ladies in the Laboratory?,* 126–27.

99. Creese, *Ladies in the Laboratory?,* 10–12, 14–16, 27–28, 35–37, 47. A number of the other Western European women botanists discussed in the present volume also specialized in cryptogamic botany—see, for example, the sections on Dutch algologist Anna Weber van Bosse and Italian bryologist Elisabetta Fiorini-Mazzanti.

100. See also the contributions in glacial geology of British women amateurs Elizabeth Hodgson and Charlotte Eyton, although their work was carried out thirty years earlier than that of the Irish women—Creese, *Ladies in the Laboratory?,* 292–93.

Chapter 3

FRANCE: OF PHYSICS, FARMS, AND PHYSICIANS

Frenchwomen and women working in France form one of the three most productive groups of nineteenth-century women scientists in continental Europe, as measured by publications indexed in the Royal Society *Catalogue*. Thirty-nine authors produced 164 papers between 1800 and 1900 (Figure 3-1). Only the Russian and Italian groups published more. The three fields in which the French contributions were most prominent (measured by paper count) were astronomy (39 papers), neurology/physiology (27), and anthropology (22) (Figure 3-2). A number of women were also working in botany and closely related areas, and in zoology, while in physics, by the late 1890s, Marie Sklodowska Curie had begun to publish the joint research on radioactivity with Pierre Curie that was to bring them the Nobel Prize they shared with Henri Becquerel in 1903.

Among the early French contributions, the mathematics papers by Sophie Germain in the 1820s and '30s are especially notable. Other early reports include an 1852 catalogue of coleoptera by the Comtess de Buzelet and a technical article on wine-making brought out by Elisabeth Gervais in 1823. Most of the French papers were published in the last two decades of the century (Figure 3-1), the five largest individual contributions coming from American-born astronomer Dorothea Klumpke Roberts, Romanian-born physiologist Mariette Pompilian, Polish-born physicist Marie Curie, and two French-born women, writer Clémence Royer and zoologist Fanny Bignon.

Medical and Biological Sciences

Of the twenty-four women working in France whose published research in the medical and biological sciences is listed in the Royal Society's index, only a few are well remembered. These include physician Blanche Edwards-Pilliet, neurologist Augusta Dejerine-Klumpke, and physiologist Marie Picot Phisalix; the story of physician and political activist Madeleine Pelletier has also fairly recently been brought to the fore. Others who were notably productive but who have received less attention from biographers or historians of women in science were zoologist Fanny Bignon and botanist Aimée Camus, both of whom worked at the Muséum National d'Histoire Naturelle in Paris (Camus after the turn of the century), agricultural writers and experimenters Cora Millet-Robinet and Marguerite Löwenhjelm, Duchesse de Fitz-James, and physiologist Mariette Pompilian.

Among the medical women discussed here the two best known to English-speaking readers are most likely Blanche Edwards-Pilliet and Augusta Dejerine-Klumpke. Dejerine-Klumpke was American by birth, although she lived most of her life in Europe; Edwards-Pilliet was the daughter of a British-born physician married to a French woman. These two were the pioneers in the battle to open to women the prestigious hospital extern- and internships, the first steps in the program of supervised hospital work during medical study that was at the heart of the French medical education system. Only those who had served an externship followed by a full-time residency or internship had full access to a career in hospital or university medicine. Because hospital programs could accommodate only a limited number of students, access was controlled by rigid competition.[1] Edwards-Pilliet and Dejerine-Klumpke succeeded against almost universal opposition from the medical establishment because of substantial backing from the republican government of the post-Franco-Prussian War period.

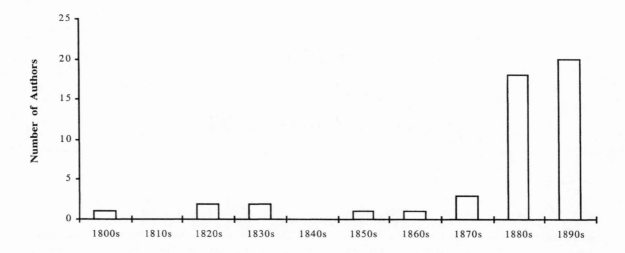

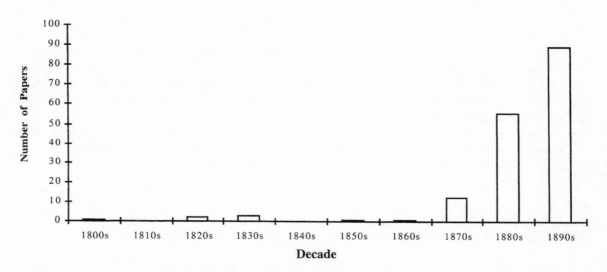

Figure 3-1.   French authors and papers, by decade, 1800–1900. Data from the Royal Society *Catalogue of Scientific Papers.*

J'eus l'honneur d'être brulée, en effigie, au Bal Bullier.[2]

—Blanche Edwards-Pilliet

The 1988 biography by two of her granddaughters presents a full and very readable account of the life and career of BLANCHE EDWARDS-PILLIET[3] (1858–1941), a leading social reformer as well as pioneering physician.

Blanche Edwards was born in Milly, about thirty miles south of Paris, near the forest of Fontainbleau, on 24 November 1858. Although times were beginning to change, with industry starting and communications improving, the Milly region was still a place of peasant farmers living under mediaeval conditions. Blanche's father was George Hugh Edwards, London-born son of a secretary to British statesman Lord Palmerston. When his father died at the age of twenty-eight George was taken to France by his mother who married the Chevalier de Gondouin. George Edwards took a medical degree and, fluent in several languages, worked in Russia for a time as tutor to one of the grand duchesses. He then settled in Milly and married Amanda Froc, twenty years his junior, the daughter of a well-to-do farmer. Lively, well-educated for her time, and practical, she was a woman of great vitality and courage, qualities she passed on to her daughter.

An only child, Blanche Edwards was taught at home by her father and was bilingual from the start. She

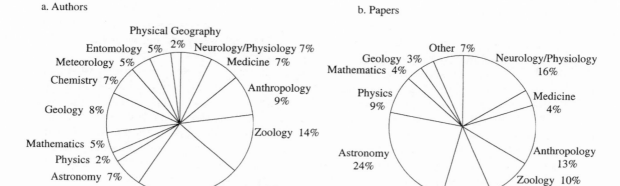

Figure 3-2. Distribution of French authors and papers, by field, 1800–1900. (In a., an author contributing to more than one field is counted in each. In b., the sector "Other" represents papers in chemistry [2 percent], meteorology [2 percent], entomology [1 percent], and physical geography [1 percent]). Data from the Royal Society *Catalogue of Scientific Papers*.

had a free, outdoor life and an education far superior to that of most girls of her time. She often accompanied her father on his professional rounds, saw the dirt and misery in which the peasants lived, and early realized the need for social change. When she was ten the family moved to Neuilly-sur-Seine, on the western outskirts of Paris near the Bois de Bologne. Her father continued her instruction, giving her a solid secondary-level training in classics, science, mathematics, and modern languages. To perfect her English she spent some time in an Anglican convent in England about 1870–1871. In general outlook she grew up in the Protestant liberal tradition of her father, but she was later to give up all conventional religious practices and adopt the views of the secular liberal section of French society. She took the *baccalauréat-ès-lettres* in 1877, the *baccalauréat-ès-sciences* the following year, and shortly before her twentieth birthday achieved her childhood goal, enrolling in the faculty of medicine in Paris.

A slight, blond girl of medium height, lively and attractive, she had a happy, enthusiastic personality. She continued to live with her parents, first at Neuilly and then in Paris near the medical school. Strictly following the proprieties, her father accompanied her to class every day; after he died in 1882 her mother walked with her. Life was challenging; the male medical students, well known for their obstreperousness, made clear their objections to the presence of women in their midst and turned the lecture theatre, as Augusta Klumpke later wrote, into a "*fosse aux ours*" (bear pit).[4] In 1882, having completed her first four years, Blanche Edwards began the process of obtaining permission to compete for a hospital externship. Accompanied by her father, she pleaded her case before *députés, senateurs,* and other government officials, making more than 300 visits; eventually she carried the day.

She specialized in surgery, still a dangerous practice at that time when the need for aseptic conditions was only beginning to be accepted. Diagnostic methods were primitive, and dirt and infection abounded; tuberculosis and typhoid were especially prevalent. One of her first publications (1887) was a paper on scarlet fever microbes; others, of which there were at least eight in the period up to 1891, dealt with women's diseases and child pathology (see bibliography). Six months of her year's externship she spent in the Salpêtrière, a huge hospice for women suffering from chronic mental and nervous disorders. She studied hysteria under the direction of the eminent Jean-Martin Charcot, internationally known for his work in neuropsychiatry. Charcot considered her one of the best students he ever had.

After an incredible campaign of soliciting government support, during which she and her mother made some 600 visits to officials, over the near unanimous objections of the medical establishment, and finally thanks only to an order from the Préfet de la Seine on the authority of the Minister of Public Instruction, she and Augusta Klumpke in 1886 took the internship examinations. Conditions were hardly ideal; students and faculty were divided into *blanchiste* and *antiblanchiste* factions, Edwards was burned in effigy on the Boulevard Saint-Michel, a main thoroughfare near the school of medicine, and crowds on the street yelled "*Sortez Blanche.*"

Accepted as a provisional intern only at l'Hôpital des Enfants Assistés, she worked in a number of different hospitals but concentrated on obstetrics and gynecological surgery. She took the internship examinations again in 1888, but again failed to win a titular position, an unhappy outcome, considering her long, almost single-handed fight to open the competition to women. After passing her final examinations in 1889 with a prize-winning dissertation prepared under the guidance of Charcot,[5] she set up a consulting room and began what would be fifty years of practice.[6]

Building this practice was not easy. Her focus was on families and her patients were mainly working-class women and children; obstetrics was a major part of her work. House calls, carried out on foot or by public transportation, initially involved someone having to come and get her, custom making it difficult for a young woman to walk through the streets alone. Her fees came from the Assistance Médicale Gratuite (L'AMG), a health service started in 1893; she never asked for payment from the uninsured poor. She also took on work in school medicine, much of it then unpaid or poorly paid; vaccination for smallpox was a particular interest. An enthusiastic teacher, she gave evening classes for hospital nurses at the Salpêtrière, where she remained on the teaching staff for most of her life. Indeed she was the only woman of her time offered a medical teaching post by the Assistance Publique. For a time she also taught at the nurses' school of the Dames de France.

In 1891, after a four-year engagement, she married Alexandre-Henri Pilliet (1861–1898), a research worker in anatomy and pathology and a man of broad cultural interests. Three children were born in the next four years, but Blanche had excellent health and the births did little to interrupt her work routine. Despite Pilliet's early death from tuberculosis and her own continuing professional commitments, she gave her children a happy, lively upbringing, having excellent help from a maid, Mimi, who became part of the family.

From 1889 Blanche Edwards was active in national organizations concerned with education, public assistance, and women's and children's issues. Herself an officer of public instruction from 1895, she worked with the Ligue de l'Enseignement (Education League), many of whose members she had met during her fight for entrance to the internship examinations. Admission of women and girls to educational institutions, the establishing of *baccalauréat* programs in girls' *lycées,* and the teaching of hygiene and childcare to girls were particular concerns. Most especially however, she gave her energies to the Ligue pour les Droits des Femmes (LDF; League for Women's Rights), one of the founding groups in the Conseil National des Femmes (National Council of Women).

Her interests spread over a vast spectrum of social reform. A close friend and colleague of feminist lawyer Marie Vérone, one of the leading figures in the LDF, she took up the women's suffrage question at an international meeting of women's organizations in Paris in 1910. She fought for daycare provision for small children and the ending of the practice of sending infants to wet-nurses in country districts; in addition she undertook legal work on divorce laws, rights of married women, and paternity claims. The Ligue des Mères de Famille, which she founded in 1901 functioned until 1940. It was one of the first NGOs (Nongovernmental Organizations), groups from which many of France's social organizations later developed.

During the First World War Blanche Edwards-Pilliet and her family were much involved in medical work. She stayed in Paris, continuing her house calls day and night as before despite bombardments, and also taking medical night duty for the first *arrondissement.* In addition, she taught first-aid courses and opened her home to British and American Red Cross workers and embassy staff. Her daughter Henriette, a second-year medical student, assisted the surgeon caring for evacuated wounded at the Hôtel-Dieu throughout the war; her son Georges also broke off medical studies, and at age nineteen went to the trenches as a stretcher-bearer; her elder daughter, a lawyer, used her bilingual abilities in a post with the American Red Cross.

After the war Edwards-Pilliet continued her medical work, in part because she had never saved for retirement. Her activities on behalf of the women's rights cause also went on and much LDF organizational work was done at meetings in her apartment. The group's social and political program was now coordinated with the efforts of those in the socialist party who supported women's suffrage, many of them people she had known before the war. A member of the party herself, she was elected vice president of one of its Paris sections about 1930. In 1924 she became Chevalier de la Légion d'honneur, an honor bestowed in recognition of her work for women's rights, her contributions to the education of nurses, and her war service.

From about age seventy she gradually reduced her professional responsibilities. In 1933 she suffered a stroke from which she partially recovered, but after that she lived with her son's family. She died in January of 1941, at the age of eighty-two.

La Première Interne des Hôpitaux

Une petite révolution s'est accomplie avant-hier, une vrai révolution, et la date du 1er février 1887 marquera dans les annales de l'Assistance publique et du corps médical. La première femme qui ait été reçue interne des hôpitaux, Mlle Klumpke, a été installée, en effet, ce jour-là, dans ses nouvelles fonctions, et l'émotion produite par cette événement n'est pas encore apaisée au quartier Latin.[7]

—Gaston Calmette

Augusta Klumpke (1859–1927),[8] the first woman intern in a Paris hospital, was born in San Francisco on 15 October 1859, the second of the six surviving children of Dutch-German immigrant Johan Gerard Klumpke and his wife Dorothea Matilda (née Tolle). Johan Klumpke, who grew up in New Orleans, studied medicine for a time but at age twenty-four went West to join the California gold rush. In late 1849, after brief experience as a prospector, he settled in the small Spanish mission of San Francisco, where he became a very successful businessman dealing in San Francisco real estate. In his later years he was known as an authority on the city's history. New York–born Dorothea Tolle arrived in California in 1853 on a visit to her sister, wife of a recently arrived San Francisco gunsmith. She married Johan Klumpke two years later.

At age seven Augusta, with her mother and sisters, traveled to Europe where they spent the years 1866 to 1868 while seeking medical help for the oldest child, Anna, somewhat crippled by a leg injury. After eighteen months at a school in Berlin Augusta spoke fluent German. When Johan Klumpke and his wife separated in 1871 Mrs. Klumpke, accompanied by all six of her children, returned to Europe, settling in Switzerland, near Lake Geneva, in 1873.

Augusta attended the Lausanne *école supérieure de jeunes filles* until 1877. The family then moved to Paris in order that Augusta could begin medical studies, Anna pursue her art training, and the younger sister Dorothea enter the faculty of science at the Sorbonne without any of the three having to forgo the support of a family environment. Augusta Klumpke later wrote of how important this home living was to her and her sisters.[9] Many students in Paris at the time led lonely, isolated lives as foreigners in a large city, but the young Klumpke women had a pleasant home on the top floor of a corner building, a bright, sunny apartment filled with flowers and books, with a view of the Luxembourg Garden on one side, the fountain by the famous sculptor Jean-Baptiste Carpeau on the other, and the dome of the Paris Observatory in the background.

Despite advice to the contrary from Alfred Vulpian, dean of the faculty of medicine, who not only opposed medical education for women but considered eighteen-year-old Augusta Klumpke too young, she went through the standard program. Like Blanche Edwards she had to put up with harassment from male fellow students but, far from discouraged, she took extra science courses at the Sorbonne and the Collége de France, attended clinical demonstrations in Paris hospitals, and worked in laboratories at the Muséum d'Histoire Naturelle. In 1880 she was accepted (as a *stagiaire,* or junior assistant) for a period of practical training at the Charité hospital; there she quickly acquired a reputation as an excellent worker who was also a good linguist, able to translate and summarize English and German publications for her group.

In 1882 she and Blanche Edwards became the first women externs in Paris hospitals, having successfully passed the required written and oral examinations. Augusta Klumpke later recalled that, notwithstanding the long struggle (fought by Blanche Edwards) to win entry to the competition, when it came to her public oral examination, the male students behaved very reasonably.[10]

She spent the first year of her externship at the Hôtel-Dieu, also attending clinics at other hospitals, including the Salpêtrière. During her second and third years she worked under the direction of Alfred Vulpian, with whom she was now on good terms despite her rejection of his earlier advice. It was at this time that she elucidated and described the condition resulting from neurological injury to the complex of nerves controlling arm movements, the brachial plexus; this condition, characterized by paralysis of the inner-arm and forearm as well as the ulnar side of the hand, is still called *Klumpke* or *Lower Radicular Syndrome.*[11]

In 1885, again over the near unanimous opposition of the medical establishment but with the backing of the government at the highest level, Augusta Klumpke and Blanche Edwards moved on to the next phase in their medical training, competing in the internship examinations. Augusta Klumpke received the top score (twenty-nine points out of a possible thirty) in the written examination, but nevertheless was awarded a provisional internship only. She tried again, however, with more success and in 1886 became the first woman to win a regular internship in a Paris hospital (the Lourcine, later Broca). The event was sensational, a milestone in medical history. Not surprisingly she was ill-received by her fellow interns. Foreseeing the arrival of many more women, the men feared the coming of a day when women would even be judges in the internship competitions, with their own priorities that could lead them to give preference to female candidates. They refrained from interfering with Klumpke's work, but they never allowed her into their quarters; she took her meals alone, prepared for her in a small kitchen next to the patients' area. Thirty years later, when she attended her daughter Yvonne's internship examination, she was nothing short of amazed at the harmony and camaraderie between men and women interns.

In her inaugural dissertation which she defended in 1889 Klumpke discussed further studies of paralysis of the inferior brachial plexus. Her series of investigations of this condition brought her the Prix Godard of the Académie de Medécine, the Médaille d'Argent des Thèses of the Paris faculty (1886), and in addition the Prix Lallemand of the Academy of Sciences (1890). In 1888 she married Joseph Jules Dejerine, a native of Savoie, whom she had met eight years before when they both worked at the Charité hospital, he as a young *chef de clinique*. She then resigned her internship and joined in the research of her husband and his students.

The Dejerine neurology laboratory was one in which a number of scientists later famous and influential in France and abroad received their training. Augusta Dejerine-Klumpke's own investigations, methodical, painstaking, and always precisely documented, were outstanding, particularly her work on the development and application of the technique of cutting successive very thin sections of the entire brain for microscope examination: "Pareille technique n'avait jamais été suivie avec une telle perfection . . . Elle fut le Maître qui connut peut-être le mieux au monde l'anatomie des centres nerveux, l'origine, le trajet et la terminaison des faisceaux et des fibres, leurs associations et leurs structures."[12]

Canadian neurologists Lecours and Caplan[13] have discussed in detail one particularly incisive and revealing contribution her exceptional knowledge of neuroanatomy made in her collaborative work with her husband. Dejerine, at the time professor of pathology and soon after professor of neurology at the Salpêtrière, was then one of the two foremost French theorists on aphasis, or loss of speech. His work led him to the conclusion that particular collections of language deficiency symptoms were associated with particular localized cerebral injury. He was opposed by professor of pathological anatomy Pierre Marie, who rejected the idea that there were distinct forms of aphasia. Three sessions of the Paris Société de Neurologie in June and July of 1908 witnessed a vigorous debate on the subject. Augusta Dejerine-Klumpke's participation in this debate provides a typical example of the kind of solid contribution she made. Focusing squarely on the crucial question of the anatomical limits of the particular region of the brain central to the discussion, she revealed the weak points in Marie's presentation, backing her arguments with evidence from her own sections, "some of the best gross anatomical material of the area ever prepared,"[14] clear proof of her deep appreciation of neuroanatomy. Her demonstration was the definitive treatment of the subject; among other things, she pointed out that one of the important sections used by Marie was much too low to reveal the relationship under discussion. Marie defended his analysis vigorously but Mme. Dejerine's won out. Lecours and Caplan have pointed out that many of the empirical issues she then raised remained unsettled more than seven decades later.[15]

Between 1884 and 1926 her name appears on fifty-six articles, many of them joint papers with her husband and his students and some her own.[16] She also coauthored with her husband a two-volume work on the anatomy of nerve centers, *Anatomie des Centres Nerveux*.[17] One of the classics of French neurological literature, the work was of special importance for research workers in neuroanatomy. In the preface to volume 1 Dejerine wrote, "Cet ouvrage est le fruit d'une collaboration assidue de plusieures années; ma chère femme, Mme. Dejerine-Klumpke, y a contribué pour une large part; aussi ai-je tenu, et ce n'est que justice, qu'il fût publié sous nos deux noms." Augusta Dejerine-Klumpke's contributions included the brain sections on which were based 2,000 anatomical drawings.

During the First World War both the Dejerines continued to work at the Salpêtrière hospital, where a large unit was set up for military casualties. Augusta's specialty was the assessment of spinal nerve injuries. After Dejerine's death in 1917 she took charge of a similar program at les Invalides for the care of soldiers with especially serious injuries. When enemy action necessitated the transfer of this program to the town of Nay in extreme southwestern France, she went with it.

Named Chevalier de la Légion d'honneur in 1913, she was awarded the further honor of Officier de la Légion d'honneur in 1921, in recognition of her war services. She belonged to a number of scientific societies, including the Société de Neurologie de Paris, which she joined as a founding member in 1901 (president, 1914–1915), and the Société de Biologie, to which she was elected as the first woman member in 1924. Although she never came forward herself for professional honor and recognition, it was well known among their colleagues that the Dejerine scientific work was joint. As their daughter put it, ". . . leurs noms furent et resteront indissolublement unis, comme ils l'avaient désiré."[18]

Augusta Dejerine-Klumpke was remembered by one of Dejerine's intern students as someone who could be depended on to provide, when called on, patient, methodical, and incisive advice, especially in the preparation and analysis of histological sections.[19] And she was often called on because Dejerine, pressed for time, sent his students to her: "Demandez à madame Dejerine." On many occasions, when the time came for publication of a thesis or original paper, a student would arrive at her house of an evening, spread a huge pile of sections on the dining-room table and ask for Mme. Dejerine's guidance in interpretation. She was crucially involved, primarily in the area of neuroanatomy, in three important theses directed by her husband.[20] A good teacher, she had a clear, precise mind that could simplify the most difficult analysis.

Always sociable and hospitable, she and Dejerine throughout the years welcomed students (often alone and far from their families) to regular Sunday evening gatherings in their home. These were occasions when not only the medical concerns of the week were examined, but many other questions of the time, scientific and nonscientific, were discussed. Augusta Dejerine-Klumpke's interests were by no means limited to neurology; art, literature, and natural history were of great importance to her. Every summer she and her family spent some time in the Swiss Alps. After the war she set up a memorial to her husband that took the form of a Société de Neurologie research fund, a prize for Salpêtrière nurses, and a museum in the faculty of medicine to house all the written materials relating to Dejerine's work. She died on 5 November 1927 at age sixty-eight, in her house on boulevard Saint-Germain, Paris, and is buried in the Père Lachaise cemetery alongside her husband. The Dejerines's only child, Yvonne, followed in her mother's footsteps, passing her internship examinations with high standing.

Augusta Dejerine-Klumpke's achievements in basic research in neuroanatomy and in clinical neurology are outstanding for a woman of her time. It is also the case that her contribution to the opening to women of the medical profession in France was second only to that of Blanche Edwards.

Madeleine Pelletier[21] (1874–1939) has the distinction among French women physicians of being the country's first woman psychiatric intern. An almost forgotten figure until rediscovered in the 1970s, she is described by her biographer Felicia Gordon as "one of the most original and talented French women of the early twentieth century."[22]

Pelletier was a rebel, first and foremost a militant and radical feminist in a country that withheld the vote from women until after the Second World War. She was a prominent figure in the Socialist Party who stood for a parliamentary seat, an outspoken campaigner for the right to contraception and abortion in a society that was conservative and Catholic, and a prolific author who set out in both expository writing and fiction the intellectual and political case for the emancipation of women. By the 1920s and '30s she was anathema to conservatives and to the pronatalists, then a powerful force in French society. In 1939 she was arrested on an abortion charge and locked up in a mental institution, where she died within six months.

One of two surviving children of Louis Pelletier and his wife Anne (née de Passavy), she was born on 18 May 1874, in the one-room living space behind the family's fruit and vegetable store at 38 rue des Petits-Carreaux. The street was one of a maze of narrow crowded thoroughfares in a working-class, republican part of Paris to the north of les Halles, the great food market. Louis Pelletier had come to Paris from the *département* of Deux Sevres to find work as a cab driver. He was republican in outlook and a religious skeptic. From the time Madeleine was four, he was paralyzed as the result of a stroke. His wife, a fervent royalist and fanatical Catholic, ran the store and dominated the family. An illegitimate child from Clermont-Ferrand in the Auvergne, Anne de Passavy Pelletier carried the brand P on her neck, the mark of her origins. She, too, had come to the capital to find work. Intelligent but totally uneducated, she was a miserable housekeeper and the family lived in poverty and squalor. Her extreme right-wing opinions, openly expressed, hardly endeared her to the neighborhood, and her unpopularity rubbed off on her daughter, who had no friends among the local children.

Madeleine was taught to read by her father and at age seven was sent to a school run by nuns. But her intelligence and obvious capabilities did not compensate for the dirt and lice on her person and, never well accepted, she left when she was twelve. About this time, she began to develop a strong and lasting distaste for what she saw as the female experience, personified in her mother. Her replacement of her given name Anne (her mother's) with her own choice, Madeleine, perhaps in part symbolized this rebellion. Until she was about twenty she "ran wild," frequenting evening meetings of largely middle-class feminist and anarchist groups. She took to wearing a modified style of men's clothing; somewhat later, she cut her hair short and switched to male dress almost entirely, a tactic that gave her the freedom to walk unmolested through the streets of Paris. By the late 1890s she had concluded that her only escape from her family and poverty was through education and so, with her mother still providing her food and lodging, she began to prepare for the *baccalauréat*.

Without instruction or encouragement and with little money for the necessary textbooks, she worked her way alone through the daunting syllabus; in 1897 she passed the examination with distinction—an extraordinary accomplishment. With the help of a professor at the School of Anthropology, she obtained a Paris municipal council scholarship for medical studies; a year later she passed the preparatory certificate in the sciences.

While a medical student during the period 1898–1903 Madeleine Pelletier also carried out research in the new and intensely active field of physical anthropology which then had very close ties with medicine; the Laboratoire d'Anthropologie at the Muséum d'Histoire Naturelle had its origins in the Laboratoire d'Anatomie Humaine. She found physical anthropology, which attempted to look at humans in terms of evolution, of especial interest because it appeared to offer a scientific basis for the study of human behaviour within which she could logically examine feminist ideas. The Société d'Anthropologie, founded in 1859 by a group of Paris physicians, was the first in the world and it enjoyed enormous international respect. Most likely because she lacked money for dues Pelletier was never a member, but between 1900 and about 1905 she regularly attended the society's meetings and published several papers in its *Bulletins* and *Mémoirs*.

Her research was in craniometry, the now almost forgotten science that attempted to correlate skull shape and capacity with intelligence. The field was already under attack as a pseudoscience and was to be essentially removed from the province of respectable scientific investigation in the first years of the twentieth century by British statistician Karl Pearson and his coworkers.[23] However, Pelletier, still in her early twenties, accepted the mainstream French anthropologists' view of the importance of work in the field.

Under the direction of Léonce Manouvrier, she carried out a detailed examination of a museum collection of fifty-five Japanese skeletons (published in 1900; see bibliography). Looking at variation in skull weight with that of other bones, she demonstrated that women's skulls, in proportion to body height and weight, were larger and heavier than men's, a fact that, by some current theories, put women evolutionarily ahead of men. The following year she published a second paper in which she put forward a new formula for evaluating cranial capacity, long a problem for craniologists. She tried to devise a series of measurements not influenced by sex variation but was unable to avoid various logical contradictions.[24] Her 1902 article reporting her study of mandibular bone structure from an evolutionary perspective was well-received.[25]

Pelletier also undertook a joint investigation with Nicholas Vaschide, at the time section head of an experimental psychology laboratory at Villejuif psychiatric asylum. They attempted to correlate skull shape and intelligence in 140 elementary school children at Villejuif, a working-class suburb of Paris. Despite the considerable amount of data collected, the study revealed little, largely because no valid intelligence test was available; what little was concluded told against the girls.[26] This study was demolished a year later by Pearson and coworkers, who considered it a good illustration of "how little can safely be argued from meager data and a defective statistical theory."[27]

Although all efforts in craniometry were soon to be recognized as scientifically worthless, the work was not without value for Pelletier because it gave her some familiarity with both the "scientific" arguments for women's inferiority and the counter-arguments, useful training for her later activities. She progressed steadily through her medical course, carrying out clinical work and serving internships in Paris hospitals. Her doctoral thesis presented in 1903 was a psychiatric study based on her work during a *stage* at the large Sainte Anne hospital. Linking normal and abnormal psychology, she suggested that the insane should not be looked on as entirely separated from the normal and that the study of abnormal psychology had relevance in the understanding of normal mental processes. The work was well received, Pelletier being awarded a bronze medal and the Prix Lorquet of the Académie de Médecine.[28] In 1904 she began a three-year appointment in hospital psychiatry at the Villejuif asylum, having competed successfully in the internship examinations, despite the fact that the medical establishment had expressed strong opposition to her being granted permission to enter. Many of the psychiatrists in the service she joined were members of the Anthropological Society, the connection between their field and physical anthropology being close.

Although working conditions in the asylums were difficult, she published a remarkable number of articles in the period up to 1906,[29] but that year failed by a narrow margin to pass the competitive examinations for a permanent post as an asylum doctor, thus losing her chance for professional security. From then on she supported herself largely as a medical officer for the Postes et Télégraphes, which paid her 1,800 francs a year, a poor salary but certainly above the poverty line. She also had a private practice, conducted first in her two-room apartment on rue de Gergovie and later in her rooms on rue Damrémont, but she failed to attract many patients and her earnings were negligible.[30]

By 1906 she was involved in a range of political activity. Until the outbreak of the First World War she concentrated especially on two issues: making her voice heard in the Socialist Party, and organizing a mass feminist movement, the latter a formidable task in Catholic France. She rose rapidly in the French Section of the

Workers International (SFIO), where she became prominent for her debating skills and organizing capability; in 1909 she was nominated to the executive committee, rapid advancement for a woman at that time; in 1910 and 1912 she stood in national elections as a socialist candidate, although she failed to gain party endorsement for a winable seat. After 1911 however, having been unable to bring about the integration of feminist goals with socialist revolutionary activity, she to a large extent switched her main focus to women's issues and social justice; she was not prepared to postpone women's emancipation until after a successful social revolution. Her advocacy of freely available contraceptive information and abortion on demand, rights she saw as fundamental to women's freedom, constituted a clear challenge to the influential pronatalist lobby that had been supporting measures to encourage France's flagging birthrate since the country's defeat in the Franco-Prussian War.

The outbreak of the First World War and the collapse of the Socialist International was a watershed for Pelletier along with other European socialists. She still attended socialist and pacifist meetings, activities recorded in police files, but she was bitterly disillusioned when the working class embraced patriotic nationalism instead of maintaining international proletarian solidarity. Her offer of service at the front was turned down; as yet there were no women doctors in the French army. She enrolled with the Red Cross but resented what appeared to her the patronizing attitude of the mainly middle-class volunteers. For distraction she took a degree at the Sorbonne in natural sciences, specializing in chemistry.

After the war she reopened her private practice, closed for the duration, and also continued her work with the Postes et Télégraphes. Like many European socialists, she was much heartened by political events in Russia; her many articles supporting the Bolshevik cause appeared in periodicals such as *La Suffragiste,* which she had long edited. A trip she made to Moscow in 1921 was described in her book *Mon Voyage aventureux en Russie communiste* (1922); although somewhat disillusioned by the various difficulties encountered during the visit, she continued to uphold Soviet communism as a superior alternative to capitalism.

In the 1920s and 1930s, her private practice improved somewhat, the number of her women patients increasing. She advertised in socialist and feminist newspapers as treating "women's illnesses," which in all probability included offering advice on contraception and abortion. She left the Communist Party in 1925, mainly because she disagreed with colleagues over feminist issues, but she remained a committed socialist in the broadest sense, continued to contribute to a variety of left-wing periodicals, and gave pro-Bolshevik public lectures. In 1932 she joined the pacifist group Mundia. About the same time, feeling the pressure of the rightist political climate of the period, she began to replace her political activism with fiction writing, building in her mind new world utopias. Between 1920 and 1933 she produced two plays, three short stories, and at least two novels,[31] one of which, *La Femme vierge,* was to a large extent autobiographical.

Even by the 1920s Pelletier had been identified as a leading neo-Malthusian, particularly dangerous because of her medical expertise and her linking of birth control with women's rights. Although from 1933 she was periodically threatened with prosecution for carrying out abortions, she continued to speak in public on contraception and women's rights until 1937 when, because of a stroke, she gave up public activities. Two years later, her midwife assistant and her cleaning woman were arrested by the police on a charge of performing an abortion under her direction. Pelletier herself was examined by a psychiatrist, pronounced irresponsible, and committed to the Perray-Vaucluse psychiatric hospital at Épinay-sur-Orge, about twelve miles south of Paris. A trial would have generated a great deal of publicity and even had a guilty verdict been rendered it would have resulted in a sentence of fixed time span; committal to an insane asylum was in effect a life sentence. In the letters she sent to friends during her period of incarceration and in the memoirs, she dictated at the time there is nothing to suggest that she was insane. She died in the asylum, alone and unnoticed, at the age of sixty-five, on 29 December 1939, a few months after the outbreak of the Second World War. Only the extreme left-wing press carried a brief notice of her passing.

Over her long career Madeleine Pelletier had produced a steady stream of articles, books, and pamphlets in which she set out a compelling case for the emancipation of women. Nevertheless she reached a relatively small audience in her own time and was for long marginalized in historical accounts of both feminism and socialist politics. Her biographer Felicia Gordon attributes her lack of recognition to her class origins as much as her militancy.[32] Her contemporaries found her hard to place; to French socialists of the early years of the twentieth century feminists were mainly middle class (*bourgeois*) and therefore suspect when they pushed their agenda. But Pelletier never recognized this split between *bourgeois* feminists and socialists; she was a socialist *and* a feminist, with a militant agenda in both areas, an unusual combination for the time. Likewise, for later historians she failed to fit any of the expected patterns and so fell through the cracks, forgotten until rediscovered in the 1970s. She is now acknowledged as the most eminent ("la plus illustre") of the French radical feminists of her time.[33]

A comparison might be made between Pelletier and Blanche Edwards-Pilliet: although Pelletier began her medical studies almost two decades after Edwards-Pilliet, both were pioneers among French women physicians, both were committed feminists and social reformers, both were religious skeptics, and both were members of the Socialist Party. Edwards-Pilliet however, was no militant rebel driven by the pain and hardship of a childhood in the Paris slums. She fought for her rights with tremendous courage, energy, and staying power but in contrast to Pelletier had the psychological assistance provided by a fully supportive family. Edwards-Pilliet's tactics were persistent persuasion in the pursuit of limited, achievable goals; coming from a middle-class background, she was at home in mainstream feminist action groups and there achieved impressive results in a variety of undertakings. Of the two she was the more successful, although her goals would have been unacceptably limited by Pelletier's ambitious standards.

Papers on medical topics by two other French women physicians—Madeleine Brès and Joséphine-Inèz Gaches-Sarraute—are listed in the bibliography.

MADELEINE BRÈS,[34] née GÉBELIN (1839–1925) was the first French woman to receive a diploma from the medical faculty of the University of Paris.[35] During the 1870–1871 Prussian siege of Paris, Brès, a medical student, asked for a post as a substitute intern in one of the overworked city hospitals. Helped by the relatively liberal-minded Paul Broca, professor of clinical surgery and a supporter of education for women, she succeeded in getting into the Pitié hospital, where she remained for the duration of the fighting, through several bombardments of the hospital. Her hard work was warmly praised by the director and a number of medical faculty members, but when at the end of hostilities she asked for permission to compete for an externship, this was denied on the basis of concern about setting a precedent. In 1921, when she was eighty-two, blind, and living in dire poverty in a tiny Paris apartment stripped of all but the barest essentials, a public appeal was made for her support. In an interview she then gave, she recounted the story of her life; she still had an excellent memory and a lively mind.

Her early childhood was spent in Nîmes, a few miles inland from the Mediterranean coast. Her father, a wheelright and carriage-maker, worked for the sisters of the Nîmes hospital and she often accompanied him when he took the sisters on their rounds, helping to carry their various poultices and decoctions. When she was seven, the hospital's head physician told her she would make a good little doctor ("Quel bon petit docteur tu serais!"),[36] a remark she never forgot. A few years later the family moved north to Lyons, the father having found a job with the new railway system. However, the parents did not like Lyons and wanted to return to the south. Madeleine at age fifteen was married off to a man twice her age, the driver of a horse-drawn carriage, working for the railway station; most of his earnings were the tips he received from his passengers, and so they had little to live on.

Rather like Madeleine Pelletier, Madeleine Brès for the most part educated herself. Until the age of ten she had attended a school run by the sisters of the Chalade in Nîmes (at a cost of two sous per month), but after the birth of her first child she began to study on her own. Her neighbor was a classics teacher who had no children and took a great liking to her handsome little son. When she confided her dream of a medical education to him he immediately gave her the practical advice that she would have to get instruction and pass the *baccalauréat* examination, something she had never even heard of. A *baccalauréat* manual she came across in a bookstore helped her find out what would be required and she went to work, learning "*pêle-mêle,*" as she put it, everything she could. Her kindly neighbor gave her some lessons and loaned her books, and her excellent memory helped her considerably. She passed the *baccalauréat* at age twenty-eight, on her second attempt, an extraordinary performance, especially considering the fact that she had ten children. Shortly after, thanks to the intervention of the Empress Eugénie who became interested in her case, she was accepted into the Paris medical faculty. Gynecology and pediatrics were her major interests. Her husband never opposed her studies but rather sympathized with her ambitions. He, too, had had his hopes and plans and had studied for the priesthood until bad luck and his own poor financial judgement brought him into trouble with the law. During the siege of Paris, while Madeleine worked in the Pitié hospital, he served as a captain in the national guard.

Madeleine Brès received her diploma in 1875 after presenting a thesis on breast feeding,[37] a subject about which she no doubt has considerable practical knowledge. Immediately afterward she opened a consulting room on rue de Rivoli from where, for almost forty years, she conducted a large practice in gynecology and pediatrics. She never made much money though; the AMG (l'Assistance Médicale Gratuite), the public service for the poor that paid for most of Blanche Edwards-Pilliet's patients (see above), did not start until 1893, eighteen years after Madeleine Brès began to practice, and even some of her patients who could afford to do so avoided paying fees. Nevertheless, for a time she provided support for her mother as well as her husband and children.

Beginning in 1883 she brought out the journal, *L'Hygiène de la Femme et de l'Enfant*. She herself was editor-in-chief and for the most part the sole contributing author; a manager conducted the business side of the enterprise and within a short time a committee of patronage was formed. The journal appeared monthly from May 1883 until December 1886 and reappeared under new administration in 1890, continuing until 1893; a final number came out in February 1895. The publication was a considerable undertaking and, viewed over the course of its eight-year existence, represents a notable contribution to public education. Issues typically ran from twelve to fifteen pages and ranged across a wide spectrum of areas related to Madeleine Brès's special interest, the health of women and infants. Articles, written in a familiar, chatty, perhaps somewhat motherly style, covered such subjects as the following: care of the skin during seaside vacations; health advice to newly married women and girls ignorant of the facts of human biology; the benefits of suckling for the infant's own mother rather than the substitution of a wet nurse (a common expedient at the time, poor women from country districts regularly being found to undertake the task); a sketch of the history of smallpox control, beginning with the story of Edward Jenner's early work in Britain in the 1770s and including an account of her own visit to Louis Pasteur in his Paris laboratory to get firsthand information on the subject.

Over the course of many years her interest had come to focus increasingly on the provision of practical, material assistance for the poor working women of her community in the form of a model nursery facility and regular instruction in infant care.[38] By 1890 her work in this area was well known to municipal officials concerned with public health. The following year, commissioned by the ministry of the interior, she traveled to Switzerland to study the organization and functioning of public crèches; a similar mission took her to England.[39] Soon after that initial steps were taken to establish a philanthropic foundation to raise funds necessary for a crèche and public school, which she would direct. This crèche, provided with a trained staff and accommodated in a fairly spacious and well-prepared converted inn at 86 rue Nollet in the seventeenth *arrondissement,* opened in 1893. Supported by a small subsidy of 2,000 francs (about one fifth of the expenses) it is said to have served some 7,000 infants per year. The children came largely from working-class families in this recently developed part of northwestern Paris, lying along the eastern side of the major railway lines linking the city to the north and west of the country. The École Populaire Madeleine Brès met once a week and presented practical, "hands-on" instruction in infant care,[40] Brès being convinced that lectures alone were not sufficient to change long-established habits. The opening of the crèche and school marked the fulfillment of a long-held dream for Madeleine Brès. She was then in her early fifties and widowed some years previously.

In 1918, when she was about seventy-nine, she became blind and had to give up her practice. At the time of her interview three years later she was living on what were essentially charitable donations of 200 francs a month, half coming from the mayor of the eighth *arondissement* and the other half from the funds of the dispensary LeVallois, where she had most recently worked. L'Assistance Publique offered her a place in the communal ward of the Salpêtrière, the hospice for the mentally ill, where she had made regular visits to care for patients. She would have accepted a single room there, but the communal ward was more than she could face.

Despite all the struggle and hard work, however, Madeleine Brès looked back with pleasure and satisfaction on the fine reputation she had earned in her time and the help she had given to great numbers of people. Her general philosophy was that if she had two problems worrying her she just tried to forget about them and waited for the third. Usually the wait was not long! She never took part in politics and, although a firm believer in cooperation and mutual help, never considered herself a feminist. "Je suis de mon temps. Il y a trois choses donc je n'ai jamais voulu discuter: la politique, la religion, l'amour."[41] She was indeed a woman of her time, but far more so than in the limited conservative sense she would seem to have meant; in a time of pioneers in the opening of medical education to women and in the provision of help for poor, working-class women, Madeleine Brès was a pathfinder. She died in Montrouge, on the south side of Paris, in 1925, when she was about eighty-six.

JOSÉPHINE-INÈZ GACHES-SARRAUTE,[42] later GACHES-BARTHÉLEMY (b. 1853), after an initial appointment in 1886 as substitute doctor at the Théâtre de l'Opéra, succeeded to an official position there. Throughout the 1890s she published a series of papers, mainly in the *Tribune Médicale,* on the harmful effects of wearing an abdominal corset (see bibliography). She also discussed her findings in her work *Le Corset.*[43] Aimed at a general audience, this set out in graphic fashion the damage to bone structure and internal organs caused by the constriction of the corset, *"cette cuirasse"* (this suit of armour). Anticipating resistance to abandoning the fashion altogether,[44] she offered a redesigned corset for special conditions (such as hernia). This "Corset Gaches-Sarraute" with its straight-fronted busk provided support for internal organs rather than simply pulling in the waist. Her book was discussed at length in the *Revue Mensuelle du Touring Club de France*; bicycle-riding, a new and popular sport for women in the 1890s, was making clear the need for a change in fashion that would permit normal functioning of the lungs. Nevertheless the Gaches-Sarraute corset never became very popular; the wish for a small waist persisted. The design is still discussed, however, in accounts of women's fashions in the twentieth century.[45] Gaches-Sarraute also published two short technical monographs, a microscopy study and a discussion of palliative treatment for uterine cancer.[46]

A paper by one additional French woman who had close connections with the Paris medical community, or was perhaps a physician herself, is listed in the Royal Society *Catalogue,* namely the report of work in physical anthropology and statistics by JEANNE BERTILLON.[47] The study was carried out in collaboration with Dr. Parrot of l'Hôpital des Enfants and was published in 1887, thirteen years before Madeleine Pelletier's first anthropology paper. Bertillon presented data assembled by Parrot over the course of many years of autopsy studies on children up to the age of six. She had worked with him and kept all the records, including brain and heart weight, height, and total weight. Following his death in 1883, she undertook an analysis of the findings and set these out, along with detailed tables and graphs, before the Société d'Anthropologie. She paid special attention to the relationship of brain weight to the other variables measured, considering the data for boys and girls separately. As she noted, the growth patterns for the organs measured closely followed those in Belgian children published somewhat earlier by the Belgian statistician Adolphe Quételet. Little difference was found between the sexes, a result that was not received with much enthusiasm by some members of the Société d'Anthropologie.[48]

Among French botanists, AIMÉE CAMUS[49] (1879–1965), who ranks among the most distinguished and productive of the "amateurs" whose careers began before 1900, was known particularly for her extensive systematic studies of the grasses of Madagascar. Born on 1 May 1879, she was the daughter of Paris pharmacist Edmond-Gustave Camus, himself considered one of the best of the nineteenth-century botanists of the Paris region. E.-G. Camus carried out wide-ranging studies of the flora of France and Switzerland and was an acknowledged authority on orchids and their hybrids; for a time he served as vice president of the Société Botanique de France.

From an early age, Aimée Camus took great interest in her father's work, accompanying him on his excursions and acquiring a sound knowledge of the techniques and methods of a field botanist. Plant studies were strong in her secondary level education acquired at courses conducted by Mme. Morot, wife of Muséum d'Histoire Naturelle botanist Louis René Morot, managing director of the *Journal de Botanique.* Later she attended courses given by botanist Gaston Bonnier at the Sorbonne and by morphologist and taxonomist Philippe van Tieghem at the Muséum d'Histoire Naturelle. Van Tieghem, one of the museum's more experimentally inclined biologists, gave her an excellent training in systematic anatomy, an area in which she later excelled. Throughout her life she was very close to her younger sister Blanche Camus (1884–1968), an artist of the impressionist school, whose paintings are still on the market.

Aimée Camus's work falls into two main divisions, her early studies with her father and their continuation following his death, and her later work, inspired by her own strong interests. She covered a wide range of subjects from the systematics of flora of both temperate and tropical zones to the physiology of species and plant anatomy; she also published studies in applied botany and brought out works for general readers. Her output was vast—close to 400 publications, including about a dozen books of major importance and several hundred notes and reports, the great majority of which were of considerable interest to the botanical community.

One of her first publications was a joint report with her father when she was a girl of only fifteen. An account of collections they made in the cantons of Vaud and Valais in southwest Switzerland, it appeared in the Société Botanique's *Bulletin* in 1894 (see bibliography). The Camus team went on to a range of studies, many involving histological work by Aimée. Among the groups she examined were ornamentals, plants important for their essential oils or perfumes (lavenders, mints, and basils), and the regional flora of Mediterranean coastal areas, subjects that remained of interest and on which she continued to publish occasional notes for many years.[50]

Her first major project was the study she embarked on jointly with her father on the taxonomy, classification, and geographical distribution of the European willows. It was a bold undertaking, the classification of the European willows then being in an extremely confused state because of the large number of hybrid species. Indeed the genus Salix, the willows, had long been a major botanical trouble spot. An extended series of joint Camus papers appeared in the period up to 1906 and the investigation was published in expanded form in a joint two-volume monograph.[51] The two-volume atlas that accompanied the text presented 1,257 illustrations of external structures by E.-G. Camus and internal morphological features (microscope sections) by Aimée Camus. These illustrations drawn by the authors themselves are impressively beautiful, perhaps appearing particularly so in this age of the photograph and computer graphics.

The Camus team's studies of primarily the flower nectary led them to the conclusion that polymorphism was less extensive than previously thought; they suggested that the willow species of France fell into fourteen divisions, a scheme that, although it differed from those adopted by earlier authorities including Swedish botanist and willows specialist Johan Andersson,[52] was accepted by Ferninand Pax in the first edition of Engler's great *Pflanzenfamilien*.[53] The Camus study paid special attention to nomenclature, each of the hybrids being given two names, a simple name and one that reflected parentage. Their work on hybrids, much of it carried out at the locations where the trees were growing to ensure greater accuracy in classification, marked new progress in the study of a complex and difficult area of European botany. Further, basic information on willows was of considerable commercial significance in France, osier willow stems being a major agricultural product, the raw material of the important wicker-work industry.[54]

A second notable jointly authored Camus monograph, an extensive study of the orchids of Europe, the Mediterranean region, and the Russian trans-Caspian provinces, appeared in preliminary form in 1908.[55] E.-G. Camus's work on orchids had begun in the 1880s, first in the environs of Paris and then throughout France.[56] The aim of the expanded collaborative study was a close examination of orchid classification based on morphology and anatomy. Distinctive characteristics for the numerous genera were investigated and the organs (roots, stems, hairs, bud clusters, stamens, and more) examined in detail and figured by Aimée Camus. The systematics of the two subfamilies and six tribes were studied, varieties carefully distinguished and hybrids named according to the principles established by orchid specialist Robert Allen Rolfe and others.[57] The Camus team found that in general the anatomy confirmed the classification based on external characters. Their 490-page work presented detailed descriptions of thirty-one genera and about 100 species, as well as subspecific forms. As with the willow studies, hybrids received special attention. A classic study, it was brought out in its three-volume final form in the period 1921–1929.[58]

For many years after the publication of these major works, studies of both orchids (particularly hybrids) and willows were a continuing interest for Aimée Camus. Notable among her later investigations of willows was a fairly extensive examination of species in Syria and Lebanon.[59]

Although she no longer had the collaboration of her father during the later stages of the orchid study, E.-G. Camus having died in 1915, Aimée Camus did have the companionship of her sister Blanche. Together they explored the entire chain of the Pyrénées from the Mediterrean to the Bay of Biscay, to the summits of the highest peaks, Aimée finding a number of new hybrid forms. The sisters' joint expeditions to the Mediterranean region included a trip to Turkey, a country whose luminous landscapes artist Blanche Camus had long wanted to capture on canvas.

From 1908 both Aimée Camus and her father (who that year gave up his pharmacy business) worked full time at the Muséum National d'Histoire Naturelle in Paris. This institution, once widely regarded as the most celebrated natural history museum in the world, had by then lost some of its former glory but it had taken to itself a mission in colonial science. Here it saw an opportunity to make an important contribution while at the same time ensuring its own future support.[60] With France becoming increasingly active in colonial expansion in the decades immediately following the Franco-Prussian war, large quantities of plant materials were being sent home; Muséum naturalists, although they lacked field experience abroad, were among the country's experts in the work of identification required. From about 1900 interest was centered on the newer colonies in the Far East (French Indochina) and Madagascar. These were huge stretches of territory; the latter island, 300 miles off Africa's southeast coast, a French protectorate from 1895, has an area greater than that of France and the Netherlands combined. Further, Madagascar, whose native grasses became the subject of much of Camus's research, has a special place in natural history studies. One of the world's most remarkable land masses, almost a microcontinent, it has a wonderfully rich and unusual flora and fauna. Although much reduced during 1,000 years of occupation by a largely cattle-herding human population, a huge variety of endemic species (flora and fauna) still awaited exploring naturalists in Camus's time. The less-accessible mountain massifs of the northeast in particular were virtually untouched and retained the rich, primitive vegetation of the island's higher elevations.

In both Madagascar and French Indochina the earlier pattern of colonial small-holder settlement typical of French Algeria was replaced by large-scale agricultural undertakings with a focus on the export trade.[61] The possible economic value of indigenous plants was therefore a matter of considerable importance. Joining in the work of plant surveys of the African and Far Eastern regions, Aimée Camus and her father undertook major studies on the Cyperaceae (aquatic monocotyledons, sedges) and Gramineae (grasses) for a multivolume general flora of Indochina.[62] Only the Cyperaceae section had been completed when E.-G. Camus died in 1915 and it fell to Aimée to continue the Gramineae, a group which soon became her favorite subject and remained so for the rest of her life.

As early as 1913 she brought out two notable contributions in applied botany: one discussed the rices of Indochina, the region's food staple; the other was her 350-page work on the bamboos.[63] Also surveyed and classified by her father,[64] the bamboos, the giants among the Gramineae, were another group of tremendous economic importance in the Far East, where they were used for a wide variety of purposes ranging from house building, to utensil manufacture, to food.

The following years saw the appearance of a great many papers and notes by Aimée Camus on the systematics of newly discovered grasses of the Far East. Among those of special note was her 1921 paper on the genus Andropogon, several of whose members were much prized, particularly in antiquity and up until mediaeval times, for the fragrant oils present in their leaves.[65] A number of the oil grasses remain well known; *Andropogon nardus* L. is the source of the insect repellant citronella oil, and *Andropogon citratus* D.C. (lemon grass) is used to make an herbal tea.

Camus's grass investigations included studies of material from many countries—French North Africa, both East and West Africa, Mauritius, Réunion, the Cormores Islands, and Taiwan, in addition to Indochina and Madagascar—but it was the tall grasses of Madagascar that she made her particular specialty.[66] The ornamentals of the genus Erianthus (the Plume Grasses), and the bamboos (Bambuseae Tribe) were groups to which she devoted considerable attention. Among the bamboos new to Madagascar that she described were members of the genera Arundinaria, Pseudocoix, and Hitchcockella. Her revised classification of the bamboos appeared in 1935.[67] While examining the grasses of Madagascar's northern and central highland regions, she discovered many other new species endemic to the island and differing from those of regions of lower elevation; a few were related to the grasses of southern and eastern Africa.[68] Her work on the grasses of the northern region of Madagascar, in particular the isolated and virtually untouched Marojejy Massif explored botanically only in the late 1940s and early 1950s by Henri Humbert, were an important contribution to the latter's monograph on the natural history of the island.[69]

In applied botany, in addition to her early work on bamboos and the rices of Indochina, her investigations included studies of the grasses of the prairie regions (secondary grasslands) of Madagascar, forage crops grown in India, grasses of Indochina used in the brewing industry, and species of rice from the Sudan.[70]

Over the course of many years Aimée Camus collaborated with A. de Cugnac in studies of the development and physiology of hybrid species of Bromus. Native to the temperate zones of northern Europe, the genus includes members that have value as forage grasses on dry soils; the hybrids were evaluated in comparison to the natural forms.[71]

Her investigations of the grasses, the main theme running through fifty years of her research, constituted a body of work whose scope and peer reception might well have more than satisfied the ambitions of a lifetime for even a fairly self-demanding scientist. Nevertheless she also carried out a considerable number of studies in other areas; trees of the genus Cupressus (the cypresses) and the Fagaceae (the beeches), including the oaks (Quercus) and the chestnuts (Castanea), were special interests. Her detailed investigations of these groups resulted in numerous notes and papers in reviews of pure and applied botany and in three important monographs, *Les Cyprès* (the cypresses), *Les Châtaigniers* (the chestnuts), and *Les Chênes* (the oaks).[72] Separate work on the beeches of the southern hemisphere appeared in 1951.[73] Anatomical investigations and painstaking examination of hybrids formed part of these studies, all of them characterized by penetrating observation and precise methodology. *Les Cyprès,* published just before the outbreak of the First World War, was a well illustrated volume with over 400 figures. At the time of its appearance it stood out for its focus on anatomy as a tool in systematics, particularly in the use of characteristics determined by examination of shoot sections and leaf structures (distinguished as cupressoid and arbor vitae–like). Studying not only external and internal morphology but also taking culture and overall biology into consideration, Camus recognized nineteen species. Publication of *Les Châtaigniers* and *Les Chênes,* with their emphasis on tree form, marked the beginning of a new period in the dendrology of these two major groups.

In the course of her tree studies Camus discovered many new species and her publications figured many more for the first time.[74] One especially noteworthy section in the concluding two-volume tome III of *Les Chênes* (1954) concerned the genus Lithocarpus. A small group of the beech family confined mainly to the Orient, Lithocarpus has affinities with both Castanopsis and Quercus; her detailed studies led her to a number of general conclusions about these two groups.[75] The work was much valued by botanists and those engaged in timber-related industries.[76]

Camus also brought out a number of morphology papers reporting studies of plant organs, particularly in the Gramineae; topics she took up included the anatomy of flower spikelets, the regularly patterned network of sap channels in leaves, and the blossoming process. In addition she examined the cotyledon junction in Quercus and Lithocarpus seedlings.[77]

Other noteworthy contributions were her popular writings and her studies on the history of botany, especially work on eighteenth- and early nineteenth-century French specialists on the grasses of North America.[78] The former included two volumes brought out by the *Encyclopédie pratique du Naturaliste,* one discussing aquatic plants, the flora of marshes, lakes, rivers, and ponds, and the other dealing with ornamental trees, bushes, and shrubs.[79] Well-illustrated books presenting new research findings in clear, precise language, readily understood by amateurs, these works combined up-to-date botanical information with practical advice in a way that made them far more than scholarly manuals.

Aimée Camus continued her research in the Laboratoire de Phanérogamie of the Muséum National until the early 1960s, her career in botany spanning more than sixty years, over half a century at the museum. Several times *lauréate* of the Institut de France and the recipient of Société Botanique de France awards, she was also Chevalier de la Légion d'honneur. In 1958 she was named *associée* of the Muséum National, a title very rarely bestowed. Latterly she held a CNRS (Centre National de Recherche Scientifique) research position. She died on 17 April 1965, shortly before her eighty-sixth birthday, two years after health difficulties caused her to give up museum work. Her important exsiccata collection, both her own and her father's material, she left to the museum's herbarium. It constituted a major contribution of about 50,000 dried plants that included several type specimens.

Among the other six French women whose botanical papers are listed in the bibliography[80] the best remembered is MARGUERITE BELÈZE[81] (1851–1913). From the district of Montfort-l'Amaury to the southwest of Paris, Belèze, like Camus, was known for her taxonomic and plant distribution studies but her work was local, on a far less grand scale than that of Camus.

Belèze investigated in particular the cryptogamic flora of her neighborhood and the nearby forest of Rambouillet, publishing long, detailed lists in the bulletins of the Association Française pour l'Avancement des Sciences and the Société Botanique as well as in the *Comptes-rendus du Congrès de Sociétés Savantes.* These appeared between 1895 and 1901. She continued to bring out botanical work until about 1906, including one or two notes on plant pathology, physiology, and dicotyledon taxonomy. Her seventy-eight-page *Catalogue des plantes nouvelles, rares ou intéressantes . . . de la forêt de Rambouillet,* the combined list taken from her 1895–1901 papers, was published in 1905.[82]

Papers on topics in agriculture and agronomy by three French women—Elisabeth Gervais, Marguerite Löwen-hjelm, Duchesse de Fitz-James, and Cora Millet-Robinet—are listed in the bibliography.

ELISABETH GERVAIS (fl. 1820s), a landowner in the south of France near Montpellier, grew grapes and was one of the early experimenters in wine quality improvement. A description of the equipment she used for carrying out the fermentation process appeared in the London journal *Philosophical Magazine* in 1823, a notably early date for a report of technical developments by a woman experimenter. Her method of using semi-closed vessels rather than the open vats then in general use gave a higher-quality product for wines, cider, and beer; two years previously a short monograph on wine production and the advantages of the semi-closed-vessel method, which had already been granted a government patent, had been published by Jean Antoine Gervais.[83]

These suggestions for improving procedures and equipment aroused considerable controversy. In a lengthy report presented to the Bordeaux Académie Royale in 1822, F. Delavau, a landowner in the Médoc region of Bordelais, famous for its fine wines, described how he had exhaustively compared results from the traditional method with those obtained using the Gervais innovations. He concluded that the difference in the product did not justify the expense of making the changes. The Académie awarded him a medal for his efforts.[84] Delavau's opinion did not reflect the general consensus, however, and the results of the Gervais improvements were sufficiently impressive to attract the attention of a number of influential figures, including the Duc de Bellune, maréchal de France, and statesman and chemist Count Jean Chaptal, already a widely known authority on methods of improving wines.[85] These men organized a company that bought the patent to ensure that the improved method was made more widely accessible throughout the country. Further refinements were worked out by several technical people, including chemist Louis Joseph Gay-Lussac. A patent was obtained in Britain also and the method adopted there with great success.

In his work *Femmes dans la Science* Rebière stated that the improved fermentation technique with which Gervais is credited was actually due to a late eighteenth-century physician, Casbois. Whether or not this is the case, it would seem clear that the Gervais family at the very least took up the idea, experimented with it, and publicized the improved results—essential developmental steps if the technique was to have any importance. Between 1820 and 1823 three short works were published concerning the method; two discussed verifications of Elizabeth Gervais's claims for an improved product and the other was a manual for grape growers and manufacturers of beer, wines, and spirits. The manual included descriptions of equipment and supplies.[86]

MARGUERITE LÖWENHJELM, DUCHESSE DE FITZ-JAMES[87] (fl. 1830s–1890s), wife of Édouard-Antoine-Sidoine, seventh duc de Fitz-James, also owned vineyards in the south of France. The Fitz-James family, several branches of which live in France, is descended from James (b. 1670), an illegitimate son of King James II of Britain and Arabella Churchill. Marguerite Löwenhjelm was widely recognized for her contributions to the work of reestablishing French viticulture following the devastating infestations of the American plant louse *Phylloxera vastatrix*; this insect, a sap-sucking aphid that attacks vine root systems, spread quickly throughout France during the 1870s and 1880s, threatening the country's whole vast wine-producing industry, an industry that accounted for one sixth of the national revenue.[88] Very active as a writer as well as an experimenter, the duchesse was much respected among academic botanists and agronomists at the nearby University of Montpellier, the institution that took the lead in phylloxera research. She was often contacted by growers seeking technical advice, such as detailed instruction on vine propagation techniques.

One of her particular concerns was the introduction to France and Algeria of resistant grapevines native to North America (or hybrids of these), an area in which a great deal of work was being done at the time. She herself carried out extensive studies of viticulture in America, the subject of one of her early publications (*Enquête viticole en Amérique 1875–1881* [1882]). However, she worked on a whole range of matters then affecting grape growers, the phylloxera and other insect infestations, anthracnose, mildew and other fungal attacks (controlled by lime and copper sulfate sprays), the choice of particular hybrids for particular soils, the increasingly complex financial aspects of the grape-production business, and the practical side of propagation by the use of small cuttings or by grafting. The latter technique, using resistant American rootstocks and French vines, was soon demonstrated to be successful for the production of phylloxera resistant plants and, with official approval, became the method of choice.[89]

An extremely energetic woman, the duchesse regularly attended viticulture congresses in France and Algeria throughout the 1870s and 1880s and was often called on to speak. Among her published works was her 648-page monograph, *La Viticulture franco-américaine (1869–1889),* brought out in Montpellier in 1889 in collaboration with the Bureau de Progrès Agricole et Viticole; in it were included detailed reports of viticulture congresses from 1879 to 1888, the last one, a report of the 1888 Oran congress, presenting a lengthy discussion of viticulture in Algeria.[90] Her paper listed in the bibliography was read before the French Academy of Sciences in 1885. It reported her experiments to combat mildew by the application of a water suspension of slaked lime, one of several of the chemical sprays then coming into use for the control of mildew-causing fungi.

Marguerite Löwenhjelm had at least one child, a son, Jacques-Gustave Sidoine de Fitz-James, born in Paris in 1852.[91]

CORA MILLET-ROBINET[92] (1798–1890) was the wife of François Millet, a military subadministrator and director of an experiment station in Poitiers for the raising of silkworms. Her own family was much involved in agricultural matters, particularly education and agricultural improvements; her brother Stephane Robinet (1796–1869) was a professor of silkworm culture; her father was most likely Joseph Robinet, a veterinarian. Along with her husband and brother, Cora Millet-Robinet coauthored a 120-page memoir on the experiments on silkworm culture they conducted in the *département* of Vienne in 1840. The work was carried out under the auspices of the Société d'Agriculture de Poitiers and included a thorough study of the eggs, the worms, the feeding of the latter, and the effects on them of such variables as heat and humidity.

Cora Millet-Robinet was herself a prolific and very successful author, bringing out an impressive collection of instructional works on agricultural, farm, and farm household matters from the 1840s on. These included her two-volume *Maison Rustique des Dames,*[93] a remarkable comprehensive manual of household and farm management, probably first published in the 1840s, that ran to at least fifteen editions; it was intended for the farmer's wife on the more well-to-do and progressive farm of the period, a time before country dwellings had plumbing, electricity, or mechanization of any kind for farm work or transportation. In the preface to the revised and expanded tenth edition (1878) she commented that the increasing popularity of the book over the years owed much to the growing importance of women's contributions to agricultural work in France. Her general aim was to improve the education of country women, the secondary-level instruction currently offered at girls' public schools (accessible to those who could travel to a town) being, in her opinion, inadequate for a future farmer's wife.

Volume 1 of *Maison Rustique* is half household management and half cookery manual. Volume 2 is more unusual; it covers three major topics: home medicine, the raising of fruits, vegetables, and flowers, and the organization and management of the parts of farm work then considered within a woman's sphere of responsibility. The latter section included a 124-page discussion on poultry raising, important for the small but steady income it brought.[94] Also covered at some length was butter production, with great emphasis on the need for hygiene in all dairy work. The chapter on sheep-rearing stops with the operations of shearing and fleece cleaning; the more traditional women's work of carding, spinning, and weaving is not discussed. Much of the household equipment described, such as the cooking stove (*fourneau économique*) or the treadle-operated sewing machine was not much different from that in use in country districts of Europe until the introduction of electricity after the Second World War. The two volumes remain of considerable general interest.

Among Millet-Robinet's other works was a fruit preservation manual, *Conservation des Fruits* (1854), a 252-page classic of French cookery entitled *Les Recettes de Cuisine de ma Grand-mère* (recently republished[95]), a work on infant and child care, *Le Livre des Jeunes Mères: la nourrice et le nourrisson* (fifth edition, 1897), and an 1866 study on migratory birds, *Étude sur les oiseaux voyageurs ou migrateurs et sur les moyens de les protéger*, also published in the Paris journal *Bulletin de la Société Protectrice des Animaux*.

Cora Millet-Robinet was a corresponding member of the Société Centrale d'Agriculture de France, of the Reale Accademia d'Agricoltura di Torino, of the Société d'Agriculture d'Ille-et-Vilaine (a *département* at the base of the Brittany peninsula), and an honorary member of the Société d'Agriculture, Science et Arts de Poitiers.

Papers on entomological topics by two French women—la comtesse de Buzelet and Mme. Errington de la Croix—are listed in the bibliography.

LA COMTESSE DE BUZELET (fl. 1850s) prepared a general catalog of a collection of insects found in the central Loire valley and the surrounding regions. A thirty-five-page extract from this catalog, listing coleoptera, was published in 1852 in the *Mémoirs* of the Angers Société d'Agriculture, Science et Arts, a notable contribution for a woman at the time.

The study by Mme. ERRINGTON DE LA CROIX of a nest of a species of ant, *Termes carbonarius*, was carried out in 1899, in Negri Sembilan, on the southwest of the Malay peninsula. Her paper in the *Bulletin* of the Muséum National d'Histoire Naturelle described the large conical nest of yellow clay, of two meters base diameter and height of more than two meters. Clearly a knowledgeable naturalist, she collected samples of the various castes of ants for entomological collections in French museums. Mme. Errington de la Croix was most likely the wife of John Errington de la Croix, who traveled extensively in the East Indies, Malaya, and North Africa and contributed geographical and geological reports on these regions to the Academy of Sciences and the Société de Géographie throughout the 1880s.[96]

Of the six French women whose papers on zoological topics are listed in the bibliography—Barthelet, Deflandre, Loyer, Bignon, Le Masson le Golft, and Thiesse—Bignon was the most notable.

FANNY BIGNON was born in Châtillon-sur-Seine,[97] about 150 miles southeast of Paris. During the 1880s she carried out a considerable amount of basic anatomical research at the Muséum National d'Histoire Naturelle, which then accommodated a number of students working for doctoral as well as *licence* degrees in the biological sciences.[98] Following some initial very detailed work on the lachrymal glands and occular structures of the giant tortoise carried out with Alexandre-Henri Pilliet (later the husband of physician Blanche Edwards—see above), Bignon undertook a long series of studies on the respiratory system of birds. These were reported in eight papers and notes published between 1887 and 1890. She was awarded a *docteur ès sciences* degree by the University of Paris in 1889.

The topic of respiration in birds had not been neglected previously, but it was only in the mid nineteenth century that the basic anatomical features of avian air systems were explored and the fundamental morphological differences between bird and mammalian lungs made apparent. From the 1860s one of the leaders in the field was Alphonse Milne-Edwards, director of the Muséum National d'Histoire Naturelle from 1891 to 1900. Further important contributions were made by museum zoologists Raoult Boulart, George Pouchet, and Henri Beauregard.[99] However, although the basic design of rigid lung and compliant air sac system had been established, details of the connections between the lung and the nine air sacs, and the size and positions of some of the latter, remained to be examined in detail.

Bignon, at the time *licenciée ès sciences naturelles* and a teacher at a Paris *l'école primaire supérieure*, undertook a detailed investigation under the direction of Beauregard and Boulart of the pneumatic systems of a large variety of birds. Among those she studied were representatives of the parrot family (Psittacidae), small song birds such as sparrows (Passeridae), long-legged water birds, including storks and herons (Ardeidae), small to large webfooted water birds (Anatidae), the rheas (Rheidae), pigeons (Columbidae), and foul-like birds of the galliforme order. She focused particularly on the cranial group of sacs, those located in the neck, head, and chest. Her papers included details of the anatomy of the head of the various species investigated, as well as the pneumatic systems; eleven beautiful figures illustrating many of her anatomical findings accompanied her major paper in volume 2 (1889) of the *Mémoirs* of the Société Zoologique de France.

Fanny Bignon was a member of the Société Zoologique by 1884. A group with a broad, open outlook, known for its friendliness and lack of formality, it welcomed the participation of students and amateurs, as well as professionals. From a small gathering of twenty people at its first meeting in 1876, its membership increased rapidly.[100] Bignon served as one of its three secretaries for several years beginning in the late 1880s and regularly participated at meetings. In 1895, she presented a paper on the teaching of natural history in the *écoles primaires* that aroused much interest (see bibliography). She suggested substantial changes in teaching methods, proposing in particular that the current practice of requiring children to memorize Latin names and dry facts be replaced with the study of actual specimens and the growing of plants.

Mlles. BARTHELET, DEFLANDRE, and LOYER were all students or laboratory workers during the 1890s.

Barthelet worked in the zoological laboratory in the faculty of science at the University of Nancy. Using white and grey mice, she studied the question of telegony, the influence of a previous sire on a subsequent sire's progeny by the same mother. Although acknowledging the results of studies on other animals that had been interpreted as showing that the phenomenon was real, she concluded that her own investigations pointed in the opposite direction.

Deflandre, who worked at the Broussais hospital, Paris, published jointly with Paul Carnot two short papers on pigmentation in skin grafts (see bibliography). Her research career continued at least for a time after the turn of the century and she brought out two lengthy reports on the physiology of fat production in a wide range of animals, vertebrate and invertebrate. The work involved both chemical analyses and histological studies.[101] Deflandre held a *docteur ès sciences* degree. Both she and Carnot, coauthor of her 1896 papers, were students and colleagues of Augustin Gilbert, known for his extensive physiological and biochemical studies, including investigations of glucose and glycogen metabolism.

Marie Loyer was a student of Louis-Félix Henneguy, a well-known professor of comparative embryology at the Collège de France, Paris, and director of the laboratory of cytology at l'École des Hautes Études. She carried out cytological studies on reptile ovaries, publishing her first paper in this area in 1900. Her work in Henneguy's laboratory at the Collège de France continued for at least a decade; between 1901 and 1909 she brought out six additional notes and papers reporting further extensive studies on ovarian cells from a variety of reptiles—lizards, snakes, and turtles. Loyer was particularly interested in the complex changes taking place in the cell nucleus following fertilization; she focused especially on the nucleoli-chromosome relationship in the nuclei of reptile ovarian cells, a problem biologists were then just beginning to explore.[102]

Naturalist MARIE LE MASSON LE GOLFT[103] (1749–1826) was born in Le Havre on 25 October 1749. In addition to a number of natural history memoirs, she published the monograph *Balance de la Nature* in 1784; a collection of her letters concerning educational matters appeared four years later.[104] Having strong interests in community affairs, she wrote articles on matters of local concern in Le Havre over a period of twelve years, from 1778 to 1790. These articles are now of considerable value to students of the history of Normandy.[105] Mlle. le Golft's description of a variety of seal, which appeared in the *Précis Analytiques* of the Rouen Académie des Sciences, Belles-Lettres et Arts in 1807, is one of the earliest papers by a woman listed in the Royal Society *Catalogue*.

Mme. THIESSE, a knowledgeable conchologist, published a note on *Helix hemonica,* of the group *Helix gobanzi,* in *Bulletins de la Société Malacologique de France* in 1884. *Helix hemonica* had not at that time been reported in France; Thiesse's specimen came from Greece (Thessalia). She provided a detailed anatomical description and pointed out the close resemblance to another member of the group (*perfecta*) found in the mountains of the south Tyrol.

Physiologist MARIE PHISALIX,[106] née PICOT (1861–1946) is remembered for her wide-ranging studies of venoms, their production in many different species, their functions, and antidotes against them.

Marie Phisalix was of Jurassien ancestry, her people coming from near the Swiss frontier. During the 1880s she studied at the École Normale Supérieure de Jeunes Filles, established in the Paris suburb of Sèvres at the beginning of the decade. Qualifying in 1889 she taught there herself for a period while also working toward a medical degree. At this time she was already married to Césaire August Phisalix, a former army doctor invalided out the military following an illness contracted during an 1881 campaign in Tunisia. After additional studies (which brought him a *doctorat ès sciences*), Césaire Phisalix became an assistant at the Muséum National d'Histoire Naturelle, where he and his colleague Gabriel Bertrand carried out outstanding research that led directly to the discovery in 1894 of snake poison antidote. Marie Phisalix joined in this work in 1895. Her prizewinning doctoral research demonstrated that the same venoms found in reptiles are also produced in amphibians, although the latter lack a delivery organ.[107] This initial observation led her to the fundamental hypothesis underlying all her later work, studies that spanned fifty years, namely the idea that the venom function is general and not specifically adapted to attack or defense.

Until her husband died in 1906, Marie Phisalix collaborated closely in his research in the Muséum's department of comparative pathology. Thereafter, having inherited enough money to live on comfortably, she carried on the work independently, never putting herself forward for any official post or soliciting any prize, subsidy, or reimbursement to cover her laboratory expenses. She was housed successively in a number of Muséum departments until she settled finally in 1910 in the laboratory of ichthyology and herpetology, chosen because she wanted particularly to study living reptiles and amphibians.

Her research interests spanned a remarkable range; they included especially the comparative anatomy of venom organs in different species, the physiology and pathology of venom delivery, the relationships between microbial toxins and the rabies virus, and the therapeutic applications of venoms. She was interested in the venom function wherever it presented itself, in protozoa, molluscs, arthropods, and vertebrates. She focused particularly, however, on lower vertebrates (fish, amphibians, and reptiles), higher vertebrates endowed with natural immunity (hedgehogs and badgers), whose blood characteristics resembled those of the first group, venomous arthropods, and parasitic protozoa (some of which function as unicellular venomous organisms themselves endowed with natural immunity).

Her underlying purpose was to uncover the general biological role of the venom function, whose widespread occurrence suggested to her that it was an exaggeration of a normal function whose purpose was primarily internal to the possessor organism. The great scope of her research and its implications for and application in therapeutics brought her the Academy of Sciences's Prix Bréant in 1916. The prize was awarded to her a second time in 1922 when her massive two-volume *Animaux Venimeux et Venins* appeared. The result of twenty years of research, the latter brought together in a systematic way all the work in the area up to that time. Her friend Alphonse Laveran (famous for his discovery of the malaria protozoan parasite and Nobel Prize–winner in medicine in 1907) wrote the preface.[108]

Marie Phisalix's subsequent research, published in a long series of papers in the *Bulletins* of the Muséum, of the Société Zoologique de France, and of the Société de Pathologie Exotique, as well as in the *Comptes rendus* of the Academy of Sciences, concentrated in particular on blood and tissue investigations of lower vertebrates, their venom and antivenom components, and the mechanisms controlling natural immunity; especially important was an understanding of the antivenom component on which depended anti-snakebite serum therapy. Phisalix demonstrated that venom production, because it is accompanied by natural immunity, acts primarily as an internal defense strategy, thereby conferring biological advantage.

Named Chevalier de la Légion d'honneur in 1923, she received the Grand Prix Lasserre (sciences) of the Ministry of Public Instruction in 1928. Although put forward for membership in the Académie de Médecine she was not elected; had she succeeded she would have been the first woman accepted.

She often spoke at Muséum meetings and before the Société Zoologique. In addition, in keeping with the Muséum's long tradition of public teaching, she lectured to groups of foresters and veterinarians of the French colonial service who came to her every year for advice and information. She especially welcomed to her laboratory people from the army medical service, members of the Corps de Santé Militaire in which her husband had served; the corps for its part long remembered the valuable work of both Césaire and Marie Phisalix. Her short book *Vipères de France: leur biologie, leur appareil venimeux et le traitement de leurs morsures,* a very readable, informative presentation, was a basic summary of her instructional program.[109]

A pleasant, energetic, spontaneous person, *de philosophie souriante,* Marie Phisalix was particularly happy to have groups of young people visit her laboratory, especially campers and scouts seeking advice about vipers. During the First World War she organized an anti-typhoid and anti-smallpox vaccination program. As many French women did during this war, she adopted as *filleuls* (godsons), a great number of young soldiers. Throughout the Second World War she remained in Paris and took responsibility for the reptile collection at the Muséum. She died in February 1946, at age eighty-five, just as the Muséum was preparing to celebrate her fifty years of uninterrupted work in its laboratories. At the time she was vice president of the Société de Pathologie Comparée and was due to assume the office of president that year.

Little information has been uncovered about Romanian-born MARIETTE POMPILIAN[110] who received a Paris medical degree in 1897. She does not appear to have gone into practice as a physician but concentrated on aspects of laboratory research, particularly the quantitative investigation of physiological and neurological processes. By the early years of the twentieth century she was well settled into the Paris medical research community. Her work for the most part involved muscular contraction studies on invertebrates.

After passing her *baccalauréat*-level examinations in Bucharest in 1890 Pompilian completed two years of medical studies there before moving to Paris. Her first published research, carried out in the laboratory of physiology and physics of the faculty of medicine, appeared in two jointly authored papers in 1896 (see bibliography); these concerned the influence of microbial toxins and temperature on muscle contraction. Her *thèse* on energy expenditure during muscle contraction presented to the medical faculty the following year was well received by the examiners.[111]

Over the next decade Mariette Pompilian published at least twenty-four papers and notes in Paris journals;[112] several discussed new apparatus and equipment for the measurement for neuromuscular function. Three papers brought out jointly with physiologist Maurice Letulle in 1902 reported their study, using graphical techniques, of pulmonary movement in subjects suffering from such diseases as emphysema, pleurisy, pulmonary tuberculosis, and nervous afflictions. A 1906 article with Letulle discussed their studies on nutrition chemistry, on particular requirements for salt and nitrogenous materials, and the relationship of variation in the supply of these to various physiological processes. The work was carried out in a laboratory for the study of nutrition chemistry organized by Pompilian and Letulle at the Boucicaut hospital, a large institution in southwest Paris. In this 1906 paper Pompilian announced her intention to establish her own laboratory for nutrition research, a facility, open to both foreign and French physiologists, that would be provided with all the necessary equipment for the study of the chemistry of the digestive process and accompanying heat energy and respiratory exchanges.

Mathematical and Physical Sciences

> *There is no doubt that her research is the most significant done by a woman before Sofia Kovalevskaia.*
>
> —Mary Gray

SOPHIE GERMAIN[113] (1776–1831), child of Paris of the revolutionary era, middle-class intellectual, and a talented and hardworking student of mathematics and philosophy, was the winner of the *prix extraordinaire* in mathematical physics of the French Academy of Sciences in 1816. She had working contacts with some of the leading mathematicians of her time, she was one of the few people to carry on a mathematical correspondence with Carl Friedrich Gauss, the greatest mathematician of the early nineteenth century, and she produced a result in number theory of lasting importance.

Sophie Germain was born in Paris, on 1 April 1776, the second of three daughters of silk merchant Ambroise-François Germain d'Orsanville and his wife Marie-Madeleine (née Gruguelu). From a prosperous *bourgeois* merchant family, Ambroise-François Germain was an educated man of liberal outlook who served briefly as an elected representative of the *tiers état* (the *bourgeoisie*) in the Constituent Assembly of 1789 and later became a director of the Banque de France. Life during Sophie's childhood was hardly tranquil. Born two years after the accession of Louis XVI, she was thirteen when the Bastille fell to the people of Paris and the social and political ferment and confusion of the years that followed were part of her daily life. Her refuge was her father's library and his mathematics books.

From Étienne Bézout's *Traité d'Arithmétique,* she went on to the works of Newton and Euler. Jean-Étienne Montucla's *Histoire des Mathématiques* was a special pleasure. Although her family later became reconciled to her interest in mathematics, unusual for a girl of her time, for a while they opposed her and much of her early studying was done at night in secret. Nevertheless, by her early twenties she was far enough advanced to tackle lecture notes from courses given at the newly opened École Polytechnique. She studied those for a course in chemistry given by Antoine François Fourcroy, one of the leading chemists of the time, and also those for Joseph-Louis Lagrange's course in advanced mathematics (analysis). Further, under the name of École Polytechnique student Antoine-August LeBlanc, she submitted to Lagrange a course evaluation essay then expected of students.

Generally considered "the keenest mathematician of the eighteenth century,"[114] Lagrange (1736–1813) was also an experienced teacher and the author of well-received textbooks needed for the updated curricula introduced with the establishment of the new schools of postrevolutionary Paris. Impressed by LeBlanc's course evaluation, Lagrange went to see this student. The resulting unmasking of Mlle. Germain caused something of a stir. Several other Paris *savants* called on her, gave her current problems to try, and over a period offered some general help and advice. This attention was hardly comparable to systematic training, however, and one might wish that Germain had been able to maintain the LeBlanc disguise longer and go on to benefit further, even if at a distance, from École Polytechnique mathematics courses. Still quite isolated, she was unable to develop the kind of contacts with scientists and mathematicians she needed, and indeed resented the attitude of one of her would-be helpers, astronomer Joseph Jérôme Lalande, who suggested that she ought to study his popular *Astronomie des Dames* (1785) before she could hope to read Pierre-Simon Laplace's *Mécanique céleste*. She considered watered-down science for ladies beneath her.

After the publication in 1797–1798 of Adrien Marie Legendre's two-volume *Essai sur la Théorie des Nombres* Germain became interested in number theory. Legendre (1753–1833) probably had more influence than anyone else on her mathematical work; from his *Théorie des Nombres*, she went on to Gauss's *Disquisitiones arithmeticae* (1801), one of the great classics of mathematical literature. Although this work brought Gauss instant recognition, readership was small for many years because of the author's difficult and austere style; Germain's keen interest in relationships between integers was sufficient to lead her to attempt a reading. Enthusiastic and remarkably ambitious, she contacted Gauss (one year her junior), then in Brunswick. She was one of the few people to do so. The correspondence between them was not extensive, but it has become quite celebrated in the history of early women mathematicians[115] and is of special interest to those exploring the emergence of women as members of the scientific community in the nineteenth century.

Germain's first letter to Gauss was sent in November of 1804. Once again she used her alias, LeBlanc, and introduced herself simply as a reader of Gauss's work. But she went so far as to enclose a contribution of her own—two demonstrations of a generalization of one of the major results Gauss had given in *Disquisitiones* and an application of this relationship to a problem previously considered by Lagrange. Gauss, who about then was very much absorbed in astronomical calculations, took six months to respond, but when he did, he indicated his considerable pleasure at her interest. He assumed she was a young male Paris mathematician. In their ensuing correspondence he entered into fairly extensive discussions of her work that related to his theorems but was sparing with the criticism she hoped for and did not become involved in the original work she sent.

In the winter of 1806–1807 Germain's real identity was revealed to Gauss. Anxious for his safety when Napoleon's army invaded Prussia, she contacted a family friend who was a high-ranking army officer. Gauss's safety was duly secured, but the incident led to Germain's somewhat embarrassed confession that she had taken the name LeBlanc for fear of "le ridicule attaché au titre de femme savante"; nevertheless she hoped the correspondence would continue.[116] Gauss responded cordially, even presenting her with three new theorems for which he invited her to supply proofs. He was clearly impressed with her efforts and commented in a letter to his friend the astronomer Heinrich Wilhelm Olbers as follows:

> Lagrange remains quite interested in astronomy and higher arithmetic; he considered the two theorems I shared with you a while ago (in which 2 is a cubic or biquadratic residue of primes) as "most beautiful and most difficult to prove." But Sophie Germain has sent me the proofs; unfortunately I have not been able to go through them yet, but I think they are good. At least she has approached the matter from the proper side; they are only a little lengthier than required.[117]

But the Germain-Gauss exchange was essentially over. In one further letter, written in January of 1808 after he had moved to Göttingen University, Gauss politely ended the correspondence. The warm tone of his last two letters to Germain, written after he knew who she was, has generally been taken to indicate that his acceptance of her as a promising young mathematician was unaffected by her identify change. However, one could wonder if the exchange might not have lasted longer had LeBlanc remained in Gauss's mind an up-and-coming young number theorist working in Paris, then the centre of scientific excellence in the Western world. It would not be particularly surprising if Gauss, a conservative person with a dislike of teaching, found his interest flagging when LeBlanc turned out to be a woman, talented and hardworking but not a genius, and constrained by the times to the fringes of the scientific community.

In April 1809 the First Class of the Institut National, the Paris Academy of Sciences's section for mathematics and physics, established a *prix extraordinaire* for a mathematical analysis of the modes of vibration of thin, flat, elastic plates. Members of the First Class, France's leading mathematicians, including Lagrange and Legendre, were ineligible to enter and a number of other major figures did not. Although vibration patterns for elastic bodies had been of great interest for centuries, this particular competition came about as the result of a presentation in Paris in 1808 by Ernst Chladni. Chladni demonstrated that when a glass plate covered with sand was made to vibrate the sand grains moved until they reached stationary nodes. The resulting patterns of lines and curves depended on the shape of the plate, the number and position of its support points, and the note produced. Though previously unrecorded, the phenomenon was clearly common in nature.

Germain, turning her attention in new directions after the loss of Gauss's companionship for her number theory studies, became interested in the problem. Her background for work on elastic surfaces was sadly inadequate, but she began by attempting a generalization of an earlier result of Leonard Euler that had enabled him to compute the displacement of a beam. Running into difficulties, she contacted Legendre, whose *Théorie des Nombres* had been her introduction to number theory ten years earlier. His response was direct and helpful, but he made clear that his interest must necessarily be limited because he was a competition judge.

In the memoir she submitted in 1811 Germain failed to derive a correct equation. However, her approach was right and Lagrange, also a judge, used her basic hypothesis to derive an equation that is correct, provided special assumptions are made. He communicated his result to the other judges and Legendre passed it on to Germain, indicating how she might derive it for herself. The new entry that she submitted to the extended competition in 1813 still lacked a satisfactory derivation but she nevertheless received honorable mention, largely because she demonstrated that the equation produced results that actually fitted Chladni's patterns in special cases. When the competition was once more renewed (1816) Germain was awarded the prize; despite a number of errors still present, her discussion was considered interesting and she presented new work (also flawed) on the difficult problem of initially curved surfaces.

Meantime however, following Germain's demonstration that the equation actually worked in practice, interest in the topic had increased. Siméon-Denis Poisson, despite being a judge, and over Legendre's objection, in 1814 read to his colleagues a memoir on elastic surfaces, deriving Lagrange's equation. He did this starting from an entirely different physical conjecture from Germain's mechanical model, namely the now largely forgotten "Molecular Hypothesis." This molecular parallel to Newtonian gravitation (chiefly due to Laplace) was a powerful concept at the time, influencing all branches of physics and chemistry; it explained elastic force in terms of attractive and repulsive forces between the molecules in the body considered.

By 1816, after five years of work on elasticity that had won her considerable notice in the Paris mathematical community, Germain returned to number theory. In her early correspondence with Gauss she had touched briefly on the subject of Fermat's Last Theorem, a problem that had attracted the attention of mathematicians, especially amateurs, for 140 years. This theorem asserts that for any integer exponent n greater than 2 and for nonzero integers x, y, and z, the equation $x^n + y^n = z^n$ has no solution. Fermat had sketched a proof for $n = 4$ and it was considered in Germain's time that Euler had proved it for $n = 3$.

Germain's approach to the problem was influenced by Legendre,[118] who, like both Fermat and Euler, attempted to prove the conjecture for just one exponent. Taking on much the same role as a present-day adviser of graduate students, Legendre suggested that Germain avoid both an attempt to prove the conjecture for some particular exponent and an attack on the theorem in its full generality (an extremely ambitious undertaking from which both Euler and Gauss had turned aside); instead he advised her to direct her efforts to possible solutions for all exponents that fall within the limits of some kind of restrictive hypothesis.

Germain showed that if a special case is made by excluding from consideration integers divisible by the exponent, then there are many exponents for which Fermat's equation has no solution. (From then on this has been referred to as Case I of Fermat's Last Theorem.) For instance, considering the equation $x^3 + y^3 = z^3$, in which the exponent is 3, her demonstration showed that there is no solution consisting of integers drawn from 1, 2, 4, 5, 7, 8 . . . (integers 3, 6, 9, 12 . . . being excluded from consideration in Case I). She was the first to give even part of Fermat's Last Theorem a proof applicable to more than one exponent.[119]

Legendre demonstrated her method to the Institut de France, where it was "greeted with great admiration,"[120] its simultaneous applicability to many exponents being recognized as an important tool for future progress. It was published by Legendre as part of the derivation of results of his own in an 1823 paper in the Institut's *Mémoirs*; he also added it to an 1825 supplement to his *Théorie des Nombres*.[121] Because Germain discovered the method and Legendre attributed it to her, the underlying result has come down to us as Sophie Germain's Theorem.[122] Using it, Legendre greatly extended the list of exponents for which Case I of Fermat's Last Theorem was known to hold.

In continuing work on Case I, Sophie Germain's Theorem was used for more than a century and a half. It provided an early, general approach to at least a portion of the study of Fermat's famous conjecture, a conjecture that, directly or indirectly, motivated a tremendous amount of mathematical research throughout the nineteenth and twentieth centuries. The finished proof of Fermat's Last Theorem was completed by British mathematician Andrew Wiles in 1995, drawing on the very considerable mathematical power developed in the preceding 100 years. Although this proof might have owed little to Germain, her theorem in its time was a considerable step forward; as late as 1977, number theorist Harold Edwards wrote, "Although it has been generalized and improved it has not been replaced since the time it was discovered."[123]

In 1821, encouraged by her mathematician friend Joseph Fourier, Germain brought out privately her work on elastic surfaces.[124] It still contained errors in the mathematical analysis and revealed her insufficient understanding of the physics involved; indeed by attempting to look at curved surfaces, she had moved into new territory with inadequate tools at her disposal. But the work did make public her early contribution to elastic plate theory, particularly her mechanical model alternative to the all-pervasive Laplace-Poisson molecular view. She thus became "part of the historical trend that was challenging the molecular mentality and moving away from it,"[125] although at the time her efforts were greeted with nothing further than formal, polite acknowledgment.

During the 1820s and 1830s, the groundwork for the modern theory of elasticity was laid, not without fierce debate. Germain continued to send memoirs to the Academy, but she could not compete with the professionals. Her early contributions were largely ignored, although not entirely forgotten; in the fierce Poisson-Navier debate on elasticity Claude Navier cited Germain's "ingenious hypothesis" when pointing out Poisson's deficient analysis and he took Poisson to task for ignoring the Lagrange contribution, anchored in Germain's hypothesis.[126] Germain's privately published *Remarques* on elastic surfaces appeared in 1826 and another memoir, written in 1824, was brought out posthumously in 1880.[127] Her 1828 *Annales de Chimie* paper (see bibliography) claimed priority in demonstrating the limitations of the molecular view, but here she avoided the technical details. Navier's widely circulated paper, "Mémoire sur la flexion des plans élastiques," published only in abstract, acknowledged her contribution to the development of the theory of elasticity.[128]

By 1829 she was ill with cancer but nevertheless put in order some of her earlier work and published two more papers, one on curvature of surfaces and one on number theory (see bibliography). When she became too ill to do mathematics she turned to more general questions, ideas about the nature of intellectual work and the functioning of human society that she had begun to note down years earlier. Her *Considérations générales sur l'état des sciences et des lettres* was edited and published by her nephew Armand-Jacques Lherbette shortly after her death; *Oeuvres philosophiques,* a more complete version of her philosophical writings, appeared in 1879.[129] Not surprisingly some of her *considérations* now appear dated, but others, such as her thoughts about characteristics common to all creative work, have worn better; she noted, for instance, that order, balance, and simplicity of presentation were common and essential ingredients in both poetry and mathematics.

Germain's mathematician friend Guillaume Libre described her in an obituary as accomplished, kindly, and thoughtful, a good conversationalist able to grasp ideas quickly and see clearly ahead to conclusions.[130] Although her work on elasticity had basic flaws, there is little doubt that she was well aware of the fundamental issue involved, namely that "she was speaking to . . . the sanctity of the molecular mentality espoused by Laplace, Biot, and Poisson."[131] In number theory she achieved more, producing an important result of lasting value. In 1830 Gauss tried to persuade the University of Göttingen to award her a degree, but without success. She died at the age of fifty-five, on 27 June 1831, at 13 rue de Savoie, Paris, now a historical landmark. Burial was in Père Lachaise, the city's main cemetery. With the publication in 1879 of *Oeuvres philosophiques* there came a renewal of interest in Sophie Germain; in 1888 the École de la rue de Jouy, a girls' school in central Paris established six years earlier, was renamed École Sophie Germain.

Except for Sophie Germain, few women working in France published journal articles in mathematics before 1900.[132] By the 1880s however, a number of women were taking degrees in the mathematical sciences in Paris. One of the most notable among them was astronomy student Dorothea Klumpke.

Votre thèse est la première qu'une femme ait présentée et soutenue avec succès devant notre Faculté pour obtenir le grade de docteur ès sciences mathématiques. Vous ouvrez dignement la voie . . .[133]

—Gaston Darboux

DOROTHEA KLUMPKE (1861–1942),[134] the first woman to receive a *docteur ès sciences mathématiques* degree from the University of Paris, later became well known as an astronomer in both Europe and the United States.

The younger sister of neurologist Augusta Dejerine-Klumpke (see above), she was born in San Francisco on 9 August 1861, the third of the six surviving children of Dutch-German immigrant Johan Gerard Klumpke and his wife Dorothea Matilda (néeTolle). Johan Klumpke grew up in New Orleans and initially studied medicine, but at age twenty-four went West to join the California gold rush. Not lucky as a prospector he settled in the small Spanish mission of San Francisco in late 1849 and soon became a very successful businessman dealing in San Francisco real estate. New York–born Dorothea Tolle went to California in 1853 to visit her sister, the wife of a recently arrived San Francisco gunsmith; she married Klumpke two years later.

At age five Dorothea, with her mother and sisters, traveled to Europe, where they spent two years (1866–1868) while seeking medical help for the oldest child, Anna, somewhat crippled from a leg injury. Dorothea attended a school in San Francisco for a year or two but the breakup of her parents' marriage and her mother's subsequent move to Europe in 1871 meant that she received most of her education on the Continent. After a short period in Göttingen and four years near Lake Geneva, Mrs. Klumpke and her children settled in Paris in 1877. Dorothea grew up speaking French, German, and English fluently.

Benefiting from the anticlerical educational reforms instituted in the 1880s by the government of the Third Republic, Dorothea Klumpke, after passing the *baccalauréat ès sciences* examinations, was able to proceed to *licence* level studies at the University of Paris and received her diploma in 1886. She then continued work in mathematics and mathematical astronomy as an *élève libre* (private student) at the Paris Observatory. In 1887 she was appointed *attachée* at the observatory, where she calculated star positions recorded on photographic plates.

That year the International Congress of Astronomers met in Paris to consider the proposal of British astronomer Sir David Gill of the Cape Observatory, South Africa, that a photographic sky chart be prepared by international cooperation. The projected huge *Carte du Ciel* was to be accompanied by a star catalogue. Dorothea Klumpke made good use of her language skills at the congress, translating foreign papers into French for the official record. With the adoption of the Gill proposal, the Paris Observatory undertook, as its share of the work, to photograph in a broad zone across the sky all stars to the fourteenth magnitude, and to prepare the corresponding charts. In addition, the French astronomers were to catalogue all stars to the eleventh magnitude appearing in the Paris zone. The work necessitated the setting up of a special *Bureau des Mesures* and for ten years, from 1891 to 1901, Dorothea Klumpke headed this bureau, where several women assistants worked under her direction.

Between 1888 and 1893 she brought out about twenty-six notes and papers, mainly in *Comptes rendus* and observatory publications, reporting her own observations of comets and minor planets. The earliest of these notes, along with her bureau work, brought her the first *Prix des Dames* awarded in 1889 by the Société Astronomique de France. In December of 1893, at the age of thirty-two, she defended her doctoral thesis, "Contribution à l'étude des anneaux de Saturne," a theoretical study. Her examining committee included astronomers Félix Tisserand and Marie-Henri Androyer as well as mathematician Gaston Darboux. Darboux, when congratulating her on her outstanding defense, recalled her predecessor Sophie Germain who, seventy years earlier, had won recognition among the great French mathematicians of the time.[135] Fortunately Dorothea Klumpke was not handicapped by the same constraints that had limited Germain's efforts. In 1893, in addition to receiving her degree, she became an officer of the Academy of Sciences and spoke at the World's Congress on Astronomy and Astro-physics at the Columbian Exposition in Chicago.

One of the best remembered of her undertakings was the balloon flight she made under the auspices of the Société Française de Navigation Aërienne, one of the three Paris-based ascents arranged in November 1899 to observe the expected return of the Leonid meteors. She described the adventure for American readers in an article in *Century Magazine*.[136] Her preparations reveal the somewhat hazardous nature of the venture; she made ready "little souvenirs, in case of no return."[137] The massive hydrogen-filled balloon *Centaur* also carried the dean of French *aëronauts,* de Fonvielle, who offered to assist Klumpke as secretary and note taker.

They ascended to about 1,600 feet over Paris an hour after midnight on 16 November, with a clear sky and bright moonlight. Drifting west over the forest of St. Germain to Caen, they crossed the base of the Cotentin peninsula and seven hours later, perilously close to the sea, touched down in a grassy meadow near the hamlet of St. Germain-sur-Ay, 176 miles from their starting point. Meteor sightings were disappointing: "From 5 to 6 a.m. six brilliant trails flashed by, coming from the Lion, the Great Bear, the little Bear and Hercules; that was all," and between 2 and 6 a.m. only twenty-six were observed in all. But she had no regrets about the trip; she felt "enriched 1000-fold by the wonderful experience . . ."[138]

In 1896 she sailed to northern Norway on the S.S. *Norse King* to observe the total solar eclipse of 9 August. Also on this trip was Isaac Roberts, retired Liverpool businessman and amateur astronomer, fellow of the Royal Astronomical Society and one of the pioneers of nebular photography. About 1890 Roberts had moved his observatory to East Sussex, rebuilding it on Crowborough Hill, a site chosen for the favorable probability of the occurrence of intervals of clear sky suitable for stellar photography; at 780 feet above sea level it was one of the highest points in the south of England. Using a twenty-inch reflecting telescope equipped with a camera, he had produced a great many photographs that showed structural and other details of sky objects previously unknown to British astronomers. In 1901, when she was forty, Dorothea Klumpke married Roberts, a widower more than thirty years her senior. Moving to Sussex, she joined in expanding Roberts's already extensive deep-sky photographs program that emphasized William Herschel's fifty-two "fields of nebulosity."

Isaac Roberts died in 1904 at the age of seventy-five but left his widow well provided for. She returned to France, taking the vast Roberts photographic plate collection with her, and took up residence with her mother and her artist sister Anna at the Château de By, near the hamlet of By-Thomery, some fifty miles south of Paris in the region of the forest of Fontainbleau.[139]

To mark the centenary of Isaac Roberts's birth in January 1829, Dorothea Roberts published the *Isaac Roberts Atlas of 52 Regions*;[140] a supplement followed in 1932. Of special use in the identification of feebly luminous sky areas, it included high-quality enlargements of fifty of the plates produced with Roberts's twenty-inch reflecting telescope. The work brought her the Hélène-Paul Helbronner prize from the Academy of Sciences in 1932. In 1934 she was elected Chevalier de la Légion d'honneur in recognition of forty-eight years of work in astronomy.[141]

By then over seventy, she retired and with her sister Anna settled in San Francisco. Over the years they had kept their American contacts, frequently visiting their father and younger relatives. Their large house on San Francisco's 14th Avenue, with an art studio at rooftop level, became one of the city's cultural meeting places where artists and musicians, as well as scientists, often gathered. Still immensely interested in astronomical research, Dorothea Roberts endowed several prizes through the Paris Observatory, the Société Astronomique de France, and the University of California; these were for undergraduates in mathematics and astronomy and for young astronomers, especially those doing distinguished work on nebulae. Her gift to the Astronomical Society of the Pacific established the Klumpke-Roberts Lecture Fund, named in memory of her parents and her husband; it now also supports the Klumpke-Roberts Award recognizing outstanding popularizers of astronomy. Yet another substantial gift went to the American Astronomical Society. Dorothea Roberts died in San Francisco, on 5 October 1942, at the age of eighty-one, a few months after the death of her sister Anna and after several years of illness.

Papers on astronomical topics by two other women working France—Clémence Royer (p. 85) and Gabrielle Vallot—are listed in the bibliography.

GABRIELLE VALLOT, née PÉRON, collaborated with her husband Joseph Vallot, director of the Mont Blanc Observatory, on high altitude observations. Both were active members of the Club Alpin Français. At least five of their joint papers appeared before 1901, mainly in the *Annales de l'Observatoire Météorologique du Mont Blanc*. These reported measurements of the fall and rise of solar radiation intensity at alpine locations during a solar eclipse and observations of chemical effects of radiation at different altitudes. The Vallots sometimes worked at different sites, one at Chamonix, Haute-Savoie, and the other at the Mont Blanc Observatory, in order to have comparative data gathered over the same time intervals. As climbers and mountaineers they were also interested in mountain water flow and cave formations.[142]

> *En tout cas, la physique se définit désormais par un nouveau défi, aller au-delà des phénomènes observables, vers un autre réalité qui permet de les interpréter.*[143]
>
> —Bensaude-Vincent and Stengers

Physicist-chemist and "mother" of atomic physics, MARIE CURIE (1867–1934)[144] was awarded a *licence ès sciences mathématiques* by the Sorbonne in 1894. Thirteen of her pre-1901 papers, seven of them joint publications, are listed in the bibliography.

Curie, whose name is as indissolubly linked with radioactivity as are those of Ampère, Volta, and Ohm with electricity, is probably still the most famous and most written-about woman scientist of all time. Works about her range from articles in biographical dictionaries and encyclopedias, to chapters in anthologies, to stories aimed at younger readers, to full-scale biographies. The latter include Marion Cunningham's *Madame Curie and the Story of Radium* (1918), Eve Curie's 1938 work *Madame Curie*, Robert Reid's *Marie Curie* (1974), and Susan Quinn's very complete *Marie Curie: A Life* (1995). The works aimed at girls include some in non-European languages; Curie's icon status as premier example of a woman scientist is worldwide. Articles attempting to provide insight into her life and work from particular perspectives continue to appear and recent analyses of her contributions to the development of science are also available.[145] The following is a brief outline of Marie Curie's life and career.

Born Marya Sklodowska in Warsaw, Poland, then part of imperial Russia, on 7 November 1867, she was the fifth and last child of Wladislaw Sklodowski and his wife Bronislawa (née Boguska). Both parents were descended from Catholic families of the Polish minor nobility and both were teachers. After receiving her early education in government schools, Marya worked for several years as a governess to earn money. In 1891 she went to Paris, where one of her sisters was already studying, and enrolled at the Sorbonne. By dint of hard work, she took her *licence* qualification in physics in 1893 (at the head of her class) and that in mathematics (in which she ranked second) the following year—a very considerable achievement. She married physicist Pierre Curie in 1895.

Although her first research was on the magnetic properties of steels (under the direction of physicist Gabriel Lippmann), for her doctoral work she moved to the new and rapidly advancing field of "radioactivity" as it came to be called. Here she had the assistance and collaboration of her husband, although he was already deeply and extensively involved in fundamental research on the magnetic properties of matter. He arranged working space for her, first at the Paris École Municipale de Physique et de Chimie Industrielle, the industrial school where he then taught, and later at the Sorbonne when he moved on to a position there. From 1900 until 1906 Marie was a physics instructor at the École Normale Supérieure de Jeunes Filles, a college for women teachers, in the Paris suburb of Sèvres. In 1905 she became *chef-de-travaux* (laboratory manager) for her husband in the faculty of sciences at the Sorbonne and in 1906, after Pierre Curie's death, she succeeded to his chair of physics, becoming the first woman to hold a teaching post at the Sorbonne. She became the first woman titular professor at that institution in 1908.

Marie Curie's doctoral research developed directly from the 1895 discovery by physicist Henri Becquerel, one of her professors, of the emission of rays from uranium minerals. Bequerel had found that these could pass through opaque materials and fog a photographic plate, as well as discharge an electroscope by making the surrounding air conductive. Marie and Pierre Curie undertook a systematic investigation of the Becquerel radiation with the aim of discovering its source. Their starting material was the residue left after the extraction of uranium from pitchblende, a uranium ore. The fact that the residue was *more* active than purified uranium oxide suggested it as a probable source of some unknown material more active than uranium; the task, a formidable one, was to isolate this unknown by chemical methods, namely group separation and fractional crystallization.

Papers discussing the Curies' work appeared steadily from 1898, some by Marie only, many joint with Pierre and one or two other collaborators.[146] English, German, and Polish translations were brought out promptly. Reports presented to the Academy of Sciences were read by Becquerel, neither of the Curies being an academy member at the time (Pierre Curie was elected in 1905, a year after being named to a newly created chair of physics at the Sorbonne).

In this work Marie painstakingly carried out the laborious chemical fractionations and Pierre established the electrical properties of the rays emitted by the fractions. Following the isolation in June 1898 (in a bismuth precipitate) of a fraction 400 times more active than uranium, they postulated the presence of a new element, strongly radioactive, that Marie named *polonium*. It was the first element discovered through its property of radioactivity. The crucial observation that the intensity of radioactivity of a sample depended only on the quantity of radioactive element it contained and not on chemical or physical state was made about the same time. In December 1898 a second new element was isolated (in a barium precipitate) and given the name radium. The still-impure radium preparation had an activity a million times that of uranium.[147] Throughout much of this early work Marie collaborated with Gustave Bémont, head of the chemistry section of the École Municipale de Physique et de Chimie Industrielle; Bémont coauthored one of the major 1898 Curie papers reporting the new-element discoveries (see bibliography).

In 1899 Marie Curie put forward the basic hypothesis that radioactivity was caused by atomic transformation:

> On pourrait, par example, rattacher la radioactivité à la théorie de Crookes sur l'évolution des éléments, en attribuant la radioactivité aux éléments à gros poids atomiques, qui se seraient formés en dernier et dont l'évolution ne serait pas encore achevée.[148]

It is worth noting that her suggestion came before the idea was taken up by physicist Ernest Rutherford and his coworkers.[149]

A major result came in 1902 with the isolation of one tenth of a gram of pure radium chloride from eight tons of pitchblende and the determination of its atomic weight (as 225). This aroused immediate interest. The experimental results formed the main part of Marie Curie's thesis for her doctorate, awarded in 1903 with the distinction "très honorable."[150] Later that year the Curies were awarded the London Royal Society's Humphry Davy Medal and then, along with Henri Becquerel, the Nobel Prize for physics for their discoveries in radioactivity. The latter honor, which received unprecedented and sensational coverage in the press, suddenly brought the unknown Curies to public attention and established Marie Curie's "legendary popular status in twentieth-century science."[151]

Marie Curie's research continued after Pierre's death in 1906 but from then on to a notable extent she stepped aside from the increasingly competitive field of atomic physics, which she had in part created.[152] She left to others, especially Rutherford and his colleagues, the theoretical development of modern atomic theory; her own work was more on the side of radiochemistry and, broadly speaking, might be summarized as investigations of the radioactive elements (including the puzzling problem of the materials later called *isotopes*) and studies of their disintegration processes and products. Rather than major new scientific theories, Curie's laboratory produced empirical data—data that formed part of the gradually accumulating body of results that later came to be fitted into and provided the foundation for the new classification of the chemical elements.

The tremendous interest in the new field and Marie Curie's international prestige drew many students and research workers to her group in the period up to the First World War, the maximum number in her group reaching twenty-two in the year 1910–1911. The availability of grants, including funds from the Carnegie Foundation, and the existence of what was virtually its own house journal were additional factors in making the laboratory attractive. A number of her coworkers made notable contributions in both radiochemistry and physics. Some had been colleagues during the period when the Curies were at the École Municipale; these included André Debierne,[153] Marie Curie's *chef-de-travaux* and her collaborator in the preparation of a sample of polonium large enough to view its spectrum (1910). Several were foreign scientists, among them Norwegian chemist Ellen Gleditsch, one of the most productive in the Curie group between 1907 and 1912.[154] Gleditsch's considerable contributions to the investigation of the ratios of elements in radioactive mineral deposits (such as the radium/uranium ratio) began with her studies in Paris—precise, quantitative chemistry in the Curie tradition. Because there was much confusion at the time over where the new elements and the substances that were later called isotopes fitted into the periodic system, the investigation of their relationships, properties, and relative abundance in nature was an important topic. Further, because the theory of radioactive transformation required that the ratio of a daughter element to its parent element be the same in any given decay series, the variability then being observed by a number of workers was a major difficulty; the problem was not finally resolved until a different measurement method became available in 1920.

Other work carried out in the Curie laboratory during the pre–First World War years included the development and improvement of electrical instrumentation for the detection of subatomic particles; efforts to increase the precision of values for radioactive constants, including Curie's own work on the half-life of radon (1910); studies on the range and energy of α-particles and the effects of α-particles on chemical processes and on organic materials important in living cells; investigations of ß-rays from radium; studies on the disintegration products in the thorium series; examination of the decay of polonium using a photographic method for counting the emitted α-particles, a new technique at the time.

Marie Curie's two-volume *Traité de Radioactivity* appeared in 1910, six years after the similar work by Rutherford.[155] She was persuaded to submit herself for election to the Academy of Sciences in 1911 but was not accepted, probably in part because of the scandal in the Paris press about the time concerning her alleged affair with her physicist colleague Paul Langevin. The same year she received her second Nobel Prize, this time in chemistry. It was awarded for her discovery of radium and polonium, the isolation of radium, and the study of its properties.

The medical applications of radiation, particularly diagnostic X-rays, had been quickly recognized and with the coming of the First World War, Curie became director of the Red Cross Radiological Service. Along with her elder daughter Irène, she worked to provide both mobile radiology units for the French army and to set up radiology stations at strategic locations. She also started a training program for X-ray technicians at the Institute of Radium.[156] The latter, built jointly by the Pasteur Institute and the University of Paris, was established to carry out research in two areas, physics and chemistry related to radioactivity (government-financed and directed by Marie Curie), and the development of medical and biological applications (supported by the Pasteur Institute). Although due to begin when the building was completed in 1914, the research programs did not start until the war was over. Curie returned to the institute in 1918, her daughter Irène accompanying her as a junior scientist (*préparateur*).

In 1921, money and materials being still in short supply in postwar France, she made a speaking tour of the United States in support of a subscription campaign to raise funds for the purchase of radium for the institute. Although by then in poor health, she also undertook fundraising tours throughout Europe and returned to the United States in 1928 to receive a gift for the Marie Sklodowska Curie Institute recently established in Warsaw. A member of the League of Nations International Committee on Intellectual Co-operation, she served for a time as its vice president. In 1922 she was elected to the French Academy of Medicine, its first female member. Beginning the following year, when she was fifty-six, the French government gave her an annual pension, but she donated the money to her laboratory and continued to work.[157] Until 1934 she lectured at the Sorbonne but gradually turned over the leadership and work of the Institute of Radium to Irène Joliot-Curie and her son-in-law Frédéric Joliot. She died on 4 July 1934, aged sixty-six, in a small sanatorium in Haute-Savoie in the French Alps, of leukemia that had been misdiagnosed as tuberculosis.

Aside from Marie Curie, very few French women or women working in France published papers in chemistry journals before 1901. The only one found listed in the Royal Society index was JOSÉPHINE CHEVALIER. She lived for several years in New York City in the 1870s and taught chemistry at the Medical College of the New York Infirmary for Women and Children. She also prepared abstracts and translations from French periodicals for the journal *American Chemist.*[158] Her 1886 paper in the *Zeitschrift für Physiologische Chemie* discussed biochemical work on nerve tissue, carried out under the guidance of Félix Hoppe Seyler at the famous Strasbourg Institute for physiological chemistry.

Also included in the French section of the bibliography are a few papers on meteorology and the earth sciences.

Two women—Déo and Bardin—wrote on sky phenomena. Both published in the journal *Astronomie,* reporting observations from the Paris region, Déo from Viroflay to the west of the city, and Bardin from Montmorency to the north. Mlle. Déo's note concerned a rare optical phenomenon preceding an unusually violent weather event in 1894. Along with her sister, she observed the true Sun with two accompanying images on one occasion and with three accompanying images on a second occasion. Mme. Bardin commented on sky mirages, recording her earlier sighting (1879) of the image of a winding river in the sky at sunset.

Five women working in France authored or coauthored papers in geology or physical geography listed in the Royal Society index—Honnorat Bastide, Peney, Royer (see p. 85), Sinard, and Vallot.[159]

Mme. HONNORAT BASTIDE and her husband Édouard, over the course of some twenty years, studied the natural history and especially the palaeontology and stratigraphy of their local region, the *département* of Basses Alpes on the western flanks of the French Alps near Digne, Provence. Building on studies of the region carried out by Edm. Hébert and A. Garnier in the 1860s and 1870s, they examined in particular beds thought to mark the divide between Lower and Middle Jurassic. On the basis of fossils they discovered in the spring of 1889, including the mollusc *Turbo capitaneus* previously considered characteristic of the Lower Jurassic, they raised the question of the classification of beds then designated upper strata of Middle Jurassic. They suggested, on the basis of both mineral and fossil content, that four of these beds fitted better into lower Middle Jurassic. The Honnorat Bastides were also interested in the exceptionally rich prehistory of their region; Édouard collected Stone Age tools and pottery fragments from ancient cave dwellings.

Mme. PENEY, née BURGER, published a brief note in the *Annuaire* of the Société Météorologique de France in 1880 reporting earth movements that occurred in southern Switzerland in December of the previous year. A widow, living in Saint-Maurice in the canton of Valais, she described a mild quake that shook her house, cracking ceilings but causing no major damage. The effects were felt over a wide area in the neighboring cantons and in Savoie.

BERTHE SINARD carried out geological studies in the region of arid limestone plateaux in the *départment* of Gard in southern France, just west of the Rhône river. Her findings appeared in the *Comptes rendus* of the Association Française pour l'Avancement des Sciences in 1891. Working out of Avignon, she investigated strata in the plateau des Angles, focusing on beds rich in echinoderms (especially *Pentacrinus*), considered to be of Miocene age. She described the stratigraphy in terms of fossil content, noting particularly changes from beds rich in crinoids to those rich in bryozoa. Mlle. Sinard clearly had colleagues but she did not record names of coworkers.

GABRIELLE VALLOT, née PÉRON, wrote on the cave formations in the limestone strata of the Cevennes, a lengthy paper appearing in the 1890 *Annuaire* of the Club Alpin Français, of which she was a member. She and her husband Joseph Vallot (1854–1925) spent three months each year at Joseph's childhood home near the town of Lodève, in the sparsely populated southeastern part of the Massif Central.[160] With one or two colleagues and assistants they carried out extensive explorations in the region. Many of the caves they investigated had been known since antiquity and local opinion held that some had been mined for their lead veins in Roman times; one of the more accessible was currently being used for cheese storage, having been fitted with shelves. Full accounts and detailed topographic maps of these cave structures were lacking, however. Throughout the explorations Gabrielle Vallot kept notes and wrote descriptions; her husband took photographs, using a magnesium lamp, and collected the data required for the preparation of maps and sections. They investigated by canvas boat a number of underground lakes and streams not previously explored and documented for the first time a great many impressive stalactite formations.

Social Sciences

Listed in the bibliography are papers in anthropology by four women working in France—Bertillon, Pelletier, Renooz, and Royer. Bertillon and Pelletier, members of the Paris medical community, are covered previously. Both Renooz and Royer were primarily writers and commentators; Royer made numerous contributions in anthropology and was well known in her time.

CLÉMENCE ROYER[161] (1830–1902), the first translator of Charles Darwin's *The Origin of Species* into French, was born in Nantes, on 21 April 1830, the daughter of Augustin-René Royer from the neighboring province of Maine. Royer married Clémence's mother, Joséphine-Gabrielle Audouard, daughter of a Breton naval officer, some years after their child was born. An army captain, fervent Catholic, and strong supporter of the Bourbon monarchy, he was for a time exiled from France for his involvement in the attempted royalist uprising of 1832. Thus Clémence lived in Switzerland during her early years.

Her education was much interrupted and fragmented. She spent some time in the convent of Sacré-Cœur du Mans, a refuge of children of Bourbon supporters, but the instruction she received there led her into mysticism and caused so much psychological strain that she had to leave the establishment. Except for help from her father with mathematics, a subject she enjoyed, she had little further guided education but studied on her own, preparing to teach piano, languages, and mathematics. She passed various examinations that gave her teaching credentials and for a year (1853–1854) taught in a private girls' boarding school in Haverfordwest, in southwest Wales. While there she learned English, and in addition rethought the tenets of her Catholic faith from within a Protestant milieu. This period of soul-searching, coupled with a program of readings of eighteenth-century French philosophers, which she undertook after returning to France, led her to turn aside from religion. Experiencing something of a second mystical crisis, she broke with her family and took the first steps toward starting out on her life's mission of teaching and writing. Moving to Switzerland, her home during her earliest years, she lived frugally at the châlet de Praz-Perez, seven miles from Lausanne. Her mother, by then a widow, thought her daughter had gone mad and had the circumstances investigated. But Clémence appeared to be all right. Over the course of two years she did a tremendous amount of reading, using mainly the Lausanne public library. She ranged across many fields, acquiring a great store of information, whether or not she gained understanding in depth. In 1857 she moved to Lausanne where, a year later, she met Pascal Duprat, a French political refugee. An economist of the liberal school, Duprat had been a professor at l'Académie de Lausanne since 1856 and was editor of two journals, one general and one specializing in the social sciences. This meeting marked the end of Clémence Royer's solitary life of self-directed study. Duprat, fifteen years her senior, was caught in an unsatisfactory marriage with no possibility of divorce; she became his mistress and remained in the relationship, openly, until his death in 1885.

About the time she moved to Lausanne Royer began her career of writer and public speaker, starting with an educational course for women in logic. Women speakers were fashionable then, and she continued in 1859–1860 with a course in natural philosophy. Because formal advanced education was not yet open to women even in Switzerland, a pioneer in this area of social progress, she had little competition and could attract considerable audiences. Her lecture program expanded, both in Lausanne and in other Swiss cities; later she went to Italy. Her wide reading enabled her to cover many subjects. She liked to combine fields, drawing no separation between science and philosophy. This habit, along with a certain amount of intellectual rashness and her lack of directed, disciplined training in any one field, led her into what, seen by a modern reader of scientific background, was very confused thinking on the topics she tackled. However, to specialists well versed in the complexity of competing philosophical and scientific theories current in Europe in the mid nineteenth century her views could perhaps seem less eccentric.

She had a special interest in the theory of taxation and its role in alleviating the effects of the worst social inequalities. Relatively well prepared by readings suggested by Duprat, she won a prize in 1860 in a canton competition for an essay in this field. Her ideas were elaborated in an ambitious two-volume work, *Théorie de l'Impôt ou la Dîme sociale,* published in Paris in 1862. In addition she brought out a number of articles in the publication *Journal des Économistes.*

The year 1862 also saw the appearance of her translation of Darwin's *Origin of Species—De l'Origine des Espèces par Sélection Naturelle, ou les Lois du Progrès chez les Êtres Organisés—*perhaps the work for which she is best remembered.[162] She was already well acquainted with the evolutionary theories put forward by French naturalist Lamarck (1744–1829) who, developing earlier ideas of Buffon (1707–1788) and others, had suggested that one species developes from another (that is, organic evolution takes place) via small inheritable modifications produced in an individual by its environment. Disturbed by the fact that Lamarckian theory was totally unacceptable to her female lecture audiences, Royer eagerly grasped the new Darwin work as a vindication of Lamarck who, for fifty years before the publication of *Origin of Species* had defended the idea of mutation, as opposed to fixity of species, against considerable opposition.

Although Royer can be criticized for failing to grasp the essential difference between Lamarck's doctrine of the inheritance of acquired characters and Darwin's theory of natural selection, it is well to remember that the development of theories of inheritance and evolution during the nineteenth century was a complex process with staunchly defended competing views. Publication of Darwin's *Origin of Species* by no means ended the arguments.[163] Darwinism was long resisted in France; the quintessentially French theories of biological transformation derived from Lamarck persisted among highly respected French biologists long past Royer's period of activity in the area in the 1860s and '70s.[164] Nevertheless she missed the thrust of Darwin's contribution,[165] never understanding the basic concept of the theory of natural selection. Consequently her translation, via its biased choice of phraseology, to a significant extent constituted a misrepresentation of Darwin's ideas. For her, *Origin of Species* was a development and concrete demonstration of Lamarck's transformation-of-species theory.[166] In fact the translation offered Royer, very much a rebel both social and religious, an opportunity to attack established political and religious doctrine. Her work had a clear propagandist function and, skewed to suit her purpose, inevitably had serious technical flaws.

Although Darwin had, with some reservations, welcomed Royer's first translation of his work, by the time the third French edition was being prepared relations between author and translator had cooled. Royer declined to incorporate additions Darwin had made to a new English edition and so he found another translator (J. J. Moulinié) for the 1873 French edition.

The first edition of Royer's translation was prefaced by a long essay of her own in which she undertook to extend the principles of Darwinism, as she understood them, to the social and political spheres, a topic of major importance to her given her primary interests in sociology and philosophy. This "social Darwinism," a prominent theme in late nineteenth-century thought, fitted well the ideas of supporters of the free-enterprise system, such as British philosopher Herbert Spencer. Spencer argued, even before the publication of *Origin of Species,* that social and economic progress would be guaranteed by allowing free-for-all struggle in which the weak would be eliminated and the fittest left unencumbered to exercise their abilities to the fullest. Further, people would learn from their mistakes and teach the next generation the need to adapt to a changing environment—clearly an analogy to lamarckian ideas.[167] Without an adequate understanding of the tremendous complexities involved, Royer indulged in a great deal of conjecture that now comes across as confused and undisciplined speculation. Using the biased social Darwinism outlined in her preface to *Origine des Espèces* as her starting place, she went on to apply the laws of biological evolution to human development, dealing, in her *Origine de l'Homme et des Sociétés* (1869), with social inequalities in terms of social biology. Fundamentally an élitist, although she selected her criteria to suit her purposes, she saw social inequality as following from biological inequality and, in company with many nineteenth-century thinkers, considered that humanity would suffer no loss if the more primitive races ("inertes et immobilisées dans leurs instincts de brutes sauvages") were forced to relinquish their living space to progressive peoples ("races progressives").[168]

In 1870, with the end of the Second Empire and the establishment of the Third Republic, Royer with Duprat and their four-year-old son René returned to Paris. For five years previously they had lived in Italy where René was born. His existence was freely acknowledged by Royer among her friends and he was legally recognized by his father, outside of marriage, as permitted in Italy at the time. Life was difficult however, mainly because of lack of money; Duprat's teaching salary sometimes was seized by the authorities to settle his legal wife's debts.

Reentering political life, Duprat served as a *député* in the National Assembly. As his hostess, Clémence Royer had considerable visibility in Paris social and political circles and from then her writings focused to a considerable extent on political problems. The period was one of continuing upheaval in France; questions of the redistribution of wealth, acceptable means of bettering the conditions of the working class, social justice in general, and the condition of women in particular occupied her attention. *Bourgeois* and anti-socialist, she wanted free universal state education but minimal interference from the state with adults; she favored democratic republican government, on condition that democracy respected "natural law" and sustained the power and influence of the intellectual élite.[169]

She became a member of the Société d'Anthropologie de Paris in 1870, following the publication of her *Origine de l'Homme.* The first anthropological society to be founded (1859), the Paris group was a lively one, much respected internationally and without a European rival until the rise of the German anthropological school in the first decades of the twentieth century. The election of Royer caused much contention and her subsequent success in being chosen for a seat on the central committee was a considerable triumph for her. She remained very active in the society until her death, presenting numerous communications. At times the views she expressed outraged her fellow members, as when in 1873 she claimed, in contradiction to all available evidence at the time, that the Aryan race originated in Europe.[170]

For a few years after Duprat's death in 1885 she had a small government pension, but this stopped when she was about sixty and she lived her remaining years in a boarding house, the Maison Galignani, which gave free accommodation to aged indigent intellectuals.[171] She continued to write throughout the 1880s and 1890s with undiminished energy, contributing to economics journals, anthropology reviews, and popular scientific reviews. In addition she submitted entries to a great many prize competitions, prepared articles for dictionaries and encyclopedias, including the *Nouveau Dictionnaire d'Économie Politique* (1891–1892), and wrote articles for feminist publications such as the new daily newspaper *La Fronde.* Her monograph, *Le Bien et la Loi Morale: Éthique et Téléogie,* appeared in 1881 and two more books were published in the last two years of her life, *Natura rerum. La Constitution du Monde, Dynamique des Atomes, Nouveaux Principes de Philosophie Naturelle* (1900), and *Histoire du Ciel* (1901); the last two suffered sadly from her lack of scientific training.

Royer became increasingly active in the feminist cause during the 1890s and by 1897, thanks to her regular contributions to *La Fronde,* was one of the major figures in the movement. That year a banquet was organized in her honor, an event that brought her great pleasure and did much to counteract her increasing isolation, especially from younger women. In 1900, supported by feminist movement leaders, she was awarded the Légion d'honneur. She died in the Maison Galignani in February 1902, shortly before her seventy-second birthday.

Although neither a scientist nor a notable generator of philosophical ideas, Clémence Royer was an extraordinarily prolific writer and essayist, passionately interested in almost the entire range of major events and concerns of her time, social, political, and scientific. Intense, ambitious, amazingly energetic, and adventurous, she attempted far more than she was competent to undertake. Her flights of fancy on scientific questions and the nonsense she sometimes published might tempt one to dismiss her as very much an eccentric whose contributions to science have been somewhat overstated; given her handicaps however, the wonder is that she accomplished what she did.

CÉLINE RENOOZ[172] (1840?–1928?), an acquaintance of Clémence Royer, with whom she corresponded at least intermittently over a period of more than twenty years,[173] was, like Royer, a prolific writer and commentator on social and scientific matters. She was also an extreme and outspoken feminist and a rebel, totally opposed to the teachings of established religion.

Born in Liège, Belgium, in the 1840s, Céline was the daughter of Emmanuel-Nicolas Renooz, a city magistrate well known for his liberal ideas and a man so out of favor with the established church that it refused him a religious burial. His daughter is said to have been much influenced by him. She spent a number of years in Spain following her marriage to an engineer by the name of Muro, the son of a prominent Spanish banker also active in the political life of his country. In 1876 however, well provided for financially, she left her husband and with her four children settled in Paris. Three of the children died of tuberculosis before reaching the age of twenty.

Céline Renooz was very interested in current scientific work and developments, particularly evolutionary and anthropological theories and how these could be tied in with the mystical and matriarchical ideas then in vogue. Fairly quickly she began to formulate her own thoughts in these areas and to try to bring her ideas to as wide an audience as she could. Her intense feelings of anticlericalism, misanthropy, and the supreme importance of motherhood inspired her to campaign for not just equality for women but for according them superior status. Matriarchy she saw as the path to salvation for the human race and, endowed with a strong missionary spirit, she felt it her duty to lead the way.

Beginning in the early 1880s she published a succession of books, many of them lengthy, on the new ideas of human and animal evolution, comparative psychology, the history of civilizations and religions, and the status of women in various societies.[174] Her writing has a certain amount in common with some of Clémence Royer's more speculative contributions, but the unusual extremes to which Mme. Renooz was prepared to go make her a less attractive subject for feminist historians.

Her major work was her massive six-volume *L'Ère de Vérité*.[175] Here she reinterpreted a great many important historical events to make clear what she saw as the true story of the leading role of women in early human communities and their subsequent ruthless suppression. This story, she held, had been essentially wiped out of the collective memory after societies became male dominated. Her criticism of the fundamental tenets of the Christian church, set out in volume 5, comes as quite a startling revelation. Relying largely on linguistic connections and current anthropological suggestions and beliefs (some of them erroneous) to support her arguments, she suggested that a woman, Johana, who is known to us as John the Baptist, was the true bringer of Christianity to the world. The story of Jesus she believed to be nothing more than a myth whose origins are rooted in the male drive for dominance and the fight of men against goddess worship and matriarchy. Hope for mankind's future lay in the late nineteenth-century reemergence of women, in the persons of the pioneers of the feminist movement.

For a short time around 1888, she brought out the journal *Revue Scientifique des Femmes*, much of whose purpose was to further the process of reorienting science in a more feminist direction. This process, she believed, would lead to a "true science" whose method was based on intuition. Although she used the review to present lengthy previews of excerpts from her 1891 three-volume work *La Nouvelle Science*, she also publicized the accomplishments of women scientists and physicians. Somewhat too militant and aggressive in tone, the review had only a small readership. In 1890 she founded a society to promote her new philosophy—the Société Néosophique.

Renooz followed closely anthropological studies and developments in evolutionary ideas although she disagreed with Darwin and with most of the leading Paris anthropologists. At least for a period in the late 1880s and early 1890s she was given a hearing by some in the academic community. The bibliography lists her long conjectural paper in an 1886 issue of the *Journal de Micrographie*, in which she presented a theory of evolution based on her studies of accounts of embryological development; these ideas were also put forward in her work *L'Origine des Animaux*.[176] Perhaps influenced by the "ontogony recapitulates phylogony" theories of German zoologist Ernst Haeckel, she considered man's ancestors were to be found in the plant kingdom (specifically the bean) rather than in the animal world.

Although much of Céline Renooz's "neosophism" or "renoozism" was invention wrapped in scientific jargon, she did have a small following of enthusiastic supporters. Further, even a feminist with solid scientific background such as Madeleine Pelletier, although she had perforce to reject Renooz's "new science," tended to treat her fairly gently; she was after all an ally in the fight against the fundamental problem of male dominance.

Like Clémence Royer, Céline Renooz is said to have passed her later years in poverty.[177] She died in Paris in the late 1920s.

Summary and Further Comments

Figure 3-1 summarizes numerical counts of papers in scientific journals indexed by the Royal Society that were published by nineteenth-century women working in France. The concentration of authors in the botanical sciences, zoology, and the medical fields (especially neurology and physiology) is brought out in Figure 3-2a. The six most important areas of activity as measured by number of articles were astronomy, neurology and physiology, anthropology, botanical sciences, zoology, and physics (Figure 3-2b).

It is worthwhile, however, to look closely at the work in these areas to assess its scientific importance. The contribution in physics (8.5 percent of the total French article count) is Marie Curie's well known early work. The 24 percent contribution in astronomy, almost entirely the work of Dorothea Klumpke Roberts, to a large extent consists of short observational notes on comets and minor planets, fairly routine astronomical studies; Klumpke Roberts's major contribution came after 1900 when she published the atlas of sky regions examined by Isaac Roberts. Both Augusta Dejerine-Klumpke and Mariette Pompilian made sizable pre-1901 contributions to medical research, Dejerine-Klumpke in neurology and Pompilian in physiology, fields that together constitute 16 percent of the French article count. Dejerine-Klumpke's work, some of it joint with Jules Dejerine, is clearly recognized as a valued contribution to basic research in the area. No recent assessment by a physiologist of Pompilian's work has been found, but she would appear to have been engaged in more routine studies. Of the twenty-two papers in anthropology (13 percent of the French total) nineteen were by Clémence Royer and one by Céline Renooz, and of these, few, if any, have much scientific significance, being largely poorly founded conjecture. The contributions in the botanical sciences and zoology (11 percent and 10 percent, respectively) result to some extent from the relatively large number of contributors in these fields (ten and six, respectively); except for the three independent agriculturalists—Fitz-James, Gervais, and Millet-Robinet—most were students in the 1880s and 1890s, carrying out creditable, although minor research projects. Zoologist Fanny Bignon, notable for her extensive studies in bird anatomy and author of eight pre-1900 papers, was something of an exception; Aimée Camus's one pre-1900 paper was but the first of her many contributions to plant geography and systematics—a foreshadowing, one might say, of good work in the future. Indeed the post-1900 work at the Muséum National d'Histoire Naturelle in Paris of the two outstandingly productive women—Camus and physiologist Marie Phisalix—is impressive; both made notable contributions to French colonial science, an important branch of the nation's research effort at the time.

Although separate and distinct from their scientific contributions, the considerable efforts of the two left-leaning social activists among the early French women doctors—Edwards-Pilliet and Pelletier—deserve special note.

Overall this is a remarkable group even though small compared to the large numbers of American and British women active in the sciences about the same time[178] (Figure 0-1). In nineteenth- and early twentieth-century France, a few enterprising and talented women participated with considerable success in a broad spectrum of the major scientific and technical activities then underway, their efforts ranging from the early work in mathematics of Germain, to the plant systematics studies of Camus, the neurological research of Dejerine-Klumpke, and the pioneering work in subatomic physics of Curie.

The four who had the most distinguished and productive research careers—Camus, Curie, Dejerine-Klumpke, and Phisalix—all had the advantage of having male relatives who were experts in the same field collaborating closely with them at some stage in their careers. Camus had a many-year apprenticeship with her father, Dejerine-Klumpke was her husband's lifelong research partner, Phisalix entered a field her husband was pioneering, and Marie Curie's acclaimed early research, the intellectual high point of her career, was her joint work with Pierre Curie. One other notably successful scientist in this group of thirty-nine was astronomer Klumpke Roberts. Here again collaboration with a male relative was crucial; although her early studies were done independently, it was her later joint work with her husband Isaac Roberts that led to her most important contribution to her field. The period of the late nineteenth and early twentieth centuries was still a time when advanced technical training for women was in its early stages and such family relationships continued to play an important role as gateways for women's entry into scientific research.

Curie and Germain have already received considerable attention in English-language accounts of nineteenth-century women in science; more recently Pelletier's story has been told. In addition, Dejerine-Klumpke and especially Klumpke Roberts have been discussed in American journals and mentioned in more general works. The career of writer and commentator Royer has also attracted the attention of feminist historians. Particularly notable among those made more prominent by this survey are Camus, Edwards-Pilliet, the duchesse de Fitz-James, Millet-Robinet, and Phisalix.

Notes

1. Thomas Neville Bonner, *To the Ends of the Earth: Women's Search for Education in Medicine* (Cambridge, Mass.: Harvard University Press, 1992), 70–71.

2. The Bal Bullier was a big hall in Paris used for popular Saturday-night dances; it was also the place where the annual interns' ball was held.

3. Claude Barbizet and Françoise Leguay, *Blanche Edwards-Pilliet: femme et médecin, 1858–1941* (Le Mans: Éditions Cénomane, 1988).

4. Yvonne Sorrel-Dejerine, "Madame Dejerine-Klumpke (1859–1927)," *La Presse Médicale* 53 (1959): 1997–99, on 1997.

5. Blanche Edwards, "De l'hémiplégie dans quelques affections nerveuses: ataxie locomotrice progressive, sclérose en plaques, hystérie, paralysie agitante" (Paris: Delahaye et Lecrosnier, 1889).

6. Her rooms, including living space, were on the third floor of a historic seventeenth-century apartment building at the corner of rue Saint-Honoré and rue Richepanse. The sisters and a younger brother of Robespierre had once lived there, and he himself had rooms in the building at the time of his arrest and execution in 1794. In the 1980s, the ground floor was occupied by a café called "Robespierre"—see Barbizet and Leguay, *Edwards-Pilliet*, and Jacques Hillairet, *Dictionnaire historique des rues de Paris*, 2 vols. (Paris: Éditions de Minuit, 1985), 8th ed., vol. 2, 436–37.

7. From *Le Figaro,* 3 February 1887, quoted in Andrée Roche Lecours and David Caplan, "Augusta Dejerine-Klumpke or 'The lesson in anatomy,'" *Brain and Cognition* 3 (1984): 166–97 on 192.

8. André-Thomas, "Augusta Dejerine-Klumpke 1859–1927," *Encéphale* 23 (1928): 75–88; Smith Ely Jelliffe, "Madame Dejerine-Klumpke, 1859–1927," *Bulletin of the New York Academy of Medicine* 4 (1928): 655–59; Sorrel-Dejerine, "Madame Dejerine-Klumpke"; Richard Satran, "Augusta Dejerine-Klumpke. First Woman Intern in Paris Hospitals," *Annals of Internal Medicine* 80 (1974): 260–64; Lecours and Caplan, "Augusta Dejerine-Klumpke"; Anna Elizabeth Klumpke, *Memoirs of an Artist,* ed. Lilian Whiting (Boston: Wright and Potter Printing Co., 1940).

9. André-Thomas, "Dejerine-Klumpke," 82.

10. Sorrel-Dejerine, "Madame Dejerine-Klumpke," 1997.

11. *Merritt's Textbook of Neurology,* ed. Lewis P. Rowland, 8th edn. (Philadelphia: Lea and Febiger, 1989), 434.

12. Sorrel-Dejerine, "Madame Dejerine-Klumpke," 1999: "That kind of technique had never before been used with such perfection. . . . She was the master who perhaps understood better than anyone else the anatomy of the nerve centers, the origins, pathways, and terminals of the bundles and fibres, their relationships, and their structures."

13. Lecours and Caplan, "Augusta Dejerine-Klumpke."

14. Lecours and Caplan, "Augusta Dejerine-Klumpke," 173.

15. Lecours and Caplan, "Augusta Dejerine-Klumpke," 184.

16. See for instance (with J. Dejerine) "Le faisceau pyramidal direct," *Revue Neurologique* 12 (1904): 253–74; (with J. Dejerine) "Contribution à l'étude des localisations motrices opinales dans un cas de désarticulation scapulo-huméral remontant à l'enfance," *Revue Neurologique* 17 (1909): 593–600; and "Distrophie osseuse par aplasie de la substance spongieuse du corps basilaire de l'occipital . . . Considérations anatomiques," *Revue Neurologique* 33, pt. 2 (1926), 281–300 and *Bulletin de l'Académie de Médecine* s.3, 96 (1926): 21–27.

17. J. Dejerine avec la collaboration de A. Dejerine-Klumpke, *Anatomie des centres nerveux,* 2 vols. (Paris: Rueff, 1895, 1901; new edn. 1980).

18. Sorrel-Dejerine, "Madame Dejerine-Klumpke," 1999: "[. . . their names were and will remain inseparably linked, as they wanted.]"

19. André-Thomas, "Dejerine-Klumpke," 83–84.

20. Lecours and Caplan, "Augusta Dejerine-Klumpke," 195.

21. Felicia Gordon, *The Integral Feminist: Madeleine Pelletier, 1874–1939. Feminism, Socialism and Medicine* (Cambridge: Polity Press, 1990); Christine Bard, *Madeleine Pelletier (1874–1939): logique et infortunes d'un combat pour l'égalité,* papers delivered at a CEDREF conference, Paris, 1991 (Paris: Côté-femme éditions, 1992), and,*Les Filles de Marianne: Histoire des feminismes 1914–1940* (Paris: Fayard, 1995).

22. Gordon, *Integral Feminist,* 1.

23. See Mary R. S. Creese, *Ladies in the Laboratory? American and British Women in Science, 1800–1900: A Survey of Their Contributions to Research* (Lanham, Md.: Scarecrow Press, 1998), 198.

24. Madeleine Pelletier, "Sur un nouveau procédé pour obtenir l'indice cubique du crâne," *Bulletins de la Société d'Anthropologie de Paris* (1901): 188–93.

25. "Contribution à l'étude de la phylogenèse du maxillaire inférieure," *Bulletins de la Société d'Anthropologie de Paris* (1902): 537–45. See also Raoul Anthony's review, "Mademoiselle Pelletier, Contribution à l'étude . . . inférieure," *Bulletins de la Société d'Anthropologie de Paris* (1902), and *L'Anthropologie* 14 (1903): 719–20.

26. Nicolas Vaschide and Madeleine Pelletier, "Contribution expérimentale à l'étude des signes physiques de l'intelligence," *Comptes rendus de l'Académie des Sciences* (1901): 1–3, and "Recherches expérimentales sur des signes physiques de l'intelligence," *Revue de Philosophie* (1903–1904): 1–63.

27. Alice Lee, Marie Lewenz, and Karl Pearson, "On the correlation of mental and physical characters in man. Pt. 2." *Proceedings of the Royal Society* 71 (1902): 106–14, on 108.

28. Jean-Christophe Coffin, "La doctoresse Madeleine Pelletier et les psychiatres," in Bard, *Madeleine Pelletier,* 51–62. Pelletier's thesis was entitled, *L'association des idées dans la manie aigüe et dans la débilité mentale* (Paris: Jules Rousset, 1903).

29. These include "L'écho de la pensée et la parole intérieure," *Bulletin de l'Institut Général Psychologique* 4 (1904): 449–73; "La parole intérieure chez les psychasthéniques et les persécutés," *La Médecine Moderne* 16 (1905): 33–34; "L'idéation chez les débiles," *La Médecine Moderne* 16 (1905): 97–100; "Les membres fantômes chez les amputés délirants," *La Médecine Moderne* 16 (1905): 161–62; "L'hérédité biologique et l'hérédité psychologique," *La Médecine Moderne* 16, (1905): 225–27; "La débilité mentale chez l'enfant," *La Médecine Moderne* 16 (1905): 329–31; (with P. Marie) "La folie, cas de divorce," *La Médecine Moderne* 16 (1905): 393–95; (with A.-A. Marie) "Action hypnotique et sédative du neuronal chez les aliénés," *Bulletin Général de Thérapeutique* 10 (1905): 17–28; (with A.-A. Marie) "Le sérum isotonique dans le traitement des maladies mentales," *Bulletin Général de Thérapeutique* 10 (1905): 628–37; (with A.-A. Marie) "Le mal perforant dans la paralysie générale," *Revue de Psychiatrie et de Psychologie Expérimentale* 11 (1905): 469–76; "Cranioectomie et régéneration osseuse," *Bulletin de la Société d'Anthropologie* 6 (1905): 369–73; "Folie et choc moral," *Archives de Neurologie* 21 (1906): 188–92; "Les mentalités inférieures," *La Médecine Moderne* 17 (1906): 145–47; and "Hérédité et intelligence," *La Médecine Moderne* 17 (1906): 189–91.

30. Gordon, *Integral Feminist,* 53, 132.

31. *In anima vili, ou un Crime scientifique. Pièce en trois Actes* (Conflans-Sainte Honorine: A. Lorulot, 1920); *Supérieur!*

Drame des Classes sociales en cinq Actes (Conflans-Sainte Honorine: A. Lorulot, 1923); *Trois Contes* (Paris: Imprimérie L. Beresniau, n.d.), *Une Vie nouvelle* (Paris: Figuière, 1932); and *La Femme vièrge* (Paris: Bresle, 1933, 1996).

32. Gordon, *Integral Feminist,* 240.

33. Bard, *Filles de Marianne,* 248.

34. *Lexikon der Frau* (Zürich: Encyclios Verlag, 1953), 2 vols., vol. 1, 520; Huguette Garnier, "Une existence d'abnégation et de travaille . . . ," *Excelsior* (Paris), 11 January 1921, 2; Mélanie Lipinska, *Histoire des femmes médecins depuis l'antiquité jusqu'à nos jours.* (Paris: G. Jacques & Cie, 1900), 417–19, 527 and, *Les femmes et le progrès des sciences médicales* (Paris: Masson, 1930), 165; Bonner, *Ends of the Earth,* 51–52; and Lucienne Mazenod and Ghislaine Schoeller, *Dictionnaire des femmes célèbres de tous les temps et de tous les pays* (Paris: Éditions Robert Laffont, 1992), 124.

35. The first woman to receive an M.D. degree from the University of Paris faculty of medicine (1870) was the Englishwoman Elizabeth Garrett.

36. Garnier, "Une existence."

37. *De la mamelle et de l'allaitement* (Paris: de E. Martinet, 1875). Brès's other publications relating to infant feeding include *L'allaitement artificiel et le biberon* (Paris: Masson, 1877) and *Analyses du lait des femmes galibis du jardin d'acclimatation* (Paris: Robert e Cie, 1882) also published in the Academy of Sciences's *Comptes rendus*—see bibliography.

38. See Brès, "Chronique," in *L'Hygiène de la Femme et de l'Enfant* (15 July 1891): 1–4.

39. Brès, "Chronique," *L'Hygiène de la Femme et de l'Enfant* (15 February 1895): 1.

40. Various authors, *L'Hygiène de la Femme et de l'Enfant* (15 June 1893): 1–12. This issue reports the opening ceremonies for the crèche. See also Garnier, "Une existence."

41. Brès, quoted in Garnier, "Une existence": "[I'm a woman of my time. There are three things I have never wanted to argue about: politics, religion, love.]"

42. Lipinska, *Histoire* (1900), 427, 529.

43. Josephine-Inèz Gaches-Sarraute, *Le Corset. Étude physiologique et pratique* (Paris: Masson, 1900).

44. In addition to fashion considerations, she expected resistance from corset manufacturers; the assembling of these garments from cloth and whalebone was a fairly important industry, employing large numbers of seamstresses.

45. See for instance Elizabeth Ewing, *Dress and Undress: A History of Women's Underwear* (New York: Drama Book Specialists, 1978), 109–10.

46. *Étude microscopique d'un lithopedion* (Paris: n.p., 1884); and *Du traitement palliatif du cancer utérin inopérable* (Paris: A. Parent, 1886).

47. Lipinska (*Histoire* [1900], 527) mentioned a Mme. Bertillon as being listed in the 1900 *Annuaire Médicale* among eighty-seven women physicians then practicing in France. She stated that Bertillon held the positions of physician to the girls' school Lycée Racine, rue du Rocher, Paris, and to the Postes et Télégraphes.

48. "Discussion," following presentation of Bertillon's paper, *Bulletin de la Société d'Anthropologie* 10 (1887): 149–58, on 157–58.

49. J. Leandri, "Aimée Camus. 1er mai 1879—17 avril 1965," *Adansonia* s. 2, 6 (1965): 3–21, and "Aimée Camus, 1879–1965," *Association pour l'Étude Taxonomique de la Flore d'Afrique Tropicale. Bulletin,* no. 17 (June 1966): 12; H. Lecomte, "Notice biographique sur Edmond-Gustave Camus," in Edmond-Gustave Camus, Aimée Camus, and Henri Lecomte, *Iconographie des Orchidées d'Europe et du Bassin Méditerranéen* (Paris: Lechevalier, 1921), 5–9; *Chronica Botanica* 6 (1940–1941): 270; and *Muséum National d'Histoire Naturelle. Bulletin* s. 2, 31 (1959): 5.

50. See for instance "Étude sur le *Mespilodaphne pretiosa,*" *Bulletin Scientifique et Industriel de la Maison Roure-Bertrand Fils,* Grasse s. 3, 2 (1910); "Étude botanique des basilics cultivées," *Bulletin Scientifique et Industriel de la Maison Roure-Bertrand Fils* s. 3, 2 (1910); "Étude botanique des menthes cultivées," *Bulletin Scientifique et Industriel de la Maison Roure-Bertrand Fils* s. 3, 4 (1911); "Étude botanique de deux Cyprès subspontanés ou plantés en France," *Bulletin Scientifique et Industriel de la Maison Roure-Bertrand Fils* s. 3, 5 (1912); *Florule de Saint-Tropez et de ses Environs Immédiats* (Paris: Lechevalier, 1912); and "Le *Popowia caprea,*" *Bulletin Scientifique et Industriel de la Maison Roure-Bertrand Fils,* Grasse, s. 3, 6 (1913). See also "Étude botanique du *Lavandula stoechas* L. et du *L. dentate* L.," *Bulletin Scientifique et Industriel de la Maison Roure-Bertrand Fils* s. 4, 4 ((Oct. 1921); "Sur quelques orchidées des environs de Saint-Tropez," *Riviera Scientifique: Bulletin de l'Association des Naturalistes, Nice et Alpes-Maritimes* 13 (1926): 75–76; "Quelques Ophrys intéressants des Alpes-Maritimes, Gattières, Carros et environs de Nice," *Bulletin de la Société Botanique de France* (hereafter *Bull. Soc. Bot. Fr.*) 74 (1927): 579–81.

51. A. Camus and E.-G. Camus, *Classification des Saules d'Europe et Monographie des Saules de France,* vol. 1 and atlas; and *Classification et Monographie des Saules d'Europe,* vol. 2 and atlas (Paris: J. Mersch, 1904–1905).

52. Nils Johan Andersson, *Monographia Salicum. Pars 1* (Holmiae [Stockholm]: Apud P. A. Norstedt, 1867).

53. H. G. A. Engler and K. A. E. Prantl, *Die naturlichen Pflanzenfamilien* (Leipzig: W. Engelmann, 1887–1909).

54. In recognition of the work, the Union of French Wickerworkers chose E.-G. Camus as their vice president (Lecomte, "Notice biographique," 9). The uses of osier willow stems, material important since pre-Roman times in a variety of crafts, including coracle construction and basket-weaving, became more and more diverse over the centuries. Willows are now used in such areas as soil conservation, environmental improvement projects, and renewable-resource fuel production, in addition to traditional manufacturing—see Christopher Newsholm, *Willows: the Genus Salix* (Portland, Ore.: Timber Press, 1992), 12–21.

55. E.-G. Camus, P. Bergon, and A. Camus, *Monographie des Orchidées de l'Europe, de l'Afrique Septentrionale, de l'Asie Mineure et des Provinces Russes Transcaspiennes* (Paris: P. Lechevalier, 1908).

56. E.-G. Camus, *Iconographie des Orchidées des environs de Paris* (Paris: Imp. Paindebled, 1885).

57. Robert Allen Rolfe, *On Biogeneric Orchid Hybrids* (n.p., 1887) and *Hybridisation viewed from the Standpoint of Systematic Botany* (n.p., 1900); and R. A. Rolfe and Charles Chamberlain Hurst, *The Orchid Stud-book: An Eexamination of Hybrid Orchids of Artificial Origin, with Their Parents . . .* (Kew: F. Leslie, 1909).

58. E.-G. Camus, *Iconographie des Orchidées d'Europe et du Bassin Méditerranéen; avec la Collaboration, pour l'Anatomie et la Biologie, de A. Camus* (Paris: P. Lechevalier, 1921–1929), 3 vols. and atlas.

59. (With R. Gombault) "Sur quelques Saules de Syrie et du Liban," *Bull. Soc. Bot. Fr.* 86 (1939): 135–40; *Bull. Soc. Bot. Fr.* 89 (1942): 24–30.

60. Camille Limoges, "The Development of the Muséum d'Histoire Naturelle of Paris, c. 1800–1914," in *The Organization of Science and Technology in France 1808–1914*, eds. Robert Fox and George Weisz (Cambridge: Cambridge University Press, 1980), 211–40, on 232–33. See also Michael A. Osborne, *Nature, the Exotic, and the Science of French Colonialism* (Bloomington, Ind.: Indiana University Press, 1994).

61. Limoges, "Development of the Muséum," 235–40.

62. H. Lecomte, H. Humbert, and F. Gagnepain, eds., *Flore Générale de l'Indo-Chine* (Paris: Masson, 1907–1934), 6 parts, plus an introductory volume with general tables published by Masson (1944) and two supplementary volumes published by the Muséum National d'Histoire Naturelle, Paris, 1938, 1950. For Aimée Camus's work on aquatic plants, see also "Potamogeton nouveau de l'Asie orientale," *Notulae Systematicae* 1 (1909): 85–89; "Note sur le genre Typha," *Notulae Systematicae* 1 (1909): 271–73; "Aponogeton asiatique nouveau," *Notulae Systematicae* 1 (1909): 273–74; "Contribution à l'étude des espèces asiatiques du genre Juncus," *Notulae Systematicae* 1 (1909): 274–83; and "Note sur les especès asiatiques du genre Aponogeton," *Notulae Systematicae* 2 (1912): 202–4.

63. "Espèces et variétés de Riz de l'Indochine," *Journal d'Agriculture Tropicale, Supplement 8* (1913): 1–146; *Les Bambusées. Encyclopédie Économique de Silviculture*, 350 pp. and atlas (Paris: P. Lechevalier, 1913).

64. E.-G. Camus, *Les Bambusées: Monographie, Biologie, Culture, principaux Usages, 1*, with atlas (Paris: P. Lechevalier, 1913).

65. "Les Andropogonées odorantes des régions tropicales," *Revue de Botanique Appliquée et d'Agriculture Tropicale* 1, no. 4 (1921): 270–306.

66. The following is only a selection of Camus's many Gramineae papers; some others dealing with particular branches of the subject or particular regions are listed in notes 67–71: "Note sur le genre Themeda Forsk (Graminées)," *Muséum National d'Histoire Naturelle. Bulletin* (hereafter *Mus. Hist. Nat. Bull.*) 26 (1920): 266–73; (with A. Chevalier) "Deux bambous nouveaux de l'Annam," *Mus. Hist. Nat. Bull.* 27 (1921): 450–54; "Espèces nouvelles d'Arundinaria malgaches," *Mus. Hist. Nat. Bull.* 30 (1924): 384–96; "Perrierbambus, genre nouveau de Bambusées malgaches," *Bull. Soc. Bot. Fr.* 71 (1924): 697; "Espèces nouvelles d'Erianthées malgaches," *Bull. Soc. Bot. Fr.* 71 (1924): 1182; "Graminées nouvelles de Madagascar," *Bull. Soc. Bot. Fr.* 73 (1926): 401–6; "Le genre Arundinaria à Madagascar," *Bull. Soc. Bot. Fr.* 73 (1926): 624–26; "Un bambou nouveau du Tonkin," *Bull. Soc. Bot. Fr.* 74 (1927): 620–22; "Graminées nouvelles de Madagascar," *Bull. Soc. Bot. Fr.* 74 (1927): 631–35; "Graminées nouvelles de Madagascar et de Nossi-Bé," *Mus. Hist. Nat. Bull.* 34 (1928): 911–16; "Quelques Graminées nouvelles pour la flore de l'Indochine," *Bull. Soc. Bot. Fr.* 75 (1929): 552–55; "Graminées nouvelles de Madagascar," *Bull. Soc. Bot. Fr.* 77 (1930): 638–41; "Sur quelques Graminées de Madagascar et des îles voisines," *Bull. Soc. Bot. Fr.* 79 (1932): 844–46; "Sur quelques Graminées africaines," *Mus. Hist. Nat. Bull.* 40, 1 (1934): 98–99; "*Humbertochloa* A. Cam. et O. Stapf., genre nouveau de Graminées malgaches," *Bull. Soc. Bot. Fr.* 81 (1934): 467–71; "Bambous nouveau des îles Salomon," *Bull. Soc. Bot. Fr.* 81 (1934): 758–60; "*Cephalostachyum Chevalieri* A. Cam., bambou de l'Indochine," *Bull. Soc. Bot. Fr.* 90 (1943): 74–75; "Graminées nouvelles de Madagascar," *Bull. Soc. Bot. Fr.* 92 (1945): 50–53; "Espèces nouvelles du genre Panicum, sous-genre Pseudolasiacis," *Notulae Systematicae* 12 (1945): 86–88; "Decaryochloa, genre noueau de Graminées malgaches," *Bull. Soc. Bot. Fr.* 93 (1947): 242–45; "Graminées nouvelles de Madagascar," *Bull. Soc. Bot. Fr.* 94 (1947): 39–42; "Quelques Graminées nouvelles de Madagascar," *Bull. Soc. Bot. Fr.* 96 (1949): 51–53; "Andropogon et Nastus nouveau de Madagascar," *Notulae Systematicae* 3 (1951): 213–15; "Graminées nouvelles de Madagascar et de la Réunion," *Bull. Soc. Bot. Fr.* 99 (1952): 142–44; "Especés et variétés nouvelles de Graminées malgaches," *Bull. Soc. Bot. Fr.* 104 (1955): 394–97; "*Chasechloa* A. Cam., genre de Graminées malgaches," *Institut de Recherche Scientifique de Madagascar. Mémoires* (hereafter *Mém. Inst. Scient. Madag.*) B-5 (1955): 201–4; "Quelques Graminées de Madagascar et de l'île Maurice," *Bull. Soc. Bot. Fr.* 102 (1956): 347–49; "Contribution à l'étude des genre américain Leptosaccharum (Graminées)," *Bull. Soc. Bot. Fr.* 103 (1956): 142–47; "Contribution á l'étude des Graminées du Cambodge et du Vietnam," *Mus. Hist. Nat. Bull.* s. 2, 29 (1957): 186–89; "Contribution à l'étude des Graminées de Madagascar," *Mus. Hist. Nat. Bull.* s. 2, 29 (1957): 274–81; "Graminées hybrides de la flore française (genre Bromus excepté)," *Bulletin du Jardin Botanique de l'État à Bruxelles* 28 (1958): 337–74; "Section, especès et sous-especès nouvelles de Graminées malgaches," *Bull. Soc. Bot. Fr.* 106 (1959): 337–40; "Schizachyrium, Poecilostachys et Panicum de Madagascar," *Notulae Systematicae* 15 (1959): 410–15; "Especès et sous-especès nouvelles de Graminées malgaches," *Bull. Soc. Bot. Fr.* 107 (1960): 205–8; and "Sur quelques Graminées de Madagascar. 1. Le genre Humbertochloa. 2. Description de Panicoideae malgaches," *Bull. Soc. Bot. Fr.* 108 (1961): 3–4, 158–63.

67. "Classification des Bambusées," *Archives du Muséum National d'Histoire Naturelle*, s. 6, 12, vol. du Tricentenaire (1935), 601–3.

68. "Les Graminées dans le domaine central de Madagascar," *Mem. Inst. Scient. Madag.* B-1 (1949): 101–12; "Sur les Graminées du massif de Marojejy et de ses satellites (Nord-Est de Madagascar) récoltées par le Professeur H. Humbert en 1948–49," *Naturaliste Malgache* 3 (1951): 79–85.

69. "Les Graminées du massif du Marojejy et de ses avant-monts," in Henri Humbert, "Une merveille de la nature à Madagascar. Première exploration botanique du massif du Marojejy et de ses satellites," *Mém. Inst. Scient. Madag.* B-6 (1954): 1–271, on 245–51.

70. "Contribution à l'étude des Graminées fourragères cultivées dans l'Inde," *Revue de Botanique Appliquée et d'Agriculture Coloniale* 5 (1925): 376; "Sur quelques Graminées d'Indochine employées dans la brasserie," *Revue de Botanique Appliquée et d'Agriculture Coloniale* 5 (1925): 594; (with R. Viguier) "Riz flottants du Soudan," *Revue de Botanique Appliquée et d'Agriculture Coloniale* 17 (1937): 201; "Sur les Graminées des prairies de Madagascar," *Revue de Botanique Appliquée et d'Agriculture Coloniale* 27 (1947): 193–203, 271–81; "Sur les Graminées des prairies de Madagascar (fin)," *Revue de Botanique Appliquée et d'Agriculture Coloniale* 27 (1947): 299–300, 377–89; "Les espèces utiles du genre Zizania (Graminées)," *Revue Internationale de Botanique Appliquée et d'Agriculture Tropicale* 30 (1950): 327–28; "Contribution à l'étude des Graminées du Maroc," *Revue de Botanique Appliquée et d'Agriculture Coloniale* 32 (1952): 139–44; "Graminées nouvelles du mont Loma (Sierra Leone)," *Journal d'Agriculture Tropicale et de Botanique Appliquée* 1 (1954): 210–13; and "Andropogonées nouvelles du Cambodge et du Vietnam," *Journal d'Agriculture Tropicale et de Botanique Appliquée* 2 (1955): 3–4, 200–3. See also "Espèces et variétés de Riz de l'Indochine"; and *Les Bambusées. Encyclopédie Économique de Silviculture* (Paris: P. Lechevalier, 1913).

71. Bromus papers include *"Un hybride nouveau de Bromus madritensis* et de *B. maximus,"* *Bull. Soc. Bot. Fr.* 76 (1929): 596–97; "Hybrides nouveaux du genre Bromus," *Bull. Soc. Bot. Fr.* 80 (1933): 38–39; (with A. de Cugnac) "Sur quelques Bromes et leurs hybrides. IV. Deux especès messicoles menacées de disparition: *Bromus (Serrafalcus) grossus* Desf. et *Bromus (Michelaria) arduennensis* Dumort.," *Bull. Soc. Bot. Fr.* 83 (1936): 47–68; (with H. Gombault), *"Bromus bikfayensis,* espèce nouvelle du Liban," *Bull. Soc. Bot. Fr.* 84 (1937): 310–12; "Un nouvel hybride du genre Bromus," *Bull. Soc. Bot. Fr.* 91 (1945): 79–80; (with A. de Cugnac) "Un hybride interspécifique nouveau, *Bromus laagi,"* *Bull. Soc. Bot. Fr.* 91 (1945): 172–74; "Un Bromus hybride des dunes du Cotentin," *Mus. Hist. Nat. Bull.* s. 2, 29 (1957): 184–85; and "Bromus hybrides de la flore française," *Bulletin du Jardin Botanique de l'État à Bruxelles* 27 (1957): 479–85.

72. *Les Cyprès (genre Cupressus). Monographie, Systématique, Anatomie, Culture, principaux Usages,* 106 pp. (Paris: P. Lechevalier, 1914); *Les Châtaigniers. Monographie des Genres Castanea et Castanopsis,* 604 pp. and atlas (Paris: P. Lechevalier, 1928); and *Les Chênes. Monographie du Genre Quercus,* 4 vols. and 3 vol. atlas (Paris: P. Lechevalier, 1934, 1936, 1954).

73. "Le genre Notofagus, hêtres de l'hémisphère austral," *Revue du Botanique Appliquée et d'Agriculture Coloniale* 31 (1951): 71–84.

74. See (with R. Hickel) "Castanopsis nouveau d'Indochine," *Mus. Hist. Nat. Bull.* 29 (1923): 534–36; "Fagacées nouvelles d'Indochine: genre Quercus L.," *Mus. Hist. Nat. Bull.* 29 (1923): 598–601; "Fagacées nouvelles d'Indochine: genre Pasania Oerst.," *Mus. Hist. Nat. Bull.* 29 (1923): 602–6; "Le *Cupressus dupreziana* A. Cam., Cyprès nouveau du Tassili," *Bulletin. Société Dendrologique de France* 58 (1926): 39–44; (with R. Hickel) "Fagacées nouvelles d'Indochine," *Mus. Hist. Nat. Bull.* 32 (1926): 398–401; "Fagacées nouvelles d'Asie orientale," *Mus. Hist. Nat. Bull.* 37 (1931): 688–91; "Quelques Chênes nouveau de l'île d'Hainan et de la Péninsule malaise," *Mus. Hist. Nat. Bull.* 38 (1932): 912–14; "Quelques diagnoses de Fagacées," *Bull. Soc. Bot. Fr.* 81 (1934): 814–18; and "Fagacées nouvelles de l'Asie orientale," *Notulae Systematicae* 6, no. 4 (1938): 178–85.

75. See also *"Lithocarpus guinieri* A. Cam., Chêne nouveau du Cambodge," *Bull. Soc. Bot. Fr.* 83 (1936): 419; "Lithocarpus nouveau de l'Annam," *Bull. Soc. Bot. Fr.* 90 (1943): 4–5; "Espèces et variétés nouvelles du genre Lithocarpus," *Bull. Soc. Bot. Fr.* 90 (1943): 198–201; "Deux espèces voisine du *Lithocarpus kunstlerei,"* *Bull. Soc. Bot. Fr.* 92 (1945): 9–10; "Espèces et variétés nouvelles du genre Lithocarpus," *Bull. Soc. Bot. Fr.* 92 (1945): 82–84; "Variétés et combinaisons nouvelles du genre Lithocarpus," *Bull. Soc. Bot. Fr.* 92 (1945): 254; and "Deux Lithocarpus nouveaux du Laos," *Notulae Sytematicae* 14, no. 3 (1951): 212–13.

76. "Les Chênes dans la production forestière indochinoise," *Revue de Botanique Appliquée et d'Agriculture Tropicale* 15 (1935): 20–25; "Produits des Chênes," *Revue de Botanique Appliquée et d'Agriculture Tropicale* 25 (1946): 24–37; "Espèces (Fagacées, Betulacées et Graminées) découvertes par Poilane en Asie orientale," *Journal d'Agriculture Tropicale et de Botanique Appliquée* 1 (1955): 394–406; and "Notes sur quelques Fagacées," *Journal d'Agriculture Tropicale et de Botanique Appliquée* 3 (1956): 1–2, 82–86.

77. "Sur la rachéole et le pédicelle des épillets dans le genre Hordeum," *Mus. Hist. Nat. Bull.* 34 (1928): 113–14; "La sourdure des cotylédons dans le genre Quercus," *Riviera Scientifique* (Nice) 23 (1936): 26–27; "Sur la floraison des Bambous," *Riviera Scientifique* 25 (1938): 16–20; "Description des épillets et biologie florale du *Briza maxima* L.," *Bull. Soc. Bot. Fr.* 88 (1941): 10; "La sourdure des cotylédons dans le genre Lithocarpus blume," *Mus. Hist. Nat. Bull.* s. 2, 14 (1942): 461–62; "Le glume des épillets latéraux dans le genre Lolium et les glumes dans les hybrides x Festulolium," *Mus. Hist. Nat. Bull.* s. 2, 15 (1943): 237; and "Sur la présence de nervures tessellées dans les feuilles de Graminées," *Société Linnéene de Lyon. Bulletin mensuel* 14 (1945): 70.

78. "Contribution française à l'étude des Graminées de l'Amérique du Nord au XVIIIe. siècle et dans la première moité du XIXe," *Colloque intern, C.N.R.S.*, Paris (11–14 September 1956), 107–21.

79. *Les Fleurs des Marais, des Tourbières, des Cours d'Eau, des Lacs et des Étangs (Plantes palustres et aquatiques),* (Paris: P. Lechevalier, 1921); and *Les Arbres, Arbustes et Arbrisseau d'Ornement* (Paris: P. Lechevalier, 1923).

80. Little information has been collected about five of these women—Juliette Chauliaguet, A. Frémont, Rachel Joffé, Amélie Leblois, and A. Mayoux. All five carried out their studies in the 1880s and 1890s, mostly at educational institutions. Chauliaguet received an M.D. degree from the University of Paris in 1897; see John Hendley Barnhart, comp., *Biographical Notes upon Botanists,* 3 vols. (Boston: G. K. Hall, 1965), vol. 1, 336; her joint paper on active principles of several members of the Aroid family reported work done in the natural history laboratory of the faculty of medicine. Frémont published two papers on root structure in the Onagraceae (the evening-primrose family) and the genus Lythrum in the Loosestrife family, both used in horticulture. Joffé's 1896 paper on plant fertilization described work done at the botanical institute of the University of Montpellier. Leblois's investigations of secretory cells and ducts in various plant families were carried out under the guidance of morphologist and taxonomist Philippe Van Tieghem in the mid 1880s in the botanical laboratory of the Muséum National d'Histoire Naturelle in Paris. Rebière states that Leblois was the daughter of an "*honorable pasteur*" (respectable shepherd) from Strasbourg and that she was the first woman to receive a *docteur ès science* degree from the Paris faculty of science—see Alphonse Rebière, *Les Femmes dans la Science. Notes recueilles,* 2nd ed. (Paris: Nony et Cie, 1897), 176. Mayoux, a student in the faculty of science at the University of Lyons, published two lengthy papers on plant morphology and physiology in the university's *Annales* in the early 1890s.

81. *Bull. Soc. Bot. Fr.* 60 (1913): 506; Rebière, *Femmes dans la Science,* 34–35; and Barnhart, *Biographical Notes,* vol. 1, 156.

82. Belèze's post-1900 works included "Liste de champignons supérieurs et inférieurs de la forêt de Rambouillet et des environs de Montfort l'Amaury (S. et O.)," *Association Française pour l'Avancement des Sciences. Bulletin. Botanique* (1901): 95–96, 127–28, 174–80; "Indication des plantes rares ou intéressantes des environs de Montfort l'Amaury et de la forêt de Rambouillet (S. et O.)," *Comptes-rendus du Congrès des Sociétés Savantes de Paris et des Départements. Section des Sciences* (1901): 251–54; "Florule calaminaire," *Comptes-rendus du Congrès des Sociétés Savantes de Paris et des Départements. Section des Sciences* (1901): 254–56; "Troisième supplément de la liste des plantes rares ou intéressantes . . . des environs de Montfort l'Amaury et de la forêt de Rambouillet (S. et O.)," *Bull. Soc. Bot. Fr.* 48 (1901): 10–11; "Quatre cas de fasciations fongiques," *Science et Nature* 1 (1902): 4; "Station anormale du *Tetragonolobus siliquosus* Roth," *C.-R. Cong. Soc. Sav.,* 1902 (1903): 138–39; "Quelques observations sur les 'criblures en grains de plomb' qui perforent les feuilles de certains végétaux cultivés et sauvages des environs de Montfort-l'Amaury . . . ," *C.-R. Cong. Soc. Sav.,* 1902, (1903): 139–42; "Notes botaniques. 1. Les roses et les rosiers," *C.-R. Cong. Soc. Sav.* (1904): 329–41; *Catalogue des plantes nouvelles, rares ou interessantes: phanérogames, cryptogames, vasculaires et cellulaires ansi que de quelques hybrides remarquables des environs de Montfort-l'Amaury et de la Forêt de Rambouillet (Seine-et-Oise)* (Le Mons: Impr. veuve Edmond Monnoyer, 1905); "La morelle noire," *C.-R. Cong. Soc. Sav.* (1906): 287–88; and "Les plantes carnivores," *C.-R. Cong. Soc. Sav.* (1906): 288–91.

83. Jean Antoine Gervais, *Opuscule sur la Vinification . . .* (Toulouse: F. Vieusseux, 1821).

84. Lacour, "Rapport sur les travaux de l'Académie Royale de Bordeaux pendant l'année 1822," *Académie Royale des Sciences, Belles-Lettres et Arts de Bordeaux. Séance Publique, 15 Déc 1822* (Bordeaux: de Brossier, 1823), 39; and Lacour, "Rapport sur le procédé vinificateur de Mlle Gervais, suivi d'expériences comparatives, par M. F. Delavau, propriétaire," in *Académie Royale des Sciences,* 69–74.

85. Harry W. Paul, *Science, Vine, and Wine in Modern France* (Cambridge: University of Cambridge Press, 1996), 123–54.

86. See *Pièces justificatives des avantages produits par la méthod de vinification inventée par Mlle. Elisabeth Gervais . . . l'expérience faite par M. le Maire de Corbeil (Seine-et-Oise) . . .* (Paris: impr. Mme. Huzard, 1820, 1821); and J.-C. Choiset, *Le guide indispensable aux propriétaires-vignerons, brasseurs, fabricans de cidre, distillateurs d'eaux-de-vie de grains, de fécules et autres materières fermentescibles, pour faire avec succès l'application de l'appareil vinificateur inventé par Mlle. Elisabeth Gervais, avec une planche* ([Paris]: n.p., 1823). See also Rebière, *Femmes dans la Science,* 127.

87. *Dictionnaire de Biographie Française,* vol. 13 (1975), cols. 1419, 1422; Rebière, *Femmes dans la Science,* 106; and *Nouveau Petit Larousse* (Paris: Larousse, 1969), 1338.

88. Paul, *Science, Vine, and Wine,* 9.

89. Paul, *Science, Vine, and Wine,* 9.

90. The duchesse de Fitz-James's other monographs on viticulture include the following: *Le Congrès de Bordeaux* (Nîmes: Dubois, 1882)—this incorporated a reprint of her early study of American viticulture; *Grande culture de la vigne américaine,* 5 vols., the last two entitled *La vigne américaine* (Nîmes: Dubois, 1881–1887); *Étude sur les dernières publications de M. Laliman, par Mme. la duchesse de Fitz James* (Nîmes: Dubois, 1883); *La pratique de la viticulture;* and *Adaptation des cépages franco-américaine à tous les sols français . . .* (Paris: Ballière, 1894); the first three dealt with resistant vine varieties, the fourth with grafting. The duchesse was also interested in the art of horse riding and brought out the work *Principes élémentaires d'équitation* (Paris: Plon, 1893).

91. Jacques-Gustave Sidoine de Fitz-James had a long military career, serving much of the time overseas in the French colonies during the last three decades of the nineteenth century; he returned to active duty for a short period in the First World War as a company commander (*Dictionnaire de Biographie Française*).

92. Information was collected from remarks in technical papers, books, and various bibliographic lists and indices.

93. *Maison rustique des dames,* 2 vols. (Paris: Librairie Agricole de la Maison Rustique, 10th ed. 1878).

94. Much of this material was republished in revised and expanded form eighty years later as *Basse-cour, pigeons et lapins* (Paris: La Maison Rustique, 1944).

95. *Les recettes de cuisine de ma grand-mère* (Nantes: J.-M. Williamson, 1995).

96. See for instance, John Errington de la Croix, "Sept mois au pays de l'étain, Perak . . . ," *Compte rendu des Séances de la Société de Géographie et de la Commission Centrale* 6 (1886): 394–432. The region of Perak is just north of Sembilan, where Mme. Errington de la Croix's observations were made.

97. Rebière, *Femmes dans la Science,* 37.

98. Although beginning to decline in importance in teaching and basic research in the biological sciences relative to the University of Paris faculty of science, the Muséum was still a leading institution for zoological research. See Limoges, "Development of the Muséum," 211–40; and Robert Fox, "La Société Zoologique de France. Ses origines et ses premières années," *Bulletin de la Société Zoologique de France* 101 (1976): 799–812, on 807.

99. See for instance A. Milne-Edwards, "Observations sur l'appareil respiratoire de quelques oiseaux," *Annales des Sciences Naturelles (Zoologie)* 3 (1865): 137–42, and 7 (1867): 12–14; and George Pouchet and Henri Beauregard, *Traité d'Ostéologie Comparée* (1889).

100. Fox, "Société Zoologique," 802, 807.

101. C. Deflandre, "La fonction adipogénique du foie dans la série animale," *Journal de l'Anatomie et de la Physiologie Normales et Pathologiques* . . . 40 (1904): 73–112, 305–36, and 41 (1905): 94–101; and C. Deflandre, "2e Partie. Étude synthétique de la fonction adipohépatique: sa signification physiologique," *Journal de l'Anatomie et de la Physiologie Normales et Pathologiques* . . . , 41 (1905): 223–35; 319–52.

102. Marie Loyer, "Sur les transformations de la vésicule germinative chez les sauriens," *Comptes rendus de l'Académie des Sciences* 133 (1901): 137–38; "Les premiers stades du développement de la vésicule germinative chez les reptiles (Sauriens et Chéloniens)," *Bulletin de la Société Philomatique de Paris* s. 9, 4 (1901–02): 63–76; "Recherches sur le développement ovarien des oeufs méroblastiques à vitellus nutritif abondant," *Archives d'Anatomie Microscopique* 8 (1905): 69–237 (Introduction et première partie), and *Archives d'Anatomie Microscopique* 8 (1906): 239–397; "Sur la vésicule germinative des reptiles et des oiseaux. (Réponse à M. Dubuisson)," *Comptes rendus hebdomadaires des Séances et Mémoires de la Société de Biologie* 62 (1907): 81–83; and "Sur la formation de la graisse dans l'oocyte d'un Saurien *Tejus monitor* Merr.," *Comptes rendus hebdomadaires des Séances et Mémoires de la Société de Biologie* 66 (1909): 225–27.

103. Rebière, *Femmes dans la Science,* 180.

104. *Balance de la nature* (Paris: Barrois l'aîné, 1784); and *Lettres relatives à l'éducation* (Paris: chez Buisson, 1788).

105. *Le Havre au jour le jour de 1778–1790* (Rouen: Société de l'Histoire de Normandie, 1999), text presented and annotated by Philippe Manneville.

106. Léon Bertin, "Marie Phisalix (1861–1946)," *Bulletin du Muséum d'Histoire Naturelle* s. 2, 18, (1946): 37–40; and Jean de Cilleuls, "Le souvenir de Marie Phisalix (1861–1946)," *Histoire des Sciences Médicales* 6 (1972): 237–41.

107. Marie Phisalix, *Researches embryologiques, histologiques et physiologiques sur les glandes à venin de la salamandre terrestre* (Paris: Schleicher, 1900).

108. Laverin, an army doctor later on the staff of the Institut Pasteur and founder of the laboratory for tropical diseases, had been one of Césaire Phisalix's professors. After Laverin's death in 1922, Marie Phisalix published an account of his long scientific career, *Alphonse Laverin, 1841–1922, sa vie, son oeuvre* (Paris: Masson et cie, 1923).

109. Published in Paris during the Second World War (Stock-Delamain et Boutelleau, 25 April 1940), it appeared as part of J. Delamain's "Livres de Nature" series, and was intended for doctors, veterinarians, and those at risk for snake bites, as well as for biologists; the bibliography lists twenty-three of Phisalix's technical articles specifically on venomous animals, venoms, antivenom serum, and vaccination published between 1913 and 1939. Included are the following: (with Félix Pasteur) "Action des rayons ultraviolet sur le venin de la vipère aspic," *Comptes rendus de l'Académie des Sciences* 186 (1928): 538–40 and *Bulletin du Muséum National d'Histoire Naturelle* 2 (1928): 143–45; "Vaccination contre le venin de vipère et la rage expérimentale par les mélanges virus-venin, avec excès de virus," *Comptes rendus de l'Académie des Sciences* 187 (1928): 1006–8; and (with Félix Pasteur) "Action destructice des ondes courtes sur les antigènes de quelques venins, la bile et la colestérine," *Bulletin du Muséum National d'Histoire Naturelle* 7 (1935): 226–33.

110. Lipinska, *Femmes et le progrès,* 554–55.

111. *La contraction musculaire et les transformations de l'énergie* (Paris: G. Steinheil, 1897).

112. Pompilian's post-1900 publications include the following: "Un nouveau myographe," *Comptes rendus des Séances et Mémoires de la Société de Biologie* 54 (1902): 488–90; "Un nouveau cardiographe," *Comptes rendus des Séances et Mémoires de la Société de Biologie* 54 (1902): 490–92; "Un nouveau sphygmographe à transmission," *Comptes rendus des Séances et Mémoires de la Société de Biologie* 54 (1902): 492–94; "Interrupteur à contacts," *Comptes rendus des Séances et Mémoires de la Société de Biologie* 54 (1902): 494–95; (with M. Letulle) "Étude graphique des mouvements respiratoires dans l'emphysème, la pleurésie et le pneumothorax," *Comptes rendus des Séances et Mémoires de la Société de Biologie* 54 (1902): 520–23; (with M. Letulle) "Étude graphique, des mouvements respiratoires dans la tuberculose pulmonaire," *Comptes rendus des Séances et Mémoires de la Société de Biologie* 54 (1902): 523–24; (with M. Letulle) "Etude graphique des mouvements respiratoire dans quelques affections nerveuses," *Comptes rendus des Séances et Mémoires de la Société de Biologie* 54 (1902): 525; "Recherches

sur les propriétés fondamentales du système nerveux," *Comptes rendus des Séances et Mémoires de la Société de Biologie* 54 (1902): 586–88; "Explication du repos compensateur et de la période refractaire," *Comptes rendus des Séances et Mémoires de la Société de Biologie* 54 (1902): 588–89; "Explication de l'inhibition," *Comptes rendus des Séances et Mémoires de la Société de Biologie* 54 (1902): 589–90; (with M. Letulle) "Chambre respiratoire calorimétrique," *Comptes rendus de l'Académie des Sciences* 143 (1906): 932; and (with M. Letulle) "Recherches sur la nutrition, bilan de l'azote et du chlorure de sodium," *Comptes rendus de l'Académie des Sciences* 154 (1906): 1188–91.

113. Louis L. Bucciarelli and Nancy Dworsky, *Sophie Germain: An Essay in the History of the Theory of Elasticity* (Dordrecht, Holland: Reidel Publishing Co., 1980); Mary W. Gray, "Sophie Germain (1776–1831)," in *Women of Mathematics: A Biobibliographic Sourcebook,* eds. Louise S. Grinstein and Paul J. Campbell (Westport, Conn.: Greenwood Press, 1987), 47–56; Amy Dahan Dalmédico, "Sophie Germain," *Scientific American* (December 1991): 117–22; *Dictionnaire de Biographie Française,* vol. 15 (1982), 1330 (entry for Ambroise-Thomas Germain d'Orsanville. The *Dictionnaire* entry for Sophie Germain herself, vol. 15, pp. 1326–27, gives her father's first names as Ambroise-François, the form accepted by both Gray and Bucciarelli and Dworsky); J. H. Sampson, "Sophie Germain and the Theory of Numbers," *Archive for History of Exact Sciences* 41 (1990): 157–61; *Sophie Germain, Oeuvres Philosophiques,* ed. H. Stupuy (Paris: Paul Ritti, 1879; new edn., Paris: Firmin-Didot, 1896. This includes many of Germain's letters to and from Gauss, Legendre, and other mathematicians; the reproductions contain numerous typographical errors); B. Boncompagnie, "Cinq lettres de Sophie Germain à Carl Friedrich Gauss," *Archiv der Matematik und Physik* 65 (1880), *Literarische Bericht* 259, 27–31, and 66 (1881), and *Lit. Ber.* 261, 6–10; Sophie Germain, *Considérations générales sur l'état des sciences et des lettres, aux différentes époques de leur culture,* ed. Jacques-Amant Lherbette (Paris: Lachevardière, 1833); G. Waldo Dunnington, *Carl Friedrich Gauss: Titan of Science* (New York: Hafner, 1955); and Kenneth O. May, "Gauss, Carl Friedrich," in *Dictionary of Scientific Biography* (New York: Scribners, 1972), vol. 5, 298–315.

114. Carl B. Boyer and Uta C. Merzbach, *A History of Mathematics,* 2nd. ed. (New York: Wiley, 1989), 547.

115. See, for example, Bucciarelli and Dworsky, *Sophie Germain*; Gray, "Sophie Germain"; and Dalmédico, "Sophie Germain."

116. Germain to Gauss, 20 February 1807, reproduced in Boncompagnie, "Cinq lettres" (1881), 6.

117. Gauss to Olbers in Carl Friedrich Gauss, *Werke,* bd. 10, abt. 1 (Leipzig: Teubner, 1863–1929), 74; English translation from Bucciarelli and Dworsky, *Sophie Germain,* 28.

118. Bucciarelli and Dworsky, *Sophie Germain,* 86.

119. When Germain took up this work, with the case $n = 4$ actually proven, the problem could be reduced by very elementary arguments to the following symmetric form: if the exponent, n, is a prime number greater than 2, then the equation $x^n + y^n + z^n = 0$ has no solution in integers x, y, z having no common factor, unless x or y or z is zero. The incorporation of Germain's exclusion into the symmetric form of Fermat's Last Theorem, referred to as Case I, along with the restriction on the exponent that $2n + 1$ be prime, allowed her to prove that for all such values of n Case I is true. It is readily seen that $2n + 1$ is prime for the prime numbers $n = 3, 5, 11, 23$; for these values Case I is therefore true. By varying her technique a little she was able to show that Case I is also true for all primes in the range $2 < n < 100$.

The following statement of the symmetric form of Fermat's Last Theorem shows the cases: if n is a prime number greater than 2, then the equation $x^n + y^n + z^n = 0$ has no solution in integers x, y, z having no common factor and such that

Case I: n is not a factor of x, or y, or z.

Case II: n is a factor of x, or y, or z.

The separation into cases was prompted by Germain's work, which showed that however difficult Case II might be, at least there was progress to be made on Case I. By the first decade of the twentieth century, Case I had been proved for n almost up to 7,000, by the middle of the century, up into the millions. By 1985 it had been shown that Case I was true for an infinite number of primes but not yet all (D. R. Heath-Brown, "The First Case of Fermat's Last Theorem," *The Mathematical Intelligencer* 7, mo. 5 (1985): 40–47, 55, reporting work of Adleman, Heath-Brown, and Fouvry). Typically, the proofs for Case I have become more and more difficult; Case II was found to be even harder.

120. Paulo Ribenboim, *Thirteen Lectures on Fermat's Last Theorem* (New York: Springer Verlag, 1979), 54–55.

121. A. M. Legendre, "Researches sur quelques objets d'analyse indéterminée et particulièrement sur le théorèm de Fermat," *Mémoirs de l'Académie Royale des Sciences de l'Institut de France* s. 2, 6, année 1823, Paris (1827): 1–60. This paper includes Legendre's illustration of the general nature of Germain's result—see especially pp. 14–17. See also A. M. Legendre, *Essai sur la Théorie des Nombres,* 2nd. ed., (Paris: Courcier, 1808), second supplement, September 1825, 1–40.

122. Legendre fully acknowledged Germain's work in a footnote in his 1823 *Mémoirs de l'Académie Royale* paper (p. 17): "Cette démonstration qu'on trouvera sans doute très ingénieuse, est due à Mlle Sophie Germain, qui cultive avec succès les sciences physiques et mathématiques, comme le preuve le prix qu'elle a remporté à l'Académie sur les vibrations des lames élastiques" ["This demonstration, which will without doubt be considered very ingenious, is due to Mlle. Sophie Germain, a successful student of the physical and mathematical sciences, as is clear from the prize she received from the Academy for her investigation of elastic plate vibrations"]. A full statement and proof of the basic theorem is given in Harold M. Edwards, *Fermat's Last Theorem: A Genetic Introduction to Algebraic Number Theory* (New York: Springer Verlag, 1977), 64; see also Gray, "Sophie Germain," 50, for a more abstract version, sufficiently powerful to imply the calculations given in Legendre's 1823 paper.

123. Harold M. Edwards, *Fermat's Last Theorem,* 59. Fermat's Last Theorem was the subject of a new competition

established by the First Class of the Institut National in 1816, reset in 1818, and finally retired because of no worthwhile entries in 1820. For the finished proof for the general case, see Andrew Wiles, "Modular elliptic curves and Fermat's Last Theorem," *Annals of Mathematics* (2) 141, no. 3 (1995): 443–551.

124. Sophie Germain, *Recherches sur la théorie des surfaces élastiques* (Paris: Mme. V. Courcier, 1821).

125. Bucciarelli and Dworsky, *Sophie Germain,* 94.

126. See Navier and Poisson papers in *Annales de Chimie et de la Physique* 37 (1828): 337–55 (Poisson); 38 (1828): 304–14 (Navier), 435–40 (Poisson); 39 (1828): 144–51 (Navier), 204–11 (Poisson); and 40 (1829): 99–107 (Navier).

127. Sophie Germain, *Remarques sur la nature, les bornes et l'étendue de la question des surfaces élastiques* (Paris: Courcier, 1826); and Sophie Germain, *Mémoire sur l'emploi de l'épaisseur dans la théorie des surfaces élastiques* (Paris: Gauthier-Villars, 1880).

128. C. Navier, "Extrait des recherches sur la flexion des plans élastiques," *Bulletin de la Société Philomatique de Paris* (1823): 92–102; a copy of the full memoir is in the Archives Bibliothèque, École Nationale des Ponts et Chaussées, Paris.

129. See note 113.

130. G. Libre, "Mlle Germain," *Journal des Débats,* 18 May 1832, reprinted in Germain, *Considérations générales* (1833), 11–16.

131. Bucciarelli and Dworsky, *Sophie Germain,* 119.

132. Two notes in the Academy of Sciences' *Comptes rendus* in the late 1880s by Mlle. L. Bortniker were the only ones found in the Royal Society *Catalogue* (see bibliography). They report studies on analytic geometry and the properties of collections of spheres. Mlle. Bortniker is said to have passed the *agrégation ès science mathematiques* (examinations for teachers) in 1885; see Rebière, *Femmes dans la Science,* 40–41.

133. Quoted by Rebière, *Femmes dans la Science,* 157–58: "[Your thesis is the first presented by a woman and successfully defended before our faculty for the doctoral degree in mathematical sciences. You lead the way with dignity . . .]"

134. Katherine Bracher, "Dorothea Klumpke Roberts: a forgotten astronomer," *Mercury* 10 (1983): 139–40; obituaries, Robert G. Aitkin, "Dorothea Klumpke Roberts—An Appreciation," *Publications of the Astronomical Society of the Pacific* 54 (1942): 217–22, and J. H. Reynolds, *Monthly Notices of the Royal Astronomical Society* 104 (1944): 92–93; Nora Moylan, "Reports of the Berkeley Meeting of the Astronomical Society of the Pacific, Feb. 20, 1937," *Publications of the Astronomical Society of the Pacific* 49 (1937): 115–17; Kenneth Weitzenhoffer, "The Triumph of Dorothea Klumpke," *Sky and Telescope* 72 (1986): 109–10; *National Cyclopedia of American Biography,* vol. 31 (1944), 403, 405–6; Rebière, *Femmes dans la Science,* 154–58; Anna Klumpke, *Memoirs;* and Lecours and Caplan, "Augusta Dejerine-Klumpke," 184–88.

135. Rebière, *Femmes dans la Science,* 157.

136. Dorothea Klumpke, "A Night in a Balloon: An Astronomer's Trip from Paris to the Sea," *Century Magazine* 60, n.s. 38 (1900): 276–84.

137. Klumpke, "A Night in a Balloon," 278.

138. Klumpke, "A Night in a Balloon," 282.

139. Anna Klumpke, Dorothea's older sister, a respected portrait painter, was the student, protégée, and companion of artist Rosa Bonheur. In 1899 she inherited Bonheur's château, a building that dated back to the fifteenth century when it had been a royal hunting lodge. When the Klumpke sisters returned to San Francisco in the 1930s, the château passed to their niece, Yvonne Sorrel-Dejerine, the daughter of Augusta Dejerine-Klumpke.

140. Dorothea Klumpke Roberts, *Isaac Roberts Atlas of 52 Regions: A Guide to William Herschel's Fields of Nebulosity* (Paris: Gauthiers-Villars, 1928, 1932). This was the third volume of Roberts's photographs published in a series, *Photographs of Stars, Star Clusters and Nebulae,* volumes 1 and 2 appearing in 1893 and 1899 respectively.

141. Dorothea's sister Augusta Dejerine-Klumpke was similarly honored in 1913 for her work in neurology.

142. See below for a note on Vallot's geological work.

143. [In any case, physics from then on defined itself in terms of a new challenge, one that went beyond observable phenomena to another reality, which would permit their interpretation.]

144. Soraya Svoronos, "Marie Sklodowska Curie (1867–1934)," in *Women in Chemistry and Physics: A Biobibliographic Sourcebook,* eds. Louise S. Grinstein, Rose K. Rose, and Miriam H. Rafailovich (Westport, Conn.: Greenwood Press, 1993), 136–44; Bernadette Bensaude-Vincent and Isabelle Stengers, *Histoire de la chimie* (Paris: Éditions la Découverte, 1993), 286–93; J. L. Davis, "The research school of Marie Curie in the Paris faculty, 1907–14," *Annals of Science* 52 (1995): 321–55; J. R. Partington, *A History of Chemistry,* 4 vols. (London: Macmillan, 1964), vol. 4, 936–41; and Helena M. Pycior, "Pierre Curie and 'His Eminent Collaborator Mme Curie': complementary partners," in *Creative Couples in the Sciences,* eds. Helena M. Pycior, Nancy G. Slack, and Pnina G. Abir-am (New Brunswick, N.J.: Rutgers University Press, 1996), 39–56.

145. See for instance, Pycior, "Pierre Curie"; and Bensaude-Vincent and Stengers, *Histoire*; Davis, "Research School."

146. In one of these early papers, the word *radioactive* is used, probably for the first time; see P. Curie and Mme S. Curie, "Sur une substance nouvelle radio-active, contenue dans la pechblend" (1898—see bibliography).

147. A third radioactive element was discovered in another precipitate by André Debierne, one of the Curies' coworkers. He named it *actinium.* A. Debierne, "Sur une nouvelle matière radio-active," *Comptes rendus* 129 (1899): 593–95, and "Sur un nouvel élément radio-actif: l'actinium," *Comptes rendus* 131 (1900): 333–35.

148. Sklodowska Curie, ["Les rayons de Becquerel et le poloniun," *Revue Générale des Sciences Pures et Appliquées* 10

(1899): 41–50, on 49: "One could, for instance, connect radioactivity to Crookes's theory of the evolution of the elements, designating radioactivity as a property of the heavy elements which would have been formed last and whose evolution is still incomplete."]

149. Ernest Rutherford, *Radio-activity* (Cambridge: Cambridge University Press, 1904), Preface.

150. "Recherches sur les substances radioactives," thèse, Paris, 1903. An English translation, "Radio-Active Substances," was published in instalments between August and December of the same year in *Chemical News* 88 (1903): 85–86, 97–99, 134–35, 145–47, 159–60, 169–71, 175–77, 187–88, 199–201, 211–12, 223–24, 235–36, 247–49, 259–61, 271–72. This translation was also brought out separately as *Radioactive Substances: Thesis presented to the Faculty des Sciences, Paris* (1904) and republished many decades after its first appearance as *Radioactive Substances: A Translation from the French of the Classic Thesis presented to the Faculty of Sciences in Paris* (New York: Philosophical Library, 1961, 1983).

151. Elisabeth Crawford, *The Beginnings of the Nobel Institution: The Science Prizes, 1901–1915* (Cambridge: Cambridge University Press, 1984), 194.

152. See also Bensaude-Vincent and Stengers, *Histoire de la Chimie*, 292–93.

153. A third radioactive element was discovered in another precipitate by André Debierne, one of the Curies' coworkers. He named it *actinium*. Debierne, "Sur une nouvelle matière radio-active"; and "Sur un nouvel élément radio-actif: l'actinium."

154. Ellen Gleditsch (1879–1968), one of the pioneers in the early development of the nuclear sciences, falls outside the set limits of this survey because her first paper (a report in organic chemistry) appeared in 1906. However, her career, remarkable for a woman chemist of her time, suggests the inclusion of a brief biographical sketch here.

The oldest of the ten children of Karl Kristian Gleditsch and his wife Petra Birgitte (née Hansen), she was born in the town of Mandal at the southern tip of Norway on 29 December 1879 but grew up mainly in Tromsø in the far north of the country. Her father, a notable educationist, was a school principal. In 1897, after completing her secondary-level education, she became an apprentice pharmacist, the choice being in part motivated by a special interest in botany. Having passed the pharmacy examinations in 1902 she continued studies, entering the university in Kristiania (now Oslo) to concentrate on chemistry. A year later she was awarded an assistantship in the chemistry laboratory. After taking the matriculation examination in 1905 and a preparatory examination in 1906 she held the position of amanuensis.

Ellen Gleditsch's work in radiochemistry began in 1907 when she joined Marie Curie's group at the Sorbonne. The Curie-Gleditsch research collaboration, which lasted for five years and resulted in more than a dozen papers, led to a close, lifelong friendship between the two and was continued between Gleditsch and the Joliot-Curies. In 1912 Ellen Gleditsch received a *licence ès sciences* diploma. The years 1913–1914 saw her in the United States on an American-Scandinavian Foundation fellowship, working with radiochemist Bertram Boltwood at Yale University on the uranium-to-actinium ratio in minerals. Smith College, Massachusetts, gave her an honorary doctorate in 1914.

In 1916 Gleditsch was appointed to a newly established docent position at the university in Kristiania; in 1929 she became Norway's first woman professor of chemistry and its second woman professor. Over the years she received many honors and awards, including the Order of St. Olaf first class in 1946 and honorary doctorates from the University of Strasbourg (1948) and the Sorbonne (1962). Her efforts to organize Norway's first purchase of radium helped to start the Kristiania Radiumsinstitutt, now the Norske Radiumhospital.

Very active in the cause of women's education and their advancement in academia and in scientific research, Ellen Gleditsch was a member of the first executive committee of the Norwegian League of Academic Women (NKAL) and its president from 1924 to 1928. She also served for a time as president of the International Federation of University Women. One of her special causes was the establishment of scholarships for women students and research workers. A member of the League of Nations International Committee on Intellectual Co-operation, she was also known for her concern for political refugees; among the latter were a number of scientists for whom she provided direct help in the form of space in her laboratory. During the Second World War she helped in Norwegian resistance organizations and, with the return of peace, served on the UNESCO committee for the international control of nuclear weapons.

Ellen Gleditsch brought out more than 150 publications. These included books on chemistry, radioactivity, and the history of chemistry as well as her many research papers. She died in Oslo on 5 June 1968 at age eighty-eight. See the excellent biography by Torleiv Kronen and Alexis C. Pappas, *Ellen Gleditsch: Et Liv i Forskning og Medmenneskelighet* (Oslo: Aventura Forlag, 1987) and also Kristi Lægreid, "Ellen Gleditsch (1897 (*sic*)—1968): Professor i skjort," in *Alma Maters Døtre: Et Århundre med Kvinner i Akademisk Utdanning*, eds. Suzanne Stiver Lie and Maj Birgit Roslett (Oslo: Pax Forlag A/S, 1995), 184, and A. D. Wadsley, "Dr Ellen Gleditsch" (obituary), *Nature* 222 (1969), 101.

155. Ernest Rutherford, *Radio-activity* (Cambridge: Cambridge University Press, 1904), Preface.

156. Marie Curie's discussion of medical radiology relating to war circumstances, *La radiologie et la guerre* (Paris: Félix Alcan) appeared in 1921. She received honorary M.D. degrees from three institutions, the University of Geneva, the Woman's Medical College of Pennsylvania, and the University of Cracow.

157. Her book *L'Isotopie et les éléments isotopes* was published in 1924 (Paris: Société de Physique).

158. *American Chemist* 5 (1874–1875): 451; ibid., 6 (1875–1876): 463.

159. For Vallot's contributions in astronomy, see above.

160. Joseph Vallot, director of the Mont Blanc Observatory, was a man of very broad scientific interests that included all aspects of the earth sciences, meteorology, and botany. He returned to his family's property near Lodève for two periods

every year, largely to oversee his work on the acclimatization to the region of exotic plants. Over a sixteen-year period, he experimented with almost 500 species—see J. Vallot, *Les plantes exotiques ornamentales que l'on peut cultiver dans la région de l'olivier* (Paris: G. Steinheil, 1902); see also entry for Vallot (Joseph) in *Qui êtes-vous? Annuaire des contemporains, 1908* (Paris: Ch. Delagrave, 1908), 473.

161. Geneviève Fraisse, *Clémence Royer: Philosophe et Femme de Sciences* (Paris: Éditions La Découverte, 1985; this includes a comprehensive bibliography of Royer's writings, 167–84); Joy Harvey, "Strangers to Each Other," in *Uneasy Careers and Intimate Lives: Women in Science 1787–1979*, eds. Pnina G. Abir-ám and Dorinda Outram (New Brunswick, N.J.: Rutgers University Press, 1987), 147–71, and *"Almost a Man of Genius": Clémence Royer, Feminism, and Nineteenth-Century Science* (New Brunswick, N.J.: Rutgers University Press (1997); Mazenod and Schoeller, *Dictionnaire des femmes célèbres*; and Claude Blanckaert, "L'anthropologie au féminin: Clémence Royer (1830–1902)," *Revue de Synthèse* 105 (1982): 23–38.

162. Twenty-three years earlier, Royer's fellow countrywoman Tullia Meulien translated another famous scientific treatise from its English original, Charles Lyell's *Elements of Geology* (1838), to *Éléments de géologie* (Paris: Pitois Levrault et Cie., 1839). Mme. Meulien followed this with a translation of Lyell's *Principles of Geology* (1830–1833)—*Principes de géologie*, 4 vols. (Paris: Langlois et Leclercq, 1843, 1848). Both projects were carried out under the auspices of astronomer and physicist François Arago.

163. Peter J. Bowler, *The Mendelian Revolution; the Emergence of Hereditarian Concepts in Modern Science and Society* (Baltimore: Johns Hopkins Press, 1989).

164. Denis Buican, "L'accueil de Darwin à l'Académie des Sciences," *Revue de Synthèse* 105 (1982): 39–52; Osborne, *Nature, the Exotic*. Even after French biologists had given up *fixism* (the doctrine of permanence of species through time), the stage was held by a recast lamarckian doctrine (neolamarckism). ". . . par la brèche ouverte grâce au darwinism dans la citadelle fixiste, le lamarckisme prit un essor tardif" [". . . the breach opened by Darwinism in the citadel of fixism let lamarckism take a late flight"], Buican, "Accueil," 51. Royer was an enthusiastic neolamarckian.

165. Yvette Conry, *L'Introduction du Darwinism en France* (Paris: Vrin, 1974); and Fraisse, *Clémence Royer*.

166. Conry, *L'Introduction*, 33. Royer herself wrote, "Si j'ai traduit Darwin . . . c'est qu'il apportait des nouvelles preuves à l'appui de ma thèse" (quoted by Blanckaert, "L'anthropologie au féminin," 29, n. 19, from an unedited letter of Royer to A. de Quatrefages, April 1891).

167. Herbert Spencer, *Social Statics* (London: John Chapman, 1851); *Principles of Biology*, 2 vols. (London: Williams and Norgate, 1864); and *The Factors of Organic Evolution* (London: Williams and Norgate, 1887).

168. Clémence Royer, "Du groupement des peuples et de l'hégémonie universelle," *Journal des Économistes* (May 1877): 5, 14.

169. Fraisse, *Clémence Royer*, 69.

170. Clémence Royer, "De l'origine des diverses races humaines," *Bulletins de la Société d'Anthropologie de Paris* 8 (1873): 905–36.

171. Her son René, a civil engineer and a junior army officer, had little with which to help her. He died in French Indo-China, a few months after his mother.

172. Bard, *Filles de Marianne*, 109–16; and "Renooz (Mme Muro, née Céline)," *Archives Biographiques Contemporaines* (Paris: n.p., 1906), 232–33. Sources differ on dates of birth and death for Renooz: Bard gives 1840–1928, and *Archives Biographiques* gives the date of birth as 7 January 1849.

173. Renooz-Royer correspondence is listed in Fraisse, *Clémence Royer*, bibliography, 185.

174. See for instance, *L'Origine des animaux: Histoire du développement primitif: nouvelle théorie de l'évolution refutant par l'anatomie celle de M. Darwin* (Paris: J. B. Baillière, 1883), 606 pp.; *La nouvelle science* (Paris: Administration de la Nouvelle Science, 1890), 3 vols.; *Psychologie comparée de l'homme et de la femme* (Paris: Bibliotheque de la Nouvelle Encyclopédie, 1898), 576 pp.; *L'Origine végétale de l'homme et des animaux aeriens. Les mammifères* (Paris: A. Maloine, 1905), 243 pp.; and *Évolution de l'idée divine (simple aperçu)* (Paris: V. Giard and E. Brière, 1908), 58 pp., résumé brochure.

175. *L'Ère de vérité. Histoire de la pensée humaine et de l'évolution morale de l'humanité à travers les âges et chez tous les peuples* (Paris: Marcel Giard, 1921–1933), 6 vols.

176. See n. 174.

177. Gordon, *Integral Feminist*, 153.

178. See Creese, *Ladies in the Laboratory?*

Chapter 4

BELGIUM AND THE NETHERLANDS:
FROM ARDENNES MOSSES TO
EAST INDIES ALGAE

Belgium

Twenty-four papers by eight women are listed in the Belgian section of the bibliography. Twenty are on botanical subjects and most of these (eighteen articles) are reports on cryptogams, including lengthy catalogues by the three authors Marie-Anne Libert, Élise-Caroline Bommer, and Mariette Rousseau. The remaining papers are in phanerogamic botany and plant geography (two), bacteriology and cell biology (three), and mathematics (one). Except for the contributions of Libert, the earliest of which appeared in 1820, all the work was published between 1879 and 1900 (Figure 4-1).

Although she brought out little in print, MARIE-ANNE LIBERT[1] (1782–1865) was very well known during her lifetime among botanists throughout Europe for her studies of the cryptogamic plants of the Ardennes.

The twelfth of thirteen children (four of whom died young) of tanner and property owner Henri-Joseph Libert and his wife Marie-Jeanne-Bernadine (née Dubois), Marie-Anne Libert was born in Malmédy, principality of Liège, in the family home on rue Devant le Vivier on 7 April 1782; she was baptized the same day at nearby Saint-Géréon. Malmédy, then a small village, lay about twenty-five miles south-east of the city of Liège on the northern edge of the Ardennes plateau near the present Belgian-German border. The Liberts had lived there since the late fifteenth century.[2]

Literate, middle-class people, Marie-Anne's parents noticed her intelligence early and arranged instruction for her. Her first teachers were the sepulchrine nuns of Malmédy, a community in which her aunt, Mère Marie-Suzanne Libert, had twice served as Superior. At age twelve she was sent to a boarding school in Prüm, some thirty miles southeast of Malmédy in the Rhineland, to learn German and arithmetic so that she might be better able to help in the family business. Being musical she also had violin lessons from a Benedictine of the Prüm abbey. All her studies progressed rapidly and the arithmetic instruction was expanded to include algebra and geometry.

On her return to Malmédy she quickly became absorbed in natural history. Unlike most girls of her time and her station in life, she was intensely interested in just about everything she saw around her. During long walks in the countryside around Malmédy she observed in detail and made extensive collections, particularly of plants and minerals.[3] These she attempted to identify and classify using her father's library. The fact that the scientific and informational works available to her were in Latin was not an insuperable barrier; without any help she learned the language, becoming very proficient.

She took her first plant collections to Alexandre Louis Lejeune (1779–1850), a physician in the neighboring community of Verviers and the most prominent botanist of the region. Lejeune had undertaken to prepare a catalogue of the plants of the *département* of Ourthe for an official survey of the flora of northern France.[4] Requesting her to collect and dry for him the mountain plants of the Malmédy region, Lejeune offered to supply her with the necessary reference works. With these in hand she quickly became an expert on the Malmédy flora. Many of the vascular plants listed in Lejeune's *Flore des environs de Spa* were found by her; notable among them were new species of brambles and roses—*Rubus arduennensis*, *Rubus montanus*, *Rosa nemorosa*, and *Rosa umbellata*.[5]

In 1810 she met the celebrated Swiss botanist Auguste-Pyrame de Candolle (1778–1841), then professor

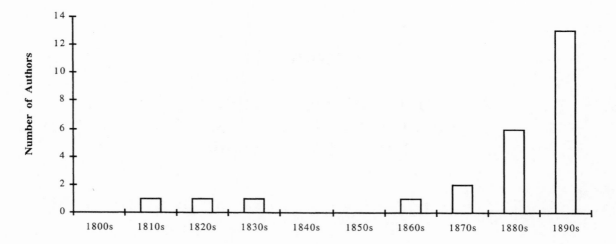

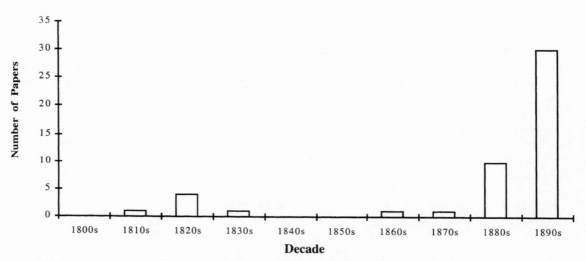

Figure 4-1.   Belgian and Dutch authors and papers, by decade, 1800–1900. Data from the Royal Society *Catalogue of Scientific Papers.*

of botany at Montpellier University, who was making a scientific tour through Belgium. Together with Lejeune she accompanied De Candolle through the high country to the north of Malmédy. De Candolle was impressed both with the knowledge and abilities of Mlle. Libert and with the exceptionally rich cryptogamic flora of the region. He suggested that she begin studies in the area, one that had hitherto received little attention. She accepted the idea and began to collect extensively in the woods, on the mountain slopes, and in the broad, upland marshes typical of the region.

In the course of her early explorations she discovered a new genus of hepatic or liverwort of almost microscopic size, which she named *Lejeunia*; it became the type for a tribe within the Jungermanniaceae family. Her first publication, a report of Lejeunia, appeared in 1820 in *Annales Générales des Sciences Physique* although, because she herself was reluctant to go into print, it was brought out on the initiative of a French refugee. Two notes published in the 1827 *Annales* of the Linnean Society of Paris reported her observations on the rare genus Inoconia and two species of the genus Asteroma. Her description of the new genus of fungus she named *Desmazierella* after her contemporary the Lille mycologist Jean Baptiste Desmazières appeared in 1829. The same year saw the publication of her short memoir on cryptogams that can be grouped into the genus Ascoxyta.

These papers, all brief, compressed reports, hardly reflected the reputation Marie-Anne Libert had by then acquired among botanists, a reputation that had led to her nomination as *associée libre* in the Paris Linnean Society in 1820. Her main work, *Plantes cryptogames des Ardennes*, or *Plantae cryptogamicae quas in Arduenna collegit M.-A. Libert*, which appeared over the years 1830–1837, fully demonstrated her impressive knowledge of the field and at the same time made clear the tremendous richness of the cryptogamic flora of this region, the site of the ancient Arduenna forest.

Plantes cryptogames comprised four volumes of *exsiccata*, each specimen labeled with a complete description. All cryptogam groups were represented in the 400 species reported—ferns, mosses, algae, fungi, and lichens—and many were new to science. Presented in the style used in two lists of fungi of neighboring regions that had preceded it, those of Jean Baptiste Desmazières and French physician and botanist Jean Baptiste Mougeot,[6] its publication constituted a very important step forward in the systematic study of the cryptogamic flora of the Ardennes. Following established tradition Libert wrote the descriptive notes in Latin. The first fascicule included, in addition to the plants, an introduction and a memoir on the Ascoxitaceae. The considerable task of editing and preparing the work for a printer was undertaken by Lejeune.

The year 1837 also saw publication of Marie-Anne Libert's last significant botanical contribution, a memoir on the Hypoxylon family in *Annales des Sciences Naturelles*. She was then at the height of her fame among European botanists. *Plantes cryptogames* brought her to the attention of several learned societies and she received a number of honors, among them a gold medal of merit and a gift of jewels from Emperor Friedrich-Wilhelm III, Malmédy having come under Prussian sovereignty by the treaties of 1815. At a scientific congress in Liège in 1836 she was unanimously elected president of the natural sciences section. Special note was taken of the fact that she had carried out her work without benefit of being close to any large scientific center or even to a large library, disadvantages that could well have isolated her in provincial mediocrity.

Marie-Anne Libert's scholarly contributions were not confined to botany. Having decided about 1837 that at age fifty-five she was too old for plant collecting, she switched her attention to local history and archaeology, also subjects that had long interested her. Her collection of artifacts included ancient coins and a Merovingian ring, the latter found in a bog by a peasant. In this area, however, she lacked access to the background materials and reports of current work that she needed. Her interpretation of the Roman monument of Igel near Triers was fairly quickly shown to be in error; she had not taken into account recent research by German specialists in Roman archaeology. Her debate with the Belgian historian Arsène de Noüe about Wibald, the celebrated twelfth-century abbot of Stavelot and Malmédy, became somewhat bitter and protracted. Relying on religious writings of 1151 from the abbey church of Schwarzheindorf in Beuel (near Bonn) that had recently been made available, she suggested that Wibald was from Lorraine, of the house of the counts of Wied, and a brother of Arnold de Wied, founder of the Beuel abbey. This suggestion caused furor among Belgian historians, who favored a local origin for Wibald.[7]

Although she brought out nothing further after this dispute, Marie-Anne Libert left a considerable amount of unpublished material on the ancient history of Stavelot. Mainly extracts and notes from historical works and manuscripts, this material was later deposited in the state historical archives, Liège.[8] She also left a 599-page manuscript that she had intended to be an expanded version of Augustin-François Villiers's *Dictionnaire Wallon-Français*; she added proverbs and sayings in French and Wallon, rare expressions, and common names of native plants. Latterly her interests turned to genealogy.

All her life Marie-Anne Libert was unshakably Belgian, throughout the territorial adjustments that altered the political map of her region of Western Europe more than once during her time.[9] She was the first woman to join the Belgian Société Royale de Botanique, being named an honorary member when the group was founded in 1862. She also held corresponding memberships in the Société d'Horticulture de Tournai, the Société des Sciences Naturelles de Liège, the Société des Sciences Médicales et Naturelles de Bruxelles, and the Institut Archéologique Liègeois. In addition she belonged to seven non-Belgian scientific societies (in France, Germany, and Luxembourg). As the years went on her connections grew and she exchanged letters or plants with correspondents in France, Germany, and Britain, as well as in Belgium. Even after her active period in collecting she remained interested in botany and often guided visiting botanists on plant excursions around Malmédy and neighboring regions.

All her steady scholarly activity did not prevent Marie-Anne Libert, a capable and enterprising woman in many areas, from doing her share of the work of managing the flourishing family business; she and her brothers greatly expanded the tannery they inherited from their parents. They nevertheless led a simple life. Of the nine surviving Libert children only three married and Marie-Anne, her sister Marie-Elisabeth-Thérèse, and four brothers stayed on in the family home, five of them living into their seventies or beyond. Upright in character and unwilling to accept injustice in any form, Marie-Anne was active in civic and community affairs. After the notice taken of her by Emperor Friedrich-Wilhelm, her opinions carried considerable weight. She died on 15 January 1865 after three days of illness, three months before her eighty-third birthday.

In 1925 a new street in Malmédy was named *Marie-Anne Libert*. On the centenary of her death the *Cercle Naturaliste* of the Malmédy region placed a plaque on the building that replaced her house and also erected in a new community park a monument bearing her medallion effigy by Stavelot sculptor vicomte Jacques de Biolley.[10] The fact that her region was separated politically from Belgium for many decades meant that she was not always given the attention she deserved in early works on Belgian botany; but this was later rectified.[11] Many species of plants and six genera are named after her.[12]

Although Libert's *Plantes cryptogames* collections established her reputation in the European botanical community, after her death it was her personal herbarium that became the particular interest of specialists. Sold to the Jardin Botanique in Brussels by her nephew Hubert-Remacle Libert of Malmédy for 2,000 francs, it included an extensive collection of cryptogams, phanerogams, and published herbaria. Specimens were well prepared and documented. The fungi and lichen collections became especially famous; parts of the collection were published by Casimir Roumeguère in *Revue Mycologique* in 1880, additional material was brought out the following year by Italian fungal taxonomist Pier Andrea Saccardo,[13] and other botanists continued the work. The material was still being used a century after Libert's death and even a few forms thought to be unknown in Belgium were found in it from time to time. This is hardly surprising because Libert worked in the early nineteenth century before extensive damage had been done to the vegetation of the area; further, she was the only person collecting there at the time and for long after.[14]

Within a decade of Libert's death two other prominent early Belgian women botanists had begun studies of the cryptogamic flora of their region—Élisa Bommer and her younger colleague Mariette Rousseau.

ÉLISE-CAROLINE (ÉLISA) BOMMER,[15] née DESTRÉE (1832–1910) was born on 19 January 1832 at Laeken, on the outskirts of Brussels in the province of Brabant. Her early years were spent near the royal *château* where her father worked and as a child she enjoyed the freedom of its large park. Lively and intelligent, she attracted the attention of one of the palace governesses who gave her some elementary instruction and taught her English, a language she later spoke fluently. At age ten she was sent to a boarding school in nearby Vilvorde. During her six years there she chafed at the loss of her freedom and the monotony of the school studies, but developed sound and well-disciplined work habits and demonstrated her considerable musical talent. Further training in music was put aside in favor of a business apprenticeship in a Brussels firm, which she joined at age twenty. She did well, but overwork and long hours affected her health and the position brought her little in the way of overall satisfaction; it lacked sufficient intellectual challenge.

About this time she began to study botany, proceeding with patience and thoroughness. Through her family physician she was introduced to botanist, fern specialist, and plant physiologist Jean-Édouard Bommer (1829–1895) professor of botany at the University of Brussels from 1872; he helped her resolve a number of specimen identification problems and provided general guidance for her studies.

In 1865 she married Bommer. They had at least two children, Charles, who became a botanist and palaeobotanist, and Jules. Despite continuing business interests and family responsibilities, she expanded her botanical investigations. In 1873 she joined forces with Mariette Rousseau, a kindred spirit who was also interested in botany. At Jean-Édouard Bommer's suggestion they undertook a study of local fungi. Very few such investigations had been carried out by Belgian botanists since the earlier work of Libert, Gerard Daniel Westendorp (1813–1868),[16] and Jean Kickx (1803–1864). Relying largely on Kickx's *Flore cryptogamique des environs de Louvain* and his *Flore cryptogamique des Flanders*, with Swedish botanist Elias Magnus Fries's *Systema Mycologicum* as a taxonomy and classification reference,[17] they found the work difficult but tremendously interesting and inspiring. Access to the holdings of specialized mycology literature in the library of the Jardin Botanique helped them considerably.

Setting themselves the goal of making known the fungal flora of their region and completing the investigations of earlier workers, they published a succession of monographs in the *Bulletins* of the Société Royale de Botanique over the course of eleven years: their 195-page catalogue of fungi observed near Brussels appeared in 1879 and was followed by a 350-page mycological flora of the Brussels district;[18] a further three-part contribution to Belgian cryptogamic flora came out over the period 1886–1890 (see bibliography), and additional work on several new species appeared in P. A. Saccardo's "Notae Mycologicae" in 1905.[19] Their joint work on Costa Rican fungi appeared in 1896 as one section of the Société Royale de Botanique memoir, "Primitiae florae costaricensis" (see bibliography). This report dealt with material, including several new species, that constituted part of the extensive collections assembled from 1887 on by Belgian botanist, geographer, and climatologist Henri Pittier and his coworkers. Costa Rican flora, richly varied because of the country's great diversity in climate and geology, had been of much interest to a succession of European botanists from the late eighteenth century. The important collections that Pittier amassed over an extended stay formed the nucleus of the Costa Rican national herbarium in San José; additional material went to the Belgian state Jardin Botanique in Brussels. The Bommer-Rousseau study of the fungae collected on the 1897–1899 Belgian antarctic expedition organized and led by Adrien de Gerlache de Gomery appeared in the section of the expedition's reports published in 1905.[20] Throughout the 1890s Élisa Bommer was also engaged in expanding the catalogue of fungi of the Netherlands, especially from the region around The Hague; her lists appeared in the journal *Nederlandsch Kruidkundig Archief.*

Her intellectual interests continued even in her last years when she was severely restricted physically. She played the piano throughout most of her life and especially enjoyed the French poets, La Fontaine as well as those of her own time; latterly she took up the painting of flowers and agarics (mushrooms). Élisa Bommer died on 17 January 1910, two days before her seventy-eighth birthday. The fungal species *Bommerella marchal* commemorates her name. Her mycological collections were left to the Brussels Jardin Botanique.

MARIETTE ROUSSEAU,[21] née HANNON (1850–1926), a self-taught mycologist, was born into a middle-class professional family. Her father, Dr. Hannon, introduced her to plant studies at an early age; her brother, poet and painter Théodore Hannon, was one of a group of Brussels-centered late nineteenth-century Belgian artists. In 1871 she married Professor Ernest Rousseau. Their son, also Ernest Rousseau, later became founding president of the group, Naturalistes Belges.

Cryptogamic plants and fungi in particular became Mariette Rousseau's special interest and, together with her friend Élisa Bommer (see p. 104), she made a notable contribution to her country's mycological collections, in her time still far from complete. The first Rousseau-Bommer publication, a catalogue of fungi found near Brussels, appeared in 1879. It was followed five years later by a second substantial monograph on the mycological flora of the Brussels region; a three-part catalogue of Belgian cryptogamic flora was brought out between 1886 and 1890 (see bibliography). Well known by then as fungi specialists, Rousseau and Bommer were invited to examine a collection of Costa Rican mushrooms sent back to Brussels by Henri Pittier (see above); their resulting list (1896, see bibliography) included determinations of several new species. Two last joint works were brought out in 1905: a contribution on Belgian fungi, again including the determination of new species, in a work by fungal taxonomist P. A. Saccardo, and a study of the fungi collected on the 1897–1899 Belgian Antarctic Expedition.[22]

From 1908 Mariette Rousseau carried out much of her work at the state Jardin Botanique in Brussels, where she was engaged in the systematic reclassification of the herbarium mushroom collection. Keen to encourage wider interest in fungi, she always welcomed at her workroom those who had questions about mushrooms and her enthusiasm for her subject provided considerable encouragement for younger workers. In addition she organized the region's first public mushroom exhibits. Although she did no more collecting after the death of Élisa Bommer in 1910, over the years she led many naturalist excursions, particularly to the Forêt de Soignes a few miles south of Brussels. In 1924, two years before her death, Mariette Rousseau received the honor of Chevalier de l'Ordre de Léopold.

The remaining Belgian botanists in this survey are Maria Goetsbloets and Fanny MacLeod.

Goetsbloets's paper on the evergreen shrub *Ledum palustris* was read before the Société Royale de Botanique in 1889. MacLeod's list of botanical literature concerning plant distribution over the period 1873–1890, together with an alphabetical list of plant names, appeared in a long paper in the *Botanisch Jaarboek* in 1891. Fanny MacLeod (*née* Maertens)[23] was the wife of Julius MacLeod (1857–1919), professor of botany at Ghent University from 1887 and a specialist in statistical and quantitative biology.

Two Belgian women, Clémence Demoor and Emma Leclercq, published papers in the medical sciences in the 1890s that are listed in the Royal Society *Catalogue*. Both worked at the University of Brussels. Demoor (*née* Everard), wife of physiologist Jean Demoors, was the first woman to graduate from the medical faculty of the university (1892).[24] Leclercq, who held a doctorate in natural sciences, was a member of the Société Belge de Microscopie. A coworker of embryologist Charles van Bambeke at the Laboratoire d'Histologie Normale at the University of Gent, she reported work on microorganisms and cellular division processes in her two 1890 papers (see bibliography). Some of her studies in the latter area were carried out at the Collège de France, Paris, in 1889.

A paper by Mme. Prime that appeared in 1893 in the journal *Mathesis* (Ghent and Paris) is also listed in the bibliography. It was one of a number of short notes by Mme. Prime presenting solutions to problems in elementary mathematics—geometry, trigonometry, and calculus—that she brought out during the 1890s, mostly as solutions to questions posed. *Mathesis* was a journal for teachers, and so Mme. Prime might have been a high school teacher.

Netherlands

Twenty-four papers by seven women from the Netherlands are listed in the bibliography, all reporting research carried out between the late 1880s and 1900. Ten were in cryptogamic botany, five in mathematics, four in zoology, and the remainder in chemistry and medicine.

One of the most distinguished of the early Dutch women scientists was algologist ANNA WEBER-VAN BOSSE (1852–1942),[25] remembered especially for her extensive studies of marine algae of the East Indies. Because she was the first person to collect in scattered and remote tropical regions and because she used dredging to obtain sublittoral material, she found and described many new genera and species.

Anna van Bosse was born in Amsterdam on 27 March 1852, the younger of two daughters in the family of five children of prosperous businessman Jacob van Bosse and his wife Jaqueline Jeanne (Reynvaan). She was to some extent brought up by her sister, ten years her senior, her mother having died when she was very young. A Swiss governess provided her education and, stimulated by frequent visits to the Amsterdam zoo, she early developed interests in botany and zoology.

In 1870 she married the painter Wilhem Ferdinand Willink van Collen and through him developed close friendships with many of the younger Dutch artists of the time. However, Willink died in 1877 and Anna returned to her father's house. Along with her sister she took up horse riding, particularly at the family country estate at Doorn, a few miles east of Utrecht.

Still very interested in natural history, she enrolled as an auditor at the University of Amsterdam in 1880, one of the first women admitted to the institution.[26] She studied under the direction of plant physiologist Hugo de Vries and botanist C. A. J. A. Oudemans. Along with two other women students, she carried out her laboratory work in a small room separate from the men but was allowed to attend the same lectures. After three years of general botanical studies she specialized in algology, collecting her first specimens of freshwater algae (colonies of the microscopic blue alga Nostoc) in the waterways around Doorn and marine algae from the North Sea in the harbor of Den Helder. In 1883 she married physician and zoologist Max Weber, professor *extraordinarius* of zoology at the University of Amsterdam from 1883 to 1884, and then for many years professor *ordinarius* of zoology and director of the zoological museum.

Anna Weber-van Bosse continued her algae studies, one of her first investigations being in response to a competition calling for a thorough examination of the algae discovered living on the hairs of sloths; her entry won a gold prize. In the early years of her marriage she accompanied her husband on several scientific trips to northern Norway, herself collecting algae. Her first visit to the East Indies came in 1888–1889 when Max Weber went there to study the little-known freshwater fauna of Java, Flores, and Celebes (Sulawesi). The greater part of the algae work from the trip was reported along with that from the Webers' later *Siboga* Expedition, but two important papers appeared in 1890 and an additional monograph in 1898 in the *Annales du Jardin Botanique de Buitenzorg* (see bibliography); these contained a description of a new genus Phytophysa and a report of a new case of symbiosis between algae and sponges. In 1894–1895 the Webers spend eight months in South Africa, Max Weber studying freshwater fauna and problems of biogeographic distribution, Anna Weber-van Bosse collecting algae from waters along the Indian Ocean coast. Two reports of her studies appeared in 1896 (see bibliography). One described a new genus, Pseudocodium; in the other she discussed the reproductive stages of *Sarcomenia miniata* (now *Platysiphonia delicata*) and noted that until then it had been known only in the Atlantic.

Three years later came the *Siboga* Expedition to the East Indies led by Max Weber. Anna Weber-van Bosse's popular book, *Een Jaar aan Boord H. M. Siboga*, was written in response to requests for an account of the expedition suitable for the nonscientific reader; a German translation by her Swiss friend Mme. Ruge-Baenziger followed soon after. In 2000, a new Dutch edition was brought out by Jaap de Visser.[27]

The flora and fauna of the region had been of much interest to students of the tropics for many decades and some famous wide-ranging biogeographical studies had already been carried out. These included the investigations of Alfred Russel Wallace in the 1850s and early 1860s, which concentrated mainly on land species; a few studies on corals had also been made. The first extensive work on deep-sea exploration came with the British *Challenger* Expedition of 1872–1876, which indeed marked the beginning of modern oceanography as a science. Deriving their impetus and support in part from the territorial ambitions and rivalries of the Western nations, other marine expeditions followed over the succeeding two decades.[28] By the 1890s the Dutch, too, felt the need to join more vigorously in the exploration of their own colonial region. The scientific purpose of the Weber expedition was to extend the work carried out on the *Challenger* and the 1874–1878 German *Gazelle*

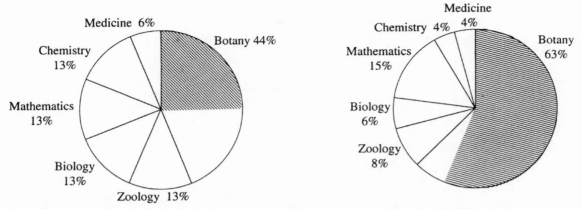

a. Authors

b. Papers

Figure 4-2.   Distribution of Belgian and Dutch authors and papers, by field, 1800–1900. Shaded sectors represent work in cryptogamic botany. (In a., an author contributing to more than one field is counted in each.) Data from the Royal Society *Catalogue of Scientific Papers.*

expeditions on the deep-sea marine flora and fauna of the eastern part of the Malaysian Archipelago. In addition Weber planned to further investigate the ocean floor of the region, a particularly complex area containing deep basins and even deeper troughs interspersed with relatively shallow banks and ridges. Anna Weber-van Bosse was responsible for collecting algae.

Leaving Holland in the autumn of 1898 and travelling via India, the Webers joined the Royal Dutch Navy's ship *Siboga* (East Indies Marine) at Surabaja on the north coast of Java in March 1899. A 790-ton coal-fired steamer, capable of over thirteen knots, she normally served as a kind of large gunboat.[29] For this trip she had a reduced complement of European officers and a crew that was largely Javan. A small cabin, crowded and usually hot, served as ship's laboratory. The region to be investigated was roughly triangular, from the southern Philippines (the Sulu Archipelago and Mindanao) in the north to Surabaja in the west, southern Timor in the south, and the Kai and Aru islands in the east—about 1,200 miles north–south and 1,500 miles east–west (Figure 4-3).

The first point of special interest was the Lombok Strait, between the islands of Bali and Lombok in the Sumba chain, which stretches east from Java. This strait was where Wallace had positioned the southern end of what became known as the *Wallace Line,* separating the flora and fauna of Asia from that more typical of Australia. A few years earlier Max Weber had questioned this positioning, having found no especially sharp biological change there; the *Siboga* Expedition now further established that the Lombok Strait did not constitute a particularly deep dividing channel.

The long trip north up the Makassar Strait between Borneo and Celebes took them by stages to the Sulu Archipelago, the chain lying along the underwater bridge between Mindanao and northeast Borneo. En route, they crossed the shallow Borneo Bank with its beautiful coral reefs, islands of fine white sand, and waters yielding rich collections of fauna and flora. The smooth seas on the bank were in sharp contrast to the rough water they ran into in the deep-basin region of the Celebes Sea immediately to the north. Here dredging and sounding operations were almost brought to a halt but nevertheless huge banks of calcareous algae (such as Halimeda and Lithothamnion) were found at considerable depths. The Sulu Islands, as part of the Philippines, had recently come under American jurisdiction, and so when the *Siboga* made a port call, she was visited by United States health inspectors. Relations with the Americans were in general very friendly, but the health officers declared themselves "horrified" at the dirty conditions on board.

Heavy seas continually handicapped the expedition on the return journey south and at times Anna Weber-van Bosse struggled with seasickness. However, criss-crossing the Halmahera Sea between the northwestern tip of New Guinea and Halmahera, she was amazed and enthralled by the myriad of tiny islands—"What a world of islands encircles the eastern part of our archipelago!"[30] Collecting was good and she obtained some rare plant specimens. Many soundings were taken in the area in order to explore the submarine relationship between the Ceram and Banda seas; the degree of isolation of the deep Banda basin from the Ceram Sea and hence from the Pacific was a topic of considerable current interest.

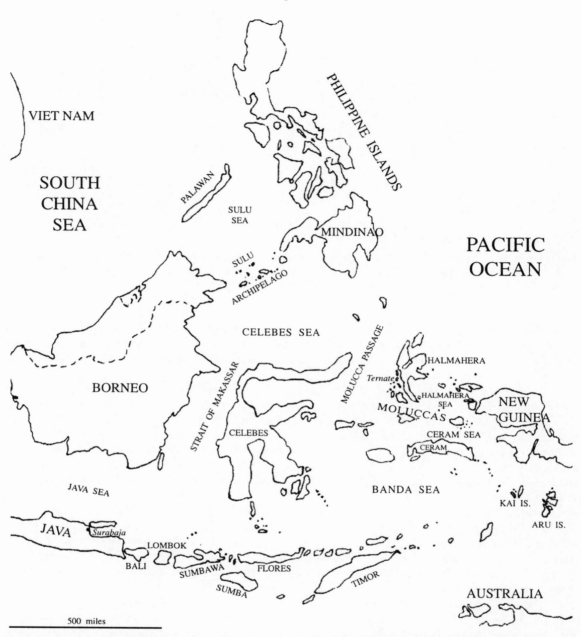

Figure 4-3. Sketch map showing the region explored during the Weber *Siboga* Expedition, 1899–1900.

By 26 February 1900 the *Siboga* was back in Surabaja, and what for Anna Weber-van Bosse had been an unforgettable year was over.

The amount of scientific information collected by the expedition—zoological, botanical, geological, and hydrographic—was such that Max Weber was occupied with arrangements for its publication until his death in 1937; his own reports on fishes became famous in the ichthyology literature. One of the major results was the establishing of a biogeographic line, known as the *Weber Line,* along the eastern side of Timor, west of the Kai Islands, through the Ceram Sea, and then north along the western side of the Ternate Moluccas. This line fixes a boundary between the Malaysian islands and those of Papuasia. The islands of eastern Malaysia between it and Wallace's line to the west (through the Macassar Strait and west of the Philippines) and the ocean channels between them have been subject to more geologic changes than the corresponding parts of the Sundaland shelf region to the west; the relative poverty and peculiarities of their fauna are ascribed to this circumstance.

Anna Weber-van Bosse's publications reporting the expedition's research on algae were numerous, her first preliminary note appearing in the *Annales* of the Buitenzorg Jardin Botanique in 1901. Particularly notable were her monograph on *Corallinaceae* (1904) and her *Liste des algues du Siboga* (issued in four volumes, 1913–1928). Also of special interest was her report on two further cases of symbiosis between sponges and algae (1910).[31] Among the new genera she found are the following: Periphykon, Exophyllum (thought by her to belong to the Rhodymeniaceae but now assigned to the Rhodomelaceae), Chalicostroma, Microphyllum, Corallophila, Aneuria (later changed to Lenormandiopsis), Ethelia, Perinema, and Tapeinodasya (Rhodophyta), Mesospora (Phaeophyta), Bryobesia and Tydemania (Chlorophyta). The distinctive tropical species *Tydmania expeditionis*, named for G. F. Tydman, Commander of the *Siboga*, is now known to be widely distributed throughout the region. Two other major works by her friends British Museum algologists Ethel Barton Gepp and Antony Gepp resulted from the expedition's collections: Ethel Gepp's monograph on the genus Halimeda (1901), and the Gepps' joint monograph on the Codiaceae (1911).[32] The importance of Weber-van Bosse's work is reflected in the fact that, from the standpoint of marine phycology, the *Siboga* Expedition is generally regarded as the most important scientific expedition to the western Pacific during the nineteenth century. In addition to her algae studies Weber-van Bosse gave her husband much assistance in the overall task of preparing for publication the monumental series of *Siboga* Expedition monographs, of which some 137 appeared during her lifetime.

As well as her accounts of the Siboga algae collections, she brought out several reports on marine algae of tropical waters collected by other expeditions.[33] These included a monograph on the Rhodophyceae collected by J. Stanley Gardiner on the British Percy Sladen Trust Expedition on the *Sealark* to the islands of the west central Indian Ocean in 1905, a monograph on material from the Danish expedition of 1914–1916 to the Kai Islands, and a shorter work on algae brought back by Prince Léopold of Belgium from a 1926–1929 expedition to the Dutch East Indies. The latter earned her a medal presented in 1938 by then King Léopold.

Anna Weber-van Bosse had a habit of modestly ranking the work of other algologists much higher than her own; she frequently stressed that her studies covered "only morphology," although she would have liked to expand into other branches of the field, particularly reproductive processes. Nevertheless she is generally recognized as one of the leading experts on marine algae of her time. Successfully integrating her own interests into her husband's wide-ranging and ambitious research program, she took full advantage of the opportunities that came her way. An ordinary member of the Nederlandsche Botanische Vereeniging from 1885, she was named an honorary member in 1924; from 1938 she was the society's oldest member. The University of Utrecht awarded her an honorary doctorate in 1910. In recognition of her work on the *Siboga* Expedition the Netherlands government nominated her Chevalier de l'ordre d'Orange-Nassau, one of the country's highest honors; in 1935 she became an *officer* of this order. On the occasion of her ninetieth birthday in 1942 the National Herbarium's journal *Blumea* published a Jubilee volume to which friends and colleagues contributed both papers dedicated to her and letters of reminiscence and appreciation.

Over the years she built up a superb algae collection, expanded from the core of *Siboga* materials by the purchase of a number of other unique holdings of European, Malaysian, American, and South African algae. These included the collections of the celebrated German algologists F. T. Kützing and F. Hauck (rich in types), the algal herbarium of Leyden professor of botany W. F. R. Suringar, and part of the herbarium of French lawyer S. R. Lenormand, all mid and late nineteenth-century workers. In 1934, when she was seventy-two, she donated her entire collection to the Netherlands National Museum, Leiden, thereby greatly enriching its phycological holdings.

Much of Anna Weber-van Bosse's work was done in a small laboratory in her home "Huis Eerbeek," an ancient manor house in the pleasant village of Eerbeek about fifty miles east of Utrecht. The manor had attached to it a considerable acreage of land that the Webers developed and managed, employing a number of agricultural workers. The extensive gardens, with fine beech avenues and ponds for carp and duck, as well as algae, had plantings of bushes and shrubs collected from many regions of the world. Exotic birds and animals were kept in the grounds from time to time, including a casowary from the *Siboga* Expedition. A lively, vigorous person whose winter exercise was skating on the Amsterdam canals, Anna Weber-van Bosse was a hostess of great charm with a tremendous store of experiences and memories that she enjoyed sharing. Many foreign botanists and zoologists came to Huis Eerbeek for visits and technical consultations, among them Ethel Barton Gepp of the British Museum and William Setchell of the University of California, Berkeley. Her practice of always being willing to lend specimens from her collections to serious algologists brought her many contacts; she was often asked to identify difficult material and in return for her help received numerous specimens as gifts.

By no means isolated from the wider social concerns of her community, particularly the needs of the less affluent, she worked in child-care centers when she lived in Amsterdam; in the village of Eerbeek, where most of her community efforts were focused, she founded a very successful Montessori school in 1921, providing the necessary building herself. Highly regarded by the people of the village, she also gave talks for agricultural workers. Anna Weber-van Bosse died in Eerbeek on 29 October 1942 at the age of ninety. She is commemorated in the names of seventeen species and genera, thirteen of them algae. Her pioneering studies of the marine algae of the East Indies constitute a major and lasting contribution to phycology.

A long-time member of the curatorial staff of the National Museum of Natural History in Leiden was CANNA MARIA LOUISE POPTA[34] (1860–1929). Born on 30 May 1860, Popta was the first woman student at the University of Leiden, where she concentrated on natural history, going as far as the intermediate-level examinations. Continuing her studies at Bern University, she carried out doctoral research on fungi (Hemiasci) and received her degree in 1898. The same year she was appointed to a position as assistant curator in the reptile and amphibian department of the Leiden museum; later she had full responsibility for this department, where she served as curator until 1911. From 1899 she published numerous articles on a variety of topics in natural history, many in the museum's *Notes*. Her two zoology papers listed in the bibliography described new species of East Indian fishes from the huge collection brought back to the Netherlands in 1860 by Dutch army doctor and ichthyologist Pieter Bleeker (1819–1878) who spent almost twenty years in Java.[35]

Popta continued to publish throughout her career, bringing out a short work on the geology of the East Indies in 1925, *Het Ontstaan van den Oost-Indischen Archipel* (The Origin of the East Indies Archipelago). She retired in 1928, when she was sixty-eight, and died on 29 October 1929.

Despite the fact that all four of the Dutch universities opened to women well before the turn of the century, relatively few candidates came forward to avail themselves of the opportunities offered in medical education until after 1900.[36] One of the earliest to do so was CORNELIA DE LANGE[37] (1871–1950), who received her license to practice in 1897.[38]

A pioneer among Dutch women physicians and medical research scientists, de Lange was born in Alkmaar, Noord Holland, about five miles inland from the North Sea coast, on 24 June 1871. After attending the Hogere Burger Schole (nonclassical high school) in Alkmaar she went to Amsterdam University where, following her parents wishes, she enrolled in 1891 as a student of chemistry. She switched to medicine in 1892 and was awarded her M.D. five years later.[39] After a period in general practice in Amsterdam, the most welcoming of the Netherlands cities to medical women, she spent some time at the children's hospital in Zurich. Thereafter she restricted herself to pediatrics and soon became one of the country's leaders in infant care and child welfare. The field was one whose development as a medical specialty that was relatively open to women physicians almost coincided with de Lange's career. In 1902 she and three other women physicians set up a clinic for women and children, one of the few in the Netherlands. Five years later she became head of a new infant care division of the Emma Kinderziekenhuis, a hospital for poor children in Amsterdam; she worked there until 1927.

From about 1909 de Lange published numerous articles in Dutch and foreign journals on diseases of children; these included reports of work on tuberculosis, infantile anaemia, and renal disease. Along with Bernardus Brower (1881–1949), one of the leading research neurologists in the Netherlands,[40] she also carried out studies on the pathological anatomy of the brain. Eight of her papers appeared before 1914 and although her publications stopped for four years during the First World War she was again bringing out results by 1918. A number of her postwar investigations were carried out jointly with her pediatrician colleague Jan Cornelis Schippers (1881–1946), medical superintendent of the Emma Kinderziekenhuis; among them was a series of studies on irregularities in blood cell production caused by disfunction of the bone marrow (leucocytosis and leucopenia).[41]

In 1927, on the death of Jacob de Bruin, professor of pediatrics at the University of Amsterdam, Cornelia de Lange was chosen to fill the position. She became professor of pediatrics in October of that year, at the age of fifty-six. Hers was the first full professorship held by a woman in the Netherlands. Amsterdam University being a municipal institution, the selection was made by the city council whose women members enthusiastically supported de Lange's appointment, sending her a telegram of congratulation on the occasion.

Her professorship and the strong positions she held in medical associations gave her considerable influence. During the eleven years of her tenure at the university she guided the next generation of pediatricians, supervising fourteen theses while herself continuing to publish at an impressive rate. There is little evidence that she had any special interest in women's issues, her views on most matters being indistinguishable from those of her male colleagues. Although many women took up pediatrics, de Lange never advocated it as a field for which women were especially well suited.

Over the course of her career she brought out more than 250 books and articles. In addition, very active in the Dutch medical association, she assisted in the management of the journal *Nederlandsch Tijdschrift voor Gneeskunde* and edited its pediatric reports. Service on the staff of the Brain Institute was another of her responsibilities. Following the death in 1938 of the woman friend with whom she lived, she decreased her work load, retiring from the university. Her writing and research continued however, two of her more general works on childcare and hygiene appearing in the 1940s.[42] In 1946 the *Nederlandsch Tijdschrift voor Geneeskunde* celebrated her seventy-fifth birthday by bringing out a special number in her honor.

Of continuing interest is de Lange's work on what is now known as the *Cornelia de Lange Syndrome* (or the *Brachmann–de Lange Syndrome*[43]), a relatively rare genetic disease causing abnormal congenital physique (including microcephaly) and mild to severe mental retardation. She had reported on two unrelated children with a distinct pattern of congenital defects and similar facial features in 1933, naming the condition "typus degenerativus Amstelodamensis." In 1941 she presented a fuller account to the neurological Society of Amsterdam. By the 1960s a number of cases had been reported in Europe and the United States. The Cornelia de Lange Syndrome Foundation (Collinsville, Connecticut), an international family support group, now organizes annual conferences for professionals and affected families.[44]

A sincere and upright person, modest and frugal in her way of life, de Lange was one of Amsterdam's most popular and admired pediatricians. Her widely known books on childcare had made her name almost synonymous with ideas of "modern motherhood." During the Second World War and the German occupation of the Netherlands she did much to help the less fortunate, work that required considerable courage. She remained in Amsterdam until her death at the age of seventy-eight on 28 January 1950.

Little information has been collected about the remaining four Dutch women whose papers are listed in the bibliography—Schilthuis, Maarseveen, Schaap, and Wythoff Kerkhoven.

L. Schilthuis was a curator at the Museum of Zoology at the University of Utrecht. Her two articles on collections of amphibia and fishes from the Congo were published in 1889 and 1891. They included descriptions of new species. Geertruida van Maarseveen is reported to have received a degree in chemistry from the University of Zurich in 1897;[45] her paper on solution processes was published that year, but she does not appear to have brought out further work in the field. J. Schaap's paper in organic chemistry was published in 1892.

Six papers and notes reporting original work in mathematics by Geertruida Kerkhoven, *née* Wythoff, (b. 1853) were published between 1893 and 1902. These were in the main solutions to problems posed, sometimes as prize competitions, in Dutch mathematics journals. Kerkhoven was an analyst; several of her papers, including her two long 1899 solutions, were in analytical mechanics, a popular area at the time.[46]

Summary

The most important contributions of Belgian and Dutch nineteenth-century women scientists were in cryptogamic botany, the greater part of their publications being in that area (Figure 4-2b). Particularly prominent workers were Anna Weber-van Bosse, known internationally for her studies of the algae of the East Indies, Marie-Anne Libert, one of Belgium's early nineteenth-century explorers of the cryptogamic flora of the Ardennes region, and the Brussels-based team of Élise-Caroline Bommer and Mariette Rousseau whose major contributions were their studies of the fungi of the Brussels district. Except for the contributions of Libert, most of the work was carried out in the last two decades of the century (Figure 4-1).

Anna Weber-van Bosse worked along with her husband, zoologist Max Weber, joining him on the wide-ranging scientific expeditions he organized and led, especially notable being the *Siboga* Expedition to the East Indies in the late 1890s. She took full advantage of the opportunities for algae studies these expeditions presented and her contributions to the field were of lasting importance. Marie-Anne Libert was very much an independent worker, although she benefited considerably from her close contacts with neighboring botanist A. L. Lejeune and from the early suggestion from the eminent De Candolle that she direct her efforts to a study of the little-known cryptogamic flora of her region. Her collections and identifications, highly regarded by her contemporaries throughout the European botanical community, remain important for two reasons—first, she worked at a time before extensive damage had been done to the region by man and many forms wiped out, and second, she was the only person collecting in the Ardennes in her time and for long after. Consequently her collections remained in use for more than a century after her death. Likewise the extensive catalogues of fungi of the Brussels region prepared by Élisa Bommer and Mariette Rousseau constituted important additions to Belgian national records of cryptogamic flora.

In mathematics the publications of Geertruida Wythoff are worthy contributions for a woman of her time; they suggest that her studies in the field were extensive and that she was familiar with current work. The most important investigations of Amsterdam pediatrician Cornelia de Lange came after 1901; only two of her early papers are listed in the bibliography.

Notes

1. B.-C. Du Mortier, "Notice sur Mlle. M.-A. Libert," *Bulletin de la Société Royale de Botanique de Belgique* (1865): 403–11; Casimir Roumeguère, "Publication des Reliquiae Libertianae," *Revue Mycologique* 2 (1880): 7–15; *Biographie Nationale* (Bruxelles: various publishers, 1866–), vol. 12 (1892–1893), 91–92; and A. Lawalree, J. Lambinon, F. Demaret, and Maurice Lang, *Marie-Anne Libert (1782–1865): Biographie, Généalogie, Bibliographie* (Malmédy: Famille et Terroir, 1965).

2. After Marie-Anne Libert's death there was considerable debate about her ancestry, some claiming that she came from an aristocratic Liège family of Liberts that had long resided in the *château* of Bévercé in the neighboring district of Stavelot (see for instance Du Mortier, "Notice"); later extensive genealogical research established that her family origins were in the villages of Malmédy and nearby Burnenville (see Lang in Lawalree, Lambinon, Demaret, and Lang, *Marie-Anne Libert*).

3. Among the minerals assembled by Libert was a remarkable collection of fine river pearls from the pearl muscles then found in abundance in the Amblève River and its tributaries.

4. Following the incorporation of the region into Napoleon Bonaparte's French empire, the *département,* a French administrative division, had recently been established.

5. A. L. S. Lejeune, *Flore des environs de Spa . . . pour servir de suite à la flore du nord de France de M. Roucel,* 2 vols., supplement, vol. 2, 311–18 (Liège: Duvivier, 1811, 1813); and *Revue de la flore des environs de Spa* (Liège: Duvivier, 1824).

6. J. B. H. J. Desmazières, *Catalogue des plantes . . . ou énumération des végétaux phanerogames et cryptogames qui croissent spontanement dans la Belgique ancienne . . . Famille des champignons* (Lille: Leleux, 1823); and Jean Baptiste Mougeot, *Stirpes cryptogamae; vogeso-rhenanae; quas in rheni superioris inferiorisque, nec non vogesorum praefecturis,* 3 vols. (Bruyerii: Vivot, 1810, 1812).

7. For Libert's historical and archaeological writings, see "Recherches faites d'après des documents du XIIe siècle sur la patrie et la famille de Wibald, XLIIe abbé des monastères de Stavelot et de Malmédy," *Bulletins de l'Académie Royale des Sciences, des Lettres et des Beaux-Arts de Belgique* 15 (1848): 176–90; and "Nouvel essai d'explication du monument d'Igel, avec planches," *Jahrbücher des Vereins von Alterthumsfreunden in Rheinland, II. Monumente* 19 (1853): 33–54. Libert also brought out two archaeological/historical articles in a local Malmédy publication: "De l'ancien village de Nova Villa," *La Semaine,* n. 36, 9 September 1849, and "Sur la fontaine de St. Remacle à Malmédy," *La Semaine,* 23 December 1849. The dispute between Libert and de Noüe concerning Libert's ideas on the family background of Abbot Wibald was also printed in *La Semaine* (1857, n. 1, 4 Jan.; n. 2, 11 Jan.; n. 3, 18 Jan.; n. 11, 15 March; n. 15, 12 May; n. 18, 3 May; n. 19, 10 May).

8. Lawalree, Lambinon, Demaret, and Lang, *Marie-Anne Libert.*

9. Malmédy remained part of Germany until after the First World War; it returned to Belgium following a 1920 plebiscite.

10. Although an oil portrait of Marie-Anne Libert was destroyed in the Christmas 1944 bombing of Malmédy (during the Battle of the Bulge), two other portraits have survived; one, in crayon, was in 1965 in the possession of Abbé Paul Libert, curé of Butgenbach (a postage stamp design was based on it); the other was bought by the Musée de la Vie Wallonne in Liège.

11. For instance, she is referred to only vaguely in Emile de Wildeman and Théophile Durand, *Prodrome de la Flore Belge* (Bruxelles: A. Gastaigne, 1898, 1907) and is omitted from their "Énumération complète de travaux publiés sur la flore belge." However, she is well documented in the *Biographie Nationale* (see n. 1), and Lawalree, Lambinon, Demaret, and Lang (*Marie-Anne Libert*) list seventy-six works published up to 1965 discussing or referring to her or her contributions.

12. The genera are Libertia C. Sprengel (1825) of the Iridaceae; Libertia Dumortier (1823) of the Lilaceae; Libertia Lejeune (1824) of the Graminae; Libertella Desmazières (1830) of the Melanconiales; Libertella Sprengel et Roumeguère (1880) of the Sphaeropsidales; and Libertina Höhn (1924) of the Melanconiales.

13. See C. Roumeguère, "Publications des Reliquiae," and P. A. Saccardo, *Reliquiae mycologicae Libertianae* (Toulouse: H. Montaubin, 1881), also published in *Revue Mycologique* (1881).

14. Marie-Anne Libert's library was sold in Brussels on 13 November 1871 by bookseller A. Bluff, 10 petit rue de l'Écuyer. The contents, known from a catalogue of sale, included works on botany, zoology, archaeology, and the classics; a number of flora; runs of botanical and general science journals; works on systematics; and many treatises on cryptogams.

15. Mme. E. Rousseau, "Madame J.-E. Bommer, née Élisa Destrée," *Bulletin de la Société Royale de Botanique de Belgique* 47 (1910): 256–61.

16. See G. D. Westendorp, *Herbier cryptogamique, ou collection des plantes cryptogames et agames qui croissent en Belgique* (Bruges: G. D. Westendorp and A. C. F. Wallays, 1845, 1859).

17. Jean Kickx, *Flore cryptogamique des environs de Louvain, ou, Description des Plantes cryptogames et agames qui croissent dans le Brabant et dans une Partie de la Province d'Anvers* (Bruxelles: Vandooren, 1835); Jean Kickx and Jean Jacques Kickx, *Flore cryptogamique des Flandres*, 2 vols. (Gand: H. Hoste, 1867); and Elias Magnus Fries, *Systema mycologicum*, 3 vols. (Lundae: Berlingiana, 1821–1832).

18. This also appeared as Élise-Caroline Bommer and Mariette Rousseau, *Florule mycologique des environs de Bruxelles* (Gand: Imprimerie C. Anncot-Braeckman and A. Hoste, 1884).

19. P. A. Saccardo, "Fungi belgici" in "Notae mycologicae," *Annales Mycologici* 3, no. 6 (1905): 507–10.

20. "Champignons," in *Expédition antarctique Belge: Résultats du voyage du S. Y. Belgica en 1897–1898–1899 sous le commandement de A. de Gerlache de Gomery: Rapports scientifiques publiés aux frais du gouvernement Belge sous la dirction de la commission de la Belgica: Botanique*, eds. Jules Cardot, E. de Wildeman, et al. (Anvers: J.-E. Buschmann, 1905.).

21. M. Beeli, "Madame Rousseau," *Naturalistes Belges. Bulletin Mensuel* 7 (1926): 18–20; H. Raab, "Bio- und bibliographischen Notizen," *Schweizerische Zeitschrift für Pilzkunde* 57 (1979): 68–69, 70; and F. A. Stafleu and R. S. Cowan, *Taxonomic Literature*, 2nd ed. (Utrecht, Antwerp: Bohm, Scheltema & Holkema, 1983), vol. 4, 942.

22. Saccardo, "Fungi belgici,"

23. John Hendley Barnhart, comp., *Biographical Notes upon Botanists*, 3 vols. (Boston: G. K. Hall, 1965), vol. 2, 429.

24. Esther Pohl Lovejoy, *Women Doctors of the World* (New York: Macmillan, 1957), 187.

25. Joséphine Th. Koster and Tera S. S. van Benthem Jutting, "Notice sur Madame Dr. A. A. Weber *née* van Bosse à l'occasion de son 90ième anniversaire," *Blumea*, supplement 2 (Dr. A. A. Weber-van Bosse Jubilee vol., 1942): 3–9; E. Ruge-Baenziger, "Lettre," *Blumea*, supplement 2 (1942): 10–11; Johanna Westerdijk, "Frau Dr Anna Weber-van Bosse, neunzig Jahre," *Blumea*, supplement 2 (1942): 12–14; Joséphine Th. Koster, "Some Preliminary Notes on the Algae Collection Weber-van Bosse," *Blumea*, 2 (1936): 229–39; M. J. Wynne, "Phycological Trail-Blazer no. 2: Anna Weber-van Bosse," *Phycological Newsletter* 30 (April 1994): 6–7; I. H. Burkill and M. A. C. Hinton, obituary for Max Carl Willem Weber, *Proceedings of the Linnean Society* (1936–1937): 218–19; and *Biological Abstracts* 21 (1947): 5049.

26. Access to university education in the Netherlands was granted to women in 1876 with passage that year of a higher education law. Girls were admitted to the Hogere Burger Scholen from the 1870s and to the gymnasia, which emphasized classical studies, from the 1880s; training in either of these prepared students for university entrance (see Hilary Marland, " 'Pioneer Work on All Sides': The First Generations of Women Physicians in the Netherlands, 1879–1930," *Journal of the History of Medicine and Allied Sciences* 50 (1995): 441–77, on 452.).

27. *Een Jaar aan Boord H. M. Siboga* (Leiden: E. J. Brill, 1904, 1905), trans. E. Ruge-Baenziger, *Ein Jahr an Bord I. M. S. Siboga* (Leipzig: W. Engelmann, 1905); and A. Weber-van Bosse and Jaap de Visser, *Een Jaar aan Boord H. M. Siboga* (Amsterdam: Atlas, 2000).

28. See *Oceanography: The Past*, eds. Mary Sears and Daniel Merriman (New York, Heidelberg, Berlin: Springer-Verlag, 1980).

29. *Jane's Fighting Ships 1930*, ed. Oscar Parkes (London: Sampson, Low, Marston, 1930), 367, 369.

30. Weber-van Bosse, *Jahr an Bord I. M. S. Siboga*, 161.

31. "Note préliminaire sur les résultats algologiques de l'expédition du Siboga; études sur les algues de l'Arch. Mal. III," *Annales du Jardin Botanique de Buitenzorg* 17 (1901): 126–41; (with M. Foslie) *The Corallinaceae of the Siboga Expedition* (Leyden: E. J. Brill, 1904—*Siboga-Expédition Monographie* 61, 1–110); "Sur deux nouveau cas de symbiose entre algues et éponges," *Ann. du Jard. Bot. Buitenzorg*, suppl. 3, 2 (1910): 587–94; "Notice sur quelques genres nouveaux d'algues de l'Archipel malaisien," *Ann. du Jard. Bot. Buitenzorg* 2e. s. 9 (1911): 25–33; and "Liste des algues du Siboga I–IV," *Siboga-Expéd. Monogr.* 59 (1913–1928): 1–533.

32. Ethel Sarel Gepp, *The Genus Halimeda* (Leiden: E. J. Brill, 1901); and Anthony Gepp and Ethel Sarel Gepp, *The Codiaceae of the Siboga Expedition, including a Monograph of the Fabellarieae and Udoteae* (Leiden: E. J. Brill, 1911). For Ethel Barton Gepp see Mary R. S. Creese, *Ladies in the Laboratory? American and British Women in Science, 1800–1900* (Lanham, Md.: Scarecrow Press, 1998), 37–38.

33. "Marine Algae, *Rhodophyceae*, of the *Sealark* Expedition, Collected by J. Stanley Gardiner," *Transactions of the Linnean Society* 8 (1913): 105–42; "The Percy Sladen Trust Expedition to the Indian Ocean, 1905, Marine Algae: *Rhodophyceae*," *Transactions of the Linnean Society* 16 (1914): 269–305; "*Rhizophyllidaceae* and *Squamariaceae*," in Frederik Børgesen, *The Marine Algae of the Danish West Indies*, 2 vols. (Copenhagen: B. Luno, 1913, 1920), vol. 2, 128–46; "Algues de l'expédition danoise aux îles Kei" (from Th. Mortense's Pacific expedition, 1914–16), *Videnskabelige Meddelelser fra Dansk Naturhistorisk Forening i Kjøbenhavn* 81 (1926): 57–155; "Algues: résultats scientifiques du voyage aux Indes Oriental Néerlandaises de L. L. A. A. R. R. le Prince et la Princesse Léopold de Belgique," in V. van Straelen, *Musée Royal d'Histoire Naturelle de Belgique: Mémoires* hors. série 6 (1932): 1–27.

34. Agatha Gijzen, *'sRyks Museum van Natuurlijke Historie, 1820–1915* (Rotterdam: W. L. and J. Brusse, 1938), 278.

35. G. A. Lindeboom, *Dutch Medical Biography: A Biographical Dictionary of Dutch Physicians and Surgeons, 1475–1975* (Amsterdam: Rodopi, 1984), 159. Bleeker was well known among European ichthyologists; his many publications included his nine-volume *Atlas Ichthyologique des Indes Orientales Néêrlandaises* (Amsterdam: F. Müller, 1862, 1878).

36. Access to university education in the Netherlands was granted to women in 1876 with passage that year of a higher-education law. Girls were admitted to the Hogere Burger Scholen from the 1870s and to the gymnasia, which emphasized classical studies, from the 1880s; training in either of these prepared students for university. During the twenty-one years

from 1879 to 1900 a total of thirteen women qualified in medicine from Netherlands universities (Marland, "Pioneer Work," 443).

37. A. Charlotte Ruys, M.D., in Cornelia C. de Lange, M.D., "Pioneer Medical Women in the Netherlands," *Journal of the American Medical Women's Association* 7 (1952): 99–101, on 101; Lindeboom, *Dutch Medical Biography,* 1134–35; E. Sluiter, obituary, in *Nederlandsch Tijdschrift voor Geneeskunde* 94 (1950): 365; and Marland, "Pioneer Work."

38. The first woman to qualify as a physician at a Dutch university was Aletta Jacobs (University of Gronigen, 1879). Jacobs (1854–1929) specialized in gynecology and pediatrics; she played a leading role in many branches of the women's movement. Eight years passed before medical qualifications were awarded to a second woman—Catherine van Tussenbroek, University of Utrecht, 1887—see Marland, "Pioneer Work." For an account of Jacobs's career see Aletta Jacobs, *Memories: My Life as an International Leader in Health, Suffrage, and Peace,* trans. Annie Wright, ed. Harriet Feinberg (New York: Feminist Press, City University of New York, 1996).

39. *Vergelijkende Asch-analyses,* doctoral thesis (Alkmaar: n.p., 1897).

40. Lindeboom, *Dutch Medical Biography,* 271.

41. de Lange's post-1900 publications include the following: "Zonnekuur en hoogetekuur bij chirurgische tuberkulose der kindern," *Nederlandsch Tijdschrift voor Geneeskunde* 2 (1909): 823–35; "Over pyelocystitis bij kindern, in het bijzonder bij zuigelingen," *Geneeskundige Bladen uit Klinick en Laboratorium vor de Praktijk* 14 (1908–1909): 233–76; "Nephritis haemorrhagica chromica cum hydroperitones," *Nederlandsch Tijdschrift voor Gneeskunde* 1 (1912): 810–14; "Infantile letale anaemie," *Nederlandsch Tijdschrift voor Gneeskunde* 1 (1912): 815–23; (with J. C. Schippers) "Familial splenomegaly; a clinical study," *American Journal of Diseases of Children* 15 (1918): 249–58; (with J. C. Schippers) "Ueber die 'spezifische Diurese' Politzers als Methode zur Funktionsprüfung der Nieren im Kinderalter," *Jahrbuch für Kinderheilkunde und physische Erziehung,* n.f., 89 (1919): 11–29; (with L. K. Wolff) ["Rat bite disease (Sodoku)"], *Nederlandsch Tijdschrift voor Geneeskunde* 65 (1921): 938–45; (with J. C. Schippers) "Verdauungsleukocytose und Verdauungsleukopenia bei Kindern," *Zeitschrift für Kinderheilkunde* 33 (1922): 169–83; and "Morbid anatomy in a case of diabetes with onset at the age of eight months," *American Journal of Diseases of Children* 31 (1926): 840–45.

42. De Lange's childcare books include the following: *De Hygiene van het oudere Kind* (Hengelo: Blenken, 1902); *De Geestelijke en lichamelijke Opvolding van het Kind* (Amsterdam: H. Meulenhoff, 1914); *Ziekteleer van den Pasgeborene* (Amsterdam: Scheltema & Holkema, 1944); and *Zieke Kinderen: Clinische voordrachten voor Artsen on Studenten,* 3 vols. (Amsterdam: Scheltema & Holkema, 1946).

43. W. Brachmann, a young physician in training, described the condition in 1916 but his case study was interrupted by his leaving for active duty in the First World War. Brachmann's report was rediscovered by John Opitz (University of Wisconsin School of Medicine) in 1963; Opitz recommended the designation "Brachmann-de Lange Syndrome" (BDLS)—see K. Patau, J. M. Optiz, and W. J. Dewey, "A multiple congenital anomaly in man presumably caused by a minute deletion in chromosome 3," *National Academy of Sciences* (autumn meeting, 12–14 Oct. 1964, Madison, Wis.); and J. M. Optiz, A. T. Segal, R. Lehrke, H. Nadler, "Brachmann/de Lange Syndrome," *Lancet* 2 (1964): 1019.

44. See Beth Fine et al., *Cornelia de Lange Syndrome: A Book for Families* (Collinsville, Conn.: Cornelia de Lange Syndrome Foundation, 1985).

45. Eleanor Shafer Elder, "A Sourcebook of Early Women Scientists," master's thesis, Louisiana State University, Baton Rouge, 1979, 67. Maarseveen's name does not appear in the Zurich University student Matriculation Register or in the available extensive excerpts from the list of women students at the Zurich Federal Polytechnikum; see Marianne Müller and Regula Schnurrenberger, "Die Philosophische Fakultät II" in *Ebenso Neu als Kühn: 120 Jahre Frauenstudium an der Universität Zürich,* Verein Feministische Wissenschaft, Schweiz (Zürich: Verein Feministische Wissenschaft Schweiz, Schriftenreihe, 1988), 153–76. Most of the women studying science or mathematics in Zurich in the 1890s were registered at the Polytechnikum.

46. Kerkhoven-Wythoff's post-1901 papers included the following: "Over de verwandering die de levende kracht van en zich vrig bewegend lichaam van onveranderlijke gedaante door het plotseling in rust brengen van en punt daarvan ondergaat" (on systems of curved surfaces), *Nieuw Archif voor Wiskunde* Amsterdam, s. 2, 5 (1902): 374–88; and (with Willem Mantel, et al.) "Waardebepaling van eenige bepaalde integralen" (on definite integrals), *Wiskundige Opgaven . . . Wiskundig Genootschap Amsterdam* 11 (1914): 381–83, 392–98, 419–23, 429–32.

Chapter 5

GERMANY: BAVARIAN LAKES,
BRAZILIAN FORESTS, A KITCHEN
IN BRAUNSCHWEIG

Thirty women authors of German birth or who were closely associated with Germany are listed in the bibliography. Their combined output of 105 papers makes them the fourth most productive national group in continental Europe between 1800 and 1901, as judged by publications indexed by the Royal Society; they follow the Russians, Italians, and French (see Figure 0-1b). This fourth place ranking is noteworthy considering that the German states were some of the last places in Europe to allow full matriculation of women at their universities. Only in 1900 did the first state (Baden) take this step, although several others soon followed (Bavaria in 1903 and Württemberg in 1904); the process was completed within a decade, the Prussian administration issuing the necessary decree in 1909.[1]

Apart from five papers published between 1860 and 1867 by botanist Johanna Lüders, all the German women's publications listed in the bibliography appeared between 1884 and 1901 (Figure 5-1). For the most part the authors were women who acquired their advanced training abroad, by independent study, or by private arrangement at German institutions. About 60 percent worked in the biological and medical sciences, their contributions forming more than 70 percent of the total German output. These were also the areas in which the first generation to be educated as regular students in their own country's universities found fewest impediments to entry.[2] Work in chemistry, physics, and anthropology/archaeology was also noticeable (Figure 5-2). Particularly outstanding as research scientists were zoologist Marianne Plehn, bacteriologist Lydia Rabinowitsch-Kempner, physicist Agnes Pockels, and archaeologist Johanna Mestorf. Chemist and social scientist Marie Baum also had a most impressive career, while biologists Maria Gräfin von Linden and Clara Hamburger, as well as traveler and naturalist Therese Prinzessin von Bayern, made creditable contributions to their chosen fields.

Biological and Medical Sciences

MARIANNE PLEHN[3] (1863–1946), now recognized as one of the cofounders of the field of fish pathology, was born on her family's estate of Lubochin, in the district of Schwetz, West Prussia, on 31 October 1863. She was the third child and the oldest daughter among the six children of gentleman farmer Anton Robert Plehn and his wife Johanna Dorothea (née Maercker), a woman remembered for her musical talents and devotion to the Protestant church. For many generations before Marianne's birth Plehns had lived in this region, which was part of Poland until the 1772 partition and again after the First World War. By the late eighteenth century they had begun to acquire sizeable landholdings; by the early nineteenth century there were so many branches of the family in the area that when Napoleon's army was marching through en route to Russia in 1812 the French had the saying, "Cette plaine est pleine de Plehn" (This plain is full of Plehns). A close-knit clan, they were very supportive of one another.

Marianne's father had studied science at Jena University but in 1860 settled on his Lubochin estate of 15,000 acres with an ancient manor house (enlarged in 1868), farm buildings, and an extensive wooded park. This estate, although later burdened with financial problems, remained in the family until the upheavals of the Second World War; only one sister lived on in the house after the parents' deaths in the late 1880s, but it continued to be an important part of the family's life, a favorite vacation place for Marianne, her brothers, and their friends.

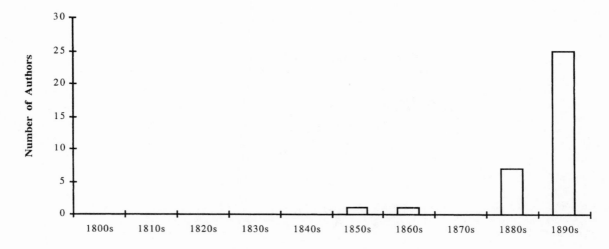

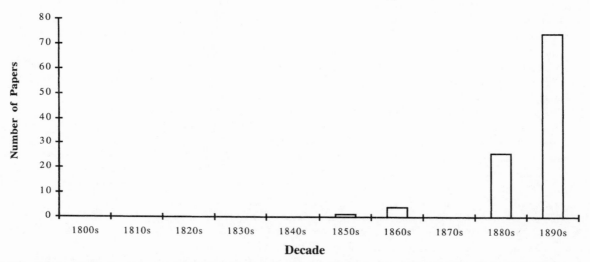

Figure 5-1.   German authors and papers, by decade, 1800–1900. Data from the Royal Society *Catalogue of Scientific Papers*.

In addition to managing his lands, Anton Plehn took his full share of public responsibilities, holding administrative posts both in his district and in the state capital of Königsberg (later Kaliningrad, Russia). He was one of the founders of the West Prussia Historical Society, the Naturalists' Society, and the Danzig (Gdánsk) Science Museum. The Plehn children were taught by private tutors, the boys then proceeding to the gymnasium in the nearby town of Marienwerder (now Kwidzyn). Marianne attended a girls' school for a year and, along with her sister Rose, spent a further year at another girls' school in Dresden. In 1888, after studies in Königsberg and Berlin, she took the women teachers' examination (*Lehrerinnenexamen*), which was then about as far as a woman could proceed academically in Germany without special arrangement.[4]

She had always been greatly interested in the scientific studies of her two older brothers[5] and, being also eager to see the world, decided to go outside of Germany to continue her education. In 1889, with financial help from her uncle, she went to Zurich, Switzerland. Within a year she had met the required academic entrance standards and enrolled in the Zurich Federal Polytechnikum, an institution closely tied to the university, which included in its divisions one that trained specialist teachers in the mathematical and natural sciences.[6] Her major subject was zoology, taught by the well-known and much respected Albert Lang (1865–1915). Because she aspired to the *Oberlehrer* examination she also studied botany and geology.

About this time she met future writer and activist in the socialist cause Ricarda Huch (from Braunschweig) and also chemistry student Marie Baum, a fellow North German (see p. 139). Spending their weekends together

a. Authors

b. Papers

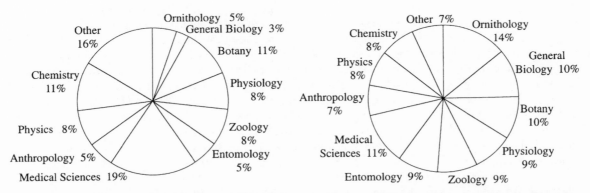

Figure 5-2.   Distribution of German authors and papers, by field, 1800–1900. (In a., an author contributing to more than one field is counted in each.) The sectors "Other" represent authors and papers in the following fields: psychology (authors 5 percent, papers 3 percent), astronomy (authors 5 percent, papers 2 percent), geology (authors 3 percent, papers < 1 percent), and geography (authors 3 percent, papers < 1 percent). Data from the Royal Society *Catalogue of Scientific Papers*.

on the lake or in the nearby mountains and sharing the same lodgings for one year, they developed close and lifelong ties. All were very active in women students' organizations, whose membership at that time included a notable number of remarkable young women who later became well known in public life.[7] Plehn, president of the Zurich All-Women Students' Association in 1892–1893, was later remembered by one of her fellow students as "a sensible, open person, the kind you can lean on, like a good tree" ("ein klüger, klarer Mensch von jener Sorte, an die man sich lehnen kann, wie an einen guten Baum").[8]

Receiving her teaching diploma (awarded with distinction) in August 1893, she began doctoral research in Lang's zoology and comparative anatomy laboratory that autumn. A year later, on Lang's recommendation, she was granted an assistantship in the zoological institute with an annual salary of 1,700 francs. The first woman to hold the post, she was well liked and respected by both men and women students. Her doctoral studies on polyclads (marine worms) brought back from German marine scientific expeditions led to the identification of three previously unknown polyclads that now bear her name: *Semonia maculata* Plehn, *Thysanoplana indica* Plehn, and *Thysanoplana marginata* Plehn. Because the polytechnikum did not then award the doctorate, her research was presented to the university that conferred the degree in January 1896; she was then thirty-three. Her main paper appeared in the *Jenaische Zeitschrift* later that year (see bibliography).

As assistant to Lang during the summer of 1896 she continued her polyclad research and brought out several additional papers.[9] However, although she greatly enjoyed Zurich life, she could barely support herself on her assistant's salary and so accepted an offer of a teaching post at a girls' gymnasium then being established in Bremen; Ricarda Huch's taking up an offer at the same gymnasium made the move from Zurich somewhat more palatable. The Bremen school was not as successful as had been expected and within two years Marianne Plehn was again looking for employment. She considered several possibilities, including going overseas. However, after a few weeks during the summer of 1898 at the Norwegian marine research laboratory at Bergen, she became an assistant at the newly established German Fisheries Association Biological Research Station for the Investigation of Fish Diseases, then housed in the zoological institute at Munich University. Arnold Lang gave her crucial help in getting the post, providing a strong recommendation.

She liked Munich, and the work. Within a short time station director Bruno Hofer (1861–1916), professor at the Munich Veterinary College and a man with great enthusiasm for the practical applications of zoology, turned over to her the examination of sick fish being sent in from all over the country. These came mainly from hatcheries. The fish-breeding industry was then expanding and acquiring greater and greater economic importance; organized scientific collaboration for disease control as well as overall research and development was much needed. To broaden her background Plehn took a university course in bacteriology, having been accepted as an "exceptional case." Her responsibilities soon expanded to helping with station organizational matters and carrying out poison investigations. Equipped with a portable microscope, she made field trips to deal with problems on site. These sometimes meant long journeys, but she valued the experience.

In 1900 the station became the Königliche Bayerische Biologische Versuchsstation für Fischerei (Royal Bavarian Biological Research Station for Fisheries) and moved to a new building. Another assistant and a technician were appointed to help her. In 1906 an urgently needed field station was established at Starnberg, about thirty miles south of Munich on Lake Starnberg. Here larger projects, including breeding, could be undertaken.

From 1899 Marianne Plehn published her findings on fish disease at an impressive rate, often bringing out several papers a year. Knowledge of fish physiology was limited at the time and very little information was available on diseases and methods for their prevention. Even by 1913 fewer than a dozen scientists in Germany and abroad were carrying out research in fish pathology. When Marianne Plehn began there was no established path to follow and often her research agenda was determined by the needs of the breeders supplying stock to lakes and streams. The work was pioneering; she was exploring new territory. Often the time factor was crucial, potential financial losses being considerable; she not infrequently worked under pressure and at times the station had to deal with criticism when diagnosis of a deadly disease and suggestions for its control could not be given quickly enough. Her most important tools were her microscope and her dissecting instruments.

Among her earliest studies was her investigation of raised scales in whitefish (1902). In 1903–1904 she identified the agent causing red disease in carp species, *Bacterium cyprinicida*, and demonstrated that more hygienic conditions reduced the problem. Also in 1903, her first investigation of protozoan parasites appeared when she described the previously unknown *Trypanoplasma cyprini* (now *Cryptobia cyprini* Plehn) she found in carp blood. In 1904–1906 she brought out five papers on stagger disease in Salmonidae (the salmon and trout group), work received with special interest by those in the field; her later investigations of the agent involved led her to the designation of a new genus, *Lentospora* (now *Myxobolus*).

Her first book, *Die Fische des Meeres und der Binnengewässer* (*Fishes of the Lakes and Inland Waters*), appeared in 1906. An illustrated work aimed more at a general audience than the specialist, it nevertheless brought her much notice.[10] Two papers in 1905 and 1908 reported studies on the trematode worm *Sanguinicola armata und inermis*; work on kidney disease followed in 1908, studies on liver disease in Salmonidae in 1909 and 1915. Her investigations of bacterial infections in Salmonidae continued over a considerable period; she examined in particular the bacteria causing epidemics of furunculoses (abscesses) and fluorescence (also open sores). Other work included studies of algal infections, especially in carp; two of the agents involved now bear her name—*Branchiomyces sanguinis* Plehn (the agent in gill rot), and *Nephromyces piscium* Plehn (now *Penicillium piscium* Plehn). In 1920 she published reports on two more skin and gill parasites—*Ichthyochytrium vulgare* and *Mucophilus cyprini* (the latter identified later as a rickettsia).

Marianne Plehn also investigated skeletal malformations in fishes and, over many years, worked on cancerous growths in fishes and other cold-blooded animals, a field that had previously received very little attention. Her demonstration that tumors in cold-blooded animals were analogous to similar growths in higher animals, including man, was followed with interest by scientists in all branches of cancer research; she spoke on the subject at an international conference on cancer in Paris in 1910[11] and later in Vienna. Two of her most important publications in the area were also brought out as short monographs soon after their initial journal appearance.[12] She was given honorary membership in the International Society for Cancer Research in recognition of her work.

Her second book, *Praktikum der Fischkrankheiten* (1924)[13], was a practical work for the use of hatchery managers, fishermen, fish biologists, and veterinarians. Although conceived by its publishers as an updating of the first book in the field, Bruno Hofer's 1904 *Handbuch der Fischkrankheiten,* it was soon realized that the field had changed so much in the intervening twenty years that a new approach was needed. Concentrating on the Salmonidae and Cyprinidae (salmon/trout and carp) of Central Europe, the major brood fish of the region, Plehn based her well-illustrated presentation on her practical experience acquired during twenty years at the Munich research station, her many consultations with workers in the field, and on lectures she had given at the Starnberg field research station. Within a year of its publication, the book became a standard work in fisheries literature and the basis of further studies on fish diseases; its illustrations, both drawings and photographs, were considered especially valuable and were used for decades.[14]

Although Marianne Plehn may not have considered her Munich position ideal, it did offer her an excellent research opportunity, perhaps the only one really available to her.[15] She often complained of overwork, and about the time of publication of her first book (1906) went through a period of depression even though her accomplishments were being recognized and acknowledged by her colleagues. In 1909 she was promoted to *Konservatorin* (curator) at the research station, and her annual salary raised to 3,000 M. Her greatest honor came in 1913 when she was named *königlich Professor* by Bavaria's last king, Ludwig III. She was one of the first German women scientists to receive the distinction and the first in Bavaria.[16] The title was purely honorary, however, not a university lectureship;[17] her teaching activities were limited to her course given at the Fisheries School at Starnberg. In 1927, when she was sixty-four, she was named *Hauptconservatorin* (chief curator) at the research station. She had for long been the foremost authority in her field, known all over Germany.[18] Having no competition and no need to put herself forward, she did her work quietly, not often appearing in public. Energetic, conscientious, and ambitious the *Fischdoktorin,* as she was known, was also cultivated and charming with a quiet sense of humor, her manner that of a Baltic lady of a bygone era. She retired on a small pension in 1928, after more than thirty years at the research station. In 1929 the Faculty of Veterinary Medicine at Munich University awarded her an honorary doctorate of veterinary medicine, the first and, at least up to 1994, the only one bestowed on a woman.

From 1909, when her salary increase somewhat alleviated the financial pinch she had struggled with over the preceding years, she lived in a two-room apartment in Öttingenstrasse in Munich. This accommodated her large library and her grand piano, and made practicable visits from her sister[19] and her many Zurich friends, among them Marie Baum and Ricarda Huch. Her friendship with Huch, who also lived in Munich for a period, remained close; she became "Tante Marianne" to Huch's daughter Marietta Ceconi. Although she frequently spent her vacations at her old Lubochin home, she also went to the Mediterranean and the coastal regions of Scandinavia. Later she was able to visit Italy. Until 1916, while Bruno Hofer was director of the research station, she always took her free time outside the summer holiday season; when her colleagues were away they relied on her to be at the station.

Marianne Plehn took no part in the women's movement (except by providing an example), although many of her friends did. She lived alone and gave her time and energy to her research and writing,[20] envying those among her friends who appeared to her to have the stamina to work harder than she did. Even official retirement did not mark the end of her research. Until 1939 she had a work room at the research station where she occupied herself with problems she had not had time for before, gave lectures and, as she had long done, put her considerable store of knowledge and experience at the disposal of her younger colleagues. Until 1942 she also worked on an expanded edition of her *Praktikum der Fischkrankheiten.* Although a harsh critic of Adolf Hitler, she was not forced to stop her activities at the station with the coming to power of the National Socialist Party. Her last publication, an overview of her studies on pancreatic necrosis in carp species, appeared in 1938.

With the outbreak of the Second World War in the autumn of 1939 and the departure of many of the staff for military service, she undertook to help with the daily management of the research station. By then, however, she was seventy-six and badly crippled by arthritis. She continued until the summer of 1943 when, too disabled to work further, she went to live with relatives in Grafrath, a quiet neighborhood outside Munich. The research station was destroyed by bombing in January 1944 and Plehn's city apartment six months later. She died on 18 January 1946 in her eighty-third year. Her urn was buried in the Munich Nordfriedhof and moved to a mass grave in 1970.

Marianne Plehn is commemorated in the names of three polyclads (see above) and twelve disease agents of fishes.[21] Although not all of her identifications have remained valid with the advent of new research methods and the accumulation of a vast amount of additional information, the tremendous breadth of her research on diseases of fishes is impressive by any standard and particularly for a woman of her time. Between 1896 and 1938 she published eighty-six papers and two books, thirty papers and her first book between 1900 and 1909, twenty-four more papers in the next decade. In addition, between 1898 and 1926 she brought out twenty-six reviews of work published in foreign journals, making in all 114 publications.[22]

Because of the turmoil at the end of the war, no obituaries were published at the time of her death. However, in 1963, on the 100th anniversary of her birth, a notice appeared in the *Allgemeine Fischerei-Zeitung,* a journal in which she had frequently published, celebrating her career and recognizing this remarkable woman as one of the founders of fish pathology.[23]

Although not a research scientist of the same standing as Marianne Plehn, MARIA GRÄFIN VON LINDEN[24] (1869–1936) also had a notable career. The first woman student at Tübingen University, von Linden was one of the first women to receive the title of professor at a German university. Her twenty pre-1901 journal publications constitute one fifth of the total contributions by German women listed in the Royal Society *Catalogue.*

Maria von Linden was born on 18 July 1869 in Schloss Burgberg, the von Linden family seat near Heidenheim in the Schwabischen Alps region of Württemberg, southern Germany. She was the second child and only daughter of Edmund von Linden and his wife Eugenie, a daughter of the family Hiller von Gärtringen, also of Württemberg. Of Catholic descent, originally from the Netherlands, the von Lindens had acquired their estates in southern Germany by the early nineteenth century. Gräfin Maria's forbears on both sides had a tradition of service to the state as privy councillors and military officers and had exerted considerable influence in diplomatic and military matters. Her father, after being invalided out of the military, occupied himself with the management of his estates.

As a child Gräfin Maria had the freedom of the woods and forest surrounding her home, and the lifelong interest in many branches of natural history that this experience awakened had a noticeable influence on her later professional work. From her mother she learned plant and animal names; fossils were a special interest. At age six she began her first formal instruction, provided by the village schoolteacher. At fourteen she went to the Victoria *pensionat* in Karlsruhe. The four-year curriculum then offered in girls' schools was not designed to prepare students for university entrance (that option not yet being formally available to women), but she had already made up her mind to work toward a doctorate,[25] if necessary by special permission.

Returning to her Burgberg home in 1887 and successfully defeating the efforts of her family to arrange a marriage for her, she spent four years studying on her own with guidance, particularly in mathematics and Latin, from a progressive-minded teacher at a boys' classical school. At the same time she carried out independent scientific work and began an enthusiastic correspondence with a number of specialists, including Tübingen geology professor Friedrich August Quenstedt. Her first paper, on geological deposits observed during boat trips she took along a local stream, appeared in 1890 when she was twenty-one; it was received with interest by workers in the field. Over the course of the next three years she brought out six biological articles, among which were her first papers in entomology. This was a field in which she continued to publish for many years, her later articles including a notable series on moths and butterflies.

With help from the principal of a *Realgymnasium* (semiclassical secondary school) in Stuttgart and with special permission from the Württemberg Minister for Church and School, Gräfin Maria took the *Reifeprüfung* examination in 1891, the first female candidate in Württemberg to do so. Although passing this test did not give her the automatic right to enter a university, it did effectively demonstrate her academic ability and competence. Even much patient effort on her behalf by her uncle, Staatsminister Joseph Freiherr von Linden, a diplomat of great tact who was not without influence, failed to win her formal admission. However, in 1892 she was accepted as a private student at Tübingen University by the professors she wanted to study with.

While taking a broad selection of basic courses including physics and mathematics, she spent as much of her time as possible in the zoological institute headed by Theodore Eimer, a convinced Lamarckian who rejected Darwin's theory of natural selection; Eimer had a considerable influence on her early scientific thinking. Presenting a dissertation on the evolutionary development of the form of the shell of the snail, she passed her oral doctoral examination in 1895, cum laude; her degree, *Scientiae Naturalis Doctor,* was awarded the following year. Until Eimer's death in 1899 she remained in Tübingen as an assistant at the zoological institute, carrying out further research on evolutionary development in gastropods and also in batrachians; five of her papers in this area were published between 1896 and 1900 (see bibliography). About this time she coedited the work *Vergleichend-anatomisch-physiologische Untersuchungen über das Skelett der Wirbeltiere* (1901), volume 3 of Eimer's three-volume work on the origin of species (*Die Entstehung der Arten . . .*). She also studied with physiologist Paul Friedrich Grützner and with physiologist and biochemist Carl Gustav von Hüfner. Von Hüfner's outstanding biochemistry teaching she was to find especially useful in her later investigations as well as in her ongoing research on moths and butterflies. In the latter work, starting from studies of wing color and pattern in 1898, she went on over the next eleven years to physiological investigations, examining particularly the metabolism of carbon dioxide by chrysalises and caterpillars.[26] The research twice earned her the Da-Gama-Machado prize from the French Academy of Sciences (1900, 1903).

In 1899, abandoning the blind alley of evolutionary research that had been a major interest until then, Maria von Linden took a post as second research assistant at the institute for zoology and comparative anatomy at Bonn University, moving to the medical faculty's institute for anatomy and biology in 1906. The same year she submitted a proposal for *habilitation* (formal admission to the faculty with the right to lecture), the second woman to do so at Bonn University.[27] Although the Bonn faculty was not overwhelmingly against her, the final decision came from the Ministry of Education in Berlin; the request was denied.[28]

However, in 1908 she became director of the newly established parasitology division of the university's hygienic institute, established for research, instruction, and the practical application of research results to medicine, land and forestry management, and fisheries. From the beginning von Linden's division was hampered by a shortage of funds, equipment, and adequate space, as well as by the fact that, because she was not allowed to lecture, her part in the instructional program was limited to demonstrations and laboratory work. Some of the difficulties were alleviated with a move to a new location in 1913 by which time the parasitology division had also been made an independent unit, concentrating on research.

Von Linden's work focused on current pressing problems in medicine and pathology, including tuberculosis in humans and a number of diseases, bacterial as well as parasitic, in cattle and other domestic animals and birds. More than 100 papers and several monographs reporting her findings appeared at regular intervals until the late 1920s.[29] Her investigations into a possible chemical treatment for tuberculosis using copper salts, conducted over the course of about ten years, were taken as far as initial animal studies; the results were disputed. As a sideline, she studied the antiseptic effect of copper in sterile bandages and suture materials, and with the collaboration of the firm of Paul Hartmann in Heidenheim was able to arrive at an acceptable product; "copper" catgut and "copper" bandages were successfully used in hospitals. The utility of copper salts for treatment of animal diseases and their effect on pathogenic bacteria were also interests. Her well-illustrated monograph on parasites and parasitic diseases, *Parasitismus im Tierreich* (1915), based largely on lectures she presented in university extension courses over many years, was intended for a general audience. It discussed the medical and economic consequences of parasitic infections in man and animals and provided fairly detailed information about the various kinds of parasites, their lifecycles, how they spread, what diseases they carry, and how they can be recognized and controlled.

In 1910, in recognition of her considerable research contributions, Gräfin Maria received a titular professorship, the first bestowed on a woman at Bonn University and one of the first in Germany.[30] By 1920 however, the state legislative assembly was moving to place the parasitology laboratory under more direct state financial control. Changes instituted in the late 1920s resulted in a downgrading of Maria von Linden's position from head of an independent unit within the university and the imposition of limits on the scope of her scientific work. In 1933, at the age of sixty-five, after thirty-four years at Bonn University, she was retired with a pension and official sanction for further research work in Switzerland (later changed to Liechtenstein). Her retirement probably resulted from the passage of the 1933 National Socialist government's law governing the reorganization of the professional civil service, administrative simplification being included as one of the grounds for removal from employment.

By then financial difficulties had required her to give up the family seat of Schloss Burgberg. Moving to Schaan, near Vaduz, Liechtenstein, Maria von Linden set up a small private laboratory where, with the cooperation of a Swiss doctor, she continued work on copper therapy for a few years. Suspected of possible political unreliability, perhaps because of her long and close association with the family of Jewish-German physicist Heinrich Hertz,[31] she was investigated by the German consulate; although in fact strongly opposed to National Socialism, she was judged harmless.

As a student Gräfin Maria had received financial help from the Allgemeine Deutsche Frauenverein (Union of German Women), a major source of funds for German women students from the mid 1880s.[32] Although committed to the cause of women's education and general advancement, she made her own contribution to the movement not as a campaigner but rather by providing an example of how a woman could effectively participate in academic scientific research. Indeed, feeling that her acceptance in the exclusively male university community depended on her remaining as inconspicuous as possible, she went so far as to adopt a masculine style of dress during her years in academia. Maria von Linden died in Liechtenstein on 26 August 1936, a month after her sixty-seventh birthday, from lung disease.

Two additional members of this group of early women research biologists were protozoa specialist Clara Hamburger, a staff member of the zoological institute at Heidelberg University for more than twenty years, and physiologist Margarethe Traube-Mengarini who did much of her work in Rome.

One of twin daughters of Jewish merchant Heinrich Hamburger, CLARA HAMBURGER[33] was born in Breslau (now Wroclaw) on 5 June 1873. After attending a Breslau city school for girls from 1880 until 1889 she continued her studies, taking further courses in science. In 1897 she entered Hermann Ludwig Cohn's plant physiology institute to complete training as a scientific illustrator, and for two years prepared drawings and related material for various scientific institutes and for research publications. At the same time, by special permission, she attended lectures at the university; a requirement for proficiency in Latin, a subject not regularly taught in girls' schools, she met with the help of private tuition. She concentrated on botany initially but then switched to zoology and studied for two years in the zoological institute under the guidance of Willy Kükenthal, a notable zoologist who, while he was in Breslau, carried out important work on whale embryology.[34] Hamburger served as his assistant for one semester. Her first publication (in *Anatomischer Anzeiger*, 1900) reported her microscopical examination of sections through teat tissue of horse and donkey embryos. A contribution to current research on the evolutionary development of the mammary organ in a range of mammals from pig through sheep and cow to man, it was undertaken at Kükenthal's suggestion. She concluded that the horse and donkey occupied positions between cow and man, as judged by the particular criteria used in the study.

In 1901 she moved to Heidelberg University in Baden, a state with a liberal social outlook and a progressive attitude toward education for women; within a year she was appointed to an assistantship in the zoological institute. Her work was carried out under the direction of Otto Bütschli (1848–1920), famous for his pioneering research in nuclear division processes and chromosomal behavior; his wide-ranging work in invertebrate zoology included studies of protoplasmic structure. Clara Hamburger's detailed investigation of the protozoan *Trachelius ovum* was published in 1903; she examined the exterior form and interior anatomy of this single-cell organism and its processes of conjugation and division.

After receiving her doctorate (3 March 1903) she stayed on as Bütschli's assistant at the zoological institute. In addition to helping students, looking after collections, and providing general assistance to Bütschli, she continued her own research on protozoa and brought out about one publication a year in the period before the First World War. Major contributions were two monographs, coauthored with her colleague Wolfgang von Buddenbrock, published in the series *Nordisches Plankton*. "Nordische Ciliata mit Ausschluss der Tintinnoidea," which constituted part 15 (1911) of the series, was essentially a handbook of northern ciliates—free-living, aquatic protozoans, so called for the threadlike processes, or cilia, that cover the exterior of the cell wall; the work presented descriptions, illustrations, and literature references for each organism. "Nordische Suctoria" appeared in part 16 (1913), which also included her shorter discussion of Flagellata.[35]

One of Clara Hamburger's early contributions of particular interest because of present-day commercial developments based on her findings is her 1905 paper "Zur Kenntnis der *Dunaliella salina*." First found in 1838 by Félix Dunal of Montpellier in the salt marshes of southern France, *Dunaliella salina* is now cultivated in brine ponds in a number of sun-rich countries as a source of ß-carotene, one of the essential growth factors in animals, which convert it to Vitamin A. Dunaliella is probably the most light-tolerant eukaryote that exists and the only photosynthetic organism that grows in salt brines, such as the Dead Sea and Great Salt Lake; ß-carotene functions in its photosynthetic (energy collecting) process.

Clara Hamburger's specimens came from the salt pits of Cagliari, Sardinia, Otto Bütschli receiving a vial of the water, colored brilliant red because of the presence of the flagellate, in early January 1905. At the time opinions differed about the classification of the organism.[36] Clara quickly realized that it did not, as some workers had thought, belong to the genus Chlamydomonas; she was of the opinion that it represented a new, as yet undetermined genus. By extremely careful observation using a good microscope and the various staining techniques then available, she was able to establish a detailed and by and large accurate picture of the inner structure, her one error being the location of the red oil drops (which contain the ß-carotene). She thought these were in the protoplast (the outer layer of cellular material), but later work established that they are confined to the chloroplast (the organelle which is the site of photosynthesis). As fate would have it, Bucarest scientist E. C. Teodoresco was also working at this time on Dunaliella, using specimens collected in the Romanian salt marshes; he published his findings first[37] and therefore has the honor of having his name associated with the organism. Hamburger read his paper in March 1905 and immediately decided to put into print the results of her own work, results she had arrived at over the course of only two months. She took pains to explain that, although she agreed with Teodoresco on many points, her observations were considerably more detailed, particularly those concerning internal structure. Indeed because Teodoresco had focused mainly on outer form and reproductive processes, Clara Hamburger's findings covered an area hardly discussed in the Romanian account and thus filled in major gaps in the description. The remarkable quality of her work has been stressed in a recent discussion of her 1905 paper.[38]

Over the course of several years she worked with Bütschli in the preparation for publication of his lectures on comparative anatomy, *Vorlesungen über vergleichende Anatomie*, a project he was persuaded to undertake by former students. She drew most of the illustrations for the section on protozoans in the volume that appeared in 1910. After Bütschli's death in 1920 she, along with Bütschli's former student F. Blochmann and her research colleague Wolfgang von Buddenbrock, brought out additional installments. Part IV, a section on digestive organs, *Vergleichende Anatomie der Metazoen: Ernährungsorgane*, to which she again contributed many drawings, was published in 1924; Part V appeared ten years later. Thereafter the publisher was required to dissolve all contracts with German Jewish authors, and the series was never completed.

In 1919 Clara Hamburger, one of the most notable of the early academic women in Baden, was considered for the title of professor; this was not granted by the government ministry concerned, although it was acknowledged that she merited recognition for her very creditable scientific work. The following year she received the official title of custodian of the collections and of the library of the Zoological Institute. When

Bütschli's private library was offered for sale to the institute after his death, it was she who made the acquisition possible; her donation of 5,000 goldmarks brought the available funds up to the required 18,000.

She gave up her post at the university in 1931, when she was fifty-seven, and not long after, because of National Socialist anti-Jewish legislation, fled the country. She and her twin sister went first to France where after some years they were arrested by the Vichy authorities and sent to Gurs, the detention camp established in 1939 in the locality of the same name about fifty miles from the Spanish border. Eventually released, they succeeded in crossing the Atlantic and settled in the United States where they had relatives. For a time Clara Hamburger lived in Berkeley, California, supporting herself as a seamstress. She died there in 1945 when she was about seventy-two.

MARGARETHE TRAUBE-MENGARINI[39] (1856–1912), one of the earliest university-trained scientists in this group, was born in Berlin on 6 April 1856, the daughter of well-known physiologist and pathologist Ludwig Traube. Married and widowed at an early age, she began in 1878 to study physiology with J. Moleschott at Rome University and was awarded a doctoral degree. She then returned to Berlin where she worked with Emil Dubois-Reymond whose recently established institute at Berlin University was known internationally as one of the foremost centres for physiological research. In 1884 she went back to Italy, having that year married Italian physicist and electrical engineer Guglielmo Mengarini, professor at Rome University.

Traube-Mengarini's research published in the 1880s and 1890s in German and Italian journals included work on fish physiology, particularly studies on the brain and swim bladder, and investigations on skin permeability (see bibliography). Later work at the Hygienical Institute of Rome University, some of it done jointly with Alberto Scala, focused on basic questions of membrane function. Biological transport processes and cell wall permeability were already areas of great research interest to people in several fields. Traube-Mengarini's work included studies of the permeability of cells to various ions, in particular the effects of isotonic salt solutions on protozoa and algae cells. She adopted a broad-based approach combining chemical and physical methods with biological techniques and she was well regarded in her field.[40] In social matters Traube-Mengarini was a strong supporter of equality for women in education and in professional opportunities. She died in Rome in 1912 when she was about fifty-six.

Among the other German women whose contributions to the biological and medical sciences are listed in the bibliography three were botanists—Lüders, Schwabach, and Widmer—three were naturalists—Princess Therese of Bavaria, Baroness Helene von Ulm zu Erbach (known especially for her ornithological writings), and Emma von Ramdohr[41]—and ten were physicians or medical research workers—Babo, Bäumler, Democh-Maurmeier, Glause, Herbig, Rabinowitsch-Kempner, Stier, Weiss, Wildenow, and Wolff.

JOHANNA LÜDERS,[42] née DEBOOR (1811–1880), whose special interest was cryptogamic botany, was born in Hamburg on 21 October 1811. In 1831 she married chief magistrate Peter Lüders of Glückstadt, Schleswig-Holstein, later adviser to the state government. On his retirement in 1851 they settled in Kiel and Johanna Lüders, at age forty, began to study botany with great energy and enthusiasm. She had the benefit of guidance from biologists at Kiel University, particularly botanist Nolte and plant physiologist Christian Hensen; Nolte helped her with local flora and Hensen taught her how to use a microscope.

Her contributions on mosses and algae to Rabenhorst's series *Kryptogamen-Flora*[43] were considerable. In addition, during the 1860s, she brought out several papers on diatoms and minute, mold-causing fungi (see bibliography). Among them were two lengthy reports published in 1866 and 1867 concerning her microscopic investigation of the development of the bacterium "*Vibrio lineola* Ehrb." and its close relationship with the spores of such fungi. These works were received with interest, not always free from criticism, by the botanical community. Until her health failed she followed developments in botany in general and in zoology and physiology as well. She died in Badenweiler, in the southern Schwarzwald, on 18 July 1880.

ELISE SCHWABACH,[44] née SALOMON (d. 1907) worked for many years in the botanical institute at the University of Berlin with Simon Schwendener. A specialist in plant anatomy and plant tissue research, Schwendener carried out notable work demonstrating the ability of certain specific tissues to confer mechanical stability to the plant body. This was also the area of Schwabach's first published work (1898), which reported studies of changes at the cellular level during the growth and development of the coiled-spring tendrils that support and anchor climbing plants, enabling them to sustain motion. The subject was one of much interest at the time, largely as the result of the publication eleven years earlier of Darwin's work on climbing plants.[45] Indeed the phenomenon of twist in both biological fibers and in thin elastic rods in general remains very much a topic of research.[46] Schwabach's subsequent papers, published between 1899 and 1902,[47] dealt with the movement of resin in conifer cells.

Active in social work in Berlin, Elise Schwabach was especially interested in helping homeless women and girls. A practical person with sound judgment and a clear view of what was needed, she took the initiative in founding a club where working women could find a safe place to stay. She died in April 1907, shortly after undergoing a major operation.

ELISE WIDMER[48] (fl. 1880s, 1890s), of Munich, carried out a notable study of European species of primula, or primrose, bringing out a monograph on the genus in 1893.[49] She was the niece and also the student of the eminent Swiss botanist Karl Wilhelm von Nägeli, a mid-century pioneer in cell division and plant physiology studies who taught in Freiburg and then Munich. It was at Nägeli's suggestion, and under his guidance, that the primula project was undertaken. Widmer's investigation was comprehensive, and included rare alpine species and intermediate forms; species, subspecies, intermediate forms, and hybrids were systematically described and their locations listed. Her 1889 *Flora* paper listed in the bibliography presented a small section of the findings.

THERESE, PRINZESSIN VON BAYERN[50] (1850–1925) was a daughter of the House of Wittelsbach, one of the most venerable of Europe's princely families, with an ancestral line that goes back to the tenth century. For more than 800 years Wittelsbachs ruled Bavaria and lands in the Rhine Palatinate as dukes, counts-palatine, electoral princes, and latterly, in the nineteenth and early twentieth centuries, as kings of Bavaria, although by Princess Therese's time the crown's political authority had been drastically reduced. The nineteenth-century Wittelsbach kings are perhaps now most widely remembered for the rich architectural and artistic legacy they left their country. Princess Therese, the only sister of Ludwig III, last king of Bavaria, made her more modest contributions in the realms of travel literature and studies in ethnography and natural history; her work on plant and animal geography was especially notable. Perhaps more than any of the other women scientists included in this survey Princess Therese stands out as a person bridging two very different worlds. Born into the old, privileged, nineteenth-century aristocracy, she was nevertheless in her scientific work a woman of the twentieth. The many writings she left would make possible a substantial study of her varied activities over the course of almost three decades; through them all there shines clearly her impressive vigor and energy. She was recognized with an honorary doctorate from Munich University and honorary membership in the Bavarian Academy of Sciences. Her story was dramatized in a 1998 German television documentary.[51] A glimpse of her remarkable career is offered here.

Born in Munich on 12 November 1850, she was the third among the four children and the only daughter of Luitpold, Prince Regent of Bavaria from 1886 until his death in 1912, a correct and unassuming man who, although his interests may have leaned more to hunting than to politics, was able and cultivated. The eccentric Ludwig II, Bavaria's *Märchenkönig* (fairy-tale king), on the throne from 1864 until 1886, was her first cousin (see Figure 5-3). Through her mother, Princess Auguste Ferdinande (Augusta) of Tuscany, also an Austrian archduchess, Therese was related to Queen Maria Theresa of Austria. Her immediate family circle was tight-knit; Therese was close to her three brothers, especially the youngest, Prince Arnulf, with whom she later shared strong geographical interests. After the death from tuberculosis of Princess Augusta in 1864 Therese, being the only remaining female member of the immediate family, managed the household for her father, help and advice being provided by her aunt. Prince Luitpold never remarried and led a somewhat withdrawn life. Therese is said to have been very like him in character, precise and conscientious but also self-willed, unconventional, and reserved, tending to avoid public appearances. From her mother she inherited great vitality, perseverance, and a strong will, along with a marked sense of purpose.[52]

Most of her education was provided by private tutors, though later she attended some public courses for ladies. She was a good student, endowed with the Wittelsbach artistic bent and aptitude for languages; over time she became fluent in twelve, both spoken and written, including modern Greek and Russian, which she learned in company with her brother Arnulf. She had a special liking for mathematics and a tremendous interest and curiosity in a whole range of natural sciences. Foreign lands, their peoples, and patterns of human culture in general were subjects that early caught her attention, sparking her intense desire to travel and see for herself distant places and other ways of life. Physically strong, she enjoyed swimming, bicycling, and long mountain walks, pursuits that undoubtedly built up the stamina she later needed in her travels.

Starting in 1871 with a visit to Italy and Greece, she made frequent journeys, exploring throughout Europe and in North Africa, the Middle East, and the Americas; she crossed the Atlantic several times, visiting Brazil in 1888, North America and Mexico in 1893, and vast stretches of South America in 1898. She took pains to be well prepared, studying each country or region, the land and its people, their languages, history, and literature, before she set out.

Kings of Bavaria

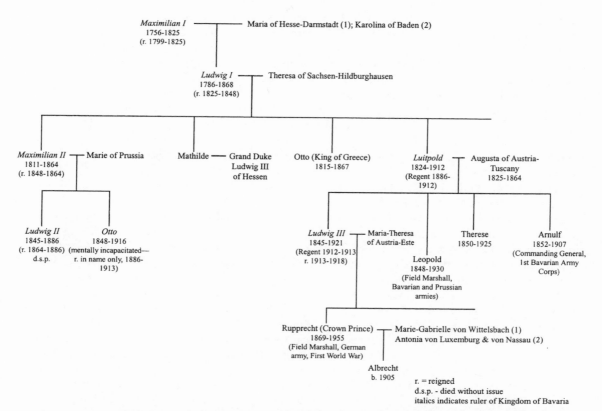

Figure 5-3.   Part of the family tree of the House of Wittelsbach, showing Therese von Bayern's immediate ancestors.

Her memoir *Ausflug nach Tunis* (*Excursion to Tunis*) appeared in 1880, but she brought out her first major published work in 1885, *Reiseeindrück und Skizzen aus Russland* (*Impressions and Sketches from Russia*), a 600-page detailed and very interesting account, dedicated to her aunt Marie, the Queen Mother, of a long exploratory journey through European Russia with a small party of companions in the late summer of 1882. Following ten years of study of the Russian language and peoples, this trip was the fulfillment of a long-held desire to see the Slavic lands. From Moscow, reached by rail from Vienna via Warsaw, she went to the Upper Volga region of Yaroslav and Kostroma. In Nizhniy-Novgorod she visited the annual summer fair, an event that attracted traders from everywhere from China to Britain as well as from all corners of the huge and varied Russian domains. Although Moscow and St. Petersburg with their art and architectural glories were carefully explored, perhaps the most interesting part of her book described her journey south from Moscow through the lands of the Don Cossacks. She wrote of the flora and fauna of the region, the already important Don basin coalfields, the wine industry, and the German settler colonies; in the Crimea she found much of interest in the Greek merchant communities and the then still very oriental character of parts of the Khanate, especially the Tatar capital of Bakhchisaray. Reaching Odessa by steamer from Sevastopol, she made a further trip north to Kiev (where a current problem concerning Jewish agricultural colonies in the region attracted her attention) and then went home via Lemberg (L'vov) and Krakow.

Ueber den Polarkreis (1889) described a journey to northern Norway in the summer of 1881. This expedition "auf das Gebiet der Mitternachtssonne," also the fulfillment of a long-held wish, was in large part the result of Princess Therese's special interest in Arctic flora and the life of the nomadic Laplanders of the northern tundra. Like her other early works the book, illustrated with her own sketches, was brought out under the pseudonym Th. v. Bayer.

Before the decade of the 1880s was over she was turning her attention to the tropics, the region where she was to carry out the work that resulted in most of her natural history reports. *Meine Reise in den Brasilia-*

nischen Tropen (1897) presented a diary-form record of her experiences during four months in Brazil in 1888. She went, she explained, to discover for herself what life in the tropics was like and to pursue her interests in ethnography and plant and animal geography.[53] Her sketch of Brazil's imperial court adds a note of unusual interest to her account because she saw here the end of an era; within a year this court had gone, swept away by the revolution that established the republic. Princess Therese was to live to witness a similar fate overtaking her own family three decades later. The following few paragraphs offer a summary of her 500-page *Reise*—the story of a most remarkable and enterprising undertaking for a woman of her time.

Traveling on the Liverpool steamer *Manauense* from Lisbon, Princess Therese's party arrived at the mouth of the Amazon on 25 June 1888. She had three companions—a servant (*Diener*) trained in taxidermy, a reliable lady of the court, and a *Kavalier* who could be depended on to protect the group. Still on the *Manauense* they proceeded upriver, threading their way through the islands of the estuary and on for about 1,000 miles through the rain forest to the inland port and trading center of Manaus on the Rio Negro, their starting point for further expeditions. Exploring up the Rio Negro by open launch, they observed and collected plants and animals, including monkeys, birds, snakes, and insects, especially butterflies, the area being exceptionally rich in lepidopterous species. With the help of their half-Spanish, half-Indian guide who spoke fifteen Indian dialects, they made the acquaintance of a number of native peoples and sometimes lodged overnight in native huts. Bargaining for ethnological materials brought them spears, barbed sticks, darts with iron tips, and beautiful long, wooden-tipped arrows, a rich collection to which they added pottery and wooden and carved utensils bought in Manaus.

From the Amazon they traveled down the coast on a Brazilian steamer to Rio de Janeiro, taking with them their sizeable collections, including the plants and live animals. Calls at port cities en route, São Luis, Recife, and Bahia (now Salvador) among others, provided opportunities for further observation and collecting in a variety of natural environments. From Rio de Janeiro they went north to the Campos country in the province of Minas Geraes, a spectacular railway trip of more than 200 miles through high mountains. Of special interest to Princess Therese were the rich mineral resources of this region. She made a considerable collection of geological and mineral specimens and visited the School of Mines in Ouro Preto, an institution that provided free education for mining engineers.

She and her party also explored the hinterland of Vitória, the capital of Espirito Santo province, a port city some 300 miles north of Rio de Janeiro. Their 150-mile trip by boat, canoe, and horseback took them in a half-circle, northwest from Vitória along the Rio Santa Maria, west and north across hilly country to the Rio Doce, and back to the coast along the latter. Camping in tents throughout the trip, Princess Therese continued her energetic collecting of plants and animals and made many contacts with native people, a number of whom she photographed.

Throughout her travels she took every opportunity to study collections in local museums and botanical gardens, particularly the large and varied ethnological, anthropological, paleontological, and mineral collections in the National Museum in Rio de Janeiro. Although she traveled incognito, her identity eventually leaked out and so she was invited to visit the royal family at their palace in Rio de Janeiro and also at their residence in Petropolis about forty miles to the north. A final trip south by train to the rich province of São Paulo took her party through one of Brazil's important coffee-growing regions; the country already produced half the world's coffee supply. By late October they were back in Europe. Although some of their tropical birds died during their twenty-three-day Atlantic crossing, their collections of both natural history materials and ethnological artifacts were sizeable.

The nine-year lapse between the end of the expedition and the publication of her account was due largely to her time being taken up by the lengthy process of analysis of the collections. Further work on the ethnological material took her back across the Atlantic in 1893, when she visited many Indian tribes from Canada through the western United States to southern Mexico.

A second South American travel book, her two-volume *Reisestudien aus dem westlichen Sudamerica* (1908), again illustrated with her own sketches and photographs, described her five-month trip to the West Indies and western South America, the most ambitious and the most rugged and demanding of all her expeditions. Again traveling incognito with three companions,[54] she left Bordeaux in late May 1898 on the steamer *Labrador* bound for Guadeloupe in the Lesser Antilles. Proceeding down the island chain, they called at Trinidad before going west along the Venezuelan and Colombian coasts to Barranquilla at the mouth of the Rio Magdalena; here sizable entomological collections were made. After exploring a considerable length of the Magdalena valley (for the most part by river steamer) Princess Therese proceeded into the Colombian interior, investigating the high country of the Cordillera and the tableland of the Bogota region. Rich collections of insects, plants, and animals, including freshwater fishes, were made in essentially all the zones visited and much anthropological material acquired in the high tablelands. Although train and steamer transportation was used whenever available, in many areas the party traveled by horse or mule; help was obtained from local inhabitants for the long rides through often very rugged country.

One of the major goals of the expedition was the collecting of Andean flora from the mountains of Ecuador and the inter-Andean valleys. Explorations started in Guayaquil (reached by steamer from Panama). Although very significantly handicapped by altitude sickness in the high country, the party nevertheless succeeded in amassing substantial collections both botanical and zoological, climbing as high as the 12,000-foot Chuquipoquio Pass and approaching to within a few miles of Mt. Chimborazo.

In Peru, which they reached by coastal steamer service from Guayaquil to Callao, the most important of Princess Therese's collections were probably her archaeological and anthropological materials from that country's rich heritage. Included were ancient skulls and a mummy she unearthed herself from a prehistoric graveyard near Ancon, north of Lima. A somewhat nerveracking journey inland from Lima to La Oroya on the world's highest railway took the party into the high Peruvian Andes, lengthy stops at small stations en route permitting collecting. A swing inland from Mollendo on the southern Peruvian coast across the Andes to Lake Titicaca and on through La Paz, Bolivia, to the high, bleak plateau region, or *puna,* brought them close to the last stage of their western journeys. Much of the route was covered by slow train, along the line still used by the present railway, the last stretch being through the Atacama Desert of northern Chile. In Bolivia as in Peru the anthropological collections made were of special interest, particularly the fine woven articles, ceremonial vessels, and musical instruments. Passage by coastal steamer to Valpariso followed by a train journey across the Andean divide and the Argentine pampas took them to Buenos Aires, their point of departure for the return trans-Atlantic voyage.

Princess Therese's last major literary work was probably the editing and publishing of the diaries and letters of her brother Arnulf, recording his hunting expedition in the Tien Shan mountains of south central Asia on the border between the Kirgiz republic and China's Sinkiang province; the prince died in 1907 on the return journey. *Des Prinzen Arnulf von Bayern Jagdexpedition in den Tian-Schan* appeared in 1910 when she was sixty.

Her broad background and her aptitude for detailed observation made her Central and South American natural history studies interesting and valuable to the scientific community. The articles listed in the bibliography reported several large collections of plants and animals, which included new material. Two papers discussed freshwater fishes from Mexican lakes,[55] two reported insect collections, one dealt with South American molluscs, and two presented botanical work. Having many contacts in the scientific community throughout Germany, Austria, Sweden, and Switzerland, she had expert help when needed with identifications for both her plants and animals. However, she did much of the determining and arranging of her collections herself, frequently visiting the Munich zoological institute's museum, a good one for its time, to compare her material with its holdings. Indeed she was a regular visitor at the institute, attending many lectures and actively participating in question sessions.[56]

Princess Therese's fish collections came from three lakes in Mexico's high interior tableland, all of them at an altitude of over 6,000 feet, which she visited during her second trans-Atlantic trip in 1893. Her vivid descriptions of these lakes and the surrounding countryside as it was more than 100 years ago make interesting reading.

She and her party made a fairly detailed exploration of Lake Texcoco, then about three miles from Mexico City, a shallow lake rapidly filling up with sand and refuse and increasing in salinity. Her Texcoco fishes were obtained from native women selling them in the city market. The other two lakes from which she obtained specimens were Cuitzeo (about 120 miles northwest of Mexico City) and Pátzcuaro (some fifty miles southwest of Cuitzeo), both in the state of Michoacán. She was able to reach the area via the Mexican state railway, a western branch of whose main Mexico City–Laredo line had only the previous year been completed as far as the old Spanish colonial town of Pátzcuaro. Lake Cuitzeo, the second biggest of the Mexican lakes, high in salt content, with no outlet, she described as a desolate place, not often visited. Only a few miserable native villages dotted its shores and she found no evidence of fishing activity, although she did see one canoe—a real Indian dugout. There was a wealth of bird life, however, with geese, ducks, and pelicans. At Lake Pátzcuaro, where she found accommodation in a hacienda on the lakeshore, she was able to make direct contact with Indian fisher people. This beautiful, much indented lake surrounded by picturesque, volcanic mountains, with potable if slightly salty water, provided a habitat for many birds, frogs, snakes, and fishes. Indian fishermen using canoes supplied her with specimens and she augmented the collection with additional species (some specimens coming from Lake Cuitzeo) bought at the Pátzcuaro town market. A day-long horseback ride to the west produced little of zoological interest but she collected some insects (spiders, butterflies, and caterpillars) in the Pátzcuaro area.

Princess Therese's 1894 preliminary communication described the four fish species in her collection that were new to science; her 1895 paper gave detailed descriptions of eight. They belonged to three genera— Algansea (of the Cyprinidae family—carp) found only in the freshwater lakes of Central Mexico; Characodon (of the family Characodontidae) also restricted to the highland waters of Mexico; and Chirostoma (of the Antheridinidae family—"silversides") eighteen species of which are found in the Mexican lakes. Those reported as species new to science were listed as *Characodon Luitpoldii, Atherinichthys albus,* and *Atherinichthys grandoculis,* all from Lake Pátzcuaro, and *Atherinichthys brevis* from Lake Cuitzeo.

The insects collected by Princess Therese in South America in 1898 and discussed in her two 1900 papers (see bibliography) included new species and varieties; new localities were recorded as well. She studied in particular myriapods (one new species, identified as *Spirostreptus baranquillinus* Attems), arachnids (scorpions and spiders; seventeen species, including a new variety identified as *Euophrys decorata* C. L. Koch), Orthoptera (twenty-six species including two new ones), and what were then classed as *Neuroptera odonata* (dragonflies and their allies; twenty-three species, four new). By far the greater part of the insect collections came from Colombia, particularly the Barranquilla region.

Her contributions on the flora of the West Indies and South America appeared in supplements of *Botanisches Centralblatt* in 1902 and 1905 and were also published independently.[57] Here she described her collections of 429 species (ninety-eight families) assembled from locations in the Caribbean and throughout the length of South America—from Guadeloupe, Martinqiue, Trinidad, Venezuela, Colombia, Ecuador, Peru, Bolivia, Chile, and Argentina. Eleven of her specimens were previously unknown. Her listing of plant communities throughout this vast region, together with her accurate records of the altitudes at which she found them, was considered a particularly valuable contribution to plant geography, a field of much interest to German botanists at the time; her discoveries of many intermediate locations in Venezuela and Peru were also important. The main plant list, occupying ninety pages in the 1902 *Botanisches Centralblatt* supplement, covered a variety of both cryptogams and phanerogams.

Princess Therese's honorary membership in the Bavarian Academy of Sciences came in 1892, the first given to a woman; the same year she became an honorary member of the Munich Geographical Society. Her 1897 honorary doctorate from Munich University was also the first awarded to a woman. She was a corresponding member of the Berlin Entomological Society.

She lived through the hardships of the First World War and the subsequent political upheavals that brought the end of the Wittelsbach dynasty; her brother was removed from the throne of Bavaria in 1918 and a republic established. Most of the war period she spent at her summer residence of Villa Amsee in Lindau, on the southeastern shore of Lake Constance near the Austrian border. Here she provided accommodation for a small hospital for wounded soldiers and, despite her freely acknowledged deficiencies in the domestic arts, took her share in the work of caring for the patients.

Her friend and fellow naturalist the Swiss psychiatrist Auguste Forel left a description of her in her later years:

> In October 1919 we had a visit from the Princess Therese of Bavaria, the sister of the now dethroned king, Ludwig III. She was in Lausanne, and came with her faithful companion, Countess Deym. We were old acquaintances, and it gave me great pleasure to show her my collection of ants from tropical America which I had dedicated to her, or which she herself had collected. We were greatly moved by the spectacle of this old lady—humble, learned, and aristocratic—always gay and courageous, despite the misfortunes of her family. She seemed to feel quite at home in our modest dwelling. . . . In her love for the natural science, Therese of Bavaria has never loved or dreamed of fame. She loved the virgin forest, the living animals and plants in their natural surroundings.[58]

Even in her last years she was never idle. In addition to continuing her writing she occupied herself with the care and improvement of her Lindau parkland and the cultivation of rare trees. Princess Therese died at the Villa Amsee in Lindau on 19 September 1925, two months before her seventy-fifth birthday. Her rich and important collection of more than 2,000 anthropological and ethnological articles from native peoples of the Americas, initially held in private royal museums, is now in the Munich Volkerkundemuseum; other materials went to Bavarian state natural sciences collections. A tropical flowering shrub that she discovered was later named *Macairea theresia* (genus *Melastoma*).

HELENE VON SIEBOLD, BARONIN VON ULM ZU ERBACH (1848–1927),[59] notable for her large contribution of fourteen pre-1900 papers on topics related to birds (see bibliography), was also of Bavarian ancestry. She was the second child and elder daughter among the five children of Philipp Franz von Siebold (1796–1866) and his wife Helene von Gagern (1820–1877).

The von Siebolds had a long tradition of service in the field of medicine. Indeed the family played such a prominent role in medical education in Würzburg from about the middle of the eighteenth century that the University of Würzburg's medical faculty was humorously referred to as "Academia Sieboldiana."[60] As a young physician in the service of the Dutch government,[61] Philipp Franz von Siebold spent six years in Japan at the Dutch trading settlement near Nagasaki in the 1820s, a time when the islands were still virtually closed to the outside world. The studies he carried out and the natural history, art, and ethnological collections he assembled (coupled with those from a later stay) are renowned. Widely considered the most important European scientist to have visited Japan at that early period, von Siebold is said to have been the "scholar who almost single-handedly put Japanese studies on the European academic map."[62]

Helene von Siebold was born on 27 September 1848 at Boppard, about ten miles south of Koblenz. The family home was a former Franciscan property, the monastery of St. Martin, that Philipp Franz von Siebold had partially rebuilt and developed, establishing an oriental garden in the grounds. Like her siblings, Helene was baptized into the evangelical faith. In 1853 the von Siebolds moved to Bonn, where they lived for eleven years before again moving, this time to Würzburg, Philipp Franz von Siebold's birthplace. Helene received a good education; her later writings suggest that she had at least a working knowledge of several European languages and an acquaintance with the classics. A strikingly handsome young woman with long dark hair, she married Maximilian, Freiher von Ulm zu Erbach (1847–1929) in 1871. From then on her home was Schloss Erbach, an ancient mediaeval fortress with drawbridge and towers surrounded by hunting forests, a few miles southwest of Ulm in the upper Danube valley; the castle had been in the possession of her husband's family for 500 years.

Much of Baroness Helene's work concerned the preservation of the part of her father's archives that came to her, a considerable undertaking in which she had the full collaboration of her husband. Her special interest was birds. Her articles which appeared in the *Mittheilungen* of the Vienna Ornithological Society between 1884 and 1891 included lists of both permanent bird residents of the Württemberg high country around Erbach and the migrant species she observed there during winter and spring months. She also wrote on various aspects of the domestication of birds, kept her own poultry yard, and was interested in the introduction of new or less common breeds; she was one of seventeen distinguished contributors to the work on systematic poultry raising compiled by Bruno Dürigen,[63] supplying material on Japanese varieties. Several of her journal communications were accounts of bird life in the Japanese islands based on her father's observations and collections; water birds were a particular interest—geese, swans, and ducks, including the miniature mandarin ducks noted for their bright plumage. She examined the place of birds in Japanese art and wrote in some detail about falconry in Japan, still a popular sport in the nineteenth century among the country's nobility, although no longer in fashion in Europe. Her last paper reported a study that traced the place of the cuckoo in historical works on ornithology from the classical legends to the seventeenth century.

Baroness Helene died in Esslingen am Neckar on 4 July 1927 in her seventy-eighth year. Because she had no children, her collection of the von Siebold archives passed to her sister Mathilde's son, Alexander von Brandenstein-Zeppelin.

Among the ten medical women listed in the German section of the bibliography—Babo, Bäumler, Democh-Maurmeier, Glause, Herbig, Rabinowitsch-Kempner, Stier, Weiss, Willdenow, and Wolff—all except Wolff are known to have taken some or all of their training at Swiss universities.[64] These ten make up less than half of the women of German birth or close association who qualified as physicians (or, as in the case of Rabinowitsch, received basic training for medical research) before 1901 outside Germany, mainly in Zurich and Bern.[65] The others, several of whom had notable careers,[66] do not appear to have published before 1901 in scientific journals indexed by the Royal Society.

Of the group, the most outstanding as a research scientist was undoubtedly bacteriologist LYDIA RABI-NOWITSCH-KEMPNER[67] (1871–1935) who, by the early years of the twentieth century, was known internationally for her research on tuberculosis and her considerable contributions in the field of public health. A left-leaning liberal in general outlook at the time when the first of the middle-class women's movements was coming to its peak of activity (the decades around 1900), Rabinowitsch was much involved in the politics of women's rights and family health issues, particularly the pressing problems of high infant mortality and the health of working women.

Born on 22 August 1871 in the garrison town and trading center of Kovno (now Kaunas), Lithuania, when the country was part of imperial Russia, Lydia Rabinowitsch was the youngest of the nine children of brewery owner Leo Rabinowitsch and his wife Minna (née Verblunsky). The family belonged to the city's polyglot Jewish community, strongly influenced by the close connections with neighboring Prussia; Jewish merchants conducted much of the city's trade and the Jewish community dominated cultural life. Thanks to the prosperous state of the brewing business, several of the Rabinowitsch children received a university education despite the accidental early death of the father. The pogrom of 1881 following the assassination of Tsar Alexander II inevitably led to greater cultural isolation of the Jews, but at the same time the stepwise russification process that was instituted early in Alexander's reign and that involved the establishment of new state schools and gymnasia brought marked educational benefits. Lydia Rabinowitsch and her sisters attended a public elementary school and then the Russian girls' gymnasium, for which fees were required. Although this school prepared girls for the teaching profession rather than university entrance, she received a solid secondary-level education with a good grounding in a range of sciences as well as in the classics and modern languages, adequate background for further study in Western Europe.

In 1889, at the age of eighteen, with her mother's encouragement, she went to Switzerland and enrolled in the philosophical faculty at Bern University. She was one of many Russian students there at the time, a considerable number of them Jewish. The heavy involvement of Jewish intellectuals in the ongoing Russian revolutionary movement had resulted in severe restriction of their opportunities for higher education at home. Further, steady and dependable university-level education for all women was then hard to find in Russia.[68] Little is recorded about the extent of Lydia Rabinowitsch's participation in the life of the large Russian colony in Bern but, given her later activities, she would hardly have been unaware of her compatriots' lively interest in political and social questions, including women's issues. In Bern there were also many students from other countries, among them a few young women from the United States.

In the gymnasium teacher-training program where she was initially enrolled, she studied German language and literature and a broad range of science subjects as well as pedagogy. Botany became a special interest and she had classes with Ludwig Fischer, professor and director of the state botanic garden, and with his son and successor from 1894 mycologist and phytopathologist Eduard Fischer. Following the common practice of spending one's student years at more than one university,[69] she moved to Zurich in 1891. There she continued to work in botany and also studied zoology with Arnold Lang. As in Bern she lived in a student community acutely aware of and indeed already involved in some of the major social and political changes then taking place in Europe. Among her fellow women students in Zurich were a number of people who later became leaders in their chosen areas of endeavor; they included zoology student Marianne Plehn (p. 116) and law students Anita Augspurg (1857–1943), later very prominent in the women's movement in Germany, and Rosa Luxemburg (1864–1919), future socialist politician. Rabinowitsch returned to Bern in 1893 to specialize in botany, working with fungi and yeasts and developing microscopic technique under the guidance of Eduard Fischer. Her dissertation on yeasts was presented in 1894 (see bibliography). A contribution to the systematics and development of several members of the Basidiomycota, the topic was initially suggested to her by Ludwig Fischer.

Immediately after receiving her doctoral degree from Bern (1894, summa cum laude) she went as an unpaid student trainee to the recently founded Royal Prussian Institute for Infectious Diseases in Berlin headed by Robert Koch (now the Robert Koch Institute).

Koch (1843–1910), the leader of the German school of bacteriology and the man often regarded as the chief founder of the field, was already widely known for his pioneering work of the 1870s and 1880s which identified the disease agents of anthrax, tuberculosis and cholera.[70] His findings, which made abundantly clear the fundamental importance to medicine of bacteriological research and brought the new field into prominence, also pointed the way to a great many new areas of investigation, including immunity studies, toxin investigations, and vaccine therapy. Lydia Rabinowitsch thus had the good fortune to enter an emerging field at a time when it had not yet acquired the rigidity of a long-established discipline but was already recognized as having tremendous potential. Under Koch's vigorous and dynamic leadership the institute in Berlin, the city that was then probably the center of European scientific life, became a magnet that attracted students and research workers from many countries. As his assistant Rabinowitsch was at the focal point of the activity, and the training and experience she received in techniques of modern bacteriology (an area Koch pioneered with his introduction of plate culture and agar surfaces) provided the sound base on which she built a lifetime of outstanding work.

The first and for a period the only female scientist at the institute, Lydia Rabinowitsch initially carried out studies involving basic investigations of types of thermophilic bacteria in earth and water samples from sites around Berlin. These were followed by work on disease-causing yeasts including animal pathogens, some of them associated with materials used in brewing and wine production. All the while she was experimenting with clean culture preparation techniques and modifications of staining procedures needed for microscopic examinations. Results appeared in two papers published in 1895 (see bibliography).

In September 1895 she left Koch's institute for Philadelphia, Pennsylvania. Why she went is not clear, although she may have needed to find a salaried position. Opportunities for further education and professional work in medicine and related areas were in general more readily available in the United States than in Germany, and she might have heard of promising openings thorough American contacts made in Switzerland. Introducing herself into Philadelphia scientific and medical circles by attending a course in bacteriology at the Laboratory for Hygiene at the University of Pennsylvania (a course covering material that must have been very familiar to her), she applied for the position of head of the bacteriological laboratory to be established at the Woman's Medical College of Pennsylvania, the oldest school of medicine for women in the United States. Selected from a field of three (the other two were male medical doctors) at a salary of $500 for the seven-month academic year, she started in December 1895; formally her position was demonstrator in bacteriology in the department of pathology and bacteriology. This appointment of Rabinowitsch, a student of Koch, constituted a milestone in the advancement of the training of women physicians in America. Further, it put the Woman's Medical College of Pennsylvania at the forefront of the transition then taking place in American medicine, namely the acknowledgment that laboratory science, and bacteriology in particular, was part of the practice of medicine; from about then nonphysician scientists had to be acknowledged as coworkers and colleagues.

Her primary task was to establish a department, an undertaking much complicated by the necessity of importing equipment, including microscopes and glassware, from Germany. During her first winter and spring she was fully occupied with organization and teaching, the latter being extended to include a summer course in 1896; promised time for research never materialized. She therefore requested leave and returned to Berlin for August and September of that year. These two months marked the start of her long involvement in tuberculosis research. Her first paper in the field, a report of her investigation of the presence of the tuberculosis bacillus in commercial butter, appeared in 1897 (see bibliography). That summer she also represented her college at the Berlin International Congress on Women's Work, a most successful meeting with 1,700 participants. Rabinowitsch presented a paper on the status of medical studies for women in a number of countries.[71]

The summer of 1897 she again spent in Berlin, returning to the Woman's Medical College for the 1897–1898 academic year; her annual salary was now increased to $1,000. "Dr. Rabby," as she was called, got on well with both students and other faculty; she was remembered as "a brilliant Russian woman," who, with her slight accent and blue-checked bib aprons, charmed all her students.[72] Her course continued to expand and, since her department was by then well established, additional laboratory facilities were opened in 1898. Early the same year the possibility was raised of establishing a professorship in bacteriology, Rabinowitsch to be appointed to the position. Not surprisingly, the proposal was controversial and the faculty remained undecided. Rabinowitsch left to attend an international hygienic convention in Madrid in April with the matter still unresolved. In addition to reluctance to giving a faculty member who lacked a medical degree the right to reject degree candidates, there was resistance from the pathology department to what could be seen as the separating off of part of its preserve. However, Rabinowitsch agreed to accept the professorship if offered and to return to the college as a full faculty member in the autumn of 1898. The offer finally made was for a professorship in bacteriology at the same salary as that paid the other professors, $1,150 for the academic year 1898–1899.

Meanwhile circumstances were changing for Lydia Rabinowitsch. Shortly after her arrival in Spain, she married Walter Kempner at the German Consulate in Madrid. In August she requested a leave extension from the Woman's Medical College until January 1899. This was not granted. A second request was also turned down and a cable followed notifying her that the offer of a professorship would be withdrawn if she did not return to Philadelphia by 15 October. When she did not, the leadership of the bacteriology department went to American physician and bacteriologist Adelaide Ward Peckham.[73]

Whether Lydia Rabinowitsch ever aspired to a career as a professor at a small American women's college or whether she took a teaching position in Philadelphia because of financial necessity (perhaps coupled with a desire to see something of the United States) remains a question. Her first choice might always have been medical research in Berlin, once again possible with the financial security her marriage brought. Walter Kempner (1864–1920), a fellow research worker in Koch's institute, came from a prominent Jewish family in Glogau, Lower Silesia (now Głogów, Poland). The Kempners, bankers and financiers, had considerable wealth derived from their very successful business interests in mortgage bonds. Walter Kempner held a medical degree from Munich University; at Koch's institute, where he had an official but unpaid assistantship, he followed his interests in a number of current bacteriological problems while at the same time holding the post of head physician in the hospital department attached to the institute. He most likely also had private financial resources.

Family life for the Kempners was overshadowed from the beginning by serious health difficulties. Walter Kempner had already contracted what was later diagnosed as tuberculosis of the throat, possibly caught, it was thought, during his work at the institute on infected milk. Tuberculosis was thus a personal, ever-present problem for the family. Lydia Rabinowitsch made it the focus of her life's work.

She returned to the institute in the summer of 1898, this time without a formal appointment but with access to facilities that allowed her to continue to work and publish. Between 1899 and 1903 her three children were born,[74] without, however, causing much interruption in her research; she had adequate domestic help and was also assisted by her widowed mother-in-law Angelika Kempner, who lived with the family.

Her research was now concentrated on tuberculosis. Koch's 1882 report on the aetiology of the disease[75] provided a new perspective on its many aspects and considerable variability but much remained to be investigated, including infection routes. Despite considerable effort by scientists in many countries, progress was slow because of the time needed to grow cultures and follow the effects in test animals. Lydia Rabinowitsch was one of a number of investigators who took up the question of the relation between human and bovine tuberculosis. Koch, who held the opinion that milk and milk products were a major source of infection for man, gave her full backing. Her initial examination of commercial butter samples had uncovered a complicating factor, namely the presence of an atypical tubercle bacillus-like organism rather than the typical pathogenic tubercle bacillus. Later referred to as the *Petri-Rabinowitsch* or *Rabinowitsch bacillus,* this atypical organism was one of the acid-fast, rapid-growing mycobacteria. Its discovery was important because it set the stage for the later search for a virus of reduced virulence for use in immunization. Her first major publication (1897) reporting the presence of virulent tubercle bacilli in commercial butter was quickly followed by further detailed investigations, some of them joint with Walter Kempner, on the transmission of infection via the milk and milk products of tubercular cows. Their joint 1899 paper reported the presence of tubercle bacilli in 28 percent of all the milk samples examined and pointed out the dangers of underestimating the infectious potential of tuberculosis; using the tuberculin diagnostic test developed by Koch, the Kempners demonstrated that even latent tuberculosis in cattle having no clinical symptoms of the disease carried the potential of making the milk unsafe for humans, a conclusion that differed from reports published by others somewhat earlier. In her short *Deutsche Medicinische Wochenschrift* article of 1900 (see bibliography) Rabinowitsch advocated that the regularly higher-priced milk sold especially for children and invalids should come only from tuberculin-tested herds. Further, she showed that the major source of tubercle bacillus contaminated butter on the Berlin market was a large dairy farm owned by Carl Bolle, a business that prided itself on the high quality of its milk produced under the most hygienic conditions with careful monitoring and all modern controls.

The explosive nature of the findings concerning milk from the Bolle dairy prompted Koch to take the step of notifying the Ministry of Religion, Educational, and Medical Affairs before publication of the results. Bolle reacted swiftly, proposing testing of his herds by his own veterinarians. Considerable controversy arose, Robert Ostertag of the Berlin veterinary college backing reports of earlier workers who claimed that clinically healthy but tuberculin-positive cattle did not produce tuberculosis-contaminated milk. He and the Kempners argued their respective cases in print, the Kempners defending themselves point by point and sticking to their initial conclusions.[76] The episode came to be known as the "Berlin milk war" (*Berliner Milchkrieg*) and was closely followed in the city newspapers. The difficulties then faced by investigators should not be underestimated. Reliable diagnosis of tuberculosis in cattle was coming to be seen by some workers as impossible without the aid of the not yet universally accepted tuberculin test. Complications arose from such factors as the presence of tuberculous bacilli in milk being dependent on the extent and location of tuberculous changes in udder tissue (bacilli were found to inhabit interstitial tissue without penetrating milk ducts), and also the frequent presence of a great variety of bacilli in tuberculous udders, some of which produce changes resembling tuberculosis.

The extent of the problem led to proposals for general pasteurization of milk and to investigations to find a practical method that resulted in an acceptable pasteurized product. The Koch institute's recommendation of heating milk at 88.1 to 88.3°C for one minute to ensure complete destruction of tuberculosis bacilli is not radically different from today's "high-temperature short time" (HTST) procedure. As early as 1900 the pasteurization of milk before it went on the Berlin market was officially ordered and the sale of unpasteurized milk and milk products by big dairy farms penalized. Producers faced serious difficulties, however; at the time fewer than one third had been able to install the equipment needed for pasteurization. Further, increasing competition from more-distant producers using the pasteurization process coupled with low-temperature transportation methods was seriously affecting the Bolle dairy and other farms that had long held a monopoly in the Berlin market. They put up considerable resistance, Bolle even going so far as to substitute pasteurized material for the required raw milk samples sent to Rabinowitsch for examination. The latter manoeuver led her to break off the testing contract she had with Bolle and sue (through her husband) for payment of the fees still owed her; she won substantial compensation. The overall effect of Rabinowitsch's tough stand on the safe milk issue and her painstaking and persistent testing is hard to assess, but it could be said that her investigations, begun in the closing years of the nineteenth century, strongly backed by Koch and quickly brought to the attention of the appropriate state authorities, were a clear wake-up call that constituted a important contribution to the research effort then being applied to one of the major public health concerns of the time.

In 1901 however, the field of bacteriology received something of a jolt. That year, at the first British Tuberculosis Conference in London in a talk entitled "The Fight against Tuberculosis," Koch unexpectedly announced that he had reassessed the human-bovine tuberculosis connection and was no longer satisfied that the causative agent was identical in the two cases.[77] Based on his findings that human tuberculosis did not measurably carry over into calves and swine and that tuberculosis-infected milk products did not cause primarily stomach and gut tuberculosis in humans, this revised opinion was in stark contrast to the view he had put forward almost twenty years earlier. He reaffirmed his new position in October 1902 at the International Congress on Tuberculosis in Berlin and held to it from then on. Such was Koch's reputation that several years of investigation by workers in a number of countries were needed before it was firmly established that the same causative agent was indeed responsible for the disease in both humans and cattle. As a result of Koch's *volte-face,* the adoption of measures against human infection via bovine tuberculosis proceeded more slowly than it otherwise might have, particularly in Germany, where the dairy industry was influential and where, especially in the period between the two world wars, the country's economic situation made the government reluctant to impose further burdens on farmers. Because Rabinowitsch never doubted the bovine-human connection, the disagreement somewhat strained the professional relationship between her and Koch. In 1903 she left the institute.[78] The precise reason is not clear but there seems to have been a certain amount of friction between her and heads of departments that caused them to ask for her removal.[79] Their request was carried out by Wilhelm Dönitz, acting head of the institute, Koch being away on a scientific expedition in Africa. Rabinowitsch's last publication from the institute was her joint paper of 1903 on trypanosomes, a report relating to Koch's investigations of tsetse fly-borne diseases in Africa.[80]

The trypanosome work was not Rabinowitsch's only nontuberculosis interest of these early years of her career. In 1899 she and Walter Kempner carried out research in the Balkans aimed at the eradication of malaria from the region, and in 1902 they spent their summer vacation in the Crimea and Odessa investigating a cholera outbreak. Their account of their trip, through the Bosporus on a small Russian trading steamer to the south coast of the Crimea and then again by ship to Odessa, is still interesting reading. The city had been officially declared "acutely infectious" and the usually busy port with its very considerable grain trade was almost at a standstill. Hotels were empty, the streets reeked of carbolic disinfectant, houses were being evacuated and some of the poorer districts burned as epidemic control measures. The faculty at the almost completed Odessa medical school gave them a warm welcome and the director of the vastly overworked Mechnikov Bacteriological Station made his samples freely available to them.

The epidemic, which dated back to October of the previous year when the first two cases had been discovered, was one of the earliest to be confirmed bacteriologically, the specific bacillus having been identified only in 1894. The sources were not known but a route for the cholera bacillus via man or rats by way of the shipping trade between Odessa and Mediterranean ports was suspected. Extensive bacteriological work carried out on the fleas on the rats coming into the city and on dead rats found in Odessa cellars strongly suggested that these were the carriers, the rats being ships' rats (*M. rattus*) and Alexandrine rats (*M. alexandrinus*). The situation was of particular concern to the Kempners because of the possibility of the epidemic spreading to Austria and Germany. However, thanks to prompt action by Odessa's bacteriologists who had followed Koch's advice and quickly instituted control measures, the outbreak was over by October 1902, fifty cases having by then been confirmed bacteriologically.[81]

After she left Koch's institute in 1903 Lydia Rabinowitsch for a time worried about where to find alternative laboratory space. However, the same year she joined pathologist and bacteriologist Johannes Orth as an assistant at the Pathological Institute at the Charité Hospital of Friedrich-Wilhelms University, Berlin (now Berlin University). As in Koch's laboratory she worked without a formal contract and without a salary. Orth, who had only the previous year succeeded the widely known and much respected scientist and politician Rudolf Virchow, had a strong interest in infectious diseases, particularly tuberculosis and its control. Further, he shared Rabinowitsch's view that the milk of infected cows was an important source of tuberculosis in children.

The research carried out by Lydia Rabinowitsch at the Pathological Institute was basic in nature and far-reaching in scope. It constituted the high point of her research career and earned her wide recognition among her fellow bacteriologists. Her primary goal was to establish a solid scientific basis for her conviction that there was a direct link between bovine and human tuberculosis, despite Koch's arguments to the contrary.

Focusing on the morphological and biological differences between various groups of *Mycobacterium tuberculosis,* she examined the disease agent in a broad sample of human and animal cases. Conscious of the fact that she could not investigate every known tuberculosis type, she concentrated on whether the differences she observed were sufficiently constant to justify a species division. Human tissue samples were obtained from the Pathological Institute and material from a variety of animals, including forty-five tuberculous monkeys and 459 infected birds, from the Berlin Zoological Garden. Most of the samples cultured showed attributes that would be classified as typical, including morphology and color that at that time were important criteria in bacteriological classification. But there was also significant variation: the bovine type was harder to culture and took longer to grow than the human forms; avian bacilli were typically easier to grow and less temperature dependent; virulence in laboratory test animals varied. A few tuberculosis-causing agents fell outside the range of standards being used and were not classifiable by their behavior as cultures and their virulence in test animals. Further, Rabinowitsch found that about 30 percent of human tuberculosis cultures deviated from at least one of the rules for "typical" behavior; these she designated as atypical and considered to be transitional forms. Similar deviation was also present in tuberculosis cultures from other mammals and from birds. These findings led her to conclude that the agent causing tuberculosis was a single species that had adapted to various animal hosts. In particular bovine and human tuberculosis bacilli were not different with constant identifiable characteristics but varieties of the same species. Her "unitary theory" opposing Koch's idea of differing species of tuberculosis bacilli was put forward a 1906–1907 paper—a publication especially valued by workers in the field of animal health. Indeed this paper along with two other major publications on human and animal types of tuberculosis that appeared about the same time were her most important and notable contributions to tuberculosis research.[82]

Among the twenty human tuberculosis cultures examined two were clearly identified as bovine-type bacilli; another had all the attributes of avian tuberculosis bacilli. Similar results were reported by other workers. Thus, although the most common way for humans to contract tuberculosis was by breathing exhalation droplets containing the bacteria, infection via bovine tuberculosis was an important factor and had to be considered a serious threat, especially to children in the form of tuberculosis of the stomach and gut. Additional work carried out jointly with Orth and Ernst Oberwarth (1908) and with Carl Dammann (1913) further demonstrated that tuberculosis initially contracted through the gut could cause general infection, including pulmonary tuberculosis, in test animals.[83] Koch's thesis was not sustainable.

Other studies by Rabinowitsch about this time included investigations of the influence of factors, such as trauma, alcoholism, and the sex of the patient on the progress of tuberculosis in humans; work on the occurrence of latent or dormant tuberculosis and immune reactions and the production of tuberculosis antibodies were additional interests.[84]

Throughout her years at the Pathological Institute Lydia Rabinowitsch continued to be very much involved in the work of protection of infants and small children from tuberculosis infection; it was an issue about which she was passionately concerned and the Bolle dairy farm proprietors were by no means the only powerful and influential opposition she ran into. Her 1905 article in the medical newspaper *Berliner Aerzte-Correspondenz*[85] uncovering the intrigues of the Society for the Fight against Infant Mortality produced a major reaction in the Berlin medical establishment. One of the main founders of the society was Otto Heubner, professor of child health and chief of the medical department at the Charité Hospital; many well-known people were active in the group, including Robert Ostertag of the veterinary college. The impetus for its establishment came from statistical data of 1902, which showed that large German cities, including Berlin, ranked well below other Western European urban centers in the survival rate of infants in the first year of life.[86] The two main goals of the society were first to persuade mothers, through an information campaign, to persist in suckling infants, thereby reducing the incidence of intestinal infections, and secondly to offer a source of clean, affordable cows milk (free to destitute mothers) in cases where suckling was not possible. The difficulty lay in the second goal. Contrary to the legal provisions of 1900, the milk was to be unpasteurized but to come from healthy animals, the herds involved being regularly monitored by the society's veterinarians. About the same time, on the basis of tests carried out by Bolle's bacteriologist in the Bolle laboratory, the society issued a warning against the consumption of imported, pasteurized, Danish milk. After extensive testing of the Danish product Rabinowitsch and others demonstrated that it had negligible bacterial content while samples of the locally produced unpasteurized milk they found to contain the tuberculosis bacillus—results in sharp contrast to the Bolle laboratory findings. The exposure led several prominent people to leave the society.

Another controversy Rabinowitsch became deeply involved in concerned a prophylactic vaccine produced and widely promoted by F. F. Friedmann. The vaccine, isolated from tortoises, was tested on fifty healthy Berlin infants and children in an orphanage in Rummelsburg, Pomerania (now Miastko, Poland) in October 1911. A Prussian government follow-up investigation in January 1913 indicated that only ten of these children did not by then have tuberculosis. Rabinowitsch, who had from the beginning taken a very critical stand against use of the vaccine, had in the meantime succeeded in obtaining a pure sample of the Friedmann culture through American friends at the laboratory for tuberculosis research at Saranac Lake, New York, Friedmann himself having declined to supply the material or much information about it. Rabinowitsch's studies showed it to be pathogenic in warm-blooded animals. She and Friedmann argued their cases in the pages of the *Deutsche Medizinische Wochenschrift* in 1914, but the controversy went on, with a break during the war years, until 1933 when use of the Friedmann vaccine was finally prohibited.[87]

Throughout the period up to the First World War Lydia Rabinowitsch was a frequent speaker at both specialist tuberculosis congresses and at meetings of German medical and biological societies (London and Moscow 1901; Breslau 1904; Paris 1905; Stuttgart 1906; Berlin 1907; Rome 1912; London 1913).[88] In 1906 she became a corresponding member of the International Central Committee for the Fight against Tuberculosis and the same year, in recognition of her animal health studies, she was named a corresponding member of the Paris Société Centrale de Médecine Vétérinaire, the first female member of that society. Membership in a number of other societies followed, including (although only in 1913) the Berliner Medizinische Gesellschaft. In 1912 Friedrich-Wilhelms University recognized her research achievements by conferring on her a titular professorship.[89] A year later she became editor-in-chief of *Zeitschrift für Tuberkulose,* the leading German journal for tuberculosis research, founded after the 1899 Berlin Tuberculosis Congress. The first woman editor of a specialist scientific journal in German, she held the position until 1933 when legislation introduced by the National Socialist government required her to relinquish it.

With the outbreak of the First World War Lydia Rabinowitsch, like many European medical women, found wider fields opening to her. The possibility of soldiers on the Eastern Front bringing back infectious diseases, including cholera, was a major fear. Rabinowitsch, well known as an expert in the area, was appointed specialist adviser to the director general of the army medical services department and given the resources to put the necessary precautions in place. This work slowed down her rate of publishing, but she nevertheless brought out several papers about this time, including important work with fellow bacteriologist Wilhelm Ceelen on the relationship between tuberculosis and lymph gland disorders and joint work with Carl Hart on what appeared to be an increase in the number of bovine-type tuberculosis cases during the war years; they concluded that the increase was due to veterinary men being diverted into military work.[90]

In 1920, when women received the official right to hold university teaching positions in Germany, the medical faculty at Friedrich-Wilhelms University declined the suggestion of the Ministry of Science, Art, and National Education that Rabinowitsch be named honorary professor; Otto Lubarsch, Orth's successor as head of the Pathological Institute, finding that the majority of the medical faculty opposed her appointment, withdrew his support. The faculty put forward a number of reasons, some questioning the lasting quality of her research, others emphasizing that they already had a full teaching staff in bacteriology. Considering the era, her tough public stand on several controversial medical issues may also have reduced her popularity with her male colleagues and damaged her chances for advancement.

Thus, instead of a professorship, Lydia Rabinowitsch in 1920 received an extra-university appointment, the directorship of the bacteriology department of the Moabit, Berlin's great municipal hospital. The Moabit's bacteriological facility had a surprisingly long history, dating back more than three decades to 1884 when the institution was only a military hospital; Robert Koch had wanted to include its patients in his work and this required some laboratory space on the premises. In 1889, Berlin city management decided that each city hospital should employ a chemist and a bacteriologist and that appropriate laboratory provision be made. Lydia Rabinowitsch's appointment as a salaried city official gave her a place where she could continue her work through this time of severe postwar inflation when, although she continued to have some foundation grant support,[91] her own financial resources were much reduced. She was now for the first time in an independent leadership position. Because the Moabit was by then a teaching hospital, she was also responsible for medical student laboratory instruction in bacteriology; doubtless much changed since she established the first bacteriological laboratory at the Woman's Medical College of Pennsylvania a quarter of a century earlier.

During her fourteen years at the Moabit Hospital, a considerable amount of her time was necessarily spent on a variety of nonresearch matters—administration, laboratory improvement, routine hospital bacteriological testing, and bacteriological testing for school doctors and the health office of the Berlin Zoological Garden. Nevertheless her research continued; reports on investigations of streptococci and on actinomycete bacteria, as well as further studies on tuberculosis, including her specialty of the human-bovine tuberculosis relationship and questions of transmission, diagnosis, and treatment, appeared regularly over the next decade.[92] With general interest moving on from the disease-causing agent to the question of immunity in individuals, she became involved in the testing and trials of the Bacille-Calmette-Guérin (BCG) vaccine, the tuberculosis prophylactic still in use today. Prepared from a highly attenuated, live but only weakly virulent form of the bovine-type bacillus by the French bacteriologists Albert Calmette and Camille Guérin of the Pasteur Institutes, this was being used in several European countries by the 1920s to confer immunity to cattle. Rabinowitsch began to test it in animal studies in 1927, finding it to be safe and effective.[93] When an accident that caused the deaths of seventy-six children occurred during BCG testing at a Lübeck hospital in 1930 Rabinowitsch backed her French colleagues. A subsequent court enquiry, where she put her test results at the disposal of the Pasteur Institute defense, clearly demonstrated that the accident was caused by negligence on the part of the Lübeck physician involved. Her work on the matter of the filterability of the tuberculosis-causing agent published in 1928 touched on the important question of the transplacental transmission of the disease.[94] Lydia Rabinowitsch's last paper, published in 1931, "Fünfzig Jahre Tuberkelbazillus," summarized each major stage in tuberculosis research beginning with Koch's discovery of the bacterium in 1882; it included a full discussion of her own contributions.[95]

During the 1920s and early 1930s she remained very visible and active nationally and internationally, attending tuberculosis conferences and congresses, including meetings in Washington, D.C. (1926), in Rome (1928 and 1934), and in Locarno (1931). Not infrequently she went as an invited guest.

Lydia Rabinowitsch's full commitment to her scientific work throughout the three and a half decades of her professional career by no means resulted in her distancing herself from the upbringing of her three children. Although various domestic servants were part of her household and she had help from her mother-in-law who lived with the family until her death in 1915, her own careful planning integrated her work into the daily routine. From 1911 the Kempners lived in a large house (which also accommodated Walter Kempner's practice rooms) near the railway station in Berlin-Lichterfelde, a pleasant district of substantial houses on the southern edge of Berlin. Lydia Rabinowitsch left for work every morning at seven and on her return at four in the afternoon was met at the station by the children. Walter Kempner always supported her work even after he had given up research himself; daily dinner table conversations tended to be about bacteria. The children, too, had their connections with their mother's research, being allowed the excitement of looking at stained bacteria through the wonderful microscope in her study and having as their playmates the rabbits, guinea pigs, and mice bred as test animals and kept under the house veranda. One of their special pleasures came through her investigations of tuberculosis in nonhuman populations, the studies in which she had the collaboration of the Berlin Zoological Garden and its physician and zoologist Oskar Heimroth. The many visits made by the whole family to the zoo were special occasions, thanks to Heimroth. Lydia Rabinowitsch herself taught the children English, a skill that all three later made good use of, Nadja in her academic studies and Robert and Walter as a practical matter.

Very much of the liberal left with an international perspective, Lydia Rabinowitsch and her family had little sympathy with the militaristic sentiments that swept much of Germany at the beginning of the First World War. At the same time, however, not wanting to see the state defeated, the Kempners believed that one did one's military duty and so in 1916, at age seventeen, the oldest son volunteered for army service. He survived his two years on the eastern front.

The immediate postwar years brought major changes. Walter Kempner died in 1920, the year Rabinowitsch moved to the Moabit Hospital as head of the bacteriological laboratory. Increasing inflation took its toll and lack of money greatly reduced her activities. Further, signs of alarming political trends were already evident; in 1919 her Zurich student friend Rosa Luxemburg was assassinated (along with Karl Liebknecht, leader of the German Communist Party) by members of the *Freicorps*.[96] Nevertheless, events were not all unhappy for the Kempners at this time. In 1923 the first grandchild, Robert Kempner's son Lucien, was born. Since his family made their home in her house, Lydia Rabinowitsch took a major part in his upbringing; she found great pleasure in his company, often having him with her in her study.

Throughout most of her life she was much involved in the early women's movement (*Frauenbewegung*). She served on the committees of several organizations, including the Union for the Protection of Mothers and Sexual Reform, the Union of German Women Physicians, the Berlin Society for Women's Health, and the

German Lyceum Club.[97] In addition she worked with Elsa Neumann (p. 145) to found the Society for Guaranteeing Interest-free Loans to Women Students and she managed the Heinrich Groburek Foundation for interest-free loans to women medical students. All these activities brought her into close contact with the leaders of the movement. Her house was a meeting place for Berlin's professional women and those working for women's rights; plans were discussed and tactics worked out at regular Sunday morning coffee gatherings.

Not all of the groups she belonged to were supported by the nationwide Union of German Women's Societies, however. As in her general political outlook, her sympathies here leaned toward the liberal left. Particularly in the course of her work with the controversial Union for the Protection of Mothers and Sexual Reform, Rabinowitsch spoke out in favor of sex education in schools and the provision of housing for unmarried mothers, contentious topics at the time. She also championed the cause of health insurance for women in the labor force, emphasizing the generally poor health of pregnant working-class women and the sickliness of their children, which, as was pointed out in a petition to the Reichstag in 1907, ultimately resulted in the poor physical quality of recruits for the military. A member of the German Lyceum Club from its founding in 1905, she was particularly involved in its educational program. Along with many other longstanding members, she left the club about 1932 because of the increasing official bias against non-Aryans.

Lydia Rabinowitsch made a special effort to emphasise what she felt was the crucial role of women, ordinary housewives as well as health professionals, in controlling tuberculosis. She saw very clearly that the social conditions and poor health, which led to impaired resistance were major factors in tuberculosis transmission, and through lectures and articles stressed the necessity of clean, hygienic, well-ventilated living conditions.[98] She strongly supported the various public health facilities founded by women's groups and the sanatoria for pulmonary diseases; the latter, although they restricted their efforts initially to sanitary measures and diet treatment, gradually developed into tuberculosis hospitals that could provide modern therapies. She stressed particularly the important role of women physicians in prevention and control counselling and recommended their getting practical experience in tuberculosis clinics.[99]

By training as a bacteriologist rather than a physician, Rabinowitsch was not accepted by the International Union of Women Doctors as the official German delegate on tuberculosis to a major five-year congress in London in 1929. Nevertheless she was undoubtedly the leading German woman research worker in the medical sciences of her time. The many messages of congratulation that appeared in Berlin newspapers and in medical journals on her sixtieth birthday in 1931 demonstrate the recognition and goodwill she called forth in scientific circles and in the women's movement.

Endowed with drive and ambition, Lydia Rabinowitsch was undaunted by the conventions and restrictions that limited women at the time—restrictions that perhaps fell even more heavily on Europeans than on Americans and handicapped Russian Jewish women especially. In her scientific work her investigations of the interrelationship between the varieties of the tuberculosis bacillus were especially notable contributions, but she is probably most widely known for her publications reporting the presence of tuberculosis bacilli in the Berlin milk and milk products supply around the turn of the century. Although not the only scientist investigating the matter of contaminated dairy products or the first to demonstrate the presence in these of tuberculosis bacteria,[100] her thorough and painstaking early reports (backed by the influential Robert Koch) and her steady and persistent campaign to alert the public about the dangers of contaminated dairy products had a lasting effect on public health measures. Overall she authored or coauthored more than ninety publications, most of them concerned with tuberculosis.

From the early 1930s, life became increasingly difficult for the Rabinowitsch-Kempner family. In 1933 Nadja Kempner died of tuberculosis at age thirty-one. The following year Lydia Rabinowitsch and several of her Jewish colleagues at the Moabit Hospital were pensioned off, following passage of the National Socialist regulations that specified that non-Aryan civil servants be retired. 1934 was also the year she had to relinquish her post as managing editor of the *Zeitschrift für Tuberkulose* because of new legislation concerning publishing. About the same time her son Robert Kempner, a lawyer working in the Berlin police department section of the Prussian Interior Ministry, was dismissed because of his strong stand against the National Socialist Party. His arrest by the Gestapo from the house in Lichterfelde in March 1935 brought on a heart attack, from which Lydia Rabinowitsch, already ill with breast cancer, never recovered. Later that summer, her younger son Walter Kempner left for the United States.[101] Knowing that she herself was too ill to leave Berlin, she spent her last days trying to arrange for the safe exit from Germany of Robert and his wife; he credited his prompt entry into professional work after he crossed the Atlantic to help from his mother's Philadelphia friends. Lydia Rabinowitsch died at her home in Lichterfelde on 3 August 1935, shortly before her sixty-fourth birthday; she is buried in the Kempner family plot in Parkfriedhof, Berlin-Lichterfelde. Short biographical sketches in a few foreign scientific journals marked her passing,[102] but beyond a number of simple death announcements, little attention was paid to the event in German publications.

Much less information has been uncovered about the remaining nine medical women in this group.

AGNES, FREIIN VON BABO was born in Seckenheim, Baden, in 1859. She studied medicine at Zurich University, graduating in 1900; her dissertation research on ovarian cystic degeneration appeared in *Archiv für Pathologische Anatomie* the same year. She received German accreditation in 1902. For thirty-four years, from 1903 until 1937, she had a practice in gynaecology and pediatrics in Dresden. Appointed the city's first school doctor in 1911, Baroness von Babo was also active in community health education.[103]

ANNA BÄUMLER (1849–1919), the daughter of Dr. J. Bäumler, a member of the Munich high court for ecclesiastical matters, was born in Munich in 1849. She trained initially as a teacher and worked in schools in India during the 1870s.[104] In 1881 she enrolled in the medical faculty in Zurich and over the next six years continued her medical training, attending courses in Paris and London as well as in Zurich. She received her degree from Zurich University in 1887. Her dissertation research on spinal chord abnormalities, published in the *Deutsches Archiv für Klinische Medicin,* was done under the guidance of the well-known internist Hermann Eichhorst. In 1890, after a short period of practice in Vienna, she went to London and qualified under the British system. She then immediately returned to India where, until her death in Calcutta in 1919, she headed in succession a number of hospitals for women.[105]

IDA DEMOCH, an East Prussian born on 27 January 1877, was educated at a girls' high school and a women teachers' seminar in Königsberg (now Kaliningrad, Russia). After qualifying in 1895 she taught for a short period but in the autumn of that year went to Zurich and resumed studies. She completed university entrance requirements and proceeded with further classes spending one year (1898–1899) as an auditor in the medical faculty at Halle University. After a further year in Zurich she passed the Swiss state medical accreditation examination. About that time changes in Prussian regulations opening physician certification to women made it possible for her to return home to present herself both for the state medical examination and as a doctoral candidate at Halle University. She was the first woman to obtain full medical certification in Germany (March, 1901).[106] Her study of spinal chord paralysis appeared in *Archiv für Psychiatrie und Nervenkrankheiten* in 1900. In 1904, following further practical experience in a university clinic, she opened a practice in obstetrics and women's and children's health in Dresden. Five years later she married lawyer Robert Maurmeier and moved to Munich, where she practiced for twenty-seven years, retiring in 1936 because of paralysis in her hand. Ida Democh was a member of the Union of German Women Doctors.[107]

Amalie Glause was from Stettin (now Szczein, Poland). She received her degree from Bern University in 1884 having studied there from 1879 to 1883. In addition to her dissertation research on heart function, carried out under the direction of physiologist Balthasar Luchsinger and published in 1884, she coauthored a joint note with Luchsinger on the physiological effects of some ammonium bases. Molly Herbig, from Marannenhof, East Prussia, took a degree in Zurich in 1894. Herbig carried out her research, published in *Archiv für Pathologische Anatomie* in 1894, at the university's Pathological Institute. (See the entry for Clara Weiss, below, for more about Molly Herbig.) Sieglinde Stier, from Zerbst (about twenty miles southeast of Magdeburg) was a student at Bern University from 1889 to 1894, specializing in physiology. Her dissertation research appeared in *Archiv für Psychiatrie* in 1896.

CLARA WEISS from Stotel, a small community in northern Hannover, was born in 1856. The wife of a Stotel physician, W. Weiss, she had acquired her secondary education at a girls' high school. She studied in the medical faculty at Zurich University in the period 1882–1884 and completed training at Bern in 1891–1893, specializing in pathology. Graduating in 1893, she published her neurological research, done under the guidance of Theodor Langhans, the following year. Both she and Molly Herbig, along with the Austrian physician Gabriele Possanner von Ehrenthal, were accepted into clinical lectures on psychiatry at the University of Vienna in 1894, a noteworthy mark of their abilities and professional promise because Austrian universities did not officially open medical studies to women auditors until 1900.[108] Herbig never practiced; she married a Swiss doctor and had two children, but died at an early age, just before the First World War.[109]

CLARA WILLDENOW (1856–1931), the daughter of a Breslau privy councillor, Dr. Willdenow, was born in Bonn on 8 October 1856. Educated privately to *Abitur* level, she enrolled in 1884 in the medical faculty at Zurich University, where she studied until July 1887. During a further nine semesters (1887–1891) in the Bern medical faculty she concentrated especially on pediatrics. Her Bern degree was awarded in 1893. Her dissertation, "Zur Kenntnis der pepsidischen Verdauung des Kaseins," reported research on the pepsin digestion of the milk protein casein. A student of chemist and pathologist Edmund Drechsel, she also carried out studies in his laboratory on a number of inorganic salts of the amino acid lysine. The work followed Drechsel's classic isolation of lysine from egg albumen (1891).

Specializing in gynaecology, Clara Willdenow conducted a practice in the Seefeld district of Zurich until about 1923. It is reported tht she also worked for a time as a volunteer doctor in a Berlin clinic. She died in Zurich on 4 July 1931, three months before her seventy-fifth birthday.[110]

ELISE WOLFF published a paper on tuberculosis bacilli in 1899 from the State Hospital, Berlin (Stadisches Krankenhaus am Urban). At the time she was an assistant (*Präparatorin*) in the private laboratory of Albert Fraenkel, well known for his work on the pathology and therapy of lung diseases, including tuberculosis. In collaboration with Leipzig physician Alice Buslik, Wolff later published a short textbook, *Histologie,* designed for students of medical technology preparing for the state examination.[111] Based on the accumulated experience of the two authors, it offered a concise and well-illustrated presentation of the basic groundwork of the field and also served as a general elementary handbook for practising histologists.

Physical Sciences

Significant contributions by German women in only two branches of the physical sciences—chemistry and physics—are recorded in the bibliography. No papers in mathematics are listed, only two in astronomy, and one in geology.[112] A few women did study mathematics at German universities and publish research before 1901, but they were frequently foreign nationals, such as those accepted as special cases by the Prussian Minister of Education Friedrich Althoff, who appears to have wanted to make a limited experiment with foreign women students before Germans came forward.[113] The case of Marie Gernet, now considered to be the first German-born woman to receive a doctorate in mathematics, was for long overlooked, the distinction going to the well-recognized Emmy Noether. Gernet, however, received her degree from Heidelberg University in 1895, thirteen years before Noether graduated from Erlangen University. Because Gernet's research was not published as a journal article, her name does not appear in the Royal Society *Catalogue*. Nevertheless, because of her special position in the history of mathematics education for women in Germany a footnote outlining her career is appended.[114]

Among the German women who received doctoral degrees in chemistry before 1901, two—Baum and Wohlbrück—studied organic chemistry, and one—Immerwahr—electrochemistry.[115] By far the most striking and influential in her overall career is Baum.

A leading figure in the German women's movement in the early years of the twentieth century, MARIE BAUM[116] (1874–1964), after her early days as a chemist, went on to a long and distinguished career as factory inspector, social and political scientist, member of the national legislature, university faculty member, and writer. Indeed Baum is now recognized as a person who made a major impact in the social, cultural, academic, and political affairs of her time. She was born in Danzig (now Gdánsk) on 23 March 1874, one of the six children (four girls and two boys) of Wilhelm Georg Baum and his wife Fanny Auguste Florentina (née Lejeune-Dirichlet). Her forebears had lived in East Prussia since at least the mid seventeenth century, latterly acquiring business interests in Danzig. Wilhelm Baum, son of the founder of Göttingen University's outstanding school of surgery, was chief of the Danzig city hospital; earlier he had served as a military doctor. His wife was the daughter of the celebrated mathematician Gustav Lejeune-Dirichlet (successor to Karl Friedrich Gauss at Göttingen) and a niece of the composer Felix Mendelssohn-Bartholdy.

The Baum family circle was large and lively, various relatives from time to time living with them in the spacious official residence near the hospital that they occupied. Politics were much discussed. Both Marie's mother and her uncle, member of parliament Walter Lejeune-Dirichlet, were strong leftists and her father, although as a former military man he supported Bismark and the Kaiser, had an equally strong social commitment that he quietly demonstrated by never charging fees in his private practice. Frau Baum was an early champion of rights for women and president of the Danzig Society for the Welfare of Women; she made sure that her daughters as well as her sons had a good education. Marie followed the *realkurse* curriculum. Mathematics was her favorite subject but she also read widely in German and English literature, enjoying in particular the novels of Charles Dickens and Sir Walter Scott. Going to Zurich in 1893 at age nineteen, she took the *Abitur* plus an additional examination in mathematics and physics required for entrance to the Zurich Federal Polytechnikum, where she enrolled in the teacher training division.[117]

She concentrated on the biological sciences, especially botany, and received her teaching diploma in that area in 1897. Then becoming interested in chemistry she began doctoral research under the direction of Eugen Bamberger at the Polytechnikum and served for two years (1897–1899) as Bamberger's assistant in the institution's analytical laboratory. A zealous and enthusiastic research chemist, Bamberger not infrequently became embroiled in heated controversies with his colleagues that swept along his students as well. Arguments over the three-dimensional structure of molecules containing a nitrogen-nitrogen (diazo) linkage went on for years among the leading chemists of the period; Baum's dissertation research on a diazo derivative of naphthalene[118] reported in a long, joint paper with Bamberger in 1899 (see bibliography), was part of his series of studies in this area. Looking back from the vantage point of forty years later, she saw chemistry of her time as a field very much constrained, the developments then taking place in nuclear physics being in the process of changing science's picture of the very nature of matter itself. Her tongue-in-cheek presentation on the work of the alchemists and the coming fulfillment of their hopes for transmutation of elements via modern nuclear chemistry[119] was not received with wholehearted approval among her fellow students, some of whom felt this weighty subject demanded more respect.

For Baum as for Marianne Plehn (p. 115), the years spent in Zurich were among the happiest and brightest of her life. She later wrote of Zurich as a city of youth, freedom, and hope.[120] In her first year she met fellow student Ricarda Huch, whose already published poetry she knew and admired. Marianne Plehn, her artist sister Rosa Plehn, Eugenie Schumann (daughter of Robert and Clara Schumann), botanist and later social worker, Margarete von Üxküll-Gyllenband, law student and later social worker, Frieda Duensing, and American Mary Whitney, who became prominent among women astronomers, were among the young women in her circle; many of them she kept contact with for the rest of her life. Several, including Baum, were members of the very active International Women Students' Association. Baum was also for two sessions president of the German Women Students' Union. The common ideals for the betterment of society that these young women held, their shared liberal, socialist outlook, and an acute consciousness of being personally and centrally involved in a major movement for fundamental social change in which women were important participants, became part of Marie Baum's primary and essential philosophy.

Having interrupted her studies to visit her parents, both of whom were terminally ill, she postponed taking her doctoral examination. The action cost her her greatly prized laboratory teaching assistantship. She was the first woman to hold the position and the appointment had only been given after energetic intervention on her behalf by Albert Heim, director of the division. The administration expected a man, preferably Swiss, to fill the post.

After being awarded her doctorate by the university in 1899, she looked in vain for an industrial research position in Switzerland; few companies were then willing to hire women laboratory workers. She therefore accepted a post as chemist in the patent department of Aktiengesellschaft für Anilinfabrikation (AGFA) in Berlin-Treptow, starting there in the autumn of 1899. The work of examining patents and translating from and into English and French was not much to her taste, however, and neither did she enjoy living in Berlin, where her eight-hour office day was considerably extended by travel time. In 1902 she moved to Karlsruhe, having obtained the position of industrial inspector responsible for women workers in the duchy of Baden. Here, she felt, she could put her technical training to use in a more satisfying way and at the same time come to grips with some of the most urgent social problems of the time. She was the second occupant of the post, which had been recently created by the Baden interior ministry, the first inspector, Dr. Else Jaffe-von Richthofen, having been obliged to resign on marriage.

Baden as a whole was densely populated, particularly compared to Baum's home region around Danzig, and heavy industry was increasing in such centers as Mannheim (also important as an inland port city). Questions of workers' rights and women's rights were very much to the fore and leaders among factory workers were agitating for laws governing working conditions. Baum was responsible for inspection of workplace conditions for 55,000 women and 17,000 young people in the manufacturing trades; from 1904 her sphere was expanded to include children in domestic industries as well. In addition she had the duty of certifying compliance with work regulations. The obvious misery, the indifference of management, and the apathy of even the workers themselves profoundly affected her. Women's rights in general and in particular the welfare of working women and their families became her cause. Publication of her pioneering study on the causes of infant mortality in the families of women workers had a powerful effect, bringing a public outcry over the social conditions of wage earners in Karlsruhe.[121] As Baum saw it, children were being made to pay the price for the Industrial Revolution.

However, this 1906 exposure, the first sociological study of the conditions of life of working women in a German-speaking country, also had the effect of antagonizing her superiors in the Baden Board of Directors for Industry and her position gradually became untenable; her working conditions compared to those of male factory inspectors became more difficult and her salary remained lower. In 1907, after a one-semester break to attend classes in philosophy at Heidelberg University, she moved on to the post of business manager of the Society for Infant Care and Welfare Work in Düsseldorf. The position was offered to her by the provincial administration in Düsseldorf, a large industrial center with many factories employing considerable numbers of women and children. Her study of infant death rates there (one in six for legitimate children and one in three for the illegitimate) led her to bring to the fore questions of birth control and family welfare. By then the pro–working class, socialist sympathies of "*rote Bäumchen*" were well known in the region. A member of the German Society for Public and Private Welfare, she worked closely with the Union of German Women's Societies.

With the coming of the First World War in 1914, Marie Baum undertook war-related welfare work in various cities as needed: in 1915 she was sent to Danzig to organize a wartime welfare administration patterned on a model already established in Düsseldorf; within a few months she was called to Brussels for a short time to help the German army of occupation set up welfare relief for Belgian women and children. At this time she also organized a huge program of visits to neutral Netherlands for German children caught in the stress and turmoil of war; about 60,000 young people were given a few weeks vacation with care and good food in Dutch families. Arranged with the assistance of her Zurich friend Margarete von Üxküll-Gyllenband, by then living in the Netherlands,[122] the program went on until 1926.

In late 1916, after a year in Düsseldorf, she went to Hamburg where, along with Gertrude Bäumer, she headed a new institute, the Soziale Frauenschule und Sozialpädagogisches Institut. Here she taught four courses covering a broad range of urgent social issues, Germany then being under the extreme conditions resulting from the Allied blockade. War welfare work, the national health situation, food supply problems and policies, employment opportunities, and government welfare obligations were among the topics she lectured on to very varied audiences, from manual workers to teachers, students, artists, and trades union leaders.[123] She remained at the Hamburg institute through the last years of the war, the collapse of the country, and the beginning of the immediate postwar period—a time of revolutionary turmoil. Sadly, none of the people who came through her courses had any chance of finding jobs. All women's positions had to be relinquished to demobilized men, even in the area of welfare work.

In 1919 Marie Baum was elected to the constituent national assembly in Weimar, one of thirty-six women delegates of the liberal, left-wing Deutsche Demokratische Partie (DDP). In 1919–1920 she served as a member of the first parliament of the new republic representing the electoral district of Schleswig-Holstein. However, discouraged and disillusioned by the increasing coarseness of political life, she turned away from a further period in the legislature and accepted a position as acting divisional head of welfare services in the newly formed Baden Ministry of Labor in Karlsruhe.

The city was much changed by the war; the ducal court was gone and so was the garrison, the region being now in a demilitarized zone. Baden, the first of the German states to call together an assembly after the nation's defeat, had particularly complex problems to solve. The social services of the transitional administration had to deal not only with the half-starved population that included hundreds of thousands of homeless families, war wounded, and destitute men still in uniform, but also a large influx of refugees from Alsace when the latter was ceded to France.

The continuation of the Allied blockade even after the signing of the Armistice put enormous pressures on relief agencies. Care of starving children was given top priority. The many large buildings that were taken over, including hotels in the Schwarzwald and the castles of the region, provided only a fraction of the needed housing, but largely due to Marie Baum's initiative, a plan was put into place to accommodate children in the huge, unoccupied, military training complex in the Heuberg valley in Württemberg, some sixty miles to the southeast of Karlsruhe. "Heuberg," the Weimar republic's model children's home, was occupied from June 1920 (when it was already able to take 1000 children) until again required for military use in 1933; over 100,000 young people spent their early years there. Operated on an all-creeds basis by the Baden-Württemberg local administration whose de facto appointee Baum was, it accepted children from all over Germany from 1923. Latterly it was used for special programs, including a training school for girls in household work and summer athletic camps for Mannheim and Stuttgart schoolchildren.

Marie Baum resigned from her post in 1926, largely to protest the squeezing of funds for her office and the increasingly inflexible rules that were making her work more difficult. Subsequently she carried out a number of fact-finding assignments for the national government. These included investigations into needs for family assistance and the provision of recreational opportunities for children and young people, as well as a comprehensive study of the severe problems confronting working families during the economic depression of the 1920s.[124]

The interwar years brought several foreign trips, often to Italy or the Austrian Tyrol with Marianne Plehn or Ricarda Huch and her daughter Marietta Ceconi. In 1928 she was appointed associate lecturer in the Institute of Social and Political Studies at Heidelberg University; in 1931 she made a successful speaking tour in the United States. Two years later however, with the introduction of new civil service regulations by the National Socialist Party and the *Säuberung* (cleansing) of the universities, she had to resign her lectureship; her Mendelssohn-Bartholdy forbears, although they had converted to Christianity three generations before Baum's time, were of Jewish blood. Writing in her memoirs fifteen years later she remarked how, still unfamiliar with the new *Rassegedanke* (racial thinking), she took the dismissal as a personal attack on her good name and reputation and required longer to recover inwardly than she had anticipated.[125] Her close ties with her Zurich friends, particularly Marianne Plehn and Ricarda Huch (who lived with her from 1932 to 1934) were a steady source of strength to her over the war years. Other friends, including writer and women's movement activist Marianne Weber and her husband the economist Max Weber also gave her valued support. She was kept under surveillance by the Gestapo, interrogated many times, and had her apartment searched in 1941. Nevertheless she worked with Heidelberg clergyman Hermann Maas to help those undergoing political persecution.

In March 1945 she was still in Heidelberg. Her memoirs contain an interesting account of the American army's advance on the city and the early days of the occupation.[126] For a short time that year she earned a livelihood by giving private English lessons, but with the full reopening of the university in January 1946, although then almost seventy-two years old, she was reinstated in her teaching position. At that time interest in the social and political questions she dealt with in her lectures was intense and she had a great deal of interaction with students from all faculties; one of the new student associations was organized at meetings in her home. In addition to her university work she was much involved in reestablishing secondary education in the region including the reorganization in Schloss Wieblingen near Heidelberg of the boarding school for girls renamed the *Elisabeth von Thadden School*.[127] In 1949, on her seventy-fifth birthday, Heidelberg University bestowed on her the honor of "*Ehrenbürgerin ausgezeichnete*," citing her pioneering contributions in practical social welfare and her far-reaching and very successful educational work.[128] For a brief period following the war she was a member of the Christian Democractic Party, but then moved on to the nonparty Heidelberg Action Group for Free Socialism. After her retirement in 1952 she stayed in Heidelberg and continued to write, bringing out a biography of her fellow social worker and child welfare activist Anna von Gierke.[129] Marie Baum died in Heidelberg on 8 August 1964 at age ninety.

Little information has been uncovered about OLGA WOHLBRÜCK[130], who began her studies at the Zurich Federal Polytechnikum nine years before Marie Baum. Wohlbrück was one of the first women to receive a doctorate in chemistry from Zurich University. From Weimar, Saxony, she enrolled in the division of technical chemistry of the Polytechnikum[131] in 1884 and was awarded her diploma in 1886. Continuing her studies, she carried out research on the structure of esters of higher fatty acids under the direction of Arthur Hantsch, professor at the Polytechnikum from 1885 until 1893. Two of her papers, including one joint with Hantsch, appeared in the German Chemical Society's *Berichte* in 1887 (see bibliography), the year she received her doctorate. She became a member of the society the following year. After a short time in Cannstatt near Stuttgart, she took a position in an oil factory in Libau on the Russian Baltic coast (now Liepago, Latvia) and was there until at least 1889.

CLARA IMMERWAHR[132] (1870–1915), the first woman to receive a doctorate from Breslau University, has fairly recently been rescued from the obscurity in which she languished during much of the eight decades immediately following her death; her tragic story has aroused considerable interest among present-day feminists, at least in Europe.

Clara was the youngest daughter among the four children of Philipp Immerwahr and his wife Anna (née Krohn). She was born on 21 June 1870 on the family estate of Polkendorf in Neumarkt (now Sroda Slaska), Silesia, about twenty miles west of Breslau (now Wroclaw) the major trade center of the region. The Immerwahrs were a prosperous and respected Jewish family with extensive commercial interests in Breslau. These included a flourishing business, with wide international connections, established in the early years of the nineteenth century by Clara's grandfather David Immerwahr. Philipp Immerwahr had studied chemistry, first in Breslau and then with Robert Bunsen at Heidelberg University but, academic careers still being largely blocked to Jews, he returned to management of the Polkendorf estate and of a sugar factory in Trachenberg (now Zmigród) about twenty-five miles north of Breslau.

Growing up in a happy family atmosphere, Clara was given her first schooling at home by a teacher from the neighboring village and by a governess. The family regularly spent the winter months in Breslau with Lina Immerwahr, Clara's grandmother, whose large establishment afforded accommodation for a girls' school that she attended. An eager student, she learned quickly; physics was a special interest and the science teaching was good, several of the instructors being men from the Breslau *Realgymnasium* (nonclassical secondary school). Sometime in her teens at a dance class in Breslau she met the future Nobel Prize winner Fritz Haber. A chemistry student at the time, Haber was doing his military service and was stationed near the city, his place of birth. The relationship was close, but the parents, not surprisingly, declined to give permission for marriage; Haber at that time would not have been able to support a wife without parental financial help.

In 1892–1893 Clara Immerwahr attended the Breslau Women Teachers' Seminar, but although she received her certificate, she never taught.[133] She would in any case have had to teach in a private school, a career in public school teaching being closed to her as a Jew.[134] But times were changing; women were being admitted as auditors into a number of German universities in increasing numbers, and Jews were finding greater acceptance in academia. In 1896, with her father's help, she obtained special permission to enter Breslau University. She was not the only woman student there at the time, official state approval having been granted the previous year for the acceptance as auditors in advanced classes of women teachers preparing for the *Oberlehrerinnenprüfung* (the advanced teachers' examination for women, instituted in Prussia in 1894).[135] Her classes, attendance at which required further special permission from the lecturers concerned, included experimental physics, taught by Oskar Meyer, and inorganic chemistry, taught by Friedrich Küster. In 1897 she passed the *Reiseprüfung* at the Breslau *Realgymnasium,* thereby completing formal university entrance requirements.

Two years later she began research under the direction of chemist Richard Abegg who succeed Küster in Breslau when the latter moved to the School of Mines in Clausthal. Abegg, soon to be well known for his investigations in many branches of solution chemistry and especially electrochemistry, was a close friend of Fritz Haber; both took doctoral degrees at Berlin University in 1891. Abegg encouraged Clara to proceed to a doctorate[136] and, following his advice, she began investigating the solubility of a series of salts of heavy metals (mercury, copper, lead, cadmium, and zinc). She examined ionic concentrations via electrochemical methods, making a special effort to produce standard electrodes and control temperature; the reversibility of copper electrodes was one of the questions of particular interest to her. Her results, published in *Zeitschrift für Anorganische Chemie* in 1900 (see bibliography) and in *Zeitschrift für Elektrochemie* the following year,[137] constituted a creditable contribution to the then very active field of electrochemistry. The work was done in part in the laboratories of the Breslau Technische Hochschule and in part at the School of Mines in Clausthal in the spring of 1900, better facilities being available in Küster's Clausthal laboratory.

In addition to her dissertation research, Immerwahr carried out a study on the dissociation of silver fluoride and another on silver bromide photographic emulsions, both joint with Abegg (see bibliography). By 1900 she had been present at the university (as an auditor) for eight semesters, two more than the six specified for male doctoral candidates. She took the required oral examination on 22 December 1900. An article in the *Breslauer Zeitung* for that date described this event—an historic one in the annals of the university: an unusually large and lively audience had assembled in the main hall, the Aula Leopoldina; many young ladies from the city who were more in the habit of attending lectures on art history or literary topics were curious to see "Unser erster weiblicher Doktor." She passed magna cum laude, and received warm praise from the dean of the philosophy department who presented her as a person who had reached her desired goal despite considerable difficulty. (He nevertheless went on to express his hope that the university would not be flooded with women students, the most sacred calling of the female sex being, in his opinion, the care of a family.)[138]

For a few months she continued work in electrochemistry in Abegg's laboratory,[139] and in April 1901 attended the Freiburg Congress of the Deutsche Gesellschaft für Elektrochemie. There she renewed her friendship with Fritz Haber, who by then held a professorship *extraordinarius* at the Karlsruhe Technische Hochschule. They were married the following August.

Thereafter Clara Haber gave up professional work; indeed there exists no real evidence to suggest that she expected to continue research after marriage. However, she frequently visited her husband's laboratory, followed his work, proofread manuscripts, and checked and verified the data for his widely acclaimed third book, *Thermodynamik Technischer Gasreaktionen* (1905).[140] After the birth in 1902 of her son Hermann, a delicate child over whom she worried, she became increasingly burdened with family and household cares. In addition she suffered more and more from periods of depression. Immersed in his research and unstinting of time given to his large group of students and coworkers, Haber worked long days. As had been his habit before marriage, he spent lunch hours at his laboratory and many evenings with his colleagues in bars—a lifestyle that left him little time at home. He had scant sympathy for the domestic problems that worried his wife, a perfectionist in her cooking and housekeeping who disliked delegating work to servants. Haber's habit of unexpectedly bringing home as house guests the many visiting scientists who came to his laboratory added to Clara's anxieties. In short, her husband's ambition, driving need for recognition in a society where anti-Semitism was still latent, tremendous energy, and commanding personality had the effect of crushing Clara Haber and shattering her self-esteem. Hers was a mild, somewhat withdrawn character, her success as a student notwithstanding. About 1906 she had treatment in a psychiatric sanitorium in Freiburg, but that improved her health and state of mind only temporarily. She became even more dispirited following the deaths about then of her father, to whom she had always remained close, and of a nephew as well. A second stay in the sanatorium was necessary in 1910.

Thus the years in Karlsruhe, a time of brilliant achievement for Fritz Haber culminating in his successful development and patenting of a process for the production of ammonia from its elements,[141] brought ever-increasing difficulties for Clara. She had little enthusiasm for Haber's alliance with industry, seeing academic science in the old, traditional way as properly being "pure science," free from commercialism and money interests. She worried that his confident anticipation of substantial financial rewards from his patent success would increase what she considered his tendency to spend more freely than his income warranted. As a result she distanced herself further and he talked with her less and less about his work and plans. About 1910 she appears to have presented a series of public lectures on "household chemistry" to a mainly female audience but in general she retreated into her domestic work. Writing about this time to her former research adviser Richard Abegg, who had remained a close friend to whom she confided her unhappiness, she spoke of her husband's overpowering attitude, the peculiarities of her own temperament, and her deepest despair about the future. Abegg's accidental death in 1910 further deepened her melancholy.

In 1911 the family moved to Berlin-Dahlem, Haber having been named director of the new Kaiser-Wilhelm Institute for Physical Chemistry, a position of very considerable prestige. The move did not help the marriage; on the contrary it appears to have increased the conflict. Clara found no pleasure in her husband's career advancement and was unsuited by nature to shoulder any further demands made on her as wife of the director of an important and sizable institute. Neither did the change of scene stimulate her into taking part in any of the women's movement actions in which a great many Berlin middle-class women and early university graduates were then involved.[142]

The coming of the First World War in 1914 brought Haber growing responsibilities and a work load that left him even less time at home than before. With the blocking of Germany's access to Chilean nitrate deposits, synthetic production of ammonia became increasingly important. Haber was put in charge of organizing and systematizing production for both agricultural use and the needs of the military, nitrates being required for the manufacture of explosives. He also started work on the development of fuel additives that allowed motorized campaigns to continue on the eastern front throughout the winter months—another major contribution to the military effort. In addition, at the suggestion of the War Ministry, he undertook the investigation of poison gas production for battlefield use.

The latter project, begun at the Kaiser Wilhelm Institute for Physical Chemistry during the first year of the war, did not proceed without accidents. Otto Sackur, one of the chemists Clara Haber had known well as a student at Breslau University, was killed in a powerful laboratory explosion the immediate aftermath of which she witnessed. It seems likely that the gas research and the animal trials that were part of it caused her deep distress; such a reaction would hardly be surprising. She is said to have felt it was nothing short of a corruption of the discipline, a perversion of science, and she did her best to bring her husband to her view. Haber however, like the vast majority of German academics, was caught up in the famous "spirit of 1914," the powerful wave of nationalistic and militaristic feeling that swept through the country and its universities early in the war.[143] He considered that his primary duty lay in placing his scientific knowledge at the service of his country, and he believed that in German hands the chemical weapon could bring quick victory and end the fighting. By March 1915 he was totally occupied with preparations for a chlorine gas attack on the Western Front and only occasionally came to Dahlem for a few days. On 22 April 1915 the attack took place under his supervision along a seven-kilometer front near Ypres. The chlorine gas cloud blown over the French trenches killed 5000 men and severely damaged the lungs of 10,000 more, effectively knocking them out of combat. The trial was viewed as a considerable success by the German military. Haber was promoted to captain and directed almost immediately to prepare a similar attack on the Eastern Front.

On the night of 1 May 1915, following a social gathering in the Habers' Dahlem villa, Clara Haber shot herself with her husband's military revolver. The *Grunewald-Zeitung* for 8 May reported the suicide, which Haber himself did not publicly acknowledge. The newspaper stated that the reason for the tragedy was unknown.[144]

After the war Haber's distinguished career continued, his dynamic leadership making the Kaiser Wilhelm Institute for Physical Chemistry world famous by the 1920s. Forced to leave the country because of the coming to power of the National Socialist Party, he died in Basle, Switzerland, in 1934. Following his instructions, Clara Haber's ashes, originally interred in Dahlem, were moved to Basle; a single gravestone, giving only names and dates of birth and death, marks the burial site of the two sets of remains in Hörnli cemetery, Basle.

Clara Haber has been depicted as a solitary female protagonist fighting a desperate battle against modern, male-devised methods of mass destruction, taking a humane, civilized stand against the forces of barbarism—an interpretation of the Immerwahr-Haber story that goes back for a number of years and that has considerable attraction for present-day feminist historians. However, as has recently been pointed out,[145] caution requires that restraint be exercised to avoid turning her into a pacifist heroine on the basis of little more than word-of-mouth tradition. There are few reliable sources of information concerning the relationship between Clara and Fritz Haber about the time of the suicide; Clara appears to have left no diaries, no illuminating correspondence, not even a farewell letter to her husband or son. Fritz Haber's recent biographers, basing their work on sober and painstaking evaluations of the large amount of available source material about him, hardly depict him as an unfeeling demon.[146] An ardent Prussian and a militarist he undoubtedly was, and a poor choice of domestic partner for a woman of Clara's mild, anxiety-prone nature. But given the complexities of the situation and the lack of information, Clara Haber's suicide might very reasonably be seen as the final step taken after years of worry, frustration, and acute depression—the cumulative effect of the daily problems that for her were overwhelming. She acted quietly and privately without making any public statement, without even leaving a word of explanation as far as is known. And this course of action, while very much in character, speaks against the interpretation of her suicide as an idealistic gesture; she had no audience other than her husband and teenage son. Whether or not she killed herself as a last desperate protest against gas warfare remains a question.

All the same, Clara's name is now clearly linked with antiwar activism. The Clara Immerwahr Award, a prize established in 1991 by the German section of the IPPNW (International Physicians for the Prevention of Nuclear War/Physicians for Social Responsibility) recognizes and honors people who have, in the course of their professional duties, worked against war, arms, and other threats to human existence.[147] Her story was the subject of a German radio program in the early 1990s, and is also told in the stage play *Square Rounds,* first performed, to considerable acclaim, at the Olivier Theatre, London, in October 1992. Fritz and Clara Haber are the major characters in this antiwar drama in verse, song, and dance (set mainly about the time of the First World War) that explores the dual creative and destructive powers of science. Here they heatedly argue out the case for and against the military use of nitrate explosives and poison gases, to the point of Clara's sensational suicide (offstage) and the chilling prediction by her ghost that fellow Germans will use Haber's form of killing against Jews.[148]

In physics one German woman—Elsa Neumann—received a doctoral degree before the turn of the century and contributions to the field by two others—Else Köttgen[149] and Agnes Pockels—are listed in the bibliography.[150] Of the three, Pockels is the best known and by far the most distinguished.

> *Agnes Pockels' researches, developed almost entirely independently, are meritorious by any standard. They show a clarity of thought and observation, a strictness of scientific approach remarkable for a girl of her years who had no formal scientific training. When examined against the background of her life they become truly astonishing.*[151]
>
> —Giles and Forrester

AGNES POCKELS[152] (1862–1935), the elder child and only daughter of Captain Theodor Pockels and his wife Alwine (née Becker), was born in Venice, on 14 February 1862. Originally from the Netherlands, Theodor Pockels's forbears had migrated to Halle, Saxony, there becoming *Halloren*—workers in the ancient city's famous and long-established salt industry. Theodor Pockels himself was from Braunschweig, Lower Saxony. The family had a notable record of church and state service; as a young man Theodor entered the Emperor's First Infantry Regiment of the Austrian army. Thus Agnes spent her earliest years at various locations in what is now northeastern Italy, but was then part of the Austrian Empire. With the unification of Venetia with the Kingdom of Italy in 1866 the regiment returned to its home base of Troppau, Moravia (now Opava, Czech Republic). The entire family suffered much from ill health, having contracted malaria during their years in northern Italy; Captain Pockels received an early discharge in 1871 and retired to Braunschweig, where Agnes and her younger brother Friedrich grew up.

For several years from age ten she attended a municipal school for girls. She was interested in the sciences, particularly physics, a subject in which there was then little instruction in girls' schools. Opportunities for university-level training being still almost nonexistent for German women at the time she most needed them (about 1880), her subsequent studies were self-directed. She always regretted her scant knowledge of mathematical physics. By the 1890s, when German universities were beginning to accept women as auditors, she had heavy responsibilities taking care of her aging and frequently ill parents. Her brother Friedrich, three years her junior, attended the Braunschweig *Realgymnasium.* Illness often kept him at home and brother and sister had plenty of time to discuss their common interests in science. Agnes's first guide was a textbook by Matthias Pouillet,[153] but by the mid-1880s, when Friedrich Pockels was a physics student at Göttingen University, she was using textbooks provided by him.

Her work on surface films began about 1880 or 1881, when she was eighteen or nineteen, and well before her brother would have been able to provide direction. The family kitchen was her laboratory. Here she made original observations, developed research methods, and invented the apparatus that, with later elaboration, became standard equipment in the field. It is said that she became interested in surface films as a result of daily dealing with greasy dishwater.[154]

In 1881 she recorded her first quantitative observations on surface currents and discovered changes in surface tension caused by these currents. Her apparatus consisted of a slightly modified apothecary's balance that had belonged to her grandfather, a recycled metal food container which served as a water trough, and some small buttons. She measured the force required to lift a button from the water surface. In 1882, when she was twenty, she developed a method of changing the surface area of the body of water under study by means of a metal strip placed over it—that is, she invented the slide trough, an apparatus later used universally in surface film studies.

In 1889 Friedrich Pockels became an assistant at the Physical Institute at Göttingen University and from about then was better able to appreciate the value of Agnes's work, to supply her with books, and perhaps to advise. There was little interest in surface film phenomena among German scientists at the time, but British physicist Lord Rayleigh was working in the area and in 1890 had published in the *Proceedings of the Royal Society* three papers reporting his initial findings.[155] The *Proceedings* were abstracted into the recently founded German review journal *Naturwissenschaftliche Rundschau,* published in Braunschweig, to which Agnes Pockels subscribed. Rayleigh's third paper, discussing changes in surface tension in the case of a water surface contaminated with a film of insoluble grease, was close to her own work. And so, on her brother's advice, although with considerable diffidence, she summoned up her courage and wrote to Lord Rayleigh in January 1891.

Then perhaps the leading figure in the physical sciences, Rayleigh had every reason to assume that he was without rival in the surface film work. A lesser man might have turned aside from an unknown amateur who had anticipated him in an area he was himself developing. Much to his credit however, and most fortunately for Agnes Pockels, he satisfied himself on a few more details by further correspondence with her and then arranged for her work to be published. It appeared two months later in the widely read general science journal *Nature* in an English translation (prepared by Lady Rayleigh). Rayleigh's introductory note addressed to editor Sir Norman Lockyer was as follows:

> I shall be obliged if you can find space for the accompanying translation of an interesting letter which I have received from a German lady, who with very homely appliances has arrived at valuable results respecting the behaviour of contaminated water surfaces. The earlier part of Miss Pockels's letter covers nearly the same ground as some of my own recent work, and in the main harmonises with it. The later sections seem to me very suggestive, raising, if they do not fully answer, many important questions. I hope soon to find opportunity for repeating some of Miss Pockel's experiments.[156]

Pockels's letter is "a landmark in the history of surface chemistry, and together with papers which Rayleigh had published shortly beforehand, it gave the subject new impetus which is still maintained."[157] Her observations laid the foundation for the quantitative method of surface layer research, outlining many of the principles later to be adopted as standard practice in the field worldwide. Her simple, rectangular tin trough, equipped with a movable tin strip to permit surface area variation, forms the basis of the trough method of surface film investigation developed especially by Irwin Langmuir in 1917 and then improved by others. Langmuir's 1932 Nobel Prize in chemistry for his investigations of monolayers (on both solids and liquids) thus relates back in part to Pockels's studies with primitive apparatus.

Among the surface layer properties that Agnes Pockels observed was the fact that the surface tension of a strongly contaminated surface varies with the size of the surface area. Thus when a monolayer of an oily substance on water is compressed, the surface tension decreases to that of the monolayer and on extension the effect is reversed, the surface tension gradually returning to that of pure water. This observation prompted Lord Rayleigh to remark that, "It is only when I have myself made experiments upon the same lines that I have appreciated the full significance of Miss Pockel's statement."[158] She considered that her apparatus could detect the presence of films down to an apparent thickness of 0.37Å and that in this state the substance was present not as a coherent film but in a finely divided state. The minimum area occupied by a monomolecular surface film is known as the "Pockel's point." She also measured the effects of wave damping by surface films. Problems of producing a clean surface and of dealing with the return current that tended to break through between the dividing partition and the side of the trough were topics she discussed at length. Her second letter to Rayleigh described her method, which later became the standard technique, of applying a water insoluble material to a water surface by allowing a benzene solution of the material to evaporate on the surface.[159]

She made a great many other observations about different kinds of surface films on water and carried out numerous quantitative studies on interfacial tension between water and water-immiscible liquids. Her additional work included the development of the ring method for surface tension measurements and investigations of the behavior of colloidal solutions on surfaces. Her main overall interest was the physics of surface forces and the nature of the water layer just below the film, a topic that was later to become very important in protein studies. She focused on these areas rather than on the more chemical questions of the nature of the film itself and the arrangement of its constituent molecules.

Rayleigh, who had some difficulty believing his correspondent was actually a woman when he received her first letter,[160] provided important initial help and encouragement when he arranged for her first report to be published. Her contacts with German physicists were established gradually. In 1893 Woldemar Voigt of Göttingen University offered her facilities at the Physical Institute; four years later she met several other German physicists at a scientific meeting in Braunschweig, and in 1901, when visiting her brother in Heidelberg (where he had received an appointment the preceding year), she talked with Rudolf Weber and Georg Quincke, both of whom had interests in her field.

After her first four publications in *Nature* (1891–1894) she brought out several additional reports in German journals discussing mainly research carried out before the First World War. The death of her brother in 1913, that of her mother the year after, the war, the difficulties of getting relevant journal articles while hostilities lasted and for several years subsequently, and the deterioration of her own health, particularly her eyesight, greatly reduced her ability to keep up with her field and continue research.[161] Nevertheless she did bring out a notable number of additional works. As well as reports of her own research, these included a translation from the English of Sir George Darwin's 1891 geophysical treatise on tidal phenomena and a philosophical paper on the random nature of things; the latter appeared in 1909, a time when this concept was coming to the fore. She also helped her brother with his work of editing *Beiblätter zu den Annalen der Physik*, writing reviews and reports on capillarity. Her last paper appeared in *Kolloid Zeitschrift* in 1933.[162]

After the war she led a quiet life. In the family she was known as "Tante Agnes." She had many friends in Braunschweig and two puzzle-solving groups regularly met in her house. During the postwar period of severe inflation she received help from relatives in America; later assistance came in the form of dividends from family investments in California, an income she shared with others. Friends and relatives were much surprised when in 1931 her early work was recognized by the scientific community. That year she received the Laura Leonard Prize of the Deutsche Kolloid-Gesellschaft for her "Quantitative investigation of the properties of surface layers and surface films." The prize was awarded jointly to her and French investigator Henri Devaux, who took up the subject after Rayleigh. On 27 January 1932, shortly before her seventieth birthday, the Carolina-Wilhelmina Hochschule in Braunschweig awarded her a well-deserved honorary doctorate. Both honors were presented during a Physical Society conference in Braunschweig; the occasion was marked with a celebratory tea at which she made an impromptu speech.

Agnes Pockel's general outlook was broad and international. When asked what facet of her early work gave her the most pleasure she replied "The idea that the recognition of this fundamental law should have been made simultaneously in Germany, France and England."[163] In 1914 when her country was swept with a wave of patriotic enthusiasm for war, she stood aside, foreseeing the likely outcome. And again in 1935, on the eve of the Second World War, she saw with apprehension the signs of trouble and destruction to come. Her thoughts were expressed in a poem, a verse of which reads:

Wir bereiten vor einen neuen Versuch,
der klares Erkennen soll bringen;

> wir schaffen Gemälde und hauen in Stein,
> was immer soll unvergessen sein—
> und über uns grollet der Flieger. . . .
> und singt seinen dröhnenden, drohenden Sang
> von der Menschheit baldigem Untergang.

Agnes Pockels (1935)[164]

Agnes Pockels died in Braunschweig on 21 November 1935 at the age of seventy-three.

Neumann, the only German woman who received a doctorate in physics before 1901 whose work is listed in the bibliography, studied at Friedrich-Wilhelms University in Berlin. Her degree was awarded in 1899, the first doctorate given to a woman by the university.

ELSA NEUMANN[165] (1872–1902) was born in Berlin on 23 August 1872, one of the younger siblings in the family of at least seven children of Maximilian Neumann and his wife Anna (née Meyer). Of the reform Jewish faith and moderately wealthy, the family was long established and respected in Berlin society. Maximilian Neumann is thought to have been a banker; he also had strong interests in zoology, probably as an amateur. One of Elsa Neumann's older brothers, Oskar Neumann, became well known internationally for his zoological studies in east and central Africa. He took part in a number of scientific expeditions and became an expert on the taxonomy of birds of the tropics. Alice Neumann, Elsa's older sister to whom she was much attached and to whom she dedicated her doctoral dissertation, was a sculptor.

Although women in Prussia could not officially take the *Abitur* until 1900 and there were no girls' gymnasia that provided pre-university education equivalent to that available to boys, Berlin had a number of private girls' schools, some of which made a special effort to provide instruction that would bring girls up to university entrance level. Elsa Neumann attended the Charlotte School, opened in 1879, and the exclusive "Crainsche höhere Mädchenschule und Elementar-Knabenschule" run by Lucie Crain. She also spent some time at a private institution in Hanover. After passing the women teachers' examination (*Lehrerinnenprüfung*) in 1890, the most advanced standard qualification open to women,[166] she continued her studies. In her 1898 request to the Ministry of Culture for special permission to take her doctoral examination without having passed the *Abitur*, she listed explicitly the men who had taught her in her pre-university studies: mathematician Immanuel Lazarus Fuchs, professor at Friedrich-Wilhelms University, physicist Hugo Hertzer, professor at the Technische Hochschule in Charlottenburg, Dr. Spies, director of Urania (a still-existing Berlin scientific society also interested in the popularization of science), and Herren Heyne and Voss, teachers of upper-level students at the Falkrealgymnasium.

In 1894 she began university studies, first at Göttingen University and then at Friedrich-Wilhelms University in Berlin.[167] She completed nine semesters, attending classes in mathematics, physics, chemistry, and philosophy. In her case as with other women students at the time, arrangements had to be made personally, her admission to lectures and laboratories being dependent on the consent of the individual professors; a number of women students had previously attended classes at Göttingen University and, from 1895, at Friedrich-Wilhelms University, but another fourteen years were to pass before they received the right to matriculate.

At Göttingen Elsa Neumann's professors included electrochemist Richard Abegg (there for a year before he went to Breslau University) and physical chemist Walther Nernst; in Berlin she studied with mathematician Lazarus Fuchs and with physicists Emil Warburg and Max Planck. Her dissertation research, directed by Warburg with Planck as second adviser, was an investigation of the polarization capacity of reversible electrodes using mercury and silver cells; the area was one in which both Warburg and Planck were extremely active at the time. Neumann focused particularly on the relationship between potential and metal ion concentration. Thanks to the strong support of Warburg, Planck, and Fuchs, all influential men, she received permission to take the degree examination, the first woman candidate at Friedrich-Wilhelms University. She passed, cum laude, on 15 December 1898 and received her diploma on 18 February 1899. The event was a notable one in the history of the university and it was reported in detail in the Berlin newspapers. Her main paper presenting her research appeared in the well-known journal *Annalen der Physik und Chemie* early the following year (see bibliography). She was proposed by Max Planck for membership in the much-respected Berlin Physical Society (later the German Physical Society) at its January 1899 meeting and accepted two weeks later, becoming the first woman member and the only one for some years. In 1901 she joined the German Chemical Society as an associate member.[168]

Elsa Neumann had little hope of employment at a university after her graduation and research posts in the electrical or chemical industries were largely unavailable to women.[169] A teaching career in a public school was also closed to her as a Jew although there were a number of private schools in Berlin where she would have been able to work. One further possibility remained.

At that time there were several private chemical laboratories in Berlin where important basic research was carried out. Indeed science and those engaged in its pursuit were very much part of the social and cultural life of the city; reports on science and science- and technology-related topics were a daily feature in Berlin's main newspapers. The private scholar, unaffiliated with any institution, was by no means unusual and the cost of a private laboratory was not prohibitive. Coming from a relatively well-off family Elsa Neumann was able to continue research in such a private laboratory, the Berlin Scientific-Chemical Laboratory N, on Chausseestrasse. Established in 1891 by Carl Friedheim and Arthur Rosenheim, the Chausseestrasse laboratory was managed from 1897 by Rosenheim and Richard Joseph Meyer, both adjunct, external professors at Friedrich-Wilhelm's University. Several doctoral candidates of Rosenheim and Meyer worked in the laboratory that also rented space to other students and to private researchers. Elsa Neumann had a room of her own and appears to have continued her work in electrochemistry. In 1900 she paid a short visit to the Cavendish Laboratory at Cambridge University, where several women had worked for periods from 1880 on.[170] No record appears to have survived of what she studied there but work in this pioneering laboratory, famous especially for the elucidation of the nature of cathode rays, included important research in Neumann's field of electrolysis.[171]

Active in the women's movement and very conscious of the need of women students for financial help in order to successfully complete university-level training, she founded, in April 1900, the Verein zur Gewährung zinsfreier Darlehen an studierenden Frauen (Society for Guaranteeing Interest-free Loans to Women Students). She served as the group's first president until March 1902 when bacteriologist Lydia Rabinowitsch (p. 135) accepted the post. A number of well-known and respected men and women of the scientific and academic communities were members and supporters of the society, which collected and dispensed a considerable sum over the course of three decades. It was essentially refounded in March 1930, by which time its funds, depleted by post–First World War inflation, were very low.

Enthusiastic about technological developments as well as purely scientific advances, Elsa Neumann had a special interest in the airships then being built by Graf Ferdinand von Zeppelin. In June 1902 she took a trip in an airship in the company of von Zeppelin and a professor from the Berlin Technische Hochschule—an adventurous undertaking. These huge ships, which were later to play an important role during the opening stages of the First World War, used hydrogen as the lifting gas, a practice that brought a significant risk of explosion and fire. At the next meeting of the Deutsche Verein für Luftschifffahrt (German Society for Airship Travel), she presented a lively and humorous account of the trip. She also undertook to prepare a detailed discussion of the potential for a hydrogen explosion.[172]

Elsa Neumann died suddenly on 23 July 1902, a month before her thirtieth birthday, in her laboratory room on Chausseestrasse. According to reports in Berlin newspapers, the cause of death was cyanide poisoning.[173]

Around the turn of the century, a considerable amount of work was being carried out using hydrocyanic acid in both inorganic and organic chemistry but the precautions necessary and the proper care needed were not always fully appreciated. The well-known German chemist Ludwig Gattermann noted in a 1907 paper that the presence of even trace amounts of hydrocyanic acid in the atmosphere could be readily detected by its effect on the taste of cigar smoke[174]—a control method of which Neumann most likely did not avail herself. Whether or not her room in the Chausseestrasse laboratory was equipped with a fume cupboard is not known, but either her own carelessness or a failure or inadequacy in the ventilation system could readily account for the accident.

In contrast to the common custom of the time, Elsa Neumann's remains were cremated, a choice that reinforces the picture of her as modern and forward-looking in her outlook, free from strict religious dogma. The procedure being still prohibited in Prussia, as in several other German states, the body was taken to a crematorium in Hamburg and the ashes buried there also; the Jewish cemetery in Berlin-Wissensee did not allow urn burial until 1909. A memorial service held at the home of her mother (by then widowed) at Potsdamerstrasse 10 was attended by Rabbi Wilhelm Kemperer, minister to reform Jews in Berlin. Several prominent members of the Berlin academic community were present and the Airship Travel Society was represented.

In 1904, two years after her daughter's death, Anna Meyer Neumann gave Berlin University the then considerable sum of 30,000 marks to establish the Elsa Neumann Foundation. Its purpose was to present an annual Elsa Neumann Prize for the best work of the year in mathematics or physics by a student under the age of thirty; the selection was to be made without regard to sex or religious affiliation. Between 1906 and 1917 twelve prizes were awarded, all to men; none were given in 1917 and 1918. The inflation that followed the First World War wiped out the funds of the foundation, and so far it has not been reconstituted. Only one of Elsa

Neumann's siblings survived the period of National Socialist government that began in the 1930s; ornithologist Oskar Neumann escaped via Cuba and died in Chicago in 1946.

Social Sciences

Papers by four German women—Johanna Mestorf and Paula Karsten (archaeology and anthropology), Elsa Köttgen and Anna Pötsch (psychology)—are listed in the bibliography.

> *Mit Stolz blicken wir auf Fräulein Mestorf welche das weibliche Geschlecht in der prähistorischen Archäologie zu einer so glanzvollen Anerkennung gebracht hat.*[175]
>
> —Rudolf Virchow

JOHANNA MESTORF[176] (1828–1909), well known in her time for her many contributions to the rich field of North German and Scandinavian archeology and ethnology, was one of nine children (five of whom died young) in the family of Jacob Heinrich Mestorf and his wife Sofia Katrina Georgina (née Körner). She was born on 17 April 1828 in the small community of Bad Bramstedt, Holstein, about twenty miles north of Hamburg, an area that was part of Denmark until the duchies of Schleswig and Holstein were annexed by Prussia in 1866. Jacob Mestorf, a former army surgeon, had practices in Bad Bramstedt and Rendsburg from 1822. In his leisure time he occupied himself with the prehistory of the region, amassing a sizable collection of archaeological materials; Johanna Mestorf's interests in prehistory may well have been kindled by an early introduction through his work. Following his premature death in 1837, his widow Sofia, daughter of lance-corporal Johan Körner of the Oldenburg Infantry Regiment and a relative of the early nineteenth-century German poet Theodor Körner, moved her family to the nearby larger town of Itzehoe. There, despite their poverty, the children were given a good basic education, Johanna attending a girls' high school.

In 1849, at the age of twenty, she accepted the post of governess and lady's companion in the family of Swedish landowner Count Axel Mauritz Piper, lieutenant of the Dragoons of the Royal Guard and chamberlain at the court of the queen mother. For the next four years she lived at Castle Ängsö on the count's estate of Engsö in Västmanland, about sixty-three miles west of Stockholm, all the while greatly expanding her knowledge of Scandinavian languages and history. Although she enjoyed being with the family, her somewhat delicate health suffered from the harsher Swedish climate and perhaps also from winters in a seventeenth-century stone castle; in 1853 she returned to Itzehoe.

Her connection with the Pipers continued however, and over the next few years she accompanied them on extended visits to France and Italy; she also spent some time in the latter country as companion to Coutness Faletti de Villa Falletto. This experience in the Mediterranean lands with their rich cultures and ancient traditions allowed her to further broaden her knowledge and horizons as well as learn other languages. Her process of self-education was well advanced by the time she returned to the north of Germany in 1859 and made her home with her mother and brother in Hamburg. After a time she was able to support herself as foreign-language secretary at the Hamburg publishing and printing house of C. Adler.

Johanna Mestorf's literary and scientific activities began within a few years of her return to the north. Her first publications were translations into German of Swedish works of fiction such as Emilie Flygare-Carlén's 1862 collection *Skuggspel* (Shadow Play). About the same time she began to write herself, bringing out her historical novel *Wibeke Kruse*.[177] Set in the time of King Kristian IV of Denmark (1577–1648) with the king's mistress, the young peasant girl Wibeke Kruse, as its main character, it also carried a message—namely the idea that the preservation of prehistoric monuments was a matter of considerable importance. Mestorf had early realized that this work, which had scarcely begun in Schleswig-Holstein, required the cooperation of ordinary people in local communities, especially farmers.

Her translation of Swedish archeologist Sven Nilsson's treatise on the original inhabitants of northern Scandinavia (*Die Ureinwohner des Scandinavischen Nordens*) was published in two sections; part I, on the Bronze Age, appeared in 1863 with supplements in 1865 and 1866, and part II, on the Stone Age, in 1868. This work, probably suggested to Mestorf by Kiel librarian and classical archaeologist Christian Petersen, marked the start of her career in archaeology that spanned nearly half a century.[178]

Her many-sided literary activity in addition to her series of public lectures for women on Nordic mythology made Johanna Mestorf a well-known figure in the Hamburg area. From 1868 she was associated with the Museum of National Antiquities in Kiel as an independent worker, a connection that undoubtedly made it easier for her to form contacts with others in her field; the following year at the Fourth Anthropological Congress in Copenhagen, she made the acquaintance of many of the best-known anthropologists and archaeologists of the time. Clear recognition of her contributions to the promotion of local archaeological knowledge came in 1871 when the Hamburg Senate sent her as its official representative to the Fifth International Congress for Prehistoric Anthropology and Archaeology in Bologna.[179]

The turning point in her career came in 1873 when she was appointed by the Prussian Ministry for Church and Education to the newly created post of custodian at the Schleswig-Holstein Museum of National Antiquities, Kiel, which, under the directorship of Heinrich Handelmann, had recently been affiliated with Christian-Albrechts University, Kiel. This official position gave her a firm base from which to develop her interests. At the International Congress in Stockholm in 1874, perhaps the most important in Europe up to that time, she was one of very few women present in her own right. Although she does not appear to have taken part in the public discussions, the meeting gave her an excellent opportunity to extend and consolidate her position within the international network of European archaeologists.

The formidable task of preserving, cataloging, arranging, and expanding the Kiel Museum of National Antiquities collections, until then little more than a disordered mass of objects, absorbed most of her time and energy. She also continued her efforts, started with the publication of *Wibeke Kruse,* to ensure that the numerous finds still being unearthed by local people were brought to the museum, where they could be preserved and, no less important, made accessible to research workers. By enlisting the help of schoolteachers, she attempted to arouse the interest of children in archaeological materials and through them their parents. In 1878 she succeeded in the difficult job of moving the museum collections to a former university building in Kattenstrasse.

Conscious of the limitations imposed by her not very robust frame and delicate health, she did not attempt much field excavation. Her preference in any case was to work on the integration of archaeological data into a wider historical context, drawing in folklore and general anthropological ideas. Strongly influenced by the theories and analytical methods developed by nineteenth-century Scandinavian workers,[180] she saw modern north European cultures as evolving directly from behavioral patterns already present in prehistoric societies. Her goal was to contribute to the uncovering of these earlier cultural trends.

The 1870s and 1880s were a time of great literary productivity for Johanna Mestorf, most of her major translations of books and articles appearing then. After about 1875 the authors of the books were invariably her colleagues at Scandinavian national museums, all of them leading figures in the field. Following publication of her rendering of C. H. Wiberg's *Der Einfluss der Klassischen Völker auf den Norden* (1867) she brought out Carl Säve's book on the Nibelungen legends, *Zur Nibelungensage: Siegfriedbilder beschreiben und erklärt* (1870—from the Swedish), to which she added an appendix of her own. Then came Hans Hildebrand's *Das Heidnische Zeitalter in Schweden* (1873—from the Swedish), particularly noted for its correct rendering of names; *Vorgeschichte des Nordens nach Gleichzeitigen Denkmälern,* the work on Scandinavian antiquities by Jens Jacob Worsaae, Denmark's first modern archaeologist, along with Sophus Müller's, *Die Nordische Bronzezeit und deren Periodentheilung,* both from the Danish, were published in 1878. Another work by Müller, *Die Thierornamentik im Norden,* followed in 1881. A year later she brought out a German version of Norwegian archaeologist Ingvald Undset's work on the earliest appearance of iron in northern Europe—a subject of much discussion at the time—*Das erste Auftreten des Eisens in Nordeuropa.* Her last contribution, her translation from the Swedish of the expanded dissertation of Bernhard Salin, *Die Altgermanische Tierornamentik* (Stockholm, 1904), was a challenging undertaking. A major study of fourth- to ninth-century Germanic metal art objects, including a comparison with Celtic art from Ireland, had a lasting influence. Her skillful and painstaking presentations, often fully annotated, on occasion included critical comments, but were generally sympathetic to the authors' theories and interpretations.

In addition to these major works Mestorf translated many scientific journal articles, prepared German versions of guide books to national collections in Copenhagen and Stockholm, and over a period of more than thirty years, between about 1872 and 1905, brought out a series of annual bibliographies of Scandinavian archaeological publications. Most of the latter appeared in *Archiv für Anthropologie.* Over the same period she wrote many reviews, most of them on Scandinavian work, but some on material by French and German authors. Her bibliographies of French and Italian archaeological literature appeared in *Magazin für die Literatur des Auslandes* in 1877.

Because Scandinavian archaeologists dominated the field in West European work in the latter half of the nineteenth century, Mestorf's German translations were crucially important in the somewhat slower development of the subject as a fully professional discipline in her own country. Further, with German becoming the major langauge of science in continental Europe by the second half of the century, the translations were of considerable value throughout a wide region.

Mestorf's original work was also extensive. Topics she discussed ranged from the earliest Iron Age in Scandinavia, to religious beliefs of the people of Greenland, to Danish Bronze Age graves, including an examination of glass beads from women's graves.[181] Among her especially notable articles were those discussing finds of Viking-era hacksilver hoards housed in the Kiel museum. These reflected the fact that her years at the museum coincided with a period of spectacular discoveries of Viking Age hoards of coins, jewelry, and ingots. An 1895 article summarizing her interpretation of the structure and function of these hoards, and hence their cultural implications, remains significant in present-day work.[182] Her urgent plea for the preservation of Schleswig-Holstein's ancient monuments appeared in 1877.[183]

One of Mestorf's particular interests was the *Moorleichen,* the bog bodies or mummified human remains (often with associated clothing) found in the peat bogs of northwestern Europe; indeed it was she who coined the term. Her 1871 *Moorleichen* catalogue, the first compiled, listed twelve finds—in Ireland, Denmark, and Germany. Updates followed in 1900 and 1907, by which time fifty-two finds were listed. Wetlands archaeology was already a field of great activity in Mestorf's time. The opportunities for preservation of unusual evidence in watery environments had already been demonstrated and the possibility of deducing a great deal of information about conditions and practices in earlier societies clearly recognized.[184]

In 1885 and 1886 she brought out two important surveys, one on prehistoric antiquities and the second on urn burials in Schleswig-Holstein.[185] The former, dedicated to the memory of her father, celebrated the Kiel museum's fiftieth anniversary.[186] It incorporated a collection of outstanding lithographs of artifacts in the museum collections, plus a few of objects in collections in nearby cities. Written not as an art book, however, but rather as a guide for working archaeologists, it falls into three sections—Stone Age, Bronze Age, and Iron Age—and depicts artifacts ranging from flint choppers to elaborate bronze jewelry, ornate Iron Age buckles, shields, and silver inlaid iron stirrups; the last page shows a collection of silver *denarii* of the time of Charlemagne. Mestorf's special interest in the Three-Age system could well have originated in her father's early work. Jacob Mestorf applied this organizational method in the ordering of his archaeological collection at a time when the basic idea was still far from widely accepted among antiquarians and archaeologists.[187] Mestorf herself concentrated particularly on the Bronze Age, but she is also credited with having set the stage for all future work on the Iron Age in Schleswig-Holstein.[188]

All this steady effort in the investigation of northern antiquities, work that in large measure constituted the foundation of North German archaeology as a separate field, led to Johanna Mestorf's appointment in 1891 to the directorship of the Kiel Museum, following the death of Heinrich Handelmann. She was then sixty-three. The choice was an event of major significance in the history of women's advancement in Germany, being the first time a woman was placed at the head of a state museum and a university institute.[189] The Berlin Society for Anthropology, Ethnology and Prehistory elected her to honorary membership later the same year. In 1899, on her seventy-first birthday, the Kaiser bestowed on her the Women's Distinguished Service Order as well as the title of honorary professor, generally considered the first awarded to a woman in Germany.

This recognition, truly remarkable for an entirely self-educated late nineteenth-century woman, was enthusiastically celebrated in the local press and widely noted throughout Germany. Many congratulatory telegrams arrived in Kiel; the Swedish Academy of Sciences and the Swedish Archaeological Society also presented their good wishes, along with a copy of an eleventh-century silver vessel. Five years later (1904) she was awarded a Swedish gold medal (perhaps a personal gold medal from the Queen).[190] Other notable tokens of recognition Mestorf received included membership in anthropological and archaeological societies of Sweden, Finland, and Vienna, and in the Swedish academy for literary history and antiquities. On her eighty-first birthday in 1909, just after she had retired from her museum position, she was given an honorary doctorate by the medical faculty at Kiel University (most likely for her work on bog bodies).[191] Johanna Mestorf died three months later, in Kiel, on 20 July 1909, after a lengthy illness. She was buried in the still-existing Mestorf family plot in the Ohlsdorfer Cemetery in Hamburg, many prominent people in the cultural, scientific, and political communities as well as titled aristocracy attending the funeral. Numerous obituaries celebrating her remarkable career appeared in German anthropological and ethnological journals.[192]

Johanna Mestorf's life and work has received attention intermittently in Schleswig-Holstein publications over several decades.[193] In addition, in his 1938 account of the development of prehistory research in Germany, Hans Gummel made many references to her writings, underlining the importance of her work to studies of the North German Bronze and Iron Ages.[194] However, throughout most of the twentieth century Mestorf's name does not appear in discussions of the pioneers of archaeology included in major histories of the field.[195] Likewise, general surveys, histories, and collections of articles on early women in science in Germany rarely mention her. Reasons for the omission from the latter are fairly obvious: not being prominent in the women's movement, Mestorf fails to fit into the usual groupings studied by historians primarily interested in social questions; secondly, being entirely self-taught she cannot be included in studies of pioneering female students at particular universities; thirdly, although anthropology was already an accepted academic field, prehistory was scarcely even a distinguishable discipline when Mestorf began her work, hardly equivalent to old, established subjects such as chemistry or mathematics. Hence in studies of women scientists by discipline she has until lately tended to slip through the net as well.[196]

However, a number of papers providing biographical information and also a closer examination of her professional career have been published fairly recently.[197] Further, a two-day International Conference marking the 100th anniversary of the conferring of her honorary professorship and the 170th anniversary of her birth took place in Bad Bramstedt on 15–17 April 1999. Organized by the Institute for Pre- and Early-history at Christian-Albrechts University, Kiel, it provided a forum for the discussion of Johanna Mestorf's work by both Scandinavian and German historians.[198]

Early accounts often emphasized Mestorf's "fragile femininity"; a diminutive figure with her small frame, graceful, elegant carriage, and large, impressive blue eyes, she was almost lost amid the museum's old urns, vessels, and stone implements. The picture presented was that of a warm, motherly, soft-spoken, unassertive Baltic lady, remote from the strident demands of the women's movement that was well underway by the time she assumed the directorship of the Kiel museum. Hers was a life dedicated to work, the careful, painstaking preparation and presentation of the objects in the museum and their arrangement and display, often a difficult and demanding task requiring a considerable amount of manual labor.

This picture is now being revised. Even in the early 1860s, well before the full blossoming of the women's movement or any significant penetration of women into scientific work, this mild Baltic lady most likely had a remarkably ambitious goal, namely the custodianship of the Kiel Museum of Antiquities. Within a few years of taking up work in the field she considered, probably rightly, that she was well on the way to being the most qualified person for the post and with dogged patience and twelve-hour working days set out to fulfill her ambition; at the same time, she cultivated a groundwork of alliances in the right places. Thus, although there is no question that Johanna Mestorf's scientific achievements were the basis of her extraordinary academic advancement and fully justified her rise in her profession, she was not a modest, unassuming recluse, but in fact was pushing steadily beyond the purview of nineteenth-century women. In a preface to her unpublished diary she clearly stated that she worked hard over the course of five years preparing for the Kiel museum custodianship, progressively building up her knowledge. Always aware of her lack of physical strength, she wondered if she was overestimating herself, but hoped she could compensate for the deficiency with energy and endurance. She wrote in her diary that only her mother and her sister Jacobina ever knew of her plans and of her constant search for ways and means to reach her goals.[199]

Mestorf's friendship with the distinguished Berlin professor Rudolf Virchow and his family probably played a significant role in her early success. Well known and much respected as a medical scientist and anthropologist, Virchow was also a powerful and influential figure in Berlin and in national politics.[200] He often accompanied Mestorf to meetings of the German Anthropological Society and was one of the first to recognize the value of her work. In the two years immediately preceding her appointment to the museum custodianship she sent him at least one long memorandum bringing his attention to serious difficulties with Schleswig-Holstein collections split during the war with Denmark and asking for his help on behalf of museum interests;[201] in the peace treaty of 1864 German archaeologists claimed important remains. Because the custodianship appointment was not made locally but by the Prussian Ministry of Religion, Education, and Medical Affairs, which regularly listened to recommendations from distinguished figures such as Virchow, Mestorf's friendship with him may well have helped her win the selection to what was at the time a somewhat sensitive post politically.

After she became custodian Mestorf's protective instincts for the museum objects and her keen appreciation of their artistic qualities were apt to lead her into an attitude of almost despotic irritability when she met with any criticism of her presentations from superiors. Relations between her and the director did not always run harmoniously. However, it was Mestorf who as custodian and later as director laid the groundwork for the exploration of the prehistory of Schleswig-Holstein. She fought for the centralized storage of archaeological artifacts, prepared a catalogue of all the Schleswig-Holstein finds, and organized a system of rescue of finds that involved nominating responsible people in each district to serve as contacts between the Kiel museum and the local communities. This system was later adopted by other regions. The rich collections now in the Schleswig-Holstein Provincial Museum in Schloss Gottorf date back to her. Deeply knowledgeable and an expert in her field, the self-taught Mestorf was acknowledged and much respected by her fellow archaeologists, German and foreign. She was one of the initiators of the move to found the Schleswig-Holstein Anthropological Society and remained the organization's secretary until her death.

There is some question about whether Johanna Mestorf was as remote from the concerns of the women's rights movement and from ideas about the need for far-reaching social change as early biographical sketches suggest. She is known to have strongly supported the nationalist revolutionary movements that swept across Germany and Austria-Hungary in 1848 and she had a lively exchange of ideas with the North Frisian writer, painter, and revolutionary Harro Harring (1798–1870).[202] A prominent figure in Schleswig-Holstein political life, Harring stood against monarchial power and for freedom and democratic ideals, including the equality of women.

Mestorf was by no means without opponents, even enemies, over the course of her career, but she never feared to fight for her rights; in arguing her position, the fragile little Baltic lady could be a tough opponent. In her later years many of her close friendships were with women of aristocratic families who provided her with connections to official authorities when needed.

In her scholarly work Mestorf did not hesitate to present views that differed from the typical male perspective of the time on the meaning and significance of archaeological objects that had been used by women. For example, in her paper on daggers in fifteen graves of Bronze Age women in the Schleswig-Holstein region, she suggested that these women, whose daggers had clearly been worn at the belt, may either have joined with men in fighting or else lived independently, ready to fight or defend when the need arose. Here perhaps were the origins, she argued, of the folk legends about the warlike spirit of the German women, the "Valkieri of the North."[203]

Throughout her life Johanna Mestorf was known in her local community as an outspoken "go-getter," a woman who, against the odds, had created for herself a career in a field almost exclusively populated by men. Although she never explicitly expressed in writing her agreement with the aims of the women's movement, her independent way of life as an unmarried intellectual and her professional career in science were unprecedented in Germany at the time; she provided a unique example of the emancipated woman.[204] By breaking through barriers and opening gates Johanna Mestorf ably demonstrated that a woman was quite capable of research and organization in a scientific field, and furthermore of research that was far too important to be brushed aside. However, in the story of women's progress toward equal access to leadership positions in scientific work, she is perhaps something of an exception rather than an example that could be followed with reasonable hope of success. The early stage of development of her field, her particular circumstances, and her own truly exceptional drive and abilities came together to allow her to succeed as she did. Women are now well represented in archaeology and prehistory studies, but many years were to elapse before another woman reached Mestorf's level of achievement.

PAULA KARSTEN,[205] traveler, writer, linguist, translator, and ethnologist, was born on 8 March 1850 in Pasewalk, northeast Germany, about twenty miles inland from the Baltic coast. From her childhood she had a strong interest in languages and literature. She left home at an early age and from the late 1880s lived in Berlin, earning her living as a companion and by teaching languages (German, English, French, Italian, and Swedish). She also gave public lectures on a variety of topics, including cremation, a custom she advocated strongly but which was opposed by the religious authorities of the time. Interested in all aspects of human cultures, she explored in many countries. The stories, songs, and ethnographic information she collected throughout Europe, North Africa, and West Africa were published in periodicals (including *Deutsche Jugend*) or as monographs. She studied in particular the customs and languages of peoples of the western Sahara and in addition to her ethnographic papers published translations of Arabic works and collections of Arabic words and idioms from regions under German control. Her study of native peoples of the German West African colonies, *"Wer ist mein Nächster?" Negertypen aus Deutschwestafrika,* appeared in 1903.

Else Köttgen and Anna Pötsch both published work in experimental psychology in the late 1890s.[206] Else Köttgen (b. 1867) had broad interests in science and is known to have audited courses in several fields, particularly chemistry and biology.[207] For a period in the 1890s she worked with Arthur König, then professor *extraordinarius* in the physics section of the Physiological Institute at the University of Berlin and a leading investigator in the field of color vision. Following a preliminary paper on the spectral composition of light from various sources, Köttgen published (jointly with Georg Abelsdorff) two articles on red vision in vertebrates. Anna Pötsch was also interested in color vision. Her long article on color blindness appeared in *Zeitschrift für Psychologie* in 1899.

Summary and Further Notes

In this small group of thirty German women, eight (about 27 percent) were especially notable. The most outstanding research scientists among them were Marianne Plehn and Lydia Rabinowitsch, internationally known for their pioneering work in, respectively, fish pathology and tuberculosis investigations. Each produced an impressive number of technical publications. The work of Plehn's fellow zoologist, protozoa specialist Clara Hamburger, was also notable and the insect metabolism and parasite studies of Maria von Linden were received with interest by her colleagues. Although German women were less prominent than some of their French, Belgian, and Dutch contemporaries in botany, that popular field for nineteenth-century women of scientific bent, the early contribution of Johanna Lüders to German studies in cryptogamic botany is worth noting. Naturalist and traveler Therese von Bayern, a striking personality, must also be ranked highly, not only for her early contributions to the plant geography of South America, but for her fine legacy of travel books.

In the physical sciences the pioneering research of Agnes Pockels on the physics of surface tension is now well recognized. Chemist Marie Baum became a nationally known figure, although her major achievements were in social work, particularly practical social welfare, a field she came to via a period as a factory inspector in the increasingly industrialized state of Baden. In the social sciences Johanna Mestorf stands out. Internationally recognized archaeologist, prehistorian, translator, and author she became director of the Kiel Museum of National Antiquities several years before the turn of the century; her achievement was remarkable for a woman of her time.

Figure 5-2 shows the distribution of papers and authors by subject for this group. The largest contributions were in ornithology, the medical sciences including bacteriology, general biology, and botany. In ornithology the publications were nearly all those of Helene von Siebold, while in general biology the work was that of Maria von Linden; relatively large numbers of authors contributed to the medical sciences and botany. Overall, the wide spread of subjects is notable.

The crucial role played by close male relatives in fostering and facilitating the work of especially successful women research scientists in France has been pointed out (see chapter 3). This kind of assistance does not appear to have been as important among the leading German women. Plehn, Hamburger, and von Linden received only the help from academic advisers normally given a student. Von Bayern had the considerable advantage of royal birth and the accompanying financial resources, but her research was carried out independently. Rabinowitsch, because she earned no salary during much of her career, depended on her husband's financial resources and general support, but her research undertakings were clearly her own responsibility. Agnes Pockels benefited to some extent from her younger brother's connections with academic physics, although that could hardly compensate for lack of formal advanced training; there is little doubt, however, that her pioneering early studies were carried out on her own initiative and resulted from her own questions and ideas. Baum's tremendous drive and energy made possible her achievements in social welfare; in many of her undertakings she succeeded despite the lack of support and sometimes in the face of active antagonism of male superiors. Rudolf Virchow's putative support of Mestorf at the turning point in her career may well have been very important, although most likely no more so than the help many younger male scientists receive from mentors; however, her advancement and success basically depended on her own outstanding enterprise and hard work.

Notes

1. James C. Albisetti, *Schooling German Girls and Women: Secondary and Higher Education in the Nineteenth Century* (Princeton, N.J.: Princeton University Press, 1988), 242–49; see also Waltraud Heindl, "I. Zur Entwicklung des Frauenstudiums in Österreich," in *"Durch Erkenntnis zu Freiheit und Gluck . . ." Frauen an der Universität Wien (ab 1897)*, eds. Waltraud Heindl and Marina Tichy (Wien: WUV-Universitätsverlag, 1990), 17–26, on 17–18.
2. Anne Schlüter, "Wissenschaft für die Frauen? Frauen für die Wissenschaft! Zur Geschichte der ersten Generation von Frauen in der Wissenschaft," in *Frauen in der Geschichte IV*, eds. Ilse Brehmer, Juliane Jacobi-Dittrich, Elke Kleinau, and Annette Kuhn (Düsseldorf: Schwann, 1983, Geschichtsdidaktik), 244–61, especially 244, 252.
3. Eva Katzenberger, "Marianne Plehn 1863–1946, eine bedeutende Fischpathologin," Ph.D. Dissertation, Ludwig-Maximillians-Universität, München, 1994 (München: Hieronymous Buchreproduktions, 1994); *Das Frauenstudium an den Schweizer Hochschulen*, ed. Schweizerischer Verband der Akademikerinnen (Zürich: Rascher & Cie, 1928), 44–45; *Wer ist's* (Leipzig: H. A. L. Degener), vol. 9 (1928), 1192.
4. A remarkable number of late nineteenth-century middle-class German women qualified as *Lehrerinnen* by attending a *Lehrerinnenseminar* (women teachers' training college) and passing the *Lehrerinnenexamen* after they had completed studies

at a girls' school. The examination might almost be seen as part of a very common educational progression for young women. Some then worked for several years as governesses or as teachers in girls' schools, an occupation that necessarily ended if they married, married women not being accepted as schoolteachers. The occupation of *Lehrerin* has been described as basically part of life experience—a stage (*Statuspassage*) between school and marriage for middle-class women. It is also the case that for some women the teacher qualification and teaching experience was, in the absence of the hard-to-obtain *Abitur* qualification, their spring-board to professional studies; see Beate Vogt, "Erste Ergebnisse der Berliner Dokumentation: Deutsche Ärztinnen im Kaiserreich," in *Weibliche Ärzte: Die Durchsetzung des Berufsbildes in Deutschland,* ed. Eva Brinkschulte (Berlin: Edition Hentrich, 1993), 159–67, on 161.

5. All three of the brothers in the vigorous and enterprising Plehn family had notable careers: Albert Plehn (1861–1935) studied medicine; after a trip to the East Indies as a ship's doctor and some time in practice near Hamburg, he spent nine years as a government physician in the German colony of Cameroun, where he carried out notable studies on malaria and blackwater fever. He later became professor of pathology at Berlin University. Friedrich Plehn (1862–1904), also a physician, likewise served in government posts in Africa, first in Cameroun and then in German East Africa (later Tanganyika). The author of many publications on tropical medicine, he took part in scientific expeditions to South America, Japan, and India, and for a short time directed a sanatorium in Egypt. Rudolph Plehn (1868–1899) studied forestry but after a period in Togo, West Africa, took a doctorate in Togo language. A lieutenant colonel, he was killed in an action against native peoples in Cameroun during a second stay in Africa.

6. From shortly after its founding in 1855, twenty-two years after the university, the Zurich Federal Polytechnikum largely provided the university's instruction in mathematics and the sciences; its senior staff held the titles and rights of *Universitätsprofessoren.* There was considerable movement of students back and fore between the Polytechnikum and the university's Philosophische Fakultät II, that is the science and mathematics part of the Philosophische Fakultät. The Polytechnikum had seven divisions: architecture; engineering; mechanical/technical studies; technical chemistry (including pharmacy); land and forestry studies; specialist teacher training in the mathematical and biological sciences; general philosophy and political economy. Courses typically lasted three or four years and led to a diploma. The teacher-training division was one of the institution's smallest. Of the fourteen women who began their studies there in the 1890s, most completed diplomas and eight went on to doctorates in the sciences in which they had specialized; several had outstanding later careers; see Marianne Müller and Regula Schnurrenberger, "Die Philosophische Fakultät II" in *Ebenso neu als kühn: 120 Jahre Frauenstudium an der Universität Zürich,* Verein Feministische Wissenschaft Schweiz (Zürich: Verein Feministische Wissenschaft Schweiz, Schriftenreihe, 1988, 153–76).

7. Among these women (in addition to Plehn, Huch, and Baum) were botanist and later social worker Margarete von Üxküll-Gyllenband, law student Anita Augspurg, later one of the outspoken German feminists, Frieda Duesing, also a law student and later outstanding as a social worker, and Adeline Rittershaus-Bjarnason, a scholar of old Scandinavian literature, who, although she failed in her attempt to win a teaching position at Bonn University in 1900, later became a lecturer (*Privatdozent*) at Zurich University; see Albisetti, *Schooling German Girls,* 73, 205, 255, 288; and Müller and Schnurrenberger, "Philosophische Fakultät II," 160–61 (for von Üxküll-Gyllenband).

8. Hedwig Bleuler-Waser, "Über Ricarda Huch," in *Frauenstudium . . . Schweizer Hochschulen,* 70. A native of Zurich, Hedwig Bleuler-Waser was later a teacher, playwright, and social activist (see Regula Schnurrenberger, "Hedwig Bleuler-Waser (1869–1940)" in *Ebenso neu,* 169.

9. See bibliography and also "Die Polycladen der Plankton-Expedition," in *Ergebnisse der Plankton—Expedition der Humboldt-Stiftung 2* (Kiel and Leipzig: Lipsius & Tischer, 1896).

10. *Die Fische des Meeres und der Binnengewässer. Bilderatlas des Tierreichs 4* (Esslingen: Schreiber, 1906; Meiland, 1908).

11. "Ueber Geschwülste bei niedern Wirbeltieren," II Conférence Internationale pour l'Étude du Cancer, Paris (1910).

12. "Über Geschwülste bei Kaltblütern," *Zeitschrift für Krebsforschung,* 4 (1906): 525–64, *Sitzungsberichte der Gesellschaft für Morphologie und Physiologie,* 22 (1906): 85–94, and as a monograph (same title, Berlin: August Hirschwald, 1906); "Über einige bei Fischen beobachtete Geschwülste und geschwulstartige Bildungen," *Berichte aus der Kgl. Bayerischen Biologischen Versuchsstation in München,* 2 (1909): 55–78, and as a monograph (same title, Stuttgart: Schweizerbartsch Verlagsbuchhandlung, 1909). See also "Über die Bedeutung der Fischgeschwülste für die allgemeine Onkologie," *Aus deutscher Fischerei* (Neudamm: Verlag J. Neumann, 1911), 43–48; "Über Geschwülste bei Kaltblütern," *Sitzungsberichte der Gesellschaft für Morphologie und Physiologie,* 32 (1920): 20–25; "Zur Kenntnis der Ovarialtumoren bei Kaltblütern," *Zeitschrift für Krebsforschung,* 21 (1924): 313–19.

13. *Praktikum der Fischkrankheiten,* in Bruno Hofer, *Handbuch der Binnenfischerei Mitteleuropas,* vol. 1, and also printed separately (Stuttgart: Schweizerbartsch Verlagsbuchhandlung, 1924); trans., *Practice of Fish Diseases* (Madison, Wis.: Wisconsin Conservation Department, Biology Division, 1941, WPA [Works Progress Administration] project no. 9027).

14. See for instance H.-H. Reichenbach, *Krankheiten und Schädigungen der Fische* (Stuttgart, New York: Gustav Fischer, 1980).

15. Katzenberg, "Marianne Plehn," 83–84.

16. See also the discussion of Maria von Linden. At least one German woman held the title of professor before von Linden. Archaeologist Johanna Mestorf, director of the Kiel Museum of National Antiquities, was given the distinction by the Prussian government in 1899 (see Mestorf).

17. The title *königlich Professor* was often bestowed by the royal house in recognition of outstanding research. The fisheries research station was not part of Munich University but a Bavarian state agency.

18. Richard B. Goldschmidt, *Portraits from Memory: Recollections of a Zoologist* (Seattle; University of Washington Press, 1956), 154.

19. Marianne Plehn was very close to her only surviving sister Rose (1865–1945). An artist who had studied in Berlin and Munich, Rose Plehn had some of her work included in an exhibition of religious art in Düsseldorf in 1909; she also painted landscapes and portraits. Along with her companion, fellow artist and poet Maria Baroness von Geyso, Rose spent most of her life in the old family home of Lubochin, where, resisting change almost completely, they lived as if in a bygone era. When West Prussia became part of Poland in 1919 Rose Plehn became a Polish citizen so as to stay on in her home. Financial necessity eventually forced her to rent the land, but she remained in the house. She died during the upheavals of the Second World War, killed by a Polish intruder.

20. It is said that she wished she could have adopted three or four children (Katzenberger, "Marianne Plehn," 85).

21. Among these, some of which are also mentioned in the text, are the following: *Bacterium cyprinicida* Plehn (1904), agent for red disease in carp; *Lentospora cerebralis* Hofer-Plehn (1904); *Ichthyophonus hoferi* Plehn and Mulsow (1911), agent for giddiness; *Branchiomyces sanguinis* Plehn (1912), agent for gillrot in carp; and *Sphaerospora tincae* Plehn (1932). For a full list see Katzenberger, "Marianne Plehn," 59, 61.

22. See Katzenberger, "Marianne Plehn," 44–57 for a full list. Among the most important of Plehn's post-1900 original articles are the following: "Die Schuppensträubung der Weissfische, verursacht durch das Krebspestbakterium," *Allgemeine Fisherei-Zeitung* (hereafter *Allg. Fisch.-Zt.*) 3 (1 February 1902), 40–44; "Die Rotseuche der karpfenartigen Fische," *Allg. Fisch.-Zt.* 11 (1 June 1903): 198–201; "*Trypanoplasma cyprini* n. sp.," *Archiv für Protistenkunde* 3/2 (1903): 175–80, *Journal of Applied Microscopy and Laboratory Methods* 6 (1903): 2706–7 (abstract); "Woher stammt die Drehkrankheit der Salmoniden [*Lentospora cerebralis* (Hofer) Plehn]," *Archiv für Protistenkunde* 5/1 (1904): 145–66; "*Bacterium cyprinicida* n. sp., der Erreger der Rotseuche der karpfenartigen Fische," *Centralblatt für Bakteriologie, Parasitenkunde und Infektionskrankheiten* (hereafter *Centralbl. f. Bakt.*) 35 (1904), 461–67; "*Sanguinicola armata und inermis* (n. gen., n. sp.) n. fam. Rhynchostomida. Ein ento-parasitisches Turbella im Blute von Cyprinidin," *Zoologischer Anzeiger* 29 (1905): 244–52; "Über den Krebs der Schilddrüse bei Fischen," *Allg. Fisch.-Zt.* 2 (15 February 1906): 27–30; "Die Drehkrankheit der Salmoniden," *Allg. Fisch.-Zt.* 22 (15 November 1906): 465–70; "Nochmals die Drehkrankheit der Salmoniden," *Allg. Fisch.-Zt.* 24 (15 December 1906): 516–19; "Über eigentumliche Drüsenzellen in Gefassystem und in anderen Organen bei Fischen," *Anatomischer Anzeiger* 7/8 (1906): 192–203; "Über eine Infektionskrankheit der Niere bei Salmonidenjährlingen," *Allg. Fisch.-Zt.* 20 (15 October 1908): 436–37; "Ein monozoischer Cestode als Blutparasit (*Sanguinicola armata und inermis* Plehn)," *Zoologischer Anzeiger* 13 (1908): 427–39; "Über die Leber der Salmoniden," *Allg. Fisch.-Zt.* 24 (15 December 1909): 525–27; "Zur Degeneration der Regenbogenforelle," *Allg. Fisch.-Zt.* 24 (15 December 1911): 530–33; (with K. Mulsow) "Der Erreger der 'Taumelkrankheit' der Salmoniden," *Centralbl. f. Bakt.* 59 (1911): 63–68; "Die Furunkulose der Salmoniden," *Centralbl. f. Bakt.* 60 (1911): 609–24; "Eine neue Karpfenkrankheit und ihr Erreger *Branchiomyces sanguinis*," *Centralbl. f. Bakt.* 62 (1912): 129–34; "Zur Kenntnis der Salmonidenleber im gesunden und im kranken Zustand," *Zeitschrift für Fischerei* 17 (1915): 1–24; (with R. Trommsdorf) "Zur Kenntnis der Furunkulose," *Allg. Fisch.-Zt.* 14 (15 July 1916): 223–28; (with R. Trommsdorf) "*Bakterium salmonicida* und *Bacterium fluorescens*, zwei wohldifferenzierte Bakterienarten," *Centralbl. f. Bakt.* 78 (1916): 142–57; "Pathogene Schimmelpilze in der Fischniere," *Zeitschrift für Fischerei* 18 (1916): 51–54; "Neue Parasiten in Haut und Kiemen von Fischen," *Centrbl. f. Bakt.* 85 (1920): 275–81; "Aufruf! An alle Hechtfischer und Hechtzüchter," *Allg. Fisch.-Zt.* 51 (15 May 1926): 159–69; "Die Hecktkrankheit im Wörtersee in Kärnten," *Allg. Fisch.-Zt.* 19 (1 October 1927): 332–37, *Österreichische Fischerei-Zeitung* 24 (1927): 165–66, 173–74; "Eine Schleienbrutkrankheit und ihr Erreger *Sphaerospora tincae* n. sp.," *Internationale Revue der gesamten Hydrobiologie und Hydrographie* 26 (1932): 265–80; and "Pankreas-Fettnekrose bei karpfenartigen Fischen (Cypriniden)," *Archiv für Pathologische Anatomie und Physiologie und für Klinische Medizin* 302/1 (1938): 9–38.

23. "Mitbegründerin der Fischpathologie," *Allg. Fisch.-Zt.* 88 (1963): 182.

24. *Maria Gräfin von Linden: Erinnerungen der ersten Tübinger Studentin*, ed. Gabriele Junginger (Tübingen: Attempto Verlag, 1991); Johanna Kretschmer, "Maria von Linden—die erste Studentin der Universität Tübingen," *Attempto* 33/34 (1969): 78–88; Suzanne Flecken, "Maria Grafin von Linden (1869–1936)," in *100 Jahre Frauenstudium. Frauen der Rheinischen Friedrich-Wilhelms-Universität Bonn,* eds. Annette Kuhn, Valentine Rothe, Brigitte Mühlenbruch (Dortmund: Edition Ebersbach, 1996), 25, 70, 117–25.

25. For an account of the German university system at this time (very different from that in America), see Goldschmidt, *Portraits*, 3–10. A student who was admitted to a German university after completing the strict nine-year gymnasium curriculum had already finished his general liberal education up to about the level of the first two years of an American college course of study. The university was therefore an institution for the training of professionals and for research, rather than a "school" where students received an education. They were in fact largely free to learn in their own way, although those studying science subjects normally had laboratories to attend. There were no examinations of any kind before the doctor's degree examination, which most took. Students frequently chose a university for a professor they wanted to work with and often changed universities to get the benefit of being with more than one scholar.

26. See bibliography and the following, "Morphologische und physiologisch-chemische Untersuchungen über die Pigmente der Lepidoptern," *Pflüger's Archiv für die gesamte Physiologie* 98 (1903): 1–89; "Der Einfluss des Stoffwechsels der

Schmetterlingspuppe auf die Flügelfärbung und Zeichnung des Falters. Ein Beitrag zur Physiologie der Varietätenbildung," *Archiv für Rassen- und Gesellschafts-biologie einschliesslich Rassen- und Gesellschafts-hygiene* 1 (1904): 477–518; "Physiologische Untersuchungen an Schmetterlingen," *Zeitschrift für wissenschaftliche Zoologie* 82 (1905): 411–44; "Die Assimilationstätigkeit bei Puppen und Raupen von Schmetterlingen," *Archiv für Physiologie* suppl., bd. 1 (1906): 1–108; "Die Veränderung des Körpergewichtes bei hungernden Schmetterlingen," *Biologisches Centralblatt* 27 (1907): 449–57; and "Der Einfluss des Kohlensäuregehaltes der Atemluft auf die Gewichtswänderungen von Schmetterlingspuppen," *Archiv für Physiologie* (1907): 162–208.

27. The first was Adeline Rittershaus-Bjarnason (see note 7).

28. The right of *habilitation* for German women came only in 1920, the first woman full professor being chemist and plant nutrition specialist Margarethe von Wrangell (1877–1932). Born in Moscow into an aristocratic Baltic-German family, von Wrangell studied in Leipzig and Tübingen taking a doctorate with chemist Wilhelm Gustav Wislicenus at Tübingen in 1909. Following assistantships in Strasbourg, in London (with Sir William Ramsay), and in Paris (with Marie Curie) and a summer of study in the agricultural faculty at Bonn, von Wrangell's major research interest changed from radio chemistry to the emerging field of agricultural chemistry. From 1912 she headed the research station of the Estonian Agricultural Society in Reval (now Tallinn), concentrating on phosphate studies. Following the 1918 revolution, she moved to Germany and for a short time worked with Fritz Haber at the Kaiser-Wilhelm-Institut for physical chemistry research in Berlin (see section on Clara Immerwahr Haber). The importance of her work being already well recognized, von Wrangell received *habilitation* in botany and chemistry at the Agricultural Hochschule in Hohenheim (near Stuttgart) in 1920; from 1923 she held the professorship of plant nutrition there and headed the institute established to accommodate her work. She died in 1932 at the age of fifty-five, after a short illness; see Birgit Formanski, "Margarethe von Wrangell (1877–1932)" in *100 Jahre Frauenstudium,* 136.

29. See for instance "Beiträge zur Chemotherapie der Tuberkulose. Die Ergebnisse des Finklerschen Heilverfahrens bei der Impftuberkulose des Meerschweins," *Beiträge zur Klinik der Tuberkulose und spezifischen Tuberkulose-forschung* 23 (1912): 201–13; "Die Entwickelung der freilebenden Generation des Lungenwurmes [*Strongylus*]," *Deutsche Tierarztliche Wochenschrift* 21 (1913): 557–60; *Parasitismus im Tierreich* (Braunschweig: Friedr. Vieweg & Sohn, 1915); "Experimentalforschungen zur Chemotherapie der Tuberkulose mit Kupfer- und Methyleneblausalzen," *Beiträge zur Klinik der Tuberkulose . . .* 34 (1915): 1–104; *Erfahrungen der Kupferbehandlung bei experimenteller Tuberkulose des Meerschweinchens und bei den verschiedenen Formen der Tuberkulose des Menschen* (Berlin: R. Schoetz, 1917); "Erfüllt das Kupfer die Forderung eines spezifisch wirkenden chemotherapeutischen Heilmittels gegen Tuberkulose?," *Berliner Klinische Wochenschrift* 55 (1918): 298–304; "Ueber die bisherigen Tatsachen und die therapeutischen Aussichen der Kupfertherapie," *Therapeutische Monatsheft* 33 (1919): 161–73; "Das Kupfer als Wurmmittel," *Reichs-medizinal-anzeiger* 43 (1918): 145–51; "Die entwicklungshemmende Wirkung von Kupfersalzen auf Krankheit erregende Bakterien," *Centralblatt für Bakterologie* abt. 1, 85 (1920): 136–66; "Entwickelungshemmende Wirkung von Kupfer-glasverbindungen auf des Wachstum von Bakterien," *Centralblatt für Bakterologie* abt. 1, 87 (1921–1922): 310–15; "Ueber Nematoden aus Grassmen und ihre Bedeutung für die Entwickelung der Lungenwürmer," *Centralblatt für Bakterologie* abt. 1, 100 (1926–27): 88; and (with Lydia Zenneck) "Untersuchungen über des Ulmensterben in Beständen der städtischen Gartenverwaltung der Stadt Bonn und anderer Orte," *Centralblatt für Bakterologie,* abt. 2, 69 (1927): 340–51.

30. At least one German woman held the title of professor before von Linden. Archaeologist Johanna Mestorf, director of the Kiel Museum of National Antiquities, was given the distinction by the Prussian government in 1899 (see Mestorf, below).

31. In Bonn, Maria von Linden had lived for thirty-four years with the widow of Heinrich Hertz (1857–1894). Her career in academic research may well have had a significant influence on the two Hertz daughters, Johanna and Mathilde. Mathilde Hertz (1891–1975) became a noted animal psychologist and sensory physiologist. After receiving a doctorate in zoology from Munich University (1926), she went on to a research post at the Kaiser-Wilhelm Institute for Biology in Berlin-Dahlem (1927–1935) and a lectureship at the University of Berlin (1930–1933), one of the few held by women at German universities at the time. Forced to emigrate in 1936, she went to Cambridge, England, but did not continue the research that had already brought her wide recognition; see Siegfried Jaeger, "Von erklärbaren, doch ungeklärten Abbruch einer Karriere: die Tierpsychologin und Sinnesphysiologin Mathilde Hertz (1891–1975)," *Passauer Schriften zur Psychologiegeschichte* 11 (1996): 229–62); and Mary R. S. Creese, "Hertz, Mathilde," *Oxford Dictionary of National Biography* (Oxford: Oxford University Press, 2004).

32. Albisetti, *Schooling German Girls,* 138, 160.

33. Clara Hamburger, biographical sketch in "Beiträge zur Kenntnis von Trachelius ovum Ehrbg," inaugural diss., Heidelberg University, 1903 (Jena: Gustav Fischer, 1903); university archives (*Signatur* PA4060), Ruprecht-Karls-Universität Heidelberg; Lothar Jaenicke, "Clara Hamburger and *Dunaliella salina* Theodoresco—A Case Study from the First Half of the XXth Century," *Protist* 149 (1998): 381–88; Goldschmidt, *Portraits,* 74–75. Clara Hamburger was a cousin of chemist and Nobel Laureate Fritz Haber (see section on Clara Immerwahr Haber) and an aunt of developmental biologist Viktor Hamburger.

34. Goldschmidt, *Portraits,* 176–77.

35. Clara Hamburger's post-1900 publications include the following: "Beiträge zur Kenntnis von *Trachelius ovum,*" *Archiv für Protistenkunde* 2 (1903): 445–74; "Die Konjugation von *Paramaecium bursaria* Fock," *Archiv für Protistenkunde*

4 (1904): 199–239; "Zur Kenntnis der *Dunaliella salina* und einer Amöbe aus Salinenwasser von Cagliari," *Archiv für Protistenkunde* 6 (1905): 111–30; "Zur Kenntnis der Konjugation von *Stentor coeruleus* nebst einigen allgemeinen Bemerkung über die Konjugation der Infusorien," *Zeitschrift für Wissenschaftliche Zoologie* 90 (1908): 423–35; "Studien über *Euglena ehrenbergii* insbesondere über die Korperhülle," *Sitzungsberichte der Heidelberger Akademie der Wissenschaften* abt. 4 (1911): 1–22; (with W. von Buddenbrock) "Nordische Ciliata mit Ausschluss der Tintinnoidea," in *Nordische Plankton, eds.*, K. Brandt and C. Apstein, (Kiel and Leipzig: Lipsius & Tischer, 1911), part 15, no. 13, 1–152; "Über einige parasitische Flagellaten," *Verhandlungen des Naturhistorisch-medicinischen Vereins zu Heidelberg* 11 (1912): 211–19; (with W. von Buddenbrock) "Nordische Suctoria," in *Nordische Plankton*, Part 16 (1913): 153–94; "Flagellata (*Protomastigina, Cystoflagellata*) und Sarcodina (*Amoebea, Heliozoa, Sticholonche*) des nordischen Planktons," in *Nordische Plankton,* part 16 (1913), 195–211. Clara Hamburger was also interested in arachnids and published at least one anatomical paper in this area—"Zur Mittledarmes der Spinnen," *Zoologischer Anzeiger* 48 (1916): 39–46.

36. The species definition of Dunaliella remains uncertain; new forms are still being reported, older definitions revised and refined, and different criteria used in classification work—see Hans R. Preisig, "Morphology and Taxonomy,"chapter 1 in *Dunaliella: Physiology, Biochemistry and Biotechnology,* eds. Mordhay Avron and Ami Ben-Amotz (Boca Raton, Florida: CRC Press, 1992), 1–15, on 12–13.

37. E. C. Teodoresco, "Organisation et développement du *Dunaliella*, nouveau genre de Volvocacée-Polyblepharidée," *Beihefte zum Botanischen Centralblatt* 18, abt. 1 (1905): 215–32.

38. Jaenicke, "Clara Hamburger." Clara Hamburger's Dunaliella paper is rarely cited in current literature, but is referenced by Preisig, "Morphology and Taxonomy."

39. *Lexikon der Frau* (Zürich: Encyclios Verlag AG, 1953), vol. 2, 605; obituary for Guglielmo Mengarini, *L'Elettrotecnica* 15 (1928): 129–32, on 131.

40. Traube-Mengarini's post-1900 publications include the following: "Sur la conjugation des amibes," *Archives Italiennes de Biologie* 39 (1903): 375–86; (with Alberto Scala) "Dell'azione del cloruro di sodio sui corpuscoli rossi del sangue della rana e sulle opaline," *Archivo di Fisiologia* 3 (1906): 572–79; (with A. Scala) "Azione del cloruro di sulle opaline," *Archivo di Fisiologia* 4 (1907): 605–18; (with A. Scala) "Soluzione di metalli allo stato colloidale ottenuta per azione dell'acqua distillata bollente," *Atti della Società Italiana per il Progresso delle Scienze* 3 (1909): 511–18; and (with A. Scala) "Ueber die chemische Durchlässigkeit lebender Algen- und Protozoenzellen für anorganischen Salze und die spezifische Wirkung letzterer," *Biochemische Zeitschrift* 17 (1909): 443–90.

41. Little information has been collected about Emma von Ramdohr. A resident of Hannover, she had a special interest in birds and reported her extensive observations on a young common swift in the Berlin journal *Ornithologische Monatsberichte* in 1897 (see bibliography). Having rescued a swift nestling that fell into her sewing basket in early July 1895 she reared it herself, a task commonly considered impossible. When she found it not yet strong enough to join its fellows in their autumn migration, she kept it over the winter, taking the opportunity to observe its habits and character with care. She took great pleasure and satisfaction in the undertaking, and was able to bring the bird to the point where it was able rejoin its own kind on their return to the Hanover region in the spring.

42. Obituaries in *Botanisches Centralblatt* 5 (1881): 255—56, and *Journal of Botany* 19 (1881): 96; and Elise Oelsner, *Die Leistungen der Deutschen Frau in den Letzten Vierhundert Jahren auf Wissenschaftlichen Gebiete* (Guhrau: M. Lemke, 1894; *Gerritsen Collection of Women's History* (1975), microfiche no. 2092, University of Kansas Libraries).

43. Ludwig Rabenhorst, *Kryptogamen-Flora von Deutschland, Oesterreich und der Schweiz* (Leipzig: Akademische Verlagsgesellschaft, 1884; later editions had other authors/editors and publishers).

44. Carl Holtermann, "Elise Schwabach," *Berichte der Deutschen Botanischen Gesellschaft* 26a (1907): 76–77.

45. Charles Darwin, *The Movements and Habits of Climbing Plants* (New York: D. Appleton, 1888).

46. For a report of recent work at the theoretical level, see Alain Goriely and Michael Tabor, "Spontaneous helix hand reversal and tendril perversion in climbing plants," *Physical Review Letters* 80 (16 February 1998): 1564–67, and references therein. This paper examines the mechanics and dynamics of the spiral twist phenomenon, particularly twist inversion, and the most stable states for the rods or fibers in terms of elastic energy.

47. See bibliography; the last of these papers was "Zur Entwickelung der Spaltöffnungen bei Coniferen," *Berichte der Deutschen Botanischen Gesellschaft* 20 (1902): 1–7.

48. Oelsner, *Leistungen*, 93.

49. Elisabeth Widmer, *Die europäischen Arten der Gattung Primula* (München: R. Oldenbourg, 1893).

50. Sophie Pataky, *Lexikon Deutscher Frauen der Feder,* 2 vols. (Berlin: C. Pataky, 1898, reprint Herbert Lang, 1971), vol. 2, 363–65; *Wer ist's* 2 (1906), 1194 and 7 (1914), 3–4; obituary, *Österreichische Botanische Zeitschrift* 74 (1925): 288; *Stieftöchter der Alma mater? 90 Jahre Frauenstudium in Bayern—am Beispiel der Universität München,* ed. Hadumod Bussmann (München: Verlag Antje Kustmann, 1993), 106–7; Irma Hildebrandt, *Bin halt ein zähes Luder: 15 Münchner Frauenportraits* (München: Diederichs, 1990), 43–54; and Adalbert Prinz von Bayern, *Die Wittelsbacher: Geschichte unserer Familie* (München: Prestel-Verlag, 1979), 348, 357, 364–65. For an English-language source on the Wittelsbach family see Robert S. Garnett, Jr., *Lion, Eagle, and Swastika: Bavarian Monarchism in Weimar Germany, 1918–1933* (New York: Garland Publishing, 1991), especially chapter 1.

51. "Therese von Bayern, Forscherin, Sammlerin, Weltreisende." Hessen Fernsehen, May 1998, online at www.hr-online.de/fs/wissenschaft/ . . . schaft-forschung/sendungen/19980526.html (last accessed 10 January 2002).

52. Hildebrandt, *Bin halt ein zähes Luder,* 43–44, 52.

53. Princess Therese was doubtless familiar with the scientific results of the 1859–1860 expedition to Brazil of her Austrian cousin Archduke Ferdinand Maximilian, the ill-starred Emperor of Mexico during the years 1863–1867. This three-month expedition, much less ambitious than Therese's, explored the hinterlands of Salvador, Ilhéus, and Rio de Janeiro. Its scientific staff included botanists F. Maly and H. Wawra and the collections brought back greatly enriched the holdings in the Schönbrunn Palace greenhouses, facilities that occupied an important place in Vienna botanical work; see the impressively illustrated folio publication by Heinrich Wawra, *Botanische Ergebnisse der Reise Seiner Majestät des Kaisers von Mexico Maximilian I nach Brasilien (1859–60)* (Wien: C. Gerold's Sohn, 1866).

54. On particularly strenuous trips such as this one, Princess Therese's group included Baronin Johanna von Malsen and Freiherr Maximilian von Speidel, court official and commanding general of the heavy cavalry regiment Prinz Karl von Bayern. She herself reguarly travelled as "Gräfin Elpen"; see Hildebrandt, *Bin halt ein zähes Luder,* 47; and *Wer ist's* 2 (1908), 1138).

55. Also published as a monograph, *Ueber einige Fischarten Mexico's und die Seen in welchen sie vorkommen* (Wien: F. Tempsky, 1895).

56. Goldschmidt, *Portraits,* 88–91.

57. Therese, Prinzessin von Bayern, "Auf einer Reise in Westindien und Südamerika gesammelte Pflanzen," *Beihefte zum Botanischen Centralblatt* 13, H1 (1902): 1–90; "Auf einer Reise in Sudamerika gesammelte Pflanzen," *Beihefte zum Botanischen Centralblatt* 18, H3 (1905): 523–26; *Auf einer Reise in Westindien und Sudamerika gesammelte Pflanzen. Mit Diagnosen neuer Arten* (Jena: G. Fischer, 1902); and *Auf einer Reise in Sudamerika gesammelte Pflanzen* (Leipzig: G. Thieme, 1905).

58. Auguste Forel, *Out of My Life and Work,* trans. Bernard Miall, from the German original *Rückblick auf mein Leben,* Zürich, 1935 (London: George Allen & Unwin, 1937), 321.

59. Eberhard Friese, *Philipp Franz von Siebold, als früher Exponent der Ostasienwissenschaften: Ein Beitrag zur Orientalismusdiskussion und zur Geschichte der Europäisch-japanischen Begegnung* (Bochum: Studienverlag Brockmeyer, 1983), 245, 268; *Aus der Vergangenheiten der Universität Würzburg: Festschrift zum 350 Jährigen Bestehen der Universität,* ed. Max Buchner (Berlin: Julius Springer, 1932), 510–36; Hans Körner, *Die Würzburger Siebold: Eine Gelehrtenfamilie des 18. und 19. Jahrhunderts, Quellen und Beiträge zur Geschichte der Universität Würzburg,* vol. 3 (Neustadt a.d. Aisch: Verlag Degener & Co., Inh. Gerhard Gessner, 1976), 432–34, 445, 469, 475, 511–12, 555, portr. opp. 552; and *Assignment Japan: von Siebold, Pioneer and Collector* (The Hague: Groenevelt, Landgraaf, 1989, Department of Oriental Manuscripts, University Library, Leiden), 1.

60. Körner, *Würzburger Siebold.* The woman who is sometimes credited with being the first to receive a medical degree from a German university (Landesuniversität Giessen, 20 March 1817) was Charlotte Heidenreich-von Siebold, whose stepfather was Damian von Siebold (1768–1828), director of the Grand-ducal Medical College of Hess in Darmstadt. Charlotte von Siebold, whose formal qualifications were in obstetrics only, had a large practice in Darmstadt. Her patients included a great many poor women, but she also was called to the houses of the nobility; in fact she was the doctor who attended the birth, in Kensington Palace, London, on 24 May 1819, of the infant who became Britain's Queen Victoria (R. Kaschade, "Charlotte Heidenreich-von Seibold, die erster Frauenärztin Deutschlands," *Janus* 42 (1938): 185–88; see also Elizabeth Longford, *Queen Victoria: Born to Succeed* (New York: Harper and Row, 1965), 21).

61. Following the occupation of the Netherlands by the French during the years of Napoleon Bonaparte, the country was sorely impoverished and men with scientific training were in short supply. Von Siebold was one of a number of Germans who came to fill the need; see P. Smit, "International influences on the development of natural history in the Netherlands and its East Indian colonies between 1750 and 1850," *Janus* 65 (1978): 45–65.

62. *Assignment Japan,* 1. Philipp Franz von Siebold and his Japanese mistress Kusumoto Sonogi had a daughter, Oine (1827–1903), who became Japan's first female physician and a famous obstetrician. Two of his sons by his German wife Helene, Alexander and Heinrich, became diplomats who served in Japan; Heinrich von Siebold also published studies in Japanese ethnology and archaeology (*Assignment Japan,* 12, 68).

63. *Die Geflugelzucht, nach ihrem Jetzigen Rationellen Standpunkt,* comp. Bruno Dürigen (Berlin: Verlag von Paul Parey, 1886).

64. Albisetti, *Schooling German Girls,* 137–38 n. 5., 204–5 n. 3; Hanny Rohner, *Die ersten 30 Jahre des medizinischen Frauenstudiums an der Universität Zürich 1867–1897* (Zürich: Juris Druck, 1972), 82, 84, 241–42; Matriculation Register, Zurich University, for Bäumler, Weiss, and Willdenow; Barbara Bachmann and Elke Bradenahl, "Medizinstudium von Frauen in Bern 1871–1914," inaugural diss., Bern University, 1990. (City of origin, years at Bern, date of graduation, and dissertation title for Glause, Stier, Weiss, and Willdenow from Bachmann and Bradenahl.)

65. For a list of these physicians, see Vogt, "Erste Ergebnisse," in *Wiebliche Ärzte,* 160.

66. Among them were Emilie Lehmus (1841–1932; degree, Zurich, 1875), Franziska Tiburtius (1843–1927; Zurich, 1876), Agnes Bluhm (1862–1943; Zurich, 1890), and Agnes Hacker (1860–1909; Zurich, 1897). These four all had practices in Berlin in gynecology, the major area of activity of early female physicians in Germany as in other countries. Lehmus and Tiburtius, the first German women physicians in the city, ran a polyclinic for poor women for several years and later a women doctors' clinic. They were joined by Bluhm in 1890. A strong proponent of women's right to higher education, Bluhm was one of the first German women physicians known for her research; this was largely in areas related to social

problems, particularly alcohol addiction and eugenics. Agnes Hacker, after graduating with a dissertation in gynaecology ("Uber abdominale Totalexstirpation des schwangeren myomatösen Uterus"—Berlin: S. Karger, 1897), went on to train in Vienna and Leipzig as a surgeon. She worked at the Berlin women doctors' clinic from 1898, her skill and efficiency in surgery admirably demonstrating that women could be as capable as men in this area. After 1905 she gave much of her time to the leadership and management of the clinic, successfully working for its expansion and modernization. She was heavily involved in almost all the social and political matters of special concern to the women's movement, including the much-debated Morality Movement. The first woman appointed police doctor by the Berlin authorities, Hacker was responsible for the medical examination of prostitutes; she also took part in the work of rehabilitation of prostitutes released from prison and the health education of young women; see Regina Bornemann, "Erste weibliche Ärzte. Die Beispiel der 'Fräulein Doctors' Emilie Lehmus (1841–1932) und Franziska Tiburtius (1843–1927); Biographisches und Autobiographisches," in *Weibliche Ärzte*, 24–32; Svenja Ludwig, "Dr. med. Agnes Bluhm (1862–1943). Späte und zweifelhafte Anerkennung," in *Weibliche Ärzte*, 84–92; Kristin Hoesch, "Eine Ärztin der zweiten Generation: Agnes Hacker: Chirurgin, Pädagogin, Politikerin," in *Weibliche Ärzte*, 58–64.

67. Thomas Schimpke, "Lydia Rabinowitsch-Kempner (1871–1935). Leben und Wirken einer tuberkulose Forscherin," inaugural diss., Bayerischer Julius-Maximilians-Universität zu Würzburg (Würzburg, 1996); Katharina Graffmann-Weschke, *Lydia Rabinowitsch-Kempner (1871–1935). Leben und Werk einer der führenden Persönlichkeiten der Tuberkuloseforschung am Anfang des 20 Jahrhunderts* (Herdecke: GCA-Verlag, 1999) and "Frau Prof. Dr. Lydia Rabinowitsch-Kempner (1871–1935). Die führende Wissenschaftlerin in der Medizin ihrer Zeit," in *Weibliche Ärzte*, 93–102; Annette Vogt, *Elsa Neumann. Berlins erstes Fräulein Doktor* (Berlin: Verlag für Wissenschafts- und Regionalgeschichte, 1999), 26–27; Lori R. Walsh and James A. Poupard, "Lydia Rabinowitsch, PhD, and the emergence of clinical pathology in late 19th-century America," *Archives of Pathology and Laboratory Medicine* 113 (1989): 1303–8; *Wer ists* 7 (1914), 1320; obituaries in *Tubercule* 16 (1935): 567; *Nature* 136 (1935): 505; and *Policlinico* (Rome) 42 (1935): 1717; and *Lexikon der Frau*, vol. 2, 1001.

68. Lydia Rabinowitsch's sister Rosa studied for several years beginning in 1883 in the philosophical faculty at Zurich University. Her brothers went to the university in Königsberg, East Prussia (later Kaliningrad, Russia); two of them studied medicine becoming gynaecologists and later heading a large clinic in Kovno, a third became a dentist, and a fourth a businessman who worked in Vladivostok.

69. See note 25.

70. Recipient of the 1905 Nobel Prize in medicine for his work on tuberculosis, Koch also carried out extensive studies on insect-borne diseases of the tropics, including work on malaria in German-held territories in the East Indies and investigations of a number of diseases, animal and human, in Africa; as leader of the 1906 German Sleeping-Sickness Commission to East Africa he made a major contribution with his studies of the lifecycle of the trypanosome that was the disease-causing agent.

71. "Das Studium der Medizin in verschiedenen Ländern," in *International Kongress für Frauenwerke und Frauenbestrebungen, Berlin, 19–26 September 1896*, eds. Rosalie Schoenflies, Lina Morgenstern, et al. (Berlin: H. Walther, 1897), 180–84.

72. Gulielma Fell Alsop, *History of the Woman's Medical College Philadelphia, Pennsylvania 1850–1950* (Philadelphia: Lippincott, 1950), 170.

73. Mary R. S. Creese, *Ladies in the Laboratory? American and British Women in Science, 1800–1900: A Survey of Their Contributions to Research* (Lanham, Md.: Scarecrow Press, 1998), 145–46.

74. The oldest child, Robert Kempner (1899–1993), godson of Robert Koch, became a lawyer who from 1923 worked in the Prussian Interior Ministry as a police department justiciary. His anti–National Socialist activities led to his dismissal in 1933. After the death of his mother in 1935 he left Germany, first going to Italy and four years later fleeing to the United States, where he became a citizen and held a post of special adviser to the United States Department of Justice; he served as deputy chief prosecutor in the United States legal team at the Nuremberg War Crimes Tribunal. Later returning to Germany, he worked for many years in Frankfurt am Main. Nadja Kempner (1901–1932) studied English at Heidelberg University, focusing on writings by the Elizabethan sailor and statesman Sir Walter Raleigh and receiving a D.Phil. degree. She died of tuberculosis shortly before completing further work in philology. Walter Kempner (1903–1997), a physician, worked at the Charité Hospital in Berlin from 1928 and also carried out research at the Kaiser Wilhelm Institute for Cellular Physiology. In 1934 he immigrated to the United States and obtained a professorship at Duke University Medical School in Durham, North Carolina. His interests included the effect of diet on various diseases, among them kidney disfunction and heart disease, although at the time conventional medicine considered diet largely irrelevant to treatment. He became famous in the 1940s as the originator of the successful salt-free "Rice Diet" for high blood pressure. Autocratic and somewhat theatrical in manner, with a strong German accent, Kempner was regarded as something of a character in Durham. He retired from the Duke faculty in 1972 and died in Durham in 1997. The Walter Kempner Distinguished Professorship at the Duke Medical School now commemorates his name (Jim Wise, "The Dr. Kempner Story," *Durham* (N.C.) *Herald*, 12 October 1999).

75. Robert Koch, "Ueber Tuberculose," *Archiv für Anatomie und Physiologie. Physiol. Abt.* (Berlin Physiol. Ges. Verh.) (1882): 190–92; "Die Aetiologie der Tuberculose," *Berliner Klinische Wochenschrift* 19 (1882): 221–30; and "Ueber die Aetiologie der Tuberculose," *Verhandlungen des Congresses für Innere Medicin, Erster Congress* (Wiesbaden: J. F. Bergmann, 1882), 56–66.

76. See bibliography and also Robert Ostertag "Rezension von: Rabinowitsch und Kempner, 'Beitrag zur Frage der Infektiosität der Milch tuberkulöser Kühe, sowie über den Nutzen der Tuberkulinimpfung,'" *Zeitschrift für Fleisch- und Milchhygiene* 9 (1899): 192–94, *Zeitschrift für Hygiene* 31 (1899): 137–52, and Lydia Rabinowitsch, "Besprechung der Ostertag'schen 'Untersuchungen über die Eutertuberkulose und die Bedeutung der sogenannten säurefesten Pseudotuberkelbacillen für die Feststellung der Eutertuberkulose,'" *Centralblatt für Bakteriologie* abt. 1, referate, 35 (1904): 174–77.

77. Robert Koch, "Die Bekämpfung der Tuberkulose unter Berücksichtigung der Erfahrung, welche bei der erfolgreichen Bekämpfung anderer Infektionskrankheiten gemacht sind," *Deutsche Medizinische Wochenschrift* 27 (1901), 549–54.

78. Walter Kempner had left the institute in 1902 in order to set up a private medical practice. Koch himself resigned as head in 1904 to have more time for his scientific expeditions.

79. An American visitor to Koch's laboratory about this time later recalled his impression of Lydia Rabinowitsch: "a slight, black-eyed, and determined Russian woman," whose manner was very direct and somewhat abrupt; see Edward R. Baldwin, "A call upon Robert Koch in his laboratory in 1902," *Journal of Outdoor Life* 16 (1919): 1–2.

80. (With Walter Kempner) "Die Trypanosomen in der Menschen- und Tierpathologie, sowie vergleichende Trypanosomenuntersuchungen," *Centralblatt für Bakteriologie* abt. 1, originale, 34 (1903): 804–22. See also note 70.

81. (With W. Kempner) "Die Pest in Odessa," *Deutsche Medizinische Wochenschrift* 29 (1903): 20–21, 51–53.

82. "Ueber spontane Affentuberkulose, ein Beitrag zur Tuberkulosefrage," *Deutsche Medizinische Wochenschrift* 32 (1906): 866–69 and *Archiv für Pathologische Anatomie und Physiologie* 190 (1907): 196–245; "Untersuchungen über die Beziehungen zwischen der Tuberculose des Menschen und der Tiere," *Arbeiten aus dem Pathologischen Institut zu Berlin,* ed. Johannes Orth (Berlin: Hirschwald, 1906): 365–436; (with M. Koch) "Die Tuberkulose der Vögel und ihre Beziehungen zur Säugetiertuberkulose," *Archiv für Pathologische Anatomie und Physiologie* 190, beiheft (1907): 246–541.

83. (With J. Orth) "Über experimentelle enterogene Tuberkulose," *Archiv für Pathologische Anatomie und Physiologie* 194, beiheft (1908): 305–67; (with E. Oberwarth) "Ueber die Resorptionsinfektion mit Tuberkelbacillen vom Magandarmkanal aus," *Berliner Klinische Wochenschrift* 45 (1908): 298–301; and (with Carl Dammann), "Ueber die Häufigkeit des Vorkommens von Rindertuberkelbazillen beim Menschen," *Zeitschrift für Tuberkulose* 21 (1913): 158–65.

84. (With J. Orth) "Zur Frage der Immunisierung gegen Tuberkulose," *Archiv für Pathologische Anatomie und Physiologie* 190 (1907): 1–58; "Zur Frage latenter Tuberkelbacillen," *Berliner Klinische Wochenschrift* 44 (1907): 35–39; and (with J. Morgenroth) "Die Immunitätsreaktionen tuberkulösen Gewebes und deren Zusammenhang mit der Theorie der Tuberkulinwirkung," *Deutsche Medizinische Wochenschrift* 33 (1907): 705–9.

85. "Zur Michfrage," *Berliner Aerzte-Correspondenz* 10 (1905): 137–38.

86. See also the work of Marie Baum about this time on behalf of women in the industrial workforce in Baden and their infants.

87. See "Beitrag zur bakteriologischen Kenntnis des Friedmann'schen Tuberkulosemittels," *Deutsche Medizinische Wochenschrift* 40 (1914): 686–88; Friedmann's reply, *Deutsche Medizinische Wochenschrift* 40 (1914), 901–4; and further comments by Rabinowitsch, *Deutsche Medizinische Wochenschrift* 40 (1914): 904–5. See also "Zur experimentellen Grundlage der Friedmannschen Behandlungsmethode der Tuberkulose," *Therapie der Gegenwart* 62 (1921): 1–6.

88. Papers by Rabinowitsch on tuberculosis published before the First World War and not already listed include: "Die Infectiosität der Milch tuberkulöser Kühe, die Sicherstellung der bakteriologischen Diagnose, sowie die praktische Bedeutung des Tuberculins für die Ausrottung der Rindertuberculose," *Zeitschrift für Hygiene und Infektionskrankheiten* 37 (1901): 439–49; English translation, "The infectiousness [infectivity] of the milk of tuberculous cows; the bacteriological diagnosis, and the practical value of tuberculin for the extermination of tuberculosis among cattle," *Lancet* 2 (1901): 838–40, *Journal of Comparative Pathology and Therapeutics* 15 (1902): 509–15, *Transactions of the British Congress on Tuberculosis, London, July 22–26, 1901,* vol. III, Report of the Pathological Section (London: William Clowes & Sons, 1902), 507–14, discussion 514–22; "Die Infektiosität der Milch tuberkulöser Kühe im Lichte der neueren Forschungen," *Centralblatt für Bakteriologie* abt. 1, 34 (1903): 225–36; "Die Beziehungen der menschlichen Tuberkulose zu der Perlsucht des Rindes," *Berliner Klinische Wochenschrift* 43 (1906): 784–88; "Neuere experimentelle Untersuchungen über Tuberkulose," *Deutsche Medizinische Wochenschrift* 32 (1906): 1809–11, and *Berliner Tierärztliche Wochenschrift* (1906): 817–19; "Zum gegenwärtigen Stand der Tuberkuloseforschung," *Weiner Medizinische Wochenschrift* 57 (1907): 1793–98; (with J. Orth) "Über Resorption korperlicher Elemente im Darm, mit besonderer Berücksichtigung der Tuberkelbacillen," *Sitzungsberichte der Königlich Preussischen Akademie der Wissenschaften zu Berlin* 39 (1908): 871–86; (with C. Dammann) "Die Impftuberkulose des Menschen, zugleich ein Beitrag zur Indentitätsfrage der von Mensch und Rind stammenden Tuberkelbazillen," *Deutsche Medizinische Wochenschrift* 16 (1908): 389–95 and *Zeitschrift für Tuberkulose* 12 (1908): 441–55; "Experimentelle Untersuchungen über die Virulenz latenter tüberkülöser Herde," *Zeitschrift für Tuberkulose* 15 (1909–10), 217–56; (with F. Jessen) "Zur Frage der Vernichtung von Tuberkelbacillen durch Flussläufe," *Berliner Klinische Wochenschrift* 47 (1910): 878; (with F. Jessen) "Zur Frage der Löslichkeit von Tuberkelbazillen," *Centralblatt für Bakteriologie* abt. 1, Originale, 54 (1910)" 454–57; "Ueber das Vorkommen von Tuberkelbazillen im kreisenden Blute und die praktische Bedeutung dieser Erscheinung," *Deutsche Medizinische Wochenschrift* 36 (1910): 1161–64; "Blutbefunde bei Tuberkulose," *Berliner Klinische Wochenschrift* 49 (1912): 110–13; "Untersuchungen zur Tuberkulosefrage," *Deutsche Klinische Wochenschrift* 39 (1913): 103–6; "Tuberkelbazillen im Herzblut" *Tuberculosis* (Berlin) 13 (1914): 321–24; (with G. Findler) "Experimentelle

Versuche über den Einfluss behinderter Nasenatmung auf das Zustandekommen der Inhalationstuberkulose," *Berliner Klinische Wochenschrift* 51 (1914): 1809–12.

89. See also the section on parasitologist Maria von Linden and that on archaeologist Johanna Mestorf, both of whom received titular professorships some years before Rabinowitsch-Kempner—von Linden in 1910 and Mestorf in 1899. Fish pathologist Marianne Plehn was awarded the distinction in 1913.

90. (With W. Ceelen) "Über Lymphogranulomatose und ihre Beziehung zur Tuberkulose," *Zeitschrift für Tuberkulose* 27 (1917): 175–209; (with C. Hart) "Beitrag zu der Frage nach der Häufigkeit der Infektion des Menschen mit dem Typus bovinus des Tuberkelbazillus in den Kriegsjahren," *Zeitschrift für Tuberkulose* 27 (1917), 334–42.

91. Throughout her work on tuberculosis, Lydia Rabinowitsch received financial support from various foundations including the Robert Koch-Stiftung, Gräfin Bose-Stiftung, Salomonsohn-Stiftung, and, in the 1920s, the Notgemeinschaft Deutscher Wissenschaft (Emergency Society for German Sciences, an association founded by universities to support German sciences during the post–First World War collapse).

92. Among these were "Die Bedeutung der Haustiere für die Verbreitung der Tuberkulose," *Zeitschrift für Tuberkulose* 34 (1921), 570–74; "Zur Serodiagnostik der Tuberkulose mit dem Extrakt Besredka," *Deutsche Medizinische Wochenschrift* 48 (1922): 379–81; (with R. Neumann) "Strahlenpilz-(Streptothrix-) Meningitis," *Zeitschrift für Klinische Medizin* 94 (1922): 215–23; (with G. Klemperer) "Zur Kenntnis der Wirkungen ultravioletter Lichtstrahlen und ozonisierter Luft," *Therapie der Gegenwart* 63 (1922): 241–47; (with G. Katz) "Spezifische Kutanreaktion, Komplementablenkung mit Besredka-Antigen und Blutkörperchen-Senkungsreaktion in ihrer Bedeutung für Diagnose und Prognose der Lungentuberkulose," *Zeitschrift für Tuberkulose* 38 (1923): 401–19; Über neuere Streptokokkenuntersuchungen," *Fortschritte der Medizin* 44 (1926): 18–22; "Die Übertragung der Tuberkulose durch Haustiere," *Fortschritte der Medizin* 44 (1926): 1398–400; "Types of tubercle bacilli in human tuberculosis," *American Review of Tuberculosis* 15 (1927): 225–34; "Transmission of tuberculosis through domestic animals," *American Review of Tuberculosis* 15 (1927): 419–28; "Übertragung der Tuberkulose durch filtrierbare Erreger," *Deutsche Medizinische Wochenschrift* 53 (1927): 1982–83; and "La tuberculose spontanée chez les animaux de laboratoire," *Annales de Médecine* 25 (1929): 287–92.

93. See "Die verschiedenen Stämme der Tuberkelbazillus," *Handbuch der Kindertuberkulose* 1 (1930): 1–9; and "Fünfzig Jahre Tuberkelbazillus," *Medizinische Welt* 5 (1931): 1629–33 and 1669–70.

94. "Zur Frage der Filtrierbarkeit des Tuberkulose-Virus," *Zeitschrift für Tuberkulose* 52 (1928): 18–25; and "Kongress und Vereinsberichte: Internationale Tuberkulosekonferenz in Rom (5–7 Oct. 1928)," *Zeitschrift für Tuberkulose* 52 (1928): 263–65.

95. See "Die verschiedenen Stämme der Tuberkelbazillus"; and "Fünfzig Jahre Tuberkelbazillus."

96. Members of the *Freicorps,* a volunteer militia group, were early adherents of what became the National Socialist Party.

97. Sabine Sander, "Nur für geladene Gäste. Der 'Deutsche Lyceum-Club,'" in *Ich bin meine eigene Frauenbewegung: Frauen-Ansichten aus der Geschichte einer Grossstadt,* ed. Bezirksamt Schöneberg, Kunstamt Schöneberg (Berlin: Edition Hentrich, 1991), 52–57. Organized along the lines of the London Lyceum Club founded two years earlier, the Deutsche Lyceum-Club was established in 1905 to promote the interests of professional women, in particular artists, writers, and scientists, and to encourage their international connections. Its facilities included a library, a legal information office, guestrooms, and space for lectures and concerts.

98. "Die Beteiligung der Frau an der Tuberkulosebekämpfung in der Familie," *Internationale Tuberkulose-Konferenz Rom, 10–14 April 1912, Bericht* (Berlin-Charlottenburg, 1912), Dritte Sitzung, 234–40, and *Wiener Medizinische Wochenschrift* 62 (1912): 1677–80; *VII Internationale Kongress gegen Tuberkulose, Rom 1913 (Atti del Congresso* 1.2), bd. II, 1, 12–17; "Die Tuberkulose, und was können die Frauen gegen dieselbe tun," *Deutscher Lyceum-Club* 9 (1913): 137–43, and *Das Rote Kreuz* 31 (1913): 227–28; and "Die Aufgabe der Frau bei der Tuberkulosebekämpfung," *Tuberculosis* 13 (1914): 285–95.

99. "Ärztinnen und Tuberkulosebekämpfung," *Vierteljahresschrift des Bundes Deutscher Ärztinnen* 1 (1924): 7–8.

100. See Rabinowitsch, "Zur Frage des Vorkommens von Tuberkelbacillen in der Marktbutter," *Zeitschrift für Hygiene* 26 (1897): 90–111.

101. See note 74.

102. See note 67.

103. Eva Brinkschultze and Beate Vogt, "Ausgewählte Biographien der Berliner Dokumentation: Ärztinnen 1876–1914," in *Weibliche Ärzte,* 169–87, on 170.

104. See note 4.

105. Brinkschultze and Vogt, "Ausgewählte Biographien," *Weibliche Ärzte,* 170; and Matriculation Register, Zurich University (n. 6313).

106. But see also note 60.

107. Brinkschultze and Vogt, "Ausgewählte Biographien," 172–73; Albisetti, *Schooling German Girls,* 241–42.

108. Heindl, "I. Zur Entwicklung," 17; Marcella Stern, "Gabriele Possanner von Ehrenthal, die erste an der Unversität Wien promovierte Frau," in *"Durch Erkenntnis zu Freiheit,"* 189–219, on 201.

109. See Ricarda Huch, *Frühling in der Schweiz* (Zürich: Atlantis Verlag, 1938), 42. Huch remembered her fellow student Herbig as acute, blonde, and possessing a good sense of humor.

110. Matriculation Register, Zurich University (n. 6980); report of work in Berlin from Oelsner, *Leistungen.*

111. Alice Buslik and Elise Wolff, *Histologie* (Berlin: C. F. Pilger, 1930).

112. The geology paper and one astronomy paper are by Maria von Linden. The second astronomy paper, reporting determinations of brightness of Mars, was by Frau von Prittwitz, who carried out her observations from her balcony in Berlin.

113. Albisetti, *Schooling German Girls,* 227. Perhaps the best known of these foreign women mathematics students were three who entered Göttingen University in 1893, Englishwoman Grace Chisholm and Americans Mary Winston and Margaret Maltby (see Creese, *Ladies in the Laboratory?,* 185–86, 192–94, 214–15, 206 n. 9).

114. Marie Gernet (1865–1924), the daughter of an army surgeon, was born in Ettlingen, a few miles south of Karlsruhe, on 1 October 1865. She attended the Höhere Töchterschule in Karlsruhe for nine years (1871–1880) and then the Prinzessin Wilhelm-Stift Seminar for women teachers, qualifying as a teacher in girls' high schools in 1883. After several years of private study in mathematics, she was accepted as an exceptional case into the Karlsruhe Grossherzogliche Technische Hochschule, where from 1888 to 1891 she attended lectures in physics, chemistry, mathematics, and botany and completed laboratory requirements as well. She entered Heidelberg University in the autumn of 1891, immediately after Baden's Ministry of Education, overriding the university senate, gave women permission to audit courses in the faculty of science and mathematics (see Albisetti, *Schooling German Girls,* 225–6). She studied mathematics and physics for two years, taking part in the mathematical seminars and working in the physics laboratories. Her research on simplifying hyperelliptic integrals was carried out under the direction of Leo Königsberger, an analyst. Unsuccessful in her first attempt to pass the oral doctoral examination in November 1894, she studied for another half year and passed in all three of her subareas (mathematics, physics, and mechanics) in July 1895. Thereafter, as a staff member in the recently organized *Gymnasium* section of her former school in Karlsruhe, she became deeply involved in the reform of the school's management, the upgrading of the curriculum to *Abitur* level, and the procuring of financial support from the city. She was also active in work for the advancement of women in postgraduate mathematics studies and in statewide curriculum planning for physics teaching in girls' high schools in Prussia—see Gustav Noodt, Marie Gernet, et al., *Leitfaden der Naturlehre für Lyzeen: nach den Ausführungsbestimmungen zu dem Erlasse vom 18. August 1908 über die Neuordnung des höheren Mädchenschulwesens in Preussen,* 2 vols. (Leipzig, Berlin: B. G. Teubner, 1911). The Karlsruhe girls' school, where Gernet spent her entire career, was an institution famous for the quality of education it provided. Renamed the *Lessingschule* in 1911, it was destroyed in 1942, but rebuilt after the war. It became coeducational in 1973—Renate Tobies, "Matematikerimnen und ihre Doktorväter," in *"Aller Männerkultur zum Trotz": Frauen in Matematik und Naturwissenschaften,* ed. Renate Tobies (Frankfurt/Main: Campus Verlag, 1997), 131–58, on 137–40; Gerhard Kaller, "Mädchenbildung und Frauenstudium. Die Gründung des ersten Mädchengymnasiums in Karlsruhe und die Anfänge des Frauenstudiums an der badeschen Universitäten (1890–1910)," *Zeitschrift für die Geschichte des Oberrheins,* 140 (NF 101), (1992): 361–75; and a biographical sketch in Marie Gernet, "Über Reduktion hyperelliptischer Integrale," inaugural diss., Heidelberg University (Karlsruhe: Friedrich Gutsch, 1895).

115. The name of S[ally] Schiff, who received a doctorate in chemistry from the University of Freiburg (Baden) in 1890 has appeared in English-language listings of early women scientists—see Eleanor Shafer Elder, "A sourcebook of early women scientists," master's thesis, Louisiana State University, Baton Rouge, 1979, 67. However, the first woman to receive a doctorate from Freiburg University was the Dutch physician Constance Auguste Gelderblom, whose degree was awarded (by examination) in February 1895; the American zoologist Elizabeth Bickford was the second, receiving a Ph.D. in December of the same year—see E. Th. Nauck, *Das Frauenstudium an der Universität Freiburg i. Br.,* 3. Heft in *Beiträge zur Freiburger Wissenschafts- und Universitätsgeschichte,* ed. Johannes Vincke (Freiburg im Breisgau: Verlag Eberhardt Albert Universitätsbuchhandlung, 1953), 30–31. Further, the dedication of Sally Schiff's inaugural dissertation makes it clear that the author was male—see Sally Schiff, "Beiträge zur Kenntniss des Acetonchloroforms und einiger seiner Derivative," Albert-Ludwigs-Universitaet zu Freiburg i. B. (Freiburg in Baden: Universitäts-Buchdruckerei von H. M. Poppen & Sohn, 1890). The dedication reads "Seinen theuren Geschwistern in Liebe gewidmet vom Verfasser." See also n. 150.

116. Marie Baum, *Rückblick auf mein Leben* (Berlin: Krolls Buchdruckerei, 1939, and Heidelberg: F. H. Kerle Verlag, 1950; the 1950 edition takes the memoirs to 1948); Wolfgang Bocks, "Baum, Marie" in *Baden-württembergische Biographien,* ed. Bernd Ottnad (Stuttgart: K. Kohlhammer Verlag, 1994), bd. 1, 9–11, and *Die Badische Fabrikinspektion: Arbeiterschutz, Arbeiterverhältnisse und Arbeiterbewegung in Baden 1879–1914* (Freiburg und München: Verlag Karl Alber, 1978), 86–88, 95, 96, 233, 342, 426, 428, 431; Barbara Guttmann, "Marie Baum: Chemikerin, Fabrikinspektorin abgeordnete," in *Blick in die Geschichte: Karlsruher stadthistorische Beiträge 1988–1993,* eds. Leonhard Müller and Manfred Koch (Karlsruhe: Stadt Karlsruhe Forum für Stadtgeschichte und Kultur, 1994), 239–40; K. H. Stuckenbrock, "Dr Marie Baum 90 Jahre alt," *Chemiker-Zeitung/Chemischer Apparatur* 88 (1964): 221; Huch, *Frühling,* 81–82; *Lexikon der Frau,* vol. 1, 347; Müller and Schnurrenberger, "Philosophische Fakultät II," 160; and university archives, Ruprecht-Karls-Universität Heidelberg.

117. See note 6.

118. *Über p-Xylylhydroxylamin. Beiträge zur Kenntnis des 1-2-Naphthalendiazooxyds* (Zürich: J. Leeman, 1899).

119. See M. Baum, "Goldmachen im Lichte alter und neuer Theorien" [Alchemy in the light of older and newer theories], *Prometheus; illustrierte Wochenschrift über die Fortschritte in Gewerbe, Industrie und Wissenschaft* 13, no. 669 (1902): 705–10.

120. Baum, *Rückblick* (1950), 39.

121. Marie Baum, *Drei Klassen von Lohnarbeiterinnen in Industrie und Handel der Stadt Karlsruhe* (Karlsruhe: G. Braunsche Hofbuchdruckerei, 1906). Among her other publications from about this period were (with Philipp Brugger and Heinrich Finkelstein) *Die Bekämpfung der Säuglingsterblichkeit* (Leipzig: Duncker & Humblot, 1905) and (with Agnes Blum and E. Jaffé) *Der Einfluss der gewerblichen Arbeit auf das persönliche Leben der Frau* (Jena: G. Fisher, 1910).

122. Margarete von Üxküll-Gyllenband (b. 1873), from Riga, took a teaching diploma at the Zurich Federal Polytechnikum in 1899 and received her doctorate in botany from Zurich University in 1901. Shortly after, during a research trip to Java, where she visited the Buitenzorg Botanical Garden, she met Dutch botanist Anton Willem Niewenhuis, later professor at Leiden University. She married Niewenhuis about 1902 and thereafter became increasingly active in social work. She also continued her research, at least until the outbreak of the war, several of her articles appearing between 1902 and 1914 (Müller and Schnurrenberger, "Philosophische Fakultät II," 160–61).

123. See Marie Baum, *Die Wohlfartspflege, ihre einheitliche Organisation und ihr Verhältnis zur Armenpflege* (München and Leipzig: Dunckler and Humblot, 1916), a discussion of public health and welfare programs and the relationship of these to charitable poor-relief efforts; *Grundriss der Gesundheitsfürsorge; zum Gebrauch für Schwestern, Kriesfürsorgerinnen, sozial Beamtinnen und andere Organe der vorbeugenden offenen Fürsorge bestimmt* (Wiesbaden: Bergmann, 1919), a manual for nurses and women welfare workers in the public health care system.

124. See for instance *Beiträge zur planmässigen Ausgestaltung der Erholungsfürsorge für Kinder und Jugendliche* (Berlin: F. A. Herbig, 1928); and *Rhythmus des Familien Lebens; das von einer Familie täglich zu leistende Arbeitspensum, mit 7 Tabellen und 38 Kartogrammen* (Berlin: F. A. Herbig, 1931).

125. Baum, *Rückblick* (1950), 276.

126. Baum, *Rückblick* (1950), 321–26.

127. Marie Baum's friend Elisabeth von Thadden (1890–1944), a well-known and innovative educationist, had founded and led this school at Schloss Wieblingen until removed from her post by the National Socialist government in 1939. She then went to France and with extraordinary dedication and efficiency worked in a soldiers' home until arrested in 1943 and taken to Ravensbrück concentration camp for women. She was executed in 1944 (*Lexikon der Frau*, vol. 2, 1430–31).

128. For comparison see the pioneering work in inspection of industrial working conditions carried out by American physician and industrial toxicologist Alice Hamilton during the early years of the twentieth century. Hamilton also had a remarkable career and latterly an academic position (at Harvard)—Creese, *Ladies in the Laboratory?*, 139–41.

129. *Anna von Gierke: ein Lebensbild* (Weinheim: J. Beltz, 1954).

130. Verein Feministische Wissenschaft Schweiz, *Ebenso neu*, 157, 208; membership lists, Deutsche Chemische Gesellschaft, *Berichte der Deutschen Chemischen Gesellschaft* 21, 1 (1888): 85; 21, 2 (1888): 3588; 22, 1 (1889): 86.

131. See note 6.

132. Gerit von Leitner, *Der Fall Clara Immerwahr: Leben für eine Humane Wissenschaft* (München: C. H. Beck, 1994; for a review in English see Jeffrey A. Johnson, "One Chemical Marriage," *Chemical Heritage* 11, no. 2 (1994): 16–17); Dietrich Stoltzenberg, *Fritz Haber: Chemiker, Nobelpreisträger, Deutscher, Jude: eine Biographie* (Weinheim: V C H, 1994), 29–30, 60–70, 352–56, 630; Ulla Fölsing, *Geniale Beziehungen: Berühmte Paare in der Wissenschaft* (München: C. H. Beck, 1999), 136–45; David Nachmanson, *German-Jewish Pioneers in Science, 1900–1933: Highlights in Atomic Physics, Chemistry, and Biochemistry* (New York: Springer, 1979); Morris Goran, *The Story of Fritz Haber* (Norman, Okla.: University of Oklahoma Press, 1967), 29–31, 71–72; Albisetti, *Schooling German Girls*, 232; J. C. Poggendorff's *Biographisch-Literarisches Handwörterbuch zur der Exacten Wissenschaften* (Leipzig: J. A. Barth and other publishers later, 1863–), band 4 (1904), abt. 1, 681–82.

133. See note 4.

134. See Vogt, *Elsa Neumann*, 22.

135. Albisetti, *Schooling German Girls*, 221. See also the case of Clara Hamburger.

136. See note 25.

137. C. Immerwahr, "Beiträge zur Kenntniss der Löslichkeit von Schwermetallniederschlagen auf elektrochemischen Wege," *Zeitschrift für Elektrochemie* 7 (1901): 477–83; 625.

138. "Unser erster weiblicher Doktor," *Breslauer Zeitung*, Abendausgabe, 22 December 1900; reproduced in von Leitner, *Der Fall Clara Immerwahr*, 66. Immerwahr's dissertation was entitled, "Beiträge zur Löslichkeitsbestimmung schwerlöslicher Salze des Queksilbers, Kupfers, Bleis, Cadmiums und Zinks."

139. About this time, Immerwahr gave a popular lecture on physics and chemistry in the household ("Physik und Chemie im Haushalt") to a large audience assembled under the auspices of the Breslau Society for the Welfare of Women. Women's education groups had been active in Breslau since 1866 when Elise Oelsner founded the Breslau Women's Education Association. By the early 1890s, this organization was conducting courses in areas ranging from cooking to kindergarten teaching to photography (Albisetti, *Schooling German Girls*, 103).

140. An English edition, *Thermodynamics of Technical Gas Reactions* (trans. Arthur B. Lamb; New York: Longman's Green & Co.), appeared in 1908. This carried a dedication to Clara "for her silent co-operation."

141. Known as the Haber Process, this procedure was tremendously important because of the growing need for nitrate fertilizer. At the turn of the century Chile, the only rich source of nitrates then known, was supplying two thirds of the world's fertilizer and the deposits were being depleted rapidly. By about 1905 both Walther Nernst, professor of physical chemistry at Berlin University, and Haber had become interested in the thermodynamics of the production of ammonia

from nitrogen and hydrogen. Haber took the process to the commercial stage, working jointly with Badische Anilin und Soda Fabrik (BASF). His patent (German Patent No. DRP238450) was taken out in 1909. The work brought him the Nobel Prize for chemistry in 1918, although his military research during the First World War made his nomination for the award a matter of considerable controversy.

142. These actions included major marches and demonstrations in 1911 for women's right to vote and the organization of a large, well-attended women's congress in 1912. See Sabine Sander, "Bürgerliche Frauen organisieren sich (1810–1914)," in *Ich bin meine eigene Frauenbewegung,* 24–30.

143. Elisabeth Crawford, *Nationalism and Internationalism in Science, 1880–1939: Four Studies of the Nobel Population* (Cambridge: Cambridge University Press, 1992), 115.

144. *Grunewald-Zeitung,* 8 May 1915, notice reproduced in von Leitner, *Der Fall Clara Immerwahr,* 215.

145. Fölsing, *Geniale Beziehungen,* 136–45.

146. See Stoltzenberg, *Fritz Haber,* and Margit Szöllösi-Janze, *Fritz Haber 1868–1934. Eine Biographie* (München: C. H. Beck, 1998).

147. Information from the Deutsche Sektion der Internationalen Ärzte für die Verhütung des Atomskrieges. Ärtze in sozialer Verantwortung (IPPNW). Körtestrasse 10, D-10967, Berlin 61. The IPPNW, founded by a small group of physicians from the United States and the Soviet Union at a meeting in Geneva in 1980, received the Nobel Peace Prize in 1985. Its work includes research, publication, advising governmental and international agencies, and organizing frequent IPPNW World Congresses.

148. Tony Harrison, *Square Rounds* (London and Boston: Faber and Faber, 1992).

149. Köttgen was primarily interested in the mechanism of color vision (see psychologists, below).

150. Berlin physics student Sally Simon, whose 1899 paper is listed in the Royal Society *Catalogue* might be assumed by English speakers to be a woman. However, Simon was male (Salomo Simon)—see "Vita" in Sally Simon, "Über das Verhältnis von elektrischer Ladung und Masse der Kathodenstrahlen," inaugural diss., Friedrich-Wilhelms-Universität zu Berlin, 1899 (Berlin: Buchdruckerei Gustav Schade, 1899; cf. also n. 115).

151. From C. H. Giles and D. S. Forrester, "The origins of the surface film balance. Studies in the early history of surface chemistry, part 3," *Chemistry and Industry,* no. 2 (9 Jan. 1971): 43–53, on 46.

152. Elisabeth Pockels (with introduction by S. Rösch), "Ein gelehrtes Geschwisterpaar. Zur Erinnerung an Agnes Pockels (1862–1935)," *Bericht der Oberhessischen Gesellschaft für Natur- und Heilkunde zu Giessen. Naturwissenschaftliche Abteilung* 24 (1949): 303–7; Giles and Forrester, "Origins"; W. Ostwald, "Die Arbeiten von Agnes Pockels über Grenzschichten und Filme," *Kolloid-Zeitschrift* 58 (1932): 1–8; M. Elizabeth Derrick, "Agnes Pockels (1862–1935)," in *Women in Chemistry and Physics: A Biobibliographic Sourcebook,* eds. L. Grinstein, R. K. Rose, M. H. Rafailovich (Westport, Conn.: Greenwood Press, 1993), 502–7; Gabriele Beisswanger, "Agnes Pockels (1862–1935) und die Oberflächenchemie: '. . . Sauberkeiten nicht nur herzustellen sondern sogar zu messen,'" *Chemie in unserer Zeit* 25 (1991): 97–101; and Hans-Joachim Bittrich, "Pockels, Agnes Luise Wilhelmine," in *ABC Geschichte der Chemie,* eds. Siegfried Engels, Rüdiger Stolz, et al. (Leipzig: VEB Deutscher Verlag für Grundstoffindustrie, 1989), 314.

153. This was probably *Pouillet's Lehrbuch der Physik und Meteorologie,* translated from the French and expanded by Johan Müller (Braunschweig: Vieweg, several eds., 1853–).

154. Pockels, "Gelehrtes Geschwisterpaar," 304.

155. Rayleigh (Lord), "On the tension of recently formed liquid surfaces," *Proceedings of the Royal Society* 47 (1890): 281–87; "Measurements of the amount of oil necessary in order to check the motions of camphor upon water," *Proceedings of the Royal Society,* 47 (1890): 364–67; "On the superficial viscosity of water," *Proceedings of the Royal Society* 48 (1890): 127–40.

156. Lord Rayleigh and Miss A. Pockels, "Surface Tension," *Nature* 43 (1891), 437.

157. Giles and Forrester, "Origins," 43. Pockels's 1891 observations were included in standard advanced textbooks of physical chemistry many decades later—see for example Samuel Glasstone, *Textbook of Physical Chemistry,* 2nd. ed. (London: Macmillan, 1955), 1210.

158. Rayleigh (Lord), "Investigations in capillarity . . . The tension of contaminated water surfaces," *Philosophical Magazine* 48 (1899): 321–37.

159. *Nature* 46 (1892): 418–19.

160. Pockels's second letter to Rayleigh (1892) contains the remark, "With regard to your curiosity about my personal status, I am indeed a lady" (quoted, in English translation, by Giles and Forrester, "Origins," 44).

161. Illness was a considerable burden on the family. Agnes Pockels was subject to periods of insomnia and depression, brought on at least in part by her own physical ailments in addition to those of the others. As early as 1907, she had a five-week stay in a sanitorium where she received treatment for her nervous condition.

162. Pockels's post-1900 publications include the following: "Ueber das spontane Sinken der Oberflächenspannung von Wasser, wässerigen Lösungen und Emulsionen," *Annalen der Physik* 8 (1902): 854–71; "Das Willkürliche in der Welt," *Annalen der Naturphilosophie* 8 (1909): 321–28; "Ueber Randwinkel und Ausbreitung von Flüssigkeiten auf festen Körporen," *Physikalische Zeitschrift* 15 (1914): 39–46; "Ueber die Ausbreitung reiner und gemischter Flüssigkeiten auf Wasser," *Physikalische Zeitschrift* 17 (1916): 142–45; "Zur Frage der zeitlichen Veränderung der Oberfächenspannung," *Physikalische Zeitschrift* 17 (1916): 441–42; "Die Anomalie der Wasseroberfläche," *Naturwissenschaften* 5 (1917): 137, 149;

"Zur Frage der Ölflecke auf Seen," *Naturwissenschaften* 6 (1918), 118; "The measurement of surface tension with the balance," *Science* 64 (1926): 304; "The dependence of wetting of solids on time of contact," *Kolloid Zeitschrift* 62 (1933): 1–2. Her German translation of G. H. Darwin's works on tides (*On Tidal Prediction* and *On the Harmonic Analysis of Tidal Observations of High and Low Water*—London: Harrison and Sons, 1891, and *Proceedings of the Royal Society* (1891), vols. 48, 49) appeared in 1902 under the title *Ebbe und Flut.*

163. See Giles and Forrester, "Origins," 50.

164. The poem appears in Pockels, "Gelehrtes Geschwisterpaar," 307. I thank Dr Michael Serafin, editor of the *Oberhessische Naturwissenschaftliche Zeitschrift: Bericht der Oberhessischen Gesellschaft für Natur- und Heilkunde zu Giessen, Naturwissenschaftliche Abteilung,* for permission to quote the verse. Dr Anna Creese helped with the following translation:

> We prepare for a new endeavour,
> that should bring clear vision;
> we paint into pictures and carve into stone
> what should never be forgotten—
> and above us the pilot roars . . .
> and sings his dull, menacing song
> of the imminent destruction of man.

165. Vogt, *Elsa Neumann*; this work includes reproductions of a great deal of archival material relating to Neuman; Elsa Neumann, "Vita" in "Über die Polarisationscapacität umkehrbarer Elektroden," inaugural diss., Friedrich-Wilhelms-Universität, Berlin (Leipzig: J. A. Barth, 1899); and Albisetti, *Schooling German Girls,* 235–36.

166. See note 4.

167. See note 25.

168. *Berichte der Deutschen Chemischen Gesellschaft* 34, 2 (1901): 1348. Elsa Neumann would seem to have been the first German woman member of the society although at least eleven from other countries, notably the United States and Russia, had joined earlier. The first was probably Lidiia Sesemann from Finland who became a member in 1877 four years after receiving a doctorate in chemistry from Zurich University (Membership lists, *Berichte der Deutschen Chemischen Gesellschaft,* 1877–1901); for Sesemann, see the chapter on Scandinavian women, section on Finland.

169. See also the section on chemist Marie Baum, above.

170. Anonymous, "A list of those who have carried out researches at the Cavendish Laboratory," *A History of the Cavendish Laboratory 1871–1910* (London: Longman's, 1910), 331. The first woman to work at the Cavendish Laboratory was Eleanor Sidgwick, who was there during the years 1880–1882; see Creese, *Ladies in the Laboratory?,* 219–20. The Cavendish Laboratory archives do not appear to have any additional records concerning Neumann.

171. *History of the Cavendish,* 149, 218.

172. Vogt, *Elsa Neumann,* 36. Neither this technical report nor Neumann's account of her trip has yet been found.

173. Obituaries, *Der Tag,* 24 July 1902, 1, and *Berliner Lokal-Anzeiger,* 24 July 1902, 1. Other Berlin newspapers (*Vossische Zeitung* and *Berliner Tageblatt*) also carried obituaries on 24 July 1902; see in addition *Allgemeine Zeitung,* n. 202, 25 July 1902, 6, and *Berichte der Deutschen Chemischen Gesellschaft* 35, no. 3, (1902): 2764.

174. See Gattermann's report of his synthesis of aromatic aldehydes using anhydrous hydrocyanic acid (prepared by the action of concentrated sulfuric acid on a cyanide salt), *Justus Liebig's Annalen der Chemie* 357 (1907): 313–83.

175. "We look with pride upon Fräulein Mestorf who has brought such brilliant recognition to women in the field of prehistoric archaeology"—remarks by Virchow at the twenty-fifth anniversary meeting of the Berlin Anthropological Society (1894), quoted by Richard Andree, "Johanna Mestorf zum 80 Geburtstag," *Globus* 95 (1909): 213–15, on 215.

176. *Eine Dame zwischen 500 Herren; Johanna Mestorf—Werk und Wirkung,* eds. Julia K. Koch and Eva-Maria Mertens, papers from the International Symposium, Christian-Albrechts-Universität, Keil, in Bad Bramstedt 15–17 April, 1999 (Münster: Waxmann, 2002)—this work includes a full listing of Mestorf's publications; Eva-Maria Mertens, "Mestorf, Johanna," in *Neue Deutsche Biographie,* ed. Bayerische Akademie der Wissenschaften, Historische Kommission (Berlin: Duncker & Humblot, 1994), bd. 17, 227–28; Gabriele Junginger, "Johanna Mestorf (1828–1909)—eine Urgeschichtsforscherin in Kiel," *Dokumentation; 17. Bundesweiter Kongress von Frauen in Naturwissenschaft und Technik, 9–12 May 1991, Kiel,* eds. Ulrike Rapp and Maarit Bebensee (Kiel: Treibgut-Verlag), 171–74; Thomas Erdmann Fischer, *Die Anfänge des Frauenstudiums in Deutschland: Das Beispiel der Universität Kiel* (Trier: Auenthal Verlag, 1996), 70–71; Karl Zimmermann, "'. . . dass ihr kostbarster Schmuck, ihre einzige Macht, ihr ganzer Zauber in der Weiblichkeit liegt.' Zum Briefwechsel zwischen Johanna Mestorf (1828–1909) und Karl Adolph von Morlot (1820–1867)," *Nordelbingen. Beiträge zur Kunst- und Kulturgeschichte* 62 (1993): 171–88; Hans Gummel, *Forschungsgeschichte in Deutschland* (Berlin: Walter de Gruyter & Co., 1938), bd. 1, appendix, 442–43; Nicolaus Detlefsen, "Johanna Mestorfs Grab auf dem Ohlsdorfer Friedhof in Hamburg," *Die Heimat (Monatsschrift des Vereins zur Pflege der Natur- und Landeskunde in Schleswig-Holstein und Hamburg* 82 (1975): 229–34; Dagmar Unverhau, "Zur Erinnerung an Johanna Mestorf," *Schleswig-Holstein,* hf. 7 (July 1986): 7–9; Andree, "Johanna Mestorf"; obituary, Alexander F. Chamberlain, *American Anthropologist* 11 (1909): 536–37; Jarno Jessen, "Professor Dr. Johanna Mestorf," in *Bahnbrechende Frauen* (Berlin-Charlottenburg: Deutsche Lyceum-Club, 1912), 179–84; and *Lexikon der Frau,* vol. 2, 613. There is some difference of opinion in the literature concerning Mestorf's dates

of birth and baptism; Zimmermann and Detlefsen give 15 April 1828 as birth date (baptismal date 17 April 1828—see Zimmermann, n. 11, 187); Junginger gives 17 April 1828 as birth date.

177. *Wibeke Kruse, eine Holsteinische Bauerntochter. Ein Blatt aus der Zeit Christians IV* [Wibeke Kruse, a Holstein Peasant's Daughter. A Tale from the Time of Christian IV] (Hamburg: O. Meissner, 1866).

178. For a comprehensive discussion of Mestorf's translation work and its importance, see Barbro Johnsen and Stig Welinder, "Johanna Mestorf. The link between Swedish and Continental Archaeology in the Golden Age," in *Eine Dame zwischen 500 Herren*, 73–101.

179. See J. Mestorf, *Der Archäologische Kongress in Bologna* (Hamburg: O. Meissner, 1871).

180. These were, in particular, the idea of the Three-Age system—the division of the prehistoric era into Stone Age, Bronze Age, and Iron Age—and the method of typological organization. A Three-Age system of chronology had been discussed by French scholars in the eighteenth century, the basic idea of an evolutionary sequence going back to the Roman philosopher Lucretius. However, no rational, practical strategy having been devised to apply and test it, it remained speculative theory that had little influence on antiquarian thought until the opening years of the nineteenth century. About then, Danish scholar C. J. Thomsen began the systematic studies that enabled him to work out a logical, chronological sequence based on stylistic variation. Typological organization, an elaboration of Thomsen's basic ideas, allows the classification of similar objects into general types, providing a mechanism for ordering and comparing artifacts from various sites and revealing cultural trends. Type is thus seen as a stage in development according to a Darwinian scheme; the concept constituted a major step in the development of archaeology as a science, and Mestorf's translations from the Swedish played a crucial role in its acceptance by German workers—see also Bruce G. Trigger, *A History of Archaeological Thought* (Cambridge: Cambridge University Press, 1989, especially 73–79, 155–61).

181. A few of Mestorf's papers presenting these topics are listed in the bibliography; for others see *Eine Dame zwischen 500 Herren*, 17–26.

182. See bibliography, and also Ralph Weichmann, "Wikingzeitliche Schatzfunde: alte Meinungen, neue Perspektiven," in *Eine Dame zwischen 500 Herren*, 197–212.

183. *Die Vaterländischen Alterthümer Schleswig-Holsteins. Ansprache an unsere Landsleute,* commissioned by the Ministry for Church, Education and Medical Affairs (Hamburg: O. Meissner, 1877).

184. See bibliography and "Moorleichen" in *42. Berichte des Schleswig-Holsteinischen Museums Vaterländischer Alterthümer bei der Universität Kiel* (Kiel, 1900); "Nachtrag zu den Moorleichen," *44. Berichte des Schleswig-Holsteinischen Museums . . .* (Kiel, 1907). See also Wijnand van der Sanden, "Bog body research since Johanna Mestorf," in *Eine Dame zwischen 500 Herren*, 195–96 (abstract only).

185. *Vorgeschichtliche Alterthümer aus Schleswig-Holstein. Zum Gedächtnis des Fünfzigjährigen Bestehens des Museums Vaterländischer Alterthümer in Kiel* (Hamburg: O. Meissner, 1885); *Urnenfriedhöfe in Schleswig-Holstein* (Hamburg: O. Meissner, 1886).

186. It is perhaps of interest to note that not long before the appearance of these major contributions Johanna Mestorf's request for auditor status for the winter semester 1884–1885 at Kiel university was rejected (Fischer, *Anfänge des Frauenstudiums,* 70). No explanation for the rejection is recorded.

187. See note 180. Jacob Mestorf explained the method in an 1828 preface to his archaeological collection. The relevant excerpt from his manuscript, by then in the Kiel museum along with his collection, was sent by his daughter to Rudolf Virchow in 1886; it was published by Virchow in the *Verhandlungen der Berliner Gesellschaft für Anthropologie, Ethnologie und Urgeschichte* (1886), 81–82.

188. M. Johanna Brather, "Johanna Mestorf, die erste Bodendenkmalpflegerin Schleswig-Holsteins: Ein Vergleich ihrer Studienergebnisse zu Urnenfriedhöfen mit unserem heutigen Kenntnisstand," in *Eine Dame zwischen 500 Herren*, 177–94.

189. Fischer (*Anfänge des Frauenstudiums,* 71) notes that at the same time an eight-man commission for the Museum of National Antiquities and Ethnology was set up that was clearly for the purpose of monitoring Mestorf.

190. Johnsen and Welinder, "Johanna Mestorf: The Link," 86.

191. See note 184.

192. These obituaries included the following: Helene Höhnk, "Frl. Prof. Dr. med. Johanna Mestorf," *Niedersachsen* (*Illustrierte Halbmonatsschrift für Geschichte . . .*) 14 (1908–1909): n. 23, 445; Friedrich Knorr, "Professor Dr. Johanna Mestorf . . . ," *Mitteilungen des Anthropologischen Vereins in Schleswig-Holstein* 19 (1909): 1–19; Gustav Kossina, *Mannus* (*Zeitschrift für Vorgeschichte*) 1 (1909): 323–24; Hubert Schmidt, *Prähistorische Zeitschrift* 1 (1909): 110–11; and Karl von den Steinen, *Zeitschrift für Ethnologie* 41 (1909): 852. For a more complete list, see Zimmermann, "Johanna Mestorf und Karl Adolph von Morlot," n. 10, 186.

193. See Gustav Schwantes, "Johanna Mestorf," *Festschrift zum 275jährigen Bestehen der Christian-Albrechts-Universität Kiel* (Leipzig: 1940), 309–31; H. B. Jessen, "Zur Jugendgeschichte Johanna Mestorfs," *Die Heimat* (*Monatsschrift des Vereins zur Pflege der Natur- und Landeskunde in Schleswig-Holstein und Hamburg*) 63 (1956): 82–83; Gustav Schwantes, "Johanna Mestorf. Ein kurzes Wort der Erinnerung an den 20. Juli, den 50. Todestag der Forscherin," *Die Heimat* 66 (1959): 274–76; Gerda Pfeifer, "Johanna Mestorf," *Heimatkundliches Jahrbuch für den Kreis Segeberg* 16 (1970): 166–73; and Detlefsen, "Johanna Mestorfs Grab."

194. Gummel, *Forschungsgeschichte.*

195. See Glyn Daniel, *A Hundred and Fifty Years of Archaeology*, 2nd ed. (London: Duckworth, 1975); Trigger, *History*

of Archaeological Thought; and Alain Schnapp, *La conquête du passé: aux origines de l'archaéologie* (Paris: Éditions Carré, 1993).

196. But see, for instance, *Excavating Women: A History of Women in European Archaeology*, eds. Margarita Díaz-Andreu and Marie Louise Stig Sørensen (London: Routledge, 1998), especially the chapter by Díaz-Andreu and Stig Sørensen, "Towards an engendered history of archaeology," 1–28, on 11–13.

197. See note 176.

198. See Koch and Mertens, eds., *Eine Dame zwischen 500 Herren.*

199. *Tagebuch der Johanna Mestorf 1873–1891*, Preface. Mestorf's *Tagebuch* is held in the archives of the Schleswig-Holsteinischen Landesmuseums für Vor- und Frühgeschichte, Schleswig. See Unverhau, "Zur Erinnerung," 8–9 for a long quotation.

200. Rudolf Virchow (1821–1902), one of Germany's most outstanding nineteenth-century men of science, although remembered particularly for his contributions to pathology, also had broad interests in all aspects of prehistory (archaeology, ethnology, and folklore). In addition he served in the German *Reichstag* and published a great many political writings; see Gunter B. Risse, in *Dictionary of Scientific Biography*, ed. C. C. Gillispie (New York: Charles Scribner's, 1976), vol. 14, 39–44.

201. Zimmermann, "Johanna Mestorf und Karl Adolph von Morlot," 182 and 188 n. 55. See also Christian Andree, *Rudolf Virchow als Prähistoriker, Bd. 1: Virchow als Begründer der neueren deutschen Ur- und Frühgeschichtswissenschaft* (Köln and Wien: Böhlau, 1976), 118–19; and *Bd. 2: Briefe Virchow's und seiner Zeitgenossen*, 313–19.

202. Knorr, "Professor Dr. Johanna Mestorf," 4.

203. "Dolche in Frauengräbern der Bronzezeit," *Correspondenz-Blatt der Deutschen Gesellschaft für Anthropologie, Ethnologie und Urgeschichte* 20 (1889): 150–54.

204. See also the examples of Marianne Plehn and Maria von Linden, who somewhat later followed similar paths in that they took no visible part in the women's movement but concentrated their efforts on their work.

205. Pataky, *Lexikon*, vol. 1, 409–10.

206. Two additional experimental psychology papers by women students at Göttingen University were published in the Leipzig journal *Zeitschrift für Psychologie* in 1900 (see bibliography, under Appendix). These were by American students Lottie Steffens and Laura Steffens (see appendix).

207. Renate Tobies, "Einführung: Einflusfaktoren auf die Karriere von Frauen in Mathematik und Naturwissenschaften," in *Aller Männerkultur zum Trotz*, 17–67, on 20.

Chapter 6

AUSTRIA-HUNGARY:
MAINLY MEDICINE

Sixteen authors who together published a total of thirty-three papers are listed in the Austria-Hungary section of the bibliography. Six, including three Welt sisters, were medical workers; three were botanists; and two were students of mathematics. The others made contributions in astronomy, chemistry, natural history, and geography. Except for the astronomy papers by the Viennese baroness Elisabeth von Matt in the period before 1820, all the work was published in the last quarter of the nineteenth century (Figure 6-1).

The early stages of the opening to women of universities and the professions in the Hapsburg empire, one of the last places in Europe to take this step, have been examined fairly extensively.[1] The traditional universities, Vienna, Graz, Innsbruck, Prague, Kraków, Lemberg (later L'vov), and Czernowitz (later Chernovtsy) led the way, opening their philosophical faculties in 1897, but many of the technical institutions remained closed to women until after the First World War. The demand for medical education and license to practice was a major factor spurring women's efforts to gain university entrance;[2] indeed it is said that the single most important event that unlocked the door to higher education as a whole for women in Austria-Hungary was the Emperor Franz Josef's granting permission, in 1890, to Russian-born and Swiss-educated Rosa Kerschbaumer to manage her own ophthalmic clinic in Salzburg.[3] The prominence of medical women among the Austrians in this survey reflects the emphasis on this area, more than a third of the Austrian papers being in the medical sciences (Figure 6-2).

ROSA (RAISSA) KERSCHBAUMER,[4] née SHLYKOVA (1854–1923), the first woman physician to practice independently in Austria, was born in Moscow on 21 April 1854, one of the two daughters of Vasilii Dmitrievich Shlykov and his wife Adelaide Aleksandrovna. Members of Russia's minor aristocracy, the Shlykovs held lands in the administrative district of Tula, south of Moscow. Vasilii Shlykov, a gentleman farmer but a man of progressive ideas, served as a council member and university official. Raissa Vasilievna could as well be classified among Russian women physicians as among Austrian, but her special place in the opening of the medical profession to Austrian women, her twenty-three years of practice in Austria, and her marriage for a period to an Austrian suggest her inclusion here.

At the time she was growing up her country was going through a period of far-reaching change. The *débâcle* of the Crimean War (1853–1855) had made very plain Russia's backwardness and there was much agitation for social, economic, and educational reconstruction. A prime concern of middle-class women was access to higher education as a means to social emancipation. Although accepted as auditors for a few years from about 1859, women were expelled from the universities in 1863, a move by the authorities that caused many to go abroad to Western Europe, particularly to Switzerland.

Raissa Shlykova's family followed the way of life traditional for Russian landowners at the time, spending summers on their country estate and winters in the city. Raissa and her sister were educated by private tutors and enjoyed the round of balls and parties usual for people of their social class. Before she was out of her teens she married Vladimir Putiata, an actor in Tula. Her sister Virginiia, more caught up in the prevailing mood of eagerness for education, wanted to continue her studies and, after first attending courses for women in Moscow, obtained her father's permission to go to Switzerland. Accompanied by her governess, who was to live with her, Virginiia arrived in Zurich in the spring of 1872 and enrolled in the science division of the university's philosophical faculty. In October of the same year, Raissa Putiata-Shlykova, now separated from her husband, also moved to Zurich; both sisters then enrolled in the medical faculty.[5]

A fellow student later wrote of Raissa Putiata-Shlykova as one of a group of serious, talented, progressive,

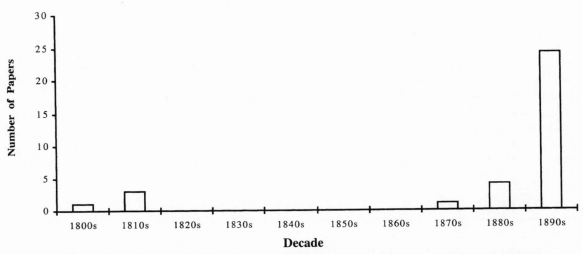

Figure 6-1.   Austro-Hungarian authors and papers, by decade, 1800–1900. Data from the Royal Society
Catalogue of Scientific Papers.

and idealistic Russian women students in Zurich at that time who were strongly inspired by the powerful movement for complete social reform in their country, but who nevertheless put their studies first and largely avoided political activity.[6] This caution notwithstanding, however, she and her sister did not have long in Zurich. In 1873 the tsarist government, worried about student involvement in the émigré revolutionary groups that then flourished in the city, ordered all Russian women students to leave Zurich. Failure to do so brought, among other penalties, the threat of future exclusion from Russian institutions of higher learning and disqualification from licensing examinations and government employment in Russia. After investigating possibilities at Leipzig University, which rejected her, and Prague, where she would not have been allowed to take examinations, Raissa continued her studies at Bern.[7] Enrolled there for seven semesters (1873–1876), she specialized in ophthalmology and received her degree in 1876 (when she was twenty-two), submitting a dissertation on tumors of the lymph glands—"Über Sarcom der Lymphdrüsen."

She practiced for a short time in an ophthalmic clinic in Vienna and in 1877 married a coworker, Friedrich Kerschbaumer, an Austrian ophthalmologist. For the next thirteen years she served as an assistant at the ophthalmic hospital her husband founded in Salzburg. In 1890 however, following the granting of her petition to Emperor Franz Josef for an official license to practice independently, she opened her own clinic in Salzburg and managed the facility for six years. Specially interested in neoplasms of the eye, she earned an enviable reputation as an exceptionally skilled ophthalmic surgeon.[8] In her 1891 *Archiv für Ophthalmologie*

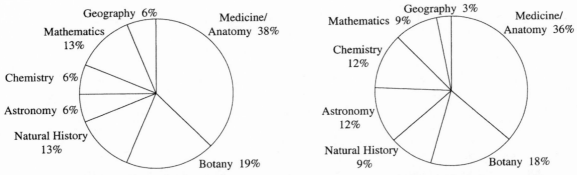

Figure 6-2. Distribution of Austro-Hungarian authors and papers, by field, 1800–1900. (In a., an author contributing to more than one field is counted in each.) Data from the Royal Society *Catalogue of Scientific Papers*.

report of cataract operations performed at the ophthalmic hospital (a continuation of previous reports—see bibliography and note 8), she noted that the total number of operations performed at the hospital between 1880 and 1888 exceeded 500. Of the 200 cases covered in her 1891 paper—those operated on over a period of nineteen months in the early 1880s—182 were restored to "good" vision and only five lost vision. These were notable results for the time; techniques and counterinfection precautions were not yet well established and in addition many of Raissa Kerschbaumer's patients were illiterate country people who did not always follow postoperative care instructions.

In 1896, having separated from her husband,[9] she returned to Russia, where she remained for the next eleven years. Under the auspices of the Tsarina Maria, she undertook organization of ophthalmic care first in the Caucasus and then at several places along the trans-Siberia railway, both regions where there was tremendous need for the service. Going back to Austria in 1907 she spent four years in Vienna before immigrating to the United States in 1911; she was then fifty-seven. After a short time in Seattle, Washington, she settled in California, passed the state medical licensing examinations (1914), and joined the Medical Society of California. At least until 1918 she conducted a practice in Los Angeles, where she died on 27 July 1923 at the age of sixty-nine.

SOPHIE VON MORACZEWSKA,[10] née OKUNIEWSKA, also Russian by birth, was the second woman to obtain a license to practice medicine in Austria by the regular examination route.[11] The daughter of physician A. Okuniewski, she was born in 1865 in Podolia, a region of southwest Russia bordering the territories of Austria-Hungary. Having lost her mother at an early age, she was brought up in the home of her uncle, Canon J. Ozavkiewicz, in a village on the river Pruth, in Galicia, then part of Austria-Hungary. The strong influence of her Russian cousin Natalie Kobzunska, a writer, and her own readings in Russian literature inspired her to find a way to acquire an education. At age sixteen she returned to her father, then a district doctor in Kimpolung, Bukovina (now Cîmpulung Moldovenesc, Romania, but at the time in Austria-Hungary). He raised no objection to the wishes of his only daughter to continue her studies, which she did first at home and then by private arrangement in Lemberg; in 1885 she was able to take and pass the school leaving certificate examinations.

Two years later Sophie Okuniewska went to Zurich University and began studies in science and medicine. She married a fellow medical student, Waclaw von Moraczewski (b. 1867 in Warsaw) in 1890. Her dissertation research on changes in the blood in cases of anemia, carried out under the direction of Hermann Eichhorst, was published in Virchow's *Archiv für Pathologische Anatomie* in 1896 and her degree conferred the same year. She took the medical degree examinations in Krakow shortly after and was then able to practice in Austria.

Calm and confident, sound and sensible in her judgments, and genuinely kindly, Moraczewska concerned herself especially with the health and welfare of women and girls. Specializing in gynecology she worked in the state hospital in Lemberg and, during the season, at Franzensbad (now Frantikovy Lázne, Czech Republic).

The Welt sisters Rosa, Leonore, and Sara all had notable careers in medicine, although all three spent most of their working lives outside Austria.

Rosa Welt Strauss[12] was born in Czernowitz, Bukovina (now Chernovtsy, Ukraine), on 24 August 1856, one of four daughters in a Jewish family. She was taught at home and for a time attended a public normal school in Czernowitz. Mainly under the guidance of her father and the writer Karl Emil Franzos she began studies at the gymnasium level, passing the school leaving certificate examinations in 1873.

In the vain hope that Rosa might be admitted to lectures in the philosophical faculty of Vienna University, the family moved to that city. In 1874 however, after her attempts to enroll in the medical faculty also failed, Rosa Welt went to Bern. She specialized in pathology and was awarded her degree by Bern University in 1878,[13] when she was twenty-two. Hers was the first medical degree conferred on an Austrian woman.

Returning to Vienna, she attended lectures on ophthalmology in the summer of 1879 and spent some months as a visiting student at the Rothschield Hospital. She served as an assistant at the Royal Maternity Hospital in Dresden for a time, but by 1882 had moved to New York City where, for thirty-seven years, from 1883 until 1920, she had a practice in ophthalmology. She married Louis Strauss of Brooklyn in 1882.

Leonore Gourfein-Welt[14] (1859–1944) was born in Sadgora, on the outskirts of Czernowitz, Bukovina, on 30 July 1859. She passed the school-leaving certificate examinations at the *Staatsgymnasium* in Czernowitz and studied for two years in the philosophical faculty at Czernowitz University. In 1882, after one semester in the medical faculty at Bern (winter, 1881), she enrolled as a medical student at Zurich University. She received her degree in 1888; her dissertation research, carried out under Hermann Eichhorst's direction and published in 1888, concerned lesions of the frontal lobes of the brain (see bibliography).

Leonora Welt married David Gourfein, ophthalmologist and professor at the University of Geneva, and for a number of years worked as an assistant in the ophthalmology clinic he directed. A popular and much-respected physician, she also conducted a large practice of her own. In addition she carried out a considerable number of basic studies in pathology, focusing particularly on inflammatory diseases of the eye and surrounding tissue. Over the years she published about twenty papers.[15]

She was active in many areas, assisting students and young research workers, promoting the welfare of women students, providing public assistance for children, especially war victims, and taking part in local, national, and international organizations that were working for the advancement of women. A charter member of the University of Geneva Women's Association, she was honorary president from 1934. Of special note was the school for laboratory workers she founded as a section of l'École d'Études Sociales to help create new career opportunities in the sciences for young women. Her gift to the university in memory of her husband established a fund for research in experimental biology; another gift, in memory of her sisters, ("Don Soeurs Welt") provided assistance for the housing of the elderly and indigent blind and promoted research in ophthalmology. She died in Geneva on 8 January 1944.

Sara Welt-Kakels[16] (1860–1943), the third of these physician sisters, was born on 12 December 1860, also in Czernowitz, Bukovina. She passed the full school leaving certificate examinations at the state gymnasium in Bern and then studied for two semesters in the Bern University faculty of medicine (1879–1880). Returning to Vienna in 1880, she spent a semester in the philosophical faculty in 1880–1881 before transferring to Zurich University. She received her Zurich medical degree in 1885. Her dissertation research on currently used medicaments for fever reduction, carried out under the guidance of Hermann Eichhorst, was published a year later (see bibliography).

Following in the footsteps of her older sister Rosa, Sara Welt then moved to New York City. In 1887 she became the first woman pediatrician at Mt. Sinai Hospital and for twenty-three years, from 1899 until 1922, she headed a children's clinic in the hospital's outpatient department. In 1894 she held a New York Academy of Medicine full Resident Fellowship,[17] one of the first women doctors to do so. Until about 1919 she published steadily. Her more than twenty papers covered a variety of topics but were mainly clinical studies in pediatric medicine.[18] A member of the New York Pathological Society from 1916, she became a fellow of the American Medical Association in 1931. She married Moses S. Kakels, surgeon at Lebanon Hospital and Rockaway Beach Hospital, New York. In 1926, three years after Moses Kakels's death, Sara Welt-Kakels retired from the post of adjunct pediatrician at Mt. Sinai Hospital that she had held since 1922; she remained an off-service member of the staff however, and also kept on her private practice at her East Sixty-first Street office and home. She died of bronchial pneumonia at Mt. Sinai Hospital on 26 December 1943, two weeks after her eighty-third birthday.

One additional medical woman is listed in the Austrian section of the bibliography—Sophie Fuchs-Wolfring. Her anatomical papers on the larynx and air tubes that appeared in *Archiv für Mikroskopische Anatomie* in 1898 and 1899 reported work done at the histological institute of Vienna University. She later became particularly interested in tuberculosis management, a public health problem of immense concern and formidable challenge at the time. For at least a decade she was a coworker of Carl Spengler at his tuberculosis clinic in Davos, Switzerland. Her critical examination and comparison of therapeutic methods for tuberculosis treatment, with special emphasis on Spengler's "J-K-Therapy" appeared in 1911;[19] she also published at least eight additional papers in this area in French and German tuberculosis journals in the period up to 1918. Several were essentially priority claims and restatements of the advantages of Spengler's particular diagnostic procedures and his immunization method.[20]

All three of the Austrian botanists in this survey—Johanna Witasek, Emma Lampa, and Emma Ott—carried out much of their research in the late 1880s and 1890s at the Botanical Institute of the University of Vienna under the guidance of the distinguished taxonomist and phylogenist Richard Wettstein; Wettstein was director of the institute and the university's botanical museum and garden whose facilities were considerably expanded in the early 1890s.

JOHANNA WITASEK[21] (1865–1910) was born in Vienna on 13 August 1865. In 1891, following some years as a teacher of special subjects in Vienna public schools, she took a post in a city school for girls. She began studies at the botanical museum in 1899 and during the next eleven years published several papers and monographs in taxonomy, geographical distribution, and nomenclature, areas in which Richard Wettsetin made major contributions. Her 1908 monograph on Solanaceae (the nightshade family) discussed results from the Austrian Academy of Science's expedition to Brazil in 1901 led by Wettstein. This was followed by another publication on Solanaceae in 1910 reporting results from the 1905 expedition to the East Indies led by Karl Rechinger. Earlier work included distribution studies on the genus Campanula (the bellflowers) and investigations of species of the genus Callianthemum.[22] Johanna Witasek died in Vienna on 5 July 1910 a month before her forty-fifth birthday.

EMMA LAMPA[23] from Rumburg, northern Bohemia, was born in 1873. A student of Wettstein from 1899 until 1909, she published her first paper in 1900, a study of leaf form in Liliaceae. This was followed by three reports of work in cryptogamic botany, including investigations of germination and development processes in ferns and mosses.[24] She later married a state councillor in Hadersdorf, forty miles west-northwest of Vienna.

Three papers by EMMA OTT reporting work carried out in the Botanical Institute are listed in the bibliography; a fourth appeared in 1902.[25] They covered a variety of topics in plant physiology and morphology including investigations of the physical properties of starches, early studies on hardness variation in plant tissues, and the relationship of morphology to taxonomy in freshwater diatoms. Emma Ott was a student in the philosophical faculty at the University of Vienna.

Two other Austrian contributors to the biological sciences whose papers are listed in the bibliography are the naturalists Schlechta and Werner.

In a report published in the *Mittheilungen* of the Vienna Ornithological Society in 1892 SIDONIE SCHLECHTA discussed her observations of the many varieties of wild birds, mainly songbirds, which visited her Vienna aviary. Baroness Sidonie, fourth child and only daughter of Freiherr Franz Xaver Schlechta von Wschehrd and his wife Catharina Gutherz, was born on 25 April 1838. Her branch of the Schlechta von Wschehrd family, which traced its ancestry back to the fifteenth century, had been established in Vienna since her grandfather's time. The best known of her generation were her brothers Camill Franz, a writer, and Ottocar Maria, a distinguished orientalist and diplomat who served in Constantinople.[26]

HELENE WERNER,[27] also from Vienna, was the daughter of businessman, later insurance agent, Franz Werner and his wife Amalia (Papacek). Her two 1892 papers in *Der Zoologische Garten* reported her studies of vipers from Dalmatia and Algeria, including observations of habits and food needs in captivity. The animals had been brought back by her brother Franz Werner, a herpetologist, later professor at the University of Vienna and a leader in his field; he made many collecting trips throughout the Mediterranean region, tropical Africa, and South America from the 1890s on. Helene Werner had earlier studied with August Bodinus, director of the Berlin Zoological Garden, and for a time until Bodinus's death in 1884 she held a position at the Zoological Garden.

Four Austrian women covered here—von Matt, Welt, Klekler, and Wendt—reported work in the physical and mathematical sciences between 1800 and 1900. Von Matt was an astronomer, Welt a chemist, and Klekler and Wendt were students of mathematics.

ELISABETH REICHSFREIIN VON MATT,[28] a Viennese baroness, was well known among late eighteenth- and early nineteenth-century continental astronomers for the observations she published, mainly in the two German journals, J. E. Bode's *Astronomisches Jahrbuch* and Franz von Zach's *Monatliche Correspondenz*. She worked from a small private observatory in Vienna that she equipped with a number of excellent instruments, including a Reichenbach transit. Many of her pre-1810 communications were published anonymously and are difficult to trace. Three of the four papers listed in the bibliography discussed latitude and longitude determinations for places in Austria; the fourth reported an occultation of 31 March 1808. Baroness von Matt died in 1814.

IDA WELT[29] (1871–1950), a younger sister of the three Welt medical women discussed previously, was born in Vienna on 23 April 1871.[30] While still a girl she moved to New York City where two of her sisters were already established as physicians.[31] She attended Vassar College (A.B., 1891) and then returned to Europe for studies in Geneva where her other sister, Leonore Gourfein-Welt, practiced ophthalmology.

After graduating from the University of Geneva in 1895 she stayed on for a further year of study while serving as an assistant in analytical chemistry. By 1894 she had already published three research papers in the *Comptes Rendus* of the Paris Academy of Sciences. These discussed investigations in physical-organic chemistry, namely specific rotation and molecular refractivity studies in series of amyl derivatives. The work was carried out in the university's chemical laboratories under the direction of Philippe Auguste Guye, well known for his contributions to this area. Ida Welt's doctoral research, published in *Annales de Chimie et de Physique* in 1895, was a continuation of these studies, completed during the winter of 1894–1895 in the organic chemistry laboratories at the Sorbonne under the guidance of Charles Friedel.

For a year or two in the period 1896–1897 she held a *privatdozent* position at the University of Geneva; she was one of the first women to do so. Also about this time she carried out research on the preparation of unsaturated compounds (olefins and acetylenes) at the University of Heidelberg in Friedrich Krafft's laboratory; her report appeared in the German Chemical Society's *Berichte* in 1897. By 1899 she had returned to New York City. She joined the American Chemical Society the same year.[32] Appointed chemistry instructor at the Girls' High School, New York, she remained on the school's teaching staff for a number of years. Sometime before the outbreak of the Second World War Ida Welt went back to Geneva where she died in 1950.

Both Cäcilie Wendt and Paula Klekler were students of University of Vienna mathematics professor Leopold Gegenbauer in the late 1890s.

CÄCILIE WENDT[33] (later BÖHM-WENDT) was born on 4 May 1875 in Troppau, Silesia (now Opava, Czech Republic). Her father, Dr. F. M. Wendt, was probably a teacher. Entering the University of Vienna in 1896, she received her doctoral degree in June 1900. Her first publication appeared in 1899; concerned with rational values of trigonometric functions, it resolved a conjecture outstanding for almost seventy years. Her dissertation research, a proof of a generalization announced earlier by Gegenbauer in the mathematical seminars he led, dealt with special functions of mathematical physics; the report appeared in 1900 (see bibliography).

Wendt went on to research at the University of Vienna's Physical Institute, a center where a number of productive women physicists (Lise Meitner among them) acquired experience during the early years of the twentieth century. Wendt collaborated with Egon von Schweidler, head of the institute and a pioneer in the emerging field of radioactivity. At that time he was investigating the radiation produced by the newly discovered elements. A joint Wendt–von Schweidler paper published in 1909 described their examination of the conductivity of liquid dielectrics (petroleum ether and vaseline oil) when subjected to radium radiation; it included an estimate of the velocity of the ions produced.[34]

PAULA KLEKLER[35] (1876–1929), one of Austria's notable women pioneers in modern schooling for girls, was born on 17 June 1876 in Fiume, then in the Austro-Hungarian empire. The daughter of the director of a *Realschule* (nonclassical secondary school), she studied at the women teachers training institute of the royal *Zivilmädchenpensionat* (state boarding school for girls), and passed the school leaving certificate examinations in 1895. Two years later, when regular enrollment in philosophical faculties of Austrian universities was first opened to women, she entered Vienna University. Her mathematical work, carried out under Leopold Gegenbauer's direction, concerned large factors of multinomial coefficients (see bibliography). The first candidate to take the qualifying examinations for teaching mathematics, physics, and natural history in girls' secondary schools, she received her public school teaching certificate in 1901. From 1902 she taught at the city secondary school for girls in Brünn, Moravia (later Brno, Czech Republic) and from 1906 headed the institution. Under her outstanding leadership it was reorganized into an eight-year, secondary-modern school with a science-based curriculum (*Reformrealschule*); from 1913 its students took the school leaving certificate examinations in nonclassical studies.

Paula Klekler was also very active in the women's movement, serving as board member, secretary, and deputy to the president of the Brünn Women's Federation, although from 1909 the strain of her educational work required her to limit her efforts to advising. During the First World War she did city welfare work, assisting refugee children. She retired in 1925 and died in Vienna on 1 July 1929, a month after her fifty-third birthday.

Of the Austrian women in this survey, there remains LEOPOLDINE VON MORAWETZ-DIERKES,[36] traveler and student of geography, who was one of the first women to address the Geographical Society of Vienna. She was born in 1861 in Krems, about fifty miles west of Vienna on the Danube, the daughter of Gustav Ritter von Dierkes, a colonel in the imperial army; her mother's maiden name was von Stöhr. Educated at a school for women teachers in Innsbruck, she also studied at a conservatory of music in Vienna. In 1877, at age sixteen, she married cavalry captain, later *Feldmarshall-Leutenant*, Karl Morawetz von Moranow, but the marriage ended in 1885.

Intensely interested in other lands and peoples, she traveled a great deal, especially in northern Europe and the Mediterranean region including North Africa. She had always enjoyed writing but the pastime was forbidden during her marriage. Once freed from that restriction, she described her experiences in foreign lands in articles in various periodicals such as the *Neue Freie Presse*. Her paper "Land und Leute in Finland" appeared in the 1898 *Mittheilungen* of the Vienna Geographical Society, of which she was a member. Finding the transition from military circles to literary society somewhat difficult, she often sheltered behind the pen name Leo von Dierkes. She is said to have published several plays and short stories in addition to her travel articles.[37]

Summary

The low number of pre-1901 scientific publications by Austrian women, resulting from their relatively late entry into the country's universities, makes generalizations of limited value. However, to summarize the information offered here, more than one third (36 percent) of the papers published by these pioneers were in the medical sciences, although less than half of the medical research was carried out in Austria, much being done in Switzerland; papers in botany and chemistry constituted 18 and 12 percent respectively, the chemical work again coming from Switzerland (Geneva University). The botanical research, carried out by three women at Vienna University's botanical museum and gardens, might be considered the earliest example of a block, albeit very minor, of scientific research by women in an Austrian academic setting. Three papers in mathematics (9 percent of the Austrian total) came from students at Vienna University, and the remaining eight papers (24 percent—in astronomy, geography, and natural history), were from independent workers.

Compared to their cousins in the neighboring states of imperial Germany, there were no specially outstanding research workers in this early Austrian group, no one of the stature of Munich zoologist Marianne Plehn or Berlin bacteriologist Lydia Rabinowitsch-Kempner, no one as productive as biologists Clara Hamburger of Heidelberg or Maria von Linden of Bonn.[38] The extreme conservative outlook that reserved higher education for men until almost the turn of the century was even stronger in Austria-Hungary than in its German neighbor.

Footnote: Medical Women in the Balkan States

Only one pre-1900 paper by a woman from the Balkans was identified in the Royal Society *Catalogue*, that by Aleksandra Steinlechner-Grechishnikova from Belgrade, who received her medical degree from Bern University in 1885.

However, by the late nineteenth century a number of women physicians worked in the region, notably in the Moslem communities of Austrian-administered Bosnia-Herzegovina. Here the need for women doctors was crucial because custom dictated that Moslem women could not be attended by male physicians. In 1892 Anna Bayer from Prague became the first Austrian woman doctor in Dolna-Tuszla; Bayer had previously practiced in Bern. By 1903 five women doctors held official posts in Bosnia. These were: Bohuslava Keck, an 1880 Zurich graduate (also from Prague) in Mostar; Theodora Krajewska in Sarajevo; Olszewska in Tuzla; Einhorn in Travnik; and Kuhn in Banja Luka.[39]

Aleksandra Steinlechner-Grechishnikova[40] probably never practiced; she appears to have died within a year of her graduation. A student at Bern University from 1881 to 1884, she carried out research in pathology at the Anatomical Institute of the Bern Veterinary College under the direction of anatomist Maximilian Flesch. The report of her work, studies on the structure of the spinal cord in microcephalics, appeared as a posthumous publication (1886; see bibliography).

Steinlechner-Grechishnikova was one of two early Serbian medical women known to have taken their degrees at Swiss universities before 1900. The other was Draga Ljocic,[41] the first Serbian woman doctor.

Born in 1854 in Šabac, about forty miles west of Belgrade, Draga Ljocic was the daughter of Djwro Ljocic of Belgrade. She entered Zurich University in 1872, carried out research in surgical gynecology under the guidance of anatomist F. Frankenhäuser, and received her degree in 1879.[42] Even before she had completed her training Ljocic worked as a medical assistant in the wars and insurrections her country was caught up in during its struggle for independence from Ottoman rule in the late 1870s. Several decades later she again took up military service, first in the wars against Turkey (1912–1913) and Bulgaria (1913), and then in the First World War when she served until the defeat of Serbia by joint German and Bulgarian forces in 1915. Ljocic is also remembered for her efforts on behalf of young people, in particular for the cofounding of a facility for abandoned children. In 1925, when she was seventy-one, Draga Ljocic was honored by the Society of Women Doctors.

The presence of these two Serbs among the early women graduates of the Swiss universities reflects the fact that Serbia, ahead of Austria-Hungary in allowing girls into its high schools,[43] was also the most open of the southern Slavic countries to the influences of the late nineteenth-century women's movements in Russia and Western Europe. However, the widespread poverty in the country and the lack of schools except in the larger cities, in addition to various cultural factors, severely limited the numbers of women receiving higher education.

Notes

1. See for instance *Frauenstudium und Akademische Frauenarbeit in Österreich,* eds. Martha Forkl and Elisabeth Koffmahn (Wien: Wilhelm Braumüller, Universitäts-Verlagsbuchhandlung G.m.b.H., 1968); *Women, State, and Party in Eastern Europe,* eds. Sharon L. Wolchik and Alfred G. Meyer (Durham, N.C.: Duke University Press, 1985); *Frauenstudium und Akademische Frauenarbeit in Österreich, 1968–1987,* Verband der Akademikerinnen Österreichs (Wien: Verband der Akademikerinnen Österreichs, 1987); and *"Durch Erkenntnis zur Freiheit und Gluck . . .": Frauen an der Universität Wien (ab 1897),* eds. Waltraud Heindl and Marina Tichy (Wien: WUV-Universitätsverlag, 1990).

2. Medical education was of special importance to women in many countries at this time—see Thomas Neville Bonner, *To the Ends of the Earth: Women's Search for Education in Medicine* (Cambridge, Mass.: Harvard University Press, 1992). Austria had a special need for women doctors to serve in its Balkan province of Bosnia-Herzegovina (see footnote at end of chapter).

3. Karen Johnson Freeze, "Medical Education for Women in Austria: A Study of the Politics of the Czech Women's Movement in the 1890s," in *Women, State, and Party,* 51–63, on 54–55.

4. *Österreichisches Biographisches Lexikon, 1815–1950* (Graz-Köln: Hermann Böhlaus Nachf., 1957–), vol. 3 (1965), 308; J. M. Meijer, *Knowledge and Revolution: The Russian Colony in Zurich (1870–1873)* (Assen: Internationaal Instituut voor Sociale Geschiedenis, 1955), 49–50, 146, 204, 211; obituaries, *Journal of the American Medical Association* 81 (1923): 594, and *Los Angeles Daily Times,* 28 July 1923, Pt. 1, 12; Marcella Stern, "Biographien von 'Pionierinnen,'" in *"Durch Erkenntnis,"* 189–219, on 216–17; Barbara Bachmann and Elke Bradenahl, "Medizinstudium von Frauen in Bern 1871–1914," inaugural dis., Medical Faculty, Bern University, 1990; *American Medical Directory* (1916, 1918); and Matriculation Register, Zurich University, entries for Raissa Putiata-Shlykova (n. 4383) and Virginie Shlykova (n. 4121).

5. The whole family, including Raissa's children, moved to Zurich, her father having by then retired from his administrative positions; see Meijer, *Knowledge,* 49–50.

6. Franziska Tiburtius, *Erinnerungen einer Achtzigjährigen* (Berlin: C. A. Schwetschke, 1929), 3rd ed., 129. Tiburtius (1843–1927), a north German from Rügen, was a medical student at Zurich from 1871 until 1876. She and her partner Emilie Lehmus later practiced in Berlin (see chapter on German women, note 66).

7. Virginiia Shlykova also continued her studies at Bern University. After taking her degree (1876), she returned to Russia for a short time and was imprisoned for her revolutionary connections. Later she went back to Switzerland, where she lived for the rest of her life. She married an Armenian chemist, C. Abeljanz, who became professor at Zurich University. See Meijer, *Knowledge,* 176, n. 8; and Daniela Neumann, *Studentinnen aus dem Russischen Reich in der Schweiz (1867–1914)* (Zürich: Verlag Hans Rohr, 1987), 125.

8. See Marlene Jantsch, "Der Aufstieg der österreichischen Ärztin zur Gleichberechtigung," in Forkl and Koffmahn, eds., *Frauenstudium,* 24–29 on 25. Rosa Kerschbaumer's publications, in addition to those listed in the bibliography, include the following: Raissa Putiata, *Ueber Sarcoma der Lymphdrüsen* (Berlin: G. Reimer, 1877; Bern dissertation); *Bericht über das Jahr 1880 und über ein zweites hundert Staar-Extraktionen nach v. Graaf's Methode von Rosa Kerschbaumer und Friedrich Kerschbaumer,* Salzburg, Augenheilanstalt (Salzburg: Maur, 1881); *Bericht über Tätigkeit in den Jahren 1883–90. Von Dr Rosa Kerschbaumer, Salzburg,* Salzburg, Augenheilanstalt (n.p.: H. Kerber, 1892); and *Das Sarcom des Auges. Von Dr R. Putiata Kerschbaumer* (Wiesbaden: J. F. Bergmann, 1900).

9. Tiburtius, *Erinnerungen,* 129. Friedrich Kerschbaumer died in 1906.

10. C. Lucerna, "Die erste Frauenärztin in Franzensbad," *Frauenleben,* no. 3 (1901): 63; Irene Bandhauer-Schöffmann, "Frauenbewegung und Studentinnen; zum Engagement der österreichischen Frauenvereine für das Frauenstudium," in

"Durch Erkenntnis," 49–78 on 65; Stern, "Biographien von 'Pionierinnen,'" in *"Durch Erkenntnis,"* 217; Hanny Rohner, *Die ersten 30 Jahre des medizinischen Frauenstudiums an der Universität Zürich 1867–1897* (Zürich: Juris Druck, 1972), 85; and Matriculation Register, Zurich University, entry n. 7855.

11. The first was Baronin Gabriele Possanner von Ehrenthal (1860–1940), who received a medical degree from Zurich University in July 1894 and a second from Vienna University in April 1897 (Stern, "Biographien von 'Pionierinnen,'" 189–215).

12. Constant von Wurzbach, *Biographisches Lexikon des Kaiserthums Österreich* (Wien, 1856–91), vol. 54 (1886), 251–52; Stern, "Biographien von 'Pionierinnen,'" 219; Bachmann and Bradenahl, "Medizinstudium"; *American Medical Directory,* 1916, 1918; and *Polk's Medicial Register of the United States and Canada,* 1900, 1912.

13. Her dissertation research, *Ueber Elephantiasis . . . ,* was published the same year (Wien: Schönberger, 1878).

14. Stern, "Biographien von 'Pionierinnen,'" 218–19; Rohner, *Ersten 30 Jahre,* 42, 82; Pia Maria Plechl, "Das Frauenstudium an den philosophischen Fakultäten" in Forkl and Koffmann, eds., *Frauenstudium,* 17–23, on 19; Bachmann and Bradenahl, "Medizinstudium;" obituary, *Journal de Genève,* 12 January 1944, 5; and *Lexikon der Frau,* 2 vols. (Zürich: Encyclios Verlag AG, 1953), vol. 1, 1260.

15. These included, "Patogenia del desprendimiento retiniano en la retinitis albuminurica," *Archivios de Oftalmologia Hispano-americanos* 4 (1904): 797–806; "Lésions oculaires dans le myxoedème spontané des adultes," *Archives d'Ophtalmologie* 27 (1907): 561–70; "Le lenticone postérieure chez l'homme, son diagnostic et sa pathologénie; recherches cliniques et anatomo-pathologiques," *Archives d'Ophtalmologie* 31 (1911): 625–50; (with Redalié) "Obere rechtseitige Quadrantenhemianopsie," *Schweizerische Medizinische Wochenschrift* 19 (1921): 1124; and "Le sérum du sang des cataracteux diffère-t-il de celui des non-cataracteux?," *Schweizerische Medizinische Wochenschrift* 55 (1925): 630.

16. Stern, "Biographien von 'Pionierinnen,'" 219; obituary, *New York Times,* 28 December 1943, 18; Rohner, *Ersten 30 Jahre,* 42, 81; *American Medical Directory,* 1906–1942; Plechl, "Frauenstudium . . . philosophischen Fakultäten," in Forkl and Koffmann, eds., *Frauenstudium,* 19; and Bachmann and Bradenahl, "Medizinstudium."

17. "Annual Report for the year 1927," *Bulletin of the New York Academy of Medicine* 4 (1928): 6.

18. See for instance "A Contribution on the Occurrence of Mental Disturbances Following Acute Diseases in Childhood," *New York Medical Journal* 57 (1893): 298–301; "Berichte eines Falles von Schwangerschaft bei Uterus duplex," *New Yorker Medizinische Monatsschrift* 10 (1898): 593–602; "Vulvovagenitis in Little Girls; A Clinical Study of 190 Cases," *New York Medical Journal* 80 (1904): 689; "Ein Fall von gummöser Schädelsyphilis bei einem 2½ jährigen idiotischen Knabe," *New Yorker Medizinische Monatsschrift* 16 (1905): 531–33; "The Indication for Stimulants in Pediatric Practice," *Archives of Pediatrics* 25 (1908): 350–57; "Inoculation Tuberculosis Following Ritual Circumcision," *American Journal of Obstetrics and Diseases of Women and Children* 59 (1909): 1075–78; "On Preliminary Examination of Children at the Dispensary as a Means of Protection against Contagious Diseases," *American Journal of Obstetrics and Diseases of Women and Children* 59 (1910): 849–52; "Hirschsprung's Disease in a Boy of Seven Years," *American Journal of Obstetrics and Diseases of Women and Children* 65 (1912): 364–66; "A Case of Polymyocitis with Multiple Lime Deposits in a Boy of 5 Years of Age," *American Journal of Obstetrics and Diseases of Women and Children* 67 (1913): 818–20; "Congenital Hypertrophy of the Left Half of the Face in a Boy Seven and One Half," *Medical Record* 86 (1914): 753–56; "Dermatitis bullosa heretaria," *American Journal of Obstetrics and Diseases of Women and Children* 88 (1915): 334; "A Case of Exophthalmic Goitre," *American Journal of Obstetrics and Diseases of Women and Children* 91 (1917): 1161; and "A Case of Complete Extrophy of the Bladder," *Archives of Pediatrics* 36 (1919), 179.

19. Sophie Fuchs-Wolfring, *Zur J-K-Behandlung* (Wiesbaden: J. F. Bergmann, 1911).

20. See "Die Muchschen Granula und die Carl Spenglerschen Splitter," *Beiträge zur Klinik der Tuberkulose und Spezifischen Tuberkulose-forschung* 10 (1908): 175–82; "Zur Carl Spenglerschen Blutzellenimmunität; Tuberkel-und Perlsuchtbazillen-Präzipitine und Autopräzipitine im Blut des Gesunden und tuberkulös kranken Menschen und deren Beeinflussung durch I. K. und Tuberkulin," *Beiträge zur Klinik der Tuberkulose und Spezifischen Tuberkulose-forschung* 14 (1909–1910): 167–257; "Die menschliche Tuberkulose also symbiotische Doppleinfektion; elektive Tuberkulinempfindlichkeit; Elektivzüchtung des Humano-longus aus Sputum: Dopplepräzipitation und Doppleagglutination," *Zeitschrift für Tuberkulose und Heilstättenwesen* 16 (1910): 351–64; "Le traitement de la tuberculose par I K (corps immunisants de Carl Spengler); comparison avec les résultats obtenus par la cure sanatoriale . . . ," *Revue de la Tuberculose* 2s., 9 (1912): 1–18; "Die diagnostische und prognostische Bedeutung der Präzipitine des Gesamtblutes bei Tuberkulose . . . ," *Zeitschrift für Tuberkulose und Heilstättenwesen* 18 (1911–12): 561–67; "Zur Bekämpfung der Volks-tuberkulose, Heilstätten oder spezifische Therapie?" *Gesundheit* (Leipzig) 37 (1912): 609, 641; "Réveil du paludisme à la suite d'une cure de tuberculine," *Revue de la Tuberculose* 3s., 10 (1913): 407–11; "Die Blutpräzipitation also Tuberkulose-Diagnostikum und Prognostikum," *Centralblatt für Bakteriologie* abt. 1, 81 (1918): 178–91.

21. Erwin Janchen, "Richard Wettstein: sein Leben und Wirken," *Österreichische Botanische Zeitschrift* 82 (1933): 190; and Th. O. B. N. Krok, *Bibliotheca Botanica Suecana* (Uppsala: Almquist & Wiksell, 1925), 769.

22. Witasek's study on Callianthemum is listed by Wettstein among noteworthy current monographs in plant geography in his chapter "Die Entwicklung der Morphologie, Entwicklungsgeschichte und Systematik der Phanerogamen in Oesterreich von 1850 bis 1900," in *Botanik und Zoologie in Österreich in den Jahren 1850 bis 1900, Festschrift, Zoologisch-Botanischen Gesellschaft in Wien,* eds. A. Handlirsch and R. von Wettstein (Wien: Alfred Hölder, 1901), 195–218, on 212. Witasek's post-1900 papers were "Bemerkungen zur Nomenklatur der *Campanula hostii* Baumgarten," *Verhandlungen der*

K.K. Zoologisch-botanischen Gesellschaft in Wien 51 (1901): 33–44; *Ein Beitrag zur Kenntnis der Gattung Campanula* (Wien; A. Hölder, 1902); *Solanaceae* (Wein: K. K. Hof- und Staats-druckerei, 1908), reprinted from *Denkschriften der Kaiserlichen Akademie der Wissenschaften, Math.- Nat. Kl.* 79, Th. 2); and "*Solanaceae,*" in Karl Rechinger, "Botanische Ergebnisse einer wissenschaftlichen Forschungsreise nach den Semoainseln, dem Neuguinea-Archipel und den Salomonsinseln von März bis Dezember 1905, Teil 3. . . ," *Denkschriften der Kaiserlichen Akademie der Wissenschaften, Math.- Nat. Kl.* 85 (1910): 175–388.

23. Janchen, "Wettstein," 189.

24. "Über die Entwickelung einer Farnprothallien," *Sitzungsberichte der Kaiserlichen Akademie der Wissenschaften. Math.- Nat. Kl.* 110, abt. 1 (1901): 25–111; "Untersuchungen an einigen Lebermoosen II," *Sitzungsberichte der Kaiserlichen Akademie der Wissenschaften. Math.- Nat. Kl.* 112, abt. 1 (1903): 779–92; and "Exogene Entstehung der Antheridien von *Anthoceros*," *Österreichische Botanische Zeitschrift* 53 (1903): 436–38.

25. "Anatomischer Bau der Hymenophyllaceenrhizome und dessen Verwertung zur Unterscheidung der Gattungen *Trichomanes* und *Hymenophyllum*," *Sitzungsberichte der Kaiserlichen Akademie der Wissenschaft, Math.-Nat. Kl.* 111, abt. 1 (1902): 879–925.

26. *Österreiches Biographisches Lexikon, 1815–1950,* vol. 9 (1990), 173–75 (entries for Franz Xaver, Camill Franz, and Ottocar Maria Schlechta von Wschehrd). See also *Deutsches Biographisches Archiv* (Munich: Saur, 1982), microfiche no. 1106, entries from Wurzbach, *Biographisches Lexikon des Kaiserthums Österreich*, vol. 30 (1875), especially the Schlechta family tree, p. 108.

27. Obituaries for Franz Josef Maria Werner, *Annalen des Naturhistorischen Museums in Wien* 51 (1941): 8–53; and for Karl August Heinrich Bodinus, *Zoologische Garten; Zeitschrift für die Gesamte Tiergartnerei* 25 (1884): 351–52.

28. J. E. Bode, *Astronomisches Jahrbuch* (1817): 252–53; J. C. Poggendorff, *Biographisch-literarisches Handwörterbuch zur Geschichte der Exacten Wissenschaften . . .* (Leipzig: J. A. Barth, and other publishers later, 1863–), band 2 (1863), 78; and Herman S. Davis, "Women Astronomers (1750–1890)," *Popular Astronomy* 6 (1898): 211–28, on 214.

29. *American Men of Science* (1910), 502; *Woman's Who's Who of America, 1914–1915,* ed. John William Leonard (New York: American Commonwealth, 1914), 867; Patricia Joan Siegel and Kay Thomas Finley, *Women in the Scientific Search: An American Bio-bibliography, 1724–1979* (Metuchen, N.J.: Scarecrow Press, 1985), 124–25; and Ida Welt, "The Jewish Woman in Science," *Hebrew Standard* 50 (1907): 4.

30. Ida Welt's *American Men of Science* (1910) entry indicates that she was born in 1876. If correct, this would mean that she received her bachelor's degree from Vassar College at age fifteen and her Ph.D. (Geneva) at age nineteen. Siegel and Finley (*Women in the Scientific Search*) state that Vassar College records give her date of birth as 1871.

31. Ida Welt's Ph.D. dissertation, *Contribution à l'étude des dérivées amyliques actifs,* (Paris: Gauthier-Villars, 1895) is dedicated to "My dear brother Louis." This suggests a close relationship between her and the family of her oldest sister, Rosa Welt Strauss; Rosa's husband was Louis Strauss.

32. Membership list, *Journal of the American Chemical Society* 26 (1904), *Proceedings,* 10–75.

33. Archives, University of Vienna.

34. Cäcilie Böhm-Wendt and Egon von Schweidler, "Über die spezifische Geschwindigkeit der Ionen in flüssigen Dielektrikas," *Physikalische Zeitschrift* 10 (1909): 379–82. See also Stefan Meyer and Egon von Schweidler, *Radioaktivität* (Leipzig: B. G. Teubner, 1927), 165.

35. *Österreichisches Biographisches Lexikon, 1815–1950,* vol. 3 (1965), 394.

36. Sophie Pataky, *Lexikon Deutscher Frauen der Feder,* 2 vols. (Berlin: C. Pataky, 1898), vol. 2, 55–56; and *Wer ist's,* 2 (1906), 801.

37. Pataky, *Lexikon.*

38. See chapter on German women.

39. Bandhauer-Schöffmann, "Frauenbewegung und Studentinnen," 53, n. 28.

40. Bachmann and Bradenahl, "Medizinstudium."

41. Matriculation Register, Zurich University (n. 4238); and Rohner, *Ersten 30 Jahre,* 81.

42. *Ein Beitrag zur operativen Therapie der Fibromyome des Uterus,* diss. (Zurich: O. Fieseli, 1878).

43. See for instance Desanka Trubuhovich-Gjurich, *Mileva Einstein: Une Vie* (Paris: Des Femmes, 1991), 27; trans. Nicole Casanova, from the German, *Im Schatten Albert Einstein: Das tragische Leben Mileva Einstein-Maric* (1988).

Chapter 7

SWITZERLAND: PHYSICIANS, BOTANISTS, AND A CHEMIST

Six Swiss women and one of Russian birth who spent much of her adult life in Switzerland are listed in the bibliography.[1] Together they published a total of eleven papers before 1901 in scientific journals indexed by the Royal Society.

The number of Swiss authors might seem surprisingly low considering the early opening of Swiss universities to women and the country's reputation as a Mecca for women aspiring to advanced academic training during the last three decades of the nineteenth century. However, although formal barriers to women's enrollment in the universities began to come down in 1867,[2] Swiss women still faced many problems in gaining access to higher education. Swiss cities, Zurich in particular, were leading centers of European liberalism, but at the same time the country's culture was male-dominated and women's role in society modest with few exceptions.[3] Consequently, for a considerable period, the majority of the female students taking advantage of the Swiss educational opportunities were foreigners.[4] Even after foreign women began receiving degrees, public opinion was by no means universally in favor of Swiss women following their example;[5] the country's gymnasia, which provided the usual preparation for entry into university studies, remained closed to girls until 1891.[6]

Nevertheless, if we consider medical studies, the area of interest of the great majority of that first generation of women trained in the Swiss universities and the field about which most information is available, there was a somewhat larger Swiss presence than this survey based on the Royal Society *Catalogue* might suggest.[7] For example, of the sixty-one Zurich female medical graduates who received their degrees between 1867 and 1897, thirteen were Swiss (compared to sixteen from the German states, thirteen from Russia[8], seven from North America, six from Austria-Hungary, four from Britain, one from Serbia, and one from Argentina).

Three of the Swiss women discussed here were physicians—Kuhn, Strub, and Schiele-Wiegandt. Kuhn and Strub graduated from Zurich University in the 1890s, Schiele-Wiegandt from Bern in 1880.

JOHANNA KUHN[9] (1870–1938), one of the three children of Johann Kuhn-Zuppinger, a pastor in the canton of Glarus, was born on 1 October 1870. When she was one year old the family moved to the parish of Rüti in the Zurich Oberland where Johann Kuhn-Zuppinger combined his pastoral work with management of a branch bank. Later he moved to Zurich. Johanna attended a teacher training college for girls in Zurich, but when her brother began medical studies she, too, became interested in the field. She prepared for the school leaving certificate examination in Geneva and in 1890 enrolled at Zurich University; further studies in Berlin and Vienna for short periods gave her additional experience. Her dissertation research, a cellular level investigation of endemic furunculosis, was carried out under the direction of Hermann Eichhorst and published in Virchow's *Archiv für Pathologische Anatomie* in 1897; she received her degree the same year.

For a time Johanna Kuhn served as an assistant at the Zurich Krankenasyl Neumünster, the first woman to hold such a post. In 1898 she started her own practice in her father's house at Hirschengraben 62, Zurich. A popular physician, she maintained this practice for almost four decades. She was well-liked and highly respected for her plain, sympathetic manner, sound judgment, and outspoken support of what was right and fair. She died at the age of sixty-eight, in Zurich, on 26 December 1938, following an operation, ten months after she had turned over most of her work to a colleague.

EMMA STRUB[10] (1865–1935) was born in Oberuzwil (St. Gallen canton) on 27 March 1865. About 1882 her father gave up his profession of teaching and bought a weaving mill in Zofinger (Aargau canton). He was not happy with his daughter's decision to study medicine but Emma overcame his opposition and began studies at Zurich at the age of eighteen in the spring of 1883. She spent all her free time on botanical work and was an enthusiastic plant collector; the considerable quantity of material she amassed during her student years was later donated to the university. In fact it would seem likely that interest in botany was her primary inspiration for medical studies. Among her student friends at this time was Anna Heer, who went on to a particularly outstanding career in Zurich in gynaecology and women's health; Straub is credited with having first interested Heer in medical studies.[11]

In the spring of 1889 Emma Strub passed the state physicians' examination with distinction and in July of the following year she completed her doctoral degree requirements, submitting a dissertation on the sterilization of milk; the research was reported in *Centralblatt für Bakteriologie* the same year. Following a period as an assistant physician in England she moved to Basel in 1893. The city's first woman physician, she was well-liked as an obstetrician. In 1896 however, she married Karl Sulzberger, an engineer from Winterthur, about twenty miles northeast of Zurich; as far as is known she never practiced after that and gradually lost interest in professional work.

For fifteen years (1902–1917) she and her husband lived in Berlin where Karl Sulzberger had been placed by his company. They had no children; Emma devoted herself to household work and took a very active part in Berlin social life. She does not seem to have made contact with any of the women doctors then practicing in the city, some of them fellow Zurich graduates. Because of the unstable political situation in Germany, the Sulzbergers returned to Switzerland in 1917, going first to Zofingen, then to Zurich in 1919, and later to Zollikoen (on the southern outskirts of Zurich). As she grew older Emma Sulzberger busied herself more and more with handiwork. She died in Zofingen on 1 January 1937 at the age of seventy-one, two years after the death of her husband.

VALÉRIE SCHIELE-WIEGANDT,[12] from Aussersihl, a suburb of Zurich, studied at Bern University from 1872 until 1882. She specialized in anatomy and graduated in 1880. Her dissertation research on the dimensions and wall thickness of human arteries, carried out under the direction of anatomist and physiologist Heinrich Quincke, appeared in Virchow's *Archiv für Pathologische Anatomie* in 1880. A lengthy extension of the study with appreciative comments on her work was published the following year in the same journal by F. W. Beneke of Marburg.[13]

Although her name does not appear in the Royal Society *Catalogue,* one additional early Swiss woman physician, CAROLINE FARNER[14] (1842–1913) is mentioned here because of her specially notable and interesting career. Born in the small town of Guntershausen (Thurgau canton) in 1842, she was the youngest in a family of seven children. Her father farmed and also operated a sawmill. Her mother, who functioned as the community's sole source of both medical help and spiritual advice, died in 1857; thereafter Caroline was brought up by an older sister. She attended a succession of schools for girls and then worked for eight years as a governess in Scotland. However, after a period of trying to assist several members of her family through illness and other serious difficulties, she became depressed and disillusioned. Seeing medical studies as a way forward she took the school-leaving certificate examination, teaching herself the necessary mathematics and Latin in record time, and entered the medical faculty at Zurich University in 1871. She was the second Swiss woman to receive a medical degree (1877). After short periods of further study in Paris, Vienna, and Budapest, she started a practice in Zurich that she conducted successfully for thirty-six years; in time it became one of the largest in the city. An outstanding public speaker and organizer, Farner became one of the leaders in the Swiss women's movement. President of the Swiss Women's Union from 1886 until 1891, she founded under its auspices a placement center in Zurich for women domestic workers, a free clinic for women, and a sanatorium for women in Urnäsch (Appenzell canton); the latter she gave to the city of Zurich as a holiday camp in 1907. In 1892 Farner and her life companion Anna Prufunder were arrested and charged with embezzling 60,000 Swiss francs. This incident was the culmination of a number of hostile actions against Farner by opponents of the women's movement, alarmed at her success. No evidence was ever produced to substantiate the charge but the women were each given sentences of seven months solitary confinement. Their treatment aroused protests from other Swiss feminists and their release in 1893 brought congratulations from leaders of the women's movement beyond the borders of Switzerland. Farner died in 1913 and Prufunder in 1925. The villa Ehrenberg, their home and Farner's office, was given on Prufunder's death to the Zurich Lyceum Club; the Anna-Carolina Foundation, a scholarship fund for women established by Farner, still exists.

Three women in this group were botanists—Maria Gugelberg von Moos, Alice Rodrigue Grintescu, and Charlotte Ternetz. Rodrigue Grintescu and Ternetz had academic training at the graduate level in the 1890s;

Gugelberg von Moos was a self-taught, independent, botanical explorer and artist of a somewhat earlier generation.

MARIA GUGELBERG VON MOOS[15] (1836–1918) was born on 6 February 1836 in Schloss Salenegg, Maienfeld, Graubünden. The Gugelberg von Moos family had been prominent in public life in the Graubünden canton for centuries. Maria was the second of eight children and the oldest daughter of Ulysses Gugelberg von Moos, a well-known civil engineer who constructed many of the region's roads, waterworks, and major buildings as well as the first railway line connecting Chur with Sargans. Her mother was Elisabeth Jecklin von Hohenrealta from the region of Domleschg some twenty miles to the south of Maienfeld.

Maria attended the Maienfeld school, where even in her early years she earned a reputation for hard work and perseverance. Later she spent about two years at an educational institution in Neuchâtel run by the Moravian brotherhood. The lifelong, deeply religious outlook her Moravian contacts gave her was always free from pedantry and doctrinal strictures; her genuine tolerance for other ideas and capacity for sound judgement could be relied on.

As the oldest daughter in the family she was much involved in the upbringing of her younger siblings; later, when her sister Nina von Flugi died, she looked after Nina's children.[16] Most of her life she spent at the old castle of Salenegg, set in the midst of its tranquil fields, meadows, and vineyards, with the high crags of the mountains in the background. Nevertheless she was intensely interested in all the events of her time, national as well as local and, perhaps especially, developments in natural history.

Although she had enjoyed botany from her girlhood, it was only in her middle years that she began to systematically collect and study plants. She worked on her own, first concentrating on vascular plants and investigating in detail the material in her neighborhood. She built up a considerable amount of information on geographical ranges and discovered a number of species previously unknown in Graubünden, including *Muscari neglectum* Guss. of the lily family, *Iris sibirica* L., *Barbarea intermedia* Bor. of the mustard family, *Euphorbia platyphyllos* L. of the spurge family, and *Aspertula tinctoria* L. of the madder family. These finds she eventually communicated to botanist Chr. Brügger of Chur. She also collaborated with Brügger in his work on hybrid forms, preparing detailed and accurate colored illustrations; her paintings of a number of these hybrids, including Primrose, Sempervivum, and Saxifraga, were considered especially valuable.[17] She did not restrict her investigations to her local region and during vacation trips with the children of her deceased sister explored the flora of other parts of Switzerland, including the Oberland in the west of the country and the valley of the Inn (Engadin district) in southeastern Graubünden. Her ambition of climbing the Falknis, the mountain mass she looked out towards from Salenegg, was never fulfilled but the botanical material collected there for her by herdsmen and mountain guides was substantial and included a number of new species.

Maria Gugelberg von Moos's most important work was her exploration of the mosses and liverworts of Graubünden. The mosses of the Rhaetian Alps region, immediately to the east of Maienfeld and Chur, had been investigated some years earlier by Brügger, but after his death in 1899 Fräulein von Gugelberg was for many years the only local person active in the area. She found many species previously unrecorded in Graubünden. As with her studies of vascular plants, she taught herself the basics of the field, but the fragmented and incomplete nature of the available reference materials, and in particular the lack of a comprehensive Swiss moss flora handicapped her considerably during her early work. Later her friendship with Brügger helped her. She also had contacts with plant physiologist Carol Correns, an expert on mosses, and with forest ecologist Johann Wilhelm Coaz, known for his work on Swiss mountain plants. Her first paper, brought out in the *Jahresbericht* (Annual Report) of the Graubünden Naturalists' Society, appeared in 1895 when she was fifty-nine (see bibliography); it discussed her four-year study of the liverworts of Graubünden canton. She found forty-seven species, of which eight were of special interest in that their distribution suggested a distinct plant-geographical division in the extreme northeast of the region. Four additional studies on the mosses and liverworts of Graubünden and the neighboring canton of St. Gallen followed between 1902 and 1912. These were an important contribution toward the compiling of a flora of Swiss cryptogams, her 122-page 1905 survey, "Übersicht der Laubmoose des Kantons Graubünden," being especially useful.[18]

Her last technical paper, a discussion of viticulture on the Maienfeld estates, appeared in 1914,[19] but she continued to publish in her other areas of interest, namely the history of Maienfeld from earliest times and the lives and experiences of her Gugelberg von Moos forbears.[20] During her final years, when failing eyesight made reading difficult, she continued to collect local plants and prepare these for the national dried flower collection in which she kept a lively interest. Maria Gugelberg von Moos was the first woman named corresponding member of the Naturforschende Gesellschaft Graubündens, a recognition of her contributions to botany. She died at Schloss Salenegg on 29 October 1918, in her eighty-third year.

ALICE RODRIGUE GRINȚESCU[21], who was born in Geneva on 18 April, 1871, was a student of algologist and systematist Robert Chodat at the institute of botany at Geneva University in the early 1890s. Her joint study with Chodat on the seed covering in the *Polygalaceae* (the milkworts, a family Chodat studied extensively) appeared in 1893; work on leaf movement and response to stimulus followed a year later (see bibliography). She also brought out in 1900 a lengthy study of variegation in leaf color. At least for a few years Alice Rodrigue taught botany at a girls' high school in Geneva—l'École Secondaire et Supérieure des Jeunes Filles. About 1903 she married Romanian botanist and pharmacologist Ioan Grintescu, also a student of Chodat.[22]

CHARLOTTE TERNETZ[23] began studies in botany at Basle University in 1895. Because she had taken only the women teachers' examination and not the usual university matriculation examination she could not enroll formally. She carried out a research project on protoplasmic movement in fungi presenting the work to the university as a doctoral dissertation; it was not accepted by the Basle faculty because of her irregular enrollment status. However, she passed the doctoral examination with distinction at Zurich University in 1900 and reported her research in a lengthy paper in *Jahrbücher für Wissenschaftliche Botanik* the same year (see bibliography).

Charlotte Ternetz then became a teacher in a secondary school for girls but also continued research intermittently, over the course of several years, at the Basle Botanical Institute where the director, A. Fischer, gave her work space and steady advice and encouragement. In the period up to 1907 she published two creditable papers on the assimilation of atmospheric nitrogen by fungi.[24] Later her teaching left no time for research, but she did bring out one further publication in 1912. The work reported, an examination of the morphology and physiology of the various forms of the fungus *Euglena gracilis* Klebs, was in large part the 1899 inaugural dissertation of a colleague who had died before being able to complete it. Charlotte Ternetz cultured the fungus and carried out additional studies on it at the Basle Botanical Institute.[25]

IRMA GOLDBERG[26] (b. 1871), the remaining member in this Swiss group, is one of the few early women organic chemists who had a sustained and successful research career. She is also one of the very few early women chemists whose research findings have been incorporated under their own names into standard textbooks of organic chemistry.[27]

Goldberg was born in Moscow in 1871 and went to Geneva as a student in the 1890s. Her first publication, a note discussing derivatives of benzophenone, appeared in 1897 (see bibliography); it was coauthored by German chemist Fritz Ullmann, then an assistant in Geneva University's organic chemistry laboratory and *Privatdozent* from 1897.[28] Further elaboration of this work formed Goldberg's dissertation research, directed by Ullmann and published in another joint paper in the German Chemical Society's *Berichte* in 1902.[29] That year she became *Privatdozentin,* a position she held until 1906.[30]

Several joint Goldberg–Ullmann papers on a process for the purification of acetylene by removal of contaminating sulfur and phosphorus compounds appeared in 1899 and 1900. In 1904 Goldberg published a short, single-author article on the preparation of a phenyl derivative of thiosalicylic acid using copper as a catalyst; a report of her work on elaborations and refinements of this method, known to chemists as the Ullmann Reaction, followed two years later. A widely applicable procedure for the condensation (coupling) of halogen-substituted aromatic compounds by refluxing with copper powder or copper bronze at high temperature, it is especially useful for laboratory-scale preparations and was a substantial improvement on an earlier method, proceeding smoothly and giving clean products. Goldberg focused particularly on the use of the procedure for the synthesis of diarylamines. A joint Ullmann–Goldberg patent for the preparation of arylanthranilic acids was taken out in 1906.

Goldberg continued her research on related preparative methods over the following two years, part of the work being done at Geneva University and part at the Technische Hochschule in Berlin, to which Ullmann moved in 1905 and where Goldberg held a regular assistantship from about 1906 until 1913. Her important modification of the Ullmann reaction was the addition of potassium carbonate to the reaction mixture; she found that practically all primary aryl amines convert smoothly to the corresponding diaryl derivatives under the conditions she detailed. Her patent for the preparation of ß-nitrodiphenylamine and some of its derivatives (using potassium carbonate and cuprous iodide as catalysts) was taken out in 1907; another patent, with Ullmann (1908), was for the alternative procedure using only cuprous iodide.[31]

The Ullmann–Goldberg collaborative work and also much of Goldberg's independent research had close links to industry, in particular to Germany's young and vigorous synthetic dye industry. Of great importance to the country from the 1870s, it was an area in which basic research was supported and the results rapidly turned to account. Ullmann had carried out his doctoral research under the direction of German chemist Carl Graebe, one of the founders of the dye industry, then on the faculty of Geneva University.[32]; Graebe's 1869 synthesis of the anthraquinone alizarin (carried out with Carl Liebermann at the Berlin Technische Hochschule) quickly led to the establishment of the synthetic alizarin industry, the manufactured product replacing the natural dye obtained from madder.[33] A short monograph brought out jointly by Goldberg and Hermann Friedmann in 1909 was to a large extent a review of the patent literature in the synthetic dye field, particularly German patents held by BASF (Badische Anilin und Soda Fabrik) and by Bayer & Co. Farbenfabriken.[34] It provided a listing with concise notes on preparative methods for 114 dyes or closely related compounds. For those for which a definite structure had yet to be determined Goldberg and her coauthor offered formulae that best fitted the available literature data.

Irma Goldberg married Fritz Ullmann in 1910. Her last technical publication would appear to have been a joint paper with her husband on derivatives of anthraquinones (1912). The family moved from Berlin back to Geneva in 1923 when Fritz Ullmann accepted a position at the university there. Irma Goldberg Ullmann lived until at least 1939, the year of death of her husband. Her name appears at the head of a list of people signing a memorial notice for Ullmann published in a Geneva newspaper that year.[35]

Notes

1. For a note on Maja Knecht, sometimes reported as Swiss, see *Appendix*.
2. Zurich University opened regular enrollment to women in 1867 and Zurich Federal Polytechnikum followed in 1871; both Bern and Geneva universities opened to women in 1872, Lausanne in 1876 and Basle in 1890—see Hanny Rohner, *Die ersten 30 Jahre des medizinischen Frauenstudiums an der Universität Zürich 1867–1897* (Zürich: Juris Druck, 1972), 90. At Zurich the question of admitting women was initially raised in the medical faculty that, with the support of professors in other faculties, advised the university's rector that general university enrollment be opened to women. Two key circumstances led to this action—the presence in Zurich of a reform-minded, liberal government that had already been in power for three decades, and the fact that there were in the city, and in particular in the university faculties, a large number of German political dissidents and refugees, sympathizers with the strong European liberal movements for reform of 1830 and 1848. "Nowhere else in Europe or America could so liberally minded and sympathetic a medical faculty have been assembled to hear the case for women's education"—Thomas Neville Bonner, *To the Ends of the Earth: Women's Search for Education in Medicine* (Cambridge, Mass.: Harvard University Press, 1992), 35. See also Gordon Craig, *The Triumph of Liberalism: Zurich in the Golden Age, 1830–1869* (New York: Scribner's, 1988); and Rohner, *Ersten 30 Jahre*, 7.
3. Craig, *Triumph of Liberalism*, 156–57.
4. Craig, *Triumph of Liberalism*, 157.
5. Bonner, *Ends of the Earth*, 42. Except for the principality of Liechtenstein, Switzerland was the last country in Europe to grant political equality to women. The step was taken in 1971, although the women's movement in Switzerland had roots that went back to the middle of the previous century—see Susanna Woodtli, *Gleichberechtigung: Der Kampf um die Politischen Rechte der Frau in der Schweiz* (Frauenfeld: Hubner, 1975).
6. Bonner, *Ends of the Earth*, 181, n. 93.
7. Although the Royal Society's *Catalogue of Scientific Papers* 1800–1900 covers medicine and the biological sciences, its major focus is on research communications that came to the attention of the international scientific community. Discussions of clinical observations and therapeutic suggestions (work published in strictly medical journals) were less likely to be indexed than articles reporting laboratory research. Thus, for medical publications as a whole the *Catalogue*, although a valuable indicator of productivity, is somewhat incomplete—see also George Weisz, "Reform and conflict in French medical education, 1870–1914," in *The Organization of Science and Technology in France 1808–1914*, eds. Robert Fox and George Weisz (Cambridge: Cambridge University Press, 1980), 61–94, especially 75. Of the thirteen pre-1900 Swiss women graduates of Zurich medical school listed by Rohner (*Ersten 30 Jahre*), the dissertation research of only three appeared in journals indexed by the Royal Society; that of at least five others published between 1888 and 1895 is listed in *Index Medicus* (Washington: Carnegie Institution, 1879–).
8. Rohner, *Ersten 30 Jahre*, 88–89. When considering the count of thirteen Russians, it should be noted that several from the very large Russian group at Zurich between 1871 and 1873 (when their own government required them to leave) finished their degrees at other Swiss universities; only one Russian woman physician graduated from Zurich during the decade of the 1880s. Not until 1886 was the well-known Russian predominance among women medical students reestablished (Rohner, *Ersten 30 Jahre*, graph on p. 77).
9. Rohner, *Ersten 30 Jahre*, 63–64; and obituary, "Lokale Chronik, Totentafel," *Neue Zürcher Zeitung und Schweizerisches Handelsblatt*, 30 December 1938, 5.
10. Rohner, *Ersten 30 Jahre*, 59–60.
11. Anna Heer (1863–1918) was one of the most notable of Zurich's early women medical graduates. A specialist in obstetrics, surgical gynecology, and social medicine, she was a cofounder and the first medical superintendent of the Schweizerische Pflegerinnenschule mit Frauenspital (Swiss School of Nursing and Hospital for Women), opened in Zurich in 1901,

a post she held until her death. A street in Zurich bears her name (Anna Heer-Strasse) and a 1963 postage stamp carried her picture. Her doctoral dissertation, "Ueber 'Schadelbasisbrüche,'" was published in the Tübingen journal *Bruns Beiträge zur Klinischen Chirurgie* 9 (1892–1893): 1–82. For biographical sketches of Heer and nine other pre-1900 Swiss women medical graduates of Zurich University who are not discussed here, see Rohner, *Ersten 30 Jahre*, 42–64.

12. Barbara Bachmann and Elke Bradenahl, "Medizinstudium von Frauen in Bern 1871–1914," inaugural diss., Medical Faculty, Bern University, 25 June 1990.

13. F. W. Beneke, "Bemerkung zu der Abhandlung von Valérie Schiele-Wiegandt aus Zürich 'Ueber Wanddicke und Umfang der Arterien des menschlichen Körpers,'" *Archiv für Pathologische Anatomie* 83 (1881): 116–23.

14. Rohner, *Ersten 30 Jahre*, 46–48; and Sabina Streiter, "Caroline Farner (1842–1913)" in *Ebenso neu als kühn: 120 Jahre Frauenstudium an der Universität Zürich*, Verein Feministische Wissenschaft Schweiz (Zürich: Verein Feministische Wissenschaft Schweiz, Schriftenreihe, 1988), 150–52.

15. Josias Braun-Blanquet, *Maria Barbara Flandrina Gugelberg von Moos, in Salenegg bei Maienfeld (1836–1918)* (Chur: Buchdruckerei Sprecher, Eggerling & Co., 1919), also published in *Bündnerischen Monatsblatt*, n. 3, 1918.

16. Another Gugelberg von Moos sister, Laura von Gugelberg von Albertini, was known for her study of handwriting; she published the book *Lehrbuch der Graphologie* (Stuttgart: Union Deutsche Verlagsgesellschaft, 6th ed. 1915), a well-known work in its time.

17. Some of these paintings were in Schloss Salenegg at the time of her death. Those in Brügger's possession were thought to be lost (Braun-Blanquet, *Gugelberg von Moos*, 3).

18. See Jules Amann (with Charles Meylan and Paul Culmann) *Flore des Mousses de la Swisse. Deuxième partie. Bryogéographie de la Suisse* (Lausanne: Imprimeries réunies S.A., 1912), Introduction, 3–7. Von Gugelberg was the only woman among thirty-five contemporary bryologists Amann listed as having done notable work in the exploration of the bryological flora of Switzerland (p. 4).

19. Maria Gugelberg von Moos's post-1900 technical papers were the following: "Beitrag zur Kenntnis der Laub- und Lebermoosflora des Engadins," *Jahresbericht der Naturforschenden Gesellschaft Graubündens* 44 (1901): 41–68; "Übersicht der Laubmoose des Kantons Graubünden," *Jahresbericht der Naturforschenden Gesellschaft Graubündens* 47 (1905): 1–122; "Nachtrag," *Jahresbericht der Naturforschenden Gesellschaft Graubündens* 49 (1907): 1–29; "Beiträge zur Lebermoosflora der Ostschweiz," in "Beiträge zur Kenntnis der Schweizerflora (13)," *Mitteilungen aus dem Botanischen Museum der Universität Zürich (60). Vierteljahresschrift der Naturforschenden Gesellschaft in Zürich* 57 (1912), also published with a short supplement, in *Jahresbericht der Naturforschenden Gesellschaft Graubündens* 54 (1913); and "Über den Weinbau in der Herrschaft Maienfeld," *Bündnerischen Monatsblatt* (1914).

20. See "Ul. Gugelberg von Moos, Erlebnisse eines Bündners im Regiment Roll (1804–1819). Auszüge aus dem Tagebuch des Hauptmanns Ulisses v. Gugelberg," *Historisch-antiquarische Gesellschaft von Graubünden. Jahresbericht* (1909); "Privat Aufzeichnungen aus den Revolutions- und Kriegsjahren 1792 bis 1801," *Bündnerischen Monatsblatt* (1914); "Salenegg," *Bündnerischen Monatsblatt* (1916); "Zur Geschichte des Schlosses Maienfeld," *Bündnerischen Monatsblatt* (1918); "Historische und kulturgeschichtliche Materialiensammlung zu einer Geschichte von Maienfeld; zusammengetragen von M. v. Gugelberg in den Jahren 1890–1911," presented to the Historisch-antiquarische Gesellschaft Graubündens; manuscript, 268 pp., in cantonal library.

21. *Das Frauenstudium an der Schweizer Hochschulen*, ed. Schweizerischer Verband der Akademikerinnen (Zürich: Rascher & Cie, 1928), 156–57; and J. H. Barnhardt, comp., *Biographical Notes upon Botanists*, 3 vols. (Boston: G. K. Hall, 1965), vol. 3, 168.

22. There is no mention of Alice Rodrigue Grintescu in any of the brief notices about Ioan Grintescu's career that have been examined; see *Chronica Botanica*, 1 (1935): 245; 3 (1937): 227; Serban N. Ionescu, *Who Was Who in Twentieth Century Romania* (Boulder: East European Monographs; New York: Columbia University Press, 1994), 134. A specialist in nutrition of green algae, Grintescu was professor at the College of Agriculture in Bucharest from 1911 to 1920, director of the Botanical Institute at the University of Cluj from 1920 to 1936, and director of the Institute of General Botany, University of Bucharest from 1936 until 1939. He died in 1963 (or 1964), but his name is absent from membership lists of the Deutsche Botanische Gesellschaft from 1939.

23. Schweizerischer Verband der Akademikerinnen, *Frauenstudium an der Schweizer Hochschulen*, 223–25.

24. "Assimilation des atmosphärischen Stickstoffs durch einen torfbewohnenden Pilz," *Berichte der Deutschen Botanischen Gesellschaft* 22 (1904): 267–74; "Ueber die Assimilation des atmosphärischen Stickstoffs durch Pilze," *Jahrbücher für Wissenschaftliche Botanik* 44 (1907): 353–408.

25. "Beiträge zur Morphologie und Physiologie der *Euglena gracilis* Klebs," *Jahrbücher für Wissenschaftliche Botanik* 51 (1912): 435–515.

26. Daniela Neumann, *Studentinnen aus dem Russischen Reich in der Schweiz (1867–1914)* (Zürich: Verlag Hans Rohr, 1987), 107.

27. See for instance E. E. Turner and Margaret M. Harris, *Organic Chemistry* (London: Longmans Green, 1952), 421, 771.

28. Ullmann became known internationally for his monumental twelve-volume *Enzyklopaedie der Technischen Chemie* (Berlin: Urban and Schwarzenberg), the first edition of which appeared over the period 1914–1923; it has been revised many times, the most recent edition appearing in 1995. He was also remembered as a strong supporter of women chemistry

students, particularly in applied areas; he supervised the dissertations of six—see Brita Engel, "Clara Immerwahr's Kolleg-innen: die ersten Chemikerinnen in Berlin," in *Geschlechterverhaltnisse in Medizin, Naturwissenschaft und Technik,* eds. Christoph Meinel and Monika Rennsberg (Bassum, Stuttgart: Verlag für Geschichte der Naturwissenschaft und der Technik, 1996), 297–304, on 301; obituaries for Fritz Ullmann, *C. R. Société de Physique et d'Histoire Naturelle, Genève* 57 (1940): 17–19; and *Helvetica Chimica Acta* 23 (1940): 93–100.

29. Irma Goldberg and Fritz Ullmann, "Zur Darstellung der Monoxybenzophenone," *Berichte der Deutschen Chemischen Gesellschaft* 35 (1902): 2811–14 (in part from I. Goldberg, *thèse,* Geneva University, 1897).

30. Goldberg was one of three Russian women *Privatdozentinnen* at Geneva University about this time; the others were Dora Pasmanjak, *Privatdozentin* in philosophy, 1902, and Lina Stern, *Privatdozentin,* medical faculty, 1906, professor from 1918, professor in Moscow from 1925; see Neumann, *Studentinnen aus dem Russischen Reich,* 107.

31. Goldberg's papers and patents, from 1904, were the following: "Ueber eine neue Darstellungsweise von Alphylthio-salicylsäuren," *Berichte der Deutschen Chemischen Gesellschaft* 37 (1904): 4526–27; "Ueber Phenylirungen bei Gegenwart von Kupfer als Katalysator," *Berichte der Deutschen Chemischen Gesellschaft* 39 (1906): 1691–92; (with F. Ullmann) "Verfahren zur Darstellung von Arylanthranilsäuren," German Patent 173523 (1906); (with Marie Nimerovski) "Über Triphenylamin und Triphenylamincarbonsäure," *Berichte der Deutschen Chemischen Gesellschaft* 40 (1907): 2448–52; (with Catherine Sissoeff) "Über Phenylierung von primären aromatischen Aminen," *Berichte der Deutschen Chemischen Gesellschaft* 40 (1907): 4541–46; "Verfahren zur Darstellung des ß-Nitrodiphenylamins und seiner Derivative," German Patent 185663 (1907); (with F. Ullmann) "Verfahren zur Herstellung von Diphenylamin sowie substitions Produkten desselben," German Patent 187870 (1908); and (with F. Ullmann) "Über Thio-diphenylamine der anthrachinon Reihe," *Berichte der Deutschen Chemischen Gesellschaft* 45 (1912): 832–34.

32. J. R. Partington, *A History of Chemistry,* 4 vols. (London: Macmillan, 1964), vol. 4, 788–89.

33. Madder plants were used since ancient times throughout India and the eastern Mediterranean as a source of the much-prized red dye that could be extracted from the roots. By the eighteenth century, madder was cultivated extensively in Europe and constituted an important agricultural product.

34. Irma Goldberg and Hermann Friedmann, *Die Sulfosäuren des Anthrachinons und seiner Derivate* (Berlin: Weidmann, 1909), also published in the German chemical industry journal *Die Chemische Industrie* (1909). The monograph includes a table of references to Paul Friedländer's huge serial collection of dye patents, published over a number of years from 1888 on.

35. "Avis Mortuaires," *Journal de Genève,* 21 March 1939.

Chapter 8

ITALY: SHELLS OF CALABRIA, MOSSES OF THE HILLS OF ROME, FISHES OF THE ALPINE LAKES

For much of the nineteenth century the Italian peninsula was occupied by a collection of independent duchies, states, and small kingdoms. The major step toward unification came in 1861 with the establishment of the Kingdom of Italy under Victor-Emmanuel II, king of Sardinia, and the process was completed in 1870 with the annexation of the last of the Papal States. The country remained one of deep social and cultural divisions, however; power and privilege were held by a small, wealthy, well-educated aristocracy, but the bulk of the population consisted of workers and peasants. Nevertheless, by the 1870s the growing liberal movement known as *Il Risorgimento* that, beginning in the 1830s and 1840s, had awakened Italian national consciousness, also ushered in a shift toward a more equitable social system.

Changes included a gradual adjustment of the general attitude toward women. Specially important to them was the opening of the teaching profession, bringing as it did a degree of independence even though work at the primary school level was poorly paid and carried low social prestige. During the last two decades of the century university training as preparation for *lицèо* teaching gradually increased; in the period up to 1880 only three women received degrees from Italian universities but 224 graduated between 1880 and 1901. Of these 224, a third (seventy-four) had degrees in scientific and medical fields—thirty in the sciences, twenty-four in medicine, and twenty in mathematics.[1]

The group of twenty Italians discussed here includes three who were especially productive during the middle years of the nineteenth century—conchologist Marchesa Marianna Paulucci, botanist Contessa Elisabetta Fiorini-Massanti, and astronomer Caterina Scarpellini. All three came from priviledged, upper-class backgrounds. Together they produced about 50 percent of the nineteenth-century scientific papers by Italian women indexed in the Royal Society *Catalogue* (Figure 8-1). Another 35 percent was contributed by three university-based women of the late nineteenth and early twentieth centuries, the post-1870 era—neurologist and bacteriologist Giuseppina Cattani, zoologist, ecologist, and limnology specialist Rina Monti, and zoologist Maria Sacchi. Indeed the productivity of five of these workers—Paulucci, Fiorini-Mazzanti, Scarpellini, Cattani, and Monti—was exceptional and it accounts for the fact that the small Italian group is second only to Russians in output of scientific papers by women in countries of continental Europe between 1800 and 1901 (Figures 0-1 and C-4). Further, with an average of about nine and a half articles each, the Italians outstrip all other national groups in productivity per person, the European average being about three and a half.[2] The major fraction of the Italian work was in the biological sciences, particularly neurology, physiology, bacteriology, and botany (Figure 8-2b).

Biological Sciences

MARCHESA MARIANNA PAULUCCI[3] (1835–1919), a well-known and much respected naturalist and collector, is sometimes referred to as the nineteenth-century "Lady of Italian malacology." Although she made a number of important contributions to botany and orthithology, her major interest, vigorously pursued over the course of more than twenty years, was the land and freshwater mollusk fauna of the Italian peninsula. Her reports appeared in about twenty-eight publications, both monographs and journal articles, many of the latter in the *Bullettino* of the Italian Malacological Society between 1871 and 1886.

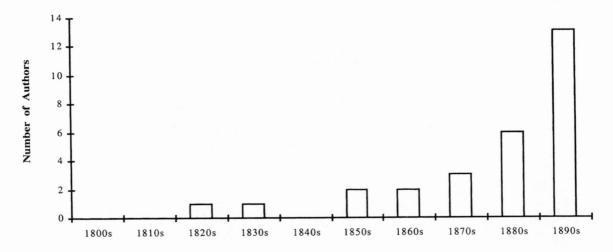

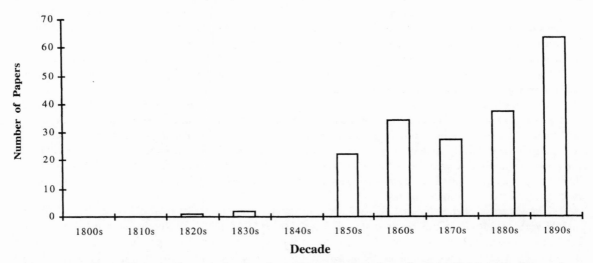

Figure 8-1.   Italian authors and papers, by decade, 1800–1900. Data from the Royal Society *Catalogue of Scientific Papers.*

Born in Firenze, in the Palazzo Panciatichi on the Via Cavour on 3 February 1835, Marchesa Marianna Panciatichi Ximenes d'Aragona was the daughter of Marchese Ferdinando Panciatichi, Honorable Knight, and his wife noblewoman Giulia De Saint Seigne. On her father's side she was descended from one of the ancient noble families of the Firenze-Pistoia region. The Panciatichis, already powerful in the eleventh century, amassed immense wealth through their trading and business enterprises, particularly in France, where, in 1301, Vinciquerra Panciatichi was knighted by Philip le Bel. He and his descendants built a number of magnificent villas throughout the Pistoia region, not the least being the Palazzo Panciatichi in the city of Pistoia, where Popes and Grand Dukes were entertained. In 1816 Marchesa Marianna's father, Ferdinando Panciatichi, being the nearest heir, inherited the very considerable property of the Ximenes d'Aragona, a family of Portuguese origin. The name was then changed to Panciatichi Ximenes d'Aragona.

Marchesa Marianna was educated in the Tuscan college of Ripoli, of which she always kept happy memories. In 1853, at age eighteen, she married Marchese Alessandro Anafesto Paulucci, a collector and botanist who successfully cultivated a wide selection of plants, common and rare, at his villa near Parma on the southern edge of the Po Valley.

Marchesa Paulucci's first shell collections were of exotic marine species but from the early 1870s she turned her attention to Italian material. For the most part her specimens were bought or were given to her but

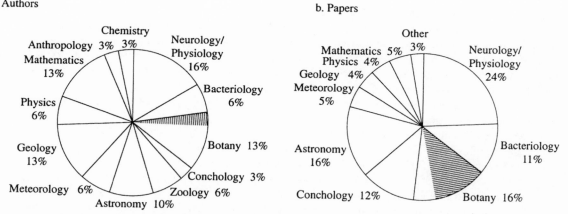

a. Authors

Chemistry 3%
Anthropology 3%
Mathematics 13%
Physics 6%
Geology 13%
Meteorology 6%
Astronomy 10%
Zoology 6%
Conchology 3%
Botany 13%
Bacteriology 6%
Neurology/ Physiology 16%

b. Papers

Other 3%
Mathematics 5%
Physics 4%
Geology 4%
Meteorology 5%
Astronomy 16%
Conchology 12%
Botany 16%
Bacteriology 11%
Neurology/ Physiology 24%

Figure 8-2. Distribution of Italian authors and papers, by field, 1800–1900. Shaded sectors represent work in cryptogamic botany. (In a., an author contributing to more than one field is counted in each. In b., the sector "Other" represents papers in the following fields: zoology [1 percent], anthropology [1 percent], and chemistry [< 1 percent]). Data from the Royal Society *Catalogue of Scientific Papers.*

careful records were kept of the acquisitions and no specimen was placed in the collection unless these details could be included on the label. Well read and informed on the field, having a good library of malacological reference works, she studied much of the material herself, classifying by current standard procedures, designating modifications in existing divisions, and proposing a few new subgenera.

Among her early publications were several monographs, including a catalogue of the Conus species in her collection and a guide for the study of Italian land and freshwater mollusks; in addition she brought out a lengthy report of an 1877–1878 scientific excursion to investigate the land and freshwater mollusks of Calabria and an 1882 work on the land and freshwater mollusks of Sardinia.[4] She described many new species and varieties, particularly from Calabria (seven new species and twenty-three varieties), Sardinia (twenty-three new species), and the Monte Argentario region (about sixty miles north of Rome; five new species and four varieties). Additional work included descriptions of rare forms—shells from seas around China, Japan, the Bering Sea, Mauritius, Siberia, New Caledonia, and Madagascar. Among these were listed *Euptychia metableta* from Madagascar, *Rapana paulucciae*, eighteen species of Neptunea, seventy-six of Chiton, 400 of Helix, and 223 of Conus, including the very rare *Conus centurio* Born.

Marianna Paulucci had an active correspondence with the leading malacologists of the time, including H. Crosse, Wilhelm Kobelt, and Paul Fischer. These experts named several species from her collections after her— *Helix paulucciae, Helix marianna, Oligomax paulucciae, Crenella paulucciae, Ostrea paulucciae, Stylifer paulucciae, Succinea paulucciae, Neritina paulucciae,* and *Conus paulucciae.* Her Italian collection exhibited at the World Exhibition in Paris in 1878 won honors and special distinctions; two years later it was shown again in Berlin.

In an 1874 report to his colleagues about malacological and palaeontological collections in Italy, the Belgian naturalist Armand Thielens described that of the Marchesa as "la plus belle et la plus remarquable de toute Italie," a country whose museums of malacology and palaeontology were exceptionally rich.[5] The entire Paulucci holding, as well as manuscripts, papers, and books, was given to the Firenze Museum of Natural History, which dedicated a room to it, the Museo Paulucciano. A very large collection, it was considered exceptionally important by the museum because of the high quality of the specimens and the many subgroupings that permitted study of the development of recent varieties of particular species. The terrestrial mollusk section was especially notable, but also included were fossil shells from the sub-Appenine areas of Tuscany, particularly the valley of the Elsa southwest of Firenze, material Marianna Paulucci herself collected. Indeed, her first paper (1866) described a fossil gastropod from that region (see bibliography).

From an early age she was also very interested in plants and she built up considerable botanical knowledge and expertise in both living forms and fossils. Her enthusiasm was most likely fostered by her father Marchese Ferdinando who, beginning in 1849 when Marianna was fourteen, established a large botanical park around his castle of Sammezzano at Reggello on the eastern slopes of the Arno valley in the Appenine foothills to the southeast of Firenze.[6] Enlarged by the acquisition of a number of surrounding properties, the park covered a circular area of about three and three quarters miles circumference, with considerable altitude variation. It was considered one of the finest in Italy. The vegetation consisted mainly of evergreen trees and bushes, many varieties of cypress, juniper, pine, laurel, ilex, some cork trees, Araucaria (Norfolk Island pine), and a few others. In 1849 Marchese Ferdinando introduced *Sequoia sempervirens,* the first in Italy; this thrived, reproducing successfully, and, within a few decades, a considerable grove was established. Marianna Paulucci's 216-page monograph describing the park, "Il Parco di Sammezzano e le sue piante," appeared in the Firenze journal *Bollettino della R. Società Toscana Orticultura* in 1889. An enthusiastic collector, she assembled an extensive herbarium of plants from the upper Arno valley. This and her fossil plant collection was later given to the Istituto Tecnico in Firenze.

Marchesa Paulucci's natural history interests were not restricted to malacology and botany; she also made a notable contribution to Italian ornithology. For much of the year she lived in the country at her villa at Pulicciano near Certaldo, some twenty miles southwest of Firenze in the Elsa valley; there she began, about 1870, to collect local bird species, mainly by trapping in nets. Gradually enlarged with specimens taken in other regions of Italy and in neighboring countries, her holding eventually comprised 1,136 specimens representing 336 Italian species: 104 birds of prey of the falconiform order, 605 small- and medium-sized birds (passeriforms and apodiforms), 255 web-footed water birds, 137 waders, and thirty-five columbiforms and galliforms (such as doves and pheasants). Riccardo Magnelli, an expert naturalist, did the work of preservation; classification was carried out according to the now classic *Manuale di Ornitologia Italiana,*[7] a work dedicated to the Marchesa by its author, her grandson ornithologist Conte Ettore Arrigoni degli Oddi, lecturer in zoology at the University of Padova. Superbly mounted and arranged, Marchesa Paulucci's specimens were displayed in natural attitudes in spacious and well-lighted surroundings. A 1908 paper by Conte Arrigoni degli Oddi described the collection, considered one of the most valuable in the country, particularly for its local Tuscan species.[8] Shortly after Marianna Paulucci's death, it was given to her local district, the Commune of San Gimignano.

Beautiful and gifted, well educated and well informed on a wide variety of subjects, lively in conversation, gracious and cultivated, in her younger years the Marchesa was often present at the grand-ducal court in Firenze and at the courts of Napoleon III in Paris and the Romanovs in St. Petersburg; she had a family connection with the Romanovs, her brother-in-law having married a member of the imperial family. She traveled across the length and breadth of Europe, from Italy to Britain and Scandinavia, and from Spain to Russia. In those days travel in the more-distant parts of the tsar's huge empire was not easy, but Marianna Paulucci explored extensively and, being a careful and sensitive observer, retained until her last years vivid memories of the customs and habits of the many communities she visited.

She had definite views on of the subject of education for young ladies and believed that at least an elementary course in natural history should be part of their instruction. She saw the subject as providing a continuing and ever new interest, something that offered relief and consolation throughout life's many trials and tribulations. Further, she saw women as particularly suited to natural history studies being, in her opinion, more careful and patient than men in investigating minute details. She felt that their smaller and more nimble hands were better adapted to successfully handling small, delicate creatures and fragile parts of plants.

A very wealthy woman, a widow from 1887, she became the owner of large estates after the death of her father in 1898. From then on, although a very capable administrator, she necessarily had to give up some of her work in natural history in order to manage the properties. These eventually passed to her three grandchildren, to whom she was greatly attached. She carried out a careful restoration of the ancestral *palazzo* in Firenze, putting in order its furnishings, books, miniatures, and other valuable contents.

In her later years, when age was limiting her activities, she took up yet one more collecting project, this time assembling a huge holding of geographical and historical picture postcards sent by her many correspondents all over Europe. These were arranged in hundreds of albums according to subject and source locality, provided with descriptive labels, and numbered. Of special interest were cards from the zone of the 1904–1905 Russo-Japanese war and those from the ruined cities and towns of Belgium, France, and Venetia during the First World War. With the coming of that war she had withdrawn to the castle of Sammezzano. Although she supported Italy's participation in the war, her last year was overshadowed by her distress over the state of her country after the conflict and the inability of the government to come to grips with the severe social and material problems then being faced by the Italian people.

Marianna Paulucci was a member of the Società Italiana di Scienze Naturali e del Museo Civico di Storia Naturale in Milano and a corresponding member of the Société Malacologique de Belgique. She died at Sammezzano on 7 December 1919, two months before her eighty-fifth birthday.

The earliest of the botanists in this group, and indeed the earliest of the Italian women in this survey, was Contessa Elisabetta Fiorini-Mazzanti[9] (1799–1879) whose scientific work spanned a period of fifty years.

The only daughter of Conte Giuseppe Fiorini and his wife Teresa (née Scirocchi), she was born on 3 June 1799 in Terracina. An ancient coastal city about sixty miles south of Rome, Terracina lay in the territory then known as the *Papal States,* not annexed into the Kingdom of Italy until 1870. Both the Fiorinis and the Scirocchis were old Terracina families; Elisabetta's grandfather Luca Fiorini, as chief magistrate, had the honor of presenting the keys of the city to Pope Pius VI. The Scirocchi family, for a time numbered among the rich, had seen its fortunes decline. Elisabetta's parents were comfortably situated but not wealthy. Her childhood was a time of great upheaval and turmoil, the recent revolution in neighboring France being followed by the rise of Napoleon, whose armies dominated much of the Italian peninsula for several years. The Fiorinis not only lost much of their modest wealth but were forced to flee the city, first to the small village of Santo Felice near Monte Circella and then to Rome. The premature death of the mother added to the family's difficulties.

These early trials gave Elisabetta Fiorini a seriousness of character that remained with her throughout her life; she had little time for the frivolous, preferring intellectual pursuits. Her father, conscious of the fact that she might well need useful skills, made sure that she had a good education, well beyond what was common for a girl of her time. She spoke French by the age of seven and also studied English, German, and Latin. History, geography, literature (both of other countries and of ancient and modern Rome), drawing, and music were included in her instruction, although she soon gave up music, preferring what she felt were more worthwhile studies.

Her love of flowers developed when she was still a girl. Somewhat frail and sickly, she was taken out of the city to regain her vitality and quickly learned to appreciate the beauty of the countryside. About this time she heard of the naturalist Giovan Battista Brocchi, famous for his work in botany, malacology, and geology. When a mutual friend introduced her to Brocchi she told him of her hopes to study some branch of natural history; he suggested botany. She became his most eager pupil, learning the Linnean system and the principles of plant classification under his guidance. Following Brocchi's move to Egypt, where his geological knowledge was in demand, she had further help from Ernesto Mauri, director of the Rome botanical garden from 1820.

Her first collections were made near Formia, a pleasant town along the coast some miles south of Terracina. These and other collections made nearer Rome were the subject of her first paper, published at Brocchi's suggestion in the *Giornale* of the Accademia Arcadica in 1823. Five years later, encouraged by naturalist Carol Luciano Bonaparte, Prince of Canino, a frequent visitor at the Fiorini residence in Rome, she brought out her appendix to previously published volumes of Sebastiani and Mauri's *Prodromo della Flora Romana*;[10] it included 100 wild plants not previously recorded in the region. Among her special interests at this time were the grapevines of Italy.

Contessa Elisabetta's finest and most important work was her investigation of the mosses of the Rome area. As she later remarked, the attractions of the microscope enticed her into this branch of botany.[11] The introduction in the early years of the nineteenth century of relatively cheap, high-quality microscopes, factory-made in Germany, Austria, France, and Britain was leading to tremendous advances in botany; Elisabetta Fiorini was well aware of the "cutting-edge" botanical research of her time. Her 1831 *Specimen Bryologiae Romanae,*[12] dedicated to her teachers Brocchi and Mauri and written entirely in Latin, not only won her wide recognition in Italy but greatly stimulated interest in Italian mosses. In Germany and France as well, the work was much appreciated and there, too, it had the effect of reinvigorating bryological studies. An important contribution to the botany of southern Europe, it brought her membership in the Torino Accademia Reale delle Scienze.

Studies on algae, lichens, and fungi followed. Contessa Elisabetta published close to thirty papers in cryptogamic botany over the course of five decades, mainly in the *Atti* of the Rome Accademia de'Nuovi Lincei. Her papers on algae included notes on identification of species of Nostoc and Collema (1857, 1858) and studies on algae from mineral waters and thermal springs. Also of special importance was her report of a new species of diatom, *Amphora bullosa* Fior. Mazz. from acidic salt water near Terracina (1861–1862), her determination of *Porotrichum Mazzantii Nob.,* and her discovery of a new species of Palmodyction (1865). A few of her more theoretical conclusions were somewhat controversial.

In 1829 she married Cavaliere Luca Mazzanti, a young lawyer with promising prospects. They had three children, of whom two died early. About this time she was much occupied with the care of her family's property, the Fiorini financial situation not having improved. She was also very involved with the upbringing and education of her one surviving child, her daughter Veneranda, a bright, intelligent girl. However, Lucca Mazzanti died in 1841. His loss was followed by that of her father and, a year or two later, by that of Veneranda (at age fifteen, of an "anemic disease"). From then on, Contessa Elisabetta's life centered largely on her botanical studies, although she was not entirely without domestic companionship. She adopted and brought up the niece of her former teacher Ernesto Mauri and the young woman, Contessa Enrichetta Fiorini, remained with her throughout her life.

She made her home for the most part in Rome moving to Terracina, where she had a house, in the summer months. Many botanists, Italian and foreign, came to see her in her Rome residence and she had numerous correspondents throughout Europe. These included the famous French cryptogamist Camillo Montagne, British botanist Philip Webb who often collected with her in the Rome countryside, the Swiss Alphonse de Candolle, and the well-known Ludwig Rabenhorst, especially prominent for his work on the cryptogamic flora of central Europe. A very cooperative naturalist, Contessa Elisabetta often exchanged specimens and was particularly pleased by gifts for her moss herbarium, a collection in which she took great pride. She frequently attended scientific gatherings, even going to the 1874 botanical congress in Firenze when she was seventy-five years old and barely able to travel. The pleasure of meeting with fellow workers was as important to her as seeing the exhibits.

Her last work, a series of reports of her many-year study of the flora of the Colosseum, was published in the *Atti* of the Rome Accademia de'Nuovi Lincei between 1875 and 1878. As she explained in an 1878 letter to French botanist Casimir Roumeguère,[13] she had started the study long before because of her worry about the loss of this flora to ongoing archaeological excavations. Publication of results was set aside during the years of her work on cryptogams but with the decline of her health and especially since failing eyesight prevented continuation of microscopical studies, she had returned to this research of her early years.

Elisabetta Fiorini-Mazzanti was a member of several scientific societies; in addition to the Reale Accademia delle Scienze di Torino, these included the Pontifica Accademia de'Nuovi Lincei in Rome, the Accademia Economia-agraria di Firenze, the Accademia di Arcadica di Scienze in Rome, the Académie d'Horticulture in Brussels, and the Leopoldino-Carolinische Deutsche Academie der Naturforscher in Dresden. During her last lengthy illness, she was looked after in her home in Rome by her adopted daughter. She died of a "gangrenous ulcer" of the tongue on 23 April 1879, two months before her eightieth birthday. At least two genera and a new species were named in her honor: the fungus genus Mazzantia by Camille Montagne, the grass genus Fiorinia by F. Parlatore, and the moss *Filotrichella Fiorini Mazzantiae* n.s. Müll., identified by C. Müller.

Little information has been collected about the other Italian contributors to the botanical literature identified in the Royal Society lists—Maria Antonietta Mirabella, Margherita Misciattelli (Marchesa Pallavicini), and Amalia Moretti-Foggia. All three were late nineteenth-century women.

ANTONIETTA MIRABELLA, who held a doctorate in natural science, studied several species of Ficus, the fig. Her 1895 paper reported chemical and cytological work on the nectar-secreting organ of the flower; in another article she discussed the above-ground root system, its latex reservoirs, and their relationship to tissues involved in transpiration processes. Her work was done using Ficus plants cultivated in the Botanical Gardens at Palermo.

MARCHESA PALLAVICINI was interested in insect galls and published four substantial papers on these in Italian journals between 1895 and 1899 (see bibliography). To a large extent she used materials in the collections of the Rome station for plant pathology; her findings were presented at Rome meetings of the Italian Botanical Society.

AMALIA MORETTI-FOGGIA published in 1895 an extensive list of the vascular plants of the forest of Fontana, near Mantova in the Po Valley.

Among the six contributors discussed here who worked in areas related to zoology, the two most productive before 1901—Monti and Sacchi—held positions at universities. Monti, one of the most active and influential Italian biologists of her time, was probably the most outstanding woman research scientist in Italy in the late nineteenth and early twentieth centuries.

RINA (CESARINA) MONTI[14] (1871–1937), the first woman in Italy to hold a full university teaching position, was born on 16 August 1871 in Arcisate, a town near Varese in the foothills of the Italian Alps. She was the daughter of Francesco Monti, a lawyer, and his wife Luigia (née Mapelli). Following her father's death when she was four the family moved to Monza, about ten miles north of Milano. She received her early education in Monza and Milano obtaining her *diploma di licenza* at the Scuola Superiore Alessandro Manzoni at age sixteen.

Especially interested in the natural sciences and encouraged by her brother Achille Monti, she enrolled at the University of Pavia, probably in 1888. As a student of biologists Leopoldo Maggi and Pietro Pavesi she received excellent laboratory training in zoology, histology, and comparative anatomy. She also studied mineralogy; one of her first two papers, published before she received her degree, was a petrographic note on rocks from the district of Brescia at the northern edge of the Po Valley (see bibliography). Graduating in natural science with highest honors in July 1892, a month before her twenty-first birthday, she immediately became assistant to the chairman of the department of mineralogy. One year later she relinquished the post to move to an assistantship in comparative anatomy with Leopoldo Maggi.

At this time the University of Pavia, then enjoying one of its most brilliant periods, was a stimulating place for a young biologist. Faculty members included Camillo Golgi whose discovery of the organelle in cell cytoplasm, now known as the *Golgi complex* (a membraneous structure involved in modification and transport of molecules within cells) won him a Nobel Prize in 1906. As an assistant in comparative anatomy Monti began research on the nerve systems of arthropods, detailed histological studies that developed into broad investigations in comparative physiology. She was the first to observe the system of myofibrils, the long, cylindrical assemblies of molecules in the cytoplasm of muscle fiber cells vital to the mechanics of muscle movement. Her findings disagreed with the generally accepted picture at the time but were later confirmed and then extended to higher animals. Having by then acquired excellent microscopic technique she went on to investigate the central nerve system in planarians and the nerve systems in the digestive tract of fishes, in the spleen of birds, and in the stomach of terrestrial gastropods. Other work included studies on marine planarians in the new area of regeneration, research done at the Naples Experiment Station.

Rina Monti's nerve system work (see bibliography), received with much interest by biologists in Italy and beyond, won her a *libera docenza* position (lecturer, nonsalaried) at Pavia University in 1899. In July of the same year she was elected corresponding member of the Regio Istituto Lombardo di Scienze e Lettere, a notable honor for a young woman who had not yet reached her twenty-eighth birthday.

About 1900, in collaboration with her brother Achille Monti, an anatomist and pathologist who also worked in Pavia, she began a series of studies on marmots to examine physiological changes occurring during hibernation. They focused particularly on the matter of osmoregulation, the process of maintaining a stable internal fluid environment and salt balance. Their results stimulated much discussion when presented at the 1903 meeting of the Istituto Lombardo di Scienze e Lettere.[15]

In 1901 and 1902 Monti acquired her first experience in competitions for university professorships, first at Messina, Sicily, and then at Bologna. Although not the winner in either attempt she was declared eligible both times and ranked third among the contestants for the professorship at Bologna. From 1902 she held the post of lecturer in comparative anatomy at Pavia, first as substitute for the ailing Leopoldo Maggi and after Maggi's death in 1905 in a regular appointment. Also in 1905 she was awarded a lectureship and the position of department head in zoology and comparative anatomy in the University of Siena's faculty of medicine, a post she held for two years. In 1908 she won the competitive examination for the position of professor *extraordinarius* in zoology, anatomy, and comparative physiology at the University of Sassari in northwest Sardinia; she became professor *ordinarius* in 1911.

Rina Monti was thus the first woman to hold a regular university professorship in the Kingdom of Italy, by then united for almost four decades. For three years, from 1912, she directed the University of Sassari's school of pharmacy in addition to her other professorial duties. She continued her research, both her hibernation studies and her work on insect nerve systems. In 1914 she published a notable paper on the Golgi complex.[16] Further, being well attuned to special local opportunities and interests, she carried out geographical distribution studies of Sardinian fauna, particularly the island's coastal species.[17] She was well liked and much admired in the Sassari community.

From about 1903 her central research interests were turning more and more to limnology, a branch of science that had caught her attention ten years previously when she studied freshwater protozoa as a student of Pietro Pavesi. It was here she made her greatest scientific contributions, and indeed she might justly be included among the pioneers of this discipline, one that was undergoing rapid development in the first half of the twentieth century. Her work focused on the biology of the Alpine and sub-Alpine lakes of Italy.

A forerunner of the present idea of ecology, limnology came to be recognized as a field in itself only in the second half of the nineteenth century, growth being assisted by several factors, including evolutionary theory, which encouraged studies of interdependence in natural systems, and the development in the 1890s of quantitative methods for the study of plankton.[18] Investigations of freshwater bodies were much stimulated by the work of F. A. Forel of the University of Lausanne on the deep-water fauna of Lake Geneva,[19] although important early research on lakes was also carried out in Scotland, Austria, and the United States. An interdisciplinary study par excellence, it is diffuse, extensive, and complex, involving the study of organisms, their interrelations with each other, and their relations with the structure and dynamics of their environment.

Following on from the early investigations of Pietro Pavesi, the discoverer of planktonic life in the Italian

Alpine lakes and the founder of limnological studies in Italy, Monti and her students continued and greatly extended Pavesi's work in a long series of studies focusing on the comparative limnology of the lakes. Mindful of the necessity of considering nonbiological factors—geology, climatology, physics, chemistry, and mineralogy—she sought the cooperation of workers in all these areas and thus built up a sound, broadly based, integrated picture. Her writings were long noted among those that led to a reduction of specialist isolation in studies of biological systems.[20]

Thus Monti's analyses of particular lake environments were supported by a solid knowledge of the geological history of the region and generally included a full geographical study of factors determining the development of the lake and therefore also of its biological communities. By painstaking comparison of the populations in small, high-Alpine lakes with those of sub-Alpine regions, she succeeded in establishing a series of stages for the postglacial colonization of lakes and put forward her hypothesis of migration of organisms, both active and passive, for the origin of lake communities. On the basis of her geohydrographical studies she suggested that migrations from the valleys to higher altitudes would have been less easy in the immediate postglacial period than in modern times and that in consequence migration in some instances would have been an active rather than a passive process. Much of this work was done in lakes of recent origin formed by the regression of glaciers in the Ruitor Massif on the Lombardia-Savoie border (in the vicinity of Mt. Blanc), extremely isolated, rugged country, difficult to travel through; she concluded that here the fauna had actively migrated from neighboring basins. Her theories of life cycles in mountain lakes won general agreement among limnologists internationally.[21]

In the course of her studies she made a great many important observations: the vertical and horizontal movement of plankton following oxygen availability, the biological balance between migrating fish and native plankton, the reasons for transparency changes in Lake Como, and the dying out of life in Lake Orta (as a result of industrial pollution) were among the topics and problems her work illuminated. Much of this research was carried out in the period 1919–1924, immediately following the interruptions caused by the First World War and after she had returned from Sassari to Pavia as professor *ordinarius* of zoology and director of the zoological institute. The undertaking was immense and complex, and the material shortages of the time were a severe handicap overcome in large part by Monti's outstanding organizational talents, efficiency, and tremendous capacity for intense work. Her major monograph on the Lake Larius basin, the first such treatment of a large Italian lake system, was published in 1924 by the Ministry of National Economy (Ministero dell' Economia Nazionale). The work was considered a milestone in Italian biology, both for its wide-ranging results and as an outstanding example of how to define and develop a complex, multifaceted research project on a large scale.[22]

Of great practical importance in the lake research was Monti's famous collapsible boat she called *Pavesia* after Pietro Pavesi. This small, portable craft had been specially constructed by the famous ship-building firm of Baglietto at Varazze near Genova and was later perfected by Monti's students and modified into a collapsible canoe for easier transport. Especially valuable in the small, high-altitude lakes, it appears in many of the illustrations included in her papers and reports.

In 1922 she was elected to full membership in the Regio Istituto Lombardo di Scienze e Lettere. Two years later she started her work of organizing the division of natural science at the new University of Milano, to which she transferred in 1925 as professor of anatomy and comparative physiology in the faculty of science and professor of zoology and comparative anatomy in the faculty of medicine.

Among the studies Rina Monti and her school carried out in the later 1920s and the early 1930s the series on the biology of the whitefish populations (genus Coregonus) of the Italian lakes is of special note. Several species of this genus are considered relic populations, cold-water fishes trapped at the end of the last glaciation in deep lakes, where bottom temperatures are always less than 6°C. Eggs of the species *Coregonus wartmanni coeruleus* Fatio from Lake Constance had been introduced into Lakes Como and Maggiore by Pietro Pavesi during the period 1859–1861. Strict control measures were lacking at the time and the possibility must be admitted of the simultaneous introduction of some eggs of other species present in Lake Constance, but nevertheless Pavesi's experiment was a biological trial on a grand scale. These early introductions were followed by others during the last two decades of the nineteenth century, the additional species brought in including *Coregonus schinzii helveticus* Fatio from Lake Zug, Switzerland.

Monti's early reports revealed a variety of morphological adaptations these whitefish populations had made over time to suit their new limnological environments and she identified specific factors (physical and biological) controlling these variations. Subsequent work involved an examination of the structural modifications undergone, modifications that were, however, mutable and reversible. Her 1933 monograph in the *Archivo Zoologico Italiano* presented the results of a detailed comparative morphological investigation of the most common Italian whitefish; combining genetic information with systematics, she showed that it had gradually acquired characters different from its ancestors and now agreed neither with *Coregonus wartmanni coeruleus* nor with *Coregonus schinzii helveticus*. She felt that it belonged to a single species, *Coregonus lavaretus,* which is remarkably plastic and capable of modifying its external form giving rise to local populations that vary appreciably in morphological characters according to the specific conditions encountered.[23] Later workers consider *Coregonus lavaretus* to have originated through the hybridization of *Coregonus wartmanni* and *Coregonus schinzii helveticus* although it has not yet been assigned a precise taxonomic status.[24]

Monti and her group also took part in the research effort underway in the mid 1920s to control May beetles, insects that were inflicting serious damage in Italian agriculture. They carried out experiments in chemical control but found that biological methods using a mold to infect the larvae proved more effective.[25]

Several of Monti's studies during her final period of research concerned the lakes of the Trentino, a region to which she had strong family connections. In part of this work she was joined by her daughter, biologist Emilia Stella. Their 1934 study of Lake Molveno, a deep glacial lake at 2,700 feet elevation, focused largely on an examination of many of the principal plankton species found, including rotifers and protozoa. The same year Monti published her analysis of limnological material collected in 1931 in the Albanian Alps by the Floridia-Allegri mission; the artificial basins where water was replaced frequently had little animal life but the small natural basins were rich in a few species. Work on populations of the cladoceran *Daphnia cucullata* Sars in several Trentino region lakes appeared in 1935; the species, one of a large group of aquatic arthropods, is of considerable importance as a fish food. Her last research (1936) concerned the action of γ-rays on the reproduction of Cladocera and the importance to Italian lake economy of the quantity of pelagic organisms living in the waters.[26]

An outstanding teacher, she had many students who went on to notable scientific careers, several of them in academia. Just before her death two projects on which she had worked long and hard came to fruition. One of these was the establishment of a limnological station equipped to support work in all branches of the field, from physical chemistry to general biology and practical fish breeding—the Italian Institute of Hydrobiology at Pallanza on Lake Maggiore. A bequest by Marco de Marchi of eminently suitable real estate properties on which this station was established was to a considerable extent inspired by the outstanding contributions of Monti and her students to Italian limnology. The second major project she undertook in her final years was the planning and acquisition of modern facilities to house the zoological institute in Milano, although the actual transfer was carried out by her students after her death.

For long an active member of the Regio Istituto Lombardo di Scienze e Lettere, she also belonged to the Accademia dei Fisiocritici di Siena, the Anatomische Gesellschaft, l'Association des Anatomistes, and the Société Zoologique de France. Over the course of her forty-four-year research career she published more than 100 papers and monographs.[27]

The portrait of Monti that accompanies her obituaries in Italian journals shows a strikingly handsome woman with an expression of almost religious calm and spirituality. Hers was a most unusual personality, complex and difficult to understand in the extreme. It was as if her fine, regular features and serene expression were a mask that confined the intense intellectual and spiritual life of the woman within, a woman dedicated to a single aim in pursuit of which were sacrificed life's common distractions and pleasures. She was remembered by her student Edgardo Baldi (later head of the zoological institute at the University of Milano) as having lived a nearly monastic existence, a personal life of almost unadorned severity. Even her style of speech and writing was sparse—clear, precise, and beautifully ordered.[28]

Nevertheless in 1903 she did marry. Her husband was geologist Augusto Stella (1863–1944), a man as dedicated to his research as she was to hers.[29] Much of Stella's work was also in the Alps, although in addition he carried out extensive research on the subterranean hydrography of the Po Valley and took part in Italian scientific expeditions to North Africa. They had two daughters, Luigia Achillea (b. 1904), who became professor of archaeology and Greek literature first at the University of Cagliari in southern Sardinia and then at the University of Trieste, and Emilia (b. 1909), a biologist specializing in limnology, who in 1948 became *docente* at the zoological institute at the University of Rome. For a time Rina Monti was associated with the Unione Femminile di Milano; this group had hailed her 1899 success in gaining an academic lectureship as an important milestone in the advancement of women in Italy and had persuaded her to join its cause. However, she later left the organization and distanced herself from its aims. In 1936, following the implementation of new government directives that changed professional arrangements, she resigned her post in Milano. She died in Pavia on 25 January 1937 at the age of sixty-five.

Histologist MARIA SACCHI[30] was born in San Pier d'Arena, Liguree, on 3 April 1863. A predecessor of Rina Monti at the University of Pavia, Sacchi, like Monti, was a student of biologist Leopoldo Maggi. She received her doctoral degree in natural science in 1885 and, after a short period as assistant in botany, moved to a similar position in Maggi's laboratory of comparative anatomy. During the 1890s, she held an assistantship in comparative anatomy at the University of Genova.

Over the course of twelve years (1886–1898), Maria Sacchi published at least nine papers reporting anatomical and morphological investigations. Among these were lengthy studies on reproductive and digestive organs in reptiles and amphibians; work on the embryonic skin structure of fishes, anatomical abnormalities in fishes, and the poison organ of scorpions followed. She also examined life-cycle processes in protists, particularly terrestrial varieties associated with mosses. She does not appear to have published further work in scientific journals after 1900.

Three additional Italian women who published papers in zoology before 1901 were identified in the Royal Society list—Zina Leardi Airaghi, Elisa Norsa, and Emma Bortolloti.[31]

ZINA LEARDI AIRAGHI of Milano worked closely with biologist Pietro Pavesi of Pavia University. Her first paper (1900) was a review of the methods then being developed for illustrating animal population distribution. Distribution and efficient ways of describing it using geographical maps, specific symbols, graphs, and tables, was then being recognized as a matter of considerable scientific importance. Examples cited by Leardi Airaghi included Pavesi's charts and maps of fish populations in Italian lakes (see also discussion of Rina Monti). In 1901 she published two papers reporting examinations of small collections of Asian arachnids brought back to Pavia some years earlier and made available to her by Pavesi. One described a collection of fifteen specimens (orders Araneae and Scorpionida) from Almora in the foothills of the Himalayas that contained one new species; several specimens were identified as arachnids considered typical of Burma. Her other paper discussed collections made at the French colony of Mahé on the Malabar coast of southeastern India and at Kandy and the surrounding region in central Ceylon (now Sri Lanka). Most of the fifty-eight specimens included were of the order Araneae but Scorpionida and Pedipalpi were also represented. Zina Leardi Airaghi held a doctoral degree and was a member of the Società Italiana di Scienze Naturali e del Museo Civico di Storia Naturale, Milano. All three of her papers appeared in the society's *Atti*.[32]

ELISA NORSA studied biology at the University of Bologna in the 1890s. Her report of her lengthy and detailed morphological study of the bone structure of birds' wings was published in 1894 (see bibliography).

The Royal Society *Catalogue* lists pre-1900 papers in bacteriology by two Italian women—Giuseppina Cattani and Maria Montessori.[33]

GIUSEPPINA CATTANI[34] (1859–1914), daughter of Tullio Cattani and his wife Teresa (née Baratta), was born in Imola on the southern edge of the Po Valley on 26 May 1859. A lively child, she attended a public elementary school, where she always ranked at the top of her classes. At the age of sixteen, after a further three years of private study, she took the school leaving certificate examinations in Bologna. She then followed the standard pattern of classical studies,[35] proceeding to *licèo* level, which qualified her for university entrance. An excellent student who had outstanding examination results, she completed the medical course at the University of Bologna and received her degree in medicine and surgery in 1884 (with commendation).[36]

Staying on in Bologna, Giuseppina Cattani worked at the university's Institute of General Pathology under the direction of Guido Tissoni, first as a student assistant and then for two years (1885–1887) in competitively won, government funded, postgraduate training appointments. In 1886, at the age of twenty-seven, with already a number of creditable histological studies of nerve structures in print (see bibliography), she ambitiously took part in a competition for the position of professor *ordinarius* of general pathology at the University of Parma. The judging commission designated her as eligible, but her competition score of thirty-eight out of a possible fifty points made her fifth among the final seven applicants. Although noting her abilities for acute observation, her outstanding microscope technique, and the clear thought processes evident from her publications, all of which suggested great promise for future success in scientific work, the judges considered that she needed to expand her interests in the wide field of normal and pathological physiology. The year being 1886, a quarter of a century before Rina Monti became the first woman in Italy to win a professor *ordinarius* appointment, Cattani was probably facing not inconsiderable resistance to the idea of a woman occupying a full faculty position.

The following year she fared better, winning both a government grant for postgraduate study abroad and the position of *libera docenza* (lecturer, nonsalaried) in general pathology at the University of Torino. After spending two semesters at the University of Zurich's Institute of General Pathology, then directed by German physiologist and pathologist T. A. E. Klebs, she taught in Torino for two years. In 1889 she transferred to the University of Bologna where, for a short time, until poor health obliged her to stop, she continued to lecture. She remained in her other post, that of assistant to Guido Tizzoni, until 1897 and for a period also had a small private practice in gynecology, conducted from a consulting room in her home.

Although Giuseppina Cattani is best known for her collaborative work with Tizzoni, she also carried out a notable amount of neurological research, investigating in particular degeneration of nerve fibres in the peripheral nervous system. Her joint work with Tizzoni focused exclusively on problems in microbiology, then a new and rapidly developing field. Their reports appeared at an impressive rate; several papers published in 1886 and 1887 discussed investigations on cholera, including work on modes of infection and organ changes brought about by the invasion of the bacterium. Cattani's last period of research, which came to a close by 1892, was devoted mainly to finding an antitoxin serum for tetanus, work that is considered her most important contribution to medical science.

Priority for the preparation of a pure tetanus culture is generally attributed to Shibasaburo Kitasato, who published his findings in 1889,[37] but Tizzoni and Cattani about the same time announced to the Torino Medical Academy that they had isolated the bacillus, now known as *Clostridium tetani*, from an anaerobic plate culture; their reports in the Academy's *Giornale* and in *Riforma Medica* (see bibliography) appeared the same year as Kitasato's. The problem of isolating and culturing the organism formed the starting point for a whole series of studies during the next few years on its biological characteristics. Experimental work with laboratory animals leading to the preparation of an antitoxin serum followed. The Tizzoni-Cattani team was one of the first to produce a serum for use in humans.[38]

Because of family needs Cattani returned to Imola, her birth place, in 1897 and there accepted the post of medical director in the hospital laboratory of the Congregation of Carita. She died in Imola on 9 December 1914, at age fifty-five. Giuseppina Cattani was the first woman member of the Società Medico-Chirurgia di Bologna, joining in 1889; her obituarist noted that among many notable male members she was by no means the least in the contributions she made to medical science.[39]

Mathematical and Physical Sciences

The already-noted pattern of Italian preeminence among nineteenth-century continental European women in the medical sciences, botany, and conchology continues in the field of mathematical research (as measured by original papers listed in the Royal Society *Catalogue*). From the late 1880s significant and gradually increasing numbers of women studied mathematics at Italian universities. This is not altogether surprising because mathematics by the latter part of the century was an area of great activity in Italy—the country's premier scientific discipline. Most of the women mathematics students were preparing for careers as teachers of the subject at *liceò* level[40] but a few went on to further academic work.[41] The four discussed here—Bortolloti, Fabri, Massarini, and Predella Longhi—were probably the only ones who published original research in mathematics journals before 1901. Among those whose contributions in the mathematical and physical sciences are listed in the bibliography, midcentury astronomer and meteorologist Caterina Scarpellini is most likely the best remembered among historians of women's history outside Italy.

CATERINA SCARPELLINI[42] (1808–1873), one of the more prominent of the earlier women whose work is catalogued by the Royal Society, published more than fifty notes and reports in Italian, French, and Belgian journals between 1853 and 1873. Many of these concerned her astronomical observations and meteorological measurements but she also wrote on electrical, magnetic, and geological phenomena.

She was born in Foligno, Perugia, on 29 October 1808. Lying in the Appenine hills, about eighty miles to the northeast of Rome, Foligno is a city known for its art and literature and its especially early ties to the Christian church. The Scarpellini family, prominent in the Foligno community, made important contributions to Italian science. Particularly notable was Caterina's uncle and godfather the astronomer Abbé Feliciano Scarpellini (1762–1840), appointed in 1816 by Pope Pius VI to a new chair of Sacred Physics in the Roman College of the Campidoglio (Capitol) and to the directorship of the Campidoglio Observatory, one of the early observatories established by the papacy. The setting up of the professorship and Abbé Scarpellini's appointment marked a turning point in the attitude of the Roman Catholic church to science. By about then the old view of science as an enemy of religion was giving way to the idea that it could instead be a useful tool in revealing the wonders of God's universe to man; the change of outlook considerably helped the development of scientific studies in Italy. Abbé Scarpellini was also noted for his efforts to reinvigorate the Lincei Academy, Rome's venerable scientific society that dated back to 1603.

Gifted and energetic, Caterina Scarpellini was interested in scientific studies from her early years. Living as she did on the Capitoline Hill next to the observatory, she developed a special interest in astronomy and was an enthusiastic observer. She married and brought up a family, but from about age twenty until her death was remarkably active in scientific work. From 1847 she was editor of *Correspondenza Scientifica in Roma,* a bulletin publishing material over a broad range of subjects.

From the late 1850s she directed the Capitoline Hill meteorological station (later incorporated into the Campidoglio station), a facility she herself to a large extent had organized. The time was one of considerable activity and development in weather studies, a field in which Italy took a prominent part starting with the establishment of Europe's first network of meteorological posts by the grand duke of Tuscany in 1653. Although initially equipped with temperature-measuring instruments only, within a few years the Duke's stations had barometers, wind vanes, and hygrometers as well. However, although statistical data could be built up, early attempts at storm forecasting failed, both in Italy and elsewhere. The lack of a rapid communication system between network stations hampered efforts in that direction until the middle of the nineteenth century when the development, mainly in Britain and the United States, of a workable electric telegraph system overcame the problem. By Scarpellini's time, meteorological stations throughout the regions of the peninsula already part of the Kingdom of Italy were being linked by telegraph, new stations were being set up, an Italian central meteorological office was established, and several international journals were available for the publication of observational data.

Her own observations, made six times daily at the Capitoline station, were reported regularly between 1856 and 1871 in *Correspondenza Scientifica* and in the news bulletin of the Société Météorologique de France. An interesting joint study with Paolo Peretti, related to observations on prevailing winds, reported a chemical analysis of sand falling in Rome over the course of three nights in February 1864; the material had been blown from the Sahara desert during a storm.

Scarpellini's astronomical notes reported observations on comets and shooting stars; she discovered a comet in 1854. Compiler of the first Italian meteor catalogue, she was also the only observer in Rome of the 1866 Leonid meteor shower. Additional topics she wrote on included sunspot periodicity, Saturn's rings, her ideas about the formation of the planets, and her hypotheses concerning celestial mechanics.

She had a strong interest in electrical and magnetic phenomena and in such topics as the speed of light and stereoscopy. Two papers she brought out in 1853 discussed the weak electrical currents associated with muscular contraction. Her writings on the influence of the moon on earthquakes brought her honors from the Moscow Imperial Society of Naturalists, the Viennese Royal Geological Institute, and other foreign societies. In 1872 the Italian government's Ministry of Education awarded her a silver medal for her considerable contributions to science. She died in Rome, on 28 November 1873 at the age of sixty-five, following a stroke. Shortly after her death a statue was erected to her memory in the Campo Verano, Rome.

Astronomical notes by Adele Acampora and Adelina di Brehm are also listed in the bibliography. Both reported meteorite observations, Acampora's from Napoli in 1885 and Brehm's from Sarezzo in 1889. Carolina Vielmi's table of temperature, rainfall, and general weather conditions data from the Breno meteorological station formed part of a comprehensive report in the University of of Brescia's 1884 *Commentari*. Presenting observations from four stations in the surrounding region, the report covered the period June 1883 to May 1884. The Breno station, about thirty miles north of Brescia in the Alpine foothills of Lombardia, was directed by Signora Vielmi.

Mathematician CORNELIA FABRI[43] (1869?–1915) was born in Ravenna into a family long prominent in the sciences. Her grandfather Santi Fabri had studied mathematics, mechanics, and hydraulic engineering at the University of Bologna and continued his education at the famous School of Civil Engineering in Rome; her father Ruggero Fabri, a member of the Rome Accademia dei Lincei, was a much-respected physicist and mathematician.

After attending the Ravenna Istituto Tecnico and passing the necessary examinations Cornelia Fabri studied mathematics at the University of Pisa for four years. The awarding of her degree (with distinction) in 1891 was a landmark in the history of the institution; hers was the first doctorate in mathematics conferred on a woman. Antonio Pacinotti, dean of the faculty of science, noted that the event pointed the way to the opening of a new era for women in scientific fields.

Fabri was closely associated with internationally recognized physicist and mathematician Vito Volterra (1860–1940), professor of mechanics at the University of Pisa from 1883 to 1893; a man of liberal, democratic outlook and a zealous promoter of science, Volterra led the Italian school of mathematics during the first quarter of the twentieth century.[44] Beginning in 1890 with a report of her generalization of some results of Volterra, Fabri brought out several notable articles in national journals, including two major papers on calculus properties of particular kinds of composite functions (1890 and 1892—see bibliography).

Encouraged by her father, she continued her mathematical research after rejoining her family in Ravenna. Her focus now was on hydrodynamics, specifically the mathematical equations whose solutions predict fluid motion; the area was one she had already become interested in while a student at Pisa.

A field of great complexity, hydrodynamics was given its first mathematical flow model by Leonhard Euler in the eighteenth century. Euler's work, however, was limited to the consideration of ideal (nonviscous) fluids. During the first half of the nineteenth century a number of workers (most notably Claude Louis Navier and George Gabriel Stokes) developed a set of very complex equations whose solution, in principle, describes flow in real fluids. Currently, although the mathematical properties of these equations remain of considerable research interest, their application is restricted to finding approximate solutions using computers, limitations being determined only by the computing power available. (The area continues to be one of great research activity, underpinning as it does such fields as aeronautical engineering, ship design, and flood control.) In Fabri's time, and indeed through the middle of the twentieth century, obtaining a solution to the Navier-Stokes equations required developing a set of functions for an explicit solution covering a specific case bounded by restrictive assumptions.

Fabri's contributions concerned vortex motion in moving fluids. Starting with early work on ideal fluids done as a student in Pisa, she went on to consider vortex motion in viscous fluids. Her 1894 and 1895 papers in the latter area (see bibliography) were especially well received by fellow mathematicians. Among her other publications were two technical reports on local projects: a study of a dam on the river Montone and a discussion of an electric signal bell installed by the Abbé Ravaglia in the port of Ravenna.

Although well known through her publications among fellow scientists, Cornelia Fabri led a quiet, solitary life. Shy and unassuming, she chose to remain largely within the bounds of her family circle and indeed is said to have never even spoken of her mathematical studies.[45] The deaths of both her parents within a period of two years deprived her of her closest companions. Beyond mathematics she had two other interests—charitable work and religious observances, to both of which she devoted a considerable amount of time, even calculating hours of prayer meticulously and precisely. She died suddenly at the age of forty-six in 1915. A study center for physics, astronomy, and mathematics established by the Ravenna Cultural Association commemorates her life and work, the Centro Studi Cornelia Fabri.

IGINIA MASSARINI, Italy's first woman mathematics graduate,[46] was awarded her degree by the University of Napoli in 1887, following presentation of her dissertation on conic surfaces—"Sul sistema di due coniche studiate sulle loro equazioni generali col sussidio delle forme invariantive, in notazione simbolica." Her first journal article on the topic appeared in 1899 (see bibliography), by which time she was living in Rome. In the interim she brought out an annotated translation of St. Petersburg mathematician Pafnuti Tchebychev's book on the theory of congruences,[47] the contribution for which she is remembered in mathematics history. Her study of wind directions and velocities in the Rome region, published in two parts in 1905 and 1918, used data from the anemometric records of the Astronomical Observatory of the University of Rome. In a detailed examination of records covering the thirty years 1876–1905, she analyzed measurements made daily throughout the period for winds from sixteen compass points, presenting the data in both tabular and graphical form.[48]

LIA PREDELLA was a student of Giulio Vivanti, who taught at the Scuola Normale Superiore in Pavia in the 1890s before moving to a professorship at the University of Messina. Predella was awarded her degree by the University of Pavia in 1894.[49] Her dissertation research on singular solutions of differential equations of the first order appeared in the *Giornale di Matematiche di Battaglini* the following year (see bibliography).

About the turn of the century Lia Predella married, becoming Lia Predella Longhi. Professor at the Reale Scuola Normale Giannina Milli in Rome from at least the late 1890s, her later publications reflected her teaching interests. Her algebra textbook for use in the introductory algebra course in teacher training institutions was well received by her colleagues and went through several editions.[50] A short work, dealing with its subject at the most basic level, it took the student as far as linear equations in one unknown and the numerical extraction of square roots and cubic roots; a generous supply of practice problems was included. Predella Longhi's other publications included an article on arithmetic properties of integer roots of integers investigated using elementary techniques and a paper on the solution of arithmetical problems by both arithmetic and elementary algebraic methods.[51] By 1917 Predella Longhi was living in Torino, where she taught at the Reale Istituto G. Sommeiller.

EMMA BORTOLLOTI published one paper in mathematics from Bologna in 1895; it reported a lengthy investigation of continued fractions. She then moved on to other fields, publishing a paper in mammalian embryology in 1896 and another on Middle Miocene marine fossils (mollusks and fishes) in 1898.

Other Areas

There remain to be discussed two women in this group of twenty—educationist Maria Montessori and anthropologist Emma Puglesi.

MARIA MONTESSORI[52] (1870–1952), whose paper on the effects of tetanus infection of the cerebro-spinal fluid is listed in the bibliography, is known internationally for her work on early childhood education. In addition to her own voluminous writings are a great many books and articles by others about her life and career and the famous pedagogical method that bears her name. The following is a brief outline of her story.

Born on 31 August 1870 in Chiaravalle, north-central Italy, about ten miles inland from Ancona, Maria was the only child of Alessandro Montessori and his wife Renilde (née Stoppani). Alessandro Montessori, decorated for his military service in the wars for the liberation of Italy, was a government finance official for the tobacco industry. His wife was a well-educated, liberal-minded woman from a landed family, niece of the distinguished scholar-priest Antonio Stoppani, professor of geology at the University of Milano, a well-known naturalist and a liberal cleric who sought to reconcile science and religion. Through her mother Maria was much influenced by Stoppani's outlook and achievements.

The family moved to Rome when Maria Montessori was five. She received her elementary education in a public school and later (1886–1890) attended the Regio Istituto Tecnico Leonardo da Vinci, where she studied modern languages, natural science, and mathematics, the latter her best subject.[53] Against her father's advice and wishes she decided to study medicine and entered the University of Rome in 1890. She successfully completed the required two years of premedical study that included courses in physics, mathematics, and natural sciences. Despite general disapproval but with her mother's encouragement she then applied for admission to the department of clinical medicine; acceptance came after a certain amount of official hesitation. In 1894 she received the prize given annually for work in general pathology and the following year won a competition for a hospital assistantship that gave her clinical experience while still a student. Pediatrics and psychiatry were the areas in which she concentrated during her last two years. She ranked high in her class and in 1896 received her degree in medicine and surgery, the first in the field awarded to a woman by Rome University's medical faculty.[54]

Montessori stayed on at the university to carry out research in the institution's psychiatric laboratory, joining the staff as a volunteer in 1897. Her assignment was to visit Rome asylums and select patients for treatment in a clinic setting. She was interested in particular in children and in possibilities for teaching the handicapped or otherwise disadvantaged. Expanding and developing her ideas, she undertook extensive studies of the writings of a number of earlier investigators who explored the process of learning in early childhood.[55] At the same time she familiarized herself with standard procedures for research in the social sciences adopting the methods of Giuseppe Sergi, professor of anthropology at Rome University.

In 1900 she became co-director of the Scuola Magistrale Ortofrenica, a medical-pedagogical institution to train teachers in the education of mentally defective children. She also started a class for twenty-two retarded children, closely observing their individual needs. Her study led her to begin devising the necessary aids and materials and developing the basic system of what is now known as the *Montessori Method*. Results were good; many of those previously considered incapable of learning began to pass the examinations of the government-run elementary schools at the same level as normal children. These findings led her to wonder if the average normal child might not be capable of achieving much more than he or she usually did when taught by current educational methods. She concluded that these methods did in fact have the effect of limiting learning.

In 1901 she abruptly resigned her post in order to have a child, her son Mario Montessori, whose father was her colleague Dr. Giuseppe Montesano, co-director of the school. After arranging for the boy's care by a family in a country district, she once again took up studies at Rome University now focusing on pedagogy, experimental psychology, and anthropology. From 1904 to 1908, she held a faculty position in the Pedagogic School. Here she gave a course for education students on "pedagogical anthropology" that laid great stress on understanding the nature of the child to be educated and the methods used to arrive at this understanding. She also taught until 1906 at the Istituto Superiore di Magistero Femminile and in that year was appointed to the board of examiners for the degree of natural science in anthropology at Rome University.

The turning point in Maria Montessori's career came in January 1907 when she established the world's first Montessori school, the Casa dei Bambini, in the Rome slum district of San Lorenzo. Concentration on individualized learning at the child's own pace with much attention in the early years to developing the sense of touch through the use of a variety of teaching materials was a key characteristic of her teaching method, a method that became increasingly successful and spread throughout other countries. At the time Montessori's ideas were revolutionary and stirred much professional debate in the pedagogical community. She became widely known and received a stream of visitors who came to observe in her classrooms. She lectured extensively and published a considerable number of articles. Her comprehensive work *Il Metodo della Pedagogia Scientifica applicato all'Educazione Infantile nei Case dei Bambini* appeared in 1909; an English translation, *The Montessori Method,* was brought out three years later. Until the mid 1930s what became known as the *Montessori Movement* flourished throughout Europe. Schools were also started in the United States where Montessori visited and lectured. She herself kept tight control over the movement and, fearful of "distractions" and "deviations," was unwilling to allow others to write about aspects of her method without her prior approval. In Italy, although the Montessori schools were for a time less successful than in several other countries, the system was reinvigorated when Benito Mussolini gave it official recognition. Montessori's control gradually diminished, however, and within a few years the schools were closed because of doubts about the loyalty of the teachers to the Fascist government.

Montessori spent some time lecturing in Spain and in England in the mid 1930s. In 1939 she and her son traveled to India, a country she had long been interested in; their aim was to set up a teacher training center. Returning to Europe after the end of the Second World War when the journey was once more possible, Montessori resumed her work, constantly moving from one country to another. She was by then close to eighty years old but nevertheless made a second trip to India and one to Pakistan as well. Her home base was Amsterdam, the location of the International Montessori Association. Managed largely by Mario Montessori until his death in 1982, the association served as the parent organization for overseeing schools and societies worldwide.

Until nearly the end of her life Maria Montessori was extremely active, presenting courses and lecturing. She died of a cerebral hemorrhage on 6 May 1952 at the age of eighty-one when visiting friends in Noordwijk aan Zee, a small village on the North Sea coast near The Hague. Although she herself was largely forgotten by the time of her death, the movement she started in the early years of the twentieth century had a powerful influence on later workers in early childhood education and in child psychology. The new ideas that she developed and taught to a wide audience had considerable impact on pedagogic theory.

EMMA PUGLIESI published a study with anthropologist Frederico Tietze in 1898 reporting their collaborative research in the then popular but soon thereafter discredited field of craniometry. With the aim of acquiring insight into the genetic background of the population of Sardinia, they examined a collection of fifteen skulls (male and female) from the period 1800–1860 obtained from an ossuary in Aristano, Sardinia, and housed in the department of anthropology at the University of Padova. A mixed background of Phoenician, Corsican, Etruscan, Carthaginian, and Balearic elements was considered likely. Puglesi's second paper, another study in craniometry comparing symmetry variations in human male and female skulls, appeared in 1899.

Further Remarks

These twenty Italians are an especially interesting and on average strikingly productive group. Their careers extend over a remarkably long time span (Figure 8-1), from the 1820s when Rome botanist Elisabetta Fiorini-Mazzanti began the work in bryology that quickly brought her to international attention, to the last decade of the century when biologist Rina Monti started her research on freshwater protozoa that led to her widely recognized work on Alpine lake ecology. A case might be made for considering the three specially productive early members of the group—Fiorini-Mazzanti, Paulucci, and Scarpellini—as representing a continuation of the notable participation of Italian women in scholarly work that dated back for many centuries.[56] However, the most outstanding of the later workers—Monti, Cattani, Sacchi, and perhaps also Fabri—fit more readily into the pattern commonly found for the careers of ambitious women research scientists of the late nineteenth and early twentieth centuries, namely formal, university-level education followed by a period of academic work that for a few developed into notable careers.

Three in this small Italian group were titled noblewomen, Fiorini-Mazzanti, Paulucci, and the later nineteenth-century botanist Marchesa Pallavicini (Margherita Misciattelli); Scarpellini also was born into a distinguished family. These four undoubtedly benefited from the social mobility and acceptance their status brought.

Fiorini-Mazzanti, Paulucci, and Scarpellini, all of whom were well-known and respected in the international scholarly community, were very much independent workers, although Scarpellini was perhaps somewhat less so than the other two in that she had close family connections with academia and the astronomy research community; she also had the use of crucial facilities in Rome.

Marchesa Paulucci is an especially interesting personality. From an aristocratic family, prominent in the Firenzi region for many generations, heiress to a large fortune including magnificent mansions and country estates, in her earlier years she was no stranger to several of the royal courts of Europe. In addition, however, her energy and intellectual abilities were such that she made very significant contributions to Italian natural history. Fiorini-Mazzanti's early cryptogamic work can be compared with that of her contemporary Marie-Anne Libert (1782–1865) discussed in the chapter on Belgian women; Libert also came to international attention by the 1830s following publication of her work on the cryptogamic plants of the Ardennes. Although from very different social backgrounds, both these women were educated well beyond the level common for girls of their time.

Among the later Italians, limnologist Monti and neurologist and bacteriologist Cattani were clearly the most notable. Both worked in academic settings. Monti was a successful research scientist, professor, administrator, and developer of departments who won an international reputation for her considerable research accomplishments in freshwater biology; Cattani, struggling to find her way into academia a decade and a half before Monti, had to settle for less, and her major contributions were the result of close teamwork with a more senior adviser and partner. Nevertheless her output of creditable research is striking and was recognized internationally. Maria Montessori's name is almost a household word; her place among twentieth-century reformers of early childhood education is well established.

Notes

1. Giuseppina Fenaroli, Fulvia Furinghetti, Antonio Garibaldi, and Anna Somaglia, "Women and Mathematical Research in Italy during the Period 1887–1946," in *Gender and Mathematics: An International Perspective,* ed. Leone Burton (London: Cassell Educational Limited, 1990), 144–55. Of the 224 women graduating from Italian universities before 1901, not all were Italians; foreign graduates included a number of Russians.

2. The tradition of notable involvement in scientific work by Italian women from mediaeval times to the eighteenth century is well known. For a sketch of the contributions to medical science of the *Mulieres Salernitanae* (Ladies of Salerno) at the school of medicine in Salerno, the work of women in the same field at other Italian universities during the late medieval period, the activities of seventeenth- and eighteenth-century Italian women mathematicians (including Laura Bassi and Maria Agnesi) at the universities of Bologna and Pavia, and more, see for instance Margaret Alic, *Hypatia's Heritage: A History of Women in Science from Antiquity to the Late Nineteenth Century* (London: Women's Press, 1986).

3. E[ttore] degli Oddi, "Delle vita e delle opere della Marchesa M. Paulucci, malacologa italiana," *Atti del Reale Istituto Veneto di Scienze, Lettere et Arti* 80 pt. 2, (1920–21): 59–70; *Enciclopedia Italiana di Scienze, Lettere ed Arti,* vol. 26 (1935), 173; and *Lexikon der Frau* (Zürich: Encyclios Verlag AG, 1953), vol. 2, 861.

4. *Catalogue des Espèces du Genre Conus de la Collection Paulucci* (Poggibonsi: Coltellini et Bassi, 1874); *Matériaux pour servir à l'Étude de la Faune Malacologique Terrestre et Fluviale de l'Italie et de ses Îles* (Paris: Librairie F. Savy, 1878); *Escursione Scientifica nella Calabria, 1877–78: Fauna Malacologica* (Firenze: tip. Arte della Stampa, 1879); and *Note Malacologiche sulla Fauna Terrestre et Fluviale dell'Isola di Sardegna* (Siena: tip. dell'Ancora di G. Bargellini, 1882).

5. Armand Thielens, "Voyage en Italie et en France. I—Italie," *Annales de la Société Malacologique de Belgique* 9 (1874): ccv–ccxv, on ccvi.

6. The Castello di Sammezzano, built on the foundations of a Roman structure, came into the possession of Ferdinando Panciatichi in 1816, when he fell heir to the Ximenes d'Aragona estate. Over a period of about forty years between 1850 and 1890, he redesigned this castle in the Hispano-Moorish style of architecture and decoration, transforming Sammezzano into a reproduction of the Alhambra of Grenada; two rooms especially are considered masterpieces, the Sala delle Stalattiti (Stalactite Hall) and the Sala dei Pavoni (Peacock Hall). Much deteriorated by the 1950s, it was sold and then restored by the new owner, who turned it into a magnificent hotel and restaurant. More recently it was sold again, the surrounding property having been divided and "developed." It is now a hotel and conference center—"Guida Turistica. "Castello di Sammezzano," available online at http://english.firenze.net/groups/6/29/65/pass_4.htm (last accessed 22 June 2000).

7. Ettore Arrigoni degli Oddi, *Manuale di Ornitologia Italiana; Elenco Descrittivo degli Uccelli Stazionario di Passaggio finora osservati in Italia* (Milano: U. Hoepli, 1904).

8. E. Arrigoni degli Oddi, "Note ornitologiche sulla collezione del monte appartenente alla signora marchesa M. Paulucci," *Atti del R. Istituto Veneto di Scienze, Lettere ed Arti* 67, pt. 2 (1907–1908): 659–77. Among the more notable specimens in the collection were the following (location of capture indicated in parenthesis): several varieties of Eurasian

buzzard, *Buteo buteo*; a rare Barbary falcon, *Falco barbarus* (southern Sardinia) and another, typical of Sardinia, Eleonora's falcon, *Falco eleonorae*; a northern hobby, *Falco subbuteo* (Tuscany); a European nightjar, *Caprimulgus europaeus* (Tuscany); a variety of Asian swift, *Apus apus murinus* (southeastern Italy); several species of bunting including the Lapland bunting, *Calcarius lapponicus* (Venetia), and Pine bunting, *Emberiza leucocephala*; the Eurasian goldfinch, *Carduelis carduelis* (Tuscany); the carrion crow, *Corvus corone* (Italian Alps); the gray partridge, *Perdix perdix*; the marbled teal, *Marmaronetta angustirostris* (Tuscany); the Arctic skua, *Stercorarius parasiticus* (Alpine foothills); and a rare Atlantic puffin, *Fratercula arctica* (Venetia). The collection also contained a number of species not usually found in Italy, such as the great thrush, *Turdus fuscatus*; Cretzschmar's bunting, *Emberiza caesia*; and the white-tailed stonechat, *Saxicola leucura*.

9. Conte Ab. Francesco Castracane, "Cenni biografica su la Contessa Elisabetta Fiorini Mazzanti," *Atti dell'Accademia Pontificia de'Nuovi Lincei* 32 (1879): 307–28; *Bulletin. Société Botanique de France* 26 (1879): 92; C. Roumeguère, "La Comtesse Elisabetta Fiorini-Mazzanti," *Revue Mycologique* 1 (1879): 104–9; "Elisabetta Fiorini-Mazzanti," *Leopoldina* 16 (1880): 13–14; G. Mazzolani, "Fiorini, Elisabetta," *Dizionario Biografico degli Italiani* (Roma: Istituto della Enciclopedia Italiana, 1960–), vol. 48 (1997), 195–96; *Enciclopedia Italiana di Scienze, Lettere ed Arti*, vol. 15 (1932), 432; and *Lexikon der Frau*, vol. 1, 1049.

10. See bibliography and also Elisabetta Fiorini, *Appendice al Prodroma della Flora Romana* (Pisa: n.p., 1828).

11. Roumeguère, "Contessa Elisabetta," 108.

12. *Specimen Bryologiae Romanae* (Roma: Typis Crispini Puccinelli, 1831; 2nd ed. 1841). See also bibliography.

13. Roumeguère, "Contessa Elisabetta," 107–8.

14. Carlo Jucci, "Rina Monti," *Festschrift für Prof. Dr. Embrick Strand* 4 (1938): 664–70; Livia Pirocchi, "In memoriam. Rina Monti," *Atti della Società Italiana di Scienze Naturali e del Museo Civico di Storia Naturale. Milano* 76 (1937): 55–69; Edgardo Baldi, "Rina Monti," *Rivista di Biologia* (1937): 347–61; Silvio Ranzi, "Ricordo di Rina Monti Stella nel cinquantenario della sua scomparsa," *Rendiconti. Istituto Lombardo di Scienze e Lettere* (hereafter *Rend. Ist. Lomb.*) 121 (1987): 173–82; anonymous, "Vittorie femminili," *Bolletino della Unione Femminili Nazionale* (February 1903): 30–1; Emilia Stella, *Fondamenti di Limnologia: Guida alla Studio delle Acque Continentali* (Rome: Ateneo, 1984); *Enciclopedia Italiana di Scienze, Lettere ed Arti*, vol. 23 (1934), 769; *Lexikon der Frau*, vol. 2, 661; and information from Pavia University library.

15. See bibliography and also "Les fonctions de sécrétion et d'absorption intestinal étudiées chez les animaux hibernants," *Archives Italiennes de Biologie* 40 (1903), fasc. 2 (also *Memorie del R. Istituto Lombardo di Scienze e Lettere*, 16 Marzo 1903); "Les glandes gastrique des marmottes durant la létargie hivernale et l'activité estivale," *Archives Italienne de Biologie* 39 (1904): 248–52; and "Le leggi del rinnovamento dell'organismo studiate negli animali ibernante," *Rend. Ist. Lomb.* 38, s. 2 (1905): 714–19.

16. "Sul sistema nervosocentrale degli insetti," *Atti della R. Accademia dei Fisiocratici in Siena* (1907); "Sur les relations mutuelles entre les éléments dans le système nerveux central des insects," *Archives d'Anatomie Microscopique* 15 (1913): 349–433; and "L'apparato reticolare interno di Golgi nelle cellule nervose dei Crostacei," *Rendiconti della R. Accademia dei Lincei* 23 (1914): 172–77.

17. "Esplorazioni talassografiche lungo le coste della Sardenga settentrionale," *Natura: Rivista di Scienze Naturali* (Milano) 1 (1910); "*Selache maxima* Gunn pescate sulla costa di Sardenga," *Rivista Mensile di Pesca e Idrobiologia* 5 (1910); and "La fisionomia biologica della Sardenga e le noeve idee circa le origini e la distribuzione geografica delle specie," *Rivista Mensile di Pesca e Idrobiologia* 6 (1915).

18. Hans-Joachim Elster, "History of Limnology," *Communications. International Association of Theoretical and Applied Limnology* 20 (1974): 7–30.

19. F. A. Forel, *Le Léman: Monographie Limnologique,* 3 vols. (Lausanne: F. Rouge, 1892–1904).

20. Elster, "History of Limnology," 9.

21. See "Sulla migrazione attiva e passiva degli organismi planctonici d'alta montagna," *Rend. Ist. Lomb.* 41, s. 2 (1908): 899–912; for a summary in English, see *Nature* 79 (1909): 466. See also "Un modo di migrazione del plancton fin qui sconosciuto," *Rend. Ist. Lomb.* 38, s. 2 (1905): 122–32; "Physiobiologische Beobachtungen an den Alpenseen zwischen dem Vigezzo und dem Onsernonetal," *Forschungsberichte aus der Biologischen Station zu Plön* 12 (1905): 63–89; "Recherches sur quelques lacs du massif du Ruiter," *Annales de Biologie Lacustre, Bruxelles* 1 (1906): 120–67; "La circolazione della vita nei laghi alpini," *Atti del Congresso dei Naturalisti Italiani* (Conference summaries) Milano (1907): 144–46, and *Rivista Mensile di Pesca* 9 (1907): 1–21; "Le migrazioni attive e passive degli organismi acquatici d'alta montagna," *Il Monitore Zoologico Italiano* (Firenze) 20 (1909): 52–53; and "Un nouveau petit filet pour les pêches plantoniques de surface à toute vitesse," *Internationale Revue der gesamten Hydrobiologie und Hydrographie* 3 (1911): 548–52.

22. *La Limnologia del Lario in Relazione al Ripopolamento delle Acque ed alla Pesa. Studi fatti sotto la direzione della prof. Rina Monti* (Roma: Ministero dell'Economia Nazionale, 1924), 507 pp. See also *L'Alimentazione dei Pesci lariani* (Roma: Ministero Ec. Naz., 1924); "Contributo alla biologia delle Dafnie lariane," *Rend. Ist. Lomb.* 7 (1924), fasc. 11–15; *Limnologia generale del Lario* (Roma: Ministero Ec. Naz., 1925); "La fioritura delle acque sul Lario," *Rend. Ist. Lomb.* 58 (1925); (with A. Monti and N. Monti) "La variazione del residuo e dei gas disciolti nelle acque del Lario, in rapporto con biologia lacustre," *Rend. Ist. Lomb* 59 (1926), fasc. 1–5; "Per l'esplorazione dei laghi alpini," *25 Annuario, 1929–30, della Società degli Alpinisti Tridentini* (Trento); and "La graduale estinzione della vita nel lago d'Orta," *Rend. Ist. Lomb.* 63 (1930): 1–22.

23. Monti's Coregonus papers include the following: "La limnologia comparata dei laghi insubrice," *Bollettino di Pesca,*

Pisicoltura e Idrobiologia 3 (1927): 51–55; "Biologia dei coregoni nei laghi italiani. Nota prima: La natura dei laghi nostri e l'introduzione dei coregoni; Nota quarta: L'alimentazione dei coregoni nei diversi laghi; Nota quinta: Le variazioni dei coregoni en relazione con l'ambiente," *Rivista di Biologia* 11 (1929), fasc. 3–4, 5–6; "L'ampiezza delle variazione presentate dei coregoni italiani," *Archivo Zoologico Italiano* 15 (1931): 83–96; and "La genetica dei coregoni italiani e la loro variabilità in relazione coll'ambiante," *Archivo Zoologico Italiano* 18 (1933): 157–202.

24. Merco Corti, Gabriele de Bonfils, Gian Luca Natili, Giovanni Arlati, and Stefano Cataudella, "Whitefishes (genus *Coregonus*) in Italy: species distinction and geographic variation," *Bollettino di Zoologia* 62 (1995): 305–12.

25. (With L. Montemarini and E. Baldi) "Per la lotta contro i maggiolini. Osservazione ed esperienza su le larve," *Atti dell'Istituto Botanico della Università e Laboratorio Crittogamico di Pavia* 3 (1927): 25–43; and "La lotta contro i maggiolini," *Nuovi Annali dell'Agricoltura Roma* 7, no. 4 (1928): 545–83.

26. (With Emilia Stella) "Il Lago di Molveno. La vita in un lago zootrofo," *Memorie Museo di Storia Naturale della Venezia Tridentina* 2 (1934): 69–101; "Contributo all'idrobiologia delle Alpi Albanesi," *Atti della Società Italiana di Scienze Naturali, e del Museo Civico di Storia Naturale, Milano* 73 (1934): 74–92; "La *Daphnia cucullata* G. O. Sars in laghi tridentini," *Memorie Museo di Storia Naturale della Venezia Tridentina* 3 (1935), fasc. 1; "L'azione dei raggi gamma sulla riproduzione dei cladoceri: raggi diretti e raggi filtrati attraverso piombo," *Festschrift für Prof. Dr. Embrik Strand* 1 (1936): 146–84; and "Numeri, grandezze e volumi degli organismi pelagici viventi nelle acque italiane, in relazione all'economia lacustre," *Mem. Ist. Lomb.*, 23 (1936), fasc. 3.

27. For more complete listings of Monti's publications, see any of the following: Jucci, "Rina Monti"; Pirocchi, "In memoriam. Rina Monti"; Baldi, "Rina Monti"; and Ranzi, "Ricordo di Rina Monte Stella" (references in note 14).

28. Baldi, "Rina Monti," 348–49.

29. Leone Testa, "Augusto Stella. 1863–1944," *Bollettino della Società Geologica Italiana* 69 (1950): 553–58.

30. Renate Strohmeir, *Lexikon der Naturwissenschaftlerinnen und Naturkundigen Frauen Europas: von der Antike bis zum 20. Jahrhundert.*

31. For Bortolloti, see mathematical and physical sciences section below.

32. See bibliography and "Arachnidi d'Almora," *Atti della Società Italiana di Scienze Naturali e del Museo Civico di Storia Naturale in Milano* 40 (1901): 85–94; "Arachnidi di Mahè e Kandy," *Atti della Società Italiana di Scienze Naturali e del Museo Civico di Storia Naturale in Milano* 40 (1901): 345–73. Zina Leardi Airaghi might have been related to palaeontologist Carlo Airaghi, who worked at the Milano Museo Civico di Storia Naturale around 1900, but I have not found a definite connection.

33. For Montessori, see Other Areas.

34. R. Gurriere, "La Dott.ssa Giuseppina Cattani," *Bullettino delle Scienze Mediche* s.9, 86 (1915): 123–28; *British Medical Journal* (27 March 1915), 578; and *Dizionario Biografico degli Italiani*, vol. 22 (1979), 503–4.

35. Italian secondary education was organized in two distinct lines, the classical and the technical. The former required five years at a *ginnasio* until the age of fifteen or sixteen, followed by three years at a *licèo*; literature and the classics were emphasized. The technical pattern consisted of seven years of modern languages, mathematics, some science, and general subjects, the first three years being at a high school and the last four at a technical institute. The curriculum was uniform throughout the country, content and standards being set by the central Ministry of Education—see Rita Kramer, *Maria Montessori: A Biography* (Reading, Mass.: Addison-Wesley, 1988), 31–32.

36. The first woman to receive a medical degree from an Italian institution was Ernestina Paper, who graduated from the Istituto di Studi Superiori, Firenzi, in 1877. Paper is in fact considered to be the first woman to graduate in Italy; see Fenaroli et al., "Women and Mathematical Research," 145.

37. S. Kitasato, "Ueber den Tetanus Bacillus," *Zeitschrift für Infektionskrankheit* 7 (1889): 225–34. A colleague of Robert Koch, Kitasato worked at Koch's Institute of Hygiene in Berlin for a period in the late 1880s; after returning to Tokyo, he founded the bacteriological research center now known as the *Kitasato Institute*.

38. A group in Germany produced an antitoxin serum for use in humans about the same time; see H. J. Parish, *Victory with Vaccines: The Story of Immunization* (Edinburgh: E. S. Livingstone, 1968), 55.

39. Gurriere, "Giuseppina Cattani," 123.

40. Fenaroli et al., "Women and Mathematical Research," 147.

41. In the thirteen-year period 1887–1899, twenty women are known to have received mathematics degrees from Italian universities; at least four of them published scientific papers; see Fenaroli et al., "Women and Mathematical Research," 154; numbers quoted from Vittore Ravà, *Le laureate in Italia. Notizie statistiche* (Roma: Cecchini, 1902).

42. *Nouvelles Météorologiques, Société Météorologique de France* 7, pt. 1 (1874): 6–7; E. Lagrange, "Les femmes-astronomes," *Ciel et Terre* (15 January 1885): 513–27 on 524–25; Herman S. Davis, "Women Astronomers (1750–1890)," *Popular Astronomy* 6 (1898): 211–20; Oscar Greco, *Bibliobiografia Femminile Italiana del XIX Secolo* (Venezia: Presso i Principali Librai d'Italia, 1875), 446–47; Alic, *Hypatia's Heritage*, 133–34; and Alphonse Rebière, *Les Femmes dans la Science. Notes recueilles,* 2nd ed. (Paris: Nony et Cie, 1897), 250.

43. Mirca Modoni and Lia Randi, "Donne ravennati tra Ottocento e Novecento," in *Storia Illustrata di Ravenna*, ed. Elio Sellino, 4 vols. (Milano: Nuova Editoriale Aiep, 1990), vol. 3 (*Tra Ottocento e Novecento*), 161–76 on 167–68 (portr.); and Rebière, *Femmes dans la Science*, 102–3.

44. Judith R. Goodstein, "The Rise and Fall of Vito Volterra's World," *Journal of the History of Ideas* 45 (1984): 607–17.

45. Modoni and Randi, "Donne ravennati," 168.

46. Fenaroli et al., "Women and Mathematical Research," 154.

47. Iginia Massarini, *Teoria delle congruenze di P. L. Tchebicheff, traduzione italiana con aggiunte e note* (Roma: E. Loescher, 1895).

48. *I venti a Roma* (Roma: Annali del R. Ufficio Centrale di Meteorologia e Geodinamica), vol. 27, 1905, part I; and *I venti a Roma*; *Memoria II* (Roma: Tipografia della R. Accademia dei Lincei, 1918).

49. Fenaroli et al., "Women and Mathematical Research" 148. Additional information about Predella Longhi was collected from notes in her publications.

50. Lia Predella Longi, *Elementi di Algebra ad uso della I Classe Normale,* 6th ed. (Torino: G. B. Paravia, 1917; first ed. 1899?; 2nd. ed., 1901).

51. "Intorno alla ricerca della cifra delle unità di una radice intera, di cui è noto il numero delle decine," *Supplemento al Periodico di Matematica* 4 (1901): 113–17; and "Intorno alla risoluzione dei problemi arithmetici," *Il Bollettino di Matematica* 1 (1902): 104–8; 128–35.

52. Kramer, *Maria Montessori*; E. Mortimer Standing, *Maria Montessori: Her Life and Work* (London: Hollis and Carter, 1958); and Gwendolyn Stevens and Sheldon Gardner, *The Women of Psychology. I. Pioneers and Innovators* (Cambridge, Mass.: Schenkman, 1982), 104–14.

53. For a sketch of the organization of secondary education in Italy, see note 35.

54. See note 36.

55. These included Jean-Jacques Rousseau, Jean Itard, Johan Pestalozzi, and Friedrich Froebel.

56. See note 2.

International Comparisons and Conclusions

In part because of the relatively late opening of universities to women in several European countries, more than two and a half times as many Americans as Europeans from the twelve countries surveyed here published research contributions in nineteenth-century scientific journals. Because the average productivity of the European group was not a great deal higher than that of the American group (3.4 papers per person in the United States compared to 3.9 in Europe), the total output of the Americans was much greater than that of the Europeans. As a whole, the Europeans had closer ties to established academic communities. The general standard of their scientific output was impressively high, reflecting solid and extensive professional training.

As measured by the Royal Society *Catalogue* entries, the most productive groups were the Italians, the French, and the Germans, followed by the Swedes and the Irish (Figure C-1).[1] The fields that received the largest numbers of contributions were botany, astronomy, zoology, and the medical sciences (here taken to include bacteriology, neurology, and physiology)—see Figure C-2. Figure C-3 makes clear the predominance of Italians in bacteriology, neurology/physiology, and botany, and their distinguished position in astronomy where they rank second only to the French in number of papers produced. Frenchwomen led the field in zoology also, with Swedes following closely.

A more detailed but condensed summary of numbers of papers, by field, produced by workers in nine of the twelve countries surveyed is presented in Figure C-4. This graph brings out a number of points: (a) in the three countries where women published the most—Italy, France, and Germany—contributions were spread over many fields; (b) contributions in botany came from all nine of the countries graphed, as well as from some

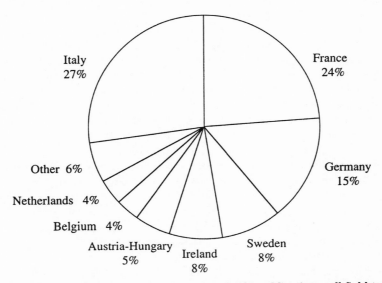

Figure C-1. Distribution of Western European women's scientific publications (all fields), by country, excluding Britain, 1800–1900. The sector "Other" represents papers from the following countries: Norway (2 percent), Switzerland (2 percent), Denmark (1 percent), Finland (< 1 percent), and Serbia < 1 percent). Data from the Royal Society *Catalogue of Scientific Papers*.

a. Authors   b. Papers

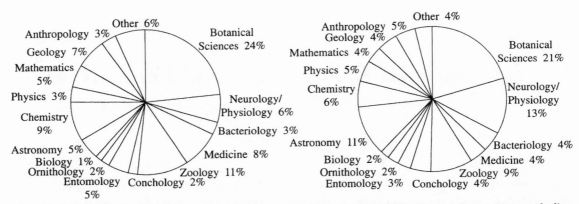

Figure C-2. Distribution of Western European women's scientific journal publications (all countries, excluding Britain), by field, 1800–1900. (In a., an author contributing to more than one field is counted in each.) The sectors "Other" represent authors and papers in the following fields: natural history (authors < 1 percent, papers < 1 percent), meteorology (authors 2 percent, papers 2 percent), geography (authors 2 percent, papers < 1 percent), and psychology (authors < 1 percent, papers < 1 percent). Data from the Royal Society *Catalogue of Scientific Papers.*

of those grouped into "Other"; (c) interest in both chemistry and zoology was widespread, although somewhat less than in botany; (d) interest was notably limited in some fields, contributions in conchology coming from only two countries—Italy and Ireland—and in anthropology from three—Italy, France, and Germany. Papers classified in the fields ornithology, general biology and natural history, meteorology, and psychology, none of which is shown separately in Figure C-4, constituted relatively minor additions to the European output.

There are a number of parallels and contrasts between the European choices of subjects and the most popular fields for early women scientists in Britain and the United States (see Figure C-5). Thus, the percentage of the total European output between 1800 and 1901 that consisted of work in the botanical sciences is somewhat lower than the corresponding percentages for the United States and Britain. However, the differences are relatively minor—21 percent in Europe compared to 28 percent and 24 percent, respectively, for the United States and Britain; the corresponding author counts are 23 percent for Europe, 27 percent for the United States, and 23 percent for Britain. In all three groups, botany was the field where women's activity was greatest. The somewhat higher percentage output in the United States could well reflect the fact that large stretches of botanically unexplored territory still awaited the attention of American workers in the late nineteenth century, especially in the western parts of the country. More than half of the United States botanical papers dealt with classification and regional studies. In Europe far less field exploration remained to be carried out; opportunities for such work tended to be in the more inaccessible regions such as the Alps and the Arctic tundra. In all three groups, cryptogamic studies formed a significant fraction of the total botany output. In Europe cryptogamic work was especially important in Italy in the middle years of the century, in Belgium in the 1820s, and in both Belgium and the Netherlands/Dutch East Indies in the 1880s and 1890s (see Figs. 4-2 and 8-2). Notable cryptogamic studies in Ireland came just after the turn of the century.

Considering medicine and its related sciences (bacteriology, neurology, and physiology), we find a considerably greater emphasis on these areas among Europeans than among the Americans and British. European papers amounted to 21 percent of the total publication output while the corresponding numbers for the Americans and British were 9 percent and 8 percent respectively. Italian bacteriologist Giuseppina Cattani and French-American neurologist Augusta Dejerine-Klumpke were leading contributors among the Europeans; Cattani's great productivity in tetanus research, in fact, determines Italy's position as the leading Western country for pre-1901 bacteriology research by women.

In astronomy, the field that ranks third in paper count for the European workers, contributions from Italy and France were again especially notable. However, in neither the continental West European countries nor Britain were there opportunities to work in astronomy comparable to those offered by several of the women's colleges and a few coeducational universities in the United States.[2] The publication counts as percentage of total

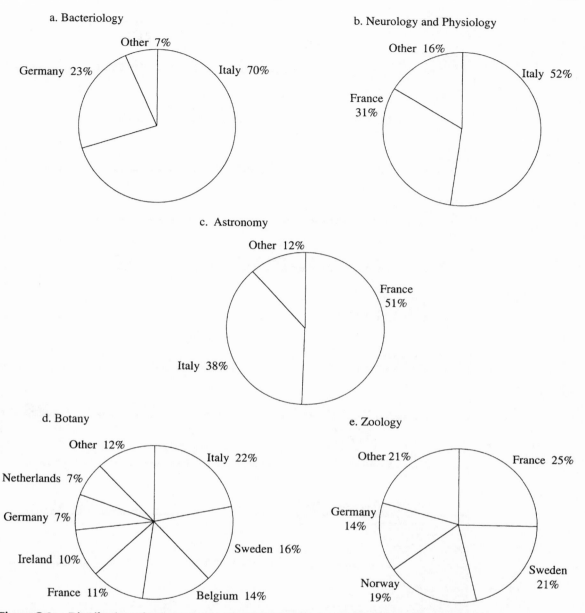

a. Bacteriology

Other 7%
Germany 23%
Italy 70%

b. Neurology and Physiology

Other 16%
France 31%
Italy 52%

c. Astronomy

Other 12%
France 51%
Italy 38%

d. Botany

Other 12%
Netherlands 7%
Germany 7%
Ireland 10%
France 11%
Italy 22%
Sweden 16%
Belgium 14%

e. Zoology

Other 21%
France 25%
Germany 14%
Norway 19%
Sweden 21%

Figure C-3.   Distribution of papers, by country, for five areas in which the most productive Western European national groups were especially active, 1800–1900. Data from the Royal Society *Catalogue of Scientific Papers.*

output for the three regional groupings are not grossly dissimilar (United States 12 percent, Europe 11 percent, and Britain 8 percent).

Continuing the three-region comparison, the greatest productivity in zoology was in the United States, contributions there constituting 15 percent of the total American output compared to 9 percent in Europe and 6 percent in Britain. The kind of work being done in Ireland, Norway, and Sweden closely paralleled that in the United States at the time; in all four of these countries, it was to a large extent concerned with analysis of material brought back by major national marine exploratory and collecting expeditions of the period and for the most part was carried out in large national museums.

Somewhat more of a contrast is evident in entomology; European papers in this field amount to only 3 percent of the total, whereas in the United States and Britain the figures are 13 percent and 14 percent respectively. There is a striking parallel between the work of the two agricultural entomologists Eleanor Ormerod in

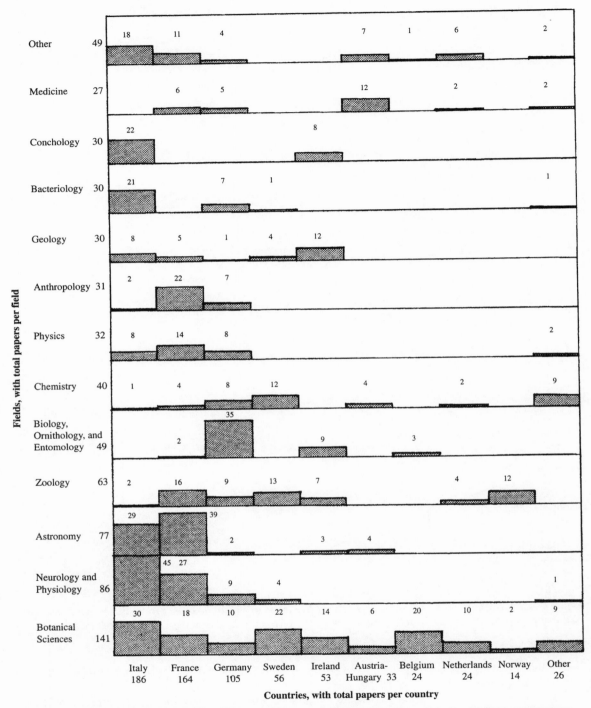

Figure C-4. Distribution of papers by field and country for Western Europe, excluding Britain, 1800–1900. The column labeled "Other" represents: Switzerland (11 papers), Denmark (8 papers), Finland (6 papers), and Serbia (1 paper). The row labeled "Other" represents: mathematics (25 papers), meteorology (12 papers), geography (6 papers), natural history (3 papers), and psychology (3 papers). Data from the Royal Society *Catalogue of Scientific Papers.*

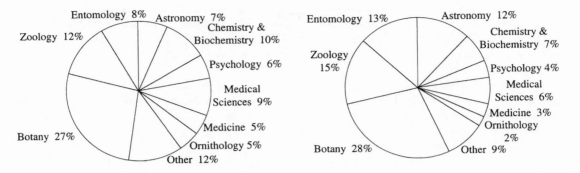

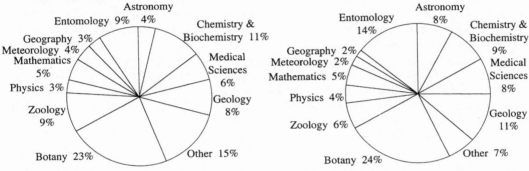

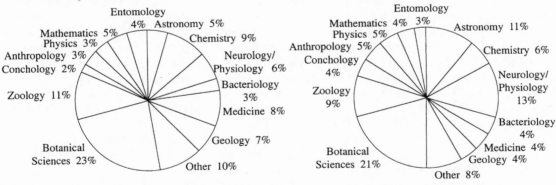

Figure C-5. Distribution of women authors and their scientific journal publications (United States, Britain, and Western Europe), by field, 1800–1900. (In a., c., and e., an author contributing to more than one field is counted in each.) The sectors "Other" represent authors and papers in the following fields where the contributions are less than 2 percent (except as noted): United States—anthropology, biology, conchology (authors 2 percent), geography, geology, mathematics, meteorology, natural history, physics, and technology. Britain—anthropology, biology, conchology, medicine (authors 3 percent), natural history (authors 4 percent), ornithology (authors 2 percent), psychology, and technology. Western Europe—biology (papers 2 percent), geography (authors 2 percent), meteorology, natural history, ornithology (authors 2 percent, papers 2 percent), and psychology. For American and British authors and papers, the sectors "Medical Sciences" include anatomy, bacteriology, neurology, physiology, and pathology. Data from the Royal Society *Catalogue of Scientific Papers.*

Britain and Sofie Rostrup in Denmark, although most of Rostrup's work came after 1900, by which time Ormerod's career had come to a close.

Interest in psychology was considerably greater in the United States than in Europe. Very few Western European women contributed to that field before 1900, even in Germany, the leader for research in the area during the latter decades of the nineteenth century. Ninety percent of all the pre-1901 papers by women were by Americans, many of whom had received their training at German universities or were students of American men who had done so.

The notable contribution of British women to geology research finds no parallel among the continental West European women, although the field was one of great activity at the time in both France and Germany as well as in Britain.[3] Indeed work in geology, making up 11 percent of all British women's research output between 1800 and 1901, stands out as a special case. The field ranks third only to botany and entomology in number of papers published.

In one other area, namely mathematics and mathematical physics, there was no Continental equivalent of the opportunity provided in Britain by Cambridge University, where a cluster of students from Newnham and Girton women's colleges trained in these fields in the late nineteenth century. Prussian universities, such as Göttingen and Berlin, then famous worldwide as centers of mathematical research, were only beginning to accept women students. In Italy, whose universities were also outstanding centers of late nineteenth-century mathematical research, increasing numbers of women were studying the subject at university level by the 1890s, but relatively few went on to publish original work.

Among the points of interest that emerge from this survey the following might be noted:

First, Stockholm Högskola, as early as the 1880s, provided important opportunities for Swedish women who aspired to a scientific education, even though considerable resistance to the employment in Sweden of able women graduates in university teaching and research persisted well past the turn of the century, the case of mathematics lecturer Sofia Kovalevskaia at the Högskola notwithstanding.

Second, of the women included in this study, a remarkable number came from the eastern borders of the region surveyed and a few were immigrants from even further east. In this eastern subgrouping, twelve were medical women (Rabinowitsch-Kempner from Lithuania, Democh-Maurmeer, Glause, Herbig, and Willdenow from areas now part of Poland, Shlykova-Kerschbaumer from Moscow, Moraczewska and three Welt sisters from a region now part of the Ukraine, Pompilian from Romania, and Steinlechner-Grechishnikova from Serbia). Two notable zoologists, Plehn and Hamburger, came from cities now in Poland. Among the chemists discussed were six from the eastern region—the fourth Welt sister, Baum from Danzig, Immerwahr-Haber from Breslau, Silesia (now in Poland), Goldberg-Ullmann and von Wrangel (of Baltic-German stock) from Moscow, and Sesemann from Finland. Two physicists, Sklodowska-Curie and Bohm-Wendt, were from, respectively, Warsaw and Troppau, Silesia (now in the Czech Republic). The powerful drive for higher education among the daughters of the Russian middle classes, widespread from the 1860s on, spilled over the borders of the empire, influencing women in neighboring states. This early push for higher education for women in Russia, strengthened by more ready access for girls to secondary-level state schools there, took place almost three decades before similar movements in the German-speaking countries.

Third, the well-known special role of the Swiss universities in providing advanced technical training for women is again very apparent. Zurich and Bern with their politically liberal faculties stand out particularly. For many women, a Swiss degree was the only route for entry to a career in scientific research or medical practice.

Who in this collection of leading women scientists in Western Europe (excluding Britain) was specially noteworthy? Aside from Nobel Prize winner Marie Curie, the following stand out as being particularly productive and influential as research workers: German fish pathologist Marianne Plehn, Italian freshwater biologist Rina Monti, Danish agricultural entomologist Sofie Rostrup, and German-Lithuanian bacteriologist Lydia Rabinowitsch-Kempner. Both Plehn and Monti made internationally recognized contributions to emerging fields, Plehn being acknowledged as one of the founders of freshwater fish pathology and Monti being seen as a leader in comprehensive, cross-disciplinary ecological studies of freshwater lake systems. Rabinowitsch-Kempner's role in early tuberculosis research is now well documented and the pioneering work of Sofie Rostrup in the Danish agricultural community acknowledged. The very productive Norwegian zoologist and geneticist Christine Bonnevie was also well known in her areas, as was Dutch algologist Anna Weber van Bosse. Swedish botanist Astrid Cleve von Euler, another very productive scientist, had a national reputation as a diatom specialist, and self-taught German physicist Agnes Pockels carried out important pioneering work in surface tension research. Three others, whose work was more in the social sciences, might be mentioned—self-taught German archaeologist Johanna Mestorf, a notable figure in early North German prehistory research, Marie

Baum, a nationally recognized pioneer in German workers' welfare and industrial health issues, and Italy's Maria Montessori, the well-known founder of the Montessori method of early childhood education. Interestingly enough, only three of these eleven specially noteworthy people were Swiss educated—Plehn, Rabinowitsch-Kempner, and Baum; two—Mestorf and Pockels—were self-taught; and the others were among the earliest women graduates of long-established universities in their own countries. Each of them had a generous endowment of ambition and talent, tremendous capacity for and enjoyment of hard, sustained work, and the confidence when young to follow a path beyond the more conventional ways for women of their time. Further, most of them were entering new fields, as yet barely existing fields, or sparsely populated areas of old fields; Montessori acquired fame by pioneering a new method.

Footnote

Although this volume is focused squarely on West Europeans, it is perhaps of interest to bring to the fore some additional points emerging from the quantitative data in the two parts of the survey now on hand—that is, data reported in *Ladies in the Laboratory?* plus the material now offered.

If we merge the data for Britain with numbers for the twelve other European countries considered here we have a combined author count of 433, compared to 409 for the United States, and a combined paper count of 1,576 compared to 1,398 for the United States. Thus the number of women in the combined British–West European group publishing work in science between 1800 and 1901 was comparable to that for the United States, but their output was measurably greater. Taking the comparison a stage further by adding Russia and Poland to the British–Western European combination, we find that the total British–Western European–Eastern European combination has an author count of 544, and an article count of 1,935, both numbers significantly higher than the counts for the United States (see Figure 0-1). This data might be of interest in United States–European comparative studies of women's activity in science during the nineteenth century.

A glance at the numbers also makes clear the fact that more than a quarter (26 percent) of the scientific journal papers published by women between 1800 and 1901 came from a relatively small island nation off Europe's western shores, namely Britain. Indeed, to a large extent this contribution came from England, the lower two thirds of that island.

Women's success in entering into scientific work at this early period depended on a fairly complex mix of circumstances. Important factors included economic conditions, particularly the existence of a reasonably prosperous middle class, the social and political structure of the country being considered, social norms on which, in general, educational opportunities depended, and, not least, the vigor of the male scientific community and the areas in which this community's activity was greatest. Compared to these factors, more obvious considerations such as the size of the country and its population are relatively irrelevant. Without detailed knowledge of the conditions in each country during the nineteenth century it is no doubt perilous to attempt generalizations. Nevertheless by the last two decades of the century, when women's participation in scientific research had reached its nineteenth-century zenith, the industrial revolution was well underway and wealth was accumulating not only in Britain but in major cities of Western Europe and the United States as well. Late Victorian Britain, however, "the workshop of the world" and the center of a large and vigorous colonial empire, stands out among other countries for the accomplishments of its women scientists. (The one area in which British women lagged markedly behind their continental sisters was in medical training.)

This remarkable success in entering into scientific work ultimately relates back to the fundamental social, political, and economic changes and upheavals that came about in Britain as it underwent its development into a world power and the world's first industrialized society. An examination of these underlying factors, with the necessary interweaving of the details of local circumstances, movements, and key personalities that engineered the women's success is beyond the scope of the present survey. The current lively interest in the history of nineteenth-century British science, and in particular the effort to bring out the roles of hitherto relatively neglected participants, including women, will undoubtedly shed new light on the subject. The story of British women's accomplishments in scientific work might be only a minor note in the overall history of late nineteenth-century British society, but it could well be necessary eventually to consider the broader underlying issues suggested above if satisfactory comparisons with women working in other countries are to be reached.

Notes

1. As pointed out in the first part of this survey (Creese, *Ladies in the Laboratory?*, Preface and Introduction, xii, n. 3), the process of producing a count of published papers, although it might at first sight appear mechanical given an appropriate

bibliographic list, is in fact not so. Choices have to be made and judgment exercised. For instance, should a preliminary note be counted when a full discussion of the same work follows a year later? Should continuations of reports in consecutive (or almost consecutive) journal issues be considered as additional publications? Should simultaneous reports published in several countries (in several languages) be counted as one publication? Reasonable answers to these questions depend on the details in each case.

Some of the numbers given in the graphs in this second part of the survey differ slightly from those offered in part 1. This is due mainly to the uncovering of more information concerning country of origin of contributors; recounts and the discovery of a few people in the Royal Society *Catalogue* missed in the main reading led to further minor adjustment.

2. A few women in both France and Britain worked, before the turn of the century, on the international photographic sky-mapping project known as *Carte du Ciel*—see chapter on French women above and Mary T. Brück, *Agnes Clerke and the Rise of Astrophysics* (Cambridge: Cambridge University Press, 2002), 175–88.

3. Mary R. S. Creese and Thomas M. Creese, "British women who contributed to research in the geological sciences in the nineteenth century," *British Journal for the History of Science* 27 (1994): 23–54, especially 52–54.

Appendix

Mentioned here are six Americans—Mary Banning, Olivia Rodham, Mary Pike Robbins, Lottie Steffens Hollister, Laura Steffens Suggett, and Harriet Richardson—eight British women—Alice Bodington, Eliza Brightwen, Sarah Bowdich Lee, Mary Morris, Rosina Zornlin, Agnes Kelly, Maja Knecht, and Edith Saunders—and one whose nationality is uncertain but who was active in the British naturalist community in Bombay, India—Mrs. Lisboa. Five of the Americans, three of the British (Knecht, Morris, and Zornlin), and Mrs. Lisboa were omitted from the first volume of this survey;[1] Bodington was incorrectly assumed to be American. Additional information has been found about Richardson, Kelly, Bowdich Lee, and Saunders. Brightwen has been added because as a naturalist she is an unusual and interesting character.

American Women

MARY ELIZABETH BANNING[2] (1822–1903), a mycologist and botanical illustrator, was born on 6 April 1822, the youngest of the nine children of Robert Banning and his second wife Mary (née Macky), also called *Maria*. She grew up on the family's small plantation not far from the town of Oxford, Maryland, on the eastern shore of the Chesapeake Bay. The Bannings were moderately well-to-do. Robert Banning was prominent in state and local affairs, serving as Collector of Customs for several years and as a member of the state general assembly during a number of sessions. He was also one of the earliest members of the Maryland Agricultural Society.

Mary Banning is thought to have had a good education for a girl of her time; either as a child or later her studies included Latin. Her interest in natural history and fungi in particular ("toad stools") began at an early age, perhaps as a result of childhood rambles through the fields and woods surrounding her home. Brought up in the Episcopal church, she remained deeply religious all her life. She was also much concerned about the education of young people.

Some time after the death in 1845 of Robert Banning, Mary, her mother, and her half-sister Catherine, her lifelong friend and companion, moved to Baltimore, taking up residence in a pleasant neighborhood of the city. Mary remained in Baltimore for more than three decades and it was during this time that she carried out the work that resulted in her book of paintings of the fungi of Maryland, her major contribution to botanical research.[3] A considerable burden of domestic duties also fell to her over these years, her mother dying in the early 1870s and her sister in 1885, both after periods of illness. Nevertheless her botanical investigations were extensive and carried out with great care and conscientiousness. Banning's initial inspiration for her undertaking appears to have come from a combining of her ideas about religion with her thoughts about the education of the young. Seeing natural history as one of the tools provided by God to teach the faith and cultivate "minds and morals," she intended her book for "educational training in a mission school."[4] As time went on, her fascination with the organisms increased and the studies became more and more a pleasure and an absorbing recreation.

Fungi of Maryland is a collection of bright, watercolor paintings, each a balanced, well-designed picture in full color with an arrangement of mosses, grasses, and small flowers surrounding the fungal form being represented. Although perhaps somewhat formal and idealized by later standards, the pictures have a brilliant and vibrant quality that makes them especially striking and attractive. Extensive field notes that accompany the paintings present detailed accounts of Banning's collecting trips in the countryside around Baltimore, not always easy expeditions, particularly those into the wilder areas where the rarer fungi were to be found. Included in the notes are descriptions of the landscape and lively anecdotes about the country people she met. Among the species depicted are *Hydnum imbricatum, Boletus luridus, Coprinus micaceus, Clitocybe illudens, Amanita nitidus, Phallus daemonum (Dictyophora duplicata),* and *Lactarius indigo.*

While she was collecting she frequently visited the library of Baltimore's Peabody Institute,[5] but the help she relied on for taxonomic determinations was that provided by Charles Peck, mycologist at the New York State Museum in Albany, New York. Probably the leading expert on North American fungi during the latter years of the nineteenth century, Peck helped and encouraged amateurs. Mary Banning never met him but they corresponded for thirty years; many of her specimens were sent to him at the museum, where they are still held. She dedicated her book to him and when, in 1890, arthritis and failing eyesight brought her studies to an end, she deposited the work at the museum. There it remained, along with her letters to Peck, undisturbed for almost a century until John Haines, a later museum mycologist, reintroduced her to the public, organizing an exhibition of the paintings at the museum in 1981 and another at the Talbot County Historical Association in Easton, Maryland, in 1986.

Banning described 175 species, twenty-three new to science. Some of the names have changed since her time but most of her descriptions can still be used for field identifications. Her published articles include three in the 1880–1881 *Botanical Gazette*; two more appeared in other semipopular journals (see bibliography). Of the new species she discovered, three are described in one of her articles and sixteen more were published by Peck in 1892 in the *Bulletin of the New York State Museum,* which also printed her catalogue of Maryland fungi.[6]

She gave up her house in Baltimore in 1890, probably for financial reasons. Much of her dried plant collection and some unfinished drawings were lost at this time. Her last years were spent in boarding houses in Winchester, Virginia. Despite increasing health difficulties and the constraints imposed by a meager income, she continued for a time to make trips into the countryside searching for fungi. However, isolated and without any close friends, she suffered considerably from depression. She died in Winchester on 28 February 1903, two months before her eighty-first birthday; burial was in St. John's churchyard, Baltimore.

A dedicated and energetic woman of remarkable talent, Mary Banning is considered a pioneer of fungus studies in Maryland. In 1994 she was elected to the Maryland Woman's Hall of Fame.

OLIVIA RODHAM[7] (1845–1920), another early American woman botanist from Maryland, was born on 17 September 1845 near Bel Aire in Huford County, about twenty miles north of Baltimore. She was one of at least two daughters in the family of Quaker farmers William Rodham and his wife Rachel (née Preston). Until about 1880 she remained on the farm, her childhood home. For a number of years she looked after her father, both her mother and her sister having died in the late 1860s, but the relationship between father and daughter gradually deteriorated and at age thirty-five Olivia Rodham abruptly left the farm.

She found work as assistant librarian and assistant in the botanical laboratory at Swarthmore College, a small, coeducational, Quaker college on the outskirts of Philadelphia, a city with a strong and closely linked Quaker community. In 1887 she became the college's acting librarian. However, having developed strong interests in botany, she resigned the following year in order to go to the University of Berlin, where she spent a year or two expanding her knowledge in the area of plant anatomy. Her paper on hitherto unreported septa in large vessels (tubelike structures) of the woody shrub *Tecoma radicans* appeared in the *Berichte* of the German Botanical Society in 1890; the *Botanical Gazette* printed a slightly abbreviated English translation the same year (see bibliography). She is said to have carried out additional botanical studies in Cambridge, England. When she returned to the United States in 1891, Swarthmore College awarded her an honorary B.A. degree.

That year she bought land, mainly rocky hill pasture, next to the village of Nelson in southern New Hampshire. Her property included a large barn, which she converted to living space and accommodation for the considerable collection of books she gradually amassed. Except during her later years, when she spent part of the winters with friends near New York, she lived in Nelson for the rest of her life. She traveled extensively throughout the United States and became very knowledgeable about the country's flora but also had strong interests in entomology and astronomy. Well read and skilled in several languages, both classical and modern, she had also studied medicine. Her linguistic abilities and broad scholarly competence brought her employment from publishing businesses, including work on the preparation of a medical dictionary and other lexicons.[8]

Olivia Rodham was the first of a number of naturalists, literary people, and artists, many of them friends from her Swarthmore College days, who bought land in the Nelson region around the turn of the century. Indeed the *Pennsylvania Settlement,* as this community was called, appears to have come into being because of Rodham's presence in the area. Over the years Headlong Hall, her renovated barn, was filled with artifacts and materials of an artistic or folk-culture nature brought back to her from many countries by her numerous friends.[9] She died in Nelson on 11 August 1920, a month before her seventy-fifth birthday, and is buried in the old

Nelson cemetery. Shortly after her death her friends and neighbors came together to build a library in Nelson to house her large collection of books. The Olivia Rodham Memorial Library now contains about 6,000 volumes.

Three papers by New England writer MARY CAROLINE ROBBINS, NÉE PIKE[10] (1842–1912) are listed in the bibliography in volume 1 of this survey,[11] but a biographical note on Robbins was not included.

The daughter of James Shepherd Pike, newspaper correspondent, editor, writer, and diplomat, and his first wife Charlotte Otis (née Grosvenor), she was born in Calais, Maine, in 1842. A coastal town on the St. Croix River that marks the boundary between the United States and New Brunswick, Canada, Calais was a place of great natural beauty; Maine's wooded hills and lake country formed its hinterland, and before it stretched fine coastal seascapes leading out to the Bay of Fundy. After attending schools in West Newton, Massachusetts, and Philadelphia, Mary Pike began to develop her special interest in art, taking up watercolor studies in New York. When she was in her early twenties, she spent several years in Europe, her father having been appointed United States minister to the Netherlands in 1861. Her art studies continued, first in the Netherlands and later (1874–1875) in Italy. After her marriage in 1881 to Harvard-trained physician James Henry Robbins (1839–1900), she lived mainly in Hingham, a Massachusetts coastal community about fifteen miles southeast of Boston. Robbins, also from Calais, Maine, was then a widower with one son who had recently established his practice in Hingham.

Mary Pike Robbins began her literary work in 1871–1872, when she coedited the short-lived, illustrated periodical *Wood's Household Magazine* with Mary Abigail Dodge.[12] However, the bulk of her writings appeared in the 1890s, a considerable fraction taking the form of articles in magazines such as *The Century Magazine, Garden and Forest,* and *The Atlantic Monthly.*

Her great interest was trees, from the character and characteristics of individuals to the mass effects of trees in woodland landscapes. This led to her concern for the development of parks and open spaces, then a matter of widespread and increasing interest throughout the country. Many of her articles described parks in New England, but she also wrote on a number of others, including Mount Royal Park, Montreal; park developments in Minnesota; and Lincoln and Jackson parks in Chicago (explored when she visited the 1893 World's Columbian Exposition). Her 1893 article "A Tree Museum" discussed the Arnold Arboretum in Boston, outlining its history and comparing it with other famous parks such as London's Kew Gardens.[13] The provision of scenic open spaces she felt should be a concern for all communities, from village improvement societies to large cities and states. Influenced by her background of study and training in art, she enthusiastically embraced the idea that America's parks might well become second to none: "The parks and park systems are the most important artistic work which has been done in the United States"; she saw the "Art of Public Improvement" as the area in which "we may hope to set an example to the world."[14] Further, at least in the smaller-scale projects, women had an active role to play in this work of environmental improvement.[15]

Mary Robbins's own considerable and sustained effort at neighborhood renewal, albeit on a limited scale, began in 1887 when she and her husband bought an abandoned farm, complete with tumbledown farmhouse, in the Hingham community. A venerable piece of property, its deed dated back two and a half centuries, to a 1634 colonial grant to one Matthew Cushing. In a series of twenty articles in *Garden and Forest,* she described how they renewed the old place, experimenting in landscape gardening with a great variety of trees, shrubs, and perennials, some grown from shoots and cuttings of plants in the original garden. Old-stock apple, pear, and plum trees were notable survivors from earlier times. Despite the initial pessimism of many of the local residents ("What does the doctor want with that forlorn old hole?"), the dilapidated farm was changed over the course of a few years from village eyesore to a neighborhood beauty spot. With the construction of a new dwelling house ("Overlea"), the site became their permanent home.[16]

Robbins's many nature-related writings of the 1890s were perhaps inspired by these "hands-on" efforts. However, during the preceding decade she had already brought out several scholarly works. Among them were her translations from the French of Eugène Fromentin's *Les maîtres d'autrefois: Beligique-Hollande* and Louis Gonse's biography of Fromentin, *Eugène Fromentin, peintre et écrivan,* the latter augmented with lengthy quotations from Formentin's writings. France's "painter of Algeria," Fromentin (1820–1876) was known for his magnificent, luminous depictions of North African landscapes but he was also a fine descriptive writer—a master of landscape painting in words. His immensely successful *Maîtres d'autrefois,* a combination of pure art criticism and descriptive writing, presented his thoughts on the Dutch and Flemish schools of painting. Robbins's English version included several excellent black-and-white reproductions of famous paintings by Rubens, Rembrandt, Vandyck, Ruysdael, and others. Her version of Gonse's biography, another competently executed translation well illustrated with black-and-white reproductions of Fromentin's North Africa sketches, remains of considerable value.[17] She also translated two fictional works—Victor Cherbuliez's *Le roman d'une honnête femme* and Henry Gréville's *Le comte Xavier.*[18]

Other articles by her include an address read before the Gaspee, Rhode Island chapter of the Daughters of the American Revolution and a joint publication with two other Massachusetts women on the question of suffrage for women.[19] Robbins was against the proposal to enfranchise women, arguing that limited voting rights were better for the country as a whole and that the great majority of women, and immigrant women in particular, were poorly qualified to exercise these rights. Mary Pike Robbins died on 5 November, 1912.

Two California women, Lottie Steffens Hollister and her sister Laura Steffens Suggett, were among a number of enterprising American women who studied psychology at German universities around the turn of the century. The group included Eleanor Gamble, Christine Ladd-Franklin, Margaret Smith, and the especially notable Lillien Martin, all of whom, along with the Steffens sisters, were students of Georg Elias Müller of Göttingen University, one of the leading experimental psychologists of the late nineteenth and early twentieth centuries.[20]

DOROTHY (LOTTIE) STEFFENS HOLLISTER[21] (1872–1956), whose paper in experimental psychology appeared in *Zeitschrift für Psychologie* in 1900 (see bibliography), has the distinction of being the first woman to be awarded a doctorate in psychology by Göttingen University.

Born on 26 October 1872 in Sacramento, California, Lottie, or *Dot* as she was also called, was the third child and second daughter of Joseph Steffens and his wife Elizabeth Louisa (née Symes). Of humble background, Canadian-born Joseph Steffens grew up in Illinois. After moving to California in 1862, he gradually worked his way up in the business world, latterly becoming a bank director and the president of the Sacramento Chamber of Commerce. A member of the Republican party, he was active in state and local politics. His British-born wife grew up in New Jersey; in the early 1860s she moved to San Francisco, where she worked as a seamstress. The best remembered of the Steffens family is Lottie's older brother Lincoln Steffens who became a journalist, editor, and author, well known as one of the "muckrakers" who exposed city and state government corruption in the early decades of the twentieth century.[22] By the late 1880s the Steffens family occupied a splendid, ornate, Victorian-style residence in Sacramento, the state capital; when sold to the state in 1903, this house became the governor's mansion.

After attending a newly established grammar school in Sacramento, Lottie Steffens and her sisters took classes at the University of California, Berkeley, and at Stanford University. She was among the first students to enroll at the latter institution, entering in 1891, the year it opened. Her A.B. degree was awarded in 1895.

Following the example of her brother who spent several years at European universities, including the University of Leipzig, Lottie, in company with her younger sister Laura, went to Leipzig in 1896. She spent a year there studying psychology, attending lectures by the distinguished Wilhelm Wundt among others. Moving to Göttingen in the spring of 1897 she became a student of Georg Müller in the Psychological Institute. Her dissertation research on the process of memorizing verse reported in her 1900 paper was an investigation of normal modes of learning, part of Müller's broad program of exploring part versus whole learning. Using a number of subjects, both German and English speakers, she studied the modifications of the normal modes that individuals adopt and the question of whether the normal mode is the most efficient.

Lottie Steffens did not use her psychology training in any professional way. Very soon after returning to California, she married John James Hollister, son of one of the early cattlemen in southern California. From then, her home was the old Hollister Adobe on Las Bolitas ranch in Goleta Valley, Santa Barbara, about ninety-five miles northwest of Los Angeles. Stock-raising had been the dominant activity in the region since the days when the large ranches were in the hands of the old, Spanish-Californian landowners; Las Bolitas was one of the most extensive land holdings in the state. Over the years, the family's interests expanded considerably, becoming the Hollister Estate Company, an important commercial enterprise. The business diversified. Lottie's son John J. Hollister (1901–1961), the oldest of her four children, developed a walnut and lemon orchard and managed the cattle operation in the section he had charge of from the 1930s. Lottie Hollister lived to see this son elected to the California State Senate in 1955. She died the following year when she was about eighty-four.

LAURA STEFFENS SUGGETT[23] (1874–1946), the youngest of the four children of Joseph Steffens and his wife Elizabeth Louisa (née Symes), was born in Sacramento, California, in 1874. As did her sister Lottie, she attended the new Sacramento grammar school and then studied at the University of California, Berkeley, and at Stanford University, which awarded her a bachelor's degree. In 1896, she and Lottie went to Germany for further studies. After a year at Leipzig University, where she concentrated on psychology, she moved to Göttingen, becoming a student of Georg Müller. Her long paper (1900; see bibliography) on the physiology and sensory psychology of weightlifting (*motorische Einstellung*) reported studies that might well have fulfilled the research requirements for a doctoral candidacy. However, she did not take the degree examination.

Two years after her return to California in 1900, Laura Steffens was appointed assistant librarian in the state library system that was then beginning to organize what eventually became the statewide network of free county libraries. Starting with a traveling library, the system gradually expanded from its base in Sacramento; for a number of years, Laura Steffens headed a section known as the *Extension Department.*

In 1918, a year after the death of her older sister Louise Steffens Suggett, Laura married her brother-in-law, Alan Suggett, a leading San Francisco orthodontist. Her work with the state county library system continued at least into the 1920s. She was also librarian at the Sutro Library in San Francisco about this time. Laura Steffens Suggett died in 1946, when she was about seventy-two.

A recent paper by D. M. Damkaer[24] provides information about marine biologist HARRIET RICHARDSON SEARLE (1874–1958) beyond that offered in the first volume of this survey.[25]

Over the course of two decades of activity in the area of isopod systematics at the United States National Museum in Washington, D.C., Harriet Richardson brought out about eighty publications, including several major monographs of lasting value; the work won her an international reputation as an isopod specialist. Nevertheless, despite her tremendous productivity and her many contacts with marine scientists both in the United States and overseas, she is a neglected figure in the annals of American women's work in science, especially when compared with her colleague Mary Jane Rathbun.[26] The fact that she gave up most of her professional work shortly after her marriage in 1913 and stopped publishing more than thirty years before her death in 1958 meant that there were no informative obituary notices. As is the case with some other notable women scientists of that era,[27] evidence of her considerable scientific contributions is for the most part to be found only in the technical literature.

The daughter of Charles F. E. Richardson and his wife Charlotte Ann (née Williamson), Harriet grew up in Washington, D.C., in the 1870s and 1880s. After attending the Friends School and Mount Vernon Seminary, both private Washington, D.C., institutions, she enrolled in 1892 at Vassar College for women in Poughkeepsie, New York. Active in student life as an undergraduate, she took part in several societies and social groups. Her contacts with her Vassar friends continued through the years and she returned to the college for many class reunions, including the fiftieth in 1946.

Harriet Richardson's work at the United States National Museum (a department within the Smithsonian Institution) began immediately after she received her B.A. degree from Vassar in 1896. Although a certain amount of work on isopods was being carried out in the United States at that time, the death of specialist William Stimpson in 1872 had left a vacuum never quite filled. Richardson moved into the area, publishing her first paper in 1897, a report of a new species of freshwater isopod from New Mexico.[28] Eight more reports followed over the next three years, including a very substantial monograph on North American Pacific Coast isopods in 1899.[29]

Awarded an M.A. degree by Vassar College in 1901, she continued her isopod studies, publishing at an impressive rate over the next thirteen years. Her reports averaged five per year, some being descriptions of new species and genera, others presenting her analyses of the many large collections she undertook to examine. In 1903 she received a Ph.D in zoology from Columbian University (now George Washington University) in Washington, D.C.; her dissertation research, a 266-page monograph "Contributions to the Natural History of Isopoda" dealing with isopods in the United States National Museum collections, was published in the institution's *Proceedings* the following year. Richardson's adviser, the eminent taxonomist Theodore Nicholas Gill, Professor of Zoology at Columbian University, continued to offer her advice and guidance throughout her succeeding undertakings. Her most important work, her 727-page "Monograph on the Isopods of North America," appeared as a National Museum *Bulletin* in 1905. One of six Richardson reports published that year, it was an outstanding survey of the systematics, distributions, habits, and literature for the terrestrial, freshwater, and marine isopods recorded in North America, including Greenland, Alaska, the West Indies, and Bermuda; a reprint issued in 1972 attests to its lasting significance.

Most of her studies dealt with isopods in collections housed in the National Museum, including the important material brought back by the United States Fish Commission steamer *Albatross.* However, she also reported on collections at the Philadelphia Academy of Natural Sciences, at the Marine Biological Laboratory in Woods Hole, Massachusetts, and at the Peabody Museum, Yale University. The international reputation she won for her remarkable output of high-quality work brought her requests to examine isopods in collections outside the United States, notably material in Dutch and French holdings. Over the course of her career at the National Museum, where she held successively the titles of collaborator in the Division of Marine Invertebrates and research associate, she examined collections made as far afield as the Antarctic, East Asia, the South Pacific, East and West Africa, and the Mediterranean. She described about seventy new genera and 300 new species of isopods and tanaids (a closely related group). More than a dozen genera and species have been named in her honor; representatives include the marine isopods *Amesopous richardsonae* Stebbing (1905), *Parionella richardsonae* Nierstrasz and Brender á Brandis (1923); *Munneurycope harrietae* Wolf (1962), and *Renocila richardsonae* Williams and Bunkley-Williams (1992).[30]

Harriet Richardson married William D. Searle, a Washington lawyer and a major in the U.S. Army, in 1913. Although she published a few more reports at intervals over the next thirteen years, her scientific work was drastically reduced from then on. From the birth in 1914 of her seriously handicapped son William, her time was given to his care. A member of the Biological Society of Washington, the Washington Academy of Sciences, and the Washington Society of Fine Arts, she was also active in the national women's organization, Daughters of the American Revolution. She died on 28 March 1958, two months before her eighty-fourth birthday. Both she and her husband, who outlived her by only half a year, are buried in Arlington National Cemetery.

British Women

Five of the women in this group—Bodington, Brightwen, Bowdich Lee, Morris, and Zornlin—are remembered now chiefly for their writing, but of these five, two—Sarah Bowdich Lee and Eliza Brightwen—were naturalists of considerable talent, Bowdich Lee making a number of original observations during her regrettably brief field experience in West Africa. Morris's essays on the early history of science-related subjects remain of considerable intrinsic interest and Zornlin's books on the earth sciences constitute notable early examples of successful introductory textbooks.

ALICE BROOKE BODINGTON[31] (1840–1897), classed as a psychologist in the first volume of this survey, is better considered a science writer and popularizer. An educated woman of English upper-class background, she had a wide range of interests. In the sciences, she particularly enjoyed biology; evolution and the tracing of evolutionary changes and adaptations though the fossil record were matters to which she gave much attention and, being a free-thinker in outlook, she was not bound by considerations of religion in her expositions.

Bodington felt strongly that scientific knowledge, "if it is to be of real service in eradicating ignorance and superstition, must be made clear and plain to many";[32] the nonspecialist writer who could present facts uncovered by specialists she considered well placed to do this work, which at the same time helped the development of science itself by creating the broader perspective necessary for there to be real progress. An enthusiastic admirer of the works of Irish writer and commentator Agnes Clerke,[33] she saw Clerke's *Popular History of Astronomy during the Nineteenth Century* (1885) as having given tremendous service to both astronomy and the public. Natural science, too, she felt, deserved to have its historians; results "should be proclaimed, not buried in the pages of scientific journals to be read only by specialists."[34] Perhaps inspired by Clerke's work, Alice Bodington, most likely in the late 1880s, began her own efforts in this area. Between about 1889 and 1897 she brought out a series of articles, some of them lengthy, on a variety of topics, but her major publication was her collection of essays, *Studies in Evolution and Biology*.[35]

Bodington's understanding of evolutionary theory was colored by her acceptance of the ideas of French naturalist Jean-Baptiste Lamarck, who postulated that organic evolution takes place via small, heritable modifications produced in an individual by its environment. Further, her writings suffered from her habit of introducing her own prejudices, such as her ideas about evolutionary "degeneracy." Nevertheless, her book presented a significant amount of generally reliable scientific information. She evidently kept abreast of research findings over a wide range of fields. Evolutionary change, especially adaptation in the animal world and the development of special features, such as the foot structure of the horse and eye position in specialized fishes, were discussed in detail. Also covered at some length was floral change through geological time, as revealed by coal measure studies; the need for an evolutionary tree for botany to match that already provided for the animal world had been the topic of one of her earliest publications (1889; see bibliography). Perhaps her most successful essay was that on recent findings in bacteriology, where she discussed the discovery in the early 1880s by Berlin scientist Robert Koch and others of the bacterial causes of infectious diseases, a matter of considerable public importance. Despite its apparent usefulness the work did not escape some severe criticism. A reviewer in the journal *Nature Notes* felt it suffered from her obvious lack of any practical scientific experience. Her treatment of fungi, which she found generally "repulsive,"[36] aroused the reviewer to remark that it "would hardly have been written by a practical naturalist" and to imply that it suggested more than a little intellectual arrogance on Bodington's part.[37]

Her notes and papers, published for the most part in the *American Naturalist, The Journal of Microscopy and Natural Science,* and *The Westminster Review,* dealt with a variety of topics from the adaptations and habits of water insects (as reported by others), to the occurrence of insanity in royal families, to her thoughts on such subjects as religion and race.

In contrast to several women science popularizers, including Rosina Zornlin (p. 228), Bodington outspokenly rejected religion; as an "evolutionist," she found religion lacked "a basis of truth on which we can firmly plant our feet . . . it can give no permanent support, no real comfort."[38] Her essay on race relations, although suggested by the much debated "Negro question" in the United States, took a form somewhat surprising to a twenty-first-century reader. For the most part, it consisted of an examination of relations between groups of European peoples from classical times on, offered as the basis of her argument in favor of the superiority of Anglo-Saxons and the desirability of a protective, paternalistic form of government for peoples of non-European origin. Here she was following closely the theories of Philadelphia-based palaeontologist Edward Drinker Cope and others. A well-known, if controversial, figure in American science at the time, Cope, on what to him were solid, scientific facts, ranked Anglo-Saxon males at the apex of the evolutionary tree. How Bodington reconciled Cope's relegation of women to an inferior role with her ideas of female equality remains obscure, but her many quotations from Cope's writings suggest considerable enthusiasm for his work.[39]

Alice Brooke Bodington was born in Athens in 1840, the only child of Francis Capper Brooke of Ufford Place, Suffolk, and his wife Juliana, who died shortly after Alice's birth. She was brought up at the Brooke family seat in Suffolk by a nurse and her paternal grandmother, a stern old lady who had strict ideas about child rearing. Married to a military man, General Bell, she had one son, but was subsequently divorced. Her writings indicate that she did some traveling in her younger years and was in Gibraltar (perhaps in her role as general's wife) in 1865 during an epidemic of Asiatic cholera among the troops of the British garrison. Later she became the second wife of George Fowler Bodington, a physician who specialized in mental disorders. With him, their three children, and one of George Bodington's daughters by his first marriage she immigrated to British Columbia in 1887.

After a year in Vancouver, the Bodingtons took up farming, moving fifty miles west along the Frazer valley to Hatzic, near Mission, where they cleared land and built a house. Contacts with local Indian people were frequent. Alice Bodington was much impressed by the songs, chants, and processions that accompanied the Indian religious observances at the nearby mission station, but she does not seem to have published her observations. Her "Notes on the Indians of British Columbia" reported information collected from British Columbia government officials on the way of life of the Indians several decades earlier when they first came into contact with European explorers and settlers. Published in the London popular journal *The Field Club* in 1893 (see bibliography), the article was prompted by her idea that knowledge of the lifestyle of these "Stone Age" peoples would provide a better understanding of the customs of Europe's Neolithic communities.

Perhaps not surprisingly, neither Alice nor her husband turned out to be suited to settler life. George Bodington was then in his sixties and Alice suffered much from neuralgia, which made her a semi-invalid for lengthy periods at a stretch. Remembered by her daughters as a cultivated woman and a delightful companion, she had no experience of housekeeping beyond directing servants. The hardships of pioneer farming pushed her into a depression that lasted throughout her remaining years. That she was able to write and publish during this period is remarkable. Although there was a regular postal connection with Britain and the Bodington household received a variety of news publications including illustrated magazines and the *British Medical Journal,* she was nevertheless considerably isolated; up-to-date science research reports must have been in short supply. However, Alice's considerable store of knowledge built up before she left England stood her in good stead; she might well have found her writing an escape from the deprivations of settler life—a link to the social and intellectual world she valued, but from which she was largely cut off.

In 1895, when George Bodington was appointed to the position of medical superintendent at the Provincial Asylum for the Insane in New Westminster, very close to Vancouver, the Bodingtons, to their great relief, sold the farm and moved back to a more urban setting. Alice died in New Westminster in 1897 at the age of fifty-seven.

Naturalist ELIZABETH ELDER BRIGHTWEN[40] (1830–1906), usually known as *Eliza Brightwen,* was born in Banff, on the northeast coast of Scotland on 30 October 1830, the fourth of six children of George Elder and his wife Margaret. At age four she was adopted by her father's brother Alexander, one of the founders of the London publishing firm of Smith, Elder and Co. From then on, she lived in the south of England and contacts with her siblings were few. Shy and timid, she had a lonely childhood; her uncle was kind but his wife, herself childless, little understood the needs of a young girl.

A few years after she arrived in London, the family moved to Thornbury Park, a ten-acre estate at Stamford Hill, Essex, then still very rural. Her formal education amounted to little more than music and drawing lessons, but she was encouraged to learn about nature. She spent most of her time in the estate's gardens, fields, and woods, and the large collection of natural history books in Alexander Elder's library supplied answers to her questions. Her special friend was a pet donkey, Shaggy Bray, given her when he was four months old. At age twelve she was sent to a nearby boarding school but she returned home after two months, ill from the effort expected of her. On Alexander Elder's retirement in 1847, the family left Thornbury Park and, after a short period exploring northern France, settled at Elderslie Lodge, Horley, Surrey.

In 1855 Eliza married George Brightwen, a clerk at a London bill broker's but within a short time co-manager of the London Discount Company. She regarded the marriage as happy but nevertheless from about then suffered increasingly from recurrences of nervous depression coupled with severe physical pain. By the standards of her social circle, she led a secluded life. But she was not inactive and did her share of voluntary parish work among the poor, undertook various social engagements with relatives and friends, and went on extended vacations with her husband, often to the Continent. About this time she came to know botanists Sir William Hooker and George Henslow. The publication in 1871 of her first book, *Practical Thoughts on Bible Study,* gave her much satisfaction; its appearance was not unconnected with the fact that her need for a formal connection with religion, unmet during childhood, was finally satisfied at her local church.

The Brightwens left their first home at Stamford Hill in 1872, George Brightwen having bought The Grove, a property of about 170 acres of woodland and lake near Stanmore on the Middlesex-Hertford boundary. At the same time however, Eliza's health difficulties intensified; she had a serious nervous breakdown accompanied by undiagnosed ailments that caused an almost complete physical collapse. Only after ten years, when her husband developed heart trouble, did she begin to recover enough to help with his care. Following his death in 1883 she began to gradually regain vitality and her early interests in natural history revived. The freedom she had as a wealthy widow and the responsibility of heading The Grove with its many resident employees and their families undoubtedly provided considerable stimulation. Her career as a naturalist might be seen as beginning at that time, when she was in her early fifties.

After exploring her estates gradually Eliza ventured further out into the surrounding woodlands. She was interested in everything in the natural world—vegetable, animal, and mineral—and slowly built up her own large museum of collections. Learning how to win the confidence of birds and animals, she acquired a vast number of animal friends and filled notebook after notebook with detailed, original observations; she considered an investigation completed only when she had uncovered the whole life history of whatever plant or animal currently held her interest and illustrated the story with finished, watercolor paintings. Birds, especially owls and lesser-known varieties, were always a great pleasure; some became household pets. Dead birds she collected for a careful study of their anatomy and she eventually placed the skulls in her museum. Among insects, coleoptera and diptera were special interests. The old woodlands of her estate were ideal hunting grounds for cryptogamic plants; the Mycetozoa, or slime moulds, particularly attracted her attention. Plant pollination by bees was another process she studied in detail. From 1889 she had help in her studies from a knowledgeable botanist, John Odell, who that year became her land steward.

Encouraged by her nephew Edmund Gosse,[41] in 1890 she offered a manuscript of her life-history stories to the publisher Fisher Unwin who immediately accepted it. *Wild Nature Won by Kindness,*[42] her first natural history book, was an instant success whose appearance changed her quiet, secluded life, bringing her correspondents from all over the country.

The great attraction of Eliza Brightwen's writing was her freshness and originality. Her "discoveries" had already been known and documented for a century but in one sense she privately and independently pioneered the field of nature study all over again, with tremendous energy and enthusiasm:

> Happily she was never aware how much had already been noted down, beyond all movement of further curi-
> osity, in the note-books of science. She set out, with brimming spirits, to do that pioneer work all over again.
> I remember hearing Sir William Flower remark, with an amusing archness, what a pity it was that so much
> was already known about the phenomena of Natural History, since it deprived Mrs Brightwen of the credit
> she deserved as a discoverer.[43]

Written in a bright, easy style and illustrated with her own excellent sketches, *Wild Nature* was widely considered the most popular natural history book published in 1890;[44] it ran to several editions and eventually sold 20,000 copies. Fisher Unwin brought out a German edition in 1892 and much of the material was later translated into Swedish. The fact that she refrained from including the moral and religious advice at that time frequently and persistently interwoven into nature study books made the work all the more acceptable to its intended audience of young readers, for whom such messages were sometimes unacceptable.[45] In addition to its biographies of wild creatures, the book offered sound, practical advice on such subjects as how best to observe nature and how to feed birds throughout the seasons.

Eliza Brightwen's second natural history work, *More about Wild Nature,* appeared in 1892; it was followed by four more (as well as a revised edition of *Wild Nature*) before her death in 1906: *Inmates of My House and Garden* (1895), *Glimpses of Plant Life,* an introduction to botany that incorporated many of her early investigations (1897), *Rambles with Nature* (1899), and *Quiet Hours with Nature* (1904). After her death Edmund Gosse brought out *Last Hours with Nature* (1908), a collection of her previously published articles and last nature-study records; the articles, many of which had appeared in *The Girls' Own Paper* and the Selborne Society's *Nature Notes,* included her writings in support of the campaign to halt the killing of birds to supply feathers for hat manufacturers. In 1909 Gosse published her autobiographical writings.[46]

The many demands made on Brightwen's time and energy after she became widely known were met with great generosity provided the cause was deserving and even though she regretted the sacrifice of work opportunities they imposed. She opened her grounds and museum to groups of poor city women and girls on holiday excursions, presented natural history talks to local organizations, lectured in local schools on such subjects as not robbing birds' nests, and answered her considerable correspondence. As the years advanced, religion became more and more important to her, markedly influencing daily life in the Grove household.[47] Parish work and church foreign missions remained major concerns throughout her life; she served as the local secretary for the Church of England Zenana Missionary Society and gave generously to its causes, supporting a bed called "The Brightwen" in St. Catherine's Hospital, Amritsar, India. Her special interest in the history of Palestine and life in the Holy Land was furthered by the close contacts she cultivated with people who knew the region well. The collection of Holy Land artifacts and fine pictures in a section of her museum attracted many visitors and her talks on Palestine drew large audiences. *Side Lights on the Bible: Scripture and Eastern Life,* her second Bible-study book, appeared in 1890. She died of cancer in the summer of 1906, in her seventy-sixth year, after a few months of marked decline; burial was in the Stanmore churchyard.

Even though her work cannot be said to have advanced knowledge in natural history, Eliza Brightwen was nevertheless a reliable observer and a capable naturalist with a remarkable breadth of interests. She was an active member of the Selborne Society, a natural history group established in 1885, and served as one of its vice presidents from 1890. She also belonged to the Entomological Society and the Zoological Society. Her very successful writings bringing natural history to a young audience and her activities in support of early wildlife protection efforts give her an honorable place in the naturalist community of the late nineteenth century.

A 1999 paper by Donald de Beaver[48] provides many additional details about the life and career of SARAH BOWDICH LEE (1791–1856) beyond the information offered in the first volume of this survey.[49]

Sarah Eglonton Wallis, the only daughter among three children of property owner Jonathan Eglonton Wallis and his wife heiress Sarah Vaughn of Colchester, Essex, was born in that town on 10 September 1791. Sometime after 1806 the family moved to London in much-reduced circumstances, Jonathan Wallis having gone bankrupt in 1802. Sarah married Bristol-born Thomas Edward Bowdich (1791–1824) in 1813, seemingly against the wishes of her parents.

Thanks to the help of an uncle, a senior officer in the British African Company, Thomas Bowdich received a commission and a writership in the company's service and in 1815 was sent to the Gold Coast (now Ghana); a year later Sarah with her infant daughter followed him only to find when she arrived on "The Coast" that he had already left for the return journey. Shortly after, on Bowdich's second West Africa assignment, the family returned to the Gold Coast and Bowdich led a successful company mission into the country's unexplored interior Ashanti region, the purpose being to establish good trading relations between the British and the then powerful Kingdom of Ashanti. His account of the venture, *Mission from Cape Coast Castle to Ashantee* was published in 1819.

Having always been more interested in geography, natural history, and all branches of culture than in commercial and administrative affairs,[50] Bowdich resigned from the African Company to devote himself to the more congenial fields of science and exploration; the great blank spaces then on the map of Africa presented an exciting challenge to Europeans. To prepare himself for the work he corresponded with the leading men in the field at the time and in 1819 moved his family to Paris to study at the Muséum National d'Histoire Naturelle, there joining other aspiring young explorers drawn by the museum's rich collections and the sizable group of *savants* in the Paris community.[51] The Bowdichs were well received, Alexander von Humboldt, then resident in the city, and Georges Cuvier becoming their mentors. Anxious to broaden their areas of competence, they also learned Arabic.

As part of their effort to find money for their planned expedition they translated several of Baron Cuvier's works into English, Sarah preparing the black-and-white illustrations with ever-increasing skill. Additional literary work included Bowdich's account of Portuguese discoveries in Angola and Mozambique[52] and their very successful *Taxidermy*, most of it written by Sarah, which appeared in 1820; reissued five times under Sarah Bowdich's name, the last revised, enlarged edition appeared in 1843. In 1820 both Bowdichs were given honorary membership in the Wetterauische Gesellschaft für die Geschichte der Naturkunde, one of the oldest natural history societies in Germany founded in 1808 in Hanau, near Frankfurt am Main. Sarah was recognized for her knowledge of botany and zoology, Thomas Edward for his research and his status as a West Africa expedition leader.

Although alleviated somewhat by grants from the Royal Literary Fund and the African Association,[53] the Bowdichs' financial difficulties remained. Nevertheless they left Lisbon for West Africa in the summer of 1822 only to be forced, because of a missed connection, to spend a year en route in Madeira. Their time there was put to good use however, and numerous natural history studies carried out. Their third and last child, daughter Eugenia, was born on the island. A month after they arrived in Gambia Sarah was left a widow, Thomas Bowdich dying in January 1824. The specimens she collected during her three-month wait for passage home with her children were lost in a storm during the voyage, wiping out her hope of raising money by their sale.

With financial help from several friends and supporters and from the Royal Literary Fund, Sarah undertook to prepare for publication her husband's records of their year in Madeira and she went to Paris to get help in the work from von Humboldt and Cuvier. *Excursions in Madeira and Porto Santo* appeared in 1825. It contained three additional sections by Sarah, including an account of the African extension of the trip, outstanding illustrations, and translations from Arabic writings. Cuvier credited the Bowdichs with the discovery of twenty-two new species and one new genus of fishes, and eight new species of birds, some of the new species undoubtedly found by Sarah after her husband's death.

Although she married Robert Lee in 1826 money difficulties continued and to augment family income she began contributing travel stories, often supplemented with full natural history notes, to various popular periodicals, such as publisher Rudolph Ackermann's annual gift book *Forget-Me-Not* and Thomas Pringle's *Friendship's Offering*. Between 1824 and 1832, she visited Paris several times, maintaining her contacts with continental naturalists, especially Baron Cuvier with whom, over the years, she became close friends. For a time she acted as a Paris journal correspondent; her nineteen-page report of Cuvier's talk to the Paris Academy of Sciences on progress in natural history during 1828 appeared in an 1829 issue of the *Magazine of Natural History* and was followed, at the editor's request, by a description of the Muséum National d'Histoire Naturelle.

Largely at the urging of publisher Ackermann, between 1828 and 1838 Sarah brought out by subscription her *Fresh-Water Fishes of Great Britain*. Fifty copies were produced, in twelve fascicules, at fifty guineas each. Each fascicule contained four watercolor plates, painstakingly prepared by hand, that were remarkable for their almost photographic quality. The undertaking represented a massive investment of time and talent; each fish was painted from life to ensure the best possible color representation and the accompanying text, which included a few original observations, was thoroughly reliable. Considerably more than exceptional art, the work remained of scientific interest for over a century.

In 1833, a year after Georges Cuvier's death, Sarah Lee published her 369-page biography, *Memoirs of Baron Cuvier*. Having been a close friend of the family, she was much affected by Cuvier's death and, well placed to discuss his contributions to natural history and describe his personality, she wished to be the first in print. The work was well received and a French translation brought out promptly.[54]

For much of 1838 and 1839 her writing activities were interrupted, her time being taken up by nursing her mother through her last illness. Because her brother was the main beneficiary from her mother's estate, her financial situation remained precarious. Consequently, from about 1840, she turned more and more to producing popular short stories, novels, and natural history works for children and young people, her output increasing markedly. These works sold well; especially successful were her *Elements of Natural History* (1844), *Anecdotes of the Habits and Instincts of Animals* (1844), and *Anecdotes of the Habits and Instincts of Birds, Reptiles and Fishes* (1853). *Elements*, officially adopted for classroom use, became well known throughout the country; a second enlarged edition appeared in 1849 with additional printings in 1853 and 1855.[55] *Anecdotes of . . . Animals,* a popular work in the United States, as well as in Britain, was augmented with a second volume in

1845 and the two volumes remained in print for almost forty years. Two other works that sold particularly well were her novels *The African Wanderers; or, The Adventures of Carlos and Antonio* . . . and *The Australian Wanderers; or, The Adventures of Captain Spencer* . . . published in the late 1840s and reissued several times on both sides of the Atlantic until at least the 1880s.

In 1854 Sarah Lee's efforts to secure a Civil List pension finally succeeded. Her award of £50 a year for her "contributions to Literature" is notable because at the time most pensions to women were granted because the recipients were dependents of eminent men rather than deserving of recognition in their own right. Advised to leave London in early 1856 because of failing health, she died in Erith, Kent, on 22 September of that year at the house of her daughter Eugenia.

Naturalist, artist, and writer of remarkable energy, talent, and initiative, Sarah Bowdich Lee wrote for a livelihood, her natural history training with her first husband and her early experience in West Africa providing her inspiration and her major themes. Her need to earn income from writing, although it led to her success as a popular author of natural history books for young audiences, most likely reduced her scientific contribution. Nevertheless her achievement was exceptional for a woman of the first half of the nineteenth century; her manual on taxidermy, her additions to Thomas Bowdich's *Excursions in Madeira and Porto Santo,* and her *Fresh-Water Fishes* remained of scientific interest for many years.

MARY MORRIS (fl. 1880s, 1890s) had a special interest in the early history of trees, in particular, fruit trees. Her series of at least eight essays in the widely read London journal *Science-Gossip* between 1889 and 1891 presented a great deal of information on the occurrence and the spreading throughout Europe of nine species; the many uses to which the trees, their timber, and their fruits were put in earlier times she discussed in considerable detail. In the process, she put forward a number of points of general historical interest. These included the fact, mentioned in her first article, that although some of the fruit trees might well have been brought to Britain by the Romans, plantings later fell into neglect and the art of fruit growing was not reintroduced until the time of William the Conquer; the monks William brought with him are said to have started English orchards with transplants from their Normandy estates. By Henry VIII's time, after the long period of civil wars, a second reintroduction was necessary and many trees and bushes, together with vegetables, were brought over from the continent, particularly the Netherlands. Morris's essay on the chestnut tree was judged to be of sufficient interest to French audiences to warrant a translation being published promptly in the *Bulletin* of the Linnean Society of the North of France (see bibliography).

A cultured, well-informed, and widely read woman, Mary Morris took as her sources the many accounts of fruit-tree cultivation and use to be found in literature from the works of the classical writers on. Thus she drew on first-century Roman naturalist Pliny the Elder for early accounts of the mulberry and the closely associated production of raw silk, long a Persian monopoly in the Mediterranean region. Later writers she referred to included the thirteenth-century English monastic historian Matthew Paris[56] and the seventeenth-century landscape authority John Evelyn, F.R.S., from whose famous *Diary* she quoted at length in her article on the chestnut. Mentioning his own large barn framed entirely of chestnut timber and undoubtedly a handsome structure, Evelyn remarked that a large forest of chestnut was said to have thrived nearby as late as the twelfth century. Morris's own house, a substantial seventeenth-century structure, had a chestnut beam pronounced by a skilled workman to be "the hardest and soundest beam he had ever met with."[57] The wood had long been dropped from use in building construction by the nineteenth century.

Evelyn's treatise on forest trees, *Sylva,*[58] one of Morris's major sources for information on the walnut tree, provided a wealth of detail on the uses of that species for both its wood (prized in carpentry and cabinet-making) and its nuts. The cold-pressed oil from the nuts was considered superior to olive oil for culinary purposes while the second, heat-pressed fraction was used by artists, ink makers, and as a lamp fuel; not even the solid residue was discarded, but made into cakes and fed to pigs, sheep, and poultry. Walnut husks and roots were also valuable being even in early times extracted to yield a dye used by cabinet-makers to stain light woods; leaves were collected and burned as a source of potash. The account offers an interesting insight into the industry and ingenuity of a labor-intensive, preindustrial society, already long gone by Morris's time.

Her interests were not confined to botanical subjects and bygone methods of agricultural production. She also wrote about the origins and evolution through the ages of some common household implements of special concern to women, in particular pins, needles, and thimbles (see bibliography). Ordinary and familiar as these items now are, the story of their gradual development and changing uses still holds considerable interest for the present-day reader. Once again drawing on a variety of ancient records and old literary sources, Morris traced the evolution of the pin from its earliest known form as a largely ornamental bronze fastener of burial clothes found in ancient grave mounds, through sixteenth-century brass pins, to the eighteenth-century, large-scale manufacture in Britain following the introduction of the art of wiredrawing. Thanks to the cooperation of the London firm of Kirby, Beard and Co., Pin and Needle Makers to H.R.H. Alexandra, Princess of Wales, she was able to present the technical details of the nineteenth-century manufacturing process, from the brass wire preparation to the "silvering" and finishing. Her research evidently included a guided tour of one of the Kirby Beard factories.

The story of needles she outlined from their earliest appearance in ancient Phrygia and Egypt, where they were used exclusively for the embroidery of robes. Tapestry-making in Europe before the introduction in the ninth century of the tapestry loom was also done by needle, still a tool used only for a few special tasks. Morris concluded that needles were not employed in garment making until the fifteenth century and were probably not produced in England for 100 years after that. By Victorian times the manufacture in Britain of pins and needles was a fairly important industry, employing thousands of people, women as well as men; British-made needles, in their many specialized forms, were considered the best available worldwide.

Morris's essay on thimbles perhaps makes the most interesting story of all. She investigated examples from Europe, dating back to bronze thimbles of the fourteenth century held in German and Swiss museums and she rounded out her knowledge by consulting accounts in old German literary works and city records. Mid-fifteenth-century records of Nürnberg, for several hundred years one of the few centers of thimble production, indicated that thimble-makers there first belonged to the brass-workers' guild but by the mid-sixteenth century were important enough to form their own guild with a constitution establishing their privileges. The ensuing altercation with the brass-workers and the technical restrictions the latter succeeded in imposing must constitute an early example of labor–union clash. It had the beneficial effect, however, of stimulating the thimble-makers to devise new techniques that circumvented the restrictions and allowed them to survive as a trade. Their products, displayed in a Nürnberg museum, included examples of great beauty and fine workmanship from the sixteenth century; among them were gold thimbles inlaid with precious stones or decorated with elaborate inscriptions, intended more as jewels than as tools. Specimens found in Britain include bronze thimbles from the fifteenth century.

Although *The Girls' Own Paper,* the popular magazine in which these articles appeared, might seem an unlikely place in which to find technically oriented material, in Morris's day such serial publications, directed largely to female readers, often presented basic scientific information.[59] Encouraging women's interests in science and mathematics was part of the ongoing effort to improve the intellectual tone of society;[60] magazine space was often given to scientific subjects that were expected to be of special interest to women—a category into which Morris's essays on pins, needles, and thimbles fit very well. With her clear and direct style and her choice of what now seem somewhat unexpected topics, Mary Morris's historical essays remain of considerable interest; she and they deserve to be rescued from their present obscurity.

Following the philanthropic practice of many better off Victorian women, Morris was active in social work among the poor. Along with some women friends she ran a "ragged school," or free school for needy children, which was subsequently expanded to provide additional classes in sewing for girls and young women; the undertaking may well have increased her broader interests in the tools involved. Because those attending the sewing classes frequently had to bring their very young charges along with them, the program was further expanded to include a crèche. Helped by private donations and volunteer assistants and consultants, but run on the bare minimum of funds, this crèche had adequate and competent staff and was deemed a considerable success. Morris's 1897 description of the school and crèche provides a vivid and shocking glimpse of the dirt, the rags, the drunkenness, and the miserable standard of infant care among the working classes in late Victorian London.

ROSINA ZORNLIN[61] (1795–1859), author of several successful educational books on scientific subjects, was born at Walthamstow, Essex, on 6 December 1795, the second of at least three daughters of successful London businessman John Jacob Zornlin and his wife Elizabeth (née Alsager). She came of distinguished ancestry, John Jacob Zornlin being descended from the Zorne family, members of the city of Strasbourg's thirteenth-century aristocracy.[62] By the late fifteenth century, the Zornlin branch had migrated to St. Gallen, Switzerland; the first of the British Zornlins, also John Jacob, settled in the City of London as a merchant about 1740. Rosina's mother's family, the Alsagers, traced their roots back to sixteenth-century farmers in the English midlands. By the mid-eighteenth century, the Alsagers were prominent in the London Clothworkers' Company. Thomas Massa Alsager, Rosina's uncle, rose to the position of master of the company, the highest Clothworker office; in addition he was an editor, later assistant manager, of *The Times* and well known in London literary circles.

An invalid for many years, Rosina lived much of her life in the family home at Clapham, Surrey. Her interest in writing, the occupation she turned to for solace, was perhaps fostered by her mother, author of a number of poetic works,[63] and was shared by her younger sister, Georgiana Margaritta Zornlin; an enthusiastic student of archaeology, Georgiana also wrote on religious issues and on heraldry.[64]

Rosina Zornlin's science writing career most likely began when she was about forty and continued until within a few years of her death. Two short books for children on astronomical topics, a discussion of comets, particularly Halley's comet, and an account of solar eclipses, appeared in the mid-1830s.[65] A keen sky watcher for many years, she published a report of her sightings of shooting stars in the *Philosophical Magazine* in 1839 and followed this two years later with a lengthy, somewhat theoretical discussion of the shooting-star phenomenon (see bibliography). The origin and periodic appearance of these sky visitors was not yet well understood; Zornlin subscribed to the idea that there was a connection between aurorae and shooting stars, the latter being linked to the electric currents causing aurorae.

Her difficulties in understanding electrical phenomena in the 1840s are not surprising. Fundamental discoveries in the field were ongoing throughout her time, starting with Alessandro Volta's demonstration in 1800 of current from a voltaic pile, through the initial work on electromagnetism by Hans Christian Ørsted reported in 1820, to Michael Faraday's electrochemical investigations in the early 1830s. This research, and the new concepts and theories it engendered, coupled with the relatively abstract nature of the subject, presented a formidable challenge to a nonspecialist writer cut off from practical scientific experience. Thus her short book for children, *What Is a Voltaic Battery?* (1842), was seen by its *Athenæum* reviewer as totally failing in its effort to present the subject in a way comprehensible to younger readers.[66]

Elementary science textbooks written by women and aimed largely at female and juvenile audiences had made their appearance by the latter half of the eighteenth century, but the rate of publication increased markedly throughout the nineteenth. Indeed some of the most celebrated of the nineteenth-century science writers and expositors were women; their contributions were of considerable importance in the dissemination of scientific information and, in a few instances, in furthering the general progress of science.[67] Among the most notable were Mary Somerville, Agnes Clerke, and Mary Ward, both Somerville and Clerke publishing works of lasting interest and value in the history of science.[68] Although they constitute a not insignificant subsection among nineteenth-century women writers and are still of much interest to those exploring the social and cultural history of nineteenth-century science, most of these women have, like their male counterparts, passed into relative obscurity. Their fate is not unlike that of many later writers of elementary texts but, unlike the latter, they in their time enjoyed wide popularity with the general public. A certain amount of contemporary criticism did come their way, however, and the occasional review might be considered somewhat harsh by twenty-first-century standards.[69] Nevertheless, despite what would seem to have been the questionable quality of a fraction of the works they produced, as a body these writers are now widely considered by historians to have significantly influenced the country's overall educational development. Britain was then industrializing rapidly and information on matters relating to science and technology was becoming of increasingly greater interest to the growing literate section of the population. By the mid-nineteenth century the market for educational materials was booming, and with London then the center of commercial book production in the English-speaking world,[70] writers, both men and women, embraced the opportunity presented and moved to satisfy the increasing demand.

Zornlin's most successful works were her books on the earth sciences—geology, the earth's waters, and, most particularly, physical geography—all of which appeared between 1839 and 1856.

Already for several decades the market for books providing basic geographical information had been brisk and lucrative, popular works selling thousands of copies and being reissued many times.[71] The subject was then of immense and growing general interest, in large part, Zornlin felt, because of the renewed possibility of overseas travel that came with the economic recovery after the long period of the Napoleonic wars. The two-volume *Physical Geography* by Mary Somerville, which appeared in 1848, is often referred to as the first advanced English-language textbook in the field; Somerville's most popular work, it ran to six editions and sold 16,000 copies.[72] Zornlin's first (1840) edition of *Recreations in Physical Geography*, which predated Somerville's comprehensive treatise by eight years, used the same didactic system as that adopted by Somerville, presenting a unified picture of the planet, the interrelations between natural phenomena, distribution patterns in the animal and vegetable kingdoms, and the factors determining these patterns. This approach, which put aside the constraints of political boundaries, was innovative at the time and anticipated modern regional studies.

Beginning with a description of the shape and motion of the planet, Zornlin went on to discuss land forms (including basic geology), the nature and distribution of the earth's bodies of water, the atmosphere, climatic zones, and plants and animals (including humans). An enthusiastic reviewer, pronouncing the title *Recreations in Physical Geography* far too modest, added that although aimed at younger readers, the large collection of facts, made with the greatest industry, and the excellent arrangement of the work, render it useful to the public in general, particularly to those (a very large class) who would like to know the general principles of the science but who have not the leisure to consult the original authorities in the subject.[73]

Special praise was bestowed on the illustrations of plant and animal distribution patterns—Mercator projections of the earth on which tiny drawings of the species in question "are placed in the localities which Providence has assigned them." Such graphical techniques for efficiently presenting population distributions were then new departures. The reviewer's reference to Providence accurately reflects the tone of all Zornlin's books, which did not neglect to point out from time to time the wisdom of the Heavenly Father and the marvels of his creations, produced and arranged specially for man's benefit; the style was valued by many teachers, if not always by the intended audience.[74] The work was brought out in Boston in 1855 in a shortened version revised by William Gage—*Physical Geography for Families and Schools.* Gage noted that it filled a gap in school texts, geographical studies being an especially neglected area in American education. Reviews were again generally favorable.[75]

Not the first of Zornlin's textbooks, *Physical Geography* closely followed her *Recreations in Geology* (1839). In the latter she introduced the subject by stressing the importance and practical applicability of this still "comparatively new science," not only in the then very active search for coal and minerals but in understanding the nature of soils and their suitability for agriculture, the successful placement of roads, the erection of tall buildings, and more. Further, in addition to these practical benefits, geology, she noted, offered an excellent recreation activity accessible to the less affluent as well as the rich and leisured; in this far from complete science, where much work remained to be done, useful observations could be made in one's local district.

Here again she was forward looking in her approach, adopting the newer way of listing strata in ascending series, although many texts still clung to the alternative descending series presentation. Although the divisions and the nomenclature for the successive geological epochs were still being formalized, her exposition was systematic and clear. A number of puzzles solved within the next few decades remained mysteries. For example, how did huge blocks of Cumbrian granite arrive on the plains of Shropshire? Particularly interesting is her short discussion of recent and ongoing changes which she illustrated by comparing present-day East Anglia with Roman Norfolk; a deeply indented island north of the Ouse and Waveney rivers in Roman times, Norfolk had long since became part of the mainland, thanks to the extensive deposition of mud flats.

Zornlin's work on the earth's waters, an equally thorough and all-encompassing presentation, included descriptions of "hydraulic engines" from ancient times, such as the Persian water-wheel and Archimedes screw from the third century B.C. but used in Egypt until relatively recently. Topics of more immediate concern included the water supplies of London and of the London Basin with its recently tapped artesian sources. In explanations of the peculiar physical properties of water she unavoidably ran into difficulties. The successful exploration of the molecular structure of water was still in the future, and the writings of the various authorities she depended on were therefore seriously flawed and confused. *Recreations in Hydrology,* like Zornlin's other two major publications, is a creditable work, the product of a great deal of detailed and painstaking investigation of original sources and skillful organization. Even the *Athenæum* reviewer who had vigorously objected to her attempt to explain the voltaic pile acknowledged that this was in a different class and quite acceptable.[76]

Twenty-first-century norms might well tempt one to see Zornlin's role (like that of many of her colleagues) as a combination of textbook author and science reporter-correspondent. However, current definitions, characterizations, and standards can hardly be applied in the emergent world of commercial educational publishing in the early nineteenth century;[77] to dismiss her work as being of minimal value in the scientific world and to deny her any originality would be unwise. At a time of great public demand for readily accessible information on scientific subjects, her contribution was considerable.[78]

Rosina Zornlin's additional publications included a number of books on religion and moral values. Her *Bible Narrative,* first published anonymously in 1838, went through at least three later editions. Patterned after a work by the Rev. George Townsend published some years earlier, it consisted of a selection of passages from the Authorized Version of the Bible arranged chronologically and was supplemented with a brief historical account of the Jewish people up to the seventh decade A.D.; in part it reflected her special interest in ancient cultures, an interest shared by her sister Georgiana. Her *Questions on the Bible Narrative* (1844) was adopted as a school textbook. In 1837 she brought out a shortened and modernized version of the very popular eighteenth-century work *Sandford and Merton.* The revision was undertaken somewhat against her own inclinations but at the urging of her publisher John William Parker, whose successful London firm specialized in "improving" works, including many on topics in religion and introductory science. *Sandford and Merton* was a moral tale, its purpose being to teach young people the emerging *bourgeois* values of independence, hard work, and the simple life. Also of didactic intent was her *Roman Catholic Chapel* (1837), a story that illustrated the mistakenness and dangers of various tenets of the Church of Rome.[79]

Rosina Zornlin died in Kenilworth, Warwickshire, on 22 May 1859, in her sixty-fourth year, after lengthy illness.

AGNES KELLY[80] (1875–?), whose 1900 mineralogical papers are listed in the first volume of this survey,[81] was the first woman to successfully apply to Munich University for permission to take the doctoral examination. She and geology student Maria Ogilvie-Gordon, her fellow Scot,[82] both took their examinations on 25 July 1900, passing with distinction. They were the first two women to be awarded doctorates by Munich University.

Born in South Australia in 1875, Agnes Kelly was brought to Scotland by her parents when she was three years old. She entered Bedford College for Women in London in 1892 at age seventeen and five years later received her University of London B.Sc. degree. A student of zoologist Richard Hertwig (also one of Ogilvie-Gordon's mentors), she worked in an area at the interface between mineralogy and zoology. Hertwig considered her work on shell formation in the animal kingdom to be a far more thorough treatment of the subject than any previous investigation.

MAJA KNECHT is sometimes reported to have been the first Swiss woman to enroll at the Zurich Polytechnikum.[83] However, the institution's register of women students gives her home address as Southport, England.[84] Knecht enrolled in the teacher training division of the Polytechnikum in 1892, concentrating on chemistry; she received her diploma in 1895. There is no indication that she went on to a doctorate. Her short paper with chemist Eugen Bamberger on the reduction of nitro groups appeared in the German Chemical Society's *Berichte* in 1898 (see bibliography).

A small amount of additional biographical information has recently come to light on plant morphologist and geneticist EDITH REBECCA SAUNDERS[85] (1865–1945) of Newnham College, Cambridge, one of the most notable British women biologists of her time.

Previous accounts have said little about Saunders's family background. However, manuscript papers of plant morphologist Richard Hauke record his 1987 interviews with Cambridge women who knew Saunders,[86] including Anna Bidder, daughter of Saunders's colleague and close friend physiologist Marion Greenwood.[87] These accounts tell us that Edith Saunders was orphaned at an early age but was brought up by an aunt who was able to give her a secure and comfortable home. She had one brother, to whom she was devoted; he is thought to have died before 1920, perhaps in the First World War. The manuscript holdings contain in addition an essay that includes a discussion of Saunders's failed theory of carpel polymorphism, now a "minor footnote" in the history of plant morphology.[88] Also touched on in the essay are Saunders's interactions with contemporary botanists, among them her Newnham colleague the distinguished plant morphologist Agnes Arber, demonstrator at the Balfour Laboratory, Newnham, from 1911 to 1914 and a research worker there until 1927. Arber, despite strong reservations about the carpel polymorphism theory, never let this difference of opinion upset her always friendly relationship with Edith Saunders.[89]

MRS. JOSÉ CAMILLO LISBOA[90] contributed two papers on the odiferous grasses of India to the Bombay Natural History Society's *Journal* in 1889 and 1891 (see bibliography). The wife of Dr. J. C. Lisboa, a graduate of the Grant Medical College in Bombay, she carried out her botanical work in company with her husband who, after retiring from medical practice, became an enthusiastic student of native grasses, especially those of the Bombay Presidency. A member of the Bombay Natural History Society, he was also a fellow of the London Linnean Society.[91]

Mrs. Lisboa, who was well versed in the literature of the flora of India, assisted her husband in his botanical work while at the same time giving special attention to members of the genus Andropogon, many varieties of which are found both wild and cultivated throughout India and Ceylon (Sri Lanka). Her collections were made mainly within the Bombay Presidency, particularly in the hills of the Deccan inland from Bombay, in the region of Thana, along the coast a few miles north of the city, and in the Satmala Hills (north of Bombay and about 100 miles inland from Surat—the district then known as *Khandesh*). Her paper of 1888 included a description of a species of Andropogon new to botanists. In 1891 she presented to the Bombay Natural History Society an exhibition of all the known scented grasses of India, some of the specimens being loaned to her by a colleague in northern India. Although the society had a number of women members before the turn of the century, Mrs. Lisboa, along with Mrs. Hart,[92] was one of the few who presented papers at its meetings during the 1880s and early 1890s.[93]

Notes

1. Creese, *Ladies in the Laboratory? American and British Women in Science, 1800–1900* (Lanham, Md.: Scarecrow Press, 1998).

2. John H. Haines, "Mushrooms to cultivate minds and morals: the works of Mary Banning," *McIlvainea* 12 (1996): 54–62 (Portsmouth, Ohio: North American Mycological Association); John H. Haines, "Mary Banning: the woman who painted mushrooms," *Maryland Naturalist* 33 (1991): 44–56 (this includes, on pp. 48–56, a reproduction of an unsigned biography of Banning believed to have been written some time after 1919 by Baltimore surgeon Howard Kelly, one of the founders of the Natural History Society of Maryland—"The biography of Mary E. Banning"); and Annette Heist, "Joyous mushrooms," *Natural History* 108, no. 7 (1999): 48–49.

3. Mary E. Banning, *The Fungi of Maryland* (unpublished manuscript held in the New York State Museum, Albany, N.Y.).

4. Banning, *Fungi*, preface, quoted in Haines, "Mushrooms," 55.

5. A librarian there remembered her as "of stout build, with fair complexion and sandy hair and with a pleasant although somewhat erratic manner." In "Biography of Mary E. Banning," in Haines, "Mary Banning," 51.

6. Charles H. Peck, "Fungi of Maryland," *Annual Report of the State Museum of Natural History* 44 (1891): 64–75; and Peck, "Fungi of Maryland," *Annual Report of the State Museum of Natural History* 44 (1892): 176–87.

7. Robbins Milbank, comp., *Olivia Rodham: 17 September 1845–11 August 1920* (Nelson, N.H.: Trustees of the Olivia Rodham Memorial Library, 1964). 18 pp.

8. Olivia Rodham's sources of income have not been identified. She may have inherited (and subsequently sold or rented) her family's Maryland farm. Her work for publishers could hardly have brought her sufficient funds for living as she did.

9. The barn was struck by lightning and destroyed some years after Rodham's death.

10. *Who Was Who in America*, vol. 1, 1897–1942 (1966), 1039; John William Leonard, ed., *Woman's Who's Who of America. 1914–1915* (New York: American Commonwealth, 1914), 691; and *James Henry Robbins, M.D., born July 22, 1839, died Aug. 21, 1900* [collected obituary notices, etc.] (Hingham, Mass.: n.p., 1900).

11. Creese, *Ladies in the Laboratory?* 378.

12. Mary Abigail Dodge ("Gail Hamilton"), an opponent of suffrage for women, was already an established writer on social questions; see *Who Was Who in America, Historical Volume, 1607–1896* (1963), 152.

13. "New England Parks: Morton Park, Plymouth, Massachusetts," *Garden and Forest* 4 (1891): 374; "New England Parks: The Lynn Woods," *Garden and Forest* 4 (1891): 482–83; "New England Parks: Forest Park, Springfield, Massachusetts," *Garden and Forest* 4 (1891): 566–67; "New England Parks: Deering's Woods and the Promenades, Portland, Maine," *Garden and Forest* 4 (1891): 602–3; "New England Parks: The Projected Park System of Providence, Rhode Island," *Garden and Forest* 5 (1892): 590–91; "A Tree Museum," *Century Magazine* 45, no. 6 (April 1893): 867–78 (see also "New England Parks: The Arnold Arboretum," *Garden and Forest* 5, [1892]: 27–29); "A Glorified Park" [Jackson Park, Chicago]," *Garden and Forest* 6 (1893): 293–94; "American Parks: Lincoln Park, Chicago," *Garden and Forest* 6 (1893): 402–3; "American Parks: Mount Royal, Montreal," *Garden and Forest* 6 (1893): 523–24; and "The Park System of Minneapolis and St. Paul, Minnesota," *Garden and Forest* 10 (1897): 162–64.

14. "The Art of Public Improvement," *Atlantic Monthly* 78, no. 470 (Dec. 1896): 742–51, quotation on 743; "Park-Making as a National Art," *Atlantic Monthly* 79, no. 471 (Jan. 1897): 86–98, quotation on 86.

15. "Village improvement societies," *Atlantic Monthly* 79, no. 472 (Feb. 1897): 212–22.

16. See the series of articles, "How we renewed an old place," I–XX in *Garden and Forest* 4 (1891)—quotation from article I, 146–47 on 147; also published as *The Rescue of an Old Place* (Boston: Houghton Mifflin, 1892).

17. Eugène Fromentin, *Les maîtres d'autrefois: Belgique-Hollande* (Paris: E. Plon, 1876), trans. Mary Caroline Robbins, *The Old Masters of Belgium and Holland* (Boston: Houghton Mifflin, 1883); and Louis Gonse, *Eugène Fromentin, peintre et écrivain* (Paris: A. Quantin, 1881), trans. Mary Caroline Robbins, *Eugène Fromentin, Painter and Writer* (Boston: J. R. Osgood, 1883).

18. Victor Cherbuliez, *Le roman d'une honnête femme*, 3rd ed. (Paris: Hachette, 1868), trans. Mary Caroline Pike, *The Romance of an Honest Woman* (Boston: W. F. Gill, 1874); and Henry Gréville [pseud. for Marie Céleste Durand], *Le comte Xavier* (Paris: Plon, Nourrit et Cie, 1886), trans. Mary Caroline Robbins, *Count Xavier* (Boston: Ticknor, 1887).

19. *Address Read before the Gaspee Chapter, D.A.R., April 19th, 1884* (n.p.: State Regent of Rhode Island, 1894); "A Few Considerations on Giving the Ballot to Women," in Caia [pseud.], M. L. W., and Mary Caroline Robbins, *Woman Suffrage* (Boston?: n.p., 1894), 38–58.

20. For biographical sketches of Gamble, Ladd-Franklin, Smith, and Martin, see Creese, *Ladies in the Laboratory?*, 348–49, 351–55.

21. Lottie Steffens, "Vita" in "Experimentelle Beiträge zur Lehre von ökonomischen Lernen," inaugural diss., Georg-Augusts-Universität zu Göttingen (Leipzig: J. A. Barth, 1900); Ilse Castas, "Zu den Anfängen des Frauenstudiums an der Universität Göttingen," *Göttingen Jahrbuch* 45 (1997): 145–56, on 152; Justin Kaplan, *Lincoln Steffens: A Biography* (New York: Simon and Schuster, 1974), especially chapter 1. Manuscript material concerning Lottie Steffens Hollister and her family is held in the archives department of the University of California, Berkeley; I have not seen this material.

22. A great deal has been written about Lincoln Steffens. See for instance Kaplan, *Lincoln Steffens.*

23. Information about Laura Steffens Suggett was collected largely from Kaplan, *Lincoln Steffens* and from Ella Winter and Granville Hicks, eds., *Letters of Lincoln Steffens*, vol. 1, 1889–1919, and vol. 2, 1920–1936 (New York: Harcourt, Brace, 1938); many of the letters were to the Steffens sisters, especially Laura.

24. David M. Damkaer, "Harriet Richardson (1874–1958), First Lady of Isopods," *Journal of Crustacean Biology* 20 (2000): 803–11 (portr.). In addition to discussing the importance of Richardson's work and its continuing value, this paper provides a broad background picture of the activity in the field at the time, including mention of the many personalities with whom Richardson would have had professional contacts. Richardson is also discussed briefly in P. A. McLaughlin and S. Gilchrist, "Women's Contributions to Carcinology," in Frank Truesdale, ed., *History of Carcinology: Crustacean Issues: 8* (Rotterdam: A. A. Balkema, 1993), 165–206, discussion on 168.

25. Creese, *Ladies in the Laboratory?*, 87, 405.

26. Creese, *Ladies in the Laboratory?*, 85–87.

27. See for instance the discussions of zoologists Julia Platt and Mary Willcox in Creese, *Ladies in the Laboratory?*, 101–3, 89–92. Platt carried out outstanding original work in vertebrate embryology, and Willcox published a series of notable papers on gasteropod anatomy. Their rediscovery as important contributors depended on the investigations of specialists in their fields.

28. The species, later designated *Thermosphaeroma thermophilum*, is now on the federal endangered species list.

29. See Creese, *Ladies in the Laboratory?*, 405, for a list of Richardson's pre-1901 publications.

30. See Damkaer, "Harriet Richardson," for a full list and for a complete bibliography of her publications.

31. Biographical information about Alice Bodington came from the 42-page manuscript by Winifred B. Irvine and Helena B. Meiklejon, Bodington's daughters, "A Family Arrives in British Columbia, 1887." The information is used with the permission of Special Collections, Vancouver Public Library, Vancouver, British Columbia, who hold the manuscript. I thank Professor Bernard Lightman, York University, Toronto, for telling me about Bodington.

32. Alice Bodington, *Studies in Evolution and Biology* (London: Elliot Stock, 1890), 142.

33. See Creese, *Ladies in the Laboratory?*, 238–41. For a full biography of Clerke, see Mary T. Brück, *Agnes Mary Clerke and the Rise of Astrophysics* (Cambridge: Cambridge University Press, 2002).

34. Bodington, *Studies in Evolution and Biology*, 143.

35. Bodington, *Studies in Evolution and Biology.*

36. Bodington, *Studies in Evolution and Biology*, 103.

37. Anonymous, "Short notices of books," *Nature Notes: The Selborne Society's Magazine* 2 (Nov.-Dec. 1891): 229–30.

38. "Religion, Reason and Agnosticism," *Westminster Review* 139 (1893): 369–80, on 379–80.

39. Bodington, *Studies in Evolution*, especially the chapter "The Origin of the Fittest," 187–206.

40. W. H. Chesson, ed., *Eliza Brightwen: The Life and Thoughts of a Naturalist*, with introduction and epilogue by Edmund Gosse (London: T. Fisher Unwin, 1909).

41. Literary critic Edmund Gosse (1849–1928) was the stepson of George Brightwen's sister Eliza, second wife of naturalist Philip Henry Gosse. Edmund Gosse liked and admired his "Aunt Lizzie" and, although often irked by her excessive religious zeal, frequently visited her at Stanmore. See Ann Thwaite, *Edmund Gosse: A Literary Landscape, 1849–1928* (London: Secker & Warburg, 1984), 104–5, 268, 423.

42. *Wild Nature Won by Kindness* (London: T. Fisher Unwin, 1890; German tr. 1892; rev. ed. 1893).

43. Gosse, "Introduction," in Chesson, *Eliza Brightwen*, xxiii.

44. Anonymous, "The Selborne Society and Its Magazine," *Nature Notes: The Selborne Society's Magazine* 2 (1891): 1–7, on 2.

45. Anonymous, "A Book for Nature Lovers," *Nature Notes: The Selborne Society's Magazine* 1 (1890): 159–60.

46. Chesson, *Eliza Brightwen.*

47. Thwaite, *Edmund Gosse*, 268.

48. Donald de Beaver, "Writing Natural History for Survival—1820–1856; The Case of Sarah Bowich, Later Sarah Lee," *Archives of Natural History* 26 (1999): 19–31. This paper also provides corrected dates for several events in Sarah Bowdich Lee's life and a corrected spelling of her (and her father's) middle name—Eglonton, rather than Eglinton, as given in early accounts. A small amount of additional information was collected from W. E. F. Ward, "Introduction to Third Edition," in T. Edward Bowdich, *Mission from Cape Coast Castle to Ashantee*, ed. W. E. F. Ward, 3rd. ed. (London; Frank Cass & Co., 1966), 11–71.

49. Creese, *Ladies in the Laboratory?*, 128–29, 396.

50. Ward, "Introduction," in Bowdich, *Mission from Cape Coast Castle*, 14.

51. Among the young naturalists preparing for work in the tropics by study at the Muséum National at the same time as the Bowdichs were Heinrich Kuhl (1797–1821) of Hanau, near Frankfurt am Main, and his colleague Johan Coenraad van Hasselt (1797–1823) of Doesburg, Gelderland Province, Netherlands. Kuhl and van Hasselt carried out notable natural history explorations in West Java from 1820 until their early deaths a few years later; see C. H. J. M. Fransen, L. B. Holthuis, and J. P. H. M. Adema, "Type-Catalogue of the Decapod Crustacea in the Collections of the Natuurhistorische Museum, with Appendices of Pre-1900 Collectors and Material," *Zoologische Verhandelingen* 311 (1997): 239–40, 256–58.

52. *An Account of the Discoveries of the Portuguese in the Interior of Angola and Mozambique*, published posthumously from original manuscripts by T. E. Bowdich prepared before he left Europe in 1822 (London: John Booth, 1824).

53. The Royal Literary Fund awarded Thomas Bowdich £40 in July 1822 (Beaver, "Writing Natural History," 28, n. 6). The aid from the London-based African Association is recorded in the publisher's note introducing Bowdich's *Discoveries of the Portuguese* (p. i). This association, also known as the *Association for Promoting the Discovery of the Interior Parts of Africa* (founded 1788), became incorporated with the Royal Geographical Society of London in 1831.

54. *Memoirs of Baron Cuvier* (London: Longman & Co., 1833; Paris: H. Fournier, 1833, trans. Théodore Lacordaire).

55. *Elements of Natural History; or, First Principles of Zoology: For the Use of Schools and Young Persons . . .* (London: Longman & Co., 1844, 2nd ed. 1849, 1853, 1855).

56. Matthew Paris, Roger of Wendover, and Henry Richards Luard, compilers, authors, and eds., *Matthaei Parisiensis, Monachi Sancti Albani, Chronica Majora* (London: Longman & Co., 1872–83). The work chronicles monastic life in the thirteenth century.

57. "Jottings Concerning Certain Fruit Trees. Pt. 6—The Chestnut Tree (*Castanea veca*)," *Science-Gossip* 26 (1890): 79–81, on 80.

58. For the works by John Evelyn (1620–1706) mentioned here, see Guy de la Bédoyère, *The Diary of John Evelyn* (Woodbridge, Suffolk, UK: Boydell Press, 1995; published in London by Henry Colburn, 1818, 1827 and many times subsequently; earlier title, *Memoirs Illustrative of the Life and Writings of John Evelyn . . . Comprising His Diary, from the Year 1641 to 1705–06 . . .*; later title, *Sylva, or, a Discourse of Forest-trees, and the Propagation of Timber in His Majesties Dominions . . .* (Brough, UK: Trollius Publications, 2001; first published in London by the Royal Society, J. Martyn, printer, 1664, and many times subsequently).

59. *The Girls' Own Paper*, brought out in London by The Leisure Hour Office from 1880 until 1908, published a remarkable variety of material, often featuring new poetry (including works by W. B. Yeats) and current musical scores as well as general and scientific articles, needlework patterns, advice, puzzles, and more.

60. Patricia Phillips, *The Scientific Lady: A Social History of Women's Scientific Interests 1520–1918* (New York: St. Martin's Press, 1990). Phillips points to the well-known example of Mary Somerville, a woman who always maintained that her interest in mathematics was awakened by her discovery of algebra in the pages of a fashion magazine.

61. Ralph Thomas, "Zornlin Family," *Notes and Queries* s. 10, 3 (27 May 1905): 402–4; and D. E. Wickham, "Thomas Massa Alsager (1779–1846): An Elian shade Illuminated," *Charles Lamb Bulletin*, no. 5 (July 1981): 45–62. For a listing of reviews of Zornlin's books, see S. A. Allibone, *A Critical Dictionary of English Literature and British and American Authors*, 3 vols. (Philadelphia: Lippincott, 1871), vol. 3, 2907. Zornlin is mentioned briefly in Barbara T. Gates and Ann B. Shteir, "Introduction," in Barbara T. Gates and Ann B. Shteir, eds., *Natural Eloquence: Women Reinscribe Science* (Madison: University of Wisconsin Press, 1997), 13–14; and in Barbara T. Gates, *Kindred Nature: Victorian and Edwardian Women Embrace the Living World* (Chicago: University of Chicago Press, 1998), 47, 48. I thank Professor James Secord, Department of History and Philosophy of Science, University of Cambridge, for helpful correspondence about Zornlin.

62. John Jacob Zornlin declined to register the Zornlin arms at the Herald's College because he considered them older than the college; to have entered them there would have implied a grant of arms.

63. See, for instance, *An Ode Written upon the Victory and Death of Lord Viscount Nelson . . .* (London: T. Boosey, 1805).

64. Thomas ("Zornlin Family," 403) lists three works by Georgiana Zornlin: *A Paper Lantern for Puseyites* (under the pseudonym, Will o' the Wisp) (London: Smith and Elder, 1842; rev. edn. 1850); Georgiana Zornlin, *Urim and Thummin, an Inquiry* (under A. Z.) (London: Shaw, 1860); and Georgiana Zornlin, *The Heraldry of the World: Observations on the Universality and Antiquity of the Seal* (Winchester: n.p., 1874; read before the Winchester Scientific and Literary Society, April 1873). The writing activities of the Alsager women continued in the next generation with Beatrice Alsager Jourdan (Rosina's niece), whose publications included *The Journal of a Waiting Gentlewoman* (London: Low, 1866) and *An Essay on the Improvements in the Education of Children and Young People during the 18th and 19th Centuries* (London: Elliot Stock, 1880; the work was awarded the Statistical Society's Howard Prize for 1879).

65. *What Is a Comet, Papa? Or, A familiar Description of Comets More Particularly of Halley's Comet: To Which Is Prefixed a Concise Account of the Other Heavenly Bodies* (London: J. Ridgeway, 3rd ed. 1835); *The Solar Eclipse, or, The Two Almanacks Containing More Enquiries in Astronomy* (London: J. Ridgeway, 1836).

66. Sir Charles Morgan, "*What Is a Voltaic Battery?* By Rosina M. Zornlin," book review, *Athenæum*, 24 September 1842, 833–34.

67. Phillips, *Scientific Lady*, 78.

68. For brief sketches of Somerville and Clerke, see Creese, *Ladies in the Laboratory?*, 201–4 and 238–41, respectively; for Ward, see chapter 2.

69. Author and surgeon Sir Thomas Charles Morgan, the *Athenæum* reviewer of Zornlin's *Voltaic Battery* (see Morgan, "*What Is a Voltaic Battery?*"), expressed the opinion that, in general, elementary presentations were often "crude, ill-digested trash" that reduced the subject under consideration to "barren generalities." See also the *Nature Notes* reviewer's comments on Alice Bodington's writing (note 37).

70. John R. Issitt, "Jeremiah Joyce: Science Educationist," *Endeavour* 26 (2002): 97–101, on 97.

71. Issitt, "Jeremiah Joyce," 99–100. Two elementary geography books Joyce published in 1803 are notable examples of very successful early textbooks in the field—*Geography Illustrated on a Popular Plan* and *An Easy Grammar of General*

Geography (London: Phillips—Longmans, after 1812); both appeared under the pseudonym, Reverend J. Goldsmith. Very popular, they remained in print until 1868, the *Grammar* selling thousands of copies annually and *Geography Illustrated* between 500 and 1,000 per year.

72. See Creese, *Ladies in the Laboratory?*, 203. Somerville's work appeared soon after the publication of the first volume of *Kosmos*, the famous treatise of Alexander von Humboldt, one of the founders of scientific geography.

73. Anonymous, "Miss Zornlin's Physical Geography," *Times*, 9 November 1840, 6.

74. See also the sketch of Eliza Brightwen, above.

75. Anonymous, "*Physical Geography for Families and Schools*. By R. M. Zornlin . . .," *North American Review* 82 (1856): 281.

76. "The World of Waters, by Rosina M. Zornlin," *Anthenæum*, 5 August 1843, 712.

77. Issitt, "Jeremiah Joyce," 100.

78. Rosina Zornlin's earth sciences books are the following: *Recreations in Geology* (London: John W. Parker, 1839–1852), 3 editions; *Recreations in Physical Geography: Or, the Earth as It Is* (London: J. W. Parker, 1840, and at least five later editions to 1855); United States edition, *Physical Geography for Families and Schools* (Boston: J. Monroe, 1855, 1856); and *The World of Waters, or, Recreations in Hydrology* (London: J. W. Parker, 1843).

79. *Bible Narrative* (London: J. W. Parker, 1838; 4th rev. ed., 1855), 504 pp.; *Questions on the Bible Narrative* (London: B. Fellowes, 1844 and later eds.), 68 pp.; *Sandford and Merton* (London: J. W. Parker, 1837), first published by Thomas Day as *The History of Sandford and Merton*, 3 vols. (London: J. Stockdale, 1783–1789). The 1783–89 edition was reprinted by Garland Publishing (1977) in their series, Classics of Children's Literature. Thomas Day (1748–1789), a disciple of Jean-Jacques Rousseau and a champion of radical political causes, wrote a number of children's books. Active in the struggle to remake English life, he was one of those challenging the power and hegemony of the old aristocracy. Day's *Sandford and Merton* went through about forty-five different editions and was one of the most widely read books in England from the 1780s until well into the Victorian age (see Isaac Kramnick, "Preface," in the Garland edition); *The Roman Catholic Chapel, or, Lindenhurst Parish* (London: J. W. Parker, 1837). J. W. Parker, who brought out no fewer than six substantial works by Zornlin, including two on religion or moral values, was the official publisher for the Society for Promoting Christian Knowledge and official printer for the Cambridge University Press. A considerable fraction of the work he did for Cambridge consisted of Bibles and editions of the Church of England's Book of Common Prayer (see Dennis R. Dean, "John W. Parker" in Patricia J. Anderson and Jonathan Rose, ed., *British Literary Publishing Houses, 1820–1880* (Detroit: Gale Publishing, 1991), 233–36 (vol. 106 of *Dictionary of Literary Biography*).

80. *Stieftöchter der Alma mater? 90 Jahre Frauenstudium in Bayern—am Beispiel der Universität München*, ed. Hadumod Bussmann (München: Antje Kunstmann, 1993), 114–17.

81. Creese, *Ladies in the Laboratory?*, 311 n. 118, 419.

82. Creese, *Ladies in the Laboratory?*, 294–96, 418–19.

83. *Das Frauenstudium an den Schweizer Hochschulen*, ed. Schweizerischer Verband der Akademikerinnen (Zürich: Verband der Akademikerinnen, 1928), 54.

84. Marianne Müller and Regula Schnurrenberger, "Die Philosophische Fakultät II," in *Ebenso new als kühn: 120 Jahre Frauenstudium an der Universität Zürich*, Verein Feministische Wissenschaft Schweiz (Zürich: Verein Feministische Wissenchaft Schweiz, Schriftenreihe, 1988), 153–76, on 157–58; see also 208 and 222, n. 11.

85. For a short account of Saunders's life and work, see Creese, *Ladies in the Laboratory?*, 43–44.

86. "Saunders, Edith Rebecca; Interviews with Anna Bidder and Delia Agar," papers of Richard L. and Kathleen A. Hauke, Msg #68, box 14, folder 72, Special Collections, University Library, University of Rhode Island, Kingston, Rhode Island. Information from the papers is used with the permission of Special Collections.

87. See Creese, *Ladies in the Laboratory?*, 147.

88. Richard L. Hauke, "Vignettes from the History of Plant Morphology," unpublished as of 2001, except in electronic form; manuscript held in Special Collections, University of Rhode Island Libraries.

89. See also the recent paper by Rudolf Schmid on Agnes Arber ("Agnes Arber, née Robertson (1879–1960): Fragments of Her Life Including Her Place in Biology and in Women's Studies," *Annals of Botany* 88 (2001): 1105–28. This paper includes a brief note on Edith Saunders as well as comments on a third notable early Cambridge woman botanist, Ethel Sargant (see Creese, *Ladies in the Laboratory?*, 44–46, for a biographical sketch of Sargant). Schmid's paper emphasizes Saunders's outstanding work in the training of several generations of science students at both Newnham and Girton colleges. Also provided is a correction of a biographical detail concerning Ethel Sargant: her burial place is specified as being in Sidmouth, Devon, not Girton, Cambridge, as stated in earlier publications (including Creese, *Ladies in the Laboratory?*, 45–46). However, there is a wall plaque commemorating Sargant in the St. Andrew's Parish Church, Girton.

90. Obituary, Dr. J. C. Lisboa, *Journal of the Bombay Natural History Society* 11 (1897): 339, and *Proceedings of the Linnean Society* (1897–98): 41.

91. Dr. J. C. Lisboa's publications include, in addition to numerous papers in the Bombay Natural History Society's *Journal*, two monographs: *Useful Plants of the Bombay Presidency* (Bombay: Government Central Press, 1886) and *List of Bombay Grasses and Their Uses* (Bombay: Government Central Press, 1896; reprinted, Delhi: Periodical Experts Book Agency, 1978).

92. See the chapter on Irish women.

93. For a sketch of the career of another woman botanist who studied the ornamental and odiferous grasses of the Far East, see the discussion of Aimée Camus, a major contributor to the field, in chapter 3.

Bibliography of Papers by West European Women (excluding British) in Scientific Periodicals, 1800–1900

Entries are from the *Catalogue of Scientific Papers* 1800–1900, 19 volumes, compiled by the Royal Society, London (Cambridge: Cambridge University Press, 1867–1925). The list has been supplemented by some additional entries, marked {}. Most of these were collected from periodicals not examined by the Royal Society indexers, typically minor journals, regional journals of short run, general-interest magazines, and journals in fields not covered in the *Catalogue* (such as some areas of clinical medicine). Papers by British and American women discussed in the appendix are listed at the end of the bibliography. For consistency, only the entries derived from the *Catalogue* are included in the paper counts given in the graphs that follow most chapters. For the most part, the *Catalogue*'s style of presentation, nomenclature conventions, and so on have been retained. A key to abbreviations follows the bibliography. (Note that page numbers here are truncated according to the format of the *Chicago Manual of Style*, 14th edition. In the corresponding bibliography of American and British papers listed in the first volume of this survey, the minimum number of digits was used.)

Austria-Hungary

Botany

Lampa, Emma
Lampa, Emma
  Untersuchungen über einige Blattformen der Liliaceen. *Oesterr. Bot. Ztschr.*, **50** (1900) 421–25
Ott, Emma
Ott, Emma
  Einige Beobachtungen über die Brechungsexponenten verschiedener Stärkesorten. *Oesterr. Bot. Ztschr.*, **49** (1889) 313–17
  Beiträge zur Kenntniss der Härte vegetabilischer Zellmembranen. *Oesterr. Bot. Ztschr.*, **50** (1900) 237–41
  Untersuchungen über den Chromatophorenbau der Süsswasser-Diatomaceen und dessen Beziehungen zur Systematik. *Wien, Ak. Sber.*, **109** (Abt.1) (1900) 769–801
Witasek, Johanna
Witasek, Johanna
  Die Arten der Gattung Callianthemum. *Wien Zool. Bot. Verh.*, **49** (1899) 316–56
  Campanula Hostii, *Baumgarten*, und Campanula pseudolanceolata, *Pantocsek. Wien Zool. Bot. Verh.*, **50** (1900) 186–90

Medicine and Anatomy

Fuchs-Wolfring, Sophie
Fuchs-Wolfring, Sophie

Ueber den feineren Bau der Drüsen des Kehlkopfes und der Luftröhre. *Arch. Mikr. Anat.*, **52** (1898) 735–61; **54** (1899) 84–87

Gourfein-Welt, Leonore
Welt, Leonore
Ueber Charakterveränderungen des Menschen infolge von Läsionen des Stirnhirns. *Deutsch. Arch. Klin. Med.*, **42** (1888) 339–90
Thrombose der Arteria centralis retinae, unter dem Bilde der sogenannten Embolie verlaufend. Mit anatomischer Untersuchung. *Arch. Augenheilk.*, **41** (1900) 355–77

Strauss, Rosa Welt
Strauss, Rosa Welt
Experiments on the germicidal properties of certain eye salves. *Arch. Augenheilk.*, **39** (1899) 388; *Arch. Ophthalm.*, **28** (1899) 40–44

Welt-Kakels, Sara
Welt, Sara
Klinische Beobachtungen über die antifebrile Wirkung des Antipyrin und Thallin nebst Bemerkungen über individuelle Antipyrese. [1885] *Deutsch. Arch. Klin. Med.*, **38** (1886) 81–121

Natural History

Schlechta von Wschehrd, Sidonie (Baronin)
Schlechta, (Baronin) Sidonie
Meine kleine Volière. *Wien Ornith. Ver. Mitth.*, **16** (1892) 205–6
Werner, Helene
Werner, Helene
Bemerkungen über den Scheltopusik und die Treppennatter. *Frankf., Zool. Garten*, **33** (1892) 38–41
Ueber die Lebensweise des Wüsten-Warans und der Hufeisennatter in Gefangenschaft. *Frankf., Zool. Garten*, **33** (1892) 304–6; 374–75

Astronomy

Matt, Elisabeth von (Baronesse)
Matt, Elisabeth (Baronesse) von
Geographische Ortsbestimmung der Kreis-Stadt Elnbogen in Böhmen, unweit Carlsbad. *Zach, Monat. Corresp.*, **22** (1810) 276–77
Sternbedeckung am 31 März, 1808, π Tauri. *Zach, Monat. Corresp.*, **23** (1811) 293–96
Längen- und Breiten-Bestimmung dreier Oerter im Unterösterreichischen (Baden, Heiligen-Kreutz, Arraberg). [1809]. *Bode, Astron. Jahrb.* (1812) 222–25
Längen- und Breiten-Bestimmungen einiger Oerter im Oesterreichischen (Bruck an der Leytha, Bergau, Fridau bei St. Pölten), nebst beobachteten Sternbedeckungen. [1811] *Bode, Astron. Jahrb.* (1814) 222–25

Chemistry

Welt, Ida
Welt, (Mlle.) Ida
Sur les hydrocarbures saturés à radicaux amyliques actifs. *Paris, Ac. Sci. C. R.*, **119** (1894) 743–47; *Paris Soc. Chim. Bull.*, **11** (1894) 1178–85
Sur l'acide amylacétique actif et quelques-uns de ses dérivés. *Paris, Ac. Sci. C. R.*, **119** (1894) 855–58; *Paris Soc. Chim. Bull.*, **13** (1895) 186–90
Contribution à l'étude des dérivés amyliques actifs. *Ann. Chim.*, **6** (1895) 115–44
Ueber das Verhalten von Dihalogeniden gegen alkoholisches Kali. *Berlin, Chem. Ges. Ber.*, **30** (1897) 1493–96; 3449

Mathematics

Böhm-Wendt, Cäcilie
Wendt, Cäcilie
    Note über die Kreisfunctionen. *Mhefte. Math. Phys.*, **10** (1899) 97–100
    Eine Verallgemeinerung des Additionstheoremes der Bessel'schen Functionen erster Art. *Mhefte. Math. Phys.*, **11** (1900) 125–31
Klekler, Pauline (Paula)
Klekler, Paula
    Note über die Polynomialcoefficienten. *Mhefte. Math. Phys.*, **10** (1899) 218–22

Geography

Morawetz-Dierkes, Leopoldine von
Morawetz-Dierkes, (Frau) Leopoldine von
    Land und Leute in Finland. [1897] *Wien Geogr. Ges. Mitth.*, **41** (1898) 219–61

Austria-Hungary—Russia

Medicine

Kerschbaumer, Rosa (Raissa; *née* **Shlykova;** later **Putiata)**
Putiata, Raissa
    Ueber Sarcom der Lymphdrüsen. *Virchow, Arch.*, **69** (1877) 245–65
Kerschbaumer, Rosa
    Ueber Altersveränderungen der Uvea. *Arch. f. Ophthalm.*, **34** (Abt. 4) (1888) 16–34; **38** (Abt.1) (1892) 127–48
    Bericht über 200 Staar-Extractionen. [1890] *Arch. Augenheilk.*, **22** (1891) 127–49; *Arch. f. Ophthalm.*, **20** (1891) 349–55
    Beitrag zur Kenntniss der leukämischen Erkrankung des Auges. *Arch. f. Ophthalm.*, **41** (Abt. 3) (1895) 99–122
Moraczewska, Sophie von (*née* Okuniewska*)*
Moraczewska, Sophie von
    Blutveränderungen bei Anämien. *Virchow, Arch.*, **144** (1896) 127–58

Belgium

Botany

Bommer, Élise-Caroline (Elisa; *née* **Destrée)**
Destrée, Caroline
    [Contributions] au catalogue des champignons des environs de la Haye. [1889–97] *Nederl. Kruidk. Arch.*, **5** (1891) 341–7; 625–32; **6** (1895) 169–94; 356–65; 594–619; **1** (1899) 127–38; 232–39
    Révision des Geaster observés dans les Pays-Bas. [Avec un avant-propos de M. F. W. van Eeden.] [1894] *Nederl. Kruidk. Arch.*, **6** (1895) 488–501
Bommer, (Mme.) E.; Rousseau, (Mme.) M.
    Catalogue des champignons observés aux environs de Bruxelles. *Belg. Soc. Bot. Bull.*, **18** (Mém) (1879) 61–219
    Florule mycologique des environs de Bruxelles. *Belg. Soc. Bot. Bull.*, **23** (Mém.) (1884) 15–365
    Contributions à la flore mycologique de Belgique. *Belg. Soc. Bot. Bull.*, **25** (Mém.) (1886) 163–85; **26** (Mém.) (1887) 187–241; **29** (Mém.) (1890) 205–302
    [Primitiae florae costaricensis.] Fungi. *Belg. Soc. Bot. Bull.*, **35** (Mém.) (1896) 151–66

Note préliminaire sur les champignons recueillis par l'Expédition Antarctique Belge. *Brux., Ac. Bull.* (1900) 640–46

Goetsbloets, Maria

Goetsbloets, Maria

Note sur le Ledum palustre, *L.*, plante signalée autrefois dans la Campine limbourgeoise. *Belg. Soc. Bot. Bull.*, **28** (C.R.) (1889) 57–60

Libert, Marie-Anne

Libert, Marie-Anne

Sur un genre nouveau d'hépatiques, Lejeunia. *Ann. Gén. Sci. Phys.*, **6** (1820) 372–74

Illustration du genre Inoconia, dans la famille des algues. *Paris Soc. Linn. Mém.*, **5** (1827) 402–3

Observations sur le genre Asteroma, et description de deux espèces appartenant à ce genre. *Paris Soc. Linn. Mém.*, **5** (1827) 404–6

Description d'un nouveau genre de champignons, nommé Desmazierella. *Ann. Sci. Nat.*, **28** (1829) 82–86

Mémoire concernant les plantes cryptogames qui peuvent être réunies sous le nom d'Ascoxylacei. *Lille Soc. Mém.* (1829–30) 174–76

Précis des observations sur la famille des Hypoxylons. [1836] *Ann. Sci. Nat.*, **7** (Bot) (1837) 121–25

Description du genre Inoconia. *Brux., Bull. Soc. Bot.*, **4** (1865) 407 (note)

MacLeod, Florence Hélène (Fanny) Maertens

MacLeod, F.

Lijst van boeken, verhandelingen, enz. over de verspreidingsmiddelen der planten van 1873 tot 1890 verschenen, met een bijvoegsel en eene alphabetische lijst der plantennamen. *Bot. Jaarb.*, **3** (1891) 192–231

Rousseau, Mariette (*née* Hannon)

Bommer, (Mme.) E.; Rousseau, (Mme.) M.

Catalogue des champignons observés aux environs de Bruxelles. *Belg. Soc. Bot. Bull.*, **18** (Mém) (1879) 61–219

Florule mycologique des environs de Bruxelles. *Belg. Soc. Bot. Bull.*, **23** (Mém.) (1884) 15–365

Contributions à la flore mycologique de Belgique. *Belg. Soc. Bot. Bull.*, **25** (Mém.) (1886) 163–85; **26** (Mém.) (1887) 187–241; **29** (Mém.) (1890) 205–302

[Primitiae florae costaricensis.] Fungi. *Belg. Soc. Bot. Bull.*, **35** (Mém.) (1896) 151–66

Note préliminaire sur les champignons recueillis par l'Expédition Antarctique Belge. *Brux., Ac. Bull.* (1900) 640–66

Biology

Demoor, Clémence Everard

Everard, (Mlle.) Clémence; Demoor, Jean; Massart, Jean

Sur les modifications des leucocytes dans l'infection et dans l'immunisation. *Ann. Inst. Pasteur*, **7** (1893) 165–212

Leclercq, Emma

Leclercq, (Mlle.) Emma

Contributions à l'étude du Nebenkern ou corpuscule accessoire dans les cellules. *Brux., Ac. Bull.*, **20** (1890) 137–48

Les micro-organismes intermédiaires aux deux règnes. *Brux., Soc. Belge Micr. Bull.*, **16** (1890) 70–131

Mathematics

Prime, (Mme.)

Prime, (Mme.)

Sur le cercle orthocentroïdal. *Mathesis*, **13** (1893) 33–36

Denmark

Botany

Hallas, Emma Dorothea Kathinka Helene
Hallas, Emma
> Om en ny Zygnema-art med azygosporer. [Sur une nouvelle espèce de Zygnema avec azygospores.] [1895] *Bot. Tidsskr.*, **20** (1895–6) 1–14 (Res. 15–16)

Rostrup, Sofie (*née* **Jacobsen**)
Rostrup, Sofie
> Danske zoocecidier. *Bot. Centrbl. Beihefte* (1896) 527–28; *Kjøbenh. Vid. Medd.* (1896) 1–64
> Grønlandske phytoptider. *Kjøbenh. Vid. Medd.* (1900) 241–49

Entomology

Rostrup, Sofie (*née* **Jacobsen**)
Rostrup, Sofie
> {Den hessiske flue (Cecidomyia destructor). *Ugeskr. f. Landm.*, **10** (1896) 487–89}
> {Fritfluen (Oscinis frit). *Ugeskr. f. Landm.*, **1** (1897), 389–90}
> {Ødelagte græsplæner. *Gartner-Tid.*, **13** (1897), 142–44}
Westh, Th. Claudi; Rostrup, Sofie
> {Fritfluen (Orscinis frit). *Hedeselsk. Tidsskr.* **17** (1897), 202–10}

Chemistry

Meyer, Kirstine Bjerrum
Meyer, (Fru) Kirstine
> Om overensstemmende tilstande hos stofferne. [1899] *Kjøbenh., Dansk. Vid. Selsk. Skr.*, **9** (1898–1901) 155–225; *Ztschr. Physikal. Chem.*, **32** (1900) 1–38

Schou, Dagmar
Schou, Dagmar
> Ueber ein neues Doppelsalz des Platosemidiammins. *Ztschr. Anorg. Chem.*, **13** (1897) 36–37

Geography

Andersen, Astrid
Andersen, Astrid
> En sommerrejse i Diskobugten og Umanaksfjorden. *Stockh., Ymer.*, **17** (1897) 21–39

Finland

Chemistry

Sesemann, Lidiia
Sesemann, (Frl.) Lydia
> {Quadrimethylirten Anilin. *Berlin, Chem. Ges. Ber.*, **6** (1873) 446}
> Ueber die benzylirte und dibenzylirte Essigsäuren. *Berlin, Chem. Ges. Ber.*, **6** (1873) 1085–87
> Ueber Dibenzylessigsäure und eine neue Synthese der Homotoluylsäure. *Zürich Vrtljschr.*, **19** (1874) 1–26; *Chem. Soc. J.*, **13** (1875) 73–74

Mathematics

Öhberg, Maria
Öhberg, Maria
    {Om lineära differensekvationers integration. *Helsingfors Läreverks*, (1894) 83–100}

Physics

Lagerborg, Ebba Louise (Nanny; Baronesse Cedercreutz)
Lagerborg, (Mlle.) Nanny
    Études sur la variation des indices de réfraction et de la densité du sel gemme sous l'influence de la tempér-
        ature. [1887] *Stockh., Ak. Handl. Bihang*, **13** (Afd. 1) (1888) No. 10, 12 pp.
    Sur le problème du mouvement d'un corps solide autour d'un point fixe. *Paris, Soc. Math. Bull.*, **18** (1890)
        118–20

Geography

Öhberg, Maria
Öhberg, Maria
    Solfläckarnas inflytande på vattenståndet vid Kronstadt. *Fennia*, **9**, No. 4 (1894) 22–26

France

Agronomy and Technology

Fitz-James, Marguerite Augusta Marie Löwenhjelm, Duchesse de
Fitz-James, (Duchesse) de
    Action de la chaux sur les vignes atteintes du mildew. *Paris, Ac. Sci. C. R.*, **101** (1885) 1049–50
Gervais, Elisabeth
Gervais, (Mme.)
    Observations on the vinous fermentation; with a description of an apparatus for the improvement of the
        process. *Tilloch, Phil. Mag.*, **61** (1823) 34–42
Millet (also Millet-Robinet), Cora Élisabeth
Millet, —; Robinet, Stéphane; Millet, (Mme.) Cora Élisabeth
    Notice sur les éducations de vers à soie, faites en 1840, dans le département de la Vienne. *[France] Soc. Agr.
        Mém.* (1840) 377–497; {*Ann. Agr. Franç.*, 4, **1** (1840) 232–46}

Botany

Belèze, Marie Louise Marguerite
Belèze, (Mlle.) Marguerite
    Liste des plantes rares ou intéressantes (phanérogames, cryptogames vasculaires et characées) des environs de
        Montfort-l'Amaury et de la forêt de Rambouillet (Seine-et-Oise). *France Soc. Bot. Bull.*, **42** (1895)
        494–509; **43** (1896) 346–52; 814; **45** (1898) 30–32; 425–78; 688
    Liste des mousses et des hépatiques de la forêt de Rambouillet et des environs de Montfort-l'Amaury (Seine-
        et-Oise). *Ass. Franç. C. R.*, (Pt.2) (1900) 621–26
Camus, Aimée Antoinette
Camus, Edmond Gustave; Camus, (Mlle.) Aimée
    Plantes recoltées à Morcles (canton de Vaud) et à la montagne de Fully (Valais). *France Soc. Bot. Bull.*, **41**
        (1894) cccxi–cccxxii

Chauliaguet, Juliette Marie Augustine Marguerite
Chauliaguet, (Mlle.) J.; Hébert, Alexandre; Heim, Frédéric
   Sur les principes actifs de quelques Aroïdées. *Paris, Ac. Sci. C. R.*, **124** (1897) 1368–70
Frémont, A.
Frémont, (Mlle.) A.
   Sur les tubes criblés extra-libériens dans la racine des Oenotheracées. *J. Bot., Paris*, **5** (1891) 194–96
   Note sur les tubes criblés extra-libériens dans la racine des Lythrum. *J. Bot., Paris*, **5** (1891) 448
Joffé, Rachel
Joffé, (Mlle.) Rachel
   Observations sur la fécondation du Bangiacées. *France Soc. Bot. Bull.*, **43** (1896) 143–46
Leblois, Louise Amélie
Leblois, (Mlle.) A.
   Sur le rôle du latex dans les composées. *France Soc. Bot. Bull.*, **31** (1884) 122–24
   Production de thylles à l'intérieur des canaux sécréteurs. *France Soc. Bot. Bull.*, **34** (1887) 184–86
   Recherches sur l'origine et le développement des canaux sécréteurs et des poches sécrétrices. *Ann. Sci. Nat. (Bot.)*, **6** (1887) 247–330; *Rev. Sci.*, **47** (1888) 643–44
Mayoux, A.
Mayoux, (Mlle.) A.
   Recherches sur la valeur morphologique des appendices superstaminaux de la fleur des Aristoloches. *Lyon Univ. Ann.*, **2** (1892) Fasc. 4, 58 pp.
   Recherches sur la production et la localisation du tannin chez les fruits comestibles fournis par la famille des Pomacées. *Lyon Univ. Ann.*, **6** (1894) Fasc. 4, 40 pp.

Entomology

De Buzelet, (Mme. la Comtesse, *née* de Boissard)
Buzelet, (Mme. la Comtess de)
   Catalogue des coléoptères de l'Anjou, trouvés dans les communes de Saint-Rémy, Blaison, Saint-Maur, les bords de la Loire, etc. *Angers, Mém. Soc. Agric.*, **3** (1852) 269–304
Errington De La Croix,—
Errington De La Croix, (Mme.)
   Observations sur le Termes carbonarius, *Haviland. Paris, Mus. Hist. Nat. Bull.*, **6** (1900) 22–23

Medicine

Brès, Madeleine (*née* Gébelin)
Brès, Madeleine
   Analyse du lait des femmes Galibis du Jardin d'Acclimatation. *Paris, Ac. Sci. C. R.*, **95** (1882) 567
Gaches-Sarraute, Joséphine-Inèz (later Gaches-Barthélemy)
Gaches-Sarraute (Mme.)
   Des dangers de l'ergot de seigle et de l'ergotine après l'accouchement. *Ass. Franç. C. R.*, (Pt. 1) (1890) 240–41
   {Étude du corset au points de vue d'hygiène du vêtement de la femme. *Rev. Méd-chir. Mal Femmes*, **17** (1895) 389–98; *Rev. Hyg.*, **17** (1895) 399–407}
   {L'hygiène du corset; étude clinique et prophylactique; déductions pratiques d'application relatives au corset le mieux approprié. *Tribune Méd.*, **18** (1896) 406–12}
   {Le corset abdominal; ses avantages dans les ptoses des vicères abdominaux dans les hernies ombilicales, les évantrations de la ligne blanche et les déplacements de l'utérus. *Tribune Méd.*, **18** (1896) 1007–9}
   {La radiographie et l'hygiène du corset. *Tribune Méd.*, **19** (1897) 226–28}
Pilliet, Blanche Edwards
Edwards, (Mlle.) Blanche
   Fracture intra-utérine des deux tibias et syndactylie ou ectrodactylie concomitante. *Paris Soc. Anthrop. Bull.*, **10** (1887) 299–302
   Les microbes de la scarlatine. *Progrès Méd.*, **6** (1887) 121; 145–46

{Adenopathie trachéo-bronchique; méningite tuberculeuse chez un enfant de 6 mois; autopsie. *France Méd.*, **2** (1888) 1063, 1073}

{La salpingite interstitielle. *Progrès Méd.*, **9** (1889) 119–22}

{Pyopneumothorax au cours de la grossesse. *Nouv. Arch. Obst. Gynéc.*, **4** (1889) 233–38}

{Suite de la discussion sur la natalité et la dépopulation en France; avortement, mortinatalité, mortalité des nouveau-nés. *Paris Soc. Anthrop. Bull.*, **1** (1890) 838–50

Quelques faits de suggestion. *Progrès Méd.*, **11** (1890) 500–502

Des cirrhoses hépatiques de l'enfance. *Progrès Méd.*, **13** (1891) 25–27

Audain,—; Edwards, (Mlle.) Blanche

{Note sur un cas de cirrhose atrophique à marche rapide. *Tribune Méd.*, **18** (1886) 255–58}

Physiology

Phisalix-Picot, Marie
Phisalix-Picot, (Mme.)

Origine mésodermique des glandes à venin de la salamandre terrestre, et travail sécrétoire du noyau. *Congr. Int. Méd. C. R.*, **1** (Histol.) (1900) 54–57

Sur les clasmatocytes de la peau de la salamandre terrestre et de sa larve. *Paris, Mus. Hist. Nat. Bull.*, **6** (1900) 72–75; *Paris, Soc. Biol. Mém.*, **52** (C.R.) (1900) 178–80

Recherches embryologiques, histologiques et physiologiques sur les glandes à venin de la salamandre terrestre. *Paris, Mus. Hist. Nat. Bull.*, **6** (1900) 294–300

Origine et développement des glandes à venin de la salamandre terrestre. *Paris, Soc. Biol. Mém.*, **52** (C.R.) (1900) 479–81

Travail sécrétoire du noyau dans les glandes granuleuses de la salamandre terrestre. *Paris, Soc. Biol. Mém.*, **52** (C.R.) (1900) 481–83

Zoology

Barthelet,—
Barthelet, (Mlle.)

Expériences sur la télégonie. *Paris, Ac. Sci. C. R.*, **131** (1900) 911–12

Bignon, Louise Augustine (Fanny)
Bignon, (Mlle.) Fanny

Sur les cellules aériennes du crâne des oiseaux. *Paris, Soc. Biol. Mém. (C. R.)*, **39** (1887) 36–37

Recherches sur les cellules aériennes cervico-cephaliques chez les psittacidés. *France Soc. Zool. Bull.*, **13** (1888) 180–81

Recherches sur les rapports du système pneumatique de la tête des oiseaux avec le système dépendant de l'appareil pulmonaire. *Paris, Soc. Biol. Mém. (C. R.)*, **40** (1888) 357–60

Contribution à l'étude de la pneumaticité chez les oiseaux. Les cellules aériennes cervico-céphaliques des oiseaux et leurs rapports avec les os de la tête. *France Soc. Zool. Mém.*, **2** (1889) 260–320; *Rev. Sci.*, **46** (1890) 180–81

Note sur les réservoirs aériens de l'urubu (Cathartes atratus). *Paris, Soc. Biol. Mém. (C. R.)*, **41** (1889) 39–40

Note sur les réservoirs aériens de Sula bassana (fou de Bassan). *Paris, Soc. Biol. Mém. (C. R.)*, **41** (1889) 90–91

Remarques sur le procédé pour la préparation des poches aériennes indiqué par M. Plateau. *France Soc. Zool. Bull.*, **15** (1890) 99

L'intelligence des oiseaux. *Rev. Sci.*, **2** (1894) 365–67

{De l'enseignement de l'histoire naturelle dans les écoles primaires. *France Soc. Zool. Bull.*, **20** (1895), 51–54}

Bignon, (Mlle.) Fanny; Pilliet, Alexandre-Henri

Sur la glande lacrymale d'une tortue géante (Chelone viridis). *France Soc. Zool. Bull.*, **10** (1885) 60–66

Deflandre, Cl.
Carnot, Paul; Deflandre, (Mlle.) Cl.

Persistance de la pigmentation dans les greffes épidermiques. *Paris, Soc. Biol. Mém.*, **48** (C.R.) (1896) 178–80
Greffe et pigmentation. *Paris, Soc. Biol. Mém.*, **48** (C.R.) (1896) 430–32

Le Masson Le Golft, (Mlle.)
Le Masson Le Golft, (Mlle.)

Description du Lompe. *Rouen, Trav. Acad.* (1807) 55–56

Loyez, Marie
Loyez, (Mlle.) Marie

Sur un têtard de Rana temporaria bicéphale. *France Soc. Zool. Bull.*, **22** (1897) 146–48
Sur la constitution du follicule ovarien des reptiles. *Paris, Ac. Sci. C. R.*, **130** (1900) 48–50

Thiesse, (Mme.) Jos.
Thiesse, (Mme.) Jos.

Nouvelle Hélice (Helix hemonica, *n. sp.*) de Thessalie. *France Soc. Malacol. Bull.*, **1** (1884) 271–72

Astronomy

Royer, Clémence (Augustine-Clémence Audouard; Clémence-Auguste Royer)
Royer, (Mme.) Clémence

Critique de l'hypothèse de Laplace et détermination de l'orbite solaire. *Ass. Franç. C. R.*, 1883 (1883) 182–88

Vallot, Gabrielle (née Péron)
Vallot, Joseph; Vallot, (Mme.) Gabrielle

Observations actinométriques faites pendant l'éclipse de Soleil du 17 juin 1890. *Mont Blanc Obs. Ann.*, **2** (1896) 71–76
Nouvelles expériences d'actinométrie solaire exécutées au Mont Blanc en 1891. *Mont Blanc Obs. Ann.*, **2** (1896) 115–47

Chemistry

Chevalier, Joséphine
Chevalier, Joséphine

Chemische Untersuchung der Nervensubstanz. *Ztschr. Physiol. Chem.*, **10** (1886) 97–105

Royer, Clémence (Augustine-Clémence Audouard; Clémence-Auguste Royer)
Royer, (Mme.) Clémence

La constitution moléculaire de l'eau sous ses trois états physiques et les propriétés des gaz d'après une nouvelle hypothèse. *Ass. Franç. C. R.*, (1889) Pt. 2, 287–328

Vallot, Gabrielle (née Péron)
Vallot, Joseph; Vallot, (Mme.) Gabrielle

Influence de l'altitude et de la chaleur sur la décomposition de l'acide oxalique par la lumière solaire. *Paris, Ac. Sci. C. R.*, **125** (1897) 857–58
Expériences d'actinométrie chimique exécutées simultanément à des altitudes différentes et à diverses températures. *Mont Blanc Obs. Ann.*, **3** (1898) 81–96

Geology

Honnorat Bastide,—
Honnorat Bastide, (Mme.); Honnorat Bastide, Éd. F.

Sur les couches indécises du Lias et du Bajocien à Digne. *Ass. Franç. C. R.*, (Pt. 2) (1890) 369–76

Peney,—(née Burger)
Peney, (Mme.)

Tremblement de terre en Suisse. *France Soc. Météorol. Annu.*, **28** (1880) 61

Royer, Clémence (Augustine-Clémence Audouard; Clémence-Auguste Royer)
Royer, (Mme.) Clémence

Le lac de Paris à l'époque quaternaire. *Paris Soc. Anthrop. Bull.*, **10** (1875) 456–94

La périodicité des phénomènes glaciaires et le creusement des vallées quaternaires. *Congr. Int. Anthrop. C. R.* (1889) 114–47

Sinard, Berthe
Sinard, (Mlle.) B.

Sur la présence du Pentacrinus dans le Miocène des Angles (Gard). *Ass. Franç. C. R.*, (Pt. 2) (1891) 402–4

Mathematics

Bortniker, L.
Bortniker, (Mlle.) L.

Sur un genre particulier de transformations homographiques. *Paris, Ac. Sci. C. R.*, **104** (1887) 771–73

Sur la théorie des cyclides. *Paris, Ac. Sci. C. R.*, **106** (1888) 824–29

Germain, Marie-Sophie (Sophie)
Germain, (Mlle.) Sophie

Examen des principes qui peuvent conduire à la connaissance de lois de l'équilibre et du mouvement des solides élastiques. *Annal. de Chimie*, **38** (1828) 123–31

Mémoire sur la courbure des surfaces. *Crelle, J. Math.*, 7 (1831) 1–29

Note sur la manière dont se composent les valeurs de y et z dans l'équation $4(x^p − 1)/(x − 1) = y^2 ± pz^2$, et celles de y′ et z′ dans l'équation $4(x^{p2} − 1)/(x − 1) = y'^2 ± z'^2$,. *Crelle, J. Math.*, 7 (1831) 201–4

Mémoire sur l'emploi de l'épaisseur dans la théorie des surfaces élastiques. [1824] *Liouville, J. Math.*, **6** (1880) Suppl. [Posth.]

Meteorology

Bardin,—
Bardin, (Mme.)

Les mirages à Paris. *Astronomie* (1890) 153–54

Déo, Marie
Déo, (Mlle.) Marie

Halos solaires et parhélies. *Astronomie* (1890) 152

[L'aurore boréale du 28 février, 1894.] *Astronomie* (1894) 144

Physical Geography

Vallot, Gabrielle (*née* Péron)
Vallot, (Mme.) Gabrielle

Grottes et abîmes (Basses-Cévennes). *Paris, Club Alpin Franç. Annu.*, **16** (1890) 145–69

Vallot, (Mme.) Gabrielle; Vallot, Joseph

Expériences sur la vitesse de la circulation de l'eau dans les torrents et sous les glaciers. *Mont Blanc Obs. Ann.*, **4** (1900) 19–34

Anthropology

Bertillon, Jeanne
Bertillon, (Mlle.) Jeanne

L'indice encéphalo-cardiaque, d'après les documents laissés par le docteur Parrot. *Paris Soc. Anthrop. Bull.*, **10** (1887) 149–57

Pelletier, Madeleine (Anne)
Pelletier, Madeleine
    Recherches sur les indices pondéraux du crâne et des principaux os longs d'une série de squelettes japonais. *Paris Soc. Anthrop. Bull. & Mém.*, **1** (1900) 514–29

Renooz, Céline (Mme. Muro)
Renooz, (Mme.) C.
    Nouvelle théorie de l'évolution basée sur le développement embryonnaire tel qu'il est. *J. Microgr.*, **10** (1886) 135–39; 333–38; 373–78; 407–12; 459–64

Royer, Clémence Augustine (Augustine-Clémence Audouard; Clémence-Auguste Royer)
Royer, (Mme.) Clémence
    Remarques sur la transformisme. *Paris Soc. Anthrop. Bull.*, **5** (1870) 265–312
    Sur la crâniologie de l'époque quaternaire. *Paris Soc. Anthrop. Bull.*, **8** (1873) 189–200
    Sur les Celtes. *Paris Soc. Anthrop. Bull.*, **8** (1873) 243–47; 254–56
    Sur l'homme tertiaire. *Paris Soc. Anthrop. Bull.*, **8** (1873) 678–84
    Sur l'homme velu de Kostroma. *Paris Soc. Anthrop. Bull.*, **8** (1873) 718–24; 746–47
    Lois mathématiques de réversion par l'atavisme convergent. *Paris Soc. Anthrop. Bull.*, **8** (1873) 725–37
    De la méthode en crâniométrie. *Paris Soc. Anthrop. Bull.*, **8** (1873) 865–69
    De l'origine des diverses races humaines et de la race aryenne en particulier. *Paris Soc. Anthrop. Bull.*, **8** (1873) 905–36
    Deux hypothèses sur l'hérédité. *Rev. d'Anthrop.*, **6** (1877) 443–84; 660–85
    Le système pileux chez l'homme et dans la série des mammifères. *Rev. d'Anthrop.*, **3** (1880) 13–26
    L'instinct social. *Paris Soc. Anthrop. Bull.*, **5** (1882) 707–27
    Comment l'homme est-il devenu droitier? *Paris Soc. Anthrop. Bull.*, **6** (1883) 657–63
    Facultés mentales et instincts sociaux des singes. *Rev. Sci.*, **38** (1886) 257–70
    L'évolution mentale dans la série organique. *Rev. Sci.*, **39** (1887) 749–58; **40** (1887) 70–79
    Les notions de nombre chez les animaux. *Rev. Sci.*, **40** (1887) 649–58
    La domestication des singes. *Rev. d'Anthrop.*, **2** (1887) 170–81
    Variabilité morphologique des muscles sous l'influence des variations fonctionnelles. [With discussion.] *Paris Soc. Anthrop. Bull.*, **10** (1887) 643–49
    Sur la phylogénie. À propos d'un lézard bipède. *Paris Soc. Anthrop. Bull.*, **1** (1890) 156–206

France—Poland

Physics

Curie, Marie Sklodowska
Curie, (Mme.) Marie Sklodowska
    Propriétés magnétiques des aciers trempés. *Paris, Ac. Sci. C. R.*, **125** (1897) 1165–69; [Tr.] *Elect. Rev.*, **44** (1899) 40–42; 75–76; 112–13
    Rayons émis par les composés de l'uranium et du thorium. *Paris, Ac. Sci. C. R.*, **126** (1898) 1101–3
    On Becquerel's rays and polonium. [Tr.] *Chem. News*, **79** (1899) 77–78
    Sur le poids atomique du métal dans le chlorure de baryum radifère. *Paris, Ac. Sci. C. R.*, **129** (1899) 760–62
    Les nouvelles substances radioactives. *Rev. Sci.*, **14** (1900) 65–71
    Sur la pénétration des rayons de Becquerel non déviables par le champ magnétique. *Paris, Ac. Sci. C. R.*, **130** (1900) 76–79
    Sur le poids atomique du baryum radifère. *Paris, Ac. Sci. C. R.*, **131** (1900) 382–84
Curie, Pierre; Curie, (Mme.) Marie Sklodowska
    Sur une substance nouvelle radio-active, contenue dans la pechblende. *Paris, Ac. Sci. C. R.*, **127** (1898) 175–78
    Sur la radioactivité provoquée par les rayons de Becquerel. *Paris, Ac. Sci. C. R.*, **129** (1899) 714–16
    Effets chimiques produits par les rayons de Becquerel. *Paris, Ac. Sci. C. R.*, **129** (1899) 823–25
    Sur la charge électrique des rayons déviables du radium. *Paris, Ac. Sci. C. R.*, **130** (1900) 647–50
    Sur les propriétés des corps radio-actifs. *Paris, Soc. Phys. Séances* (1900) 10*–11*
    Radiations diverses des corps radio-actifs. *Paris, Soc. Phys. Séances* (1900) 20*–21*

Curie, Pierre; Curie, (Mme.) Marie Sklodowska; Bémont, G.

    Sur une nouvelle substance fortement radio-active, contenue dans la pechblende. *Paris, Ac. Sci. C. R.*, **127** (1898) 1215–17

France—Romania

Physiology

Pompilian, Mariette
Pompilian, (Mlle.) M.

    Influence du poids tenseur sur la chaleur dégagée par le muscle pendant la contraction. *Paris, Ac. Sci. C. R.*, **124** (1897) 1175–77

    Automatisme, période réfractaire et inhibition des centres nerveux des insectes. *Paris, Soc. Biol. Mém.*, **51** (C.R.) (1899) 400–401

    Sur la contraction musculaire de l'escargot. *Paris, Soc. Biol. Mém.*, **51** (C.R.) (1899) 489–90

    Temps de réaction nerveuse chez les mollusques. *Paris, Soc. Biol. Mém.*, **51** (C.R.) (1899) 490–92

    Accélération et inhibition des mouvements automatiques de la sangue. *Paris, Soc. Biol. Mém.*, **51** (C.R.) (1899) 574–75

    Automatisme de la moelle du Triton et automatisme des éléments nerveux en général. *Paris, Soc. Biol. Mém.*, **51** (C.R.) (1899) 575–76

    Nouveau cardiographe clinique. *Paris, Soc. Biol. Mém.*, **51** (C.R.) (1899) 702–3

    Automatisme des cellules nerveuses. *Paris, Ac. Sci. C. R.*, **130** (1900) 141–44

    Automatisme, période réfractaire et inhibition chez les insectes. *Congr. Int. Méd. C. R.*, **1**, *Physiol* (1900) 99–108

    Un nouveau pneumographe. *Paris, Soc. Biol. Mém.*, **52** (C.R.) (1900) 184–85

    Cellules nerveuses du coeur de l'escargot. *Paris, Soc. Biol. Mém.*, **52** (C.R.) (1900) 185–87

Charrin, Albert; Pompilian, (Mlle.) M.

    Influence des toxines microbiennes sur le contraction musculaire. *Paris, Soc. Biol. Mém. (C. R.)*, **48** (1896) 962–63

    Dissociation fonctionnelle des oreillettes et des ventricules. *Paris, Soc. Biol. Mém. (C. R.)*, **51** (1899) 704–7

Coleman, (Mlle.) A.; Pompilian, (Mlle.) M.

    Influence de la température sur la contraction musculaire des animaux à sang froid: grenouille, écrevisse. *Paris, Soc. Biol. Mém.*, **48** (C.R.) (1896) 696–98

Letulle, Maurice; Pompilian, (Mlle.) M.

    Respiration de Cheyne-Stokes. Théorie cérébrale de ce phenomène. *Paris, Soc. Biol. Mém.*, **51** (C.R.) (1899) 692–94

France—United States

Neurology and Physiology

Dejerine-Klumpke, Augusta
{Klumpke, A.

    Contribution à l'étude des paralysies radiculaires du plexus brachial. *Rev. Méd.*, **5** (1885) 591–616, 739–90}

Klumpke, (Mlle.) A. (Mme. Dejerine)

    Les fibres àberantes de la voie pédonculaire. *Congr. Int. Méd. C. R.*, **7** (1900) 193–95

Balzer, Félix; Klumpke, (Mlle.) A.

    Recherches expérimentales sur les lésions nécrosiques causées par les injections sous-cutanées des préparations mercurielles insolubles. *Paris, Soc. Biol. Mém.*, **40** (C.R.) (1888) 604–7

Dejerine, Jules; Klumpke, (Mlle.) A. (Mme. Dejerine)

    Contribution à l'étude de la dégénérescence des fibres du corps calleux. *Paris, Soc. Biol. Mém.*, **44** (C.R.) (1892) 579–85

    Sur les connexions du noyau rouge avec la corticalité cérébrale. *Paris, Soc. Biol. Mém.*, **47** (C.R.) (1895) 226–30

Sur les connexions du ruban de Reil avec la corticalité cérébrale. *Paris, Soc. Biol. Mém.*, **47** (C.R.) (1895) 285–91; 328

Sur les dégénérescences secondaires consécutives aux lésions de la circonvolution de l'hippocampe, de la corne d'Ammon, de la circonvolution godron née et du pli rétro-limbique (trigone cérébral, commissure antérieure, faisceau inférieur du forceps du corps calleux, tapetum et faisceau occipitofrontal). *Paris, Soc. Biol. Mém.*, **49** (C.R.) (1897) 587–90

Astronomy

Roberts, Dorothea Klumpke

Klumpke, (Mlle.) Dorothée

Observations des comètes faites à l'équatorial de la Tour de l'Est. [1896] *Paris Obs. Ann. (Obsns.)* (1888) F. 37–F. 40

Observations de la nouvelle comète Barnard (1889 mars 31), faite à l'Observatoire de Paris (équatorial de la Tour de l'Est.) *Paris, Ac. Sci. C. R.*, **108** (1889) 846–47

Observation de la comète Swift (1889; nov. 17), faite à l'équatorial de la Tour de l'Est. *Paris, Ac. Sci. C. R.*, **109** (1889) 792

Observations faites à l'équatorial de 38 cm. (Tour de l'Est). [1898–1907] *Paris Obs. Ann. (Obsns.)* (1889) F. 33–F. 42

Beobachtungen des Cometen 1890 . . . (Coggia Juli 18). *Astr. Nachr.*, **125** (1890) 77–78

Observations de la comète 1890 . . . (Coggia juillet 18) faites à l'Observatoire de Paris (équatorial de la Tour de l'Est). *Astr. Nachr.*, **125** (1890) 89–90

Observations de la nouvelle planète Luther (Hambourg, 24 février 1890), faites à l'Observatoire de Paris (équatorial de la tour de l'Est). *Paris, Ac. Sci. C. R.*, **110** (1890) 452

Observations de la comète Brooks (19 mars 1890), faites à l'Observatoire de Paris (équatorial de la Tour de l'Est). *Paris, Ac. Sci. C. R.*, **110** (1890) 747

Observations de la comète Coggia (18 juillet 1890, Marseille), faites à l'Observatoire de Paris (équatorial de la Tour de l'Est). *Paris, Ac. Sci. C. R.*, **111** (1890) 224

Observations de la nouvelle planète Palisa (Vienne, 17 août 1890), faites à l'Observatoire de Paris (équatorial de la Tour de l'Est). *Paris, Ac. Sci. C. R.*, **111** (1890) 356

Observation de la nouvelle comète Zona (Palerme, 15 novembre 1890) faite à l'Observatoire de Paris (équatorial de la Tour de l'Est). *Paris, Ac. Sci. C. R.*, **111** (1890) 782; 853

Sur l'étude des spectres stellaires faite aux Observatoires de Hastings et de Cambridge (É. U.). *Bull. Astr.*, **7** (1890) 287–94

Observations des comètes 1889 II, 1889 V et de la planète (107), faites à l'Observatoire de Paris (équatorial de la Tour de l'Est). *Bull. Astr.*, **7** (1890) 304–5

Observations faites à l'équatorial de 38 cm. (Tour de l'Est). [1898–1907] *Paris Obs. Ann. (Obsns.)* (1890) F. 21–F. 32

Observations de la planète Charlois (Nice, 11 février 1891), faites à l'Observatoire de Paris (équatorial de la Tour de l'Est). *Paris, Ac. Sci. C. R.*, **112** (1891) 377; 451

Observations de la planète Millosevich (Rome, 1891, mars 1), faites à l'Observatoire de Paris (équatorial de la Tour de l'Est). *Paris, Ac. Sci. C. R.*, **112** (1891) 511–12

Observations de la planète Millosevich (304) [(303)], faites à l'Observatoire de Paris (équatorial de la Tour de l'Est). *Paris, Ac. Sci. C. R.*, **112** (1891) 606–7

Observation de la nouvelle planète Charlois (Nice, juin 11, 1891), faite à l'Observatoire de Paris, équatorial de la Tour de l'Est. *Paris, Ac. Sci. C. R.*, **112** (1891) 1353

Observation de la comète Tempel-Swift, faite à l'Observatoire de Paris (équatorial de la Tour de l'Est). *Paris, Ac. Sci. C. R.*, **113** (1891) 456

Observations de la planète Borrelly (Marseille, 27 novembre 1891), faites à l'Observatoire de Paris (équatorial de la Tour de l'Est). *Paris, Ac. Sci. C. R.*, **113** (1891) 838

Observations faites à l'équatorial de 38 cm. (Tour de l'Est). [1898–1907] *Paris Obs. Ann. (Obsns.)* (1891) C. 21–C. 31

Beobachtungen des Cometen 1892 . . . (Swift März 6). Auf der Sternwarte in Paris. *Astr. Nachr.*, **129** (1892) 245–46

Beobachtungen des Planeten (325) (Wolf März 4) auf der Sternwarte in Paris. *Astr. Nachr.*, **129** (1892) 277–78

Observations de la comète Swift (Rochester, 6 mars 1892) et de la planète Wolf (Vienne, 18 mars 1892) faites à l'Observatoire de Paris (équatorial de la Tour de l'Est). *Paris, Ac. Sci. C. R.*, **114** (1892) 725–26

Observations des nouvelles planètes (Wolf, 28 mars 1892), Charlois, 1er avril 1892), faites à l'Observatoire de Paris (équatorial de la Tour de l'Est.) *Paris, Ac. Sci. C. R.*, **114** (1892) 826–27

The Bureau of Measurements of the Paris Observatory. *Astr. & Astrophys.*, **12** (1893) 783–88; 857

Contribution à l'étude des anneaux de Saturne. *Paris Obs. Ann. (Mém.)*, **21** (1895) C. 60 pp.

Éléments définitifs de la comète 1885 III. *Bull. Astr.*, **13** (1896) 329–37

Notes du voyage relatif à l'éclipse totale de Soleil (9 août 1896). *Bull. Astr.*, **14** (1897) 36–48

Note sur l'orbite de la comète 1886 V. *Bull. Astr.*, **14** (1897) 305–7

Observations de quelques étoiles filantes apparues dans les nuits des 9, 10, 12, 13, 14, 16, 18 août. *Paris, Ac. Sci. C. R.*, **127** (1898) 383–85

Observations des Perséides de 1899. *Paris, Ac. Sci. C. R.*, **129** (1899) 381–82

The work of women in astronomy. *Observatory, London*, **22** (1899) 295–300

Éclipse de Soleil du 28 mai 1900, observée en ballon. *Paris, Ac. Sci. C. R.*, **130** (1900) 1529–31

Observations d'étoiles filantes, faites du 11 au 14 août 1900 à l'Observatoire de Paris. *Paris, Ac. Sci. C. R.*, **131** (1900) 439–40

Sur les éclipses. Ascension de l'*Aéro-Club* à l'occasion de l'éclipse du 28 mai 1900. *Aéronaute* (1900) 174–79

Germany

Bacteriology

Wolff, Elise
Wolff, Elise
Ueber Celloïdineinbettung und Färbung von Tuberkelbacillen in Celloïdinschnitten. *Ztschr. Wiss. Mikr.*, **16** (1899) 427–31

Biology

Linden, Maria von (Gräfin)
Linden, Maria (Gräfin) von
Bilder aus dem Tierleben. *Humboldt*, **9** (1890) 281–82; 351
Bildung von Kalktuff unter Mitwirkung von Phryganeen-Larven. *Wien, Nat. Hist. Hofmus. Ann.*, **5** (Not.) (1890) 81–83
Das Schwimmen der Schnecken am Wasserspiegel. *Biol. Centrbl.*, **11** (1891) 763–66
Beiträge zur Biologie der Phryganeiden. *Biol. Centrbl.*, **12** (1892) 523–27
Die Selbstverstümmlung bei Phryganeidenlarven. *Biol. Centrbl.*, **13** (1893) 81–83
Die Entwicklung der Skulptur und der Zeichnung bei den Gehäuseschnecken des Meeres. *Ztschr. Wiss. Zool.*, **61** (1896) 261–317
Unabhängige Entwicklungsgleichheit bei Schneckengehäusen. *Biol. Centrbl.*, **18** (1898) 697–703; *Ztschr. Wiss. Zool.*, **63** (1898) 708–28
Beobachtungen über die Ontogenie unserer einheimischen Tritonen. *Württemb. Jhefte.*, **55** (1899) 31–35
Die ontogenetische Entwicklung der Zeichnung unserer einheimischen Molche. *Biol. Centrbl.*, **20** (1900) 144–67; 226–41
Die Färbung und Zeichnung der Landplanarien. *Biol. Centrbl.*, **20** (1900) 556–60

Botany

Lüders, Johanna Elisabeth De Boor
Lüders, Joh. E.
Einige Bemerkungen über Diatomeen-Cysten und Diatomeen-Schwärmsporen. *Bot. Ztg.*, **18** (1860) 377–80

Die unterirdische Saamenbildung der Oxalis acetosella, *Lin. Harz, Naturw. Ver. Ber.* (1861–2) 5–6

Beobachtungen über die Organisation, Theilung, und Copulation der Diatomeen. *Bot. Ztg.*, **20** (1862) 41–53; 49–52; 57–61; 65–69

Ueber Abstammung und Entwickelung des Bacterium Termo, *Duj.* = Vibrio lineola, *Ehrb.* [1865] *Bot. Ztg.*, **24** (1866) 33–39; 41–46; *Arch. Mikr. Anat.*, **3** (1867) 317–41

Schwabach, Elise Salomon

Schwabach, (Frau) E.

Ueber die Vorgänge bei der Sprengung des mechanischen Ringes bei einigen Lianen. *Bot. Centrbl.*, **76** (1898) 353–61

Zur Kenntniss der Harzabscheidungen in Coniferennadeln. *Deutsch. Bot. Ges. Ber.*, **17** (1899) 291–302

Bemerkungen zu den Angaben von A. Tschirch über die Harzabscheidungen in Coniferennadeln. *Deutsch. Bot. Ges. Ber.*, **18** (1900) 417–21

Widmer, Elise

Widmer, E.

Beitrag zur Kenntniss der rothblühenden Alpen-Primel. *Flora*, **72** (1889) 69–74

Entomology

Linden, Maria von (Gräfin)

Linden, Maria (Gräfin) von

Aus dem Insektenleben. *Biol. Centrbl.*, **11** (1891) 71–73

Die Artbildung und Verwandschaft bei den Schmetterlingen. Nach G. H. Th. Eimer. *Biol. Centrbl.*, **17** (1897) 179–90; 213–26

Neue Untersuchungen über die Entwickelung der Schuppen, Farben und Farbenmuster auf den Flügeln der Schmetterlinge und Motten. *Biol. Centrbl.*, **18** (1898) 229–239

Untersuchungen über die Entwickelung der Zeichnung des Schmetterlingsflügels in der Puppe. *Ill. Ztschr. Ent.*, **3** (1898) 321–23; 370–72; **4** (1899) 19–22; *Ztschr. Wiss. Zool.*, **65** (1899) 1–49

Versuche über den Einfluss äusserer Verhältnisse auf die Gestaltung der Schmetterlinge. Eine vorläufige Mitteilung. *Ill. Ztschr. Ent.*, **4** (1899) 225–27; 261–63; 321–23; 339–41; 369–72

Theresia Charlotte Maria Anna, Prinzessin von Bayern

Therese, (Prinzessin) von Bayern

In Südamerika gesammelte Myriapoden und Arachnoideen. [Nebst Bemerkungen von Dr. Penther.] *Zool. Anz.*, **23** (1900) 279–86

Von ihrer königl. Hoheit der Prinzessin Therese von Bayern auf einer Reise in Südamerika gesammelte Insekten. [Fortsetzung]. II. Orthopteren. [Mit Diagnose zweier neuer Orthopteren von Brunner.] *Berlin. Ent. Ztschr.*, **45** (1900) 253–68

Medical Sciences

Babo, Agnes von

Babo, Agnes von

Ein Fall von kleincystischer Entartung beider Ovarien. *Virchow, Arch.*, **161** (1900) 311–28.

Bäumler, Anna

Bäumler, Anna

Ueber Höhlenbildungen im Rückenmark. *Deutsch. Arch. Klin. Med.*, **40** (1887) 443–543

Democh-Maurmeer, Ida

Democh, Ida

Ein Beitrag zur Lehre von der spastischen Spinalparalyse. *Arch. Psychiatr.*, **33** (1900) 188–205

Herbig, Molly

Herbig, Molly

Beiträge zur Histogenese der Lungeninduration. *Virchow, Arch.*, **136** (1894) 311–27

Stier, Sieglinde
Stier, Sieglinde
    Experimentelle Untersuchung über das Verhalten der quergestreiften Muskeln nach Läsionen des Nerven-
    systems. *Arch. Psychiat.*, **29** (1896) 249–98

Ornithology

Ramdohr, Emma von
Ramdohr, Emma von
    Ueberwinterung einer jungen Turmschwalbe. *Ornith. Mber.*, **5** (1897) 156–60
Ulm zu Erbach, Olga Margarete Ida Helene (Baronin von; *née* von Siebold))
Ulm-Erbach, Helene (Baronin) von
    Einführung neuer Hühner-Rassen aus Japan. *Wien Ornith. Ver. Mitth. (Beibl.)*, **1** (1884) 36–37; 41–44;
    49–51
    Die Locken oder Zottelgans. *Wien Ornith. Ver. Mitth. (Beibl.)*, **1** (1884) 163–64
    Die Entenrassen. *Wien Ornith. Ver. Mitth. (Beibl.)*, **1** (1884) 209–12
    Die Geflügelzucht in Japan. *Wien Ornith. Ver. Mitth.*, **8** (1884) 7–11
    Skizzen aus dem Vogelleben in Japan. *Wien Ornith. Ver. Mitth.*, **9** (1885) 25–29
    Das schwanzlose Huhn. *Wien Ornith. Ver. Mitth.*, **10** (1886) 88–90
    Falkenjagd in Japan. *Wien Ornith. Ver. Mitth.*, **10** (1886) 114–17
    In Erbach bei Ulm im Donauthal vorkommende Vögel. *Wien Ornith. Ver. Mitth.*, **10** (1886) 171–73
    Beobachtungen über die Ankunft der Zugvögel in der Umgegend von Erbach, im württembergischen Ober-
    lande. *Wien Ornith. Ver. Mitth.*, **11** (1887) 23; 88
    Beschreibung der aus Japan importirten Kampf-Hühner: Chamo. *Wien Ornith. Ver. Mitth.*, **11** (1887) 49–50
    Beobachtungen aussergewöhnlicher Nistplätze einiger Vogelarten. *Wien Ornith. Ver. Mitth.*, **12** (1888)
    88–89; 132–34
    Ueber verschiedene neue Hühnerrassen. *Wien Ornith. Ver. Mitth.*, **12** (1888) 89–90
    Zur Verbesserung der Hühnerzucht aus dem Lande. *Wien Ornith. Ver. Mitth.*, **12** (1888) 162–64
    Aus dem 1610 erschienenen Werke über Ornithologie von Ulysses Aldrovandus. *Wien Ornith. Ver. Mitth.*,
    15 (1891) 206–7; 216–19; 227–28

Physiology

Glause, Amalie
Glause, Amalie
    Zur Kenntniss der Hemmungsmechanismen des Herzens. *Bern Mitth.*, (Heft 2, Abh.) (1884) 3–43
Glause, Amalie; Luchsinger, Balthasar
    Zur Kenntniss der physiologischen Wirkungen einiger Ammoniumbasen. *Fortschr. Med.*, **2** (1884) 276–77
Traube-Mengarini, Margarethe
Traube-Mengarini, Margherita
    Experimentelle Beiträge zur Physiologie des Fischgehirnes. *Arch. Anat. Physiol. (Physiol. Abt.)* (1884) 553–65
    Ricerche sui gas contenuti nella vesica natatoria dei pesci. *Roma, R. Acc. Lincei Rend.*, **3** (Sem. 2) (1887)
    55–62; **4** (Sem. 1) (1888) 89–94; 313–16
    Ueber die Gase in der Schwimmblase der Fische. *Arch. Anat. Physiol. (Physiol. Abt.)* (1889) 54–63
    Ricerche sulla permeabilità della pelle. *Roma, R. Acc. Lincei Rend.*, 7 (Sem. 2) (1891) 171–75; **5** (Sem. 1)
    (1896) 14–19
Weiss, Clara
Weiss, Clara
    Ueber endoneurale Wucherungen in den peripherischen Nerven des Hundes. *Virchow, Arch.*, **135** (1894)
    326–55

Zoology

Hamburger, Clara
Hamburger, Clara
    Studien zur Entwickelung der Mammarorgane. 1. Die Zitze von Pferd und Esel. *Anat. Anz.*, **18** (1900)
    16–26

Plehn, Marianne

Plehn, Marianne

[Semon's zoologische Forschungsreisen in Australien und dem Malayischen Archipel.] Polycladen von Ambon. [1896] *Jena Denkschr.*, **8** (1894–1903) 327–34

Neue Polycladen, gesammelt von Herrn Kapitän Chierchia bei der Erdumschiffung der Korvette *Vettor Pisani*, von Herrn Prof. Dr. Kükenthal im nördlichen Eismeer und von Herrn Prof. Dr. Semon in Java. *Jena. Ztschr.*, **30** (1896) 137–76

Drei neue Polycladen. *Jena. Ztschr.*, **31** (1898) 90–99

[Ergebnisse einer zoologischen Forschungsreise in den Molukken und Borneo, im Auftrage der Senckenbergischen Naturforschenden Gesellschaft ausgeführt von Dr. Willy Kükenthal.] Polycladen von Ternate. *Senckenb. Natf. Ges. Abh.*, **24** (1898) 145–46

{Über die Vertilgung von Fischeglen. *Allg. Fisch.-Zt.*, 21 (1898) 370–72}

{Über die Schädlichkeit von Carbolineum für Fische. *Allg. Fisch.-Zt.*, 20 (1899) 349–50}

Ergebnisse einer Reise nach dem Pacific (Schauinsland 1896–97). Polycladen. *Zool. Jbüch. (Syst.)*, **12** (1899) 448–52

Theresia Charlotte Maria Anna, Prinzessin von Bayern

Therese, (Prinzessin) von Bayern

Vorläufige Mittheilung über einige neue Fischarten aus den Seen von Mexico. *Wien, Anz.*, **31** (1894) 147–49

Im Jahre 1898 auf einer Reise in Südamerika gesammelte Mollusken. *Deutsch. Malakozool. Ges. Nachrbl.*, **32** (1900) 49–56

Therese, (Prinzessin) von Bayern; Steindachner, Franz.

Ueber einige Fischarten Mexico's und die Seen, in welchen sie vorkommen. *Wien, Ak. Denkschr.*, **62** (1895) 517–30

Astronomy

Linden, Maria von (Gräfin)

Linden, Maria (Gräfin) von

Beobachtung eines Meteors. *Württemb. Jhefte.*, **48** (1892) 264–65

Prittwitz, F. (K.) von

Prittwitz, (Frau) F. von

Helligkeitsmessungen des Planeten Mars. *Astr. Nachr.*, **150** (1899) 43–46

Chemistry

Baum, Marie

Bamberger, Eugen; Baum, Marie

Ueber die Naphtalendiazooxyde $C_{10} H_6 N_2 O$. [1899] *Zürich Vrtljschr.*, **43** (1898) 327–39

Bamberger, E.; L'Orsa, T.; Tschirner, F.; Baum, M.

{Ueber die Einwirkung von Formaldehyd auf ß-Arylhydroxylamin. *Berlin, Chem. Ges. Ber.*, **33** (1900) 941–55}

Haber, Clara Helene Immerwahr

Immerwahr, C.

Potentiale von Kupferelektroden in Lösungen analytisch wichtiger Kupferniederschläge. *Ztschr. Anorg. Chem.*, **24** (1900) 269–78; **25** (1900) 112

Abegg, Richard; Immerwahr, C.

Notiz über das elektrochemische Verhalten des Fluorsilbers und des Fluors. *Ztschr. Physikal. Chem.*, **32** (1900) 142–44

Ueber den Einfluss des Bindemittels auf den photochemischen Effekt in Bromsilberemulsionen und die photochemische Induktion. [1900] *Wien, Ak. Sber.*, 109, Abt. 2a (1900) 974–80; *Mhefte. Chem.* (1901) 88–94

Willdenow, Clara

Willdenow, Clara

Ueber Lysursäure und ihre Salze. *Ztschr. Physiol. Chem.*, **25** (1898) 523–50

Wohlbrück, Olga
Wohlbrück, Olga
 Ueber die Einwirkung von Natrium auf höher moleculare Fettsäureäther. *Berlin, Chem. Ges. Ber.*, **20** (1887)
  2332–40
Hantzsch, Arthur; Wohlbrück, Olga
 Ueber den sogen. Propiopropionsäureäther. *Berlin, Chem. Ges. Ber.*, **20** (1887) 1320–25

Geology

Linden, Maria von (Gräfin)
Linden, Maria (Gräfin) von
 Die Indusienkalke der Hürbe. *Oberrhein. Geol. Ver. Ber.*, (1890) 14–20

Physics

Köttgen, Else
Köttgen, (Frl.) Else
 Untersuchung der spectralen Zusammensetzung verschiedener Lichtquellen. *Ann. Phys. Chem.*, **53** (1894)
  793–818
Neumann, Elsa
Neumann, Elsa
 Polarisationskapazität umkehrbarer Elektroden. [1898] *Ztschr. Elektroch.*, (1898–9) 85–88
 Ueber die Polarisationskapazität umkehrbarer Elektroden. *Ann. Phys. Chem.*, **67** (1899) 500–534
Pockels, Agnes Luise Wilhelmine
Pockels, Agnes
 Surface tension. [Communicated in a letter to Lord Rayleigh.] [Tr.] *Nature*, **43** (1891) 437–39
 On the relative contamination of the water-surface by equal quantities of different substances. *Nature*, **46**
  (1892) 418–19
 Relations between the surface-tension and relative contamination of water surfaces. *Nature*, **48** (1893)
  152–54
 On the spreading of oil upon water. *Nature*, **50** (1894) 223–24
 {Beobachtungen über die Adhäsion verschiedener Flüssigkeiten an Glas. *Nat. Rund.*, **13** (1898) 190}
 {Randwinkel gesättiger Lösungen an Kristallen. *Nat. Rund.*, **14** (1899) 383}
 Untersuchung von Grenzflächenspannungen mit der Kohäsionswaage. *Ann. Phys. Chem.*, **67** (1899) 668–81

Anthropology and Archaeology

Karsten, Paula Franziska Wilhelmine
Karsten, (Frl.) Paula
 Einiges über die Araber von Nord-Africa. *Ztschr. Ethnol.*, **29** (1897) (372)–(376)
 {Der Vorabend des muselmanischen Sabbaths bei den 'Aīsâwa (einer Art von Derwischen). *Ztschr. Ethnol.*,
  29 (1897) (376)–(379)}
Mestorf, Johanna
Mestorf, (Frl.) Joh.
 {Das ältere Eisenalter in Scandinavian. *Deutsch. Ges. Anthrop. Ethnol. Urgeschichte, Corres.-Bl.*, 7, (1870)
  53–56; **8** (1870) 58–60}
 {Die altgrönländische Religion und die religiösen Begriffe der heutigen Grönlander, Teil I–V. *Globus*, **19**
  (1871) 11–14, 23–26, 38–39, 55–56, 70–71}
 {Über die Holstein und anderwärts gefundenen Moorleichen. *Globus*, **20** (1871) 9}
 {Die dänischen Gräber der Bronzezeit in ihren Beziehungen zu denen der Steinzeit. *Deutsch. Ges. Anthrop.
  Ethnol. Urgeschichte, Corres.-Bl.*, 1 (1872) 4–7; 2 (1872) 9–13; 5 (1872) 37–39}

{Funde in Holstein aus der letzten heidnischen Zeit. Krinkberg, Frestedt, Vaale, Bendorf, Immenstedt. *Ztschr. Ges. Schlesw.-Holst.-Lauen. Geschichte*, **16** (1886) 411–14}

Die Hacksilberfunde im Museum vaterländischer Alterthümer zu Kiel. [1895–96] {*Mitth. Anthrop. Ver. Schlesw.-Holst.*, 8 (1895) 1–2}; *Arch. Anthrop. Geol. Schlesw.-Holst.*, **1** (1896) 3–12; **2** (1897) 14

Bronzemesser mit figürlichen Darstellungen. [1896] *Arch. Anthrop. Geol. Schlesw.-Holst.*, **2** (1897) 9–13

Die holsteinischen Gürtel. *Arch. Anthrop. Geol. Schlesw.-Holst.*, **2** (1897) 189–201

Steinaltergräber. *Arch. Anthrop. Geol. Schlesw.-Holst.*, **3** (1900) 94–104

Glasperlen aus Frauengräbern der Bronzezeit. *Arch. Anthrop. Geol. Schlesw.-Holst.*, **3** (1900) 160–71

{Moorleichen. *Globus*, 78 (1900) 18}

Geography

Theresia Charlotte Maria Anna, Prinzessin von Bayern

Therese, (Prinzessin) von Bayern

Zwecke und Ergebnisse [ihrer] im Jahre 1898 nach Südamerika unternommenen Reise. *München Geogr. Ges. Jber.*, **18** (1900) 1–7

Psychology

Köttgen, Else

Köttgen, (Frl.) Else; Abelsdorff, Georg

Die Arten des Sehpurpurs in der Wirbelthierreihe. *Berlin Ak. Sber.* (1895) 921–26

Absorption und Zersetzung des Sehpurpurs bei den Wirbeltieren. *Ztschr. Psychol.*, **12** (1896) 161–84

Pötsch, Anna

Pötsch, Anna

Ueber Farbenvorstellungen Blinder. *Ztschr. Psychol.*, **19** (1899) 47–62

Germany—Russia

Botany

Rabinowitsch-Kempner, Lydia

Rabinowitsch, Lydia

Beiträge zur Entwicklungsgeschichte der Fruchtkörper einiger Gastromyceten. *Flora*, **79** (1894) 385–418

Bacteriology

Rabinowitsch-Kempner, Lydia

Rabinowitsch, Lydia

Ueber die thermophilen Bakterien. *Ztschr. Hyg.*, **20** (1895) 154–64

Untersuchungen über pathogene Hefearten. *Ztschr. Hyg.*, **21** (1896) 11–24

Zur Frage des Vorkommens von Tuberkelbacillen in der Marktbutter. *Ztschr. Hyg.*, **26** (1897) 90–111; {*Deutsche Med. Wschr.*, **23** (1897) 507}

{Weitere Untersuchungen zur Frage des Vorkommens von Tuberkelbacillen in der Marktbutter. *Deutsche Med. Wschr.*, **25** (1899) 5–6}

{Befund von säurefesten tuberkelbacillenähnlichen Bacterien bei Lungengangrän. *Deutsche Med. Wschr.*, **26** (1900) 257–58}

{Ueber Tuberkelbacillen in Milch und Molkereiprodukten. *Ztschr. Untersuch. Nahr. Genuss.*, **12** (1900) 801–9}

{Ueber die Gefahr der Uebertragung der Tuberkulose durch Milch und Milchproduckte. *Deutsche Med. Wschr.*, **26** (1900) 416–18}

Rabinowitsch, Lydia; Kempner, Walter

   Beitrag zur Kenntniss der Blutparasiten, speziell der Rattentrypanosomen. *Ztschr. Hyg.*, **30** (1899) 251–94

   Beitrag zur Frage der Infektiosität der Milch tuberkulöser Kühe, sowie über den Nutzen der Tuberkulinimpfung. *Arch. Wiss. Prakt. Thierheilk.*, **25** (1899) 281–97; *Ztschr. Hyg.*, **31** (1899) 137–52

   {Bemerkung zu Prof. Ostertag's Arbeit "Ueber die Virulenz der Milch von Kühen, welche lediglich auf Tuberkulin reagirten, klinischen Erscheinungen der Tuberkulose aber nicht zeigen," sowie Erwiderung auf seine unseren diesbezüglichen Untersuchungen gegenüber gemachten Einwände. *Centrbl. Bakt.* (Abt. 1, Originale, **26** (1899) 289–92}

Beck, M.; Rabinowitsch, Lydia

   {Ueber der Wert der Courmont'schen Serumreaction für die Frühdiagnose der Tuberkulose. *Deutsche Med. Wschr.*, **26** (1900) 400–403}

Ireland

Botany

Glascott, Louisa S.

Barrett-Hamilton, G. E. H.; Glascott, (Miss) L. S.

   Plants found near New Ross, Ireland. *J. Bot.*, **27** (1889) 4–8

   Plants found near Kilmanock, Co. Wexford. *J. Bot.*, **28** (1890) 87–89

Hart, J. B.

Hart, J. B. (Mrs. W. E.)

   Note on a supposed root-parasite found at Mahabelshwar in October, 1885. *Bombay Nat. Hist. Soc. J.*, **1** (1886) 75–77

   Note on some branching palms. *Bombay Nat. Hist. Soc. J.*, **3** (1888) 250–55

Hensman, Rachel

Johnson, Thomas; Hensman, (Miss) R.

   [Report of the conference and excursion held at Galway, July 11th to July 17th 1895.] Algae. *Irish Natlist.*, **4** (1895) 241–42

   Algae from the north side of Belfast Lough. (Dredged by the B. N. F. C. Expedition, 4th July 1896.) *Irish Natlist.*, **5** (1896) 252–53

   A list of Irish Corallinaceae. [1898] *Dublin Soc. Sci. Proc.*, **9** (1899–1902) 22–30

Johnson, Thomas; Hanna, Henry

   Irish Phaeophyceae. (Report of the Fauna and Flora Committee). [Assisted by Miss R. Hensman and Miss M. C. Knowles.] [1899] *Irish Ac. Proc.*, **5** (1898–1900) 441–61

Joyce, Margaret Elizabeth

Joyce, Margaret E.

   Neotinea intacta in Co. Galway. *Irish Natlist.*, **8** (1899) 143

   Botanical notes from east Galway. *Irish Natlist.*, **8** (1899) 181

   {Geranium pyrenaicum in South-east Galway. *Irish Natlist.*, **8** (1899) 206}

Knowles, Matilda Cullen

Knowles, (Miss) M. C.

   Flowering plants of Co. Tyrone. *Irish Natlist.*, **6** (1897) 83–84

Johnson, Thomas

   {Seaweeds from S. E. Ireland. (Collected for the Flora and Fauna Committee). [Assisted by Miss M. C. Knowles.] *Irish Natlist.*, **6** (1897) 139–40 [abstract]}

Johnson, Thomas; Hanna, Henry

   Irish Phaeophyceae. (Report of the Fauna and Flora Committee). [Assisted by Miss R. Hensman and Miss M. C. Knowles.] [1899] *Irish Ac. Proc.*, **5** (1898–1900) 441–61

Leebody, Mary Isabella

Leebody, (Mrs.) M. I.

   Spiranthes romanzoviana in Co. Londonderry. *Irish Natlist.*, **2** (1893) 228

   Stachys betonica in Donegal. *J. Bot.*, **37** (1899) 273

Swan, Lilian M.

Swan, Lilian M.

   Sisyrinchium angustifolium in Co. Cork. *J. Bot.*, **36** (1898) 442

Conchology

Hensman, Rachel
Hensman, (Miss R.)
{Some causes of the disintegration of shells. *Irish Natlist.*, **4** (1895) 137–41}

Galwey, Honoria
Galwey, (Miss) Honoria
On the marine shells of Magilligan Strand, County Tyrone. [1887] *J. Conch.*, **5** (1886–88) 267–70

Massy, Annie Letitia
Massy, Annie L.
Land shells from Co. Limerick. *Irish Natlist.*, **8** (1899) 143

Tatlow, Emily M.
Tatlow, Emily M.
Marine shells from southwest Donegal. *Irish Natlist.*, **8** (1899) 235–38
Tatlow, Emily M.; Praeger, Robert Lloyd
[Impressions of Achill by members of an Easter party]. Marine Mollusca. *Irish Natlist.*, **7** (1898) 139–40

Warren, Amy
Warren, Amy
The land and freshwater Mollusca of Mayo and Sligo. *Zoologist*, **3** (1879) 25–29
Contributions towards a list of the marine Mollusca of Killala Bay, Ireland. [1892] *J. Conch.*, **7** (1892–94) 98–107
{Limax flavus in the west of Ireland. *Irish Natlist.*, **1** (1892) 126}
{Rare molluscs from County Sligo. *Irish Natlist.*, **1** (1892) 170–71}
Trochus duminyi and Odostomia delicata on the Irish coast. *Irish Natlist.*, **2** (1893) 252–53
{Helix rufescens in the North of Ireland. *Irish Natlist.*, **2** (1893) 301}
Donax vittatus, *var.* truncatus, *Marshall, MS. Irish Natlist.*, **4** (1895) 18
{Lepton sykesil, *Chaster*, in Killala Bay. *Irish Natlist.*, **4** (1895) 384}
{Spiralis retroversus in Killala Bay. *Irish Natlist.*, **5** (1896) 248}

Entomology

Ball, Mary
Ball, Robert
On the noise made by Corixa striata, *Curtis* under water. *Ann. Nat. Hist.*, **17** (1846) 135–36 [all but the first paragraph by Mary Ball]

Hart, J. B.
Hart, J. B. (Mrs. W. E.)
Notes on a caterpillar farm. *Bombay Nat. Hist. Soc. J.*, **4** (1889) 277–89
Protective mimicry. *Bombay Nat. Hist. Soc. J.*, **6** (1891) 410–16

O'Connor, Frances Sarah
O'Connor, Frances Sarah
Spider carrying snail-shell. *Irish Natlist.*, **5** (1896) 299

Thompson, Mary
Thompson, (Mrs.) Mary
Stridulation of Corsica. *Irish Natlist.*, **3** (1894) 114; **4** (1895) 224

Ward, Mary King (Hon. Mrs.)
Ward, (Hon. Mrs.)
{A windfall for the microscope. *Intell. Observer*, **5** (1864) 13–17}
The Humming-bird Hawk-moth: Macroglossa stellatarum. *Intell. Observer*, **9** (1866) 39–45

Ornithology

Christen, Sydney Mary Thompson
Thompson, (Miss) Sydney M.
Feathered pensioners. *Irish Natlist.*, **5** (1896) 118–19

Gyles, Lena
Gyles, Lena
    The wryneck in Ireland. *Irish Natlist.*, **7** (1898) 16–18

Zoology

Glascott, Louisa S.
Glascott, (Miss) L. S.
    A plea for the Rotifera. *Irish Natlist.*, **2** (1893) 191–94
    A list of some of the Rotifera of Ireland. [1892] *Dublin Soc. Sci. Proc.*, **8** (1893–8) 29–86
Maguire, Katherine
Maguire, Katherine
    Notes on certain Actiniaria. [1898] *Dublin Soc. Sci. Proc.*, **8** (1893–8) 717–31
Shackleton, Alice M.
Haddon, Alfred Cort; Shackleton, (Miss) Alice M.
    Reports on the zoological collections made in Torres Straits by Prof. A. C. Haddon, 1888–1889. Actiniae I. Zoantheae. [1890] *Dublin Soc. Sci. Trans.*, **4** (1888–92) 673–701
    Revision of the British Actiniae, Part II. The Zoantheae. [1891] *Dublin Soc. Sci. Trans.*, **4** (1888–92) 609–72
    Description of some new species of Actiniaria from Torres Straits. [1892] *Dublin Soc. Sci. Trans.*, **8** (1893–8) 116–31
Ward, Mary King (Hon. Mrs.)
Ward, (Hon. Mrs.)
    The Natterjack toad (Bufo calamita) in Ireland. *Intell. Observer*, **5** (1864) 227–33

Astronomy

Ward, Mary King (Hon. Mrs.)
Ward, (Hon. Mrs.)
    Observations on Comet II. 1862. *Intell. Observer*, **2** (1863) 205–19
    The auroral arch of 20th March 1865, as seen in Ireland. *Intell. Observer*, **7** (1865) 382–85
    The November shooting-stars. *Intell. Observer*, **10** (1867) 449–59

Geology

Andrews, Mary K.
Andrews, (Miss) Mary K.
    Denudation at Cultra, County Down. [1892] *Irish Natlist.*, **2** (1893) 16–18; 47–49; *Belfast Field Club Rep.*, **3** (1893) 529–32
    Dykes in Antrim and Down. *Irish Natlist.*, **3** (1894) 93–96
    Notes on Moel Tryfaen. [1894] *Belfast Field Club Rep.*, **4** (1901) 205–10
Christen, Sydney Mary Thompson
Thompson, (Miss) Sydney M.
    A plea for Irish glaciology. *Irish Natlist.*, **3** (1894) 30–34
    The Belfast Field Club in Donegal. *Irish Natlist.*, **3** (1894) 226–30
    [Report of the conference and excursion held at Galway, July 11th to 17th, 1895]. II. Geology. *Irish Natlist.*, **4** (1895) 235–37
    Glacial geology of Kerry. *Irish Natlist.*, **8** (1899) 61
    {A bit of foreshore. [1894] *Belfast Field Club Rep.*, **4** (1901) 210–14}
    On the supposed occurrence of a patch of white Lias or Rhaetic rock on the shore N. of Macedon Point, Belfast Lough. [1900] *Belfast Field Club Rep.*, **4** (1901) 566–69; *Irish Natlist.*, **9** (1900) 154 [summary]
    Report of the Geological Committee. [1893–98] *Belfast Field Club Rep.*, **4** (1901) 114–25; 229–35; 302–10; 386–90; {501–2 [Glacial geology]}

Hart, J. B.
Hart, J. B. (Mrs. W. E.)
    Note on some Post-Pleistocene molluscs from the Byculla Flats. *Bombay Nat. Hist. Soc. J.*, **1** (1886) 183–94

Archaeology

Knowles, Matilda Cullen
Knowles, M. C.
    {Kitchen middens—County Clare. *Limerick Field Club, J.*, **1** (1897–1900), 34–35}

Italy

Bacteriology

Cattani, Giuseppina
Cattani, Giuseppina
    Action de la température sur le bacille du choléra. [1887] *Arch. Ital. Biol.*, **9** (1888) 41
    {L'ematoterapia nel tetano. *Riforma Med.*, **8**, Pt. 2 (1892) 769–73}
    {Ancora sulla ematoterapia nel tetano. *Gazz. degli Osped.*, **13** (1892) 1118–21}
Tizzoni, Guido; Cattani, Giuseppina
    Untersuchungen über Cholera. *Centrbl. Med. Wiss.*, **24** (1886) 769–71
    Ricerche sperimentali sulla generalizzazione dell'infezione colerica. Terza comunicazione. *Bologna Acc. Sci. Mem.*, **8** (1887) 121–23
    Ueber die Uebertragungsfähigkeit der Cholera-Infection von der Mutter auf den Fötus. *Centrbl. Med. Wiss.*, **25** (1887) 131–32
    {Alcune ricerche sulla tenacità der virus colerica. *Riforma Med.*, (1887) 1616; [Cattani only] *Congr. Ass. Med. Ital.*, 1887, Pavia, **1** (1888) 247}
    Versuche über die Cholera-Ansteckung und -Vergiftung. Vorläufige Mitteilung. *Centrbl. Med. Wiss.*, **25** (1887) 529–32; 976
    Untersuchungen über die Cholera-Ansteckung durch das Blut. Vorläufige Mitteilung. *Centrbl. Med. Wiss.*, **25** (1887) 609–13
    Ueber die histologischen Veränderungen der Organe bei Cholera-Infection und über das Vorkommen von Kommabacillen in denselben. *Centrbl. Med. Wiss.*, **25** (1887) 721–24; 740–42
    Recherches sur le choléra asiatique. *Beitr. Path. Anat.*, **3** (1888) 189–237
    {Ricerche batteriologiche sul tetano. Prima comunicazione. *Riforma Med.*, **5** (1889) 512; 848; 885; 968; *Torino, Giorn. R. Acc. Med.*, **37** (s. 3) (1889) 230–32}
    {Sui caratteri morfologici del bacillo di Rosenbach e Nicolaier. *Riforma Med.*, **5** (1889) 752; *Torino, Giorn. R. Acc. Med.*, **37** (s. 3) (1889) 257–61}
    Sulla resistenza del virus tetanico agli agenti chimici e fisici. Comunicazione preventiva. [1890] *Bologna Acc. Sci. Mem.*, **10** (1889) 617–20
    {Sul veleno del tetano. Comunicazione preventiva. *Arch. Ital. Biol.*, **14** (1890) 101–5; *Riforma Med.*, **6** (1890) 764}
    Ueber das Tetanusgift. *Centrbl. Bakt.*, **8** (1890) 69–73
    Sul modo di conferire ad alcuni animali l'immunità contro il tetano. [1891] *Bologna Acc. Sci. Mem.*, **1** (1890) 311–14; *Arch. Ital. Biol.*, **15** (1891) 148–52; 164; [Tr.] *Centrbl. Bakt.*, **9** (1891) 189–92
    Untersuchungen über das Tetanusgift. *Arch. Exper. Path.*, **27** (1890) 432–50
    Sull'attenuazione del bacillo del tetano. *Roma, R. Acc. Lincei Rend.*, **7** (Sem. 1) (1891) 249–57; {*Riforma Med.*, **7**, Pt. 2 (1891) 157; 315; 601}
    Sulle proprietà dell'antitossina del tetano. *Roma, R. Acc. Lincei Rend.*, **7** (Sem. 1) (1891) 333–37; {[Tr.] *Centrbl. Bakt.*, **9** (1891) 685–89}
    Sur le poison du tétanos. Communication préventive. [1890] *Arch. Ital. Biol.*, **14** (1891) 101–5
    Ueber die Widerstandsfähigkeit der Tetanusbacillen gegen physikalische und chemische Einwirkungen. [1890] *Arch. Exper. Path.*, **28** (1891) 41–60

Ulteriori ricerche sull'antitossina del tetano. *Roma, R. Acc. Lincei Rend.*, **7** (Sem. 1) (1891) 384–90; {[Tr.] *Centrbl. Bakt.*, **10** (1891) 33–40}

{L'immunità contro il tetano studiata negli animali molto recettivi per questa infezione: cavia, coniglio, topo. *Riforma Med.*, **7**, Pt. 3 (1891) 385; 397}

Sull'importanza della milza nell'immunizzazione sperimentale del coniglio contro il tetano. [1892] *Bologna Rend.* (1891–92) 65–68; {*Riforma Med.*, **8**, Pt. 1 (1892) 554; **9**, Pt. 3 (1893) 457; [Tr.] *Centrbl. Bakt.*, **9** (1892) 325–27}

{Terzo caso di tetano traumatico curato coll'antitossina del tetano. *Riforma Med.*, **8**, Pt. 1 (1892) 39–42}

Sulla transmissione ereditaria dell'immunità contro il tetano. Comunicazione preventiva. *Roma, R. Acc. Lincei Rend.*, **1** (Sem. 1) (1892) 232–33; {*Riforma Med.*, **8**, Pt. 2 (1892) 219; [Tr.] *Deutsche Med. Wschr.*, **18** (1892) 394}

{Alcune questioni relative all'immunità del tetano. *Riforma Med.*, **8**, Pt. 3 (1892) 495; 505}

{Esperienza sulla vaccinazione del cavallo contro il tetano. *Riforma Med.*, **9**, Pt. 2 (1893) 661–65}

{Ulterior recerche sperimentali sulla immunita contro il tetano. *Riforma Med.*, **9**, Pt. 4 (1893) 289; 301; 313; 325; [Tr.] *Berlin. Klin. Wschr.*, **30** (1893) 1185; 1215; 1265; **31** (1894) 64}

{The treatment of tenanus by antitoxin; new experiments, with case and instructions for use. *London, Med. Press Circ.*, 58, n.s. (1894) 155–57}

{Erwiderung auf die Arbeit von Dr Hübener über das Tizzonische Tetanusantitoxin. *Deutsche Med. Wschr*, **20** (1894) 772}

{Nuove esperienze sulla vaccinazione del cavallo contro il tetano; relazione 2.a al Ministero di Agricoltura, Industria e Commercio. *Gazz. degli Osped.*, **15** (1894) 505–7}

Tizzoni, Guido; Cattani, Giuseppina; Baquis, Elia

Bakteriologische Untersuchungen über den Tetanus. *Beitr. Path. Anat.*, **7** (1890) 567–612

Montessori, Maria

Montesano, Giuseppe; Montessori, Maria

Ueber einen Fall von Dementia paralytica mit dem Befunde des Tetanusbacillus in der Cerebrospinalflüssigkeit. *Centrbl. Bakt. (Abt. 1)*, **22** (1897) 663–67

Botany

Fiorini-Mazzanti, Elisabetta (Contessa)

Fiorini-Mazzanti, (Contessa) Elisabetta

Notizia sopra poche piante da aggiungersi al Prodromo della flora Romana. *Giorn. Arcad.*, **18** (1823) 161–68

Specimen bryologiae Romanae. *Giorn. Arcad.*, **51** (1831) 3–26; *Poliografo*, 10 (1832) 181–89

Sopra una nuova diatomea (Colletonema bullosum). *Roma, N. Lincei Atti*, **10** (1856–57) 10

Sulla identità del Nostoc con il Collema. *Roma, N. Lincei Atti*, **11** (1857–58) 1–10; 103–13

Nota sulla crittogama degli Olivi. *Roma, N. Lincei Atti*, **13** (1859–60) 202–3

De vovis microphyceis. *Roma, N. Lincei Atti*, **13** (1859–60) 259–60

Microficee osservate nelle acque minerali di Terracina. *Roma, N. Lincei Atti*, **14** (1860–61) 239–40; **16** (1862–3) 631–33

Rettificazione di una nuova diatomea (Amphora bullosa). *Roma, N. Lincei Atti*, **15** (1861–62) 83–84

Osservazione sulla materia colorante della Calothrix janthiphora e diagnosi di una nuova microficea. *Roma, N. Lincei Atti*, **17** (1864) 101–3

Sopra una nuova specie di Palmodictyon (P. lubricum) e sovra un singolare organismo di alga unicellulare. *Roma, N. Lincei Atti*, **18** (1865) 377–79

Microficee delle acque minerali di Terracina. *Roma, N. Lincei Atti*, **20** (1867) 133–35

Sulla Cladophora viadrina, *Kützing. Roma, N. Lincei Atti*, **22** (1869) 1–2

Cenno sulla vegetaziona della Caduta delle Marmore. *Roma, N. Lincei Atti*, **22** (1869) 143–44

Nota critica sull' anormalità di un organismo crittogamico: lichen atypicum latebrarum. *Roma, N. Lincei Atti*, **24** (1871) 190–92

Fisiologia del Mucor romanus e specie affini. *Roma, N. Lincei Atti*, **25** (1872) 287–92

Sovra due nuove specie crittogamiche. [Amblystegium formianum; Beggiatoa foetida]. *Roma, N. Lincei Atti*, **27** (1874) 101–3

Florula del Colosseo [1874–78]; *Roma, N. Lincei Atti*, **28** (1875) 8–13; 127–33; 254–61; 305–7; 397–400; **29** (1876) 8–15; 54–58; 122–25; 236–39; 366–69; 457–66; **30** (1877) 97–105; **31** (1878) 155–67

Mirabella, Maria Antonietta

Mirabella, Maria Antonietta

I nettari extranuziali nelle varie specie di Ficus. *Nuovo Giorn. Bot. Ital.*, **2** (1895) 340–47

Contribuzioni alla conoscenza dei colleteri. *Contrib. Biol. Veg.*, **2** (1897–99) 13–40

Sui laticiferi delle radici aeree di "Ficus." *Contrib. Biol. Veg.*, **2** (1897–99) 131–36

Misciattelli, Margherita (Pallavicini—Marchesa)

Misciattelli, Margherita, [nata Princ.] Pallavicini (Marchesa)

Zoocecidii della flora italica, conservati nelle collezioni della R. Stazione di Patologia Vegetale in Roma. *[Italia], Soc. Bot. Bull.* (1894) 216–23; 275–81; (1895) 84–93, 111–22

Contribuzione allo studio degli Acarocecidii della flora italica. *[Italia], Soc. Bot. Bull.* (1895) 18–20

Nuova contribuzione all'acarocecidiologia italica. *Malpighia*, **13** (1899) 14–34

Moretti-Foggia, Amalia

Moretti-Foggia, Amalia

Florula delle piante vascolari del bosco Fontana nei dintorini di Mantova. *Modena Soc. Nat. Atti*, **14** (1895) 47–72

Conchology

Paulucci, Marianna (Marchesa; *née* Marianna Panciatichi Ximenes d'Aragona—Marchesa)

Paulucci, (Marchesa) Marianna

Osservazioni critiche sulla Cyclonassa italica, *Issel. Bull. Malacol. Ital.*, **4** (1871) 23–25

Osservazioni critiche sopra le specie del genere Struthiolaria, *Lamarck. Bull. Malacol. Ital.*, **2** (1876) 223–32; **3** (1877) 49–53

Nuova stazione della Clausilia lucensis, *Gent. Bull. Malacol. Ital.*, **3** (1877) 9–12

Di una specie di Helix [H. micropleuros, *Paget*], (nuova per la fauna d'Italia) raccolta nella provincia di Lucca. *Bull. Malacol. Ital.*, **3** (1877) 13–15

Fauna italiana. Comunicazioni malacologiche. Articolo I. [Introduttorio.] *Bull. Malacol. Ital.*, **3** (1877) 165–66

Note sur l'identité du Conus spirogloxus, *Deshayes*, avec le C. generalis, *Linné. J. de Conch.*, **25** (1877) 274–75

Remarques sur quelques espèces d'Helix de la collection Férussac, appartenant à la faune italienne. *J. de Conch.*, **26** (1878) 247–50

Étude critique sur l'Helix balmei, *Potiez et Michaud. J. de Conch.*, **27** (1879) 6–15

Étude critique sur quelques Hyalina de Sardaigne et description d'une nouvelle espèce, [H. libysonis, *Paulucci*]. *J. de Conch.*, **27** (1879) 15–21

Fauna . . . Articolo II. Descrizione di alcune nuove specie del genere Pomatias. *Bull. Malacol. Ital.*, **5** (1879) 13–21

Fauna . . . Articolo III. Studio sopra alcune specie del genere Unio. *Bull. Malacol. Ital.*, **5** (1879) 107–11

Replica alle osservazioni critiche dei signori Pini, De Stefani e Tiberi sopra alcune recenti pubblicazioni malacologiche. *Bull. Malacol. Ital.*, **5** (1879) 164–200

Fauna . . . Articolo IV. Studio sulla Helix instabilis, *Ziegler*, e le sue varietà. *Bull. Malacol. Ital.*, **5** (1879) 204–12

Lettre [au sujet de Bythinia saviana, *Issel.] Deutsch. Malakozool. Ges. Jbüch.*, **6** (1879) 64–67

Fauna . . . Articolo V. Rivista delle specie appartenenti ai generi Sphærium, *Scopoli*, Calyculina, *Clessin*, Pisidium, *Pfeiffer*, e loro distribuzione geografica. *Bull. Malacol. Ital.*, **6** (1880) 159–81

Fauna . . . Articolo VI. Studio sulla Helix (Campylæa) cingulata, *Studer*, e forme affini. *Bull. Malacol. Ital.*, **7** (1881) 5–55

Contribuzione alla fauna malacologica italiana. Specie raccolte dal Dr. G. Cavanna negli anni 1878, 1879, 1880 con elenco delle conchiglie abruzzesi, e descrizione di due nuove Succinea: [S. benoiti, S. incon-cinna.] *Bull. Malacol. Ital.*, **7** (1881) 69–180

Fauna . . . Articolo VII. Descrizione di una nuova specie del genere Acme, [A. delpretei]. *Bull. Malacol. Ital.*, **7** (1881) 221–25

Note malacologiche sulla fauna terrestre e fluviale dell'Isola di Sardegna. *Bull. Malacol. Ital.*, **8** (1882) 139–381

Fauna . . . Articolo VIII. Sull' Acme moutoni, *Dupuy*, e l'Acme veneta, *Pirona*. Su due paludine italiane. *Bull. Malacol. Ital.*, **9** (1883) 5–10

Fauna italiana, comunicazioni malacologiche. Articolo IX. Conchiglie terrestri e d'acqua dolce del Monte Argentaro e delle isole circostanti. *Bull. Malacol. Ital.*, **12** (1886) 5–64

Anatomy, Physiology, Neurology, Pathology

Cattani, Giuseppina

Cattani, Giuseppina

{Ricerche interno alla normale tessitura ed alle alterazioni sperimentali dei corpuscoli Pacinici degli uccelli (corpuscoli dell'Herbst). *Arch. Ital. Biol.*, **6** (1884) 6–34}

Studio sperimentale intorno alla distensione dei nervi. [1884] *Arch. Sci. Med.*, **8** (1884) 365–416; *Torino Acc. Sci. Mem.*, **37** (1886) 91–95

Sulla degenerazione e neoformazione delle fibre nervose midollari periferiche. [1886] *Bologna Acc. Sci. Mem.*, **6** (1884) 743–68; *Arch. Sci. Med.*, **11** (1887) 175–94

Sulla distensione incruenta del nervi. *Torino Acc. Sci. Atti*, **20** (1885) 1077–80; *Arch. Sci. Med.*, **9** (1886) 261–81

Sull'apparecchio di sostegno della mielina nelle fibre nervose midollari periferiche. [1886] *Torino Acc. Sci. Atti*, **21** (1885) 553–68; {*Arch. Ital. Biol.*, **7** (1886) 345–56}

{Sulla pneumonite catarrale da pneumotorace. *Roma. R. Acc. Med. Atti*, **3**, s. 2 (1886–87) 25–32}

Ueber die Reaction der Gewebe auf specifische Reize. *Beitr. Path. Anat.*, **7** (1890) 171–88

Monti, Cesarina (Rina)

Monti, (Signorina) Rina

Ricerche microscopiche sul sistema nervoso degli insetti. Nota preventiva. *Milano, Ist. Lomb. Rend.*, **25** (1892) 533–40; 654

Ricerche microscopiche sul sistema nervoso degli insetti. [1893–1894] *Boll. Sci.*, **4** (Ann. 15) (1894) 105–22; (Ann. 16) (1894) 6–17

Contributo alla conoscenza dei nervi del tubo digerente dei pesci. *Milano, Ist. Lomb. Rend.*, **28** (1895) 688–95

Innervazione del tubo digerente dei pesci ossei. Nota preventiva. [1895] *Boll. Sci.*, **5** (Ann. 17) (1898) 14–15

Sulle granulazioni del protoplasma di alcuni ciliati. [1895] *Boll. Sci.*, **5** (Ann. 17) (1898) 16–24

Sulle colture delle amebe. [1895] *Boll. Sci.*, **5** (Ann. 17) (1898) 24–26

Sul sistema nervoso dei dendrocœli d'acqua dolce. [1896] *Boll. Sci.*, **5** (Ann. 18) (1898) 46–57

Contribuzione alla conoscenza dei plassi nervosi nel tubo digerente di alcuni sauri. [1897] *Boll. Sci.*, **5** (Ann. 19) (1898) 99–106

Osservazioni ad alcune recensioni al [suo] lavoro "Sul sistema nervoso dei dendrocœli d'acqua dolce." *Boll. Sci.*, **5** (Ann. 20) (1898) 9–11

Ricerche anatomo comparative sulla minuta innervazione degli organi trofici nei cranioti inferiori. *Boll. Sci.*, **5** (Ann. 20) (1898) 16–20; *Milano, Cagnola Atti*, **16** (1898) No. 2, 146 pp.

Su la morfologia comparata dei condotti escretori delle ghiandole gastriche nei vertebrati. *Boll. Sci.*, **5** (Ann. 20) (1898) 33–39; 65–75; 101–8

Su la fina distribuzione e le terminazioni dei nervi nella milza degli uccelli. *Boll. Sci.*, **5** (Ann. 20) (1898) 114–17; (Ann. 21) (1899) 6–12

I Protisti delle risaie. *Milano, Ist. Lomb. Rend.*, **32** (1899) 159–64

Le ghiandole salivari dei gasteropodi terrestri nei diversi periodi funzionali. [1899] *Milano, Ist. Lomb. Mem.*, **18** (1896–1900) 115–33; *Milano, Ist. Lomb. Rend.*, **32** (1899) 534–35

Su la fina struttura dello stomaco dei gasteropodi terrestri. *Milano, Ist. Lomb. Rend.*, **32** (1899) 1086–97

L'eteromorfosi nei dendrocœli d'acqua dolce ed in particolare nella "Planaria alpina." *Milano, Ist. Lomb. Rend.*, **32** (1899) 1314–21

Su le ghiandole salivari dei gasteropodi nei diversi periodi funzionali. Nota preventiva. *Boll. Sci.*, (Ann. 21) (1899) 19–25

Studî sperimentali sulla rigenerazione nei rabdoceli marini (Plagiostoma Girardii, *Graff*). *Milano, Ist. Lomb. Rend.*, **33** (1900) 915–17

La rigenerazione nelle planarie marine. [1900] *Milano, Ist. Lomb. Mem.*, **19** (1900–4) 1–16

Monti, (Signorina) Rina; Monti, Achille

Osservazioni su le marmotte ibernanti. *Milano, Ist. Lomb. Rend.*, **33** (1900) 372–81

Su l'epitelio renale delle marmotte durante il sonno. *Anat. Anz.*, **18** (1900) (*Anat. Ges. Verh.*) 82–87

Norsa, Elisa

Norsa, Elisa

Alcune ricerche sulla morfologia dei membri anteriori degli uccelli. [1894] *Roma Lab. Anat. Norm. Ric.*, **4** (1894–95) 137–56

Sacchi, Maria Cattaneo

Sacchi, Maria

Contribuzioni all'istologia ed embriologia dell'apparecchio digerente dei batraci e dei rettili. *Milano, Soc. Ital. Atti*, **29** (1886) 361–409

Sulla morfologia delle glandule intestinali dei vertebrati. *Boll. Sci.*, (Ann. 8) (1886) 46–56

Contribuzione all'istologia dell'ovidotto dei Sauropsidi. *Milano, Soc. Ital. Atti*, **30** (1887) 273–309

Sulla struttura del tegumento negli embrioni ed avannotti del Salmo lacustris. *Milano, Ist. Lomb. Rend.*, **20** (1887) 642–49

Intorno ai protisti dei muschi ed al loro incistamento. *Boll. Sci.*, (Ann. 10) (1888) 35–56; {[Tr.] *J. Microgr.*, **12** (1888) 340–47; 376–80; 405–9}.

I protozoi terricoli. Nota preventiva. *Boll. Sci.*, (Ann. 11) (1889) 65–68; [Tr.] *J. Microgr.*, **14** (1890) 107–9

Sulle minute differenze fra gli organi omotipici dei Pleuronettidi. *Genova, Soc. Ligust. Atti*, **4** (1893) 356–69

Sulla struttura degli organi del veleno della Scorpena. *Genova, Soc. Ligust. Atti*, **6** (1895) 89–98; 234–37

Su di un caso d'arresto dell'emigrazione oculare, con pigmentazione del lato cieco in un Rhombus maximus. *Genova, Soc. Ligust. Atti*, **9** (1898) 449–51

Scarpellini, Caterina

Scarpellini, Caterina

Esperienze conformative a quelle del Sign. Dubois-Reymond relative allo sviluppo della elettricità per la contrazione muscolare del Prof. Buff. *Roma, Corrisp. Scient.*, **2** (1853) 138–39

Legge della corrente muscolare ed influenza della contrazione sopra questa corrente. *Roma, Corrisp. Scient.*, **2** (1853) 153–54; 169–71

Zoology

Bortolotti, Emma

Bortolotti, Emma

Rudimenti di corazza cutanea indicati da pieghe della pelle in alcuni embrioni di Mammiferi. [1896] *Roma Lab. Anat. Norm. Ric.*, **5** (1895–96) 275–85

Leardi Airaghi, Zina

Leardi Airaghi, Zina

I metodi grafici nello studio della distribuzione degli animali. *Milano, Soc. Ital. Atti*, **39** (1900) 93–105

Astronomy

Acampora, Adele

Acampora, Adele

[Bolide del 16 ottobre 1885, Napoli.] *Moncalieri Oss. Boll.*, **5** (1885) 187

Brehm, Adelina di

Brehm, Adelina di

Bolide del 3 ottobre [1889, Sarezzo]. *Moncalieri Oss. Boll.*, **9** (1889) 190

Scarpellini, Caterina

Scarpellini, Caterina

Sulle onde atmosferiche dell' astronomo Quetelet. *Roma, Corrisp. Scient.*, **2** (1853) 338–39

Sul ritorno della cometa di Pons nel Luglio del 1855. *Roma, Corrisp. Scient.*, **3** (1855) 406–7

L'etere come mezzo insensibilmente resistente al movimenti degli astri. *Roma, Corrisp. Scient.*, **4** (1856) 43–44

Bolide osservata sul Campidoglio. *Roma, Corrisp. Scient.*, **4** (1856) 129

Undecimo ritorno della cometa di Pons. *Roma, Corrisp. Scient.*, **4** (1856) 215

Importanti osservazioni sopra Saturno e suoi anelli. *Roma, Corrisp. Scient.*, **4** (1856) 237

Bolide osservata in Roma. *Roma, Corrisp. Scient.*, **5** (1859) 137

Ipotesi sulla fisica e meccanica celeste, secondo il sistema fluidale elettro-magnetico. *Roma, Corrisp. Scient.*, **5** (1859) 253–56

Intorno i bolidi, gli asteroidi, i satelliti e le comete. *Roma, Bull. Naut. Geogr.*, **1** (1860–61) 90–92

Sulla grande cometa del 30 Giugno 1861. *Roma, Bull. Naut. Geogr.*, **1** (1860–61) 119–20; *Nuovo Cimento*, **14** (1861) 69–72

Qualque nuova considerazione su la formazione dei pianeti maggiori. *Roma, Bull. Naut. Geogr.*, **1** (1860–61) 124–26

Ecclisse solare del 31 Decembre 1861. *Roma, Bull. Naut. Geogr.*, **1** (1860–61) 127–28

Sur les étoiles filantes du mois d'août 1861, observées à Rome. *Brux., Ac. Bull.*, **12** (1861) 180–85

Sur les étoiles filantes du 10 août 1862. *Brux., Ac. Bull.*, **14** (1862) 273–77; *Roma, Bull. Naut. Geogr.*, **2** (1862–63) 17–19

Sulle stelle cadenti periodiche del 10 Agosto 1863, osservate in Roma. *Roma, Bull. Naut. Geogr.*, **2** (1862–63) 69–70

Del grande ecclisse solare del 18 Luglio 1860. *Roma, Corrisp. Scient.*, **6** (1863) 229–31; 241

Sul periodo delle macchie solari. *Roma, Corrisp. Scient.*, **6** (1863) 353–55

La luna osservata in Roma nella sua ecclisse totale nel 1 Giugno del 1863. *Roma, Corrisp. Scient.*, **6** (1863) 469–71

Sur les étoiles filantes du 10 août 1863. *Brux., Ac. Bull.*, **16** (1863) 297–305

Étoiles filantes observées à Rome le 10 août 1865. *Les Mondes*, **12** (1866) 95

Étoiles filantes périodiques du mois d'août. *Les Mondes*, **12** (1866) 288

Observations des étoiles filantes périodiques de novembre 1866. *Brux., Ac. Bull.*, **22** (1866) 468–69

Observations des étoiles filantes faites à Rome du 9 au 10 août 1867. *Brux., Ac. Bull.*, **24** (1867) 295–97

Observations des étoiles filantes du mois d'août 1868, faites à Rome. *Brux., Ac. Bull.*, **26** (1868) 274–75

[Stelle cadenti del periodo di agosto (1871).] [1871] *Riv. Sci.-Ind.*, **3** (1872) 97(bis)–98(bis)

Chemistry

Scarpellini, Caterina

Peretti, Paolo; Scarpellini, (Mme.) Caterina

La sabbia caduta in Roma nelle notti del 21 e 23 febbraio 1864 confrontata con la sabbia del deserto di Sahara; investigazioni fisico-chimiche. *Nuovo Cimento*, **19** (1863) 353–56

Geology

Bortolotti, Emma

Bortolotti, Emma

Contribuzione alla conoscenza dei fossili del Miocene Medio nel Bolognese. *Riv. Ital. Paleont.*, **4** (1898) 55–61

Monti, Cesarina (Rina)

Monti, (Signorina) Rina

Appunti petrografici sopra alcune rocce della provincia di Brescia. *Giorn. Min. Crist. Petr.*, **3** (1892) 262–66

Studî petrografici sopra alcune rocce della Valle Camonica. Nota preventiva. *Milano, Ist. Lomb. Rend.*, **26** (1893) 605–12

Studî petrografici sopra alcune rocce della Valle Camonica. *Giorn. Min. Crist. Petr.*, **5** (1894) 44–71

Paulucci, Marianna (Marchesa; *née* Marianna Panciatichi Ximenes d'Aragona—Marchesa)
Paulucci,—
   Description d'un Murex (M. Veranyi) fossile du terrain tertiare subapennin de la vallée de l'Elsa (Toscane). *J. de Conch.*, **14** (1866) 64–67
Scarpellini, Caterina
Scarpellini, Caterina
   Sugli terremuoti avvenuti in Roma negli anni 1858 e 1859. *Roma, Corrisp. Scient.*, **6** (1863) 236–41
   Colpo d'occhio sopra i terremuoti avvenuti in Roma negli anni 1858–62, relativamente alla influenza della luna. *Roma, Corrisp. Scient.*, **6** (1863) 349–50; *Wien, Ak. Sber.*, **47** (Abt. 2) (1863) 137–42

Mathematics

Bortolotti, Emma
Bortolotti, Emma
   Sulle frazioni continue algebriche periodiche. *Palermo Circ. Mat. Rend.*, **9** (1895) 136–49
Fabri, Cornelia
Fabri, Cornelia
   Sopra alcune proprietà generali delle funzioni che dipendono da altre funzioni e da linee. *Torino Acc. Sci. Atti*, **25** (1889–90) 654–74
   Sui moti vorticosi nei fluidi perfetti. [1892] *Bologna Rend.* (1891–2) 116–21
   Sulla teorica dei moti vorticosi nei fluidi incompressibili. *Nuovo Cimento*, **31** (1892) 135–45; 221–27
   Sopra le funzioni di iperspazi. *Venezia, Ist. Atti* (1892–3) 283–95
   I moti vorticosi di ordine superiore al primo in relazione alle equazioni pel movimento dei fluidi viscosi. *Bologna Acc. Sci. Mem.*, **4** (1894) 383–92
   I moti vorticosi di ordine superiore in relazione alle equazioni pel movimento dei fluidi viscosi compressibili. *Nuovo Cimento*, **1** (1895) 281–91
Massarini, Iginia
Massarini, Iginia
   Intorno alle coniche rispetto alle quali due attre sono tra loro polari reciproche. *Giorn. Mat.*, **37** (1899) 23–40
Predella Longhi, Lia
Predella, Lia
   Sulle soluzioni singolari della equazioni differenziali ordinarie di 1 ordine. *Giorn. Mat.*, **33** (1895) 31–56; 183–209

Meteorology

Scarpellini, Caterina
Scarpellini, Caterina
   Osservazioni ozonometriche istituite in Roma nell' Agosto 1856. *Giorn. Arcad.*, **145** (1856) 177–82; *Roma, Corrisp. Scient.*, **4** (1856) 393–95
   Osservazioni ozonometriche meteorologiche fatte in Roma. *Roma, Corrisp. Scient.*, **6** (1863) 147–48; 204; 228; 244; 292–93; 402–3; 408–2
   Sulla nuova serie delle osservazione ozonometriche meteorologiche. *Roma, Corrisp. Scient.*, **6** (1863) 367–69; 376–77; 460–62
   [La description d'un altimètre à réflexion.] *France Soc. Météorol. Nouv. Météorol.*, **2** (1869) 171
   [Notes météorologiques.] Rome [Campidoglio]. *France Soc. Météorol. Nouv. Météorol.*, **4** (1871) 124; 160; 179; **5** (1872) 41; 78; 99; 139; 154; 165; 188; 200; 210; 223; **6** (Pt. 2) (1873) 11; 23; 72–73
Vielmi, Carolina
Vielmi, Carolina
   [Osservazioni termopluviometriche in Breno.] *Brescia Ateneo Comment.* (1884) 322–23

Physics

Monti, Cesarina (Rina)
Monti, (Signorina) Rina
Della forma cristallina e dei caratteri ottici della fenacetina $C_6H_4.OC_2H_2.NHCOCH_3$. *Giorn. Min. Crist. Petr.*, **4** (1893) 241–43; *Milano, Ist. Lomb. Rend.*, **27** (1894) 196–97

Scarpellini, Caterina
Scarpellini, Caterina
Sopra una esperienza relativa alla celerità di propagazione della luce. *Roma, Corrisp. Scient.*, **2** (1853) 126–27
Osservazioni sulla elettricità dell' aria. *Roma, Corrisp. Scient.*, **2** (1853) 136–38
Sulla conduttibilità degli acidi e sullo sviluppo della elettricità nella combinazione degli acidi e delle base. *Roma, Corrisp. Scient.*, **2** (1853) 147–48
Stato magnetico e diamagnetico dei gaz. *Roma, Corrisp. Scient.*, **2** (1853) 205–6
Sulla influenza dell elettricità sulle altezze barometriche. *Roma, Corrisp. Scient.*, **2** (1853) 212–13
Il monostereoscopio di Boblin. *Roma, Corrisp. Scient.*, **5** (1859) 137

Anthropology

Pugliesi, Emma
Pugliesi, Emma
Studî sulla simmetria del cranio nei due sessi. [1899] *Padova Soc. Sci. Atti*, **4** (Fasc.1) (1900) 48–76
Pugliesi, Emma; Tietze, Federico
Contributo all'antropologia fisica di Sardegna ed alla teoria dei pigmei d'Europa. *Padova Soc. Sci. Atti*, **3** (1898) 401–19

Netherlands

Botany

Popta, Canna Maria Louise
Popta, Canna Maria Louise
Beitrag zur Kenntniss der Hemiasci. *Flora*, **86** (1899) 1–46

Weber, Anne (Anna) Antoinette van Bosse
Weber van Bosse, (Mevr.) Anna
[Bijdragen] tot de Algenflora van Nederland. [1886–87] *Nederl. Kruidk. Arch.*, **4** (1886) 363–68; **5** (1891) 67–70
Études sur des algues de l'Archipel Malaisien. *Buitenzorg Jard. Bot. Ann.*, **8** (1890) 79–94; 165–88
Notes on Sarcomenia miniata, *Ag. J. Bot.*, **34** (1896) 281–85
On a new genus of siphonean algae – Pseudocodium. [1895] *Linn. Soc. J. (Bot.)*, **32** (1896) 209–12
Monographie des Caulerpes. *Buitenzorg Jard. Bot. Ann.*, **15** (1898) 243–401
Sur une nouvelle espèce d'Ochlochæte. Ochlochæte gratulans, *n. sp. Buitenzorg Jard. Bot. Ann.*, Suppl. **2** (1898) 1–4
Note sur quelques algues rapportées par le yacht *Chazalie*. *J. Bot., Paris*, **13** (1899) 133–35
Étude sur les algues parasites des Parasseux. [1887] *Haarlem, Hollands. Maatsch. Nat. Verh.*, **5** (1903) Stuk 1, 23 pp.

Medicine

de Lange, Cornelia Catharina
Lange, Cornelia de
Die Zusammensetzung der Asche des Neugeborenen und der Muttermilch. *Ztschr. Biol.*, **40** (1900) 526–28
Zur normalen und pathologischen Histologie des Magendarmcanals beim Kinde. *Jbuch. Kinderheilk.*, **51** (1900) 621–49

Zoology

Popta, Canna Maria Louise
Popta, Canna Maria Louise
  A new species of Arius. *Leyden Mus. Notes,* **22** (1900–1) 71–74
  On a small Monacanthus. [1900]. *Leyden Mus. Notes,* **22** (1900–1) 126–28
Schilthuis, L.
Schilthuis, (Miss) L.
  On a small collection of amphibia from the Congo with description of a new species. *Nederl. Dierk. Ver. Tijdschr.,* **2** (1889) 285–86
  On a collection of fishes from the Congo; with description of some new species. [1891] *Nederl. Dierk. Ver. Tijdschr.,* **3** (1890–92) 83–92

Chemistry

Maarseveen, Geertruida van
Maarseveen, Geertruida van
  Over de betrekking tusschen oplossingswarmte oplosbaarheid en dissociatiegraad. *Maandbl. Nat.,* (1897) 149–65
Schaap, J.
Schaap, (Miss) J.
  The separation of salicylic acid from benzoic acid. [Tr.] *Chem. News,* **66** (1892) 435–37

Mathematics

Kerkhoven, Anna Geertruida (*née* Wythoff)
Wythoff, (Mej.) A. G. (Mevr. Kerkhoven)
  Afleiding der bewegingsvergelijkingen in bipolaire coördinaten voor een punt, dat zich in een vlak beweegt, met toepassing op eenvoudige krachtvormen. *Nieuw Arch. Wisk.,* **20** (1893) 26–62; *Fortschr. Math.* (1893–4) 1399
  Over de stabiliteit van elliptische banen, beschreven onder de werking van drie centrale Krachten. *Fortschr. Math.* (1896) 613
  On the dynamical stability of a system of particles. *Nieuw Arch. Wisk.,* **3** (1898) 95–110
  On the dynamical stability of a system of four particles. *Nieuw Arch. Wisk.,* **4** (1899) 7–21
  On the case of small oscillations of a system about a position of equilibrium. *Nieuw Arch. Wisk.,* **4** (1899) 205–25

Norway

Botany

Møller, Sophie
Møller, Sophie; Binstead, (Rev.) C. H.
  Mosses collected at and in the neighbourhood of Maristuen in the summer of 1886. *Nyt Mag. Naturvid.,* **31** (1890) 200–13
Holmsen, Thekla Susanne Ragnhild Resvoll
Resvoll, Thekla R.
  Nogle arktiske Ranunklers morfologi og anatomi. *Nyt Mag. Naturvid.,* **38** (1900) 343–67

Zoology

Arnesen, Emily
Arnesen, Emily
  Beiträge zur Anatomie und Histologie von Ulocyathus arcticus, Cariophyllia Smithii, Dendrophyllia ramea und Cladocora cespitosa. *Arch. Math. Naturvid.,* **20** (1898) No. 9, 31 pp.

Spongier fra den norske kyst. I. Calcarea. Systematisk katalog med bemerkninger og bestemmelsestabel. (Bestimmungstafel in deutscher Sprache.) [1901] *Bergens Mus. Aarb.* (1900) No. 5, 46 pp.

Bonnevie, Kristine Elisabeth Heuch
Bonnevie, (Frøken) Kristine
Neue norwegische Hydroiden. [1899] *Bergens Mus. Aarb.*, (1898) No. 5, 15 pp.
Zur Systematik der Hydroiden. *Ztschr. Wiss. Zool.*, **63** (1898) 465–95
En eiendommelig ny molluskart der lever syttende paa tarmkanalen hos en almindelig forekommende sjøpølse (Stictiopus tremulus). *Nyt Mag. Naturvid.*, **37** (1900) 355
Hjort, Johan; Bonnevie, (Frøken) Kristine
Ueber die Knospung von Distaplia magnilarva. *Anat. Anz.*, **10** (1895) 389–94

Esmark, Birgithe Elise
Esmark, Birgithe
Bidrag til kundskaben om udbredelsen af Norges land- og ferskvandsmollusker i forskjellige egne af landet. *Nyt Mag. Naturvid.*, **25** (1880) 215–23
Die Pisidien des südlichen Norwegens. *Malakozool. Blätter*, **5** (1882) 1–6
Land and fresh-water Mollusca in the arctic regions of Norway. *Tromsø Mus. Aarsh.*, **5** (1882) 93–104
Nyt bidrag til kundskaben om Norges land- og ferskvandsmollusker. *Nyt Mag. Naturvid.*, **27** (1883) 77–110
On the land and freshwater Mollusca of Norway. [1887] *J. Conch.*, **5** (1886–88) 90–131
Esmark, Birgithe; Hoyer, Z. Aug.
Die Land- und Süsswassermollusken des arktischen Norwegens. *Malakozool. Blätter*, **8** (1886) 84–123

Serbia

Neurology

Steinlechner-Grechishnikova, Aleksandra
Steinlechner-Grecinikov, (Frau) Alexandra
Ueber den Bau des Rückenmarkes bei Microcephalen. Ein Beitrag zur Kenntniss des Einflusses des Vorderhirnes auf die Entwickelung anderer Thiele des centralen Nervensystems. [Posth.] *Arch. Psychiatr.*, **17** (1886) 649–90

Sweden

Bacteriology

Almquist, Gerda Troili-Petersson
Troili-Petersson, Gerda
Studien über saure Milch und Zähmilch. *Ztschr. Hyg.*, **32** (1899) 361–74

Botany

Cleve von Euler, Astrid Maria
Cleve, (Fröken) Astrid
En röd Bulbochaete. *Bot. Notiser* (1895) 247
On recent freshwater diatoms from Lule Lappmark in Sweden. [1895] *Stockh., Ak. Handl. Bihang*, **21** (Afd.3) (1896) No. 2, 44 pp
En bienn form af Linum catharticum, *L. Bot. Notiser* (1897) 61–64
[Undersökningar öfver fjällfloran.] *Bot. Notiser* (1898) 277
Notes on the plankton of some lakes in Lule Lappmark, Sweden. *Stockh., Öfvers.* (1899) 825–35
{Något om skogsregionerna i södra Frankrike. *Tidskr. Skogshush.*, **28** (1900) 3–13}

Klercker, Edla Hedwig Sofia Söderström af
Söderström, Edla
Ueber den anatomischen Bau von Desmarestia aculeata (*L.*) *Lam.* [1888] *Stockh., Ak. Handl. Bihang*, **14** (Afd. 3) (1889) No. 3, 16 pp.

Lewin, Maria

Lewin, Maria

Beitrag till hjertbladets anatomi hos monokotyledonerna. [1886] *Stockh., Ak. Handl. Bihang*, **12** (Afd. 3) (1887) No. 3, 28 pp.

Ueber spanische Süsswasseralgen. [1888] *Stockh., Ak. Handl. Bihang*, **14** (Afd. 3) (1889) No. 1, 24 pp.

Rissler, Sigrid Alfhild Elisabeth Andersson

Andersson, (Fröken) Sigrid

Om de primära kärlsträngarnes utveckling hos monokotyledonera. [1887] *Stockh., Ak. Handl. Bihang*, **13** (Afd. 3) (1888) No. 12, 23 pp.; *Bot. Centrbl.*, **38** (1889) 586–87

Santesson, Hedvig Carolina Lovisa Lovén

Lovén, Hedvig

Om utvecklingen af de sekundära kärlknippena hos Dracaena och Yucca. [1887] *Stockh., Ak. Handl. Bihang*, **13** (Afd.3) (1888) No. 3, 12 pp.

Något om luften i Fucaceernas blåsor. *Stockh., Öfvers.* (1892) 107–17

Några rön om Algernas andning. [1891] *Stockh., Ak. Handl. Bihang*, **17** (Afd.3) (1892) No. 3, 17 pp.

Wester, Alida Olbers

Olbers, Alida

Om fruktväggens anatomiska byggnad hos Rosaceerna. *Stockh., Öfvers.* (1884) No. 4, 97–111

Bidrag till kännedomen om fruktväggens byggnad. *Stockh., Öfvers.* (1885) No. 5, 95–119

Ueber den Bau der Geraniaceenfrüchte. [1884] *Bot. Centrbl.*, **21** (1885) 318

Om fruktväggens byggnad hos Borragineerna. [1887] *Bot. Centrbl.*, **33** (1888) 88–91; *Stockh., Ak. Handl. Bihang*, **13** (Afd. 3) (1888) No. 2, 33 pp.

Om fruktväggens byggnad hos Labiaterna. [1890] *Stockh., Ak. Handl. Bihang*, **16** (Afd. 3) (1891) No. 4, 20 pp.

Bidrag till kännedomen om kärlsträngsförloppet hos Silenéblomman. *Stockh., Öfvers.* (1895) 387–411

Ett abnormal fall af utbildning af jordstammar hos potatisplantan. *Bot. Notiser* (1895) 119–20

Wester, Alida Olbers

Bidrag till kännedomen om Alsinéblommans morfologi och anatomi. *Stockh., Öfvers.* (1899) 341–64

Physiology

Brinck, Julia

Brinck, (Frl.) Julia Maria

On the nutrition of skeletal muscle. *J. Physiol.*, **10** (1889) ix–x

Ueber synthetische Wirkung lebender Zellen. *Ztschr. Biol.*, **25** (1889) 453–73

Brinck, (Frl.) Julia; Kronecker, Hugo

Ueber synthetische Wirkung lebender Zellen. *Arch. Anat. Physiol. (Physiol. Abt.)* (1887) 347–49; *Bern Mitth.* (1887) xviii–xxii

Zoology

Carlsson, Albertina

Carlsson, (Fröken) Albertina

Beiträge zur Kenntniss der Anatomie der Schwimmvögel. [1883] *Stockh., Ak. Handl. Bihang*, **9**, (1884–85) No. 3, 44 pp.

Die Extremitätenreste bei einigen Schlangen. *Anat. Anz.*, **1** (1886) 189

Untersuchungen über Gliedmassen-Reste bei Schlangen. [1885] *Stockh., Ak. Handl. Bihang*, **11** (1887) No. 11, 85 pp.

Zur Anatomie des Hyperoodon diodon. [1887] *Stockh., Ak. Handl. Bihang*, **13** (Afd. 4) (1888) No. 7, 25 pp.

Untersuchungen über die weichen Teile der s.g. überzähligen Strahlen an Hand und Fuss. [1890] *Stockh., Ak. Handl. Bihang*, **16** (Afd. 4) (1891) No.8, 40 pp.

Ueber die Zahnentwicklung bei einigen Knochenfishen. [1894] *Zool. Jbüch. (Anat.)*, **8** (1895) 217–44

Ueber den Zahnersatz bei Agama colonorum. *Anat. Anz.*, **11** (1896) 758–66

Ueber die Schmelzleiste bei Sterna Hirundo. *Anat. Anz.*, **12** (1896) 72–75

Ueber Zahnentwicklung der diprotodonten Beutelthiere. *Zool. Jbüch. (Anat.)*, **12** (1899) 407–24

Ueber die systematische Stellung der Nandinia binotata. *Zool. Jbüch. (Syst.)*, **13** (1900) 509–28

Christie-Linde, Augusta Maria Ärnbäck-Andersson

Ärnbäck-Christie-Linde, Augusta

Zur Anatomie des Gehirnes niederer Säugetiere. *Anat. Anz.*, **18** (1900) 8–16

Westling, Charlotte

Westling, Charlotte

Beiträge zur Kenntniss des peripherischen Nervensystems. [1884] *Stockh., Ak. Handl. Bihang*, **9** (1884–85) No. 8, 48 pp.

Anatomische Untersuchungen über Echidna. [1889] *Stockh., Ak. Handl. Bihang*, **15** (Afd.4) (1890) No. 3, 71 pp.

Chemistry and Chemical Analysis

Almquist, Gerda Troili-Petersson

Troili-Petersson, Gerda

Pettersson-Palmqvist's Kohlensäureapparat modifiziert für Ventilationsuntersuchungen. *Ztschr. Hyg.*, **26** (1897) 57–65

Ueber den Kohlensäuregehalt der Atmosphäre. [1897] *Stockh., Ak. Handl. Bihang*, **23** (Afd. 2) (1898) No. 6, 17 pp.

Zur Methode der Kohlensäurebestimmung. *Ztschr. Hyg.*, **28** (1898) 331–34

Cleve von Euler, Astrid Maria

Cleve, (Fröken) Astrid

Ueber einige Phenyltriazole. *Berlin, Chem. Ges. Ber.*, **29** (1896) 2671–77; **30** (1897) 2433–38

Om några fenyltriazder. [1899] *Stockh., Ak. Handl. Bihang*, **25** (Afd. 2) (1900) No. 4, 33 pp.

Widman, Oskar; Cleve, (Fröken) Astrid

Om oxitriazol och några acidylsemikarbazider. [1899] *Berlin, Chem. Ges. Ber.*, **31** (1898) 378–81; *Stockh., Ak. Handl. Bihang*, **25** (Afd. 2) (1900) No. 3, 13 pp.

Palmqvist, Augusta

Palmqvist, A.

Hydrografiska undersökningar i Gullmarfjorden sommaren 1890. [1891] *Stockh., Ak. Handl. Bihang*, **17** (Afd. 2) (1892) No. 5, 19 pp.

Undersökningar öfver atmosferens kolsyrehalt. [1892] *Stockh., Ak. Handl. Bihang*, **18** (Afd. 2) (1893) No. 2, 39 pp.; *Fortschr. Phys.*, (Abt. 3) (1895) 252

Pettersson, Sven Otto, Palmqvist, A.

Ein tragbarer Apparat zur Bestimmung des Kohlensäuregehalts der Luft. *Berlin, Chem. Ges. Ber.*, **20** (1887) 2129–34

Apparat zur Bestimmung des atmosphärischen Kohlensäuregehalts. *Forsch. Agr.-Phys.*, **16** (1893) 173–76

Geology

Rudbeck, Sofia

Rudbeck, Sofia

Om en kromhalting vesuvian från Ural. [Chromhaltiger Vesuvian von Ural.] *Stockh. Geol. För. Förh.*, **15** (1893) 607–8; viii; *Neues Jbuch. Min.*, (Bd. 1, Ref.) (1895) 260

Sahlbom, Naima

Sahlbom, (Fröken) Naima

Analysen einiger Ganggesteine aus dem Nephelinsyenitgebiete der Insel Alnö. *Neues Jbuch. Min.*, (Bd. 2) (1897) 97–101

Andersson, Johan Gunnar; Sahlbom, (Fröken) Naima

Sur la teneur en fluor phosphorites suédoises. [1898] *Upsala Geol. Inst. Bull.*, **4** (1900) 79–88

Switzerland

Bacteriology

Strub, Emma
Strub, Emma
Ueber Milchsterilisation. *Centrbl. Bakt.*, **7** (1890) 665–70; 689–94; 721–32

Botany

Grinţescu, Alice Jenne Pierrette Rodrigue
Rodrigue, (Mlle.) A.
Contribution à l'étude des mouvements spontanés et provoqués des feuilles des légumineuses et des oxalidées. *France Soc. Bot. Bull.*, **41** (1894) cxxviii–cxxxiv
Sur la structure des organes sensibles chez les légumineuses et les oxalidées. *Arch. Sci. Phys. Nat.*, **32** (1894) 625–27
Chodat, Robert; Rodrigue, (Mlle.) A.
Recherches sur le tégument séminal chez les polygalacées. *Arch. Sci. Phys. Nat.*, **29** (1893) 319–21
Gugelberg von Moos, Maria Barbara Flandrina
Gugelberg, Marie von
Beitrag zur Kenntniss der Lebermoos Flora des Kantons Graubünden. *Graubünden Natf. Ges. Jber.*, **38** (1895) 1–7
Ternetz, Charlotte
Ternetz, Charlotte
Protoplasmabewegung und Fruchtkörperbildung bei Ascophanus carneus, *Pers. Pringsheim, Jbüch. Wiss. Bot.*, **35** (1900) 273–312

Medical Sciences

Kuhn, Johanna
Kuhn, Johanna
Ein Beitrag zur Kenntniss der Histologie der endemischen Beulen. *Virchow, Arch.*, **150** (1897) 372–87
Schiele-Wiegandt, Valérie
Schiele-Wiegandt, Valérie
Ueber Wanddicke und Umfang der Arterien des menschlichen Körpers. *Virchow, Arch.*, **82** (1880) 27–39

Switzerland—Russia

Chemistry

Ullmann, Irma Goldberg
Goldberg, (Mlle.) Irma
Purification de l'acétylène. *Arch. Sci. Phys. Nat.*, **10** (1900) 288–89
Ullmann, Fritz; Goldberg, (Mlle.) I.
[Dérivés de la benzophénone.] *Arch. Sci. Phys. Nat.*, **4** (1897) 95–96
Purification de l'acétylène. *Arch. Sci. Phys. Nat.*, **7** (1899) 590–1; *Moniteur Sci.*, **14** (1900) 334–37

Appendix
United States

Botany

Banning, Mary Elizabeth
Banning, Mary E.
{Notes on the fungi of Maryland. *Field and Forest*, 3 (1877) 42–47, 59–63}

Notes on fungi. [1880] *Bot. Gaz.*, **5** & **6** (1880–81) 5–10; 23
New species of fungi found in Maryland: [Agaricus (Tricholoma) cellaris, A.(T.) brownei; Russula cinna-
    momea, R. variata]. [1881] *Bot. Gaz.*, **5** & **6** (1880–81) 165–66
Maryland fungi. [1881] *Bot. Gaz.*, **5** & **6** (1880–81), 200–2, 210–13
{Preservative for fungi. *Torrey Bot. Club Bull.*, 9 (1882), 153}

Rodham, Olivia
Rodham, Olivia
   Observations on netted septa in vessels of Tecoma radicans. *Bot. Gaz.*, **15** (1890) 122
   Zur Kenntniss der Gefässquernetze. *Deutsch. Bot. Ges. Ber.*, **8** (1890) 188–90

Psychology

Hollister, Dorothy (Lottie) Steffens
Steffens, Lottie
   Experimentelle Beiträge zur Lehre vom ökonomischen Lernen. *Ztschr. Psychol.*, **22** (1900) 321–82; 465
Suggett, Laura Steffens
Steffens, Laura
   Ueber die motorische Einstellung. Experimentelle Beiträge. *Ztschr. Psychol.*, **23** (1900) 241–308

Great Britain

Botany

Morris, Mary B.
Morris, Mary B.
   {Concerning certain fruit trees. No. 1.—The cherry tree. *Sci.-Gos.*, **24** (1889) 194–96}
   {Concerning certain fruit trees. Part 2.—The quince tree. *Sci.-Gos.*, **24** (1889) 217–18}
   {Concerning certain fruit trees. No. 3.—Apple and pear trees. *Sci.-Gos.*, **25** (1889) 241–42}
   {Jottings concerning certain fruit trees. Part 4.—The mulberry tree. *Sci.-Gos.*, **26** (1890) 11–12}
   {Jottings concerning certain fruit trees. Part 5.—The peach tree. *Sci.-Gos.*, **26** (1890) 32–33}
   {Jottings concerning certain fruit trees. Part 6.—The chestnut tree (*Castanea vesca*). *Sci.-Gos.*, **26** (1890)
       79–81}
   {Jottings concerning certain fruit trees. No. 7.—The walnut tree. *Sci.-Gos.*, **26** (1890) 136–39}
   Notes sur quelques arbres à fruit. Le châtaignier (*Castanea vesca*). [Tr.] [1890] *N. France Soc. Linn. Bull.*, **10**
       (1890–91) 119–25
   {Jottings concerning certain fruit trees. The apricot. *Sci.-Gos.*, **27** (1891) 49–50}

Natural History

Brightwen, Elizabeth Elder (Eliza)
Brightwen, Eliza
   {Seedling trees. *Nature Notes*, **3** (1892) 143–45}
   {A visit to Selborne. *Nature Notes*, 4 (1893) 101–4}
   {A talk about birds. *Mothers and Daughters*, **1** (1893) 59–60; *Nature Notes*, **5** (1894) 89–90; repr., Leaflet
       No. 9, Society for the Protection of Birds}
   {How to protect birds. *Nature Notes*, **5** (1894) 41–44}
   {Asnapper, the owl. *Nature Notes*, **5** (1894) 161–63}
   {Imitating autumn leaves. *Nature Notes*, **5** (1894) 193–94}
   {The clothes moth. *Nature Notes*, **6** (1895) 66–70}
   {Autumn leaves in 1895. *Nature Notes*, **7** (1896) 8}
   {An Egyptian pet. *Nature Notes*, **7** (1896) 146–47}
   {In memory of Mungo. *Nature Notes*, **7** (1896) 226–27}

{A trio of vocalists. *Nature Notes*, **8** (1897) 1–4; 78}
{Wild nature at the Grove. *Nature Notes*, **8** (1897) 87–88}
{Crowborough Beacon. *Nature Notes*, **8** (1897) 204–6}
{My sanctuary. *Nature Notes*, **9** (1898) 24–25}
{A "Fairy" story continued. *Nature Notes*, **10** (1899) 31–32}

Astronomy

Zornlin, Rosina Maria
R. M. Z.
   {Observations of shooting stars on the nights of 10th and 11th August, 1839. *Phil. Mag.*, **15** (1839) 441–42}
Zornlin (Miss)
   On the periodical shooting stars, and on shooting stars in general. *Phil. Mag.*, **19** (1841) 347–57

Chemistry

Knecht, Maja
Bamberger, Eugen; Knecht, Maja
   Ueber die Reduction der Nitro- zur Hydroxylamingruppe. *Berlin, Chem. Ges. Ber.*, **29** (1896) 863–64

Sociology and History of Technology

Morris, Mary B.
Morris, Mary B.
   {Womanly weapons. *Girl's Own Paper*, **7** (1895–96) 77–78; 229–30; 428–29}
   {How we managed our crèche. *Girl's Own Paper*, **8** (1897) 518–19}

Great Britain—Canada

Biology

Bodington, Alice Brooke
Bodington, Alice
   The parasitic protozoa found in cancerous diseases. *Amer. Natlist.*, **28** (1894) 307–15

Natural History

Bodington, Alice Brooke
Bodington, Mrs
   {The flora of the past. Pts. 1–4. *Sci-Gos.*, **24** (1889) 83–84; 97–99; 122?–23; 147–48}
Bodington, Alice
   {Strange phenomena of reproduction in "Ficus Roxburghii". *J. Micr. Nat. Sci.*, (Oct. 1891) 302–?}
   {Leaves from my note-book. No. 1—Courtship of Amazons. *J. Micr. Nat. Sci.*, (Nov., 1891) 326–28}
   {Some instances of the influence of the environment in producing race peculiarities. *J. Micr. Nat. Sci.*, (Apr., 1895) 155–60.}
   {Leaves from my note-book.—Natural history. *J. Micr. Nat. Sci.*, (Jan., 1896) 45–?; (Oct., 1896) 329–?}
   {Leaves from my note-book.—Water insects. *J. Micr. Nat. Sci.*, (Apr., 1897) 133–?}

Psychology, Sociology, and Anthropology

Bodington, Alice Brooke
Bodington, Alice
   {The marriage question from a scientific standpoint. *Westminster Rev.*, **133** (1890) 172–80}
   {Mind in man and animals. *Westminster Rev.*, **134** (1890) 251–58}
   {The importance of race and its bearing on the negro question. *Westminster Rev.*, **134** (1890) 415–27}
   {The hidden self. *Open Court*, **4** (1890–91) 2621–22}
   {Prehistoric man in Europe. *J. Micr. Nat. Sci.*, **67** (1891) 70–74; 147–53}
   Mental evolution in man and the lower animals. *Amer. Natlist.*, **26** (1892) 482–92; 543–606
   {A modern view of ghosts. *Open Court*, **6** (1892) 3090–97; 3103–6}
   {Notes on the Indians of British Columbia. *Field Club*, (1893) 89–92; 104–7}
   {Facts and arguments against the vegetarian theory. *J. Micr. Nat. Sci.*, (Apr., 1894) 131–?}
   Insanity in royal families. A study in heredity. *Amer. Natlist.*, **29** (1895) 118–29; 408
   A study in morbid psychology, with some reflections. *Amer. Natlist.*, **30** (1895) 510–18; 599–605
   Mental action during sleep, or sub-conscious reasoning. *Amer. Natlist.*, **30** (1896) 849–54

Great Britain—India

Botany

Lisboa, (Mrs. José Camillo)
Lisboa, (Mrs. J. C.)
   Short notes on the odiferous grasses (Andropogons) of India and Ceylon, with a description of a supposed
   new species. *Bombay Nat. Hist. Soc. J.*, **4** (1889) 118–24; **6** (1891) 64–71

Periodical Title Abbreviations Key

Abbreviations follow the Royal Society *Catalogue* usage. For periodicals not included in the *Catalogue* but added to the bibliography, a similar style of title abbreviation has been adopted.

Aéronaute	L'Aéronaute. Paris.
Allg. Fisch.-Zt.	Allgemeine Fischerei-Zeitung. München.
Amer. Natlist.	The American Naturalist, Salem, Mass., Philadelphia, and New York.
Anat. Anz.	Anatomischer Anzeiger. Jena.
Angers, Mém. Soc. Agric.	Mémoires de la Société d'Agriculture, Sciences, et Arts. Angers.
Ann. Agr. Franç.	Annales de l'Agriculture Française. Paris.
Annal. de Chimie	Annales de Chimie. Paris.
Ann. Chim.	Annales de Chimie et de Physique. Paris.
Ann. Gén. Sci. Phys.	Annales générales des Sciences Physiques; par Bory de St. Vincent, Drapiez, et Van Mons. Bruxelles.
Ann. Inst. Pasteur	Annales de l'Institute Pasteur. (Journal de Microbiologie.) Paris.
Ann. Nat. Hist.	Annals of Natural History, or Magazine of Zoology, Botany, and Geology. London.
Ann. Phys. Chem.	Annalen der Physik und Chemie. Leipzig.
Ann. Sci. Nat.	Annales des Sciences Naturelles. Paris.
Ann. Sci. Nat. (Bot.)	Annales des Sciences Naturelles. Botanique. Paris.
Arch. Anat. Physiol. (Physiol. Abt.)	Archiv für Anatomie und Physiologie. Physiologische Abtheilung. Archiv für Physiologie. Leipzig.
Arch. Anthrop. Geol. Schlesw.-Holst.	Archiv für Anthropologie und Geologie Schleswig-Holsteins und der benachbarten Gebiete. Kiel.
Arch. Augenheilk.	Archiv für Augenheilkunde. In deutscher und englischer Sprache. Wiesbaden. [For English edition, see Arch. Ophthalm.]
Arch. Exper. Path.	Archiv für experimentelle Pathologie und Pharmakologie. Leipzig.
Arch. f. Ophthalm.	Albrecht von Graefe's Archiv für Opthalmologie. Berlin. Leipzig.
Arch. Ital. Biol.	Archives Italiennes de Biologie. Turin.
Arch. Math. Naturvid.	Archiv for Mathematik og Naturvidenskab. Kristiania. Kjøbenhavn.
Arch. Mikr. Anat.	Archiv für Mikroskopische Anatomie [und Entwickelungsgeschichte]. Bonn.
Arch. Ophthalm.	Archives of Ophthalmology. Edited in English and German. New York. [For German edition, see Arch. Augenheilk.]
Arch. Psychiatr.	Archiv für Psychiatrie und Nervenkrankheiten. Berlin.
Arch. Sci. Phys. Nat.	Bibliothèque Universelle. Archives des Sciences Physiques et Naturelles. Genève.
Arch. Wiss. Prakt. Thierheilk.	Archive für Wissenschaftliche und Praktische Thierheilkunde. Berlin.
Ass. Franç. C. R.	Association Française pour l'Avancement des Sciences. Compte Rendu. Paris.

Astr. & Astrophys.	Astronomy and Astro-Physics. Northfield, Minn.
Astr. Nachr.	Astronomische Nachrichten. Kiel.
Astronomie	L'Astronomie. Paris.
Beitr. Path. Anat.	Beiträge zur Pathologischen Anatomie und zur Allgemeinen Pathologie. Jena.
Belfast Field Club Rep.	Annual Reports and Proceedings of the Belfast Naturalists' Field Club. Belfast.
Belg. Soc. Bot. Bull.	Bulletin de la Société Royale de Botanique de Belgique. Bruxelles.
Bergens Mus. Aarb.	Bergens Museums Aarbog. Bergen.
Berlin Ak. Sber.	Sitzungsberichte der Königlich Preussischen Akademie der Wissenschaften zu Berlin. Berlin.
Berlin, Chem. Ges. Ber.	Berichte der Deutschen Chemischen Gesellschaft. Berlin.
Berlin. Ent. Ztschr.	Berliner Entomologische Zeitschrift (1875–1880: Deutsche Entomologische Zeitschrift). Berlin.
Berlin. Klin. Wschr.	Berliner Klinische Wochenschrift. Berlin.
Bern Mitth.	Mittheilungen der Naturforschenden Gesellschaft in Bern. Bern.
Biol. Centrbl.	Biologisches Centralblatt. Erlangen. Leipzig.
Bode, Astron. Jahrb.	Astronomisches Jahrbuch, nebst einer Sammlung der neuesten in die astronomischen Wissenschaften einschlagenden Abhandlungen, Beobachtungen, und Nachrichten; von J. E. Bode. Berlin.
Boll. Sci.	Bollettino Scientifico. Milano. Pavia.
Bologna Acc. Sci. Mem.	Memorie della [R.] Accademia delle Scienze dell'Istituto di Bologna. Bologna.
Bologna Rend.	Rendiconti delle Sessioni dell'Accademia Reale delle Scienze dell'Istituto di Bologna. Bologna.
Bombay Nat. Hist. Soc. J.	The Journal of the Bombay Natural History Society. Bombay.
Bot. Centrbl.	Botanisches Centralblatt. Referirendes Organ für das Gesammtgebiet der Botanik des In- und Auslandes. Kassel.
Bot. Centrbl. Beihefte	Beihefte zum Botanischen Centralblatt. Referirendes Organ für das Gesammtgebiet der Botanik des In- und Auslandes. Kassel.
Bot. Gaz.	The Botanical Gazette. Crawfordsville, Ind. Indianapolis.
Bot. Jaarb.	Botanisch Jaarboek uitgegeven door het Kruidkundig Genootschap Dodonaea te Gent. Gent. Leipzig.
Bot. Notiser	Botaniska Notiser. Lund.
Bot. Tidsskr.	Botanisk Tidsskrift udgivet af den Botaniske Forening i Kjøbenhavn. Kjøbenhavn.
Bot. Ztg.	Botanische Zeitung. Berlin.
Brescia Ateneo Comment.	Commentari dell' Ateneo di Brescia. Brescia.
Brux., Ac. Bull.	Bulletins de l'Académie Royale des Sciences, des Lettres et des Beaux-Arts de Belgique. Bruxelles.
Brux., Bull. Soc. Bot.	Bulletins de la Société Royale de Botanique de Belgique. Bruxelles.
Brux., Soc. Belge Micr. Bull.	Bulletin[s des Séances] de la Société Belge de Microscopie. Bruxelles.
Buitenzorg Jard. Bot. Ann.	Annales du Jardin Botanique de Buitenzorg. Leiden.
Bull. Astr.	Bulletin Astronomique publié sous les Auspices de l'Observatoire de Paris. Paris.
Bull. Malacol. Ital.	Bullettino della Società Malacologica Italiana. Pisa.
Centrbl. Bakt.	Centralblatt für Bacteriologie und Parasitenkunde. Jena.
Centrbl. Bakt. (Abt. 1)	Centralblatt für Bakteriologie. Erste Abteilung. Jena.
Centrbl. Med. Wiss.	Centralblatt für die Medicinischen Wissenschaften. Berlin.
Chem. News	The Chemical News and Journal of Physical Science. London.
Cong. Ass. Med. Ital.	Atti del XII Congresso dell'Associazione Medico Italiano. Pavia, 1887.

Congr. Int. Anthrop. C. R.	Congrès International d'Anthropologie et d'Archéologie préhistoriques. Compte Rendu . . . Paris.
Congr. Int. Méd. C. R.	XIIIe Congrès International de Médecine . . . Comptes Rendus. Paris.
Contrib. Biol. Veg.	Contribuzioni alla Biologia Vegetale. Palermo. Torino.
Crelle, J. Math.	Journal für die Reine und Angewandte Mathematik [Fortsetzung des von A. L. Crelle und C. W. Borchardt herausgegebenen Journals.] Berlin.
Deutsch. Arch. Klin. Med.	Deutsches Archiv für Klinische Medicin. Leipzig.
Deutsch. Bot. Ges. Ber.	Berichte der Deutschen Botanischen Gesellschaft. Berlin.
Deutsch. Ges. Anthrop. Ethnol. Urgeschichte, Corres.-Bl.	Correspondenz-Blatt der Deutschen Gesellschaft für Anthropologie, Ethnologie und Urgeschichte. Braunschweig.
Deutsch. Malakozool. Ges. Jbüch.	Jahrbücher der Deutschen Malakozoologischen Gesellschaft. Frankfurt am Main.
Deutsch. Malakozool. Ges. Nachrbl.	Nachrichtsblatt der Deutschen Malakozoologischen Gesellschaft. Frankfurt am Main.
Deutsche Med. Wschr.	Deutsche Medizinische Wochenschrift. Leipzig. Stuttgart.
Dublin Soc. Sci. Proc.	The Scientific Proceedings of the Royal Dublin Society. Dublin.
Dublin Soc. Sci. Trans.	The Scientific Transactions of the Royal Dublin Society. Dublin.
Elect. Rev.	The Electrical Review. London.
Fennia	Suomen Maantieteellinen Seura. Sällskapet för Finlands Geografi. Fennia. Bulletin[s] de la Société de Géographie Finlandaise [de Finlande]. Helsingfors.
Field and Forest.	Field and Forest. Washington, D.C.
Field Club	The Field Club, with which is incorporated The Gardner. A Magazine of General Natural History for Scientific and Unscientific Readers. London.
Flora	Flora oder Allgemeine Botanische Zeitung. Regensburg. Marburg.
Forsch. Agr.-Phys.	Forschungen auf dem Gebiete der Agrikultur-Physik. Heidelberg.
Fortschr. Math.	Jahrbuch über die Fortschritte der Mathematik. Berlin.
Fortschr. Med.	Fortschritte der Medicin. Berlin.
Fortschr. Phys.	Die Fortschritte der Physik im Jahre . . . Berlin.
France Méd.	France Médical. Paris.
[France] Soc. Agr. Mém.	Mémoires d'Agriculture, d'Économie rurale et domestique publiés par la Societé d'Agriculture. Paris.
France Soc. Bot. Bull.	Bulletin de la Société Botanqiue de France. Paris.
France Soc. Malacol. Bull.	Bulletins de la Société Malacologique de France. Paris.
France Soc. Météorol. Annu.	Annuaire de la Société Météorologique de France. Paris.
France Soc. Météorol. Nouv. Météorol.	Nouvelles Météorologiques publiées sous les Auspices de la Société Météorologique de France. Paris.
France Soc. Zool. Bull.	Bulletin de la Société Zoologique de France. Paris.
Frankf., Zool. Garten	Der Zoologische Garten. [(Zoologischer Beobachter.)] Zeitschrift für Beobachtung, Pflege und Zucht der Tiere . . . Herausgegeben von der "Neuen Zoologischen Gesellschaft" in Frankfurt a. M. [unter Mitwirkung von Fachgenossen]. Frankfurt a. M.
Gartner-Tid.	Gartner-Tidende (Almindelig Dansk Gartnerferening). Kjøbenhavn.
Gazz. degli Osped.	Gazzetta degli Ospedali. Genova.
Genova, Soc. Ligust. Atti	Atti della Società Ligustica di Scienze Naturali e Geografiche. Genova.
Giorn. Arcad.	Giornale Arcadico di Scienze . . . Roma.
Giorn. Mat.	Giornale di Matematiche. Napoli.
Giorn. Min. Crist. Petr.	Giornale di Mineralogia, Cristallografia e Petrografia. Milano.

Girl's Own Paper	The Girl's Own Paper. London.
Globus	Globus. Hildburghausen.
Graubünden Natf. Ges. Jber.	Jahresbericht der Naturforschenden Gesellschaft Graubündens. Chur.
Haarlem, Hollands. Maatsch. Nat. Verh.	Natuurkundige Verhandelingen van de Hollandsche Maatschappij der Wetenschappen, te Haarlem. Haarlem.
Harz, Naturw. Ver. Ber.	Berichte des Naturwissenschaftlichen Vereins des Harzes zu Blankenburg. Wernigerode.
Hedeselsk. Tidsskr.	[Danske] Hedeselskab Tidsskrift. Viborg.
Helsingfors Läreverks	Helsingfors Läreverks för Gosser och Flickor Ärsredogörelse. Helsingfors.
Humboldt	Humboldt. Monatsschrift für die Gesamten Naturwissenschaften. Stuttgart.
Ill. Ztschr. Ent.	Illustrierte Zeitschrift für Entomologie. Internationales Organ für die Interessen der allgemeinen und angewandten Entomologie wie der Insekten-Biologie. Neudamm.
Intell. Observer	The Intellectual Observer; a Review of Natural History, Microscopic Research, and Recreative Science. London.
Irish Ac. Proc.	Proceedings of the Royal Irish Academy. [Science.] Dublin.
Irish Natlist.	The Irish Naturalist. Dublin. Belfast. London.
[Italia], Soc. Bot. Bull.	Bullettino della Società Botanica Italiana. Firenze.
J. Bot.	The Journal of Botany, British and Foreign. London.
J. Bot., Paris	Journal de Botanique. Paris.
J. Conch.	The Journal of Conchology. Leeds.
J. de Conch.	Journal de Conchyliologie. Paris.
J. Micr. Nat. Sci.	The Journal of Microscopy and Natural Science. London.
J. Microgr.	Journal de Micrographie. Paris.
Jbuch. Kinderheilk.	Jahrbuch für Kinderheilkunde und physische Erziehung. Leipzig. Berlin.
Jena Denkschr.	Denkschriften der Medicinisch-Naturwissenschaftlichen Gesellschaft zu Jena. Jena.
Jena. Ztschr.	Jenaische Zeitschrift für Naturwissenschaft. Jena.
J. Physiol.	The Journal of Physiology. Cambridge. London.
Kjøbenh., Dansk. Vid. Selsk. Skr.	Det Kongelige Danske Videnskabernes Selskabs Skrifter. Kjøbenhavn.
Kjøbenh. Vid. Medd.	Videnskabelige Meddelelser fra den Naturhistoriske Forening i Kjøbenhavn. Kjøbenhavn.
Les Mondes	Cosmos. Les Mondes. Revue hebdomadaire des Sciences et de leurs Applications aux Arts e à l'Industrie. Paris.
Leyden Mus. Notes	Notes from the Leyden Museum. Leyden.
Lille Soc. Mém.	Mémoires de la Société [Royale] des Sciences, de l'Agriculture et des Arts de Lille. Lille.
Limerick Field Club, J.	Journal of the Limerick Field Club. Limerick.
Linn. Soc. J. (Bot.)	The Journal of the Linnean Society. Botany. London.
Liouville, J. Math.	Journal de Mathématiques pures et appliquées, fondé en 1836 et publié jusqu'en 1874 par Joseph Liouville. Paris.
London, Med. Press Circ.	Medical Press and Circular. London.
Lyon Univ. Ann.	Annales de l'Université de Lyon. Paris.
Maandbl. Nat.	Maandblad voor Natuurwetenschappen. Amsterdam.
Malakozool. Blätter	Malakozoologische Blätter. Kassel.
Malpighia	Malpighia. Rassegna mensuale di Botanica. Messina. Genova.
Mhefte. Chem.	Monatshefte für Chemie und verwandte Theile anderer Wissenschaften. Gesammelte Abhandlungen aus den Sitzungsberichten der kaiserlichen Akademie der Wissenschaften. Wein.
Milano, Cagnola Atti	Atti della Fondazione Scientifica Cagnola dalla sua istituzione in poi. Milano.

Milano, Ist. Lomb. Mem.	Memorie del Reale Istituto Lombardo di Scienze e Lettere. Classe di Scienze Mathematiche e Naturali. Milano.
Milano, Ist. Lomb. Rend.	Reale Istituto Lombardo di Scienze e Lettere. Rendiconti. Milano. Napoli. Pisa.
Milano, Soc. Ital. Atti	Atti della Società Italiana di Scienze Naturali. Milano.
Mitth. Anthrop. Ver. Schlesw.-Holst.	Mittheilungen. Anthropologischer Verein in Schleswig-Holstein, Kiel. Kiel.
Modena Soc. Nat. Atti	Atti della Società dei Naturalisti di Modena. Modena.
Moncalieri Oss. Boll.	Associazione Meteorologica Italiana . . . Bollettino Mensuale pubblicato per cura dell' Osservatorio Centrale del Real Collegio Carlo Alberto in Moncalieri. Torino.
Moniteur Sci.	Le Moniteur Scientifique. Journal des Sciences pures et appliqées. Paris.
Mont Blanc Obs. Ann.	Annales de l'Observatoire météorologique du Mont-Blanc. Paris.
Mothers and Daughters	Mothers and Daughters. London.
München Geogr. Ges. Jber.	Jahresbericht der Geographischen Gesellschaft in München. München.
München Geogr. Ges. Jber. 1894 (Festschr.)	Festschrift der Geographischen Gesellschaft in München . . . München. 1894.
Nat. Rund.	Naturwissenschaftliche Rundschau. Braunschweig.
Nature	Nature. A weekly illustrated Journal of Science. London. New York.
Nature Notes	Nature Notes, the Selborne Society's Magazine. London.
Nederl. Dierk. Ver. Tijdschr.	Tijdschrift der Nederlandsche Dierkundige Vereeniging. Leiden.
Nederl. Kruidk. Arch.	Nederlandsch Kruidkundig Archief. Verslagen en Mededeelingen der Nederlandsche Botanische Vereeningen. Nijmegen.
Neues Jbuch. Min.	Neues Jahrbuch für Mineralogie, Geologie und Palaeontologie. Stuttgart.
N. France Soc. Linn. Bull.	Bulletin de la Société Linnéenne du Nord de la France. Amiens.
Nieuw Arch. Wisk.	Nieuw Archief voor Wiskunde. Amsterdam.
Nouv. Arch. Obst. Gynéc.	Nouvelles Archives d'Obstétrique et de Gynécologie. Paris.
Nuovo Cimento	Il Nuovo Cimento. Torino. Pisa.
Nuovo Giorn. Bot. Ital.	Nuovo Giornale Botanico Italiano. Memorie della Società Botanica Italiana. Firenze.
Nyt Mag. Naturvid.	Nyt Magazin for Naturvidenskaberne. Christiania.
Oberrhein. Geol. Ver. Ber.	Bericht[e] über die . . . Versammlung des Oberrheinischen Geologischen Vereins. Stuttgart.
Oesterr. Bot. Ztschr.	Oesterreichische Botanische Zeitschrift. Wien.
Open Court	The Open Court. Chicago.
Ornith. Mber.	Ornithologische Monatsberichte. Berlin.
Padova Soc. Sci. Atti	Atti della Società Veneto-Trentina di Scienze naturali residente in Padova. Padova.
Palermo Circ. Mat. Rend.	Rendiconti del Circolo Matematico di Palermo. Palermo.
Paris, Ac. Sci. C. R.	Comptes Rendus hebdomadaires des Séances de l'Académie des Sciences. Paris.
Paris, Club Alpin Franç. Annu.	Annuaire du Club Alpin Français. Paris.
Paris, Mus. Hist. Nat. Bull.	Bulletin du Muséum d'Histoire Naturelle. Paris.
Paris Obs. Ann. (Mém.)	Annales de l'Observatoire de Paris. Mémoires. Paris.
Paris Obs. Ann. (Obsns.)	Annales de l'Observatoire de Paris. Observations. Paris.
Paris Soc. Anthrop. Bull.	Bulletins de la Société d'Anthropologie de Paris. Paris.
Paris Soc. Anthrop. Bull. & Mém.	Bulletins et Mémoires de la Société d'Anthropologie de Paris. Paris.
Paris, Soc. Biol. Mém.	Comptes Rendus [hebdomadaires] des Séances et Mémoires de la Société de Biologie. Paris.

Paris Soc. Chim. Bull.	Bulletin de la Société Chimique de Paris. Paris.
Paris Soc. Linn. Mém.	Mémoires de la Société Linnéenne de Paris. Paris.
Paris, Soc. Math. Bull.	Bulletin de la Société Mathématique de France. Paris.
Paris, Soc. Phys. Séances	Séances de la Société Française de Physique. Paris.
Phil. Mag.	The London and Edinburgh Philosophical Magazine and Journal of Science. London. Continued as The London, Edinburgh, and Dublin Philosophical Magazine and Journal of Science. London.
Poligrafo	Il Poligrafo: Giornale di Scienze, Lettere, ed Arti. Verona.
Pringsheim, Jbüch. Wiss. Bot.	Jahrbücher für Wissenschaftliche Botanik. Herausgegeben von Dr. N. Pringsheim. Berlin. Leipzig.
Progrès Méd.	Le Progrès Médical. Journal de Médecine, de Chirurgie et de Pharmacie. Paris.
Rev. d'Anthrop.	Revue d'Anthropologie. Paris.
Rev. Hyg.	Revue d'Hygiène et de Police Sanitaire. Paris.
Rev. Méd.	Revue de Médecine. Paris.
Rev. Méd.-Chir. Mal. Femmes	Revue Médico-Chirurgicale des Maladies des Femmes. Paris.
Rev. Sci.	Revue Scientifique [de la France et de l'Étranger. Revue des Cours Scientifiques]. Paris.
Riforma Med.	Riforma Medica: Giornale Internazionale Settimanale de Medicina, Chirurgia e Scienze affini. Naples.
Riv. Ital. Paleont.	Rivista Italiana di Paleontologia. Bologna. Parma.
Riv. Sci.-Ind.	Rivista Scientifico-Industriale delle principali Scoperte ed Invenzioni fatte nelle Scienze e nelle Industrie. Firenze.
Roma, Bull. Naut. Geogr.	Bullettino Nautico e Geographico di Roma. Appendice all Corrispondenza Scientifica di Roma. Roma.
Roma, Corrisp. Scient.	Corrispondenza Scientifica in Roma. Roma.
Roma Lab. Anat. Norm. Ric.	Ricerche fatte nel Laboratorio di Anatomia Normale della R. Università di Roma. Roma.
Roma, N. Lincei Atti	Atti dell' Accademia Pontificia de' Nuovi Lincei. Roma.
Roma, R. Acc. Med. Atti	Atti della R. Accademia Medica di Roma. Roma.
Roma, R. Acc. Lincei Rend.	Atti della R. Accademia dei Lincei. Rendiconti. (Classe di Scienze Fisiche, Matematiche e Naturali.) Roma.
Rouen, Trav. Acad.	Précis analytique des Travaux de l'Académie des Sciences, Belles-Lettres, et Arts de Rouen. Rouen.
Sci.-Gos.	Hardwicke's Science-Gossip. London.
Senckenb. Natf. Ges. Abh.	Abhandlungen herausgegeben von der Senckenbergischen Naturforschenden Gesellschaft. Frankfurt a. M.
Stockh., Ak. Handl. Bihang	Bihang till Kongl. Svenska Vetenskaps-Akademiens Handlingar. Stockholm.
Stockh. Geol. För. Förh.	Geologiska Föreningens i Stockholm Förhandlingar. Stockholm.
Stockh., Öfvers.	Öfversigt af Kongl. Vetenskaps-Akademiens Förhandlingar. Stockholm.
Stockh., Ymer.	Ymer. Tidskrift utgifven af Svenska Sällskapet för Antropologi och Geografi. Stockholm.
Tidskr. Skogshush.	Tidskrift för Skoghushållning. Upsala.
Tilloch, Phil. Mag.	The Philosophical Magazine (edited by A. Tilloch.) London.
Torino Acc. Sci. Atti	Atti della R. Accademia delle Scienze di Torino. Torino.
Torino Acc. Sci. Mem.	Memorie della Reale Accademia delle Scienze di Torino. [Classe di Scienze Fisiche, Matematiche e Naturali.] Torino.
Torino, Giorn. R. Acc. Med.	Giornale della R. Accademia di Medicina di Torino. Torino.
Torrey Bot. Club Bull.	Bulletin of the Torrey Botanical Club. New York.
Tribune Méd.	Tribune Médical. Paris.
Tromsø Mus. Aarsh.	Tromsø Museums Aarshefter. Tromsø.
Ugeskr. f. Landm.	Ugeskrift for Landmaend. Kjøbenhavn.
Upsala Geol. Inst. Bull.	Bulletin of the Geological Institution of the University of Upsala. Upsala.

Venezia, Ist. Atti	Atti del Reale Istituto Veneto di Scienze, Lettere ed Arti. Venezia.
Virchow, Arch.	Archiv für Pathologische Anatomie und Physiologie und für Klinische Medicin. Herausgegeben von Rudolf Virchow. Berlin.
Westminster Rev.	The Westminster Review. London.
Wien, Ak. Denkschr.	Denkschriften der kaiserlichen Akademie der Wissenschaften. Mathematisch-Naturwissenschaftliche Classe. Wien.
Wien, Ak. Sber.	Sitzungsberichte der kaiserlichen Akademie der Wissenschaften. Wien. Mathematisch-Naturwissenschaftliche Classe.
Wien, Anz.	Anzeiger der kaiserlichen Akademie der Wissenschaften. Mathematisch-Naturwissenschaftliche Classe. Wien.
Wien Geogr. Ges. Mitth.	Mittheilungen der kais. königl. Geographischen Gesellschaft in Wien. Wien.
Wien, Nat. Hist. Hofmus. Ann.	Annalen des k. k. Naturhistorischen Hofmuseums. Wien.
Wien Ornith. Ver. Mitth.	Mittheilungen des Ornithologischen Vereins in Wien. [Die Schwalbe.] Wien.
Wien Ornith. Ver. Mitth. (Beibl.)	Mittheilungen des Ornithologischen Vereins in Wien. Beiblätter. Wien.
Wien Zool. Bot. Verh.	Verhandlungen der kaiserlich-königlichen Zoologisch-Botanischen Gesellschaft in Wien. Wien.
Württemb. Jhefte.	Jahreshefte des Vereins für vaterländische Naturkunde in Württemberg. Stuttgart.
Zach, Monat. Corresp.	Monatliche Correspondenz zur Beförderung der Erd- und Himmels-Kunde; von Franz von Zach.
Zool. Anz.	Zoologischer Anzeiger. Leipzig.
Zool. Jbüch. (Anat.)	Zoologische Jahrbücher. Zeitschrift für Systematik, Geographie und Biologie der Thiere. Abtheilung für Anatomie und Ontogenie der Thiere. Jena.
Zool. Jbüch. (Syst.)	Zoologische Jahrbücher. Zeitschrift für Systematik, Geographie und Biologie der Thiere. Abtheilung für Systematik, Geographie und Biologie der Thiere. Jena.
Zoologist	The Zoologist. London.
Ztschr. Anorg. Chem.	Zeitschrift für anorganische Chemie. Hamburg. Leipzig.
Ztschr. Biol.	Zeitschrift für Biologie. München. Leipzig.
Ztschr. Elektroch.	Zeitschrift für Elektrochemie. Organ der Deutschen Elektrochemischen Gesellschaft. Halle a. S.
Ztschr. Ethnol.	Zeitschrift für Ethnologie. Berlin.
Ztschr. Ges. Schlesw.-Holst.-Lauen. Geschichte	Zeitschrift der Gesellschaft für Schleswig-Holstein-Lauenburgische Geschichte. Kiel.
Ztschr. Hyg.	Zeitschrift für Hygiene. Leipzig.
Ztschr. Physikal. Chem.	Zeitschrift für Physikalische Chemie, Stöchiometrie und Verwandtschaftslehre. Leipzig.
Ztschr. Physiol. Chem.	Zeitschrift für Physiologische Chemie. Stuttgart.
Ztschr. Psychol.	Zeitschrift für Psychologie und Physiologie der Sinnesorgane. Hamburg. Leipzig.
Ztschr. Untersuch. Nahr. Genuss.	Zeitschrift für Untersuchung der Nahrungs- und Genussmittel.
Ztschr. Wiss. Mikr.	Zeitschrift für wissenschaftliche Mikroskopie und für mikroskopische Technik. Braunschweig. Leipzig.
Ztschr. Wiss. Zool.	Zeitschrift für wissenschaftliche Zoologie. Leipzig.
Zürich Vrtljschr.	Vierteljahrsschrift der naturforschenden Gesellschaft in Zürich. Zürich.

Selected Bibliography

Albisetti, James C. *Schooling German Girls and Women: Secondary and Higher Education in the Nineteenth Century.* Princeton, N.J.: Princeton University Press, 1988.

Arrigoni degli Oddi, Ettore. "Delle vita e delle opere della Marchesa M. Paulucci, malacologa italiana." *Atti del Reale Istituto Veneto di Scienze, Lettere ed Arti* 80, pt. 2 (1920–1921): 59–70.

Bachmann, Barbara, and Elke Bradenahl. "Medizinstudium von Frauen in Bern 1871–1914." Inaugural diss., Bern University, 1990.

Baldi, Edgardo. "Rina Monti." *Rivista de Biologia* (1937): 347–61.

Barbizet, Claude, and Françoise Leguay. *Blanche Edwards-Pilliet: Femme et Médecin, 1858–1941.* Le Mans: Éditions Cénomane, 1988.

Bard, Christine. *Les Filles de Marianne: Histoire des Feminismes 1914–1940.* Paris: Fayard, 1995.

———. *Madeleine Pelletier (1874–1939): Logique et Infortunes d'un Combat pour l'Égalité.* CEDREF, Paris 1991. Paris: Côté-femme éditions, 1992.

Baum, Marie. *Rückblick auf mein Leben.* Berlin: Krolls Buchdruckerei, 1939; Heidelberg: F. H. Kerle, 1950.

Beisswanger, Gabriele. "Agnes Pockels (1862–1935) und die Oberflächenchemie: '. . . Sauberkeiten nicht nur herzustellen sondern sogar zu messen'." *Chemie in unser Zeit* 25 (1991): 97–101.

Bensaude-Vincent, Bernadette, and Isabelle Stengers. *Histoire de la Chimie.* Paris: Éditions la Découverte, 1993.

Bezirksamt Schöneberg/Kunstamt Schöneberg, ed. *Ich bin meine eigene Frauenbewegung: Frauen-Ansichten aus der Geschichte einer Grosstadt.* Berlin: Edition Hentrich, 1991.

Bonner, Thomas Neville. *To the Ends of the Earth: Women's Search for Education in Medicine.* Cambridge, Mass.: Harvard University Press, 1992.

Bowler, Peter J., and Nicholas Whyte, eds. *Science and Society in Ireland: The Social Context of Science and Society in Ireland 1800–1950.* Belfast: Institute of Irish Studies, Queen's University of Belfast, 1997.

Brehmer, Ilse, Juliane Jacobi-Dittrich, Elke Kleinau, and Annette Kuhn, eds. *Frauen in der Geschichte IV.* Dusseldorf: Schwann, 1983.

Brinkschulte, Eva, ed. *Weibliche Ärzte: Die Durchsetzung des Berufsbildes in Deutschland.* Berlin: Edition Hentrich, 1993.

Broch, Hjalmar. *Zoologiens Historie i Norge: till Annen Verdenskrieg.* Oslo: Akademisk Forlag, 1954.

Bucciarelli, Louis L., and Nancy Dworski. *Sophie Germain: An Essay in the History of the Theory of Elasticity.* Dordrecht, Holland: Reidel Publishing Co., 1980.

Bussmann, Hadumod, ed. *Stieftöchter der Alma Mater? 90 Jahre Frauenstudium in Bayern—am Beispiel der Universität München.* München: Antje Kustmann, 1993.

Craig, Gordon. *The Triumph of Liberalism: Zurich in the Golden Age, 1830–1869.* New York: Scribner's, 1988.

Creese, Mary R. S. *Ladies in the Laboratory? American and British Women in Science, 1800–1900: A Survey of Their Contributions to Research.* Lanham, Md.: Scarecrow Press, 1998.

Dansk Biografisk Leksikon. Købenkavn, J. H. Schultz, 1933–44.

Dansk Biografisk Leksikon. Købenkavn: Glydendal, 1979–1984.

Davis, J. L. "The Research School of Marie Curie in the Paris Faculty, 1907–1914." *Annals of Science* 52 (1995): 321–55.

de Cilleuls, Jean. "Le souvenir de Marie Phisalix (1861–1946)." *Histoire des Sciences Médicales* 6 (1972): 237–41.

Dictionnaire de Biographie Française. Paris: Letouzey et Ané, 1933–.

Dizionario Biografico degli Italiani. Roma: Istituto della Enciclopedia Italiana, 1960–.

Du Mortier, B.-C. "Notice sur Mlle. M.-A. Libert." *Bulletin de la Société Royale de Botanique de la Belgique* (1865): 403–11.

Eckblad, Finn-Egil. "Thekla Resvoll og Hanna Resvoll-Holmsen, to glemte?—pionerer i norsk botanikk." *Blyttia* 49 (1991): 3–10.

Enciclopedia Italiana di Scienze, Lettere ed Arti. Roma: Istituto Giovanni Treccani, 1929–1939.

Fenaroli, Giuseppina, Fulvia Furinghetti, Antonio Garibaldi, and Anna Somaglia. "Women and Mathematical Research in Italy during the Period 1887–1946." In Leon Burton, ed., *Gender and Mathematics: An International Perspective*, 144–55. London: Cassell Educational Limited, 1990.

Florin, Maj-Britt. "Astrid Cleve von Euler." *Svensk Botanisk Tidskrift* 62, no. 4 (1968): 549–64.

Fölsing, Ulla. *Geniale Beziehungen: Berühmte Paare in der Wissenschaft.* München: C. H. Beck, 1999.

Forkl, Martha, and Elisabeth Koffmahn, eds. *Frauenstudium und Akademische Frauenarbeit in Österreich.* Wien: Wilhelm Braumüller, Universitäts-Verlagsbuchhandlung G.m.b.H., 1968.

Fox, Robert, and George Weisz, eds. *The Organization of Science and Technology in France 1808–1914.* Cambridge: Cambridge University Press, 1980.

Føyn, Bjørn. "Minnetale over Professor Kristine Bonnevie." In *Det Norske Videnskaps-Akademie i Oslo. Årbok 1949,* 71–84. Oslo: Jacob Dybwad, 1950.

Fraisse, Geneviève. *Clémence Royer: Philosophe et Femme de Science.* Paris: Éditions la Découverte, 1985.

Giles, C. H., and D. S. Forrester. "The Origins of the Surface Film Balance. Studies in the Early History of Surface Chemistry, Part 3." *Chemistry and Industry,* no. 2 (9 Jan. 1971): 45–53.

Goldschmidt, Richard B. *Portraits from Memory: Recollections of a Zoologist.* Seattle: University of Washington Press, 1956.

Gordon, Felicia. *The Integral Feminist: Madeleine Pelletier, 1874–1939. Feminism, Socialism and Medicine.* Cambridge: Polity Press, 1990.

Graffmann-Weschke, Katharina. *Lydia Rabinowitsch-Kempner (1871–1935). Leben und Werk einer der führenden Persönlichkeiten der Tuberkuloseforschung am Anfang des 20 Jahrhunderts.* Herdecke: GCA-Verlag, 1999.

Grinstein, Louise S., and Paul J. Campbell, eds. *Women of Mathematics: A Biobibliographic Sourcebook.* Westport, Conn.: Greenwood Press, 1987.

Grinstein, Louise S., Rose K. Rose, and Miriam H. Rafailovich, eds. *Women in Chemistry and Physics: A Biobibliographic Sourcebook.* Westport, Conn.: Greenwood Press, 1993.

Harvey, Joy. *"Almost a Man of Genius": Clemence Royer, Feminism, and Nineteenth-Century Science.* New Brunswick, N.J.: Rutgers University Press, 1997.

Heindl, Waltraud, and Marina Tichy, eds. *"Durch Erkenntnis zu Freiheit und Gluck . . ." Frauen an der Universität Wien (ab 1897).* Wien: WUV-Universitätsverlag, 1990.

Henriksen, Kai L. "Oversight over dansk entomologisk historie." *Entomologiske Meddelelser* 15, Hf. 1–12 (1922–37): 1–578.

Hildebrandt, Irma. *Bin halt ein zähes Luder: 15 Münchner Frauenportraits.* München: Diederichs, 1990.

Hutchinson, George Evelyn. "The Harp that Once . . . a Note on the Discovery of Stridulation in the Corixid Water-Bugs." *Irish Naturalists' Journal* 20 (1982): 457–66.

Jaenicke, Lothar. "Clara Hamburger and *Dunaliella salina* Theodoresco—a Case Study from the First Half of the XXth Century." *Protist* 149 (1998): 381–88.

Johansson, Sif. "Stockholms Högskola för 100 år sedan—ett naturvetenskapligt universitet med plats för Kvinnor." *Kvinnovetenskaplig Tidskrift,* no. 4 (1984): 42–47.

Junginger, Gabriele, ed. *Maria Gräfin von Linden: Erinnerungen der ersten Tübinger Studentin.* Tübingen: Attempto Verlag, 1991.

Katzenberger, Eva. *Marianne Plehn 1863–1946, eine bedeutende Fischpathologin.* München: Hieronymous Buchreproduktions, 1994.

Koch, Julia K., and Eva-Maria Mertens, eds. *Eine Dame zwischen 500 Herren: Johanna Mestorf—Werk und Wirkung;* papers from the International Symposium, Christian-Albrechts-Universität, Kiel, in Bad Bramstedt, 15–17 April 1999. Münster: Waxmann, 2002.

Körner, Hans. *Die Würzburger Siebold: Eine Gelehrtenfamilie des 18. und 19. Jahrhunderts, Quellen und Beiträge zur Geschichte der Universität Würzburg.* Vol. 3. Neustadt a.d. Aisch: Verlag Degener, 1976.

Koster, Joséphine Th., and Terra S. S. van Benthem Jutting. "Notice sur Madame Dr. A. A. Weber *née* van Bosse à l'occasion de son 90ième anniversaire." *Blumea,* supp. 2 (1942): 3–9.

Kramer, Rita. *Maria Montessori: A Biography.* Reading, Mass.: Addison-Wesley, 1988.

Krok, Th. O. B. N. *Bibliotheca Botanica Suecana.* Uppsala: Almqvist and Wiksell, 1925.

Kronen, Torleiv, and Alexis C. Pappas. *Ellen Gleditsch: Et Liv i Forskning og Medmenneskelighet.* Oslo: Aventura Forlag, 1987.

Kuhn, Annette, Valentine Rothe, and Brigitte Mühlenbruch, eds. *100 Jahre Frauenstudium. Frauen der Rheinischen Friedrich-Wilhelms-Universität Bonn.* Dortmund: Edition Ebersbach, 1996.

Lawalree, A., J. Lambinon, F. Demaret, and M. Lang. *Marie-Anne Libert (1782–1865): Biographie, Généalogie, Bibliographie.* Malmédy: Famille et Terroir, 1965.

Leandri, J. "Aimée Camus. 1er mai 1879–17 avril 1965." *Adansonia* s. 2, 6 (1965): 3–21.

Lecours, Andrée Roche, and David Caplan. "Augusta Dejerine-Klumpke or 'The lesson in anatomy.'" *Brain and Cognition* 3 (1984): 166–97.

Lexikon der Frau. 2 vols. Zürich: Encyclios Verlag AG, 1953.

Lie, Suzanne Stiver, and Maj Birgit Roslett, eds. *Alma Maters Døtre: Et Århundre med Kvinner i Akademisk Utdanning.* Oslo: Pax Vorlag A/S, 1995.

Lindeboom, G. A. *Dutch Medical Biography: A Biographical Dictionary of Dutch Physicians and Surgeons, 1475–1975.* Amsterdam: Rodopi, 1984.

Lipinska, Mélanie. *Histoire des Femmes Médecins depuis l'Antiquité jusqu'à nos Jours.* Paris: G. Jacques & Cie, 1900.

———. *Les Femmes et le Progrès des Sciences Médicales.* Paris: Masson, 1930.

Marland, Hilary. "'Pioneer Work on All Sides': The First Generation of Women Physicians in the Netherlands, 1879–1930." *Journal of the History of Medicine and Allied Sciences* 50 (1995): 441–77.

Martens, Eva-Maria. "Mestorf, Johanna," in *Neue Deutsche Biographie,* bd. 17, 227–28. Bayerische Akademie der Wissenschaften; Historische Kommission. Berlin: Duncker & Humblot, 1994.

Mazenod, Lucienne, and Ghislaine Schoeller. *Dictionnaire des Femmes Célèbres de tous les Temps et de tous les Pays.* Paris: Éditions Robert Laffont, 1992.

McKenna-Lawlor, Susan. *Whatever Shines Should Be Observed.* Samton Historical Studies. Dublin: Samton Ltd., 1998.

Meijer, J. M. *Knowledge and Revolution: The Russian Colony in Zurich (1870–1873): A Contribution to the Study of Russian Populism.* Assen: International Instituut voor Sociale Geschiedenis, 1955.

Nordhagen, Rolf. "Minnetale over amanuensis Thekla Resvoll." In *Det Norske Videnskaps-Akademie i Oslo. Årbok 1949,* 29–37. Oslo: Jacob Dybwad, 1950.

Norsk Biografisk Leksikon. Kristiania: H. Aschehoug, 1921–1983.

Norsk Biografisk Leksikon. Oslo: Kunnskapsforlaget, 1999–.

Nudds, J. R., N. D. McMillan, D. L. Weaire, and S. M. P. McKenna-Lawlor, eds. *Science and Tradition in Ireland 1800–1930: Tradition and Reform.* Dublin: Trinity College Dublin, 1988.

O'Cleirigh, Nellie. *Valentia. A Different Irish Island.* Dublin: Portobello Press, 1992.

Oelsner, Elise. *Die Leistungen der Deutschen Frau in den Letzten Vierhundert Jahren auf Wissenschaftlichen Gebiete.* Guhrau: M. Lemke, 1894; reproduced in Gerritson Collection of Women's History, University of Kansas Libraries, microfiche, 1975.

Ogilvie, Marilyn, and Joy Harvey, eds. *The Biographical Dictionary of Women in Science: Pioneering Lives from Ancient Times to the Mid-20th Century.* 2 vols. New York: Routledge, 2000.

Osborne, Michael A. *Nature, the Exotic, and the Science of French Colonialism.* Bloomington: Indiana University Press, 1994.

Österreichisches Biographisches Lexikon, 1815–1950. Graz-Köln: Hermann Böhlaus Nachf., 1957–.

Pataky, Sophie. *Lexikon Deutscher Frauen der Feder.* 2 vols. Berlin: C. Pataky, 1898. Reprint, Bern: H. Lang, 1971.

Pihl, Mogens. "Kirstine Meyer." *Fysisk Tidskrift* 40 (1942), 175–91.

Pockels, Elisabeth, and S. Rösch. "Ein gelehrtes Geschwisterpaar. Zur Erinnerung an Agnes Pockels (1862–1935)." *Berichte der Oberhessischen Gesellschaft für Natur- und Heilkunde zu Giessen. Naturwissenschaftliche Abteilung* 24 (1949): 303–7.

Praeger, R. Lloyd. *Some Irish Naturalists: A Biographical Notebook.* Dundalk: W. Tempest, 1949.

Rebière, Alphonse. *Les Femmes dans la Science. Notes recueilles.* 2nd ed. Paris: Nony et Cie, 1897.

Rohner, Hanny. *Die ersten 30 Jahre des medizinischen Frauenstudiums an der Universität Zürich 1867–1897.* Zürich: Juris Druck, 1972.

Schimpke, Thomas. "Lydia Rabinowitsch-Kempner (1871–1935). Leben und Wirken einer tuberkulose Forscherin," Inaugural diss., Bayerischer Julius-Maximilians-Universität zu Würzburg, Würzburg, 1996.

Schweizerischer Verband der Akademikerinnen, ed. *Das Frauenstudium an der Schweizer Hochschulen.* Zürich: Rascher & Cie, 1928.

Stoltzenberg, Dietrich. *Fritz Haber: Chemiker, Nobelpristräger, Deutscher, Jude: Eine Biographie.* Weinheim, VCH, 1994.

Svenska Män och Kvinnor: Biografisk Uppslagsbok. Stockholm: Alb. Bonniers Boktryckeri, 1942–1955.

Svenskt Författarlexikon, 1900–1940. Stockholm: Svenskt Författarlexikons Förlag, Rabén & Sjögren, 1942.

Thomsen, Mathais. "Sofie Rostrup: in memorium." *Tidsskrift for Landøkonomie* 3 (1940): 176–80.

Tiburtius, Franziska. *Erinnerungen einer Achtzigjährigen.* Berlin: C. A. Schwetschke, 3rd ed., 1929.

Tobies, Renate, ed. *"Aller Männerkultur zum Trotz": Frauen in Matematik und Naturwissenschaften.* Frankfurt/Main: Campus Verlag, 1997.

Verband der Akademikerinnen Österreichs. *Frauenstudium und Akademische Frauenarbeit in Österreich, 1968–1987.* Wien: Verband der Akademikerinnen Österreiches, 1987.

Verein Feministische Wissenschaft Schweiz. *Ebenso neu als kühn: 120 Jahre Frauenstudium an der Universität Zürich.* Zürich: Verein Feministische Wissenschaft Schweiz, Schriftenreihe, 1988.

Vogt, Annette. *Elsa Neumann. Berlins erstes Fräulein Doktor.* Berlin: Verlag für Wissenschafts- und Regionalgeschichte, 1999.

von Leitner, Gerit. *Der Fall Clara Immerwahr: Leben für eine Humane Wissenschaft.* München: C. H. Beck, 1994.

Weber-van Bosse, Anna. *Een Jaar aan Boord H. M. Siboga.* Leiden: E. J. Brill, 1904. German ed., trans. E. Ruge-Baenziger, *Ein Jahr an Bord I. M. S. Siboga.* Leipzig: W. Engelmann, 1905.

Wer ist's. Leipzig: H. A. L. Degener, 1905–.

Wolchik, Sharon L., and Alfred G. Meyer, eds. *Women, State, and Party in Eastern Europe.* Durham, N.C.: Duke University Press, 1985.

Women in Technology & Science (WITS). *Stars, Shells and Bluebells: Women Scientists and Pioneers.* Dublin: Women in Technology & Science, 1997.

Zimmermann, Karl. "' . . . dass ihr kostbarster Schmuck, ihre einzige Macht, ihr ganzer Zauber in der Wieblichkeit liegt.' Zum Briefwechsel zwischen Johanna Mestorf (1828–1909) und Karl Adolf von Morlow (1820–1867)." *Nordelbingen. Beiträge zur Kunst- und Kulturgeschichte* 62 (1993): 171–88.

Index

Names listed in the index are those used in the subject's main entry in the text and are generally those to which the subject is usually referred. Complete names, as far as have been determined, are given in author headings in the bibliographic list of the subject's publications; these are often married names.

About the Author and Contributor

Mary Creese (née Weir) was born in Orkney, Scotland, in 1935. After almost thirty years as a research chemist, she turned to the subject of women's contributions to scientific work, particularly in the nineteenth century. Since 1990 she has published more than 40 articles on early women scientists. She holds a B.Sc. degree from the University of Glasgow and a Ph.D. from the University of California, Berkeley (both in chemistry), and has coauthored some 20 technical publications. She has lived in Kansas since 1964, nearly all of the time working at the University of Kansas, most recently as an associate at the Hall Center for the Humanities. She is married to Thomas Creese, and they have two daughters.

Thomas Creese was born in New York in 1934 and grew up in New Jersey. He holds degrees in mathematics from Massachusetts Institute of Technology and the University of California, Berkeley. Since 1964, he has been a member of the Department of Mathematics at the University of Kansas and has coauthored both a textbook and a research monograph. He and Mary Creese have collaborated on projects in computational chemistry and history of women in science.